IFIP Advances in Information and Communication Technology 647

Editor-in-Chief

Kai Rannenberg, Goethe University Frankfurt, Germany

IFIP – The International Federation for Information Processing

IFIP was founded in 1960 under the auspices of UNESCO, following the first World Computer Congress held in Paris the previous year. A federation for societies working in information processing, IFIP's aim is two-fold: to support information processing in the countries of its members and to encourage technology transfer to developing nations. As its mission statement clearly states:

IFIP is the global non-profit federation of societies of ICT professionals that aims at achieving a worldwide professional and socially responsible development and application of information and communication technologies.

IFIP is a non-profit-making organization, run almost solely by 2500 volunteers. It operates through a number of technical committees and working groups, which organize events and publications. IFIP's events range from large international open conferences to working conferences and local seminars.

The flagship event is the IFIP World Computer Congress, at which both invited and contributed papers are presented. Contributed papers are rigorously refereed and the rejection rate is high.

As with the Congress, participation in the open conferences is open to all and papers may be invited or submitted. Again, submitted papers are stringently refereed.

The working conferences are structured differently. They are usually run by a working group and attendance is generally smaller and occasionally by invitation only. Their purpose is to create an atmosphere conducive to innovation and development. Refereeing is also rigorous and papers are subjected to extensive group discussion.

Publications arising from IFIP events vary. The papers presented at the IFIP World Computer Congress and at open conferences are published as conference proceedings, while the results of the working conferences are often published as collections of selected and edited papers.

IFIP distinguishes three types of institutional membership: Country Representative Members, Members at Large, and Associate Members. The type of organization that can apply for membership is a wide variety and includes national or international societies of individual computer scientists/ICT professionals, associations or federations of such societies, government institutions/government related organizations, national or international research institutes or consortia, universities, academies of sciences, companies, national or international associations or federations of companies.

More information about this series at https://link.springer.com/bookseries/6102

Ilias Maglogiannis · Lazaros Iliadis ·
John Macintyre · Paulo Cortez (Eds.)

Artificial Intelligence Applications and Innovations

18th IFIP WG 12.5 International Conference, AIAI 2022
Hersonissos, Crete, Greece, June 17–20, 2022
Proceedings, Part II

 Springer

Editors
Ilias Maglogiannis
University of Piraeus
Piraeus, Greece

Lazaros Iliadis
Democritus University of Thrace
Xanthi, Greece

John Macintyre
University of Sunderland
Sunderland, UK

Paulo Cortez
Universidade do Minho
Guimaraes, Portugal

ISSN 1868-4238   ISSN 1868-422X (electronic)
IFIP Advances in Information and Communication Technology
ISBN 978-3-031-08339-6   ISBN 978-3-031-08337-2   (eBook)
https://doi.org/10.1007/978-3-031-08337-2

This Springer imprint is published by the registered company Springer Nature Switzerland AG
The registered company address is: Gewerbestrasse 11, 6330 Cham, Switzerland

Preface

Artificial intelligence (AI) is a relatively new scientific area that emerged from the efforts of a handful of scientists from diverse fields approximately 70 years ago. The achievements of AI in the era of the 4th Industrial Revolution are amazing and the expectations are continuously rising. Today AI applications are found in almost all areas of human activities. Healthcare, finance, industry, security, robotics, molecular biology, and autonomous vehicles are only a small sample of the domains that have been influenced by artificial intelligence. However, serious ethical matters have emerged (e.g., privacy, surveillance, bias-discrimination, elimination of entire job categories) requiring corrective legislative actions.

The 18th International Conference on Artificial Intelligence Applications and Innovations (AIAI 2022) offered insight into all timely challenges related to technical, legal, and ethical aspects of intelligent systems and their applications. New algorithms and potential prototypes employed in diverse domains were also introduced.

AIAI is a mature international scientific conference that has been held all over the world and it is well established in the scientific area of AI. Its history is long and very successful, following and propagating the evolution of intelligent systems.

The first event was organized in Toulouse, France, in 2004. Since then, it has had a continuous and dynamic presence as a major global, but mainly European, scientific event. More specifically, it has been organized in China, Greece, Cyprus, Australia, and France. It has always been technically supported by the International Federation for Information Processing (IFIP) and more specifically by the Working Group 12.5, which is interested in AI applications.

Following a long-standing tradition, this Springer volume belongs to the IFIP AICT series and it contains the papers that were accepted to be presented orally at the AIAI 2022 conference. An additional volume collates the papers that were accepted and presented at the workshops which were held as parallel events. The event was collocated with the 23rd International Conference on Engineering Applications of Neural Networks (EANN 2022) and held during June 17–20, 2022, in Crete, Greece. The diverse nature of papers presented demonstrates the vitality of AI algorithms and approaches. It certainly proves the very wide range of AI applications as well.

The response of the international scientific community to the AIAI 2022 call for papers was more than satisfactory, with 158 papers initially submitted. All papers were peer reviewed by at least two independent academic referees. Where needed, a third referee was consulted to resolve any potential conflicts. A total of 72 papers (45.5%) of the submitted manuscripts were accepted to be published as full papers (12 pages long) in the proceedings. Owing to the high quality of the submissions, the Program Committee also decided to accept 11 manuscripts as short papers (10 pages long). The accepted papers cover the following thematic topics and application areas:

- Adaptive Modeling
- Adversarial Neural Networks

- AI and Energy Modeling
- Anomaly Detection Modeling and AI
- Autonomous Shuttles Modeling and AI
- Classification
- Cloud Data Modeling and AI
- Clustering
- Convolutional Neural Networks
- Cybersecurity and AI
- Deep Learning in Medical Applications
- Deep Learning and Fraud Detection
- Deep Learning Models for Face Mask Detection
- Environmental AI Modeling
- Evolutionary and Genetic Algorithms
- Explainable AI
- Feature Selection
- Financial Applications of AI
- Fuzzy Modeling
- Graph Representation of AI Models
- Intrusion Detection Using AI
- IoT
- Industry 4.0
- Learning
- Machine Learning
- Medical AI Modeling
- Metaheuristics
- Molecular Biology AI Modeling
- Natural Language
- Neural Networks Modeling
- Object Detection-Tracking and AI
- Pruning and AI
- Recommendation Systems
- Recurrent Modeling of the Primary Visual Cortex
- Reinforcement Models for Cryptocurrency
- Sentiment Analysis
- Speech and Emotion Recognition
- Text Mining and AI
- Timeseries AI Modeling
- Trading
- Transfer Learning Modeling
- Unsupervised Modeling

The authors of the accepted papers are based in 28 different countries all over the globe, namely, Austria, Brazil, Cyprus, the Czech Republic, Denmark, France, Germany, Greece, Hungary, India, Ireland, Italy, Japan, Lebanon, the Netherlands, Norway, China, Pakistan, Poland, Portugal, South Africa, Saudi Arabia, Serbia, Singapore, Spain, Turkey, the UK, and the USA.

The following seven scientific workshops on timely AI subjects were organized under the framework of AIAI 2022.

- The 11th Mining Humanistic Data Workshop (MHDW 2022)

MHDW 2022 was organized by the University of Patras and the Ionian University, Greece. It aimed to bring together interdisciplinary approaches that focus on the application of innovative as well as existing artificial intelligence, data matching, fusion and mining, and knowledge discovery and management techniques to data derived from all areas of humanistic sciences.

- The 7th Workshop on 5G-Putting Intelligence to the Network Edge (5G-PINE 2022)

The 7th 5G-PINE workshop was organized by the research team of the Hellenic Telecommunications Organization (OTE) in cooperation with many major partner companies. The 5G-PINE workshop was established to disseminate knowledge obtained from ongoing EU projects, as well as from any other action of EU-funded research, in the wider thematic area of "5G Innovative Activities – Putting Intelligence to the Network Edge" and with the aim of focusing on artificial intelligence in modern 5G telecommunications infrastructures. This is achieved by emphasizing results, methodologies, trials, concepts and/or findings originating from technical reports/deliverables, related pilot actions, and/or any other relevant 5G-based applications intending to enhance intelligence to the network edges.

- The 2nd Workshop on Artificial Intelligence and Ethics (AIETH 2022)

The 2nd AIETH workshop was coordinated and organized by John Macintyre (University of Sunderland, UK). It aimed to emphasize the need for responsible global AI. The respective scientific community must be preparing to act preemptively and ensure that our societies will avoid negative effects of AI and of the 4th Industrial Revolution in general. This workshop offered an extensive discussion on potential major ethical issues that might arise in the near future.

- The 2nd Workshop on Defense Applications of AI (DAAI 2022)

The 2nd DAAI workshop was organized by the European Defense Agency (EDA), a European Union (EU) organization. Defense and security systems are becoming more and more complicated and at the same time equipped with a plethora of sensing devices which collect an enormous amount of information both from their operating environment as well as from their own functioning. Considering the accelerating technology advancements of AI, it is likely that it will have a profound impact on practically every segment of daily life, from the labor market to business and service provision. The security and defense sectors will not remain idle or unaffected by this technological evolution. On the contrary, AI is expected to transform the nature of future defense and security domains, because by definition defense and security forces are highly dependent on (accurate) data and (reliable) information. DAAI 2022 aimed at presenting recent evolutions in artificial intelligence applicable to defense and security applications.

- The 1st Workshop on AI in Energy, Buildings and Micro-Grids (AIBMG 2022)

This workshop was organized by Center for Research and Technology (CERTH), Greece. Sustainable energy is hands down one of the biggest challenges of our times. As the EU sets its focus on reaching its 2030 and 2050 goals, the role of artificial intelligence in the energy domain at the building, district, and micro-grid level becomes more prevalent. The EU and member states are increasingly highlighting the need to complement IoT capacity (e.g., appliances and meters) with artificial intelligence capabilities (e.g., building management systems, proactive optimization, prescriptive maintenance). Moreover, moving away from the centralized production schema of the grid, novel approaches are needed not just for reducing energy consumption but also for the optimal management and/or balancing of local (or remote aggregated net metering) generation and consumptions.

The aim of the AIBMG workshop was to bring together interdisciplinary approaches that focus on the application of AI-driven solutions for increasing and improving energy efficiency of residential and tertiary buildings without compromising the occupants' well-being. Applied directly at either the device, building, or district management system level, the proposed solutions should enable more energy efficient and sustainable operation of devices, buildings, districts, and micro-grids. The workshop also welcomed cross-domain approaches that investigate how to support energy efficiency by exploiting decentralized, proactive, plug-n-play solutions.

- The 2nd Workshop on Artificial Intelligence in Biomedical Engineering and Informatics (AIBEI 2022)

Artificial intelligence (AI) is gradually changing the routine of medical practice, and the level of acceptance by medical personnel is constantly increasing. Recent progress in digital medical data acquisition through advanced biosignal and medical imaging devices, machine learning, and high-performance cloud computing infrastructures push health-related AI applications into areas that were previously thought to be only the province of human experts. Such applications employ a variety of methodologies, including fuzzy logic, evolutionary computing, neural networks, or deep learning, for producing AI-powered models that simulate human physiology.

- The 1st Workshop/Special Session on Machine Learning and Big Data in Health Care (ML@HC 2022)

In the present era, machine learning (ML) has been extensively used for many applications to real-world problems. ML techniques are very suitable for big data mining, to extract new knowledge and build predictive models that, given a new input, can provide in the output a reliable estimate. On the other hand, healthcare is one of the fastest growing data segments of the digital world, with healthcare data increasing at a rate of about 50% per year. There are three primary sources of big data in healthcare: providers and payers (including EMR, imaging, insurance claims, and pharmacy data), -omic data (including genomic, epigenomic, proteomic, and metabolomic data), and patients and non-providers (including data from smart phone and Internet activities, sensors, and monitoring tools).

The growth of big data in oncology, as well as other severe diseases (such as Alzheimer's Disease) can provide unprecedented opportunities to explore the biopsychosocial characteristics of these diseases and for descriptive observation, hypothesis generation, and prediction for clinical, research and business issues. The results of big data analyses can be incorporated into standards and guidelines and will directly impact clinical decision making. Oncologists and professionals from related medical fields can increasingly evaluate the results from research studies and commercial analytical products that are based on big data, based on ML techniques. Furthermore, all these applications can be Web-based, so are very useful for the post-treatment of the patients.

The aim of this workshop/special session was to serve as an interdisciplinary forum for bringing together specialists from the scientific areas of computer and web engineering, data science, semantic computing, and bioinformatics-personalized medicine, along with clinicians and caregivers. The focus of this special session was on current technological advances and challenges regarding the development of big data-driven algorithms, methods, and tools; furthermore, it sought to investigate how ML-aware applications can contribute towards big data analysis on post-treatment follow up.

In addition to the paper presentations and workshops, five invited speakers gave keynotes on timely aspects or state-of-the-art applications of artificial intelligence. The keynote presentations were held jointly with EANN 2022. Hojjat Adeli from Ohio State University, USA, gave a speech on "Machine Learning: A Key Ubiquitous Technology in the 21st Century". Riitta Salmelin from Aalto University, Finland, addressed "What neuroimaging can tell about human brain function". Elisabeth André from the University of Augsburg, Germany, discussed "Socially Interactive Artificial Intelligence: Perception, Synthesis and Learning of Human-like Behaviors". Verena Rieser from Heriot-Watt University, UK, gave a speech on the subject of "Responsible Conversational AI: Trusted, Safe and Bias-free" and John Macintyre from the University of Sunderland, UK, addressed the wider AI and ethics area in his talk "Is Big Tech Becoming the Big Tobacco of AI?".

On behalf of the organizers, we would like to thank everyone involved in AIAI 2022, and we hope that you find the proceedings interesting and insightful.

June 2022

Ilias Maglogiannis
Lazaros Iliadis
John Macintyre
Paulo Cortez

Organization

Executive Committee

General Co-chairs

Ilias Maglogiannis   University of Piraeus, Greece
John Macintyre   University of Sunderland, UK

Program Co-chairs

Lazaros Iliadis   Democritus University of Thrace, Greece
Konstantinos Votis   Information Technologies Institute, Greece
Vangelis Metsis   Texas State University, USA

Steering Committee

Ilias Maglogiannis   University of Piraeus, Greece
Lazaros Iliadis   Democritus University of Thrace, Greece

Advisory Co-chairs

Panagiotis Papapetrou   Stockholm University, Sweden
Paulo Cortez   University of Minho, Portugal

Publication and Publicity Co-chairs

Antonios Papaleonidas   Democritus University of Thrace, Greece
Anastasios Panagiotis   Democritus University of Thrace, Greece
Psathas

Liaison Chair

Ioannis Chochliouros   Hellenic Telecommunication Organization (OTE), Greece

Doctoral Consortium Chairs

Antonios Papaleonidas   Democritus University of Thrace, Greece
Harris Papadopoulos   Frederick University, Cyprus

Workshops Co-chairs

Panagiotis Kikiras   European Defense Agency, Belgium
Phivos Mylonas   Ionian Univesity, Greece
Katia Kermanidis   Ionian University, Greece

Special Sessions and Tutorials Co-chairs

Spyros Sioutas	University of Patras, Greece
Christos Makris	University of Patras, Greece

Program Committee

Aiello Salvatore	Politecnico di Torino, Italy
Aldanondo Michel	IMT Mines Albi, France
Alexandridis Georgios	University of the Aegean, Greece
Alexiou Athanasios	Novel Global Community Educational Foundation, Australia
Aloisio Angelo	University of L'Aquila, Italy
Alonso Serafin	University of León, Spain
Amato Domenico	University of Palermo, Italy
Anagnostopoulos Christos-Nikolaos	University of the Aegean, Greece
Badica Costin	University of Craiova, Romania
Bezas Napoleon	Centre for Research and Technology Hellas, Greece
Bobrowski Leon	Bialystok University of Technology, Poland
Bozanis Panayiotis	International Hellenic University, Greece
C. Sousa Joana	NOS Inovação SA, Portugal
Campos Souza Paulo Vitor	Federal Center for Technological Education of Minas Gerais, Brazil
Caridakis George	National Technical University of Athens, Greece
Cavique Luis	University of Aberta, Portugal
Chamodrakas Ioannis	National and Kapodistrian University of Athens, Greece
Chochliouros Ioannis	Hellenic Telecommunications Organization S.A. (OTE), Greece
Delibasis Konstantinos	University of Thessaly, Greece
Demertzis Konstantinos	Democritus University of Thrace, Greece
Dimara Asimina	Centre for Research and Technology Hellas, Greece
Diou Christos Harokopio	University of Athens, Greece
Dominguez Manuel	University of Leon, Spain
Drakopoulos Georgios	Ionian University, Greece
Drousiotis Efthyvoulos	University of Liverpool, UK
Ferreira Luis	Polytechnic of Porto, Portugal
Fiannaca Antonino	National Research Council, Italy
Frittoli Luca	Politecnico di Milano, Italy
Fuertes Juan J.	University of León, Spain
Gaggero Mauro	National Research Council, Italy
Georgopoulos Efstratios	University of Peloponnese, Greece
Giancarlo Raffaele	University of Palermo, Italy
Giarelis Nikolaos	University of Patras, Greece
Giunchiglia Eleonora	University of Oxford, UK

Gonzalez-Deleito Nicolas	Sirris, Belgium
Grivokostopoulou Foteini	University of Patras, Greece
Hága Péter	Ericsson Research, Hungary
Hajek Petr	University of Pardubice, Czech Republic
Haralabopoulos Giannis	University of Nottingham, UK
Hatzilygeroudis Ioannis	University of Patras, Greece
Hichri Bassem	GCL International, Luxembourg
Hristoskova Anna	Sirris, Belgium
Humm Bernhard	Darmstadt University of Applied Sciences, Germany
Iakovidis Dimitris	University of Thessaly, Greece
Iliadis Lazaros	Democritus University of Thrace, Greece
Ishii Naohiro	Aichi Institute of Technology, Japan
Islam Shareeful	University of East London, UK
Ivanovic Mirjana	University of Novi Sad, Serbia
Jeannin-Girardon Anne	University of Strasbourg, France
Kalamaras Ilias	Centre for Research and Technology Hellas/Information Technologies Institute, Greece
Kallipolitis Athanasios	University of Piraeus, Greece
Kanakaris Nikos	University of Patras, Greece
Kanavos Andreas	University of Patras, Greece
Kapetanakis Stelios	University of Brighton, UK
Karacapilidis Nikos	University of Patras, Greece
Karatzas Kostas	Aristotle University of Thessaloniki, Greece
Karpouzis Kostas	National and Kapodistrian University of Athens, Greece
Kassandros Theodosios	Aristotle University of Thessaloniki, Greece
Kefalas Petros	CITY College, Greece
Kermanidis Katia Lida	Ionian University, Greece
Kokkinos Yiannis	University of Macedonia, Greece
Kollia Ilianna	IBM/National Technical University of Athens, Greece
Kontos Yiannis	Aristotle University of Thessaloniki, Greece
Koprinkova-Hristova Petia	Bulgarian Academy of Sciences, Bulgaria
Korkas Christos	Democritus University of Thrace/Centre for Research and Technology, Greece
Kosmopoulos Dimitrios	University of Patras, Greece
Kotis Konstantinos	University of the Aegean, Greece
Kotsiantis Sotiris	University of Patras, Greece
Koukaras Paraskevas	Centre for Research and Technology Hellas, Greece
Koussouris Sotiris	Suite5 Data Intelligence Solutions Ltd., Cyprus
Koutras Athanasios	University of Peloponnese, Greece
Krejcar Ondrej	University of Hradec Kralove, Czech Republic
Krinidis Stelios	Centre for Research and Technology Hellas, Greece
Kyriakides George	University of Macedonia, Greece
La Rosa Massimo	National Research Council, Italy
Lalas Antonios	Centre for Research and Technology Hellas/Information Technologies Institute, Greece

Lazaridis Georgios	Centre for Research and Technology Hellas/Information Technologies Institute, Greece
Lazic Ljubomir	UNION University, Serbia
Lederman Dror	Holon Institute of Technology, Israel
Leon Florin	Technical University of Iasi, Romania
Likas Aristidis	University of Ioannina, Greece
Likothanassis Spiros	University of Patras, Greece
Livieris Ioannis	University of Patras, Greece
Lo Bosco Giosuè	University of Palermo, Italy
Logofatu Doina	Frankfurt University of Applied Sciences, Germany
Longo Luca	Technological University of Dublin, Ireland
Maghool Samira	University of Milan, Italy
Maglogiannis Ilias	University of Piraeus, Greece
Magoulas George	University of London, Birkbeck College, UK
Magri Luca	Politecnico di Milano, Italy
Makris Christos	University of Patras, Greece
Malialis Kleanthis	University of Cyprus, Cyprus
Maragoudakis Manolis	Ionian University, Greece
Marano Giuseppe Carlo	Politecnico di Torino, Italy
Margaritis Konstantinos	University of Macedonia, Greece
Martins Nuno	NOS Inovação SA, Portugal
Melnik Andrew	Bielefeld University, Germany
Menychtas Andreas	University of Piraeus, Greece
Mezaris Vasileios	Centre for Research and Technology Hellas, Greece
Michailidis Iakovos	Centre for Research and Technology Hellas, Greece
Mitianoudis Nikolaos	Democritus University of Thrace, Greece
Morán Antonio	University of León, Spain
Moutselos Konstantinos	University of Piraeus, Greece
Muhr David	Johannes Kepler University Linz, Austria
Müller Wilmuth	Fraunhofer IOSB, Germany
Munk Michal	Constantine the Philosopher University in Nitra, Slovakia
Mylonas Phivos	National Technical University of Athens, Greece
Nikiforos Stefanos	Ionian University, Greece
Ntalampiras Stavros	University of Milan, Italy
Oprea Mihaela	Petroleum-Gas University of Ploiesti, Romania
Papadopoulos Symeon	Centre for Research and Technology Hellas/Information Technologies Institute, Greece
Papadourakis Giorgos	Hellenic Mediterranean University, Greece
Papaioannou Vaios	University of Patras, Greece
Papaleonidas Antonios	Democritus University of Thrace, Greece
Papastergiopoulos Christoforos	Centre for Research and Technology Hellas/Information Technologies Institute, Greece
Papatheodoulou Dimitris	KIOS Research and Innovation Center of Excellence, Cyprus
Passalis Nikolaos	Aristotle University of Thessaloniki, Greece

Paulus Jan	Nuremberg Institute of Technology, Germany
Pérez Daniel	University of León, Spain
Perikos Isidoros	University of Patras, Greece
Pimenidis Elias	University of the West of England, UK
Pintelas Panagiotis	University of Patras, Greece
Prada Miguel Ángel	Universidad de León, Spain
Pradat-Peyre Jean-François	Paris Nanterre University and LIP6, France
Psathas Anastasios	Panagiotis Democritus University of Thrace, Greece
Racz Andras	Ericsson Research, Hungary
Rankovic Dragica	UNION University, Serbia
Reitmann Stefan	TU Bergakademie Freiberg, Germany
Rosso Marco Martino	Politecnico di Torino, Italy
Ryjov Alexander Lomonosov	Moscow State University, Russia
Sarafidis Michail	National Technical University of Athens, Greece
Scheele Stephan	Fraunhofer IIS/University of Bamberg, Germany
Scherrer Alexander	Fraunhofer ITWM, Germany
Seferis Manos	National Technical University of Athens, Greece
Serrano Will	University College London, UK
Shi Lei	Durham University, UK
Siccardi Stefano	University of Milan, Italy
Spyrou Evaggelos	Technological Educational Institute of Sterea Ellada, Greece
Staiano Antonino	University of Naples Parthenope, Italy
Stamate Daniel	Goldsmiths, University of London, UK
Stefanopoulou Aliki	Centre for Research and Technology Hellas, Greece
Stucchi Diego	Politecnico di Milano, Italy
Stylianou Nikolaos	Aristotle University of Thessaloniki, Greece
Theocharides Theo	University of Cyprus, Cyprus
Theodoridis Georgios	Aristotle University of Thessaloniki, Greece
Timplalexis Christos	Centre for Research and Technology Hellas/Information Technologies Institute, Greece
Trakadas Panagiotis	National and Kapodistrian University of Athens, Greece
Treur Jan	VU Amsterdam, The Netherlands
Trovò Francesco	Politecnico di Milano, Italy
Tsadiras Athanasios	Aristotle University of Thessaloniki, Greece
Tsaknakis Christos	Democritus University of Thrace, Greece
Van-Horenbeke Franz Alexander	Free University of Bozen-Bolzano, Italy
Versaci Mario	University of Reggio Calabria, Italy
Vidnerová Petra	Czech Academy of Sciences, Czech Republic
Vilone Giulia	Technological University Dublin, Ireland
Vonitsanos Gerasimos	Ionian University, Greece
Votis Kostas	Centre for Research and Technology Hellas, Greece

Contents – Part II

Machine Learning Modeling /Feature Selection

Social Media, Sentiment Analysis/Natural Language - Text Mining

Time Series Modeling/Transfer Learning

Contents – Part I

Deep Learning - Convolutional

Deep Learning - Recurrent/Reinforcement

Energy Streams Modeling

Evolutionary/Biologically Inspired Modeling and Brain Modeling

Fuzzy Modeling and IoT

A Communication Data Layer
for Distributed Neuromorphic Systems

András Veres⬤, Péter Hága$^{(\boxtimes)}$⬤, András Rácz⬤, Tamás Borsos⬤,
and Zsolt Kenesi⬤

Ericsson Research, Budapest, Hungary
{andras.veres,peter.haga,andras.racz,tamas.borsos,
zsolt.kenesi}@ericsson.com

Abstract. The proliferation of AI into everyday devices is a major trend today. This trend combined with the increasing amount of different AI hardware architectures and software frameworks imposes significant challenges when we want to interconnect such AI-based devices into single, large AI-driven distributed system. This paper addresses one key challenge which is around the problem of sharing AI encoded information among components of vastly heterogeneous nature. For that end we propose a new concept called Neuromorphic Data Layer, which can bridge various internal AI data representations in a communication channel-friendly way. The proposed methods are also stress tested in a distributed industrial robotic control & training use-case where all components are state-of-the-art devices, have some form of AI computation and they are interconnected over wireless technologies using the proposed Neuromorphic Data Layer.

Keywords: Neuromorphic computing · Distributed AI · IoT · Wireless networks · Vector symbolic architectures

1 Introduction

Distribution of AI systems into communicating, but physically separate components is going to be a major step in the evolution of AI. This trend is driven by the penetration of AI into edge devices, as well as data centers. Distribution will enable new types of applications, where distinct AI sub-tasks, including sensing, reasoning, planning and control will no longer need to be physically integrated to the same device. Another benefit of distribution is that computation can be scaled-out into large number of devices potentially.

Such distribution brings significant challenges to the interconnecting communication technologies. The most straightforward solution would be to encode neuron activations of an AI component's output layer into data packets and add a packet header pointing to the destination AI component's input neural layer. In case of a neuromorphic system, that means that the output spikes of a neuron population are transmitted with some addressing, like Address Event

© IFIP International Federation for Information Processing 2022
Published by Springer Nature Switzerland AG 2022
I. Maglogiannis et al. (Eds.): AIAI 2022, IFIP AICT 647, pp. 3–16, 2022.
https://doi.org/10.1007/978-3-031-08337-2_1

Representation (AER). While such method offers high level of flexibility and has the obvious benefit of being transparent to the AI logic, in practice, it is more suitable as a chip-to-chip rather than a device-to-device protocol.

This paper introduces a concept for an AI-specific communication layer called the Neuromorphic Data Layer (NDL) in Sect. 2. This new layer is compatible with various AI frameworks and it can be implemented using neuromorphic computing and can be integrated with the application logic natively. NDL should allow various types of information representations, here we propose two interfaces or APIs. One is a raw event communication API (E-API) and the other is a so-called symbolic representation API (S-API). The symbolic representation API is based on the concepts of High-Dimensional Computing and Vector Symbolic Architectures [1,2]. We argue that the symbolic S-API has numerous benefits, from allowing to interconnect heterogeneous frameworks, as well as offering ways for the application to adapt to communication impairments.

A real-life, distributed prototype based on the proposed NDL concept is presented in Sect. 3. The demonstrated application is an industrial use-case, where a person trains a robot using hand gestures in-front of an event camera emitting spikes. The camera input is processed by an Intel Loihi neuromorphic chip, which also implements the S-API of the NDL to interface over a wireless connection with a neuromorphic component representing a central control logic built using Neural Engineering Framework (NEF) [3]. To show the flexibility of the NDL concept, we use the NDL S-API to control an industrial robotic arm using symbolic-encoded commands and we also integrate raw spike communication from a small neuromorphic IoT sensor. For all inter-device communication we used wireless technologies.

Practical considerations for implementing parts of the application and the NDL on Intel Loihi architecture [4] are presented in Sect. 4. We conclude the paper with empirical observations and numerical results about the performance of the system in Sect. 5.

2   Neuromorphic Data Layer

Besides the actual application logic and the communication layer there are numerous tasks a distributed neuromorphic system needs to implement. We can collect many of these tasks into a single layer called the Network/IoT Layer (Fig. 1), and should include security, device management, orchestration, data sharing, etc. In a neuromorphic system these should be implemented in neuromorphic computation friendly fashion.

In this paper we focus on the problem of data sharing between components and introduce the Neuromorphic Data Layer (NDL). For the purpose of our distributed neuromorphic application, we defined two types of data APIs for the NDL: a raw event E-API and a symbolic representation S-API.

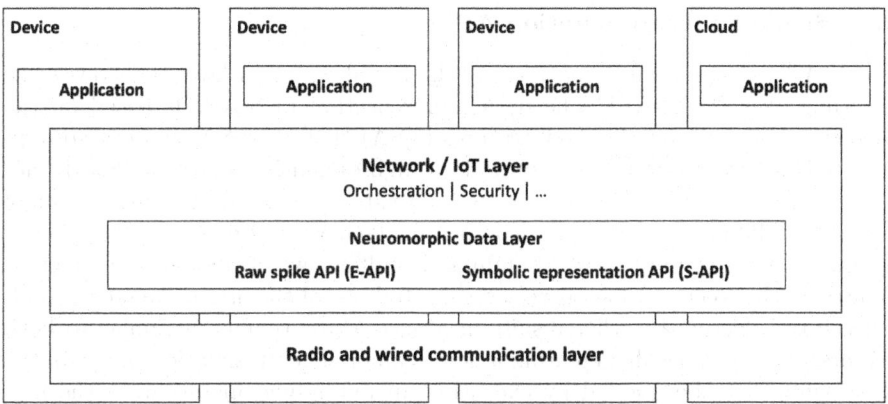

Fig. 1. Conceptual architecture of a wireless distributed neuromorphic system. The physically separated devices share information by using the two representation APIs offered by the Neuromorphic Data Layer.

2.1 Raw Spike API

The E-API interconnects two endpoints of communicating neural networks in a completely application transparent way. Neurons are identified by addresses, and the timing can be implicitly defined as the time of transmission, similar to Address Event Representation (AER). Spikes generated at the same time can be bundled together to reduce packetization overhead.

One drawback of raw spike transmission is that it requires both the sending and the receiving AI components to encode spike patterns exactly the same way. In reality, there are numerous ways how different AI frameworks, chips, sensors encode information, and they have good reasons to differ significantly. For example, a simple motion sensor may encode information as a rate of spikes, but an event camera encodes visual information in a spatio-temporal way. Other frameworks, for example the NEF [3], uses a specific way of encoding values as a combination of postsynaptic current activities of an entire neuron ensemble (via so-called tuning curves).

Another aspect of raw spike-based communication is the impact on the communication medium itself. A radio-based technology can operate best if the traffic is predictable and the application can tolerate some level of loss, jitter or latency [5]. In contrast, a real-time neuromorphic system can show high degree of burstiness due to its event driven nature and can be sensitive to either losses or delays. There may need to be some kind of adaptation to network conditions on the application-side similar to the one TCP/IP provides as well. The network may also have mechanisms to request the application's preferred way of treatment by the network.

2.2   Symbolic Representation API

The S-API represents information on a higher abstraction level than raw spike encoding over the E-API. The data representation in S-API is based on the theory of Vector Symbolic Architectures (VSA) [1,2]. In VSA symbols are represented as (usually random) vectors in a high-dimensional space. VSA defines a similarity metric, such that any two unrelated (randomly assigned) symbol vectors will be highly non-similar (perpendicular). VSA also defines a number of operations such as binding and bundling. Bundling two symbol vectors together creates a third vector, which is very similar to both of the original vectors. Binding the two vectors together results in a new vector that is dissimilar to both vectors, thereby basically, creating a new symbol. The information pieces in the new symbol can be queried by executing an unbinding operation on the new symbol. VSAs have been used in the context of robotics [6] and visual analysis [7].

In the context of communicating AI agents, we apply VSA as a means of a) representing information to be communicated as symbols, b) creating communication data structures as a single VSA symbol from various pieces of VSA encoded information (via binding). On the other end of the communication link the receiving AI agent reverses the previous steps by disassembling the VSA symbol into pieces (unbinding) and decodes the information from individual VSA encoded symbols.

When the sender agent wants to send a piece of data, it uses an internal representation E. The internal representation may depend on the hardware and software frameworks used. For example, an internal state variable may be a represented as the spiking rate of a neuron, delay between spikes or even a collective spiking pattern of a population of neurons.

Regardless of the type of internal representation, there needs to be a function G, which translates the internal representations E_i to a distinct symbolic representations S_i in the symbolic space:

$$S_i = G(E_i). \tag{1}$$

The sender packs symbolic encoded data pieces into a single VSA vector: $V = H(S_1, ..., S_n)$, which is then used for transmission. If both G and H are invertible, the receiver is able to decode each internal state. H can be implemented in various ways, it may for example, use a unique symbol T for each data type. For example T_{temp} to represent temperature, T_{pos} to represent positions. Then H may take the following form:

$$V = H(S_1, ..., S_n) = \sum (T_i \otimes S_i), \tag{2}$$

where $\otimes$ represents the VSA binding operator, and $\sum$ represents the repetitive use of the VSA bundling operator $\oplus$.

The destination agent receives V', which may include errors introduced by the communication channel. Such errors may manifest as bit erasures or additions or in case of non-binary VSA representations, it may add real or complex valued noise on the VSA vector dimensions, e.g., when using HRR or F-HRR [1]. If the communication channel errors can be modeled as a random error symbol Z bundled (e.g., dimension-based add, or phase shift) on top of the original symbol, then the received symbol will still be VSA-similar to the original due to the nature of the bundle operation:

$$V' = V \oplus Z \approx V \tag{3}$$

This way the receiver can unbind individual T_i data types and recover the sent symbol S_i:

$$R_i = T_i \oslash V' \quad \text{and} \quad R_i \approx S_i, \tag{4}$$

where $\oslash$ is the VSA unbinding operator and "$\approx$" means that the decoded vector R_i is similar to the encoded S_i when compared using the VSA similarity metric (e.g., Hamming-distance or cosine similarity). At this step the receiver can use an associative clean-up memory [8] to remove noise.

In practice, there are limitations of how much communication error can be tolerated without symbol misinterpretation. We present an empirical study in Sect. 5 showing the impact of radio channel errors in a testbed.

In the final step, the receiver decodes the information stored in S_i into its own format of representation. With notation:

$$E_i^{rec} = G^{rec}(S_i). \tag{5}$$

Even though the information encoded in E_i and E_i^{rec} are the same, their way of representation may be different: G^{rec} may be a completely different function than G. This last step is another important feature of the S-API, as it allows devices using various computational architectures to use the same S-API for communication, they only need to implement their respective G and G^{rec} functions.

2.3 Encoding of Integer Valued State Variables

Probably the most typical data type that applications exchange are integer valued variables, or data structures constructed from integer values. If using the S-API, the application needs to encode its internal integer representation to S-API compatible VSA symbols. Considering that applications may use different internal frameworks, such encoding and decoding may have very different implementation complexities.

From a theoretical point of view there are multiple ways an x integer value may be mapped to a VSA vector. We consider three different assignment methods: Spatial Semantic Pointers (SSPs) [9], VSA permutation and random assignment. In case of SSPs, S_x symbols can be derived from a single basis vector B by self-binding it $x - 1$ times:

$$S_x = B \otimes B \otimes ... \otimes B \qquad (B \text{ appears x times}) \tag{6}$$

The above calculation can be extended to encode fractional values as well [10].

The permutation based transformation also requires a single basis vector B, on which a VSA binding operation is performed multiple times.

$$S_x = p^x B. \tag{7}$$

Since permutation can take the form of circular shifting of B, this method is fairly simple to implement on neuromorphic hardware. From a communication point of view both SSP and permutation methods have the advantage that only the B basis vector has to be shared between the sender and the receiver.

The third way is probably the simplest which involves defining a random vector for each integer value. This method provides greater flexibility in customizing the used symbol vectors according to the requirements of the used communication channel. For example, we can restrict the vectors to have exactly n number of 1s randomly placed ($n << L$):

$$S_x \in \{0,1\}^L, \quad \text{where} \quad S_x^T \times S_x = n. \tag{8}$$

The downside of this method is that all the symbols need to be shared (instead of a single basis vector) between the sender and receiver before starting their communication.

2.4 Practical Integer Encoding and Decoding on Neuromorphic Hardware

In case of our Loihi-based spiking neural network (SNN) implementation we apply the following method to encode and decode x to and from S_x. First we encode the x number into a one-hot encoded X vector (i.e., in a form of $X = [0,0,\ldots,0,1,0,\ldots,0]$, where all the values are 0 except the 1 standing in the xth position of the vector). In this case the x number can be encoded into S_x simply by:

$$V = M \times X = S_x, \quad \text{where} \quad M = [S_1, S_2, \ldots, S_n]. \tag{9}$$

The one-hot encoded X selects the appropriate S_x symbol from the M encoding matrix or, in other words, selects the xth column of the M matrix that represents the x number. In our Loihi-based implementation x is one-hot encoded by a neuron layer, so the M encode matrix can be directly mapped to the neural connectivity matrix between the neuron layer representing x and an output neuron layer representing the encoded value V. The V vector can be transmitted directly or as part of a complex symbol, see Eq. (2).

As the destination agent receives V' (instead of V) due to transmission errors the decoding process has to select the best candidate out of the possible S_i symbols. By applying the M^T transpose of the encode matrix to the received V' vector we get

$$D = M^T \times V', \tag{10}$$

where D vector contains the complementary Hamming-distance values of the received V' and all the possible S_i symbols. Elements of D indicate a weight of how many 1s are matching between the V' received vector and the S_i symbols. The best candidate for the transmitted x value is the index of the maximum value of elements of D according to our X definition. By selecting the most similar symbol

$$x = \arg\max(D) \tag{11}$$

we receive the transmitted x value.

The presented decoding method can be easily implemented on the Loihi hardware by using a single neural layer connected to the neurons representing the received vector V' elements where the connection matrix is defined by the M^T matrix and a winner take all algorithm is used to select the neuron with highest activity.

3   Distributed Neuromorphic Prototype System

Using the previously defined Data Layer APIs we built an end-to-end distributed neuromorphic industrial use-case prototype. Our motivation was to prove that E-API and S-API can be used in a practical real-life scenario, and also to be able to perform empirical studies and gain experience. For that purpose, our prototype system was designed to contain highly heterogeneous components: sensors, compute resources, actuators. We also selected various AI platforms and also non-AI components to show that the Data Layer can solve the interconnection of such components efficiently. The overall architecture of the system and photos showing parts of the end-to-end system are shown in Fig. 2.

3.1   End-to-End Use-Case

In the implemented use-case a human operator trains a robotic arm by using hand gestures. First, the operator shows the robot what position to take (for simplicity limited to a 2D plane), and the robot mirrors the operator's hand in real-time. Rotation of the palm is translated into the robot gripper's similar orientation. When the desired position and pose are achieved, the operator can command the system (using a gesture) to store the exact position and pose in its memory. The operator can switch among real-time tracking, storing and replaying at any time.

The implementation is distributed into several, wirelessly interconnected components. The operator holds a small IoT device containing an LED active marker emitting sequences of high-rate (several kHz) light impulses and an inertial measurement unit (IMU). The IMU feeds a small neuromorphic network on board and transmits spike-encoded orientation data over the air using E-API.

The LED marker impulse trains are picked up by an iniVation DVXplorer DVS camera [11], which feeds a Kapoho Bay neuromorphic compute device containing 2 Intel Loihi chips [4,12]. The Loihi logic identifies the LED marker impulse trains, determines the operator's hand position, encodes the 2D coordinates as a bundle of two-coordinate VSA symbols and transmits them using the symbolic S-API. The Loihi logic integrates all these functions into a single

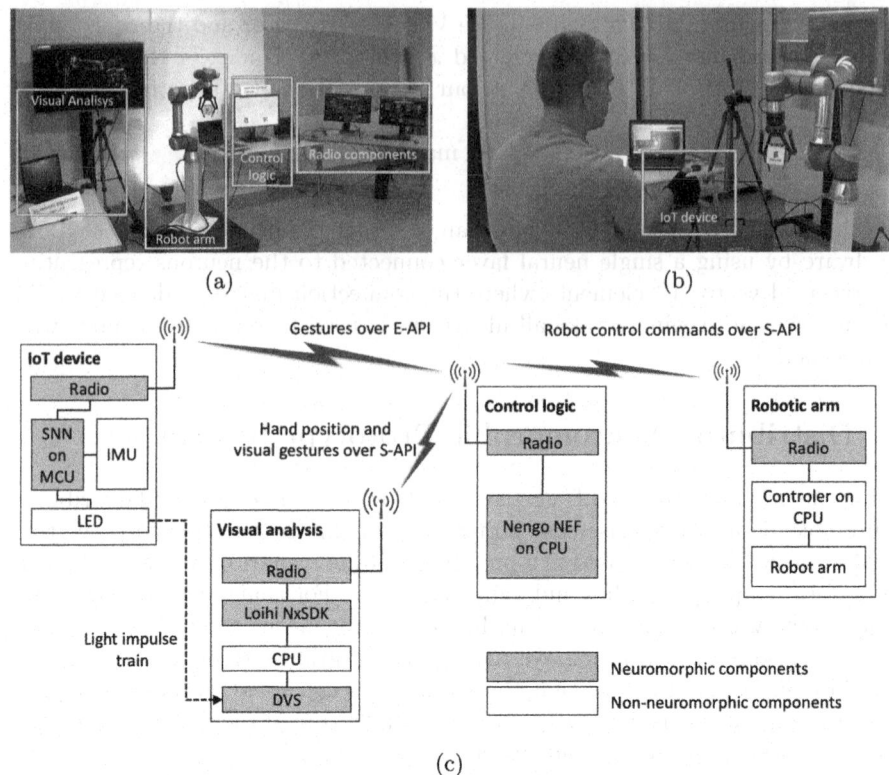

(a)   (b)

(c)

Fig. 2. The architecture of the end-to-end demonstration system and its physical realization in our lab: (a) the system overview with the main components highlighted, (b) a snapshot when the robot is controlled by the operator. The IoT device is embedded into the operator's glove, and (c) the system architecture is which the components running neuromorphic code are denoted with grey color. The content and the representation API of the radio messages are presented.

neural network. The S-API part was based on the description we explained in Sect. 2.2.

A central control logic receives both the IMU data as well as the position data in real-time. This central control logic runs a complex Nengo [13] based code. The Nengo logic architecture is shown in Fig. 3. The principle of operation takes ideas from Spaun, a functional large-scale model of the brain [14]. The position, IMU and other inputs received over S-API are placed on a state ensemble ("data bus") first. Action selection is performed by weighing the utility of possible actions and selecting one using the basal-ganglia-thalamus circuit model [15]. The actions are gated on the "bus" and buffered on the output using gated associative memory circuits. The output control parameters (arm position and

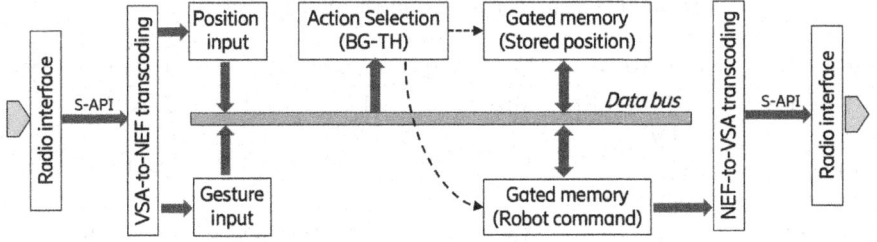

Fig. 3. Control logic in Nengo.

manipulator orientation) are then encoded symbolically and transmitted towards the robotic arm using the S-API.

The robotic arm is an industrial grade Universal Robots UR5 robot arm [16], which decodes the parameters and issues the commands directly to the arm hardware controller. The arm does not contain AI components (except an S-API capable radio and decoder), it exemplifies a traditional device communicating with neuromorphic counterparts.

3.2 Heterogeneity Aspects of the Prototype System

The system contains several devices and functional components (Table 1). These components show high degree of heterogeneity regarding their way of operation, complexity, communication requirements and internal architecture as well.

The first column lists the physically separate devices. Each contains several sub-components, but from a Data Layer point of view, they can be seen as one (albeit complex) device.

The second column shows the principal way of operation of the devices. The IoT device and the robot are regular non-AI components, even though they may send and receive AI encoded data. On the other hand, the visual analysis device contains two neuromorphic components: DVS and Loihi. The control logic is based on the Nengo Neuromorphic Framework [13] running on a PC. The robotic arm contains a regular PC-based controller and the physical UR5 robotic arm. The third column shows the component's way of operation, in particular whether the device's primary computational mode is neuromorphic or not. The fourth column shows that information is encoded in different ways in all components.

Finally, the last column shows how the component communicates with its peers. The control logic is the most complex in this regard, as it uses both the E and S-APIs, and it sends and also receives data over these APIs.

Table 1. Components used in the demonstration.

Device	Operation	Neuromorphic	Encoding	Data layer API
IoT device	MCU + LED + IMU	Mixed	Delay based spike	E-API
Visual analysis	DVS + Loihi NxSDK	Yes	Raw spike, one-hot	S-API
Control logic	Nengo NEF	Yes	NEF ensembles	E/S-API
Robotic arm	CPU + UR5	No	Cartesian coord. system	S-API

4   Visual Analysis and Data Layer on Loihi

The compute part of the visual analysis component presented in the previous section is implemented on the Intel Loihi neuromorphic chip. Our implementation ranges from the injection of the event camera spikes into the Loihi, through the computing of the position of the IoT device, to the transforming of the position data into the radio conform VSA vector. The resulting VSA vector is then transmitted to the control logic component by a radio unit.

Implementing a concrete algorithm in the Loihi chip needs practical considerations to fit the problem with the chip's resource constraints like the total number of neurons assigned to a neurocore or the total number of synaptic states mapped to the cores [4].

The details of the implementation logic is presented in Fig. 4. The input data and the processing logic are distributed into separated neurocores. To fit the processing logic into a Loihi chip the full camera resolution (640×480) is re-scaled and cropped to 120×120 pixels. The input data is then split into 36 sub-regions containing 20×20 pixels each and their processing is mapped to separated neurocores. Each sub-region determines the estimated position of the LED by integrating the incoming spikes per pixel. The integrated pixels are connected into a regional R_x and R_y flattening neuron layer (residing on the same neurocores). These regional R_x and R_y layers are connected to a global X and Y flattening layer (located on a dedicated neurocore). The global flattening layer is responsible to compute the final numerical result (the x and y coordinates of the LED) needs to be communicated to the other devices. In these flattening layers (containing 120 neurons each) we use lateral inhibition between the neurons to shape the resulting information into a one-hot encoded representation of the coordinates. By the construction of the neural layers we ensure that neurons representing the x, y coordinate values belonging together are spiking simultaneously.

The neurons of the x and y global flattening layers are mapped to the single S-API neural layer consisting 1000 neurons matching the dimension number of the VSA space we use in the communication. This way we create a multi-dimensional S-API interface in which we simultaneously encode and transmit both coordinate values. We generate M_x and M_y encoding matrices for both

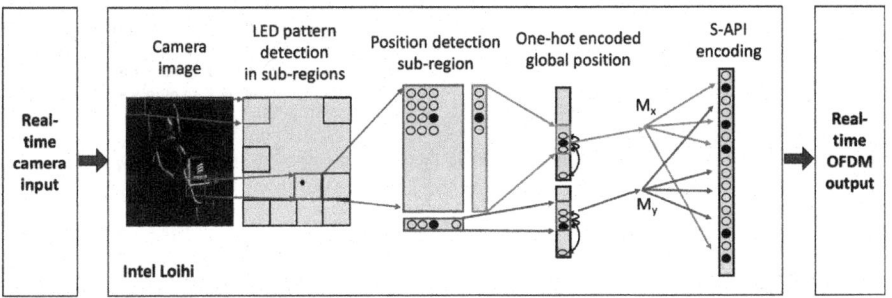

Fig. 4. Processing flow from the real-time camera input through the neuromorphic compute steps running on the Loihi chip to the real-time radio output.

the x and y coordinates separately in which each one-hot encoded coordinate is mapped to a vector containing altogether 20 pieces of 1s at randomly selected positions as we discussed in Sect. 2.4. The one-hot encoded coordinate values correspond to the single neurons of the x or y flattening layer, the joint VSA space corresponds to the S-API neural layer. The M_x and M_y encode matrices, as the connection matrices, map the x and y flattening neural layers to the same S-API neural layer.

Finally the activity of the S-API neurons are collected and translated into a binary representation to be transmitted in a communication channel. The collection of the neural activities can rely on a timer that starts counting from the first spike after the last message transmission or on counting the spiking neurons and use this as a trigger to start the transmission and to reset the spike counters to zero. The parameters of the neurons of the S-API layer are set in a way that the information is carried by only a single spike firing per neuron and the spikes fired by different neurons are firing at the same time (in the same time-step) synchronously. Thus the communication component will be able to transmit these matching spikes simultaneously.

On the receiver side, the radio module decodes the radio signal as a received joint VSA symbol and injects that over the S-API to a Loihi input layer containing 1000 neurons (the received VSA vector). The receiver neurons are configured to have fast decay to ensure that the neurons are spiking simultaneously on each received VSA vector and consecutive transmissions do not mix. The receiving S-API neural layer is connected to two application level neural layers (one for processing x and one for y coordinate values) through their pre-shared M_x^T and M_y^T matrices used as connection matrices between the neural layers. This way the x and y values are retrieved separately after a winner take all algorithm selects the most similar symbols to the received ones.

5   Empirical Results

Next, two performance related aspects are investigated of the end-to-end prototype. One aspect was the symbol decoding error over various radio physical layer

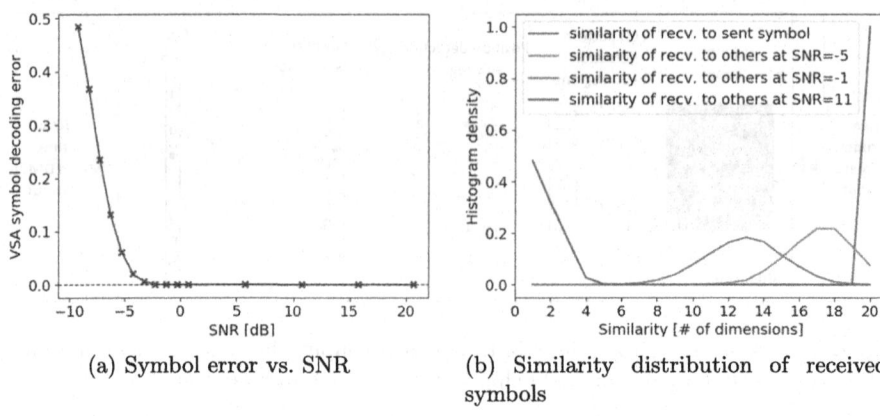

(a) Symbol error vs. SNR

(b) Similarity distribution of received symbols

Fig. 5. VSA symbol decoding performance

implementations. We custom built two physical layers specifically for the transmission of E-API and S-API data: an Orthogonal Frequency-Division Multiplexing (OFDM) and an Ultra-Wideband (UWB) radio. The VSA symbol decoding error at different measured Signal to Noise Ratio (SNR) levels are shown in Fig. 5a for the case of binary encoded VSA over OFDM. This communication link is used to transfer the human hand's coordinates as detected by the neuromorphic camera and sent towards the central control logic. If a symbol decoding error happens over this link, it can result in a wrong position, impacting the complete robot control application. As we see in Fig. 5a the detection is completely error free in a large part of the SNR range and starts to degrade only when operating well below the noise level.

The reason for the decoding degradation can be observed in Fig. 5b, which shows that the similarity of the received symbol to all other symbols increases as the SNR decreases making it more difficult to decide on the correct symbol.

The other investigated aspect was the latency budget in the system. The visual analysis in the Loihi implementation can be subdivided into several latency contributors: the LED light train integration took 10 ms, the position decision and VSA encoding was done in 5 ms, altogether the Loihi component took approximately 15 ms. The OFDM radio transmission took around 10 ms, while the UWB was slower, around 50 ms. For the Nengo based code we could not use HW accelerator (we only had one Loihi), so we had to trade-off between position noise and latency, due to the relatively large size of the Nengo network.

Overall, our observation was that the system was fairly robust. Symbol decoding errors were rare, and the control-loop felt fairly responsive even though we did not have the resources and time to optimize for neither in this early prototype. We argue that NDL is flexible enough to build a wide range of practical distributed neuromorphic systems.

6   Conclusion

The Neuromorphic Data Layer serves as a native communication layer for distributed and heterogeneous neuromorphic applications by defining two APIs E and S-API. Devices based on heterogeneous architectures can use these APIs to exchange information regardless of their internal data representation. We presented a practical Loihi-based implementation of the S-API for integer variables. Our end-to-end industrial prototype demonstrates the feasibility of the proposed concepts. We believe that such a common data layer among the vastly heterogeneous neuromorphic and AI applications will be essential in the future in order to open the way to many new and interesting neuromorphic applications.

Acknowledgements. The authors would like to thank the INRC [17] making us the Loihi cloud and the Kapoho Bay device available.

References

1. Plate, T.A.: Holographic reduced representations. IEEE Trans. Neural Netw. **6**(3), 623–641 (1995)
2. Schlegel, K., Neubert, P., Protzel, P.: A comparison of vector symbolic architectures. Artif. Intell. Rev. (2021)
3. Eliasmith, C., Anderson, C.H.: Neural Engineering: Computation, Representation, and Dynamics in Neurobiological Systems. MIT Press (2004)
4. Davies, et al.: Loihi: a neuromorphic manycore processor with on-chip learning. IEEE Micro **38**(1), 82–99 (2018)
5. Borsos, T., Condoluci, M., Daoutis, M., Haga, P., Veres, A.: Resilience analysis of distributed wireless spiking neural networks. IEEE Wirel. Commun. Netw. Conf. (2022)
6. Neubert, P., Schubert, S., Protzel, P.: Learning vector symbolic architectures for reactive robot behaviours. Workshop on Machine Learning Methods for High-Level Cognitive Capabilities in Robotics Held in Conjunction with the International Conference on Intelligent Robots and Systems (IROS) (2016)
7. Neubert, P., Schubert, S., Schlegel, K., Protzel, P.: Vector semantic representations as descriptors for visual place recognition. In: Proceedings of the Robotics Science and Systems (RSS) (2021)
8. Stewart, T., Tang, Y., Eliasmith, C.: A biologically realistic cleanup memory: autoassociation in spiking neurons. Cognit. Syst. Res. (2011)
9. Komer, B., Eliasmith, C.: Efficient navigation using a scalable, biologically inspired spatial representation. In: Proceedings of the 42nd Annual Meeting of the Cognitive Science Society (2020)
10. Komer, B., et al.: A neural representation of continuous space using fractional binding. CogSci. (2019)
11. iniVation DVXplorer DVS Camera. https://inivation.com/wp-content/uploads/2021/08/2021-08-iniVation-devices-Specifications.pdf
12. Davies, et al.: Advancing neuromorphic computing with Loihi: a survey of results and outlook. Proc. IEEE **109**(5), 911–934 (2021)
13. Bekolay, T., et al.: Nengo: a python tool for building large-scale functional brain models. Front. Neuroinformatics **7** (2013)

14. Eliasmith, C., Stewart, T.C., Choo, X., Bekolay, T., DeWolf, T., Tang, Y., Rasmussen, D.: A large-scale model of the functioning brain. Science **338**, 1202–1205 (2012)
15. Stewart, T., Choo, X., Eliasmith, C.: Dynamic behaviour of a spiking model of action selection in the Basal Ganglia. In: 10th International Conference on Cognitive Modeling (2010)
16. Universal Robots UR5. https://www.universal-robots.com/products/ur5-robot/
17. Intel Neuromorphic Research Community. https://newsroom.intel.com/news/intel-announces-neuromorphic-computing-research-collaborators/

Brainstorming Fuzzy Cognitive Maps
for Camera-Based Assistive Navigation

Georgia Sovatzidi and Dimitris K. Iakovidis$^{(\boxtimes)}$

University of Thessaly, Papasiopoulou Street 2-4, 35131 Lamia, Greece
{gsovatzidi,diakovidis}@uth.gr

Abstract. Motivated by the brainstorming process of human beings, a novel learning Fuzzy Cognitive Map (FCM) model named Brainstorming Fuzzy Cognitive Map (BFCM) is proposed. The proposed model is based on a state-of-the-art optimization algorithm, named Determinative Brain Storm Optimization, which is utilized to automatically adapt the weights of the FCM structure. In this study, BFCM is applied for safe outdoor navigation of visually impaired individuals. This application ensures the avoidance of static obstacles in an unknown environment, by taking into consideration the output of an obstacle detection system based on a depth camera. The simulation results show that the proposed model can effectively assist the users to avoid static obstacles and safely reach a desired destination, and they promise a wider applicability of the model to other domains, such as robotics.

Keywords: Camera-based navigation · Fuzzy cognitive maps · Brain storm optimization · Visually impaired individuals

1 Introduction

Fuzzy Cognitive Maps (FCMs) are mathematical models introduced by Kosko [10] and contribute to model dynamic systems with uncertain information. The design of an FCM relies mostly on the input given about a decision-making problem, usually by experts, relying on their experience and knowledge on the complex system. The main advantage of this method is that they enable a qualitative description of the degree of causality among the concepts, without requiring providing accurate numerical experiments. The simplicity of FCMs has enabled their usage in numerous applications in different fields, such as in healthcare for medical decision making [7], in economics for banking purposes and business management [5], in agriculture for planting issues [8]. In addition, FCMs have been used successfully in artificial emotion research [18], in pattern recognition applications [17], in mathematics for decision analysis and operation research. The numerous model variations of FCMs are concisely reviewed in [4].

The development of an FCM model almost always relies on human knowledge [1]. To avoid dependency on human intervention, different approaches for automated learning of FCMs have been used. These learning approaches can be categorized into three

© IFIP International Federation for Information Processing 2022
Published by Springer Nature Switzerland AG 2022
I. Maglogiannis et al. (Eds.): AIAI 2022, IFIP AICT 647, pp. 17–28, 2022.
https://doi.org/10.1007/978-3-031-08337-2_2

main types: Hebbian-based, population-based and hybrid learning approaches, which are evoked from the combination of the Hebbian and population-based approaches [15]. Population-based algorithms, aiming to perform the training of FCMs, have gained the interest of many researchers. Indicative examples of such algorithms used include Evolutionary Strategies (ES), Particle Swarm Optimization (PSO), Genetic Algorithm (GA), Simulated Annealing (SA), Tabu Search (TS), Immune Algorithm, Game-based learning model, along with their modifications. Fuzzy logic, and more specifically FCMs, plays a decisive role in the formation of navigation tasks. In [12, 20], groups of autonomous mobile robots were tuned, using fuzzy logic techniques, in order to explore semi-unknown environments in simulated applications of rescue missions. In [25], FCMs were used to depict the causal relations between ship navigational risk factors, aiming to improve navigational safety. In [23], the Particle Swarm Optimization (PSO) algorithm was utilized for parameter adaptation of the presented navigational FCM, in order to reach the goal of keeping a robot moving within a specified bounded path. A Dynamic FCM combined with the Ant Colony Optimization algorithm (DFCM-ACO) was developed in [13] and evaluated in a simulation application, where adjusted robots aim to detect and rescue victims in unknown environments.

In this paper, a novel learning FCM model is introduced based on a state-of-the-art population-based algorithm named Determinative Brain Storm Optimization (DBSO) [21]. The proposed FCM, named Brainstorming Fuzzy Cognitive Map (BFCM), is inspired from the human brainstorming process. DBSO is used for the automatic adaptation of the weights of the FCM. Another novelty aspect of this work is that BFCM is applied in the context of a wearable camera-based assistive system for visually impaired individuals (VIIs) [3]. That system incorporates a depth camera and an obstacle detection system based on deep neural networks and fuzzy logic. The proposed BFCM application aims to assist VIIs to navigate safely in outdoor environments by giving them directions on how to avoid the static obstacles detected by the obstacle detection system. The remaining of this paper is organized in three sections. Section 2 provides a theoretical background description of FCMs and DBSO algorithm. Section 3 describes the BFCM camera-based navigation approach that is proposed, and the simulation results are presented in Sect. 4. Finally, Sect. 5 presents the conclusions derived from this study.

2   Theoretical Background

2.1   Fuzzy Cognitive Maps

An FCM is a fuzzy directed graph that is constructed with a series of steps. Initially, information about a knowledge domain is collected by different experts in that domain, aiming to identify the appropriate N concepts $C = \{C_1, C_2, \ldots, C_N\}$, define the weights, $w_{ij} \in E$ of the arcs connecting these concepts for $i, j \epsilon [1, N]$ and $E = [-1, 1]$, and the causal relationships among them. This process can benefit from a brainstorming process among the involved experts, as it could optimize the resulting FCM model.

The effect of one concept to the others can be negative or positive, with a fuzzy degree of causation [9]. The determination of the sign and the description of the causal relationships, using a linguistic notion follows, and then linguistic weights, such as "strong", "weak" etc., corresponding to fuzzy sets, are assigned to each arc. After that, all the linguistic values are combined by aggregation of the respective fuzzy sets, and a final single linguistic weight emerges. Finally, the real weight values are obtained, by defuzzification, which transforms the linguistic weights to a numerical value within the range $[-1, 1]$ [11].

Each concept is modeled as a linguistic variable $C_i, i = 1, 2, \ldots N$ and expresses the degree to which the concept occurs. The formulation of the calculation rule that is used to determine and update iteratively, at each time step, the values of concept is given by (1):

$$a_i^{l+1} = \mathcal{F}\left(a_i^l + \sum_{\substack{j=1 \\ j \neq i}}^{N} a_j^l \cdot w_{ij}\right) \tag{1}$$

where a^l is a state vector that represents the current state of the FCM, l counts the iterations; w_{ij} represents the weight value from node i to node j. Function $\mathcal{F}$ is sigmoidal with saturation levels -1 and 1, normalizing a_i^{l+1} within $[-1, 1]$, and contributing to the convergence of the FCM to a steady state [2, 22].

2.2 Determinative Brain Storm Optimization

Learning algorithms are mainly used to compute the fittest weights of FCMs that increase the efficiency of the model. In this paper, the proposed navigational FCM model is developed, using a state-of-the-art swarm-based algorithm, named Determinative Brain Storm Optimization (DBSO) algorithm [21], which is used for the first time for the adaptation of FCMs. DBSO is inspired from the human brainstorming process, particularly the fact that during a successful brainstorming process, a consensus is reached between participants that have similar ideas, and as a result the most appropriate solution for a given problem is determined.

DBSO algorithm proceeds in the following steps: **Step 1** represents the initialization of parameters needed and the generation of N potential solutions, called individuals and for our problem are the potential weight values. In **step 2**, k-means algorithm clusters the N individuals into $M < N$ groups. For each cluster, in **step 3**, the individual with the best fitness values (best individuals) are recorded as cluster centers and sorted ascendingly, in order to calculate the Euclidean distance and the corresponding similarity in **step 4**. Then, in **step 5** the best two individuals are identified and, their corresponding clusters are merged. In **step 6**, a new individual is generated based on one or two clusters, according to predefined criteria. In **step 7**, the generated individual is compared with the existing ones, and the one with the fittest value is kept and recorded as the most appropriate solutions to the given problem. The algorithm repeats until convergence.

3 Brainstorming Cognitive Maps

The learning approach for BFCM is performed based on the training of the weight matrix W. For that reason, the state-of-the-art DBSO algorithm is used for the minimization of

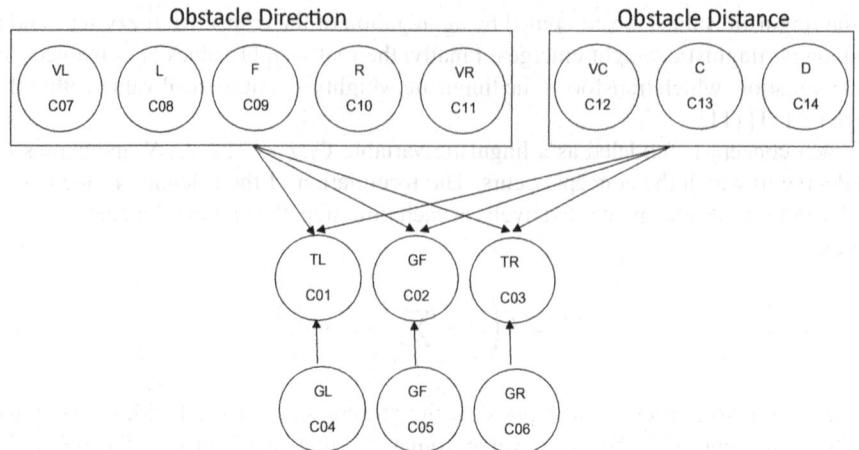

Fig. 1. Proposed BFCM structure for camera-based navigation.

the function given by (2) [16], which consequently leads to the acquisition and definition of an optimal weight matrix, proper for the design of the BFCM model.

$$\mathcal{M}(W) = \sum_{i=1}^{m} H\left(a_i^{min} - a_i\right) \left| a_i^{min} - a_i \right| + \sum_{i=1}^{m} \mathcal{H}\left(a_i - a_i^{max}\right) \left| a_i^{max} - a_i \right| \quad (2)$$

where $a_i, i = 1, \ldots, m$ are the steady state values of the output concepts, which are restricted by the user, in bounds $a_i^{min} \le a_i \le a_i^{max}, i = 1, \ldots, m$ and $\mathcal{H}$ represents the Heaviside function, given by (3):

$$\mathcal{H}(x) = \begin{cases} 0, & x < 0 \\ 1, & x \ge 0 \end{cases} \quad (3)$$

BFCM, which models the camera-based navigation for VIIs, is illustrated in Fig. 1. As it is observed, BFCM consists of fourteen concepts which are defined as follows: C01-Turn Left (TL); C02-Go Forward (GF); C03-Turn Right (TR); C04-Goal Left (GL); C05-Goal Forward (GF); C06-Goal Right (GR); C07-Very Left (VL); C08-Left (L); C09-Forward (F); C10-Right (R); C11-Very Right (VR); C12-Very Close (VC); C13-Close (C); C14-Distant (D). It has to be clarified that in Fig. 1, there is a connection between all the concepts related to Obstacle Direction (C07–C11) and the output concepts (C01–C03), as well as, between all the obstacle distance concepts (C12–C14) with the output concepts.

Considering the obstacle avoidance problem, which is under investigation, the partition of an image is presented in Fig. 2(a), along with the corresponding membership functions. The depth information of the scene is also defined, as it contributes to a greater awareness of the environment along with the risks that exist [3]. Thus, the membership functions that describe the distance between the navigator and the obstacles are presented in Fig. 2(b), where the linguistic values used are: Very Close (VC), Close (C), and Distant (D).

In order to perform the desired camera-based navigation for obstacle avoidance, an initial weight matrix (Table 1), was defined for the design of the FCM model, according to the standard approach described in Sect. 2. A. Specifically, the values of the initial weight matrix were empirically determined by opinion aggregation of experts on the assistance of VIIs, using the algebraic sum operator, and the Center of Gravity (CoG) defuzzification method. The sign and value of the causal relations, between the concepts, depend on the influences and intensity among them, and are tuned in such a way as to provide VIIs with safe directions, minimizing the risk of collision with obstacles. Thus, in the BFCM model, C04–C06 have positive weight values, related to the output concepts (C01–C03), and they are equal to 1. This means that when a destination is set, VIIs are advised to move straight forward to that destination. The relationships between (C07–C11) and (C01–C03) have both negative and positive causality; if an obstacle is detected towards a direction, BFCM proposes VIIs to avoid that direction (negative causality) and move towards another direction, which is safer, given that there is not a high risk of collision with obstacles (positive causality). For obstacle distance concepts (C12–C14) related to (C01–C03), they have negative weight values, for the same reason mentioned above, whereas the degree of causation depends on the type of distance, *e.g.*, when the obstacle is detected very close, then it has a greater negative effect to the output concepts, than being at a distance.

A part of the initial weight matrix (Table 1) is selected aiming to define the fittest optimized weight matrix that is needed for the adaptation of the BFCM and it is presented in a dashed box. This dashed box that represents the examined weight matrix includes only the non-zero input weights that are connected to each other and to the output codes; thus, they play the most decisive role to the design of the proposed FCM, and consequently to the determination of the position of VIIs. The values from the input and output concepts of the proposed model lie within the desired prespecified ranges presented in Table 2. Generally, these bounds are problem dependent.

The main goal of the paper is to ensure a safe navigation for VIIs, who have to travel from a starting point up to a predefined destination. Thus, the direction to be followed is considered to be known and given by a GPS. The new position of the entity is defined as (x', y') using basic trigonometric calculations:

$$x' = x + \cos(\varphi) \tag{4}$$

$$y' = y + \sin(\varphi) \tag{5}$$

where x, y are the previous positions and φ is the output direction angle of the BFCM, which is relative to the horizontal axis x and drives the entity towards the desired target goal, while avoiding possible obstacles, as it is presented in Fig. 3.

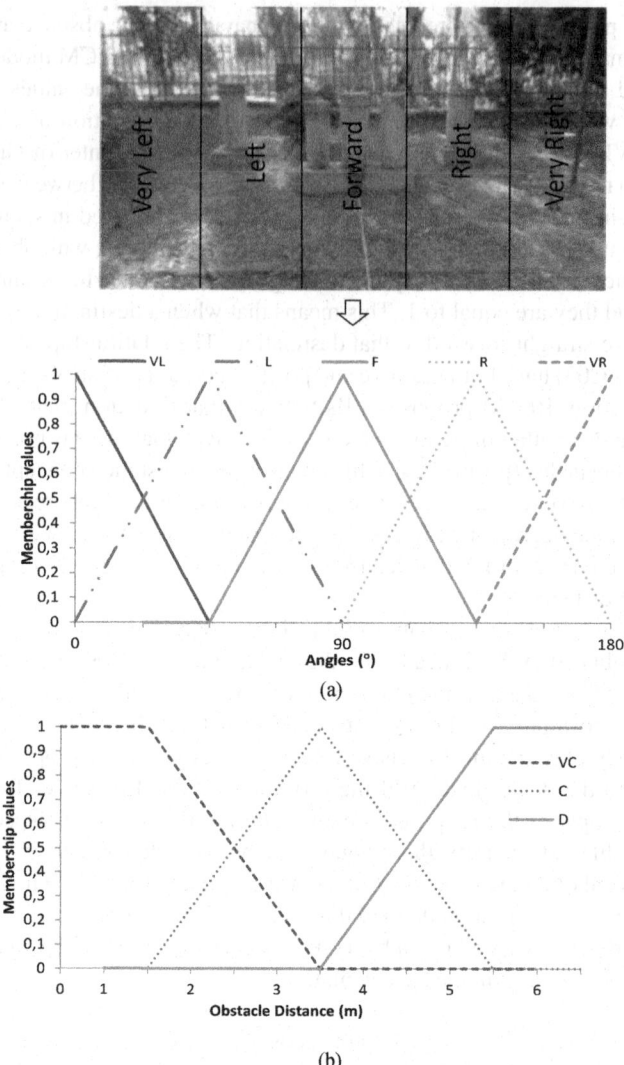

Fig. 2. Membership functions used to determine: (a) the partition of the image (upper figure) for obstacle avoidance, with linguistic values: Very Left (VL), Left (L), Forward (F), Right (R), Very Right (VR); (b) the depth information; the distance between navigator and obstacles in meters (m), using the linguistic values: Very Close (VC), Close (C), Distant (D).

DBSO is a population-based, swarm algorithm that is applied to optimize the proposed model of Fig. 1, and enhance the navigation, by defining the trajectories of a VII, after updating the nonzero weight values of the examined weight matrix, presented with a dashed box in Table 1. In this study, DBSO is performed with a population of 20 individuals, for 50 iterations, whereas the rest of the parameters of DBSO were set as suggested in [21]. DBSO tuned the weight matrix and converged to a set of optimum

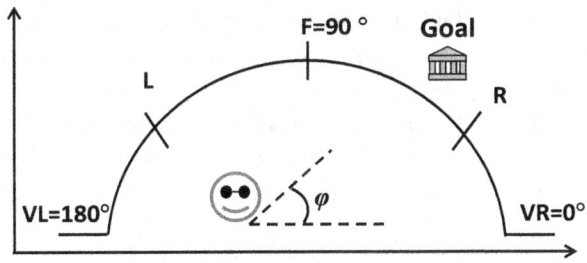

Fig. 3. The target direction concepts of BFCM.

weights, minimizing (2). As a result, an optimal weight matrix was obtained (Table 3). In addition, as it is observed, all the generated weights of Table 3 are within the ranges determined in the previous section. Compared to the initial matrix, there are differences between some weight values. In particular, the majority of weights have been modified except from $w_{10\to1}$, $w_{10\to3}$, $w_{11\to1}$, $w_{12\to2}$, $w_{12\to3}$, $w_{13\to2}$, which remained the same, as the initial ones.

Table 1. Initial weight matrix of BFCM

w	1	2	3	4	...	14
1	0	0	0	0	...	14
2	0	0	0	0	...	0
3	0	0	0	0	...	0
4	1.00	0	0	0	...	0
5	0	1.00	0	0	...	0
6	0	0	1.00	0	...	0
7	−0.45	−0.20	0.60	0	...	0
8	−0.65	−0.30	0.90	0	...	0
9	0.60	−0.90	0.60	0	...	0
10	0.90	−0.30	−0.85	0	...	0
11	0.90	−0.30	−0.55	0	...	0
12	−0.50	−0.45	−0.50	0	...	0
13	−0.60	−0.45	−0.60	0	...	0
14	−0.75	−0.70	−0.75	0	...	0

Table 2. Examined weight matrix.

$-0.75 \leq w_{7\to1} \leq -0.35$	$-0.60 \leq w_{11\to2} \leq -0.20$
$-0.50 \leq w_{7\to2} \leq -0.10$	$-0.75 \leq w_{11\to3} \leq -0.35$
$0.40 \leq w_{7\to3} \leq 1.00$	$-0.60 \leq w_{12\to1} \leq -0.20$
$-1.00 \leq w_{8\to1} \leq -0.60$	$0.40 \leq w_{12\to2} \leq 0.80$
$-0.60 \leq w_{8\to2} \leq -0.20$	$-0.60 \leq w_{12\to3} \leq -0.20$
$0.60 \leq w_{8\to3} \leq 1.00$	$-0.60 \leq w_{13\to1} \leq -0.20$
$0.55 \leq w_{9\to1} \leq 0.95$	$-0.50 \leq w_{13\to2} \leq -0.10$
$-1.00 \leq w_{9\to2} \leq -0.60$	$-0.60 \leq w_{13\to3} \leq -0.20$
$0.55 \leq w_{9\to3} \leq 0.95$	$-0.85 \leq w_{14\to1} \leq -0.45$
$0.60 \leq w_{10\to1} \leq 1.00$	$-0.85 \leq w_{14\to2} \leq -0.45$
$-0.60 \leq w_{10\to2} \leq -0.20$	$-0.85 \leq w_{14\to3} \leq -0.45$
$-0.60 \leq w_{10\to3} \leq -1.00$	$0.60 \leq w_{11\to1} \leq 1.00$

Table 3. Optimized weight matrix

w	1	2	3
7	−0.70	−0.49	0.89
8	−0.95	−0.55	0.77
9	0.71	−0.80	0.74
10	0.90	−0.49	−0.85
11	0.90	−0.47	−0.73
12	−0.38	−0.22	−0.48
13	−0.55	−0.70	−0.75
14	−0.46	0.50	−0.58

4 Experiments and Simulation Results

Simulation experiments were performed to evaluate the capacity of BFCM to provide guidance for obstacle avoidance. To assess the effect of the optimization process performed by DBSO in the navigation of the VIIs, the results of BFCM are compared to those obtained without the use of DBSO. The unoptimized model will be referred to simply as FCM. The difference between these two models relies solely on their weight matrices, as the first approach is designed in terms of the initial weight matrix, whereas the second model uses the weights presented in Table 3. The safety of the proposed model is estimated using a collision avoidance metric $c(t)$ commonly used in related studies [14, 19]:

$$c(t) = \begin{cases} 0, d_{min} \geq d_s \\ \frac{1}{d_{min}} - \frac{1}{d_s}, d_{min} < d_s \end{cases} \tag{6}$$

where d_{min} represents the closest distance of a VII to an obstacle, and d_s represents the distance to an obstacle that poses no danger for collision. For our experiments, $d_s = 2$, as the desired detection distance for the early avoidance of an obstacle according to the requirements of the visually impaired users is up to 2 m [6]. Moreover, in order to quantify the safety of $c(t)$, the first norm ($p = 1$) is calculated, according to (7), and taken as a performance criterion.

$$\|c(t)\|_p = \sqrt[p]{\left(\int c(t)^p dt\right)} \tag{7}$$

The effectiveness of the proposed method has been tested on 16 different scenarios, *i.e.*, for 16 different unknown environments that consist of static obstacles. Each scenario included a different starting position and different directions and routes with static obstacles. The results, with respect to collision avoidance metric, are summarized in Fig. 4. BFCM in Fig. 4 is represented with red-color bars, whereas green-color bars show the results of the FCM. It can be observed that BFCM is safer in all cases than original-FCM, in terms of the norm of the defined metric, with an average collision norm equal to 0.19, while FCM results to 0.33. Thus, BFCM is 73.68% safer than the original FCM.

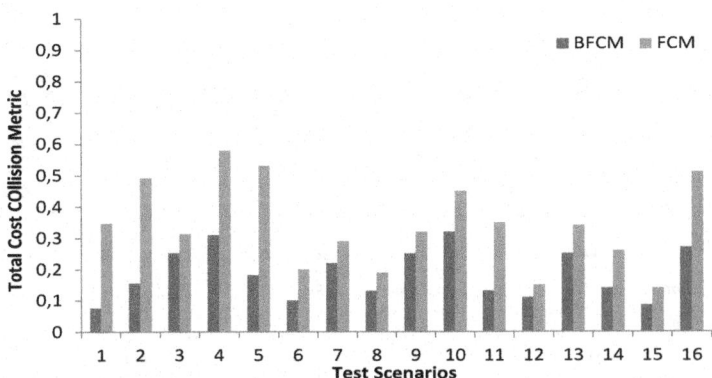

Fig. 4. Total cost of collision metric for different scenarios.

In addition, indicative simulation results of BFCM are illustrated in Fig. 5, for the first four out of the 16 different scenarios, with different starting points and destinations with target goals, which are known a priori. The results show that a VIIs efficiently manage to avoid all the obstacles and reach the final destination, which is symbolized with a miniature of a monument, in all the scenarios. However, concerning the navigation based on BFCM Fig. 5(a–d), the tuned, by the DBSO algorithm, weights contribute to a safer camera-based navigation, compared to the FCM Fig. 5(e–h), as the proposed indicates the correct directions of a route, after taking into consideration the distance between the position of the VIIs and the obstacles. On the contrary, the FCM model navigates the VII to the desired destination, with a less adaptable distance of the existing obstacles that results in the moving person approaching the obstacle very close, with the risk of colliding with it. Consequently, the navigation based on the FCM model is not so safe, as it has a higher collision risk, regarding both the calculated collision metric (Fig. 4), as well as the illustrated results of Fig. 5.

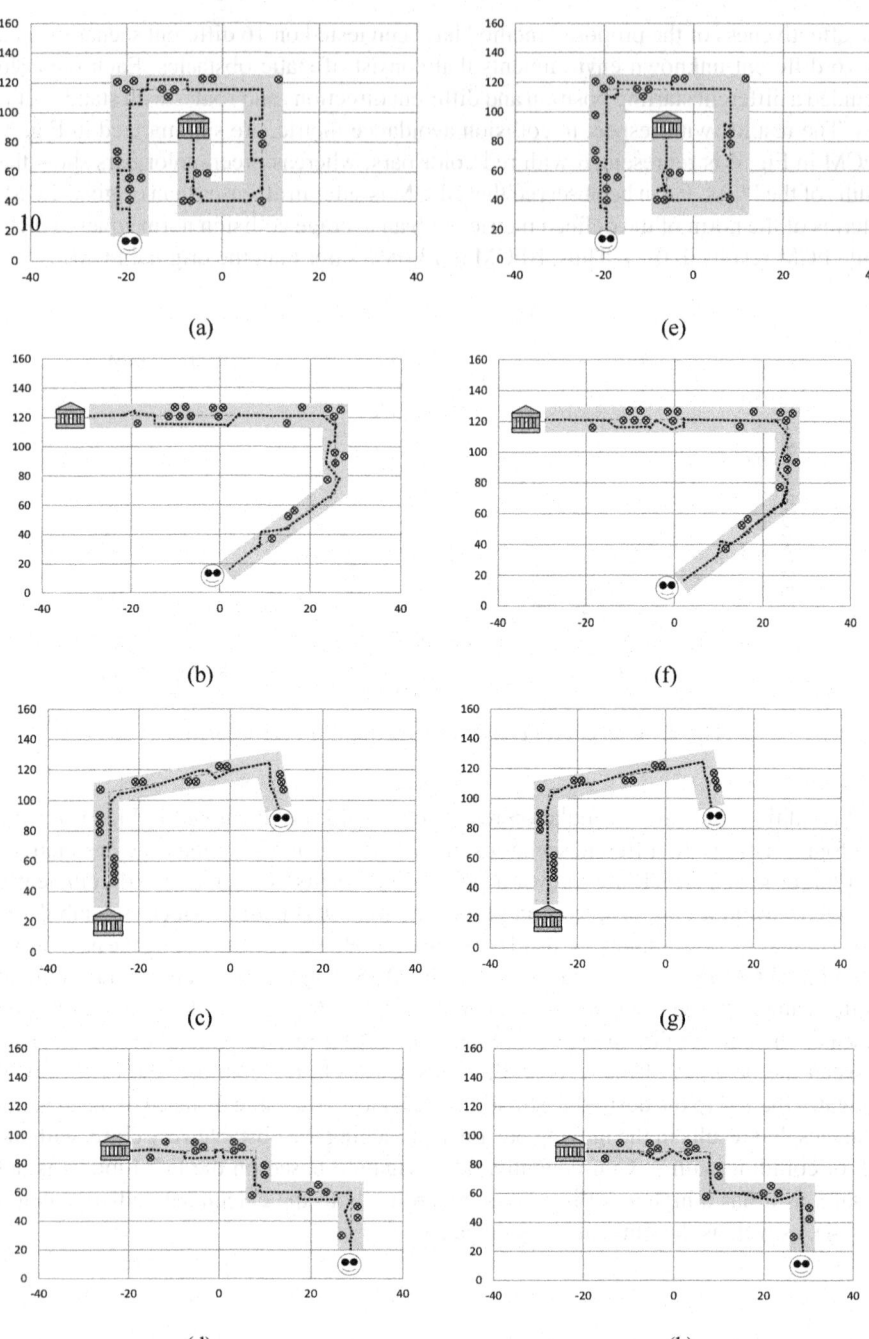

Fig. 5. Simulation results using BFCM (left) and FCM (right)

5 Conclusion

In this paper, a novel learning FCM applied as a navigational tool named Brainstorming Fuzzy Cognitive Maps (BFCM) was introduced. BFCM was created based on a state-of-the-art algorithm named Determinative Brain Storm Optimization (DBSO). The proposed model was applied for outdoor navigation of visually impaired individuals. This application contributes to the avoidance of static obstacles in unknown environments, after taking into consideration the output of an obstacle detection system based on a depth camera. The simulation results showed that the proposed approach can be used by the VIIs to effectively avoid obstacles and reach a desired destination safely. Further investigation of BFCM is needed mainly towards its capacity to adapt in dynamic scenarios, with moving obstacles, and validation of the results by human subjects in different outdoor environments. Future research directions, emerge by the application of the proposed model to other domains, where navigation is necessary for obstacle avoidance, *e.g.*, for obstacle avoidance by robots, autonomous vehicles *etc.* Further improvement of the proposed methodology could be achieved by considering additional components enhancing its robustness to uncertainties originating from different sources, *e.g.*, in the image processing stage [24].

Acknowledgment. This research has been co-financed by the European Union and Greek national funds through the Operational Program Competitiveness, Entrepreneurship and Innovation, under the call RESEARCH—CREATE—INNOVATE (project code: T1EDK-02070).

References

1. Aguilar, J.: A survey about fuzzy cognitive maps papers. Int. J. Comput. Cogn. **3**(2), 27–33 (2005)
2. Bueno, S., Salmeron, J.L.: Benchmarking main activation functions in fuzzy cognitive maps. Expert Syst. Appl. **36**(3), 5221–5229 (2009)
3. Dimas, G., Diamantis, D.E., Kalozoumis, P., Iakovidis, D.K.: Uncertainty-aware visual perception system for outdoor navigation of the visually challenged. Sensors **20**(8), 2385 (2020)
4. Felix, G., Nápoles, G., Falcon, R., Froelich, W., Vanhoof, K., Bello, R.: A review on methods and software for fuzzy cognitive maps. Artif. Intell. Rev. **52**(3), 1707–1737 (2017). https://doi.org/10.1007/s10462-017-9575-1
5. Glykas, M.: Fuzzy cognitive strategic maps in business process performance measurement. Expert Syst. Appl. **40**(1), 1–14 (2013)
6. Iakovidis, D.K., Diamantis, D., Dimas, G., Ntakolia, C., Spyrou, E.: Digital enhancement of cultural experience and accessibility for the visually impaired. In: Paiva, S. (ed.) Technological Trends in Improved Mobility of the Visually Impaired. EICC, pp. 237–271. Springer, Cham (2020). https://doi.org/10.1007/978-3-030-16450-8_10
7. Iakovidis, D.K., Papageorgiou, E.: Intuitionistic fuzzy cognitive maps for medical decision making. IEEE Trans. Inf. Technol. Biomed. **15**(1), 100–107 (2010)
8. Jayashree, L.S., Palakkal, N., Papageorgiou, E.I., Papageorgiou, K.: Application of fuzzy cognitive maps in precision agriculture: a case study on coconut yield management of southern India's Malabar region. Neural Comput. Appl. **26**(8), 1963–1978 (2015). https://doi.org/10.1007/s00521-015-1864-5

9. Kim, H.S., Lee, K.C.: Fuzzy implications of fuzzy cognitive map with emphasis on fuzzy causal relationship and fuzzy partially causal relationship. Fuzzy Sets Syst. **97**(3), 303–313 (1998)

10. Kosko, B.: Fuzzy cognitive maps. Int. J. Man-Mach. Stud. **24**(1), 65–75 (1986)

11. Lin, C.-T., Lee, C.G.: Neural Fuzzy Systems: A Neuro-Fuzzy Synergism to Intelligent Systems. Prentice Hall, Hoboken (1996)

12. Mendonça, M., Kondo, H.S., de Souza, L.B., Palácios, R.H.C., de Almeida, J.P.L.S.: Semi-unknown environments exploration inspired by swarm robotics using fuzzy cognitive maps. In: 2019 IEEE International Conference on Fuzzy Systems (FUZZ-IEEE), pp. 1–8 (2019)

13. Mendonça, M., Palácios, R.H., Papageorgiou, E.I., de Souza, L.B.: Multi-robot exploration using dynamic fuzzy cognitive maps and ant colony optimization. In: 2020 IEEE International Conference on Fuzzy Systems (FUZZ-IEEE), pp. 1–8 (2020)

14. Nair, S., Kobilarov, M.: Collision avoidance norms in trajectory planning. In: Proceedings of the 2011 American Control Conference, pp. 4667–4672 (2011)

15. Papageorgiou, E.I.: Learning algorithms for fuzzy cognitive maps—a review study. IEEE Trans. Syst. Man Cybern. Part C (Appl. Rev.) **42**(2), 150–163 (2011)

16. Papageorgiou, E.I., Parsopoulos, K.E., Stylios, C.S., Groumpos, P.P., Vrahatis, M.N.: Fuzzy cognitive maps learning using particle swarm optimization. J. Intell. Inf. Syst. **25**(1), 95–121 (2005)

17. Papakostas, G.A., Boutalis, Y.S., Koulouriotis, D.E., Mertzios, B.G.: Fuzzy cognitive maps for pattern recognition applications. Int. J. Pattern Recogn. Artif. Intell. **22**(08), 1461–1486 (2008)

18. Salmeron, J.L.: Fuzzy cognitive maps for artificial emotions forecasting. Appl. Soft Comput. **12**(12), 3704–3710 (2012)

19. Sezer, V., Gokasan, M.: A novel obstacle avoidance algorithm: "Follow the Gap Method." Robot. Auton. Syst. **60**(9), 1123–1134 (2012)

20. Soares, P.P., de Souza, L.B., Mendonça, M., Palácios, R.H., de Almeida, J.P.L.S.: Group of robots inspired by swarm robotics exploring unknown environments. In: 2018 IEEE International Conference on Fuzzy Systems (FUZZ-IEEE), pp. 1–7 (2018)

21. Sovatzidi, G., Iakovidis, D.K.: Determinative brain storm optimization. In: Tan, Y., Shi, Y., Tuba, M. (eds.) ICSI 2020. LNCS, vol. 12145, pp. 259–271. Springer, Cham (2020). https://doi.org/10.1007/978-3-030-53956-6_24

22. Tsadiras, A.K.: Comparing the inference capabilities of binary, trivalent and sigmoid fuzzy cognitive maps. Inf. Sci. **178**(20), 3880–3894 (2008)

23. Vaščák, J., Zolotová, I., Kajáti, E.: Navigation fuzzy cognitive maps adjusted by PSO. In: 2019 23rd International Conference on System Theory, Control and Computing (ICSTCC), pp. 107–112 (2019)

24. Versaci, M., Calcagno, S., Morabito, F.C.: Fuzzy geometrical approach based on unit hyper-cubes for image contrast enhancement. In: 2015 IEEE International Conference on Signal and Image Processing Applications (ICSIPA), pp. 488–493 (2015)

25. Wang, L., Liu, Q., Dong, S., Soares, C.G.: Effectiveness assessment of ship navigation safety countermeasures using fuzzy cognitive maps. Saf. Sci. **117**(2019), 352–364 (2019)

Creating a Bridge Between Probabilities and Fuzzy Sets and Its Impact on Drought Severity Assessment

Nikos Mylonas⬤, Mike Spiliotis$^{(\boxtimes)}$ ⬤, and Basil Papapdopoulos⬤

Department of Civil Engineering, DUTH, Xanthi, Greece
{mspiliot,papadob}@civil.duth.gr

Abstract. In hydrology and water resources management problems the theoretical probability distribution functions are widely used with the aim of the empirical probability function. However, it is difficult to exploit the probability functions in case that algebraic operations between random variables are required. A solution should be the motivation from the probability functions to fuzzy sets by using the fuzzy estimators. Finally based on the possibility theory the authors conclude that based on a probability distribution, a possibility distribution with the maximum specificity can be produced, that is near to the probability measure. The Reconnaissance Drought Index (RDI) was proposed to assess meteorological drought severity based on the precipitation to potential evapotranspiration ratio (P/PET). However it is difficult to express the bivariate probability density function for this ratio. Hence based on the fuzzy estimators, the analysis can be concluded to fuzzy sets, and the extension principle of fuzzy sets can provide the required ratio as fuzzy sets.

Keywords: Reconnaissance Drought Index (RDI) · Drought · Theoretical probability density function · Normal distribution · Possibility distribution · Fuzzy estimators · Consistency principle · Maximal specificity

1 Introduction

In hydrology and water resources management problems the theoretical probability distribution functions are widely used. An advantage of the probabilistic approach, as a choice to deal with the uncertainty, is the exploitation of the cumulative empirical (observed) probability distribution in order to test the goodness-of-fit for an examined theoretical probability distribution with respect to the historical sample [1].

The use of theoretical probability distribution instead of the empirical function arises from the fact that historical sample contains no many years (e.g. 40 years in Greece) whilst an event with higher return period can be included within the sample and hence, finally, probability density function are used.

© IFIP International Federation for Information Processing 2022
Published by Springer Nature Switzerland AG 2022
I. Maglogiannis et al. (Eds.): AIAI 2022, IFIP AICT 647, pp. 29–40, 2022.
https://doi.org/10.1007/978-3-031-08337-2_3

However, it is difficult to exploit the probability functions in case that algebraic operations between random variables are required. This is very useful, since the probability associated with the precipitation to potential evapotranspiration ratio (P/PET) can provide a useful information about the severity of drought.

The Reconnaissance Drought Index (RDI) can be characterized as a general meteorological index for drought assessment [2–4] with many applications. Compared with the SPI index it incorporates both precipitation and potential evapotranspiration, which are directly affected by climate change [3]. Also a strong advantage of RDI is that it offers a rational comparison of drought conditions between areas with different climatic characteristics [4]. Vangelis et al., 2011 [4] proposed a rather probabilistic approach to characterize the drought whilst the majority of the Reconnaissance Drought Index (RDI) applications used mainly simple algebraic operations. The approach of [4] can be applied only in case that normal distribution is used.

In this work a correspondence between the fuzzy sets and theoretical probability function is proposed and furthermore, this assumption is applied in order to estimate the severity of drought based on both the precipitation and the potential evapotranspiration.

Compared with work of Papadopoulos et al., 2021 [5] instead of the estimation of the mean and the standard deviation of the examined hydrological variable, here the direct transformation from probabilistic to fuzzy sets is developed.

2 Fuzzy Methodology

2.1 Fuzzy Sets

In general, if A is a function from U into the interval [0, 1], then A is called a fuzzy set.

A is convex if and only if, for every $t \in [0, 1]$ and $x_1, x_2 \in X$ it holds:

$$A(tx_1 + (1 - t)x_2) \geq \min\{A(x_1), A(x_2)\} \tag{1}$$

A is normalized if there exists $x \in X$, such that $A(x) = 1$. If A is a fuzzy set, by α-cuts $a \in (0, 1]$ we define the crisp sets:

$$A[\alpha] = \{x \in X : A(x) \geq \alpha\} \tag{2}$$

Considering the 0-cut, this can be defined as previously (Eq. 2), without the equality, that is, the zero-cut contains all the elements of the general set X, which have a membership function greater than zero.

A special kind of fuzzy sets is the fuzzy numbers. The definition of fuzzy numbers can be found in Klir and Yuan, 1995 [6]. It is proved that the membership function of a fuzzy number can be expressed as:

$$A(x) = \begin{cases} 0 & \text{for } x < \omega_1 \\ A_L(x) & \text{for } \omega_1 \leq x \leq \alpha_1 \\ 1 & \text{for } \alpha_1 \leq x \leq \alpha_2 \\ A_R(x) & \text{for } \alpha_2 \leq x \leq \omega_3 \\ 0 & \text{for } x > \omega_3 \end{cases} \tag{3}$$

where $A_L : [\omega_1, a_1] \rightarrow [0, 1]$ and $A_R : [a_2, \omega_2] \rightarrow [0, 1]$ are the left and right membership functions of the fuzzy number A. In addition, A_L is increasing and continuous from the right, and A_R is decreasing and continuous from the left [6].

The interval $[\alpha_1, \alpha_2]$ can be an interval or a point but it can not be an empty set.

Let now A and B denote fuzzy numbers and let * denote any of the four basic arithmetic operations. Then, we define a fuzzy set on $\Re$, $A*B$, by defining its α-cut, $(A*B)[a]$ as:

$$(A*B)[a] = A[a] * B[a] \qquad \text{for any} \quad a \in [0, 1]. \tag{4}$$

Among the binary arithmetic operations between the α-cuts, the interval arithmetic is applied. Here, from the fuzzy algebra we use the division and the subtraction operations

$$[\alpha, \beta] - [c, d] = [\alpha - d, \beta - c] \tag{5}$$

$$[\alpha, \beta]/[c, d] = [\alpha, \beta] \cdot \left[\frac{1}{d}, \frac{1}{c}\right] \tag{6}$$

and

$$[\alpha, \beta] \cdot [c', d'] = [\min(\alpha c', \alpha d', \beta c', \beta d'), \ \max(\alpha c', \alpha d', \beta c', \beta d')] \tag{7}$$

Finally, in conjunction with the fuzzy decomposition theorem, the following equation holds for all the fuzzy sets of the fuzzy operation (e.g. [6, 7]):

$$A * B = \cup_\alpha (A * B) \tag{8}$$

In fact, we select a significant discrete number of α-cuts, and thus, the Eq. (4) can be effectively approximated.

The question between the fuzzy sets and its relation with the conventional probability theory can be found in the field of possibility theory.

2.2 Fuzzy Estimators

Let X be a variable which takes values in a universe U and N a fuzzy set of U. Then the truth value of the fuzzy proposition "X is N" when $X = u$, $u \in U$ is defined as the value N(u) of the membership value of the fuzzy set N (see [8]),

$$T(\text{"X is N}|X=u\text{"}) = \mu_N(u).$$

Therefore, the fuzzy proposition "X is N" associates the variable X with a possibility distribution. The possibility distribution function associated with X is denoted by π_X and is defined to be the membership function μ_N of N.

$$\Pi_X \equiv \mu_N$$

So, the possibility $\Pi_X(u)$ that $X = u$ is postulated to be equal to the value $\mu_N(u)$ of the membership function of N at u,

$$\Pi_X(u) = \mu_N(u)$$

Definition 1. *The possibility measure or simply the possibility of a subset $A \subset U$ for a possibility distribution Π_X associated with the variable X with universe U is defined as the supremum of the possibilities of its elements* (see [8, 9]).

$$\Pi_X(A) = sup\{\Pi_X(u), \quad u \in A\} \tag{9}$$

In the case of finite sets, the possibility measure is the maximum of the possibilities of its elements

$$\Pi_X(A) = max\{\Pi_X(u), \quad u \in A\} \tag{10}$$

The degree of necessity of A for the possibility distribution Π_X is defined as (see [9]),

$$Ness_X(A) = 1 - \Pi_X(A') \tag{11}$$

According to Zadeh [10] from this definition follows that $Ness_X(A)$ is a measure of its "*certainty*". According to [9]:

Proposition 1. *For a continuous possibility distribution Π_X for which*

$$\Pi_X(u) = 1 \leftrightarrow u = u_0, u_0 \in U$$

(the possibility distribution function Π_X is a triangular shaped fuzzy number), the degree of necessity of the α-cut $\Pi_X[\alpha]$ of the possibility distribution function Π_X, is $1-\alpha$,

$$Ness_X(\Pi_X[\alpha]) = 1 - \alpha, \quad \alpha \in [0, 1] \tag{12}$$

According to [9]:

Definition 2. *A possibility distribution Π_X for a variable X is defined as consistent with the probability distribution Π_X of X, if and only if the possibility $\Pi_X(A)$ of any subset A of the universe U of X is greater or equal to its probability $\Pi_X(A)$,*

$$\Pi_X(A) \geq p_X(A), \quad \forall A \subseteq U \tag{13}$$

This inequality is refereed as consistency principle.

Definition 3. *A possibility distribution Π_X^* consistent with the probability distribution P_X is defined as maximally specific if it is more specific than any possibility distribution Π_X consistent with the probability distribution P_X, that is, if*

$$\Pi_X^*(x) < \Pi_X(x), \quad \forall x \in U \tag{14}$$

If the possibility distribution Π_X is consistent with the probability distribution P_X, then according to (13) the possibility $\Pi_X(A')$ of the complement A' of any subset A of U fis greater or equal to the probability of A', so because of (11).

$$p_X(A') \leq \Pi_X(A') \leftrightarrow 1 - p_X(A) \leq 1 - Ness_X(A) \leftrightarrow p_X(A) \geq Ness_X(A) \tag{15}$$

Therefore because of (13):

Proposition 2. *For a possibility distribution Π_X consistent with the probability distribution P_X of a variable X, the probability $p_X(A)$ of any subset A of the universe of X is greater or equal to its necessity $Ness_X(A)$ and less or equal to its possibility,*

$$Ness_X(A) \leq p_X(A) \leq \Pi_X(A) \tag{16}$$

From Proposition 1 and (16) follows that:

Proposition 3. If the possibility distribution function Π_X of a possibility distribution Π_X consistent with the probability distribution P_X is a triangular shaped fuzzy number, then the probability of its α-cut is greater or equal to $1-\alpha$,

$$P(\Pi_X[\alpha]) \geq 1 - \alpha \tag{17}$$

so the α - cuts of Π_X are confidence intervals of X of degree of confidence greater or equal to $1-\alpha$.

Let X a continuous random variable with universe U, unique mode m, probability density $p_X(u)$, symmetric about m and distribution function F_X and $\tilde{X}^* \subseteq U$ a fuzzy subset of U with membership function $\mu_{X^*}(u)$, $u \in U$, the α - cuts of which are intervals in which the probability of a value of X is $1-\alpha$. If $F_X^{-1}(\alpha), 0 \leq \alpha \leq 1$ the inverse distribution function of X, then it holds that [11]:

$$P\left(F_X^{-1}\left(\frac{\alpha}{2}\right) < X < F_X^{-1}\left(1 - \frac{\alpha}{2}\right)\right) = F_X(F_X^{-1}\left(1 - \frac{\alpha}{2}\right) - F_X(F_X^{-1}\left(\frac{\alpha}{2}\right)$$
$$= 1 - \frac{\alpha}{2} - \frac{\alpha}{2} = 1 - \alpha \tag{18}$$

Therefore the α - cuts of the fuzzy set $\tilde{X}^*$ are

$$X^*[\alpha] = \left[F_X^{-1}\left(\frac{\alpha}{2}\right), F_X^{-1}\left(1 - \frac{\alpha}{2}\right)\right], \quad 0 \leq \alpha \leq 1 \tag{19}$$

According to [9]:

Proposition 4. *The possibility distribution $\Pi_{\tilde{X}^*}$ induced by the fuzzy proposition "X is X^*", the possibility distribution function of which $\Pi_{X^*}(x)$ is the membership function $\mu_{X^*}(x)$ of $\tilde{X}^*$ with α - cuts given in (19), is consistent with the probability distribution P_X, that is, it satisfies the consistency principle.*

$$\Pi_{X^*}(A) > p_X(A), \forall x \in U \tag{20}$$

The fuzzy set $\tilde{X}^*$ is called fuzzy estimator of X.

Also, if the probability density $p_X(x)$ of X is symmetric about the mode, then the intervals of (18) are the shortest intervals in which the probability to find a value of X is $1-\alpha$. Therefore, for any possibility distribution Π_X consistent with the probability distribution P_X it is true that

$$\Pi_X(x) > \Pi_X^*(x), \forall x \in U \tag{21}$$

In this case, $\Pi_{\tilde{X}^*}$ is the most specific possibility distribution consistent with the probability distribution P_X and the fuzzy set $\tilde{X}^*$ is *called fuzzy estimator of maximal specificity* of X. Therefore, the triangular shaped fuzzy number $\tilde{X}^*$ which is produced putting one above the other the confidence intervals in which a value of X is found with a given probability is estimator (of maximal specificity) of X.

It is true that (F_X (x) the distribution function of X).

for $x \leq m$,

$$x = F_X^{-1}(\frac{\alpha}{2}) \leftrightarrow \frac{\alpha}{2} = F_X(x) \leftrightarrow \alpha = 2F_X(x) \qquad (22)$$

for $x > m$,

$$x = F_X^{-1}(1 - \frac{\alpha}{2}) \leftrightarrow 1 - \frac{\alpha}{2} = F_X(x) \leftrightarrow \alpha = 2(1 - F_X(x)) \qquad (23)$$

so the membership function of the fuzzy set $\tilde{X}^*$ is

$$\mu_{\tilde{X}^*}(x) = \begin{cases} 2F_X(x), & x \leq m \\ 2(1 - F_X(x)), & x > m \end{cases} \qquad (24)$$

where $F_X(x)$ the distribution function and m the mode of X. Therefore:

Proposition 5. *The membership function of the fuzzy estimator $\tilde{X}^*$ of a random variable X, the α - cuts of which are given in (19), is*

$$\Pi_X^*(x) = \mu_{\tilde{X}^*}(x) = \begin{cases} 2F_X(x), & x \leq m \\ 2(1 - F_X(x)), & x > m \end{cases} \qquad (25)$$

From Proposition 1 follows that the degree of necessity of the α - cuts of the fuzzy number $\tilde{X}^*$ of (19) is $1-\alpha$,

$$Ness\left(\tilde{X}^*[\alpha]\right) = 1 - \alpha \qquad (26)$$

Also because of (18) and (19), the probability of finding X in the α - cut $\tilde{X}^*[\alpha]$ of $\tilde{X}^*$ is

$$P\left(\tilde{X}^*[\alpha]\right) = 1 - \alpha \qquad (27)$$

so:

Proposition 6. *The degree of necessity of the α - cuts of the fuzzy estimator $\tilde{X}^*$ defined by (19) is equal to its probability,*

$$Ness\left(\tilde{X}^*[\alpha]\right) = P\left(\tilde{X}^*[\alpha]\right) = 1 - \alpha \qquad (28)$$

so that the α-cuts of are confidence intervals of X of degree of confidence $1-\alpha$.

Definition 4. *As fuzzy estimator $\tilde{X}$ of a random variable X is defined any fuzzy number such, that the possibility distribution Π_X induced by the fuzzy proposition "X is $\tilde{X}$" to be consistent with the probability distribution P_X of X.*

The membership function $\mu_{\tilde{X}^*}(x)$ of the fuzzy estimator $\tilde{X}^*$ of X (or the possibility distribution function $\Pi_{\tilde{X}^*}(x)$) is below the membership function $\mu_{\tilde{X}}(x)$ of any other fuzzy estimator $\tilde{X}$ of X (any possibility distribution function Π_X consistent with the probability distribution P_X), i.e.

$$\mu_{\tilde{X}^*}(x) \le \mu_{\tilde{X}}(x), \forall x \in U \tag{29}$$

or equivalently the α-cuts of the fuzzy estimator $\tilde{X}^*$ are subsets of the α - cuts of any other fuzzy estimator $\tilde{X}$, i.e.

$$\tilde{X}^*[\alpha] \subseteq \tilde{X}[\alpha], \forall \alpha \in [0, 1] \tag{30}$$

Consequently, the intervals $\tilde{X}[\alpha]$ are wider than $\tilde{X}^*[\alpha]$, so that according to Propositions 3 and 6 it is true that:

Proposition 7. *The probability of the α-cuts $\tilde{X}[\alpha]$ of any fuzzy estimator $\tilde{X}$ of X is greater or equal to $1-\alpha$.*

So, the α - cuts $\tilde{X}[\alpha]$ re confidence intervals of X of degree of confidence greater or equal to $1-\alpha$. Especially, the α - cuts $\tilde{X}^*[\alpha]$ of the fuzzy estimator $\tilde{X}^*$ are confidence intervals of X of degree of confidence $1-\alpha$.

The Definition 4 and the Proposition 7 have no value for a random variable with known probability distribution, since for this there is the fuzzy estimator of maximal specificity $\tilde{X}^*$ with α - cuts given in (19), but they are useful in cases of random variables for which is not easy to find the probability distribution, as presented in next section.

Example 1. *We plot the membership function of the fuzzy estimator of maximal specificity $\widetilde{Prec}^*$ of a normal variable Prec (precipitation) with mean* $m = 360.15$ mm *and standard deviation* $s = 111.4$ mm.

Since the probability density of the normal distribution is symmetric about the mode, according to Proposition 4, the α - cuts of the fuzzy estimator of maximal specificity $\widetilde{Prec}^*$ of Precipitation are given by (19)

$$Prec^*[\alpha] = [F_{Prec}^{-1}\left(\frac{\alpha}{2}; m, s\right), F_{Prec}^{-1}\left(1 - \frac{\alpha}{2}; m, s\right)], 0 \le \alpha \le 1 \tag{31}$$

where $F_{Prec}^{-1}(\alpha; m, s)], 0 \le \alpha \le 1$ the inverse distribution function of Prec (normal distribution with mean m and standard deviation s). Implementing the α - cuts of (21), in Fig. 1 the membership function of the fuzzy estimator $\tilde{P}rec^*$ is plotted, where F_{Prec} the distribution function of Prec.

Hence, with the use of the *fuzzy estimator of maximal specificity* random variable X*, a bridge between the probabilities and the fuzzy sets can be achieved.

If a random variable Y is a function of the random variables $X_1, X_2, \ldots, X_n$, which take values in the universe U ($Y = g(X_1, X_2, \ldots, X_n)$), then from the fuzzy proposition

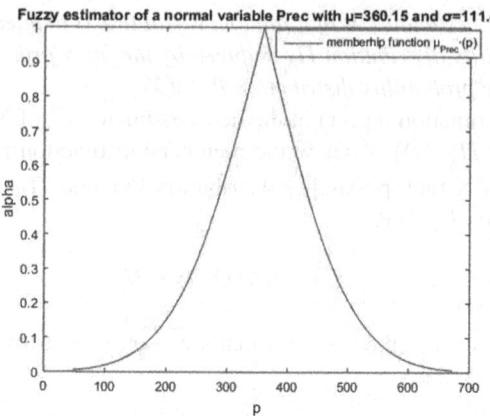

Fig. 1. The *fuzzy estimator of maximal specificity* random variable Prec*, in case that the precipitation is normally distributed.

($\tilde{Y}^*$ is a fuzzy number with α - cuts the intervals of (19) for the inverse distribution function of Y).

$$\hat{Y} \text{ is } \tilde{Y}^{*\prime\prime}$$

is induced the possibility distribution $\Pi_{\hat{\Upsilon}^*}$ for which according to Proposition 3 is true that:

Proposition 8. *Let* $\Pi_{\underset{\Upsilon}{\sim}*}$ *the possibility distribution induced by the fuzzy proposition* "$\hat{Y}$ *is* $\tilde{Y}^*$" *which has as possibility distribution function* $\Pi_{\underset{\Upsilon}{\sim}*}(y)$ *the membership function* $\mu_{\tilde{Y}*}(y)$ *of* $\tilde{Y}^*$, *the* α - *cuts of which (according to (19) with* F_Y *the distribution function of Y) are*

$$\Pi_{\underset{\Upsilon}{\sim}*}[\alpha] = \tilde{Y}^*[\alpha] = \left[F_Y^{-1}(\frac{\alpha}{2}), F_Y^{-1}(1 - \frac{\alpha}{2}) \right], 0 \le \alpha \le 1, \tag{32}$$

$\Pi_{\hat{\Upsilon}^*}$ is consistent with the probability distribution P_Y, i.e. it satisfies the consistency principle (20), so $\tilde{Y}^*$ is a fuzzy estimator of Y.

Also, if the probability density $p_Y(y)$ of Y is symmetric about the mode, then according to Proposition 3 $\Pi_{\hat{\Upsilon}^*}$ is the most specific possibility distribution consistent with the probability distribution P_Y and the fuzzy set $\tilde{Y}^*$ is called fuzzy estimator of maximal specificity of Y.

If the probability density $p_Y(y)$ of Y is not known, then the membership function of the fuzzy estimator of maximal specificity $\tilde{Y}^*$ of Y can not be found.

Even if the probability distributions of these random variables are known, in general it is difficult to determine the combined probability distribution. A choice is to use the fuzzy transformation, based on the concept of *fuzzy estimator of maximal specificity* random variable X*. Hence by exploiting the extension principle, the shape of the dependent variable Y can be determined. In such cases another fuzzy estimator of Y is constructed as follows [11]:

Proposition 9. *The α - cuts of a fuzzy estimator $\tilde{Y}$ of the variable.*
$Y = g(X_1, X_2, \ldots, X_n)$ *are*

$$\tilde{Y}[\alpha] = g\left(\tilde{X}_1^*[\alpha], \tilde{X}_2^*[\alpha], \ldots, \tilde{X}_n^*[\alpha]\right) \tag{33}$$

where

$$\tilde{X}_i^*[\alpha] = \left[F_i^{-1}(\frac{\alpha}{2}), F_i^{-1}(1 - \frac{\alpha}{2})\right], i = 1, 2, \ldots, n, 0 \le \alpha \le 1$$

the α - cuts of the fuzzy estimators $\tilde{X}_i^*$ of X_i and $F_i^{-1}(\alpha)$ the inverse distribution functions of X_i.

The α - cuts $\tilde{Y}[\alpha]$ are confidence intervals of Y of degree of confidence greater or equal to $1-\alpha$.

2.3 Proposed Methodology

Step 1: The annual precipitation and the annual potential evapotranspiration are calculates for each meteorological station.

Step 2: The individual theoretical probability distribution function is examined for both the precipitation and the potential evapotranspiration. Statistical tests can be used to check the suitability of the used theoretical probability density function. In this work the normal probability were used.

Step 3: By using the individual *fuzzy estimators of maximal specificity* regarding random variable, we translate the information into fuzzy sets regarding the annual precipitation and the annual evapotranspiration. Practically the fuzzy sets can be achieved by using a significant number of α-cuts.

Step 4: The extension principle is used in order to find the α-cuts of the annual precipitation to potential evapotranspiration ratio. This will be the fuzzy estimator:

$$\tilde{Y}[a] = \frac{\widetilde{Prec}^*[a]}{\widetilde{PET}^*[a]} \tag{34}$$

where

$$\widetilde{Prec}^*[\alpha] = \left[F_i^{-1}(\frac{\alpha}{2}), F_i^{-1}(1 - \frac{\alpha}{2})\right], \widetilde{PET}^*[\alpha] = \left[F_i^{-1}(\frac{\alpha}{2}), F_i^{-1}(1 - \frac{\alpha}{2})\right] \tag{35}$$

3 Application and Discussion

For the application of the proposed methodology the data of annual precipitation and average monthly temperature from four meteorological stations in Greece were used (Helliniko (Athens), Larissa, Heraklion and Naxos were used. Monthly values of PET were then calculated using the Hargreaves method, a method based on average monthly temperatures [4, 12].

According to [4] the Aridity Index is calculated 0.34 for Helliniko (Athens), 0.33 for Larissa, 0.47 for Heraklion and 0.42 for Naxos. The aridity index equals to mean precipitation to potential evapotranspiration ratio. Both the precipitation and the potential evapotranspiration are normally distributed regarding the examined samples [4].

Let us study the Naxos meteorological station. Assuming that the random variables Precipitation (Prec) and PET follow normal distributions.

$$Prec \sim N(m_1, s_1) \text{ and } PET \sim N(m_2, s_2)$$

where $m_1 = 360.15$, $s_1 = 111.40$ and $m_2 = 854.83$, $s_2 = 29.85$.

By using the individual *fuzzy* estimator of maximal specificity and the fuzzy arithmetics according to Proposition 9, the α - cut of the fuzzy estimator $\widetilde{Y}$ of the random variable: $Y = \frac{Prec}{PET}$ is formulated as follows:

$$
\begin{aligned}
\tilde{Y}[a] &= \frac{\widetilde{Prec}^*[a]}{\widetilde{PET}^*[a]} \\
&= \frac{\left[F^{-1}\left(\frac{\alpha}{2}; m_1, s_1\right), F^{-1}\left(1 - \frac{\alpha}{2}; m_1, s_1\right)\right]}{\left[F^{-1}\left(\frac{\alpha}{2}; m_2, s_2\right), F^{-1}\left(1 - \frac{\alpha}{2}; m_2, s_2\right)\right]} \\
&= \left[\frac{F^{-1}\left(\frac{\alpha}{2}; m_1, s_1\right)}{F^{-1}\left(1 - \frac{\alpha}{2}; m_2, s_2\right)}, \frac{F^{-1}\left(1 - \frac{\alpha}{2}; m_1, s_1\right)}{F^{-1}\left(\frac{\alpha}{2}; m_2, s_2\right),}\right]
\end{aligned}
\tag{36}
$$

where $F^{-1}(\alpha; m_1, s_1)$ and $F^{-1}(\alpha; m_1, s_1)$ the inverse distribution functions of the normal random variables Prec and PET. Hence, by using a significant number of α-cuts the fuzzy number can be constructed as in Fig. 2.

This procedure is repeated for each meteorological station and the results are depicted in Fig. 2.

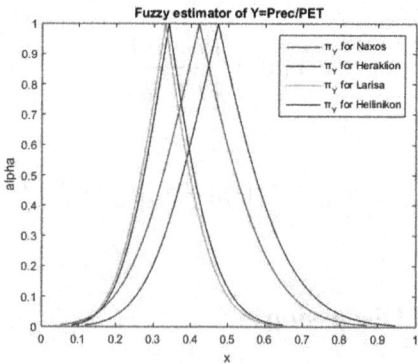

Fig. 2. The *fuzzy estimator of the ration Prec/PET regarding the four examined stations.*

A similar behavior can be considered in case of both the Hellinikon and the Larisa station. As it is descripted in the theoretical part of the manuscript the transformation from probability to fuzzy is achieved by using the *fuzzy* estimator of maximal specificity. By exploiting these individual fuzzy estimator of maximum specificity a fuzzy estimator of the ration Prec/PET can be achieved.

Unfortunately this cannot be considered as the fuzzy estimator of maximum specificity for the examined ratio. However the proposed methodology based on Eq. (36) can be applied for several probability distributions and not only for normal distributions as in [4] (as an approximation). The conventional thresholds of drought levels can be used also in the proposed possibilistic formulation based on the following approximation: the α-cuts corresponds to the $1-\alpha$ cumulative probability with the lower and upper tails of the $1-\alpha$ confidence interval. The correspondence based on the probability threshold of the extreme hydro meteorological analysis, that is, without the dry and the wet phenomena (e.g. [2, 3]) and the corresponding possibilistic approach via α-cuts are shown in Table 1:

Table 1. Correspondence between probability levels and α-cut regarding the Naxos station

Description	Probability $(1-\alpha)$ %	α-cuts
Without extremely phenomena	95.4%	[0.151, 0.732]
Without severe or more extreme cases	86.6%	[0.215, 0.651]
Without moderate or more extreme cases	68.2%	[0.281, 0.571]

4 Concluding Remarks

In hydrology and water resources management problems the theoretical probability distribution functions are widely used with the aim of the empirical probability function. However, it is difficult to exploit the probability functions in case that algebraic operations between random variables are required. A solution should be the motivation from the probability functions to fuzzy sets by using the fuzzy estimators. Based on the Possibility and the Necessity measures theory the authors conclude that based on a theoretical probability distribution we can move to the possibility distribution with the maximum specificity, near to the probability measure. The Reconnaissance Drought Index (RDI) was proposed to assess meteorological drought severity based on the precipitation to potential evapotranspiration ratio (Prec/PET). However it is difficult to express the bivariate probability density function for this ratio. Hence based on the fuzzy estimators, the analysis can be concluded to fuzzy sets, and the extension principle of fuzzy sets can provide the ratio as fuzzy sets. Unfortunately this approach cannot be considered as the fuzzy estimator of maximum specificity but it can be seen as a first approximation.

References

1. Spiliotis, M., Angelidis, P., Papadopoulos, B.: A hybrid probabilistic bi-sector fuzzy regression based methodology for normal distributed hydrological variable. Evol. Syst. **11**(2), 255–268 (2019). https://doi.org/10.1007/s12530-019-09284-7
2. Tsakiris, G.: Uni-dimensional analysis of drought for management decisions. Eur. Water **23**(24), 3–11 (2008)
3. Tsakiris, G., Vangelis, H.: Establishing a drought index incorporating evapotranspiration. Eur. Water **9**(10), 3–11 (2005)
4. Vangelis, H., Spiliotis, M., Tsakiris, G.: Drought Severity assessment based on bivariate probability analysis. Water Resour. Manage. **25**, 357–371 (2011). https://doi.org/10.1007/s11 269-010-9704-y
5. Spiliotis, M., Papadopoulos, C., Angelidis, P., Papadopoulos, B.: Classifying hydrological drought through fuzzy sets. Eur. water **71**(72), 41–61 (2020)
6. Klir, G., Yuan, B.T.: Fuzzy Sets and Fuzzy Logic Theory and its Applications. Prentice Hall, New York (1995)
7. Tsakiris, G., Spiliotis, M.: Uncertainty in the analysis of urban water supply and distribution systems. J. Hydroinform. **19**(6), 823–837 (2017)
8. Zadeh, L.A.: Fuzzy sets as a basis for a theory of possibility. Fuzzy Sets Syst. **1**, 3–28 (1978)
9. Dubois, D., Foulloy, L., Mauris, G., Prade, H.: Probability possibility transformations, triangular fuzzy sets and probabilistic inequalities. Reliab. Comput **10**, 273–297 (2004). https://doi.org/10.1023/B:REOM.0000032115.22510.b5
10. Zadeh, L.A.: Fuzzy sets and information granularity. In: Gupta, M.M., Ragade, R.K., Yager, R.R. (eds.) Advances in Fuzzy Set Theory and Applications, pp. 3–18. North Holland, Amsterdam (1979)
11. Mylonas N.: Applications of approximate reasoning and fuzzy statistics. Ph.D. thesis. Department of Civil Engineering, Democritus University of Thrace, Xanthi (2022)
12. Hargreaves, G.H., Samani, Z.A.Q.: Estimating potential evapotranspiration. ASCE J. Irrig. Drain Div. **108**(3), 225–230 (1982)

SAF: A Peer to Peer IoT LoRa System for Smart Supply Chain in Agriculture

Aristeidis Karras[1]([✉]) [ID], Christos Karras[1] [ID], Georgios Drakopoulos[1,2] [ID],
Dimitrios Tsolis[3] [ID], Phivos Mylonas[2] [ID], and Spyros Sioutas[1]([✉]) [ID]

[1] Decentralized Systems Computing Group, Computer Engineering and Informatics
Department, University of Patras, Patras, Greece
{akarras,c.karras,sioutas}@ceid.upatras.gr
[2] Humanistic and Social Informatics Laboratory, Department of Informatics,
Ionian University, Corfu, Greece
{c16drak,fmylonas}@ionio.gr
[3] Department of History and Archaeology,
University of Patras, Agrinio, Greece
dtsolis@upatras.gr

Abstract. In the dairy industry farming as well as transportation conditions are paramount to product quality and to the overall supply chain resiliency. However, modern farms are complex installations with a broad spectrum of factors such as atmospheric conditions, including rain and humidity, ground composition, and highly irregular animal motion making difficult the deployment of digital telemetry systems. These conditions in turn translate to technical requirements including easy maintenance, scalability, wide coverage, low power consumption, strong signal resiliency, and high spatial resolution. Perhaps the best way to meet them is an LPWAN based IoT deployment. Along this line of reasoning, here is presented the architecture of SAF, an integrated IoT system built on LoRa technology for monitoring the supply chain of a dairy farm ensuring livestock and food safety with emphasis placed on monitoring the states of sheep, milk refrigerator, and milk trucks. LoRa was selected after an extensive comparison between the major latest generation LPWAN protocols. SAF is slated to be implemented in a local cooperative to monitor the production of protected designation of origin products.

Keywords: Internet of Things · Smart agriculture · Supply chain management · Event detection · Trajectory modeling · LPWAN · LoRa

1 Introduction

Dairy product management presents some of the hardest challenges in smart agriculture due to the volatile nature of milk and the temperatures required to maintain it, which are close to those at the core of *unbroken cold chains* for handling the transportation of medical supplies. Moreover, the protected designation of origin (PDO) food and wine producers across the EU are obliged to

© IFIP International Federation for Information Processing 2022
Published by Springer Nature Switzerland AG 2022
I. Maglogiannis et al. (Eds.): AIAI 2022, IFIP AICT 647, pp. 41–50, 2022.
https://doi.org/10.1007/978-3-031-08337-2_4

satisfy additional quality restrictions. As a result, dairy production stakeholders have focused their attention to farm automation and manufacturing process automation in order to boost farm productivity, ensure the safety of dairy goods, and maintain acceptable well being conditions for the animals [2].

Past attempts to introduce high tech solutions to dairy farming have had limited success [26] due to a number of factors such as atmospheric conditions including dust and humidity, irregular farm geometry preventing effective coverage unless a prohibitive number of monitoring equipment was employed, interference from nearby mountains and hills, and even in certain documented cases signal scattering attributed to high concentration of gases such as methane and ammonia caused by heated animal excrement. In this context and based on lessons from earlier attempts, integrating Internet of Things (IoT) with operations and the supply chain is the principal motivation behind this work.

The primary research objective of this paper is the presentation of the architecture and intended functionality of SAF, a system for monitoring milk production and distribution safety. The initials of SAF stand for *safe for animal and food*. The system will be based on LoRa functionality for data transmission and collection, differentiating itself from the majority of previous smart farming approaches which rely on short range protocols.

The remainder of this paper is structured as follows. In Sect. 2 the scientific literature for smart farming is overviewed. The SAF architecture, the criteria for selecting LoRa, and the intended functionality are described in Sect. 3 and the analytics implemented over SAF in Sect. 4. This work concludes in Sect. 5. Technical acronyms are explained the first time encountered in the text. Finally the notation of this work is summarized in Table 1.

Table 1. Notation of this paper.

Symbol	Meaning	First in
$\overset{\Delta}{=}$	Definition or equality by definition	Eq. (1)
$\langle p \| q \rangle$	Kullback-Leibler divergence between p and q	Eq. (2)

2   Related Work

Animal identification and traceability are in continual demand driven by quality control and welfare management requirements [19]. Additionally, infectious diseases like the bovine spongiform encephalopathy (BSE), popularly known as mad cow disease, have prompted the creation of such systems [15]. Safety and quality considerations developed over the past decade provide yet another reason to utilize computerized methods of farmed animal identification [21]. Radiofrequency identification (RFID) technology has been among the first to be utilized to monitor both domestic and wild animals, however RFID tag techniques have yet to be standardized [22]. Moreover, RFID technology despite its wide adoption in smart farming [26] falls short on performance factors as it is affected by animals and the environment [1]. More recently Arduino systems for tracking cattle position and speed have been proposed [5] as well as concurrent actuator networks assessing environmental variables such as temperature and humidity for remote vineyard irrigation [7]. Blockchain for smart farming is explored in [9] and smart contracts for vineyards in [27]. LoRa systems gather vital signals from grazing cattle as in [18]. In particular, portable nodes with STM32 microcontrollers equipped with accelerometers and GNSS position collect data and communicate them to a Raspberry gateway. LoRa is also used in [20] to regulate ammonia diffusion coefficient in pig farms with gas concentration values being processed by a neural network for event detection.

Sampling is a crucial process across every discipline. With random sampling as indicated in [17], elements are taken in a probabilistic way for further processing. While sampling across complex geometric objects as in [16] with the use of Markov Chain Monte Carlo methods appears to be a successful approach.

Streaming applications such as sensor-based deployments can often be considered as graph signal processing methods as in [10] in which, the data associated within two graphs is processed in a compressed way. In the modern era, IoT as well as cloud, edge, and fog computing have recently gained popularity [8] where the latter paves the way for more research. Numerous research communities are vested in the study of spatio-temporal events. Trajectories have been employed in a variety of disciplines, among social sciences, genetics, pharmacy, geology, and data mining. The robustness of each attribute trajectory can be evaluated by stacking-based visualizations [25] or graph structural resiliency methods [12]. With the rapid emerge of Industry 4.0, graph analytics and multi-layer graphs have developed in order to aid in process mining [11].

3 SAF Description

3.1 Objectives and Design

SAF as stated earlier is designed for facilitating agribusiness and ensuring food and animal safety by monitoring in real time critical variables of the primary entities of the milk supply chain. The latter along with the associated variables and the respective monitoring frequency are listed in detail in Table 2.

The system proposed here can contribute to the dairy product quality in two ways. First, by the timely discovery of ill animals, either by measuring its temperature or by predicting an imminent abnormality through neural networks, any disease can at best have a limited spread in the farm. Second, predictive analytics can reveal hidden defects along the milk production process. In either case, identifying and solving problems early in the supply chain frequently translates to saving considerable costs, downtime, and personnel efforts.

SAF architecture can be represented as a pyramid as shown in Fig. 1 where higher layers are related to management and analytics, whereas lower ones to data collection and communication. The role of each layer is as follows:

- **Sensors and microcontrollers:** This is the physical layer of SAF. It includes the sensors and actuators attached to farm animals or to the other entities transmitting the appropriate data to a LoRa gateway and subsequently to upper layers through the SAF API.
- **SAF API:** It is the system middleware for communication between the physical and the upper layers. Each API call fetches the data from the sensors and creates an HTTP post request to the database for each parameter.
- **Database:** In this layer data obtained from the SAF API in a serialized JSON format is transformed to and stored as key-value pairs in a local NoSQL database for short- and mid-term analysis purposes.
- **Cloud:** The cloud service complements the database as a reliable storage space and additionally makes the overall project available worldwide for registered farmers. Communication takes place through Google Firebase.
- **App:** The mobile application displays all monitored instances in real-time to interested parties. This allows the easy localization of problems in the supply chain and consequently their early correction.

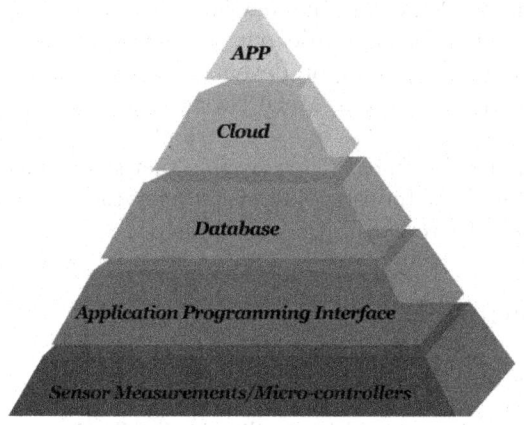

Fig. 1. SAF layers.

SAF constantly monitors the variables shown in Table 2 along with the respective monitor frequency. For farm animals temperature is a primary health indicator and hence measurements for it are taken in real time. Moreover, as certain patterns in their respective trajectories may denote agitation, declining health, or any other abnormality, herd motion is tracked at regular intervals. Heat stress levels, caused by temperature, humidity, sun radiation, wind direction, and precipitation, is evaluated through indicators [3]. The same holds for hunger stress levels since affected animals produce significantly less [6].

Regarding the farm living conditions including temperature, humidity, and methane concentration are crucial for livestock well being and they are monitored in real time. Milk tanks have certain operating profiles determined by temperature, humidity, milk pH, and the weight and level of milk. The latter two are relative and

Table 2. SAF variables.

SAF variables, intervals and technologies			
Entities	Variables	Intervals	Technologies
Sheep	Temperature	5 m	LoRa and GPS
	Daily average	24 h	
	Location	Varies	
Farm	Temperature	5 m	WiFi and RFID
	Humidity	5 m	
	Methane	5 m	
Milk tank	Temperature	5 m	WiFi and Arduino
	Humidity	5 m	
	pH	1 m	
	Level	30 m	
	Weight	Varies	
Milk truck	Temperature	10 m	GSM and GPS
	Humidity	10 m	
	Level	30 m	
	Location	Varies	

they are recorded only at the start of milk production process. Finally, milk trucks must provide viable transportation environments by having low temperatures and low humidity. GPS and GSM technologies provide real time measurements with the latter consuming a significantly less energy.

For the sheep monitoring and management, the system is built around a Lilygo T-Beam LoRa transceiver module with an integrated GPS and a battery holder. The ability to either receive or transmit with a single chip reduces the complexity to one per farm animal plus one more chip acting as a stationary gateway to the cloud. This results in a p2p IoT network where each farm animal is uniquely identified by its respective chip id. In the farm itself the measurements are transferred to the cloud via a static WiFi component.

Figure 2 depicts the four instances being posted to the API and fetched through the mobile application. Initially, data is gathered from ESP32 chips. Then, HTTP post requests publish data to the cloud. The JSON objects carrying sensor data are marked by timestamps. JSON has been selected since it is a common standard for text information exchange [13]. The JSON values supplied to the Firebase API vary depending on the instance. For example, for a sheep are reported its id, temperature, latitude and longitude, and timestamp.

```
 - doc["SheepID"] = ESP.getChipId();
 - doc["SheepTemperature"] =< temperature_sensor >;
 - doc["SheepLat"] = GPS_x;
 - doc["SheepsLon"] = GPS_y;
 - doc["Timestamp"] =< current_time >;
```

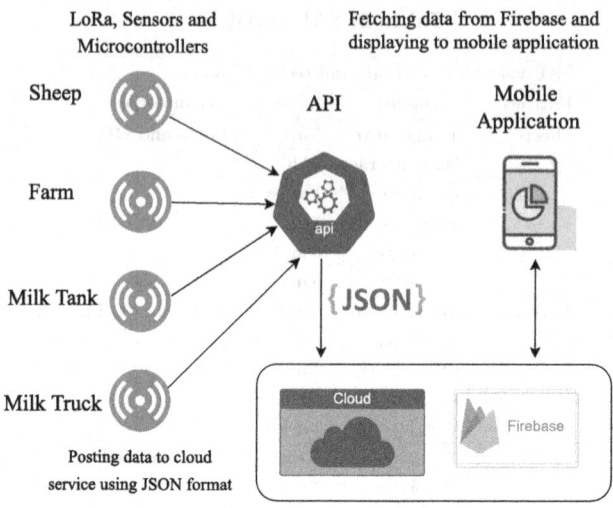

Fig. 2. SAF system data flow.

The above information is shown in the pop-up notification along with the location and temperature once an animal is identified as being ill. Additionally, beeper linked to the animal sounds to indicate its position. As a result, the affected animal will be swiftly isolated from the herd and will not be milked.

3.2   Wireless Network Protocol Comparisons

The protocols suitable for livestock management are shown in Table 3. Having successfully analysed all available network protocols, we select the LoRa technology for this particular use case due to high range and low-power consumption.

The main disadvantage of current animal tracking systems is the short battery life span. Given that farm animals continuously move and may well roam up to a few kilometers, the microcontroller must be power-efficient. LoRa chips besides being able to operate with few recharges can be put into a deep sleep mode for hours, thereby prolonging system life. Because of the same reasons, a long range network must be employed. LoRa provides the best combination of range, signal resilience and simultaneously free to use, which is important given the volatile conditions of large animal farms. For this case, LoRa is the superior alternative in terms of cost-effectiveness, deployment, and maintenance. Moreover, it benefits from a free world license in contrast to the SigFox subscription.

4   Analytics and Events

Event detection is crucial in IoT deployments. Since in the proposed architecture data comes in a streaming format, it makes sense to rely on reservoir approaches to collect samples for event detection [17].

Table 3. Comparison of LPWAN technologies (Compiled from [14, 23, 24]).

Parameter	LoRa	SigFox	NB-IoT
Standard	LoRa Alliance	SigFox/ETSI LTN	3 GPP Release 13,14
Bandwidth	250 kHz	100 Hz	200 kHz
Modulation	FSS/CSS	D-BPSK	QPSK
Spectrum	1175 kHz	200 kHz	200 kHz
Frequency band	EU: 868 MHz	EU: 868 MHz	7–900 MHz
Range (urban)	2–5 km	3–10 km	1–5 km
Range (rural)	20 km	50 km	10–15 km
Max data rate	50 kbps	100 bps	200 kbps
Throughput	50 kbps	–	–
Energy Consumption	Very low	Very low	Low
Security	AES 128b	Optional encryption	L2 security
Localization	TDOA	RSSI	–
Topology	Star-of-stars	Star	Star
Battery Life	∼ 10 years	∼ 10 years	∼ 10 years
Cost	Moderate	Moderate	High

Under ideal operating conditions each chip will consume the same amount of energy. Still the actual distribution of the N chips of (1) may well be different.

$$p_k \triangleq \frac{e_k}{\sum_j e_j}, \qquad 1 \leq k \leq N \tag{1}$$

The Kullback-Leibler divergence can quantify this difference as shown in (2).

$$\langle p \,\|\, r \rangle \triangleq \sum_{k=1}^{N} p_k \log \left(\frac{p_k}{\frac{1}{N}} \right) = \sum_{k=1}^{N} p_k \log p_k + \log N \tag{2}$$

The way animals move can denote conditions such as agitation or illness depending on certain characteristics. To this end, trajectory analytics will be used. In particular, n GPS measurements are taken per a reference time interval T in latitude and longitude pair format. First, the average velocity v of each farm animal is computed as in Eq. (3).

$$v \triangleq \frac{n-1}{T} \sum_{k=1}^{n-1} \sqrt{(x_{k+1} - x_k)^2 + (y_{k+1} - y_k)^2} \tag{3}$$

The least squares (LS) reference line for the i-th animal during T can be computed by the LS solution of the system (4) by any standard method.

$$\begin{bmatrix} y_1 \\ \vdots \\ y_n \end{bmatrix} = \begin{bmatrix} x_1 & 1 \\ \vdots & \vdots \\ x_n & 1 \end{bmatrix} \begin{bmatrix} a_i \\ b_i \end{bmatrix} \tag{4}$$

Once the LS coefficients a_i and b_i are computed, then the deviation of each animal from the respective reference line is the residual error r_i defined as in (5):

$$r_i \triangleq \sum_{k=1}^{n} |y_k - (a_i x_k + b_i)| \tag{5}$$

Once the direction coefficients a_i are computed for each animal, then the general herd direction a_0 can be defined as the average or median value. Then the deviation angle ϑ_i for the i-th animal can be found as in (6).

$$\vartheta_i \triangleq \arctan a_i - \arctan a_0 \tag{6}$$

Finally, the temperature-humidity index (THI) of (7) is a major indicator of the farm condition where T is the farm temperature is Celsius degrees and R is the percentage of relative humidity [4].

$$\text{THI} \triangleq (1.8\,T + 32)\,(0.55 - 0.0055\,R)\,(1.8\,T - 26) \tag{7}$$

Note that the above analytics are indicative and can be enriched should the need arise. The events of interest in the context of SAF are listed in Table 4. For each such event, an event notification is generated and sent to the mobile app.

Table 4. SAF events of interest.

Entity	Farm event
Animals	Deviation from the herd
	Unusual temperatures
	Large percentage of slow animals
	Incoherent herd move
Farm	Milk production drop
	High methane concentration
	Low air humidity
Tank	Unusual temperatures
	Unusual milk level
	Unusual pH values
Truck	Unusual pH values
	Large route deviation

5   Conclusions

This paper focuses on the design specifications and architecture for SAF, an integrated IoT system for monitoring milk production and ensuring dairy product quality while being as less invasive as possible. To this end, SAF will monitor the status of the main entities of the milk supply chain including the livestock, the farm, the milk collection tank, and the milk trucks. The data collected will be transmitted over a p2p network to a central point where a range of analytics like animal trajectories and location clustering will be computed. SAF will be based on the emerging LoRa technology, which was selected among competing LPWAN wireless communication protocols according to performance criteria such as range, coverage, signal resilience, and ease of maintenance. These are major technical specifications designed to overcome adverse geographical and environmental factors such as irregular farm geometry, high humidity, low temperatures, and high altitude. Once completed, SAF is scheduled to be deployed to a local cooperative for the production of milk and PDO cheese.

Acknowledgment. This paper was completed in the framework of the project: "SAF: Safe for Animal and Food: Integrated System for Interactive Monitoring, Recording and Optimization of Animal Health and for the Safety and Quality of Animal Food", Case Study: Feta Cheese of Kalavryta (Designation of Origin). Contract No M16ΣYN − 00452, Agricultural Development Programme, Measure 16, Sub-Measure 16.1, Action 1.

References

1. Angeles, R.: RFID technologies: supply-chain applications and implementation issues. Inf. Syst. Manag. **22**(1), 51–65 (2005)
2. Bhat, S.A., Huang, N.F., Sofi, I.B., Sultan, M.: Agriculture-food supply chain management based on blockchain and IoT: a narrative on enterprise blockchain interoperability. Agriculture **12**(1), 40 (2022)
3. Correa-Calderon, A., Armstrong, D., Ray, D., DeNise, S., Enns, M., Howison, C.: Thermoregulatory responses of holstein and brown swiss heat-stressed dairy cows to two different cooling systems. Int. J. Biometeorol. **48**(3), 142–148 (2004)
4. Council, N.R., et al.: A Guide to Environmental Research on Animals. National Academies (1971)
5. Cousin, P., et al.: IoT, an affordable technology to empower Africans addressing needs in Africa. In: 2017 IST-Africa Week Conference (IST-Africa), pp. 1–8. IEEE (2017)
6. Das, R., et al.: Impact of heat stress on health and performance of dairy animals: a review. Veterinary World **9**(3), 260 (2016)
7. Davcev, D., Mitreski, K., Trajkovic, S., Nikolovski, V., Koteli, N.: IoT agriculture system based on lorawan. In: 2018 14th IEEE International Workshop on Factory Communication Systems (WFCS), pp. 1–4. IEEE (2018)
8. De Donno, M., Tange, K., Dragoni, N.: Foundations and evolution of modern computing paradigms: cloud, IoT, edge, and fog. IEEE Access **7**, 150936–150948 (2019). https://doi.org/10.1109/ACCESS.2019.2947652
9. Drakopoulos, G., Kafeza, E., Al Katheeri, H.: Proof systems in blockchains: a survey. In: SEEDA-CECNSM. IEEE (2019). https://doi.org/10.1109/SEEDA-CECNSM.2019.8908397
10. Drakopoulos, G., Kafeza, E., Mylonas, P., Iliadis, L.: Transform-based graph topology similarity metrics. Neural Comput. Appl. **33**(23), 16363–16375 (2021). https://doi.org/10.1007/s00521-021-06235-9

11. Drakopoulos, G., Kafeza, E., Mylonas, P., Sioutas, S.: Process mining analytics for Industry 4.0 with graph signal processing. In: WEBIST, pp. 553–560. SCITEPRESS (2021). https://doi.org/10.5220/0010718300003058
12. Drakopoulos, G., Mylonas, P.: Evaluating graph resilience with tensor stack networks: a Keras implementation. Neural Comput. Appl. **32**(9), 4161–4176 (2020). https://doi.org/10.1007/s00521-020-04790-1
13. Drakopoulos, G., Spyrou, E., Voutos, Y., Mylonas, P.: A semantically annotated JSON metadata structure for open linked cultural data in Neo4j. In: PCI. ACM (2019). https://doi.org/10.1145/3368640.3368659
14. Hossain, M.I., Markendahl, J.I.: Comparison of LPWAN technologies: cost structure and scalability. Wirel. Person. Commun. **121**(1), 887–903 (2021). https://doi.org/10.1007/s11277-021-08664-0
15. Johnson, R.T., Gibbs, C.J., Jr.: Creutzfeldt-Jakob disease and related transmissible spongiform encephalopathies. New Engl. J. Med. **339**(27), 1994–2004 (1998)
16. Karras, C., Karras, A.: DBSOP: an efficient heuristic for speedy MCMC sampling on polytopes. arXiv preprint arXiv:2203.10916 (2022)
17. Karras, C., Karras, A., Sioutas, S.: Pattern Recognition and Event Detection on IoT Data-streams. arXiv preprint arXiv:2203.01114 (2022)
18. Li, Q., Liu, Z., Xiao, J.: A data collection collar for vital signs of cows on the grassland based on lora. In: 2018 IEEE 15th International Conference on e-Business Engineering (ICEBE), pp. 213–217. IEEE (2018)
19. Lin, J., et al.: Blockchain and IoT based food traceability for smart agriculture. In: Proceedings of the 3rd International Conference on Crowd Science and Engineering, pp. 1–6 (2018)
20. Liu, X., Huo, C.: Research on remote measurement and control system of piggery environment based on lora. In: CAC, pp. 7016–7019. IEEE (2017)
21. McKean, J.: The importance of traceability for public health and consumer protection. Rev. Sci. Techniq. Off. Int. Des Épizoot. **20**(2), 363–369 (2001)
22. Ntafis, V., Patrikakis, C., Xylouri, E., Frangiadaki, I.: RFID application in animal monitoring. In: The Internet of Things: From RFID to the Next-Generation Pervasive Networked Systems, pp. 165–184 (2008)
23. Qin, J., et al.: Industrial Internet of Learning (IIoL): IIoT based pervasive knowledge network for LPWAN-concept, framework and case studies. CCF Trans. Pervas. Comput. Interact. **3**(1), 25–39 (2021)
24. Singh Bali, M., et al.: Towards energy efficient NB-IoT: a survey on evaluating its suitability for smart applications. Mater. Today: Proc. **49**, 3227–3234 (2022). https://doi.org/10.1016/j.matpr.2020.11.1027
25. Tominski, C., Schumann, H., Andrienko, G., Andrienko, N.: Stacking-based visualization of trajectory attribute data. IEEE TVG **18**(12), 2565–2574 (2012). https://doi.org/10.1109/TVCG.2012.265
26. Trevarthen, A., Michael, K.: The RFID-enabled dairy farm: towards total farm management. In: ICMB, pp. 241–250. IEEE (2008)
27. Voutos, Y., Drakopoulos, G., Mylonas, P.: Smart agriculture: an open field for smart contracts. In: SEEDA-CECNSM. IEEE (2019). https://doi.org/10.1109/SEEDA-CECNSM.2019.8908411

Machine Learning Classification

A Multi-label Time Series Classification Approach for Non-intrusive Water End-Use Monitoring

Dimitris Papatheodoulou[1] [iD], Pavlos Pavlou[1] [iD], Stelios G. Vrachimis[1,2] [iD],
Kleanthis Malialis[1,2(✉)] [iD], Demetrios G. Eliades[1] [iD],
and Theocharis Theocharides[1,2] [iD]

[1] KIOS Research and Innovation Center of Excellence, University of Cyprus,
Nicosia, Cyprus
{papatheodoulou.dimitris,pavlou.v.pavlos,vrachimis.stelios,
malialis.kleanthis,eldemet,ttheocharides}@ucy.ac.cy
[2] Department of Electrical and Computer Engineering, University of Cyprus,
Nicosia, Cyprus

Abstract. Numerous real-world problems from a diverse set of application areas exist that exhibit temporal dependencies. We focus on a specific type of time series classification which we refer to as aggregated time series classification. We consider an aggregated sequence of a multi-variate time series, and propose a methodology to make predictions based solely on the aggregated information. As a case study, we apply our methodology to the challenging problem of household water end-use dissagregation when using non-intrusive water monitoring. Our methodology does not require a-priori identification of events, and to our knowledge, it is considered for the first time. We conduct an extensive experimental study using a residential water-use simulator, involving different machine learning classifiers, multi-label classification methods, and successfully demonstrate the effectiveness of our methodology.

Keywords: Time series classification · Multi-label classification · Water monitoring · Household end-use disaggregation

1 Introduction

The ever-increasing volume of data that is accumulated in various application areas in recent years has accelerated the development of time series methods for forecasting or classification purposes. Examples include critical infrastructure systems, such as, water distribution networks and power load balancing, as well

This work has been supported by the European Union Horizon 2020 program under Grant Agreement No. 739551 (TEAMING KIOS CoE) and the Government of the Republic of Cyprus through the Deputy Ministry of Research, Innovation and Digital Policy, and the FLOBIT project co-funded by the Research and Innovation Foundation of Cyprus, the European Regional Development Fund and Structural Funds of the European Union in Cyprus.

as areas such as healthcare, finance, environmental monitoring, and retail. What real-world problems from the aforementioned areas have in common is the existence of temporal dependencies. One unique attribute of time series data underlies in the chronological order of the observations which constitutes a challenging factor in their analysis. Thus, time series modelling has significant importance as it needs to account for trends, seasonality and abrupt changes that are often exhibited in time series data [9].

Time series classification is a general task which is useful in numerous areas and applications. It is a type of a supervised machine learning problem, where time series data are described by a class label. The difference with other classification problems is that the natural temporal order in the data is significant, and a learning algorithm has to identify and exploit the temporal characteristics.

In this work, we consider the problem of non-intrusive water usage monitoring in households as our case study [13]. As water scarcity is increasingly affecting the world, the development of new strategies focusing on water conservation has become crucial. To this direction, many investments have been made the last years in data and information technologies to facilitate the use of smart water meters for domestic use. Smart metering of domestic water consumption to continuously monitor the usage of different water fixtures and appliances has been shown to have an impact on people's behavior towards water conservation [7]. However, the installation of multiple sensors to monitor each appliance may have a high initial cost and there is currently no simple and cost-effective method to monitor end-use water consumption. This work aims to address this issue by identifying active water consuming fixtures and appliances using only data from the main water flow meter, measuring the total household consumption.

Towards this direction, studies have focused on using measurements of the total domestic consumption with Machine Learning (ML) methods to disaggregate water usage into each appliance [14]. Identifying which appliances are in use through ML is challenging since their operation may be overlapping, while specific appliances may operate with intermittent flow, making individual consumption events hard to distinguish. Decision trees and Machine learning algorithms with a combination of unsupervised learning with feature extraction and clustering evaluation have been identified as the major disaggregation techniques to classify water end-use appliances using total consumption data [6]. The authors in [10] used a Bayesian approach coupled with a template classifier, a language model, grammar and prior probabilities to classify water events, using however additional measurements from pressure sensors. The study achieved 90% and 94% accuracy at fixture level based on data collected form five sites during a five-week period. An adaptable neuro fuzzy network called Anfis has been proposed in [15] using two approaches to estimate each class: the space and the mean values and standard deviation of each class. This method achieved a 91% score on classifying water end-uses using a limited dataset of flow measurement from one point in a single house. The authors in [13] propose a rule-based methodology for end-use disaggregation, by prioritizing the identification of appliances with comparably regular behavior. The methodology was applied to a sample of four households in Italy where detailed water-use data were collected at the inlet point and at each end-use over a period of 2 months. The results were consistent with those obtained in similar studies making use of synthetic data [5]. In [3], the authors examine the use of a novel flow indicator to deal with simultaneous water consumption events. Six water usage features are extracted from each event: duration, volume, flow peak, mode, time of day, and day of week. A Random Forest classifier is used to identify the category of each event based on the extracted features. It is a common characteristic of the aforementioned studies to use pre-processing algorithms to identify consumption events before classification. This work makes two key contributions as follows:

1. We consider a specific type of time series classification which we refer to as aggregated time series classification. This setting is largely unexplored in the literature, and considers an aggregated sequence of a multi-variate time series. We propose a methodology to make predictions based solely on the aggregated information.
2. As a case study we consider the challenging problem of non-intrusive water end-use monitoring, where the proposed methodology, which uses only a sliding window of measurements and does not require *a-priori* identification of events, is considered for the first time, to the authors knowledge.

The paper is organised as follows. We formulate the problem in Sect. 2. The experimental setup is described in Sect. 3. An empirical analysis of the proposed methodology is provided in Sect. 4, while in Sect. 5 we compare the performance of various learning algorithms. We conclude in Sect. 6.

2   Problem Formulation

We consider a data generating process that provides at each time step t a sequence of instances $S = \{(x^t, y^t)\}_{t=1}^T$ from an unknown probability distribution $p^t(x, y)$, where $T \in [1, \infty)$.

The input $x^t = \{x_i^t\}_{i=1}^d \in \mathbb{R}^d$ is a d-dimensional vector belonging to input space $X \subset \mathbb{R}^d$. The instances constitute a **multivariate** time series with d number of time series, and each corresponds to a **univariate** time series defined as $z_i = \{x_i^t\}_{t=1}^T \in \mathbb{R}^T$.

The label (i.e., the ground truth) of the classification task is denoted by $y^t \in Y$. When $Y = \{1, ..., K\}$, $K \geq 2$, it is termed **multi-class** classification, that is, it refers to a task with more than two classes. When $Y \in \{0, 1\}^K$ it is termed **multi-label** classification, i.e., it assigns to each instance a set of labels. Each digit corresponds to the inclusion (1) or absence (0) of the relevant label.

A classifier h receives a new example x^t at time step t and makes a prediction $\hat{y}^t$ based on a concept $h : X \to Y$ such that $\hat{y}^t = h(x^t)$. We refer to this as **time series classification**. To capture the temporal aspects of the data, it is possible to introduce a memory component, such as, a sliding window to facilitate with the prediction task, i.e., $\hat{y}^t = h(x^t, x^{t-1}, ..., x^{t-W})$, where W is the window size.

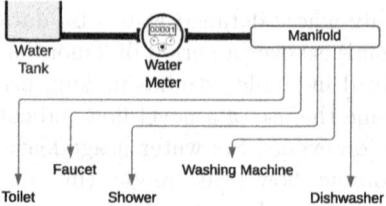

Fig. 1. Piping connectivity in a domestic water system.

Let us define the aggregated sequence $x^{*t} = \{x_1^t \otimes x_2^t \otimes ... \otimes x_d^t\}$, where the classifier makes a prediction based solely on the aggregated sequence x^{*t} at time step t, where $\otimes$ is an aggregation operator depending on the application. We refer to this as **aggregated time series classification**.

We formulate the non-intrusive water end-use monitoring problem as an aggregated time series classification task. For the generation of the dataset, we use a residential water demand simulator [5] (descibed below) that synthesises a sequence of instances S at each time step t based on the water consumption profiles of appliances in U.S. households.

The generated time series consists of five signals, that correspond to the water flow consumption of the toilet (z_1), shower (z_2), faucet (z_3), clothes washer (z_4) and dish washer (z_5). From the consumption of these five appliances, we compose an aggregated sequence x^{*t}, by summing the water flow consumption from each sequence z_i at time step t. The aggregated sequence x^{*t} is described by a set of binary labels that correspond to the appliances that were active (1) or inactive (0) at each time step t. To improve the efficacy of the predictions, we use a sliding window approach that allows the classifier to capture information from previous time steps, thus extracting underlying temporal patterns.

3   Experimental Setup

3.1   Simulator and Dataset

This case study uses the STochastic Residential water End-use Model (STREaM) [5], a modelling software developed to generate synthetic time series data of a household with resolution of up to 10 s. STREaM generates time series of each water end-use fixture characterised by its signature (i.e., typical consumption pattern), as well as its probability distributions of number of uses per day, single use durations, water demand contribution, and time of use during the day. STREaM takes into consideration the number of house occupants in the calculation of total household water demand. STREaM was calibrated on a large dataset including observed and disaggregated water end-uses from over 300 single-family households in nine U.S. cities [8]. The following water end-uses were considered in this dataset: toilet, shower, faucet, clothes washer, dishwasher. The end-uses are further distinguished in standard and high efficiency appliances, which have different consumption characteristics. Each fixture can be activated only once

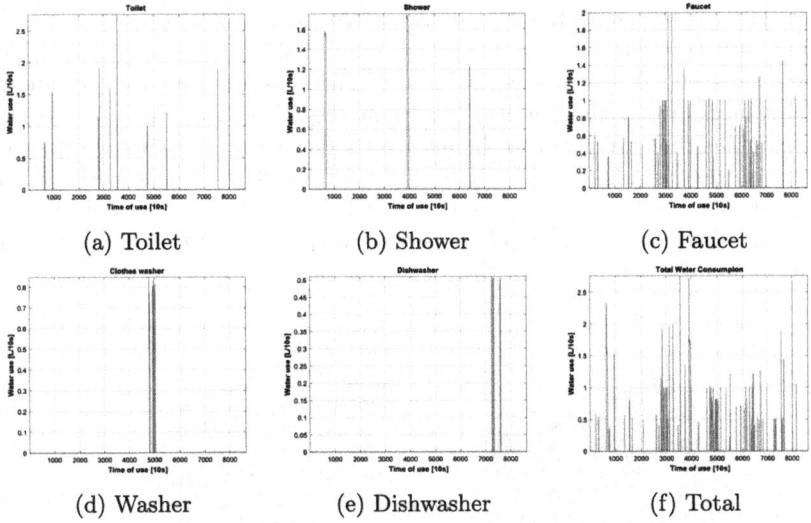

Fig. 2. Household water consumption per appliance

during each time step but multiple fixtures can be active during the same time. The dataset provides the water flow reading at each time step for each fixture and their sum as the total consumption. Figure 1, illustrates the connectivity of a domestic water system. The main flow meter is located at the outflow of a domestic house water tank thus allowing us to measure water flow for each time step. The system consists of the main water tank, the main water pipe connecting the tank to the manifold, the manifold which distributes the water to the house piping system and the end-use appliances.

The dataset used in this study considers the use of standard toilet, standard shower, standard faucet, high efficiency clothes washer and standard dishwasher in a 2-person household for a period of 180 days (6 months) and it has a resolution of 10 s. Figures 2a-2e depict the household water consumption for each appliance for a random day. Figure 2f shows the total water consumption. Figure 3 displays each class' size (i.e., time series records), where it is clear that imbalance is severe.

We split the dataset into three subsets, 3-months worth of data are held for training, and two sets of 1.5 months of historical data are reserved for validation and test sets. That equates to a set of 777600 samples for the training and 388800 samples for both validation and test sets. The training subset consists of the samples that are given to the model, to identify and learn any underlying patterns of the data. The validation subset contains data that is used for evaluation purposes in order to optimize the model. Lastly, the test subset is a set of unseen samples that are used only to assess the performance of the algorithms, to determine how well the algorithms can generalize on unseen data.

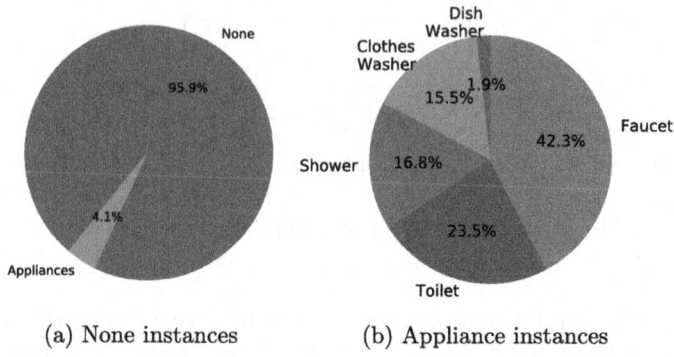

(a) None instances   (b) Appliance instances

Fig. 3. Dataset's class sizes

3.2   Classification Algorithms

Random Forest (RF) [1]: It is a tree-based, ensemble learning algorithm, i.e., it depends on multiple tree-based learners which make individual predictions that are then averaged together. Typically, the more trees it has, the more robust model it is as its performance does not rely on a single tree.

Extreme Gradient Boosting (XGBoost) [4]: It is a machine learning technique that produces a prediction model in the form of an ensemble of weak prediction models, which are typically tree-based. This technique builds a model in a stage-wise fashion and combines weak learners into a single strong learner. As each weak learner is added, a new model is fitted to provide a more accurate estimation. The XGBoost classifier is a tree-based ensemble machine learning algorithm with Gradient Boosting as its main component. Moreover, XGBoost has the ability to handle missing values on its own and it is very effective and efficient in terms of performance as well as training time even on large datasets.

Multilayer Perceptron (MLP) [1]: It is a feed-forward neural network that consists of an input and an output layer, and can have multiple hidden layers. MLP uses the backpropagation algorithm for training which computes the gradient of the loss function with respect to the weights of the neural network.

3.3 Multi-task Classification Methods

Multi-task classification [2] combines (related or unrelated) tasks by using the principles of transfer learning. It focuses on the preservation of the knowledge gained while solving a particular task and then applying it to a different task. It improves the generalisation by associating information of multiple tasks. The learning process happens simultaneously across all tasks while using shared representation, which may lead to performance improvements. In this work we use the terms multi-task and multi-label classification interchangeably.

Meta-estimators have the flexibility to appropriately leverage all the characteristics of a base estimator in multiple forms. They can utilize the information of each individual base estimator in a way that extends their capabilities. The following meta-estimators describe how they can consolidate a multi-class binary classification problem into a more generalised version, a multi-task problem.

- **Binary Relevance (BR)** [12]: It is a problem transformation technique, where each label is treated separately, as a binary classification problem. Thus, the multi-task problem is split into binary classification sub-tasks, where any type of supervised classification algorithm can be defined as the base-estimator. Subsequently, the meta-estimator is constructed that fits each individual base-estimator in order to optimize its loss function. The predictions are then combined into a multi-output format.
- **Classifier Chain (CC)** [16]: It operates similarly to Binary Relevance, however, it is capable of exploiting correlations among target variables. The difference between this approach and BR is that in a multi-label classification setting with N-classes, N-binary classifiers are assigned a number that corresponds to their order in the classifier's chain. The training process follows the order of the models in the chain, where each binary classifier is fit on the available training data with the addition of the actual target labels of the classes whose models were assigned a lower order in the chain.

3.4 Evaluation Metrics

Classifiers are typically evaluated using the **accuracy** metric. However, this metric becomes unsuitable as it is biased towards the majority (normal) class. A widely accepted metric which is less sensitive to imbalance is **F1-Score**, defined below as the harmonic mean of the model's precision and recall [11]. For multi-label classification, we will use the micro-averaging F1-score or **F1-Micro**.

$$F1 = 2 \times \frac{precision \times recall}{precision + recall} \tag{1}$$

4 Empirical Analysis

4.1 Hyper-Parameter Tuning

We have tuned all the algorithms (RF, XGBoost, MLP) using both multi-task methods (BR, CC). We have also used four different sliding windows that capture the previous 60, 120, 240 and 480 time steps that correspond to 10, 20,

40 and 80-minute intervals respectively. To facilitate the reproducibility of our results, this section provides the values of the hyper-parameters after tuning. Due to space restrictions, we present the hyper-parameter values using the CC multi-label method. Table 1 shows the hyper-parameters which yield the best performance for the Random Forest using the CC multi-task method. Table 2 shows the hyper-parameters which yield the best performance for XGBoost using the CC multi-task method. Table 3 shows the hyper-parameters which yield the best performance for MLP using the CC multi-task method.

4.2   Role of the Sliding Window Size

We now examine the role of the window size. Four different sliding window sizes are examined that capture the previous 60, 120, 240 and 480 time steps that correspond to 10, 20, 40 and 80-minute intervals respectively. In all experiments, we have used the models that yielded the best performance after tuning. Due to space constraints, we present the results only for the CC method.

Random Forest: Table 4 shows the RF's performance using the CC multi-task method for different window sizes. It can be observed that the performance of the Random Forest declines as the sliding window size becomes larger. The best performance is obtained when the window size is 60.

Table 1. Tuned hyper-parameter values for RF (CC)

	Window 60	Window 120	Window 240	Window 480
Number of estimators	325	225	475	375
Criterion	Gini	Gini	Gini	Entropy
Max depth	8	8	9	9
Max features	Auto	Auto	Sqrt	Sqrt
Class weight	Balanced	Balanced	Balanced	Balanced

Table 2. Tuned hyper-parameters values for XGBoost (CC)

	Window 60	Window 120	Window 240	Window 480
Number of estimators	275	100	275	125
Max depth	3	10	3	6
Learning rate	0.05	0.03	0.05	0.03
Booster	Dart	Dart	Gbtree	Gbtree
Subsample	0.4	0.1	0.7	0.2
Colsample by tree	0.3	0.7	0.7	0.7
Colsample by level	0.8	0.4	0.5	0.6
Colsample by node	0.9	0.7	0.6	0.8
L1 Regularisation	0.03	0.06	0.02	0.03
L2 Regularisation	0.05	0.05	0.02	0.0006

XGBoost: Table 5 shows the XGBoost's performance using CC for different window sizes. Its performance improves as the sliding window grows, for instance, the highest performance in Table 5 is obtained when the window size is 480. XGBoost can better capture the time correlations in the time-series data.

MLP: Table 6 show the MLP's performance using CC for different window sizes. As with XGBoost, the models' performance increases when the window size becomes larger, however, after some point its performance declines. The best performance is obtained when the size is 120.

Overall, the role of the sliding window is very important as it appears to affect the performance of all models. Overall, a larger window size helps a model capture time correlations in time-series data, however, the performance may start to decline after very large windows as in the case of MLP. Moreover, some models fail to capture time correlations in this domain area despite the increase in the window size; this has been the case with the RF model. While the above serve as guidelines, tuning the sliding window size is necessary.

Table 3. Tuned hyper-parameters values for MLP (CC)

	Window 60	Window 120	Window 240	Window 480
#hidden layers	2	2	3	2
#hidden units	32	32	16	64
Activation	Tanh	Tanh	Tanh	Tanh
Epochs	100	75	175	125
Optimizer	Adam	SGD	SGD	SGD
Learning rate	0.01	0.05	0.09	0.04
Batch size	256	256	128	32
L2 Regularisation	0.04	0.07	0.06	0.01

Table 4. Performance of random forest (CC)

	Window 60	Window 120	Window 240	Window 480
Accuracy	96.51	96.43	96.18	96.44
F1-Micro	55.75	54.22	52.39	48.60

Table 5. Performance of XGBoost (CC)

	Window 60	Window 120	Window 240	Window 480
Accuracy	98.80	98.86	98.78	98.76
F1-Micro	68.91	71.94	71.98	72.38

Table 6. Performance of MLP (CC)

	Window 60	Window 120	Window 240	Window 480
Accuracy	98.48	98.62	98.47	98.31
F1-Micro	62.70	65.82	64.87	61.58

Table 7. Comparison of multi-task methods with RF

	Random Forest (BR) - Window 60	Random Forest (CC) - Window 60
Accuracy	97.04	96.51
F1-Micro	49.92	55.75

4.3 Role of the Multi-label Classification Method

We examine now the role of the multi-task methods Binary Relevance (BR) and Classifier Chain (CC). We set the window sizes that yielded the best performance earlier, and we compare which method is more effective. For the Random Forest, we set the window size to 60. For the MLP, we set the window size to 120. For the XGBoost, we set the window size to 240, even though one of the models achieved better performance on larger window size (Table 5). This decision was based on the negligible difference of the two models, and due to the lower dimensionality of the dataset which results in a more simplified and efficient model.

Random Forest: Table 7 compares the performance of the Random Forest with a fixed sliding window size of 60, using BR and CC. The results indicate that CC outperforms BR with a considerable performance improvement.

XGBoost: Table 8 presents the role of the multi-task method using XGBoost on the dataset with a fixed sliding window size of 240. Similarly, with the Random Forest model, the XGBoost using CC achieves a better performance.

MLP: Table 9 shows the comparison between the Binary Relevance and the Classifier Chain methods using the MLP model with a dataset that has a fixed sliding window size of 120. Likewise, with the previous models, the Classifier Chain approach proves to be more effective using the MLP classifier.

Table 8. Comparison of multi-task methods with XGBoost

	XGBoost (BR) - Window 240	XGBoost (CC) - Window 240
Accuracy	98.37	98.78
F1-Micro	70.14	71.98

Table 9. Comparison of multi-task methods with MLP

	MLP (BR) - Window 120	MLP (CC) - Window 120
Accuracy	98.29	98.62
F1-Micro	64.21	65.82

Overall, we can conclude that the Classifier Chain approach proved to be more effective on all occasions that were tested. It had a drastic impact on the improvement of the performance of the Random Forest method, but it also demonstrated a noticeable improvement for both XGBoost and MLP models.

Table 10. Comparison of different classifiers

	Random Forest (CC) - Window 60	XGBoost (CC) - Window 240	MLP (CC) - Window 120
Accuracy	96.51	98.78	98.62
F1-Micro	55.75	71.98	65.82

5   Comparative Study

We now examine the performance of each classifier. We keep the same window sizes identified previously, and we set the multi-task method to the Classifier Chain as it outperformed the Binary Relevance method on every experimental series. Table 10 compares the performance of each classifier, where it is evident that the XGBoost model significantly outperforms the other classifiers.

Figures 4a - 4e, depict the confusion matrices of XGBoost (CC) with a window of 240-time steps. The confusion matrices are computed in a class-wise fashion. The multi-class data are treated as if they were binarised under a one-versus-rest transformation. The y-axis includes the actual class labels and the x-axis shows the algorithm's predictions. Notice that the different colours represent the percentage range, with white being 100% and black 0%.

Figure 4a presents the confusion matrix of the class label Toilet versus the rest of the classes. The model has difficulty identifying this class as it manages to correctly identify when the toilet was used approximately half of the time. On the other hand, it manages to identify almost all the other events correctly, while misclassifying as "Toilet" only 573 samples.

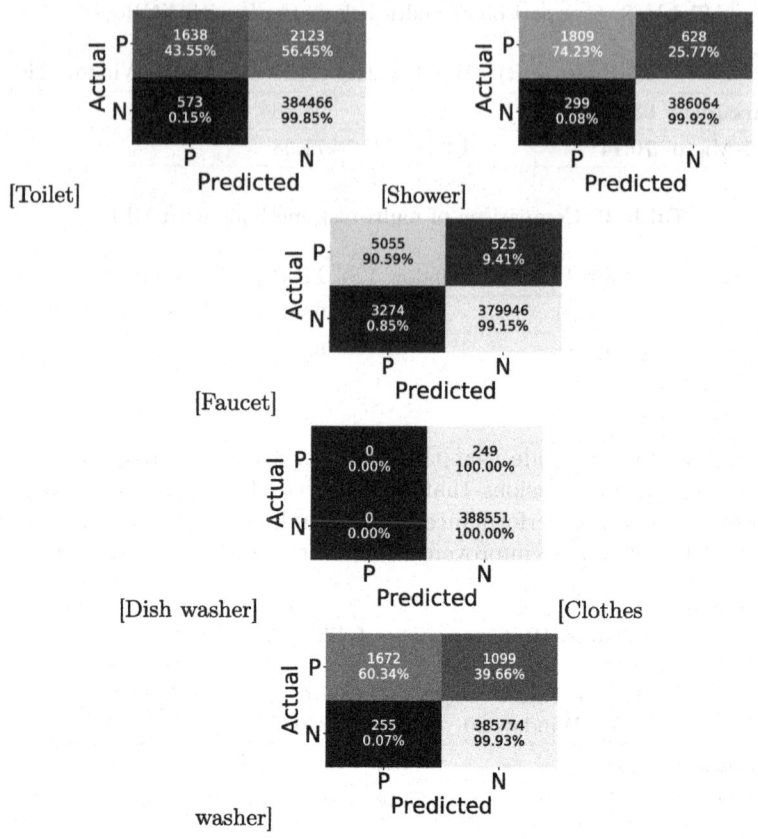

[Toilet]　　[Shower]

[Faucet]

[Dish washer]　　[Clothes

washer]

Fig. 4. Confusion matrices

In Fig. 4b we examine the predictions for the class "Shower". The model identifies correctly almost 75% of the samples that are labelled as a shower. Also, it has very few false positives as it distinguishes the rest of the samples with ease. Figure 4c, depicts the performance for the class Faucet. We observe that the classifier learnt to identify cases where the faucet was in operation with high accuracy, as it was classified correctly approximately 90% of the time.

In Fig. 4d, we examine the performance of the classifier when identifying the cases where the dish washer was active. As it is evident, the model struggles to classify correctly any of the dish washer samples. Specifically, in 235 (out of the 249) cases only the dishwasher is operating, from which 211 cases are predicted as faucet. In 14 (out of the 249) cases the dishwasher is operating simultaneously with another appliance. In 9 cases (out of the 14) the dishwasher and shower are operating, and the model correctly predicts only the shower. This is attributed partly to the fact that the dishwasher constitutes the minority class with just 1.9% relative to the other class as shown in Fig. 3, and partly to the fact that the dish washer cycle exhibits intermittent behavior, thus making it harder for the model to distinguish between the dishwasher and faucet. The results from the predictions for the clothes washer appliance are presented in Fig. 4e. We can observe that the classifier correctly identifies cases where the clothes washer was in operation. Also, we can see that there are very few cases that were misclassified as clothes washers by the model.

Overall, the problem of identifying active appliances from the aggregated water consumption is challenging. We conclude that there are cases which the model performs well, while in others it fails to give accurate predictions. This inconsistency in the performance for some classes can be attributed to three key reasons: (1) Class imbalance constitutes a key challenge. Recall that the majority of the samples constitute cases where none of the appliances was active (Fig. 3). Moreover, the imbalance among the appliances has a significant role, especially for the underrepresented appliances, such as the dish washer. (2) Another key factor lies in the aggregated sequence, where some consumption profiles might look similar, especially in the case of appliances, e.g., the dishwasher which has a long and intermittent cycle. The use of a sliding window and the absence of an event detection algorithm to specifically search for these intermittent events, misleads the classifier during inference. (3) The simultaneous use of multiple appliances could also yield a water consumption profile which is similar to another.

6   Conclusions and Future Work

In this work, we have considered an aggregated sequence of a multi-variate time series, and propose a methodology to make predictions based solely on this aggregated information. As a case study, we have considered the challenging problem of non-intrusive water monitoring. The proposed methodology has been demonstrated to be very effective. Identified difficulties are the class imbalance, and the noisy information as a result of the time series aggregation. Future work will attempt to better capture longer temporal correlations using deep neural models, such as, LSTMs and convolutional neural networks [9].

References

1. Bishop, C.M.: Pattern Recognition and Machine Learning (Information Science and Statistics). Springer-Verlag, Berlin (2006)
2. Caruana, R.: Multitask learning. Mach. Learn. **28**(1), 41–75 (1997)
3. Charalampous, A., Papadopoulos, A., Hadjiyiannis, S., Philimis, P.: Towards hydro-informatics modernization with real-time water consumption classification. In: IEEE AFRICON Conference (2021)
4. Chen, T., Guestrin, C.: Xgboost: a scalable tree boosting system. In: Proceedings of the 22nd ACM SIGKDD International Conference on Knowledge Discovery and Data Mining, pp. 785–794 (2016)
5. Cominola, A., Giuliani, M., Castelletti, A., Rosenberg, D.E., Abdallah, A.M.: Implications of data sampling resolution on water use simulation, end-use disaggregation, and demand management. Env. Model. Softw. **102**, 199–212 (2018)

6. Cominola, A., Giuliani, M., Piga, D., Castelletti, A., Rizzoli, A.E.: Benefits and challenges of using smart meters for advancing residential water demand modeling and management: a review. Env. Model. Softw. **72**, 198–214 (2015)

7. Cominola, A., et al.: Long-term water conservation is fostered by smart meter-based feedback and digital user engagement. npj Clean Water **4**(1), 1–10 (2021)

8. DeOreo, W.B.: Analysis of water use in new single family homes. For Salt Lake City Corporation and US EPA, By Aquacraft (2011)

9. Ismail Fawaz, H., Forestier, G., Weber, J., Idoumghar, L., Muller, P.-A.: Deep learning for time series classification: a review. Data Min. Knowl. Disc. **33**(4), 917–963 (2019). https://doi.org/10.1007/s10618-019-00619-1

10. Froehlich, J., Larson, E., Saba, E., Campbell, T., Atlas, L., Fogarty, J., Patel, S.: A longitudinal study of pressure sensing to infer real-world water usage events in the home. In: Lyons, K., Hightower, J., Huang, E.M. (eds.) Pervasive 2011. LNCS, vol. 6696, pp. 50–69. Springer, Heidelberg (2011). https://doi.org/10.1007/978-3-642-21726-5_4

11. He, H., Garcia, E.A.: Learning from imbalanced data. IEEE Trans. Knowl. Data Eng. **21**(9), 1263–1284 (2009)

12. Luaces, O., Díez, J., Barranquero, J., del Coz, J., Bahamonde, A.: Binary relevance efficacy for multilabel classification. Progress in AI **1**(4), 303–313 (2012)

13. Mazzoni, F., Alvisi, S., Franchini, M., Ferraris, M., Kapelan, Z.: Automated household water end-use disaggregation through rule-based methodology. J. Water Resour. Plan. Manag. **147**(6), 04021024 (2021)

14. Nguyen, K.A., Stewart, R.A., Zhang, H.: An intelligent pattern recognition model to automate the categorisation of residential water end-use events. Env. Model. Soft. **47**, 108–127 (2013)

15. Ojeda Magaña, B., Andina de la Fuente, D., Nakamura, C., Ruelas, R.: Classification of domestic water consumption using an anfis model (2008)

16. Read, J., Pfahringer, B., Holmes, G., Frank, E.: Classifier chains for multi-label classification. Mach. Learn. **85**(3), 333–359 (2011)

A Primer for tinyML Predictive Maintenance: Input and Model Optimisation

Emil Njor$^{(\boxtimes)}$ ⓘ, Jan Madsen ⓘ, and Xenofon Fafoutis ⓘ

DTU Compute, Technical University of Denmark, Kongens Lyngby, Denmark
{emjn,jama,xefa}@dtu.dk

Abstract. In this paper, we investigate techniques used to optimise tinyML based Predictive Maintenance (PdM). We first describe PdM and tinyML and how they can provide an alternative to cloud-based PdM. We present the background behind deploying PdM using tinyML, including commonly used libraries, hardware, datasets and models. Furthermore, we show known techniques for optimizing tinyML models. We argue that an optimisation of the entire tinyML pipeline, not just the actual models, is required to deploy tinyML based PdM in an industrial setting. To provide an example, we create a tinyML model and provide early results of optimising the input given to the model.

Keywords: tinyML · Predictive maintenance · Optimisation · Embedded machine learning · Resource-constrained systems

1 Introduction

Predictive Maintenance (PdM) is a promising maintenance paradigm where models are used to predict equipment failure. PdM is expected to replace reactive maintenance and preventive maintenance [23]. In reactive maintenance, equipment is repaired after a failure which, e.g. in factories can lead to expensive production downtime. In preventive maintenance, equipment is replaced according to a predefined schedule. This can be wasteful as perfectly working equipment might be replaced. It also provides no guarantee that failures do not occur before maintenance. Assuming a perfect model, PdM can predict a failure before it occurs, and maintenance can be planned and conducted in advance to avoid the failure [23].

There are three general approaches to implementing PdM systems. The first is a knowledge-based approach, which uses e.g. rules or physical models to predict failures. The second and third are traditional Machine Learning (ML) and Deep Learning approaches respectively [23]. The output of PdM models generally come in three different forms. One is a binary prediction, where the model outputs whether there is an impending equipment failure. A second form is anomalous behavior detection. In this form, the model flags equipment behaviour as normal or anomalous. The third form of predictions is a Remaining Useful Life (RUL) prediction, where the RUL of some equipment is estimated [23].

© IFIP International Federation for Information Processing 2022
Published by Springer Nature Switzerland AG 2022
I. Maglogiannis et al. (Eds.): AIAI 2022, IFIP AICT 647, pp. 67–78, 2022.
https://doi.org/10.1007/978-3-031-08337-2_6

At the moment, most PdM systems are deployed either in the cloud or on powerful computers. The data used by such models, however, are often generated by small sensor devices. Therefore, using current approaches, data has to be collected and sent over a network for processing. This has a couple of drawbacks e.g.: (i) Security and privacy of data can be compromised when sent over a network. (ii) Network communication induces a non-zero and often unpredictable latency, which can be intolerable in some use cases. (iii) The system will be less reliable as it relies on a working network connection and cloud. This is especially a problem for systems deployed in rural areas or at sea. (iv) Using network modules on sensor devices requires a significant amount of energy. This is especially a problem for battery-driven sensor devices. The alternative to sending data over a network for processing is to process data directly on the sensor device. This has been popularized as the concept of tinyML [8].

According to the tinyML Foundation [8], tinyML is broadly defined as: *"A fast growing field of machine learning technologies and applications including hardware, algorithms and software capable of performing on-device sensor data analytics at extremely low power, typically in the mW range and below, and hence enabling a variety of always-on use-cases and targeting battery operated devices."* tinyML thus provides a solution to the drawbacks of sending data over a network to be processed. tinyML has its own challenges, however, and it is therefore heavily dependent on the use case whether a tinyML or a cloud solution is the better choice. The following are some challenges of tinyML: (i) The micro controllers embedded in sensor devices have few computational resources, so inference of models will take significantly longer than in the cloud or on desktops. (ii) Micro controllers also have a limited amount of memory, so the size of the models deployed with tinyML will have to be small. (iii) Microcontrollers often have little to no operating system, which means that tinyML can not rely on standard operating system features such as dynamic memory allocation. (iv) There are a wide variety of microcontrollers on the market, and the hardware and their software tools are heterogeneous.

The field of tinyML is still in its infancy, and work has to be put into making it ready for industrial adaptation. The contribution of this work is twofold. We first provide the background of how to apply tinyML based PdM in a tutorial style, and a short (yet – to the best of our knowledge – comprehensive) survey of known optimisation techniques for tinyML models. Secondly, we argue that it is important to optimise the entire PdM pipeline and not just the tinyML models to mature tinyML based PdM As an example, we create a tinyML based PdM model and show that by optimising the input to the model we can further reduce the compute and memory requirements for running inference of the model. We show the tinyML optimisation pipeline that we argue for in Fig. 1.

2   Related Work

While the field of tinyML is still in its infancy, it has received much attention in recent years. Several surveys have been published on the topic. The surveys,

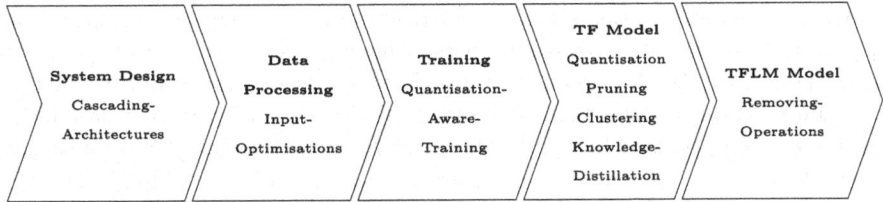

Fig. 1. The tinyML optimisation pipeline. Pipeline stages in bold followed by optimizations that are possible at the respective stages. More information about each optimisation is given in Sects. 4 and 5. TF and TFLM are abbriviations to TensorFlow and TensorFlow Lite Micro respectivly. See Sect. 3 for more information about TF and TFLM.

however, mostly investigate tinyML for any ML application, and not specifically PdM. In doing so, they tend to focus on common supervised learning techniques and cases. These techniques and cases differ from PdM in especially two areas. Firstly, as we shall discuss later, PdM datasets are often imbalanced or unlabeled. Secondly, PdM is a bit unique as late failure predictions in many cases should be penalised more heavily than early failure predictions. One tinyML survey is focused on anomaly detection [28]. This survey is focused on the types of anomaly detection systems and the techniques that are used to reduce the size of the ML models. It does not go into depth with the applications, libraries, hardware or datasets that are typically used for tinyML based anomaly detection. In this paper, we touch on these specifically for anomaly detection for PdM.

A survey by R. Sanchez-Iborra and A. Skarmeta [26] investigates general tinyML benefits, challenges, applications, libraries and models. The survey concludes with a case study, for which a decision tree model is deemed the best tinyML model choice [26]. The data for the case study is synthetically constructed, however, and is arguably constructed using decision tree-like logic, so the great performance of the decision tree is not surprising. It does not comment on common datasets or hardware for tinyML. It also does not go into depth about optimising tinyML models. Another survey by L. Dutta et al. [5] describes the benefits of tinyML, and compares tinyML to other approaches to processing sensor data. It also touches on the hardware-software co-design, optimisation techniques, libraries and tools, recent advances and the role of the industry in tinyML research. A few example datasets and tinyML results on these datasets are also presented [5]. Lastly, a survey from P. Ray [25] describes hardware, libraries, optimisations and use cases. It also includes the authors' ideas for a future roadmap of tinyML. This is a quite comprehensive survey, but does not comment on common tinyML datasets.

A book on tinyML using Tensorflow Lite Micro [32] acts as a tutorial for deploying several types of ML applications on ARM-based microcontrollers. The book contains a comprehensive overview of the background of tinyML and Optimisation techniques, however, it does not investigate PdM or anomaly detection.

Apart from investigating tinyML, this paper also tackles optimisations of the input to tinyML models. To our knowledge, this has not yet been investigated in the domain of tinyML based PdM. It has, however, been applied in other fields. For example, a publication by X. Fafoutis et al. describes how a cloud-based ML system can be optimised by conducting feature extraction directly on a sensor device. This is shown to reduce the required compute and networking by several orders of magnitude [7]. Another paper by A. Khan et al. found that sampling rates used in the literature are up to 57% higher than needed [14].

3   Background of Applying tinyML

In this section, we present the background knowledge required to apply tinyML, with a focus on tinyML for PdM. The section can be regarded as a mini-survey of the libraries, hardware, datasets and models which are used in tinyML and PdM research; and can serve as a tutorial for individuals that enter the field.

Libraries. Several software libraries have been introduced to ease the development of tinyML applications. The most popular is arguably the open-source TensorFlow Lite Micro (TFLM) library, whose primary contributor is Google [4]. We base this on the tinyML book being focused on this library [32]. Furthermore, the online learning platform "edX" has a course on tinyML that focuses on the library [6].

The TFLM library is split into two parts. One part is a converter which converts (TF) models to the TFLM model format. TF is an open-source framework for creating, training and inferring Neural Network (NN) models also spearheaded by Google. The second part is an interpreter written in C++, which runs on a microcontroller and interprets the TFLM model. As the TFLM interpreter is designed for microcontrollers, it has low compute and memory requirements and does not rely on an operating system. TFLM does not support training and only supports a subset of the operations supported by TF. The library is also able to take advantage of efficient implementations of common neural network functions on ARM-based microcontrollers described in [17].

Alternatives to using TFLM include Microsoft's Embedded Learning Library, ARM-NN, sklearnporter and µTensor [26]. Most of these libraries are made for NNs as opposed to traditional ML, suggesting that the current focus of tinyML is leaning heavily towards NNs.

Hardware. This section describes some of the hardware that can be used for doing PdM inference using tinyML. We focus our attention on what we see as the current standard systems for deploying tinyML - that is ARM-based microcontrollers, but also comment on alternative hardware platforms. ARM-based microcontrollers can be split into two sub-groups - those building on the ARM Cortex-M platform and those building on the ARM Cortex-A platform. The ARM Cortex-M platform is the most energy-efficient of the two, while the ARM

Cortex-A platform provides superior performance [1]. The Cortex-A platform is used in devices like smartphones and the Raspberry Pi, whereas the Cortex-M platform is mainly used in embedded devices such as sensors. TFLM as discussed in Sect. 3 is made for the Cortex-M platform, and confirmed supported for a number of devices listed on the TFLM webpage [30]. One of the supported devices is the Arduino Nano 33 BLE Sense. The device has an ARM Cortex-M4 processor, 256 KB of SRAM and 1 MB of flash memory. It furthermore has a wide array of internal sensors, which allows the device to be used as a prototype for several applications.

The literature proposes many alternatives to using ARM-based microcontrollers. One approach is to use the open-source processor platform PULP to speed up tinyML inference [9]. A paper shows that this platform can complete inference on a CIFAR-10 network in up to 30x fewer clock cycles than the current state of the art ARM-based microcontrollers [9]. Other publications propose completely new hardware such as BinarEye, which is a processor optimized for efficient processing of Convolutional Neural Networks (CNNs) [20]. Some papers even propose alternative ways to encode data in hardware to improve the processing energy efficiency [31].

Datasets. In order to implement tinyML based PdM appropriate data is needed. It is unfortunately notoriously difficult to find good datasets for predictive maintenance. One reason is that failures can lead to financial and reputational loss, especially in industry, and we often go to great lengths to avoid failures. Paradoxically it is also the goal of PdM to avoid failures. Even when a failure occurs, the data about the failure is often not released publicly.

We have identified three suitable datasets for tinyML based PdM. The first is the ToyADMOS dataset, which contains audio recordings of toys in normal and anomalous operating conditions [15]. A subset of the ToyADMOS dataset is used in the MLPerf Tiny benchmark, which to our knowledge is the only current benchmark targeting tinyML [2]. Similarly, we have the MIMII dataset that contains audio recordings of industrial machines in normal and anomalous operating conditions [22]. The third dataset is the Turbofan Engine Degradation dataset which contains sensor readings of simulated turbofan engines as they degrade towards failure [27].

An issue in many PdM datasets is the imbalance of observations. By their nature, normal operating conditions are more frequent than anomalous, and thus the data includes a majority of normal observations. The literature proposes to use generative models or transfer learning to solve these problems [23].

Models. The right model to choose for tinyML based PdM depends on the hardware and the data that is available for the PdM application. If the hardware capabilities are extremely limited, such as in the ATMega328P Microcontroller, which has only 2 KB RAM, then simple traditional ML methods, such as decision trees could be the right choice. For example, while the size of the TFLM interpreter used for NNs varies by the model that it needs to interpret, even the smallest example in the TFLM paper takes up 1.3 KB of RAM [4]. In a 2 KB RAM microcontroller, this would not leave much room for the model, data and remaining logic. More specialised models can also be considered in this case, e.g. the bonsai model, which is derived from decision trees [16]. In other microcontrollers such as the Arduino Nano 33 BLE Sense with 256 KB of RAM, NNs, especially for image processing, might be the better choice.

If the data is labelled, either with impending failure labels or RUL labels, then supervised learning approaches are likely the best choice. There are many supervised learning approaches [23], but Decision Trees, Support Vector Machines (SVMs), Artificial Neural Networks (ANNs) or CNNs can in our opinion all be good choices. The actual decision depends on other factors. CNNs are NNs that contain convolutional layers. Convolutional layers train a filter to pass over a tensor, usually an image, to extract features that help the classification/regression.

If the data is unlabeled then we need to turn to unsupervised learning. When this is the case we are often trying to do PdM anomaly detection. There are a few ML models that are suitable for making anomaly detection. Two of the most popular models are k-Nearest Neighbor (KNN) and autoencoders [23]. A KNN model is a traditional ML model which clusters observations based on features derived from the observations. The idea is that an anomalous sample will diverge from the cluster(s) of normal observations and that it can thereby be stamped as an anomaly. An autoencoder model is a deep learning model, which we train to compress and decompress normal observations. We also say that the autoencoder is "reconstructing" its input. The idea for this model is that the autoencoder will learn to reconstruct normal observations, but that it will struggle to reconstruct anomalous observations. Just as with other NNs we can introduce convolutional layers to autoencoders to improve their capabilities in image processing. In this case, we call the model a convolutional autoencoder. Using a loss function we can quantify the difference between the input and the output, which we expect to be higher for anomalous observations. For both models, a loss threshold should be set for when to classify a sample as normal or abnormal [23].

A significant step towards deploying convolutional models e.g. CNNs and convolutional autoencoders on small devices such as smartphones, but also microcontrollers, are depthwise separable convolutions. These were first proposed in [29], and popularized in MobileNets [12].

4   Model Optimisations

Most disadvantages of tinyML that we listed in Sect. 1 come from microcontrollers being much less powerful than desktop or server computers. Therefore it is natural to apply optimisations to a tinyML pipeline that we want to run in microcontrollers. Section 3 explained that the focus of tinyML at this point seems to be NN models, so we will focus on optimisations for these models. Overall we describe six ways to optimise the performance of NN based models for tinyML. These are quantisation, pruning, clustering, knowledge distillation, removing operations and cascading architectures.

Quantisation. Most NNs represent their weights, biases and activations as 32-bit floats. This poses two problems for deploying them on microcontrollers. Firstly, not all microcontrollers have hardware support for floating-point units. Secondly, the many 32-bit values can take up a large part of the memory of microcontrollers. For example the Arduino Nano 33 BLE Sense, mentioned in Sect. 3, has 256 KB of RAM. That leaves room for 64.000 weights, biases, and activations. While that might sound like a lot, many modern NNs have much more. E.g. AlexNet and Resnet-50 both contain more than one million weights, biases and activations [3]. That is without even considering the memory required for the model structure, the input data, or the remaining application.

Fortunately, research has shown that it is possible to quantise NNs, while still retaining a good model [21]. For most hardware, operations using 8-bit integers are some of the fastest operations, and as such many tinyML models are quantised from 32-bit floats to 8-bit integers. This quantisation is typically done by taking the minimum and maximum 32-bit floating-point weights and mapping them and the intervals between them to 8-bit integers. Note that after full 8-bit integer quantisation, multiplying or adding two 8-bit integers can easily create an overflow situation. This is due to the minimum and maximum 32-bit floating-point weights being mapped to the minimum and maximum values for 8-bit integers. Consider that applying just the smallest multiplication or addition to the largest 32-bit floating-point weight after quantisation will result in an overflow. Therefore some approaches only quantise weights and biases (or only weights, as they grossly outnumber biases), and let the remaining activations (and biases) stay as 32-bit floats. A way to achieve full 8-bit integer quantisation is to compute the 8-bit integer computations and store the result in 16-bit/32-bit integers. This can then be scaled down to 8-bit integers again for the next computation. By using quantisation we can therefore reduce both the model size, increase inference speed, and make the model run on an even larger range of devices. The downside is a potential loss in accuracy [28]. This potential accuracy loss can be reduced using quantisation aware training. In this method, a model is trained with the knowledge that it will be quantised later [13]. Note that a 4 times reduction in the number of weights, biases and activations will make neither AlexNet nor Resnet-50 fit in the Arduino that we are considering. To achieve that we require further optimisations or smaller models.

Researchers have also been looking into further quantisation and even binarisation of NNs, which can further decrease the size by up to 32 times and inference time of the networks by up to 52 times [24].

Pruning. It is common in NNs that some weights are more relevant than others. After quantisation, some weights might even be zero and not contribute to the inference at all. In such cases, we can prune the connections associated with these weights. All incoming connections to a neuron might be pruned using such an approach. In that case, we can also prune that neuron and any outgoing connections. This will further reduce the model size and make it faster to compute. It is also an option to prune non-zero weight connections. In this case, some rules should be set for when to prune a connection. This could e.g. be pruning connections when their associated weights are below a threshold [18]. Such an approach is used in [10], where pruning reduces the size of a NN by 9 to 13 times.

Clustering. An approach that is closely related to both quantisation and pruning is clustering. In this optimisation technique, weights are clustered into groups, where all weights in one group are assigned the same weight. Similarly to pruning, this technique reduces the model size, however, the computation is not sped up. The paper that initially introduced clustering claims that their approach reduced the size of a NN by 27 to 31 times [10]. This is after pruning has reduced the size by 9 to 13 times as reported above in Sect. 4.

Knowledge Distillation. Larger NN models are often better at learning the structure of a complicated dataset. However, as discussed earlier, it might be infeasible to deploy large models on microcontrollers. A solution is to "distil" the knowledge of a large model into a smaller model. This is known as knowledge distillation. The idea is to train a small model, not just using the ground truths but also using the predictions of a larger model [11]. Consider the following example. We want to create a small model that can classify the contents of an image. Normally this would be done by training the network to make the same classification as the ground truth labels. In knowledge distillation, we first train a larger model on our data. We then have the larger model give its classifications for all images in the dataset. Then we train the small classifier, not just to classify the ground truth, but to also make similar classifications as the larger model. This can be done by altering the loss function of the smaller model. Often the larger model is referred to as the "teacher", and the small model as the "student".

Removing Operations. A technique that is specific to the TFLM interpreter is the option to decide which NN operations the interpreter can execute. By removing operations from the interpreter, it is possible to reduce its size [4].

Cascading Architectures. Another approach to reducing the size and inference speed of a model is to split the model into two or more models of increasing size. Typically the idea is to use a small model as a filter before activating the larger model. E.g. when using a Google Home device, a small model is running locally, which listens for the "Hey Google" keywords. Once it detects these keywords, it sends the remaining speech to a larger model in the cloud to further process the request [32]. While the idea of cascading architectures is usually restricted to model size and alternative systems, research has looked into a cascading use of internal hardware in a system [33].

5   Input Optimisations

While there has been much research into optimising ML models for tinyML, there has, to our knowledge, been little work into optimising model inputs. Therefore in this section, we describe preliminary work that we have done on optimising the input for a PdM tinyML model.

We choose to work with the ToyADMOS dataset, as it is the benchmarking dataset for tinyML. From the dataset, we use the recordings of one microphone from one case of the ToyConveyor part of the ToyADMOS dataset. This dataset is targeted towards unsupervised anomaly detection and contains normal and anomalous sound recordings. Due to this, and that tinyML is focused on NNs, we create a convolutional autoencoder model. The reason for choosing a convolutional autoencoder, above a standard autoencoder, is that it is common to generate images (spectrograms) from audio, and input this to the NN model [19]. We implement this model using TF and TFLM. We train the convolutional autoencoder on Mel spectrograms of the normal sound samples of the dataset. Thus the model learns to reconstruct a Mel spectrogram of a normal sound sample. After training the model, we mix a few normal Mel spectrograms (not used in training) and anomalous Mel spectrograms to create a test set. Generating a TFLM model from the convolutional autoencoder shows that the model takes up ~172 KB before applying model Optimisations. This suggests that the model will be able to fit in the Arduino Nano 33 BLE Sense microcontroller.

The autoencoder architecture can be divided into an encoder and a decoder. The first layer of the encoder is a convolutional layer of 32 3×3 filters. The second layer is a max-pooling layer with a pooling size of 2×2. The third and fourth layers are a convolutional layer of 64 3×3 filters and a max-pooling layer, with a pooling size of 2×2, respectively. The first layer of the decoder is a convolutional layer with 32 3×3 filters. The second layer is an upsampling layer with a size of 2×2. The third and fourth layers of the decoder contain a convolutional layer of 16 3×3 filters and an upsampling layer of size 2×2. Lastly, the decoder contains a convolutional layer with one 3×3 filter to reproduce the spectrogram shape. All convolutional layers use the rectified linear unit activation function.

We evaluate the model using a Receiver Operating Characteristic (ROC) Area Under Curve (AUC) score calculated on the test set. A ROC AUC score of 1 means that there is a threshold for which the model can completely separate the normal and anomalous samples. A model that would take random actions, also known as a no-skill model, would on average get a ROC AUC score of 0.5.

At a sample rate of 24000 Hz of the sound files, we can train and run a model that in five out of five runs have a ROCAUC score of 1. We treat this sample rate as a benchmark and investigate the effects of reducing it. The idea is that the lower the sample rate, the lower the processing and storage capability is required to run inference on the files, which would be a useful optimisation for tinyML. We conduct experiments where we reduce the sample rate by a factor of two until reaching 375 Hz. Note that we do not cross-optimise the parameters of the Short Time Fourier Transform (STFT) used to create Mel spectrograms to the sampling frequency. The results are shown in Table 1, and are plotted in Figs. 2 and 3 As this experiment is preliminary work, we measure the inference time on an M1 Pro chip with 10 CPU cores and 16 GPU cores. We expect to see a similar decrease in inference time on the Arduino Nano 33 BLE Sense.

Table 1. Mean and standard deviation of results from 5 training rounds.

Sample rate (Hz)	ROC AUC score	Inference time (s)
24000	1.000 ± 0.0000	5.20 ± 0.022
12000	0.999 ± 0.0004	1.65 ± 0.015
6000	0.993 ± 0.0054	0.97 ± 0.041
3000	0.972 ± 0.0133	0.55 ± 0.011
1500	0.766 ± 0.0488	0.39 ± 0.013
750	0.649 ± 0.1110	0.28 ± 0.030
375	0.483 ± 0.0294	0.21 ± 0.001

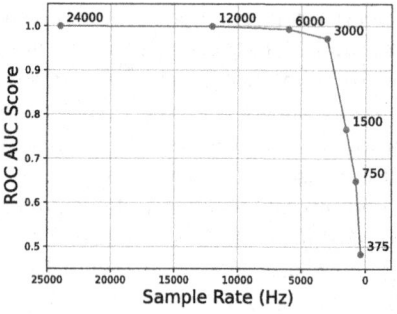

Fig. 2. AUC score by sample rate   **Fig. 3.** Inference time by sample rate

The results suggest that we can reduce the sample rate from 24000 Hz to about 6000 Hz while still retaining a respectable ROC AUC score. This shows that we can reduce the input size by four times and speed up inference about five times by optimising the input in this example. The reduced inference time is a clear proxy for reduced computational requirements. By lowering the sample rate, we also reduce the dimensions of Mel spectrograms, and in turn reduce the input and output dimensions of the convolutional autoencoder. Thus both the input and model memory requirement is reduced when lowering the sample rate. We furthermore expect that these reductions translate to a reduction in energy consumption, both due to lower compute and memory requirements, but also due to lower sensing requirements at lower sampling rates.

6   Conclusion

In this paper, we presented the background behind deploying tinyML based PdM. We furthermore investigated the optimisations that can be used to achieve PdM using tinyML. We started by describing the model optimisations that are proposed in tinyML research. Lastly, we expressed our idea that optimisations should be considered throughout the ML pipeline, and that especially optimising input to tinyML is a promising research direction. An example of input Optimisation was done for an industry-standard dataset for a convolutional autoencoder that fits in the memory of a tinyML device. The results suggest that there is a great potential for input optimisation to help achieve PdM using tinyML.

Acknowledgement. This work is supported by the Innovation Fund Denmark for the project DIREC (9142-00001B).

Resources. The source code used for the experiments is publicly accessible on GitHub: https://github.com/Ekhao/ToyADMOSTinyAutoencoder.

References

1. ARM: Processor ip for the widest range of devices. https://www.arm.com/products/silicon-ip-cpu
2. Banbury, C., Reddi, V.J., Torelli, P., Jeffries, N., Kiraly, C., et al.: MLPerf tiny benchmark. In: Thirty-fifth Conference on Neural Information Processing Systems Datasets and Benchmarks Track, Round 1 (2021)
3. Bernstein, L., Sludds, A., Hamerly, R., Sze, V., Emer, J., Englund, D.: Freely scalable and reconfigurable optical hardware for deep learning. Sci. Rep. **11**(1), 1–12 (2021)
4. David, R., et al.: Tensorflow lite micro: embedded machine learning for tinyml systems. Proc. Mach. Learn. Syst. **3**, 800–811 (2021)
5. Dutta, D.L., Bharali, S.: TinyML Meets IoT: a comprehensive survey. Internet of Things **16**, 100461 (2021). https://doi.org/10.1016/j.iot.2021.100461
6. edX: Professional certificate in tiny machine learning (tinyml). https://www.edx.org/professional-certificate/harvardx-tiny-machine-learning
7. Fafoutis, X., Marchegiani, L., Elsts, A., Pope, J., Piechocki, R., Craddock, I.: Extending the battery lifetime of wearable sensors with embedded machine learning. In: IEEE 4th World Forum on Internet of Things, WF-IoT, pp. 269–274 (2018)
8. tinyML Foundation: About us tinyml. https://www.tinyml.org/
9. Garofalo, A., Rusci, M., Conti, F., Rossi, D., Benini, L.: Pulp-NN: accelerating quantized neural networks on parallel ultra-low-power RISC-v processors. Phil. Trans. R. Soc. A **378**(2164), 20190155 (2020)
10. Han, S., Mao, H., Dally, W.J.: Deep compression: compressing deep neural networks with pruning, trained quantization and huffman coding (2015). arXiv preprint, arXiv:1510.00149
11. Hinton, G., Vinyals, O., Dean, J., et al.: Distilling the knowledge in a neural network 2(7) (2015). arXiv preprint, arXiv:1503.02531
12. Howard, A.G., et al.: Mobilenets: efficient convolutional neural networks for mobile vision applications (2017). arXiv preprint, arXiv:1704.04861
13. Jacob, B., et al.: Quantization and training of neural networks for efficient integer-arithmetic-only inference. In: Proceedings of the IEEE Conference on Computer Vision and Pattern Recognition, pp. 2704–2713 (2018)
14. Khan, A., Hammerla, N., Mellor, S., Plötz, T.: Optimising sampling rates for accelerometer-based human activity recognition. Pattern Recogn. Lett. **73**, 33–40 (2016)

15. Koizumi, Y., Saito, S., Uematsu, H., Harada, N., Imoto, K.: Toyadmos: a dataset of miniature-machine operating sounds for anomalous sound detection. In: IEEE Workshop on Applications of Signal Processing to Audio and Acoustics, WASPAA, pp. 313–317 (2019)
16. Kumar, A., Goyal, S., Varma, M.: Resource-efficient machine learning in 2 kb ram for the internet of things. In: International Conference on Machine Learning, pp. 1935–1944 (2017)
17. Lai, L., Suda, N., Chandra, V.: CMSIS-NN: Efficient neural network kernels for arm cortex-m cpus (2018). arXiv preprint, arXiv:1801.06601
18. LeCun, Y., Denker, J., Solla, S.: Optimal brain damage. Adv. Neural Inf. Proc. Syst. **2**, 598–605 (1989)
19. Marchegiani, L., Newman, P.: Listening for sirens: locating and classifying acoustic alarms in city scenes. IEEE Trans. Intell. Transp. Syst. 1–10 (2022). https://doi. org/10.1109/TITS.2022.3158076
20. Moons, B., Bankman, D., Yang, L., Murmann, B., Verhelst, M.: Binareye: an always-on energy-accuracy-scalable binary CNN processor with all memory on chip in 28nm cmos. In: IEEE Custom Integrated Circuits Conference, CICC, pp. 1–4 (2018)
21. Nagel, M., Fournarakis, M., Amjad, R.A., Bondarenko, Y., van Baalen, M., Blankevoort, T.: A white paper on neural network quantization (2021). arXiv preprint, arXiv:2106.08295
22. Purohit, H., et al.: Mimii dataset: Sound dataset for malfunctioning industrial machine investigation and inspection (2019). arXiv preprint, arXiv:1909.09347
23. Ran, Y., Zhou, X., Lin, P., Wen, Y., Deng, R.: A survey of predictive maintenance: Systems, purposes and approaches (2019). arXiv preprint, arXiv:1912.07383
24. Rastegari, M., Ordonez, V., Redmon, J., Farhadi, A.: Enabling AI at the edge with xnor-networks. Commun. ACM **63**(12), 83–90 (2020)
25. Ray, P.P.: A review on tinyml: state-of-the-art and prospects. J. King Saud Univ. Comput. Inf. Sci. **32**(4), 1595–1623 (2021)
26. Sanchez-Iborra, R., Skarmeta, A.F.: Tinyml-enabled frugal smart objects: challenges and opportunities. IEEE Circuits Syst. Mag. **20**, 4–18 (2020)
27. Saxena, A., Goebel, K.: Turbofan engine degradation simulation data set. In: NASA Ames Prognostics Data Repository, pp. 1551–3203 (2008)
28. Siang, Y.Y., Ahamd, M.R., Abidin, M.S.Z.: Anomaly detection based on tiny machine learning: a review. Open Int. J. Inf. **9**(Special Issue 2), 67–78 (2021)
29. Sifre, L., Mallat, S.: Rigid-motion scattering for texture classification (2014). arXiv preprint, arXiv:1403.1687
30. TensorFlow: Tensorflow lite for microcontrollers. https://www.tensorflow.org/lite/ microcontrollers
31. Tzimpragos, G., Madhavan, A., Vasudevan, D., Strukov, D., Sherwood, T.: In-sensor classification with boosted race trees. Commun. ACM **64**(6), 99–105 (2021)
32. Warden, P., Situnayake, D.: TinyML. O'Reilly Media, Incorporated (2019)
33. Zalewski, P., Marchegiani, L., Elsts, A., Piechocki, R., Craddock, I., Fafoutis, X.: From bits of data to bits of knowledge-an on-board classification framework for wearable sensing systems. Sensors **20**(6), 1655 (2020)

Allocating Orders to Printing Machines for Defect Minimization: A Comparative Machine Learning Approach

Angelos Angelopoulos[1], Anastasios Giannopoulos[1(✉)], Sotirios Spantideas[1],
Nikolaos Kapsalis[1], Chris Trochoutsos[2], Stamatis Voliotis[1], and Panagiotis Trakadas[1]

[1] National and Kapodistrian University of Athens, 34400 Psachna, Evia, Greece
{a.angelopoulos,angianno,sospanti,svoliotis,ptrakadas}@uoa.gr,
ncapsalis@pms.uoa.gr
[2] Pressious Arvanitidis, 15232 Chalandri, Athens, Greece
chtrox@pressious.com

Abstract. Zero-Defect Manufacturing (ZDM) is continuously emerging as the most critical target of the Industry 4.0 era. Minimization of the defected products in the industrial production chain can contribute towards significant improvements of the operational costs, the production efficiency and speed, as well as the environmental footprint. This work proposes a Machine Learning (ML) based scheme for intelligently and proactively allocating orders to printing machines, so as to ensure minimization of the defected products. Based on a historical dataset extracted by a printing company, ten supervised learning regression models were trained to estimate the machine-specific defect ratio of new orders, given their multi-feature requirements. To optimize the machine selection policy, several widely-used ML schemes were compared in terms of their performance on unseen data samples. Extensive simulations were carried out to stabilize the hyperparameters of the ML models, including single-model, ensemble and Deep Learning based regressors. Results showed that Multi-Layer Perceptron (MLP) outperform the rest of the benchmarking regressors in accurately predicting the defect rate of each machine, with the ensemble methods presenting also enhanced accuracy. Finally, the misclassification ratio of the proposed algorithm was assessed by quantifying the number of optimally allocated orders to printing machines, exhibiting that the majority of orders are correctly classified.

Keywords: Machine Learning · Industry 4.0 · Zero-defect-manufacturing · Supervised learning

1 Introduction

From the early eras of the industrial revolution, the problem of defected manufacturing (due to human errors, material deficiencies or manufacturing processes misconfigurations) still remains unsolved. In the framework of Industry 4.0, conventional methods

© IFIP International Federation for Information Processing 2022
Published by Springer Nature Switzerland AG 2022
I. Maglogiannis et al. (Eds.): AIAI 2022, IFIP AICT 647, pp. 79–88, 2022.
https://doi.org/10.1007/978-3-031-08337-2_7

for reducing defected products are gradually converted towards proactive and predictive measures in the industrial production chain, involving the digitization of the manufacturing process [1]. The emerging concept of Zero-Defect Manufacturing (ZDM) primarily aimed to detect the defects in the production chain and identify required corrective actions to minimize the loss of the raw materials and the associated cost, while in parallel optimizing the resource allocation and management in the production chain [2]. Importantly, the wasted resources involved in the production of defected products have additionally a significant contribution to the environmental footprint of the manufacturing industry.

Although the digital revolution was a crucial step towards expediting the digitalization of the manufacturing process, the emergence of Artificial Intelligence (AI) solutions is considered the substantial breakthrough towards ZDM. AI-assisted solutions and Machine Learning (ML) algorithms have been developed to monitor and manage the manufacturing production, targeting to optimize the available resources and the usage of raw materials [3]. The extensive utilization of AI/ML methods has therefore boosted the manufacturing industry towards decreasing the occurrence of defected products, eliminating the wasted resources and costs of the defects and minimizing its environmental footprint [2].

The majority of the ML algorithms that are typically employed in the manufacturing domain require vast amounts of historically gathered data. Through data processing and analysis, ML models are trained based on a specific dataset and are then able to provide estimations and predictions or find hidden patterns, complex correlations and irregularities [4, 5]. The ML algorithms can be categorized in: (i) Supervised Learning (SL) algorithms that require labeled data in the form of input and labeled output data pairs. SL algorithms can be used for classification or regression problems, depending on whether the output takes discrete values (classes) or continuous values; (ii) Unsupervised Learning (UL) methods that do not require labeled output dataset; instead, they use the input data to find clusters that exhibit similar features; (iii) Reinforcement Learning (RL) algorithms that are based on a trial and error process of an agent interacting with the environment [6].

It is worth noting that although the ML deployment methods are well-established in the manufacturing domain, ML models abide by the following constraints: (i) as aforementioned, these algorithms require huge amounts of data in order to provide efficient solutions and predictions; (ii) the quality of the collected data has a direct impact on the training procedure of ML models (for instance well-known overfitting or underfitting issues [4]). In this way, each trained ML model is data-dependent and may possibly lead to inaccurate estimates in case of insufficient or noisy dataset; (iii) ML models that are trained to optimize the parameters of an individual machine or to enhance the efficiency of a specific manufacturing process cannot be easily generalized to other pieces of equipment or different processes.

Offset printing is a widely-used printing process for multiple products including, amongst others, newspapers, magazines, labels and books. The offset printing process consists of three phases, namely the pre-press, press and post-press. In each one of these three phases, several (raw, organic, chemical and recycled) materials are used, including paper, water, ink, aluminum, alcohol solutions, having a direct impact on the environmental footprint of the printing process. It is estimated that over the course of a year, the production-related CO_2 emissions of a regular offset printing press amount to around 7,100 metric tons for 36 million printed sheets per year, while the paper waste accounts for 230 metric tons [7].

Despite the efforts spent on the formalization and standardization of the different procedures across the various offset printing processes, as well as on providing incentives to the personnel to provide products of high quality, defective products appear along the manufacturing production chain. The main issues that are currently faced within the offset printing production chain include: (i) lack of digitalization of physical processes that would enable real time decision making; (ii) plethora and diversity of production characteristics that do not allow direct process standardization; (iii) defected products are identified at the latest stages of the offset printing production chain, resulting in overdue a-posteriori manual corrective actions; (iv) the environmental footprint of the offset printing industry is considerable, since various waste materials are produced throughout the production chain [8].

The present paper outlines the implementation and comparison of SL algorithms in a labeled dataset from the offset printing industry, targeting to demonstrate the potency of ML-assisted methods towards ZDM. The purpose of the SL modeling is to link the specific characteristics of the received customer orders with the amount of defects in the printing process. The accurate correlation of order features with the defected products will result in beneficial machine selection policy, which in turn will contribute to the enhancement of the production efficiency, the minimization of defected products and the reduction of the company's environmental footprint. In summary, the contributions of this work can be identified as: (i) the exploitation of historical knowledge extracted by a real printing industry environment to obtain accurate and machine-specific supervised learning models, (ii) the proposition of a machine selection policy targeting at minimizing the printing defects by proactive allocation of orders to machines, (iii) the training, testing and comparison of multiple regression models (namely 10) to properly map the regressors to machine-specific datasets, (iv) the implementation of both single-model and multi-model (or ensemble) regressors to investigate potential accuracy benefits in using combinations of multi-predictors and (v) the utilization of both classical ML and Deep Learning based schemes to estimate the printing accuracy of multi-feature orders.

2   Methodology and Algorithmic Approach

2.1   Available Dataset

The methodology presented in the current work is based on a labelled dataset, incorporating both historical (last 3 years) and recently collected data that will allow accurate training and verification of the developed ML tools, as well as comparison of the results with the actual historical events. Each of the collected data samples follows the press process of a particular printing order with specific characteristics. In order to maintain a balanced dataset amongst the five printing machines, 10K orders for each individual machine were selected as a representative subset of raw data, leading to a total of 50K historical samples. The order-specific characteristics include:

i.   *Associated machine ID:* The ID of the machine (1–5) that the particular order was forwarded for printing.
ii. *Quantity:* The amount of paper pieces requested in this specific order. *Quantity* takes integer values extending to up to 1000 pieces, depending on the type of the printing assignment (e.g. newspaper, poster, etc.).
iii. *Quality:* The quality of the paper associated with the specific printing order. The *Quality* parameter takes discrete values (1, 2 or 3) depending on the properties of the requested paper. In this context, class 1 stands for 'Velvet' paper quality (the most-frequently used), whereas categories 2 and 3 represent the 'Uncoated' and 'Illustration/Gloss' paper quality respectively.
iv. *Color:* This categorical variable denotes the color requirements of the particular printing assignment. The most requested color requirement is the 4-color printing (class 1), followed by 4 + 1 color printing (class 2 involving the use of gold and/or silver colors) and grayscale printing (class 3 entailing only black and white colors).
v.   *Ink:* The estimated consumed ink level per paper piece (typically 0.1 to 1 gr).
vi. *Type:* Type 1 designates that the order shall follow the 'Book' printing process, type 2 describes the 'Poster' requirements, while type 3 determines the 'Journal' specifications.
vii. *Accuracy* ratio: The amount of satisfactory printed paper pieces are reported against the required *Quantity*. The ratio between them indirectly reveals the percentage of defected products, ranging from 0–1.

2.2 Machine Selection Framework

The proposed SL modeling framework involves the training of machine-specific ML models based on the described dataset, i.e. the orders that have been historically executed in the five printing machines. For these purposes, the order characteristics (*Quantity, Quality, Color, Ink* and *Type*) are considered as the input features of the ML modeling methods, while the *Accuracy* ratio is the labeled output variable.

Once these machine-specific ML models have been adequately trained and validated via testing data (not encountered during the training), they can be used for inference purposes on previously unseen orders. Figure 1 illustrates the machine selection framework. A new arriving order is accompanied by specific order characteristics. Then, these order features are used as input parameters to all five ML models for each individual machine, enabling the prediction of the machine-specific *Accuracy* ratio for the new order. The ML model of the machine that exhibits the maximum *Accuracy* ratio specifies the selection of the machine that will yield the minimum number of defects during the printing process of the particular order.

2.3 ML Algorithms for Accuracy Prediction

In principle, ML algorithms can be employed to create a regression model for each machine, using historical order-specific features as inputs and the respective accuracy score (good amount divided by the total amount) as labels. To find the best regressor for each machine, several ML regression algorithms were employed and tested on each machine-specific datasets [4, 9, 10]:

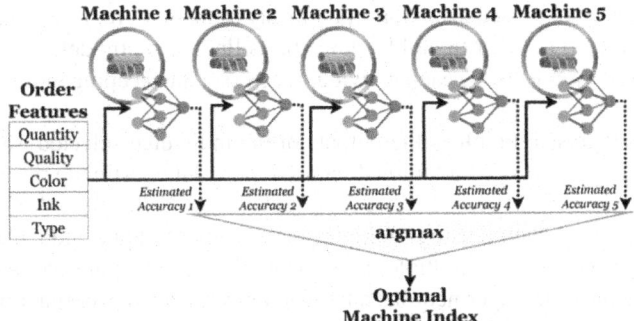

Fig. 1. ML-assisted framework for selecting the best printing machine. During the inference phase, the features of the new order pass through all machine-specific regression models and the printing machine exhibiting the best estimated Accuracy is selected.

i.   *Linear Regression (LR)* assumes that the target variable can be predicted through a weighted linear combination of the N independent variables. It results into a linear model with coefficients w_i ($i = 1, 2, \ldots N$), graphically represented by a straight line that minimizes the residual sum of squares between the actual and predicted *Accuracy* values.

ii. *Decision Tree (DT)* regressor is a non-parametric ML model that decides where and how to split the feature space, so as to ensure high information entropy in each decision area. As a result, a rule-based tree is constructed based on the previous separations of the feature space until no further splitting is required.

iii. *Support Vector Regression (SVR)* uses an ε-insensitive tube to allow for more flexibility in errors. Unlike *Linear Regression*, *SVR* penalizes only the data points that have at least ε distance from the fitting curve. The target of the SVR is to fit the best line within a threshold value (ε), reflecting the distance between the hyperplane and boundary line.

iv. *Stochastic Gradient Descent (SGD)* regression is actually an optimization method that produces a linear model by minimizing a regularized empirical loss. The method relies on the calculation of the loss gradient of each sample, whereas the model parameters are gradually updated depending on the selected learning rate.

v.   *Random Forest (RF)* regression is an ensemble learning model that is constructed by fitting N decision trees in N subsets of the whole dataset. Given a new data point, the final prediction is obtained by averaging the individual prediction of each tree.

vi. *AdaBoost* regression is a meta-estimator that creates multiple copies of a base estimator (for instance, *Decision Tree* regressor already fitted on the original dataset). Each copy adjusts its weights according to the prediction error of the base estimator and new predictions can be performed by inferring the ensemble of these models.

vii. *Bagging* ensemble method is a meta-estimator constructed by randomly picking N different subsets of the original dataset, each one being trained on an initial base estimator. The individual predictions of the base regressors are the averaged to form the final output.

viii. *Voting* regressor is used to combine previously trained ML regressors (even ensemble estimators) in order to build a powerful collaborative model. New predictions are derived by consulting each individual regressor and keeping the average output value.

ix. *Stacking* regressor employs the outputs of the individual selected estimators and uses them as input in an additional regression model to estimate the final output.

x. *Multi-Layer Perceptron (MLP)* or *Artificial Neural Networks (ANNs)* is a supervised learning scheme using multiple stacked layers (input, hidden and output). Each layer consists of multiple units (neurons) that compute the weighted sum of all the previous-layer neurons and then apply an activation function (e.g. softmax, ReLu, etc.). MLP properly adjusts the weights of the network so as to ensure minimization of the prediction error (or loss function).

3 Numerical Results

For each of the following models, a 90/10% training/test split was performed for each machine-specific dataset. Notably, to account for large variations of the features values during the training, the scalar order features (*Ink* and *Quantity*) were scaled before training so as to range between [0,1] using Min-Max scaler. All algorithmic implementations were conducted in Python 3.0 using the scikit-learn ML library [11].

3.1 Training of the Multi-layer Perceptron

The performance of the MLPs is strongly influenced by the network depth (number of hidden layers) and the considered learning rate. In this section, the optimal hyper-parameters of the MLP are fine-tuned for each machine. To stabilize the values of the learning parameters, we conducted extensive simulations with varying learning rates ($\alpha = 0.1, 0.01, 0.001, 0.0001, 0.00001$) and number of hidden layers ($H = 1, 2, 3, 4, 5$). The number of neurons in the ith hidden layer is $2^i \times 10$. For each (α, H) combination, the validation metric was the mean squared error (MSE) between the actual and predicted *Accuracy* on the testing samples. The optimal (α, H) combination corresponded to the minimum convergence loss. Figure 2 illustrates the training loss curves for the optimal (α, H) configuration for each individual machine (Fig. 2A–E), as well as the validation MSE per machine (Fig. 2F).

3.2 Ensemble Learning Techniques

In this section, we illustrate the convergence validation loss of the ensemble learning algorithms as a function of the number of the estimators used in the ensemble models. Specifically, we investigated the impact of the number of estimators on the performance of *RF*, *AdaBoost* and *Bagging* regressors. Figure 3 depicts the validation MSE loss for varying (10–200) number of individual estimators in each printing machine. The optimal number of estimators for (*RF*, *AdaBoost*, *Bagging*) was (180, 10, 180), (180, 10, 180), (80, 10, 80), (180, 10, 180) and (180, 10, 170) for machines 1–5, respectively. Generally, we noticed that *RF* and *Bagging* regressors become more accurate with increasing number of estimators, whereas *AdaBoost* was insensitive to the considered dataset splits.

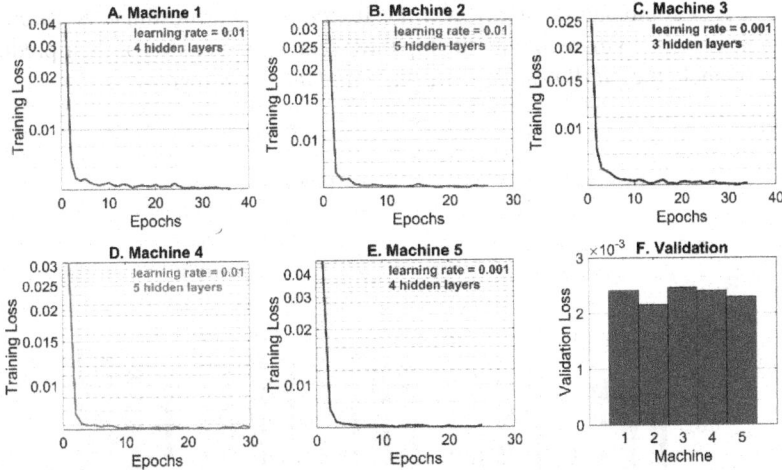

Fig. 2. Training insights of ANNs. **A–E.** Training loss curves for machines 1–5 employing the optimal learning rate and number of hidden layers. **F.** Performance of the derived models in terms of validation MSE on the testing data.

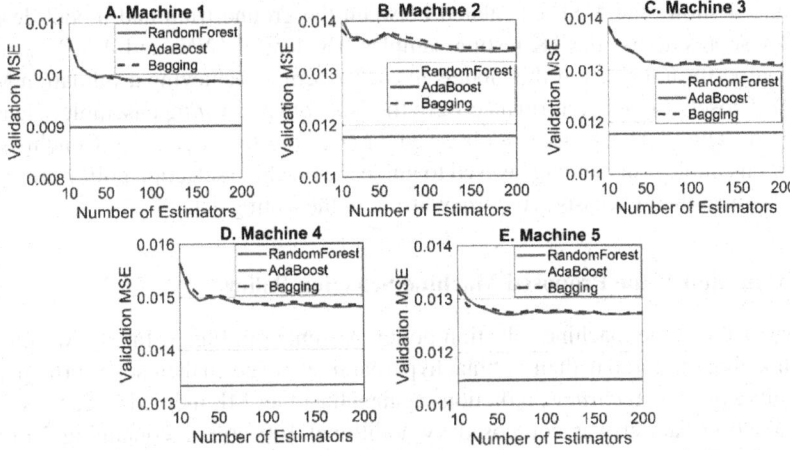

Fig. 3. Impact of the number of estimators on the validation MSE loss of the Ensemble Learning Schemes (*RF, AdaBoost, Bagging* regressors).

3.3 Comparison Between ML Methods

In this section, the regression performance is compared across 10 machine-specific ML models, namely *Linear Regression, Decision Tree, Support Vector Regression, Stochastic Gradient Descent, Random Forest, AdaBoost, Bagging, Voting, Stacking* and *Multi-Layer Perceptron* (ANNs). Note that, to guarantee optimal performance in each individual model, ensemble learning schemes have been configured in their optimal number of estimators (see Sect. 3.2), whereas the Neural Networks have been inferred using the optimal (α, H) combination (see Sect. 3.1). In addition, meta-estimators *Voting* and *Stacking* have been configured with the top three regressors in terms of their prediction accuracy, namely the *AdaBoost, Bagging* and *Random Forest* regressors.

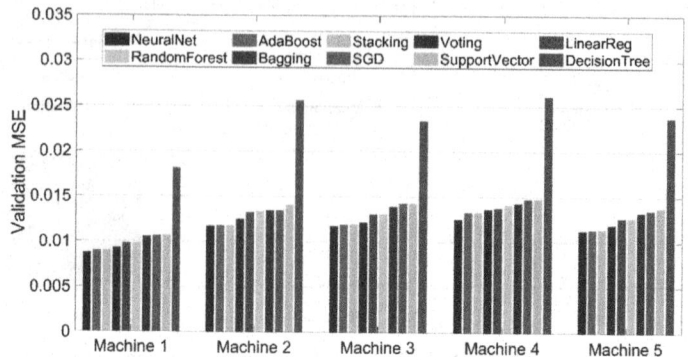

Fig. 4. Comparison of all developed ML algorithms in terms of validation MSE between actual and predicted *Accuracy* values.

Figure 4 shows the MSE calculated between the ground-truth and model derived *Accuracy* scores across the 1K testing samples. Evidently, *ANNs* and *AdaBoost* constantly outperform the rest of the models in each machine, achieving a validation MSE of ~0.01. Closely to this performance were the *Stacking* and *Voting* ensemble schemes, whereas the worst performance was observed for *Decision Tree* regressors. Conclusively, *ANNs* or ensemble schemes can be used to guide the machine selection policy presented in Fig. 1, given their excessive *Accuracy* fitting in the testing data.

3.4 Evaluation of the Proposed Machine Selection Policy

Here we evaluate the machine selection policy presented in Fig. 1. Firstly, we use the ANN models configured in their optimal hyperparameters, given their superiority in providing more precise *Accuracy* predictions against the other ML methods (see Sect. 3.3). The evaluation dataset was composed by additional 100 orders, containing 20 order for each machine (i.e. 20 × 5) that have perfectly executed at the respective machine (*Accuracy* values > 98.5%). In this sense, it is known a-priori that the first 20 samples have to be classified in machine 1, the second 20 samples to machine 2, and so on. The goal of the presented evaluation scheme is (i) to validate whether the proposed machine selection policy (see Fig. 1) properly classifies the orders to machines and (ii) to quantify the true positive rate (i.e. number of correctly allocated orders to the respective machine) of each machine. Figure 5 illustrates the confusion matrix of the classification scheme, with the element (i, j) reflecting the number of orders the were predicted to be executed in machine j when the optimal selection was the machine i. As evidently shown by the non-diagonal elements of each row, a misclassification rate of 3/20, 6/20, 0/20, 5/20 and 4/20 was derived for machines 1–5, respectively.

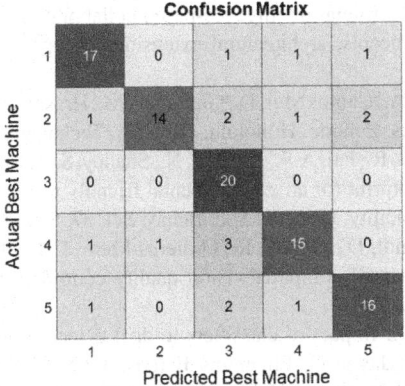

Fig. 5. Confusion Matrix of the Machine Selection policy on the evaluation dataset. Diagonal elements represent the number of orders that were correctly classified to the respective machine.

4 Conclusion

In this paper, an ML-based policy for assigning orders to printing machines is proposed. Using a real dataset from an offset printing company, we trained a machine-specific multi-feature regression model to accurately predict the defect ratio for new orders, targeting at proactively selecting the proper machine to execute a given order. In addition, ten different regression schemes were contrasted for comparative purposes, including classical ML, ensemble and Deep Learning methods. Towards minimizing the defects, numerical outcomes confirmed that the proposed machine selection scheme can efficiently provide order accuracy predictions, with the ANN and ensemble methods outperforming the rest of the regression algorithms. Results can be used for further validating experiments as benchmark.

Acknowledgment. This work has been partially supported by the project Offspring, under the open call of EFPF project, funded by the European Commission under Grant Agreement number 825075 through the Horizon 2020 program.

References

1. Dalenogare, L.S., Benitez, G.B., Ayala, N.F., Frank, A.G.: The expected contribution of Industry 4.0 technologies for industrial performance. Int. J. Prod. Econ. **204**, 383–394 (2018)
2. Psarommatis, F., Sousa, J., Mendonça, J.P., Kiritsis, D.: Zero-defect manufacturing the approach for higher manufacturing sustainability in the era of industry 4.0: a position paper. Int. J. Prod. Res. **60**, 1–19 (2021)
3. Angelopoulos, A., et al.: Tackling faults in the industry 4.0 era—a survey of machine-learning solutions and key aspects. Sensors **20**(1), 109 (2020)
4. Caiazzo, B., Di Nardo, M., Murino, T., Petrillo, A., Piccirillo, G., Santini, S.: Towards Zero Defect Manufacturing paradigm: a review of the state-of-the-art methods and open challenges. Comput. Ind. **134**, 103548 (2022)

5. Trakadas, P., et al.: An artificial intelligence-based collaboration approach in industrial IoT manufacturing: key concepts, architectural extensions and potential applications. Sensors **20**(19), 5480 (2020)

6. Kaloxylos, A., Gavras, A., Camps Mur, D., Ghoraishi, M., Hrasnica, H.: AI and ML—enablers for beyond 5G networks. Zenodo, Honolulu, HI, USA, Technical report (2020)

7. Amon-Tran, I., Anayath, R., Pai, A.S., Kamath, N., Shenoy, S., Harikrishnan, A.: An approach to minimize carbon footprint for an environmental friendly printing by optimizing an offset machine in a printing facility. Procedia Soc. Behav. Sci. **37**, 514–527 (2012)

8. Villalba-Diez, J., Schmidt, D., Gevers, R., Ordieres-Meré, J., Buchwitz, M., Wellbrock, W.: Deep learning for industrial computer vision quality control in the printing industry 4.0. Sensors **19**(18), 3987 (2019)

9. Angelopoulos, A., et al.: Impact of classifiers to drift detection method: a comparison. In: Iliadis, L., Macintyre, J., Jayne, C., Pimenidis, E. (eds.) EANN 2021. PINNS, vol. 3, pp. 399–410. Springer, Cham (2021). https://doi.org/10.1007/978-3-030-80568-5_33

10. Dengler, S., Lahriri, S., Trunzer, E., Vogel-Heuser, B.: Applied machine learning for a zero defect tolerance system in the automated assembly of pharmaceutical devices. Decis. Support Syst. **146**, 113540 (2021)

11. Pedregosa, F., et al.: Scikit-learn: machine learning in Python. J. Mach. Learn. Res. **12**, 2825–2830 (2011)

Bias in Face Image Classification Machine Learning Models: The Impact of Annotator's Gender and Race

Andreas Kafkalias[1], Stylianos Herodotou[1], Zenonas Theodosiou[1],
and Andreas Lanitis[1,2]([⊠])

[1] CYENS Center of Excellence, Nicosia, Cyprus
z.Theodosiou@cyens.org.cy
[2] Visual Media Computing Lab, Department of Multimedia and Graphic Arts,
Cyprus University of Technology, Limassol, Cyprus
andreas.lanitis@cut.ac.cy

Abstract. An important factor that ensures the correct operation of Machine Learning models is the quality of data used during the model training process. Quite often, training data is annotated by humans, and as a result, annotation bias may be introduced. In this study, we focus on face image classification and aim to quantify the effect of annotation bias introduced by different groups of annotators, allowing in that way the understanding of the problems that arise due to annotation bias. The results of the experiments indicate that the performance of Machine Learning models in several face image interpretation tasks is correlated to the self-reported demographic characteristics of the annotators. In particular, we found significant correlation to annotator race, while correlation to gender is less profound. Furthermore, experimental results show that it is possible to determine the group of annotators involved in the annotation process by considering the annotation data provided by previously unseen annotators. The results emphasize the risks of annotation bias in Machine Learning models.

Keywords: Machine learning · Annotation bias · Face images

1 Introduction

Over the last decade, the use of Machine Learning (ML) has increased dramatically [11] as numerous daily tasks are accomplished based on ML models. For example, ML has been used in recommendation systems, speech recognition, robot control, medical diagnosis, natural language processing, weather forecast, biometric authentication, text/image synthesis and for many other applications.

This project is funded by the Cyprus Research and Innovation Foundation under grant EXCELLENCE/0918/0086 (DESCANT) and by the European Union's Horizon 2020 Research and Innovation Programme under Grant Agreement No. 739578 (RISE).

© IFIP International Federation for Information Processing 2022
Published by Springer Nature Switzerland AG 2022
I. Maglogiannis et al. (Eds.): AIAI 2022, IFIP AICT 647, pp. 89–100, 2022.
https://doi.org/10.1007/978-3-031-08337-2_8

At its core, an ML model will only be as good as the data used for training the model. The main issue that relates to the quality of a training dataset is how well training samples represent the classes to be classified, in terms of quality and quantity. Furthermore, an important aspect of the training data is the quality of the annotation, as imperfections in the annotation process can influence the training data quality. Quite often, the annotation process requires human expertise, and as a result it is subjected to the expression of social stereotypes. This is because as social beings, humans are continuously engaged in a process of interpreting and forming impressions of others. However, cognitive heuristics often lead us to make trait inferences and evaluations of others that are based on very little concrete evidence (i.e., social stereotyping) [12]. For example, political candidates whose facial appearance is regarded as more accomplished, have a higher chance of winning the elections [20]. The process of data annotation can be influenced by social stereotyping and introduce bias in ML models, that eventually affects their performance.

In this study, we aim to quantify the effect of annotation bias, in terms of the performance of ML models, allowing in that way the understanding of the problems that arise due to the expression of social stereotypes in the annotation process. In particular, we compare the performance of ML models trained using data annotated by male annotators, female annotators, and annotators belonging to different (self-reported) racial groups. All groups of annotators annotated face images in relation to the classification tasks of gender recognition, race classification, attractiveness estimation, and trustworthiness estimation of subjects shown in face images. The comparison of the performance of ML models trained using data annotated by different annotator groups, allows the derivation of conclusions related to the effects of social bias (stereotyping) in ML. To further emphasize the extent of the annotation bias problem, we also present results that show that it is possible to determine the group of annotators involved in the annotation process, by considering the annotation data provided.

2   Background and Literature Review

Since the main classification tasks considered in this paper relate to face image interpretation, a brief review of the relevant literature of this topic is provided, followed by a review of the work related to bias in ML.

2.1   Face Image Interpretation

Zhao et al. [24] provide a thorough survey of the conventional methods used for face recognition where they present the main steps that include the tasks of face detection and feature extraction. They also elaborate on the methods used in the face recognition step which they divide into three categories: holistic matching methods, feature-based matching methods and hybrid methods. More recent surveys on face recognition focus on the use of deep networks by introducing different dedicated network architectures used for face image recognition [9, 15].

Apart from the face recognition task, other surveys focus on different face image interpretation tasks such as emotion recognition [14], age estimation [18], and pose estimation [16].

In this paper, we focus on the tasks of gender recognition, race recognition, attractiveness estimation and trustworthiness estimation. While for the case of gender and race recognition, a plethora of techniques were reported in the literature [8,17], only few attempts were recorded for the problems of attractiveness estimation and trustworthiness estimation. Todorov et al. [21] build a model for representing face trustworthiness using a computer model for face representation. Using this model, they generated novel faces with an increased range of trustworthiness. Xu et al. [23] propose the use of the Hierarchical Multi-task Network (HMTNet) network, that performs gender, race and facial attractiveness estimation simultaneously. Experimental results reported for the combined gender, race and attractiveness estimation tasks, outperform the results obtained by other deep architectures.

2.2   Bias in Computer Vision Algorithms

Fabbrizi et al. [6] present an overview of the major biases encountered in computer vision tasks that include selection, framing and label biases. Selection bias can be characterised as "any disparities or associations created as a result of the process by which subjects are included in a visual dataset" [6]. Selection bias is encountered in numerous ML models. For example Kay et al. [13] examined the representation of men and women in different occupations, in order to demonstrate that selection bias exists in search engines. More specifically, they were able to show that in male-dominated occupations, the male gender dominance is even more present in the Google's image search engine. However, for the respective female-dominated occupations, the results are more balanced. This showcases systematic selection biases in their retrieval algorithms and proves the importance of data gathering processes.

Framing biases in Computer Vision can arise by selecting or choosing specific characteristics and aspects in visual datasets which mislead and cause interpretation issues for the image portrayed. According to Coleman [5], this is usually achieved by manipulation of an image through editing, cropping or selecting a particular view/angle. The work of Heuer et al. [10] on the depiction of obesity in US online news websites demonstrate how framing biases can affect the meaning of a picture. Their analysis shows how obese people are portrayed with negative characteristics such as cropped heads, while non-obese people are portrayed without such characteristics. Such cruel effects will influence the opinion of the common viewer and therefore the meaning of the image.

Label bias is usually introduced during the annotation process, where different annotators may produce misleading labels. For example, social factors, such as the global pandemic of COVID-19 or the Black Lives Matter movement, or even personal circumstances may influence the annotation process. Christoforou et al. [4] focus on label bias and the limitations of crowdsourced data. They address this issue by clustering annotated data for face images collected before and after the COVID-19 pandemic. Using the Chicago Face Database they created two clusters based on health-related and identity tags. They demonstrated that temporal variations affect the annotation of data based on crowdsourcing. Christoforou et al. [4] points out the limitations that emerge with crowdsourced data based on the influence of consequential events around the globe, which is something that the requester must recognise, manage and ensure to raise awareness to the annotators. Torralba and Efros [22] suggest that label biases can also come up as different annotators can think up a variety of labels for a single object. This usually appears within enormous datasets where an object can take multiple names. Even though face classification is not very complex, the process of annotating a face dataset can be affected by the bias and viewpoint of the annotators. Previous attempts to create face datasets based on the opinion of annotators have shown that their opinion will reflect heavily on the labelling. For example, Liang et al. [7] showcased the bias of the annotators that participated in the study by creating a facial beauty dataset based on features such as attractiveness.

3   Face Database and Annotation

The data used for the project are images from the Chicago Face Database (CFD) [1] and more precisely, the main CFD image set that consists of 597 face images of unique individuals. The CFD includes images of men and women, belonging to four racial groups. Figure 1 shows typical samples of images from the CFD used in our experiments. All images in the CFD were annotated on average by 47 annotators and the mean among all annotations provided is considered as the ground truth, as is common practice in the field. Ground truth includes labels for the classification tasks considered in this work such as the gender of each subject (Male/Female), race (Latino, Asia, Black White, and additional mixed races), attractiveness (scale 1 to 7, where 1 means lowest attractiveness), and trustworthiness (scale 1 to 7, where 1 means lowest trustworthiness).

| (a) Asian Female (AF-209) | (b) Black Male (BM-213) | (c) Latino Female (LF-249) | (d) White Male (WM-038) |

Fig. 1. Sample of images used in modelling from the CDF. The tags in the brackets represent the gender, race and their ID in the Database.

For the needs of this work, a dedicated annotation process was set up through Clickworker [2]. Clickworker is an online platform where freelancers in their own free time, get paid for micro jobs such as image annotation. Annotators from different racial groups, different genders and different ages were invited to participate. During the annotation process, annotators had to specify the gender, race (Asian, Black, Latino, White, Multi-race or Other), level of attractiveness (scale 1 to 7), and the level of trustworthiness (scale 1 to 7) of each subject shown in an image. Furthermore, annotators were asked to provide information about their own gender, race, age, and employment status.

Three hundred eighty-eight annotators participated in the experiment. Among the annotators 52% identified themselves as males, 47% as females and 1% as other. Regarding their race, 69% identified themselves as White, 12% as Black, 9% as Asian, 6% as Latino, and 2% as Multi-racial and the rest 2% as other.

Every image in the CFD was labelled by at least four different annotators, resulting in a dataset of 2370 different entries. This implies that some of the images were not annotated by all different genders and races. The label of an image under any race or gender was chosen by the majority of the corresponding category. In the case of race, although annotators could indicate six different labels (Asian, Black, Latino, Mixed, Other or White), only the labels Asian, Black, Latino, and White were considered as only in very few occasions the labels Mixed and Other were indicated by annotators. Furthermore the ratings of trustworthiness and attractiveness provided were mainly in the range of 3 to 5, rather than receiving values covering the full 1 to 7 scale. For this reason, responses for the ratings of the two quantities were re-scaled to cover the whole range of 1 to 7. Given the uncertainly in providing an exact value for trustworthiness and attractiveness, the corresponding ratings were divided into the three categories of low, medium and high. Within this context data within the range of 1 to 3 was assigned to the low value, ratings of 4 was given the medium and ratings in the range of 5 to 7 were given a high value. As a result, the trustworthiness and attractiveness estimation problems were posed as three-class classification problems.

4   Experiment 1: Comparing the Performance of Annotator-Specific Classification Models

The aim of this experiment is to compare the performance of ML models trained using the collected data, as to quantify the extent of possible bias introduced by different groups of annotators.

4.1   Model Training

During the process of model training, nine different Deep Learning Models were trained for each of the four tasks of gender, race, attractiveness and trustworthiness classification. For each model trained, the training data used is the one provided by the six groups of annotators (Male, Female, Asian, Black, Latino, White). Furthermore, for each classification task a model was trained based on the ground truth provided with the Chicago Face Database, and an additional model was trained based on randomly annotated data. To compensate for the fact that the vast majority of the annotated samples were attributed to White annotators, a randomly selected subset of samples annotated by White annotators was selected, where the number of observations in that case was on par with the numbers of observations from Asian, Black and Latino annotators. The model trained using the subset of white annotators was called "Reduced White" (RWh).

Model training was done using the lobe.ai tool [3]. By using open-source Machine Learning Architectures, the lobe.ai tool is able to automate Deep Learning classification tasks without the need to perform a rigorous manual model optimisation process, ensuring that all models under comparison are trained using exactly the same training and model optimisation procedures. Furthermore, the lobe.ai tool is able to achieve an excellent performance at low computational costs. However, although lobe.ai allows the export of trained models for use in conjunction with the most popular deep learning libraries, it does not provide explicit details of the model architecture and/or the training algorithms used for training the models. After loading the data with the appropriate labels, the lobe.ai tool needs approximately around 10–15 min in training and optimizing the models when the model training procedure was run on an AMD Ryzen 3600 6-Core Processor with 16 GB RAM.

4.2   Results and Discussion

Details of all models trained in terms of the number of samples and the performance achieved on the train and test data is shown in Table 1.

Table 1. Models' train and test accuracy for each classification tasks divided by the respective annotation categories. [3]

Model	Num of samples	Gender		Race		Attractiveness		Trustworthiness	
		Train	Test	Train	Test	Train	Test	Train	Test
Ground Truth (GT)	597	99	97	93	91	77	76	62	60
All Annotators (AA)	597	99	98	86	80	62	53	56	36
Male (Ma)	596	92	94	72	32	66	53	59	39
Female (Fe)	592	93	95	84	76	68	50	56	38
Asian (As)	106	94	88	90	65	36	28	44	27
Black (Bl)	165	95	81	80	56	74	36	75	36
Latino (La)	114	89	86	75	76	49	23	70	34
White (Wh)	597	94	93	82	69	70	47	57	39
Reduced White (RWh)	128	92	88	79	65	79	45	62	31
Random (Ra)	597	67	37	54	17	47	27	62	36

As expected models built using the ground truth data outperform the rest of the models. On the other hand, in most cases models built on random data have the worst performance. Apart from the race classification task, models trained using data annotated by male and female annotators have similar performance indicating that, for the tasks considered, the annotation process by male and female annotators leads to models with similar performance. However, models trained using data annotated by annotators belonging to different racial groups display increased diversity in performance.

With the introduction of deep learning and convolutional networks, tasks such as gender classification are now considered trivial for ML problems with expected accuracy of around 95%. However, models trained using data annotated by annotators from different racial backgrounds resulted in worse performance compared to the models built using data from annotators of different genders. Among the classification problems considered, the task of trustworthiness estimation received the lowest classification rates, implies that trust cannot be easily determined based only on facial appearance. For the attractiveness task, the models trained based on the Asian and Latino annotators achieve the worst performance, on par with the performance achieved by the models based on random annotations. This observation can be linked to different attitudes related to attractiveness cultivated in different cultures [19].

Comparing the results of the models built from the entire dataset of the White annotators ('White' model) against the models built with a randomly selected subset of images annotated by White annotators ('Reduced White' model), it is observed that although the models trained using reduced samples achieved lower performance, no major differences in relation to the comparison against models trained using Asian, Latino and Black narrators is observed. Therefore, we can conclude that the results related to the performance of the model trained using White annotators, are not attributed to the higher number of samples used during the training process.

The correlation matrices shown in Fig. 2 demonstrate the percentage agreement between the classification performance achieved by different models, for each task considered in the evaluation. For the tasks of gender and race classification (Fig. 2.(a) and Fig. 2.(b)) most of the models achieve high percentage agreement between each other, with an average of around 90% and 75% respectively. Excluding the models based on Black annotators and random models, the rest of the models have a similar agreement. Even though models based on Black annotators have a high percentage of test accuracy, it is clear that they disagree the most with the rest of the models with an average of 80% for gender and 50% for ethnicity. The contradiction between the agreement of models is attributed to label bias introduced during the annotation process. Based on data from Fig. 2, it is evident that Black annotators classify ethnicity and gender in a different way and this impacts the result of the respective models.

All models built for the trustworthiness estimation task, have very low agreement with each other. Furthermore, classification results for the task of trustworthiness estimation display high diversity among different groups of annotators, indicating the perception of those attributes varies from gender to gender and race to race. The results clearly demonstrate that trustworthiness estimation is subjected to bias due to the annotation process, hence a proper annotation procedure that involves annotators from different groups need to be employed to produce training data suitable for this challenging task. Except for the task of trustworthiness estimation, the models trained based on all white annotators and the models trained using the reduced subset of white annotators have high level of agreement. This indicates that when compared with the annotation bias introduced by annotators from different backgrounds, the bias introduced by different sizes of training samples is less important for the tasks of gender, race and attractiveness classification.

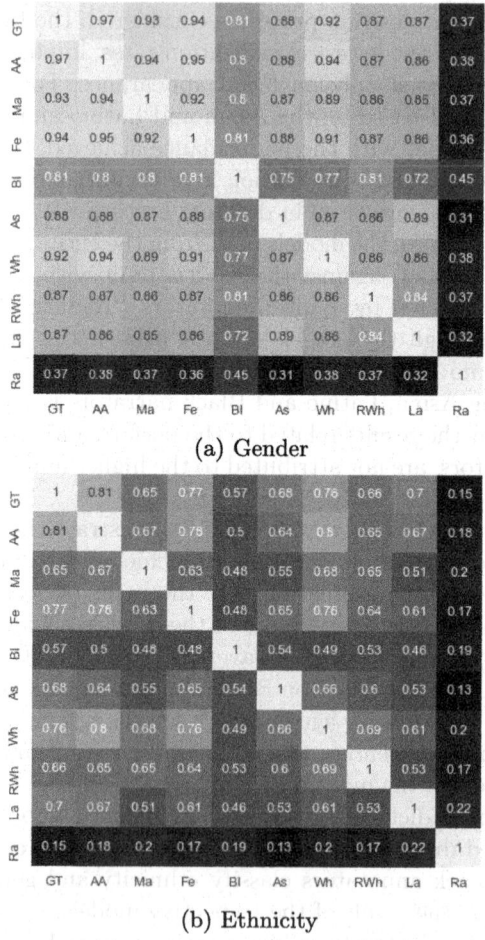

Fig. 2. Correlation Matrices between the models of each category. Light colour indicates high percentage agreement while darker colours low percentage agreement.

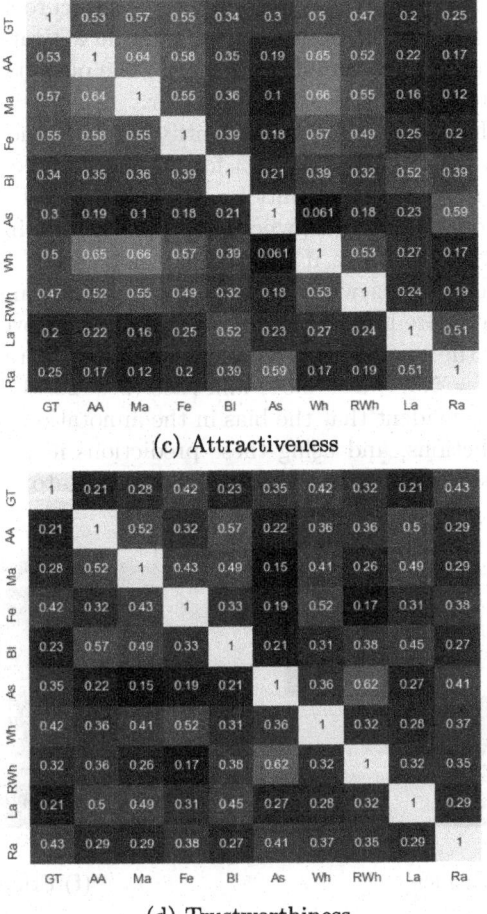

(c) Attractiveness

(d) Trustworthiness

Fig. 2. (*continued*)

5   Experiment 2: Predicting Annotator Groups Based on Annotations

The results of experiment 1 show clear differences in performance, and disagreement between models trained using data annotated by different groups of annotators. To further investigate this phenomenon, the possibility of predicting the gender and the race of an annotator, based on their respective annotations was examined. In this context two classification models were trained. Each of those models take as input the ground truth values of gender, race, attractiveness and trustworthiness for each sample, along with the annotation provided by each annotator, using the data collected through the clickworkers platform (see Sect. 3). The models trained use a Multilayer Perceptron (MLP) architecture with eight inputs, four fully connected layers of 128 neurons with relu activation, a fully connected layer with 64 neurons and relu activation, and an output fully connected layer with a sigmoid activation. The outputs of the model corresponds to the gender and race of an annotator.

Once trained, the models are able to identify correctly the gender with a test accuracy of 70% for the ethnicity and 66% for the gender. The confusion matrices below in Fig. 3 demonstrate the results for the prediction of the annotators.

A cross validation with K folds, where K = 30, was run, in combination with a hypothesis z-test, to examine if the trained models can be used to predict the attributes of annotators with better accuracy than random guesses. The results indicate that there is a statistically significant improvement between the predicted labels of the trained models when compared to random guesses, for both the gender ($z = 5.57 \mid a = 0.01$) and race ($z = 20.54 \mid a = 0.01$). Based on these results, it is evident that the bias in the annotations is reflected as bias in the models predictions, and using these predictions it is possible to reverse engineer the process and identify attributes of an annotator.

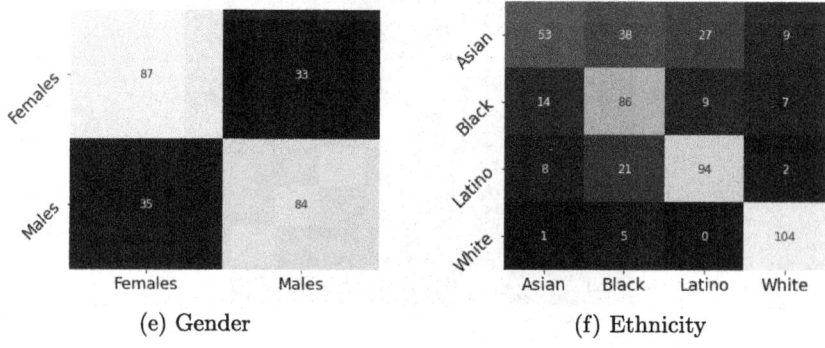

(e) Gender   (f) Ethnicity

Fig. 3. Confusion matrices for both models created for predicting the features of the annotators. Light colour indicates a high prediction count while darker colours a lower prediction count.

6   Conclusions and Future Work

Experimental results presented in this paper demonstrate that the perception of characteristics such as attractiveness and trustworthiness vary as a function of annotator demographics (gender and race). In fact, sometimes machine learning models trained to classify those attributes have higher levels of agreements with models based on random data instead of another category of annotators. Even binary gender classification, which can be considered trivial in face interpretation, show different results when models are trained on data from annotators from different racial backgrounds. Furthermore, the bias in the models predictions makes it possible to reverse engineer and identify attributes of an annotator.

Based on the results obtained, it is evident that computer vision tasks that rely on training data annotated by humans could be heavily influenced by social stereotyping, that can cause biased performance. The work presented in this study provides quantitative results indicating the extend of the problem in several classification tasks, against the groups of annotators used, providing in that way useful insight for researchers involved in similar classification tasks.

The results of this study are demonstrated through an interactive tool at http://descant.cyens.org.cy/, so that the results of this project can be used by Machine Learning practitioners and students, as training material to anticipate the dangers of annotation bias.

In the future, we plan to extend our work to additional classification tasks, and test the extend of stereotype thread bias in different network architectures. Furthermore, we plan to use the lessons learned as part of this effort, to provide ways in which machine learning models can be trained to eliminate the effects of social bias, through a dedicated machine learning process.

Acknowledgements. This project is partially funded by the Cyprus Research and Innovation Foundation under grant EXCELLENCE/0918/0086 (DESCANT) and by the European Union's Horizon 2020 Research and Innovation Programme under Grant Agreement No 739578 (RISE). We would like to thank Dr. Jahna Otterbacher and Dr. Evgenia Christoforou for their contribution in formulating the experiment and for setting up the data collection process.

References

1. Chicago Face Database. https://www.chicagofaces.org/. Accessed 22 Feb 2022
2. Clickworker crowdsourcing. https://www.clickworker.com/. Accessed 22 Feb 2022
3. Lobe.ai webpage. https://www.lobe.ai/. Accessed 22 Feb 2022
4. Christoforou, E., Barlas, P., Otterbacher, J.: It's about time: a view of crowdsourced data before and during the pandemic. In: Proceedings of the 2021 CHI Conference on Human Factors in Computing Systems, pp. 1–14 (2021)
5. Coleman, R.: Framing the pictures in our heads: exploring the framing and agenda-setting effects of visual images. In: Doing News Framing Analysis, pp. 249–278. Routledge (2010)
6. Fabbrizzi, S., Papadopoulos, S., Ntoutsi, E., Kompatsiaris, I.: A survey on bias in visual datasets. arXiv preprint arXiv:2107.07919 (2021)
7. Fei-Fei, L., Fergus, R., Perona, P.: Learning generative visual models from few training examples: an incremental Bayesian approach tested on 101 object categories. In: 2004 Conference on Computer Vision and Pattern Recognition Workshop, p. 178. IEEE (2004)
8. Fu, S., He, H., Hou, Z.G.: Learning race from face: a survey. IEEE Trans. Pattern Anal. Mach. Intell. **36**(12), 2483–2509 (2014)
9. Guo, G., Zhang, N.: A survey on deep learning based face recognition. Comput. Vis. Image Underst. **189**, 102805 (2019)
10. Heuer, C.A., McClure, K.J., Puhl, R.M.: Obesity stigma in online news: a visual content analysis. J. Health Commun. **16**(9), 976–987 (2011)
11. Jordan, M.I., Mitchell, T.M.: Machine learning: trends, perspectives, and prospects. Science **349**(6245), 255–260 (2015)

12. Jussim, L., Nelson, T.E., Manis, M., Soffin, S.: Prejudice, stereotypes, and labeling effects: sources of bias in person perception. J. Pers. Soc. Psychol. **68**(2), 228 (1995)

13. Kay, M., Matuszek, C., Munson, S.A.: Unequal representation and gender stereotypes in image search results for occupations. In: Proceedings of the 33rd Annual ACM Conference on Human Factors in Computing Systems, pp. 3819–3828 (2015)

14. Ko, B.C.: A brief review of facial emotion recognition based on visual information. Sensors **18**(2), 401 (2018)

15. Masi, I., Wu, Y., Hassner, T., Natarajan, P.: Deep face recognition: a survey. In: 2018 31st SIBGRAPI Conference on Graphics, Patterns and Images (SIBGRAPI), pp. 471–478. IEEE (2018)

16. Murphy-Chutorian, E., Trivedi, M.M.: Head pose estimation in computer vision: a survey. IEEE Trans. Pattern Anal. Mach. Intell. **31**(4), 607–626 (2008)

17. Ng, C.-B., Tay, Y.-H., Goi, B.-M.: A review of facial gender recognition. Pattern Anal. Appl. **18**(4), 739–755 (2015). https://doi.org/10.1007/s10044-015-0499-6

18. Panis, G., Lanitis, A.: An overview of research activities in facial age estimation using the FG-NET aging database. In: Agapito, L., Bronstein, M.M., Rother, C. (eds.) ECCV 2014. LNCS, vol. 8926, pp. 737–750. Springer, Cham (2015). https://doi.org/10.1007/978-3-319-16181-5_56

19. Rhodes, G., et al.: Attractiveness of own-race, other-race, and mixed-race faces. Perception **34**(3), 319–340 (2005)

20. Said, C.P., Sebe, N., Todorov, A.: Structural resemblance to emotional expressions predicts evaluation of emotionally neutral faces. Emotion **9**(2), 260 (2009)

21. Todorov, A., Baron, S.G., Oosterhof, N.N.: Evaluating face trustworthiness: a model based approach. Soc. Cogn. Affect. Neurosci. **3**(2), 119–127 (2008)

22. Torralba, A., Efros, A.A.: Unbiased look at dataset bias. In: CVPR 2011, pp. 1521–1528. IEEE (2011)

23. Xu, L., Fan, H., Xiang, J.: Hierarchical multi-task network for race, gender and facial attractiveness recognition. In: 2019 IEEE International Conference on Image Processing (ICIP), pp. 3861–3865. IEEE (2019)

24. Zhao, W., Chellappa, R., Phillips, P.J., Rosenfeld, A.: Face recognition: a literature survey. ACM Comput. Surv. (CSUR) **35**(4), 399–458 (2003)

Decision Tree Induction Through Meta-learning

Caique Augusto Ferreira$^{(\boxtimes)}$ⓘ, Adriano Henrique Cantãoⓘ,
and José Augusto Baranauskas$^{(\boxtimes)}$ⓘ

Department of Computer Science and Mathematics, Faculty of Philosophy,
Sciences and Letters at Ribeirao Preto, University of Sao Paulo,
Bandeirantes Avenue, 3900, Ribeirao Preto, SP 14040-901, Brazil
{caiqueaugustoferreira,cantao,augusto}@usp.br
https://www.usp.br/

Abstract. Symbolic or explainable learning models stand out within the Machine Learning area because they are self-explanatory, making the decision process easier to be interpreted by humans. However, these models are overly responsive to the training set used. Thus, even tiny variations in training sets can result in much worse precision. In this research we propose a meta-learning approach that transforms a Random Forest into a single Decision Tree. Experiments were performed on classification datasets from different domains. Our approach using precision (positive reliability) performs as good as a Random Forest with no statistically significant differences. Yet, its advantage is the interpretability provided by a single decision tree. Results indicate that it is possible to obtain a resulting model which is easier to interpret than a Random Forest, still with higher precision than a standard Decision Tree.

Keywords: Meta-learning · Model combination · Random forest · Meta-decision tree

1 Introduction

Machine Learning (ML) algorithms can be categorized as symbolic and non-symbolic. The symbolic category, also known as interpretable or Explanatory Artificial Intelligence (XAI), is characterized by representations of knowledge that can be easily interpreted by humans on a scale of understanding that can range from the common sense level to the expert level. The non-symbolic category, also known as the black-box, is characterized by representations that are not easily interpreted by humans. For this category, the algorithm develops its own knowledge representation, which generally does not provide any clarification, thus making it difficult to understand [8]. Symbolic learning algorithms contribute a lot to the understanding of induced knowledge (model) needed in many applications [12].

For non-critical applications such as movie, product and digital content recommendations, not understanding how the model achieves the result does not

© IFIP International Federation for Information Processing 2022
Published by Springer Nature Switzerland AG 2022
I. Maglogiannis et al. (Eds.): AIAI 2022, IFIP AICT 647, pp. 101–111, 2022.
https://doi.org/10.1007/978-3-031-08337-2_9

offer significant risks or impacts if the result obtained is not good. However, there are areas, such as medicine and healthcare, where the impact of a wrong prediction can cause great harm [10,17]. Even though the resulting model is used only to support the decision process, the fact of not understanding how the result was obtained is a factor that makes its use unfeasible [23]. The spread of Machine Learning has also led to the emergence of new regulatory laws to control its use towards XAI. For instance, the European Union created the General Data Protection Regulation (GDPR) and its Article 22 defines the right of explanation, and guarantees that anyone affected by the decision of an algorithm has the right to know how that decision was made [6]. Interpretable models are important for human experts and to ensure the model work as expected [4].

The machine learning literature is recently trying to produce interpretable models from black-box models, with new algorithms emerging [20]. LIME (Local Interpretable Model-Agnostic Explanations) is an agnostic and locally linear; it finds a linear model in the neighborhood of the instance to be explained using black-box model decision boundaries [23]. LORE (Local Rule-based Explanations), also an agnostic and local algorithm, tries to explain the decision of a black-box for a given instance by generating a symbolic surrogate model (a Decision Tree) [13]. A Decision Tree is an inherently interpretable model. Each path from the root to a leaf of the decision tree can be easily converted into a rule. Detailed surveys on the explainability of models can be found in [3,14,19].

However, symbolic models are generally less accurate than non-symbolic ones. The ensemble model combination strategy is an alternative to improve the precision and stability of models [1,2,7,22]. Although ensembles, in general, improve individual model precision, for symbolic algorithms, the resulting ensemble model is not symbolic anymore: even considering that each individual model is interpretable, the process of interpreting the resulting ensemble model becomes humanly difficult or infeasible, even for domain experts.

Combining a set of models resulting from the ensemble strategy into a single model is an alternative to minimize the difficulty of interpretation. In this study, we present an algorithm to combine decision trees generated by the Random Forest algorithm into a single decision tree using meta-learning.

The remaining of this work is organized as follows: In Sect. 2 we describe our methodological approach to generate a Meta Decision Tree from a Random Forest. Section 3 shows the empirical setup used to evaluate the proposed algorithm; Sect. 4 shows the experiments and discusses the results; finally, Sect. 5 shows the leaf weighting metrics with better performance of this study, the main contributions and some possible approaches for future work.

2   A Meta Decision Tree Algorithm

The proposed meta-learning approach is represented by Algorithms 1 and 2, where:

- Each attribute in the original set of instances corresponds to a column in the decision table.

- Each leaf in the decision tree corresponds to a single decision table row.
- In the representation of a leaf, the decision table columns assume the values contained in the branches of the subtrees.
- For attributes that are not in the leaf representation, the respective columns assume the value '?', representing the absence of a value or that the test on this attribute is unnecessary.
- A direct way to represent the weight of each leaf is to use the number of instances that reached the respective leaf. However, in this work, were used the metrics described in Sect. 2.1 as leaf weight.

  • If the tree is a single leaf, then the table contains a single row. In the decision table, the attribute columns assume the value '?', the class column assumes the same class as the leaf.

  • If the tree has multiple leaves, for each leaf, a row is generated in the decision table based on the subtree branches from the root to the respective leaf.

According to Algorithm 1, initially, a Random Forest is generated containing decision trees based on the set of instances D (line 2). The number of decision trees was set to $\mathcal{L} = 128$ [21].

Then, each decision tree in the Random Forest is transformed into a decision table (lines 4–7). The Algorithm 2 is responsible for this transformation, it identifies each leaf contained in the decision tree, considering the following information: the subtree branches from the root to the leaf, the class and the number of instances contained in the respective leaf (lines 4–12). For each leaf identified in the decision tree, a new row r is created to store this information (lines 6–10). Thus r represents a row in the resulting decision table R (line 11). In this way, each leaf contained in the decision tree corresponds to a single row in the resulting decision table.

Considering that all $\mathcal{L}$ decision trees contained in the Random Forest were converted to decision tables and merged into Z, the Table 2Instances method (line 8 of the Algorithm 1) transforms Z into a new training set D_{new}, which will be used as input to the Meta Decision Tree inducer. In this step, the meta-learning happens, where the learning acquired by the decision trees contained in the Random Forest is used as a training set for the induction of a Meta Decision Tree, transforming all decision trees into a single decision tree. The Table 2Instances method is responsible for formatting the rows contained in the decision table Z to the format expected by the algorithm used to induce the Meta Decision Tree.

2.1 Leaf-Weighting Metrics

Each path in the decision tree from the root to a leaf corresponds to a rule, which can be seen as having two components $L \rightarrow R$, where L represents the conditions (attribute tests) until reaching that leaf, and R is the class present in that leaf.

Algorithm 1. Meta Decision Tree Induction algorithm

Input: D (set of n classified instances $\{(\mathbf{x}_i, y_i), i = 1, 2, \ldots, n\}$ containing m attributes $\{X_1, X_2, \ldots, X_m\}$), $\mathcal{L}$ (number of decision trees in the Random Forest, where $\mathcal{L} = 128$)
Output: Meta Decision Tree Model

1: **function** MetaDecisionTreeInduction(D, $\mathcal{L}$)
2:   $F = $ buildRandomForest(D, $\mathcal{L}$)
3:   $Z = []$
4:   **for** $i \in \{1, 2, \ldots, \mathcal{L}\}$ **do**
5:     $t = $ Tree2Table(F_i, $\mathcal{L}$, n)
6:     $Z = Z \cup t$
7:   **end for**
8:   $D_{new} = $ Table2Instances(Z)
9:   $T = $ buildDecisionTree(D_{new})
10: **return** T

Algorithm 2. Tree to Table algorithm

Input: T (decision tree), n (number of instances), $\mathcal{L}$ (number of decision trees in the Random Forest)
Output: Decision Table

1: **function** Tree2Table(T, $\mathcal{L}$)
2:   $R = []$
3:   $W = \sum_i w_i$
4:   **for** each leaf $l \in T$ with class C and weight w **do**
5:     $r = []$ {Structure of values $[X_1, \ldots, X_m, Y, \text{Weight}]$}
6:     **for** each attribute X_j with threshold O_j from root to leaf l in T **do**
7:       $r[X_j] = O_j$
8:     **end for**
9:     $r[Y] = C$
10:    $r[\text{Weight}] = \frac{nw}{W\mathcal{L}}$
11:    $R = R \cup r$
12: **end for**
13: **return** R

From this point of view, it is possible to define the corresponding contingency matrix of a leaf (or a rule), shown in Table 1 [18]. In this table, L denotes the set of instances for which the rule condition is true (instances is covered by the rule) and its complement $\bar{L}$ denotes the set of examples for which the rule condition is false (instances is not covered by the rule), and analogously for R and $\bar{R}$. LR denotes the set of instances $L \cap R$ in which L and R are both true (the rule correctly classifies the instances), $L\bar{R}$ denotes the set of instances $L \cap \bar{R}$ where L is true and R is false (the rule misclassifies instances) and so on.

The cardinality of a set A is denoted as $a = |A|$. Thus, l denotes the number of instances in the set L, that is, $l = |L|$, r denotes the number of instances in

Table 1. Contingency matrix for a leaf (rule) $L \to R$

	L	$\bar{L}$	
R	lr	$\bar{l}r$	r
$\bar{R}$	$l\bar{r}$	$\bar{l}\bar{r}$	$\bar{r}$
	l	$\bar{l}$	n

the set R, that is, $r = |R|$, lr denotes the number of instances in the LR set with $lr = |LR|$ and so on; $n = l + \bar{l} = r + \bar{r}$ indicates the total number of instances.

The relative frequency $|A|/n = a/n$ associated with the subset A is denoted by $p(A)$, where A is a subset of the n instances. In this way, the relative frequency is used as a probability estimate. The notation $p(A|B)$ follows its usual definition in probability, given by (1), where A and B are both subsets of the n instances.

$$p(A|B) = \frac{p(A \cap B)}{p(B)} = \frac{p(AB)}{p(B)} = \frac{\frac{|AB|}{n}}{\frac{|B|}{n}} = \frac{\frac{ab}{n}}{\frac{b}{n}} = \frac{ab}{b} \tag{1}$$

Many measures can be used to evaluate the performance of a leaf. Precision (positive reliability) is the most common. However, with new problems to be dealt with, new measures such as novelty, simplicity and ease of human understanding may be interesting [24]. Based on the contingency matrix, it is possible to define most measures about rules. Of special interest in this work will be used the positive reliability metrics *prel* (2), novelty *nov* (3), satisfaction *sat* (5) and Laplace precision *lacc* (6).

Positive reliability corresponds to the ratio between the number of instances correctly classified by the rule and the total number of instances covered by the rule. Assumes values in the range $[0, 1]$.

$$prel(L \to R) = p(R|L) = \frac{lr}{l} \tag{2}$$

$$nov(L \to R) = p(LR) - p(L)p(R) = \frac{lr}{n} - \frac{l \cdot r}{n^2} \tag{3}$$

$$nov4(L \to R) = 4 \times nov(L \to R) \tag{4}$$

$$sat(L \to R) = \frac{p(\bar{R}) - p(\bar{R}|L)}{p(\bar{R})} = 1 - \frac{n \cdot l\bar{r}}{l \cdot \bar{r}} \tag{5}$$

$$lacc(L \to R) = \frac{lr + 1}{l + k} \tag{6}$$

Considering L and R, the novelty is defined by checking whether LR is independent of them. This can be obtained by comparing the observed result lr against the expected value under the independence consideration $\frac{l \cdot r}{n}$. The more the observed value differs from the expected value, greater the probability that there is a true and unexpected association between L and R. This metric takes values in the range $[-0.25, 0.25]$. It can be shown that the higher a positive value (close to 0.25), the stronger the association between L and R, while the smaller a negative value (close to -0.25), the stronger the association between L and $\bar{R}$. In this work, the value of the novelty metric was multiplied by four to in order to place the metric in the range $[-1, +1]$, which leads to (4).

Satisfaction is the relative increase in precision between the rule $L \to true$ and the rule $L \to R$. According to [18], this measure, whose values vary in the range $[-1, +1]$, is suitable for tasks aimed at discovering knowledge, being able to promote a balance between rules with different conditions and conclusions.

As can be seen, the novelty and satisfaction metrics can take on negative values. As the purpose of this work is to represent a decision tree containing rules whose conclusion is the class (and not its complement, that is, all other classes), rules with negative values for these two metrics will not be considered.

Laplace's precision does not fit directly into the frequency/probability notation proposed by [18] but fixes the problem of rules with few errors covering many examples of positive reliability [5]. In (6), k represents the number of classes in the training set. This metric takes values in the range $(0, 1)$.

2.2   Tree Leaves Weights Normalization

In the induction process of the Meta Decision Tree, it is expected that such tree reflects the number of examples provided in the training set, in a way analogous to the generation of a single tree without the use of meta-learning. The approach adopted for this in this research is described below.

Let T_i be a Random Forest Tree in which the leaves' weights without normalization are $\{w_{i1}, w_{i2}, \ldots\}$. Let the sum of weights of a tree T_i given by $W_i = \sum_j w_{ij}$. The weights for the tree T_i must be adjusted to sum 1, given by $\{\frac{w_{i1}}{W_i}, \frac{w_{i2}}{W_i}, \ldots\}$. Now, for the tree T_i to represent the total number of instances n of the training set, the bootstrap sample size n_i to generate each tree is equal to the number of instances n in the training set. The weights of each tree are given by $\{n\frac{w_{i1}}{W_i}, n\frac{w_{i2}}{W_i}, \ldots\}$. Considering that there are $\mathcal{L}$ trees in the forest $\{T_1, T_2, \ldots, T_{\mathcal{L}}\}$, it is necessary to adjust the weight of the meta decision tree as being $\{n\frac{w_{i1}}{\mathcal{L}W_i}, n\frac{w_{i2}}{\mathcal{L}W_i}, \ldots\}$ for each decision tree, such as $\{\{n\frac{w_{11}}{\mathcal{L}W_1}, n\frac{w_{12}}{\mathcal{L}W_1}, \ldots\}, \ldots, \{n\frac{w_{\mathcal{L}1}}{\mathcal{L}W_{\mathcal{L}}}, n\frac{w_{\mathcal{L}2}}{\mathcal{L}W_{\mathcal{L}}}, \ldots\}\}$

2.3   Example

Figure 1 presents a simple example of the implementation our algorithm using data from Table 2. The number of instances in each leaf was used to represent the weight of the respective row in the decision table for ease of reading. To start the process, consider a Random Forest that contains only two trees. For the creation of this Random Forest consider the set of instances represented in the Table 2. The process ① is responsible for transforming decision trees into decision tables (Algorithm 2). The process ② performs the union of decision tables, thus forming, after the necessary formatting, a new set of instances. The process ③ performs the induction of the Meta Decision Tree based on the new set of instances.

Table 2. Toy dataset containing instances about friendly and enemy robots described by four attributes (Head, Body, Hold and Smile) and two classes (friend and enemy).

Instance	Head	Body	Hold	Smile	Class
z_1	round	square	flag	no	enemy
z_2	triangular	triangular	balloon	yes	friend
z_3	round	round	flag	yes	friend
z_4	square	triangular	sword	no	enemy
z_5	square	square	balloon	yes	friend
z_6	triangular	round	sword	yes	enemy

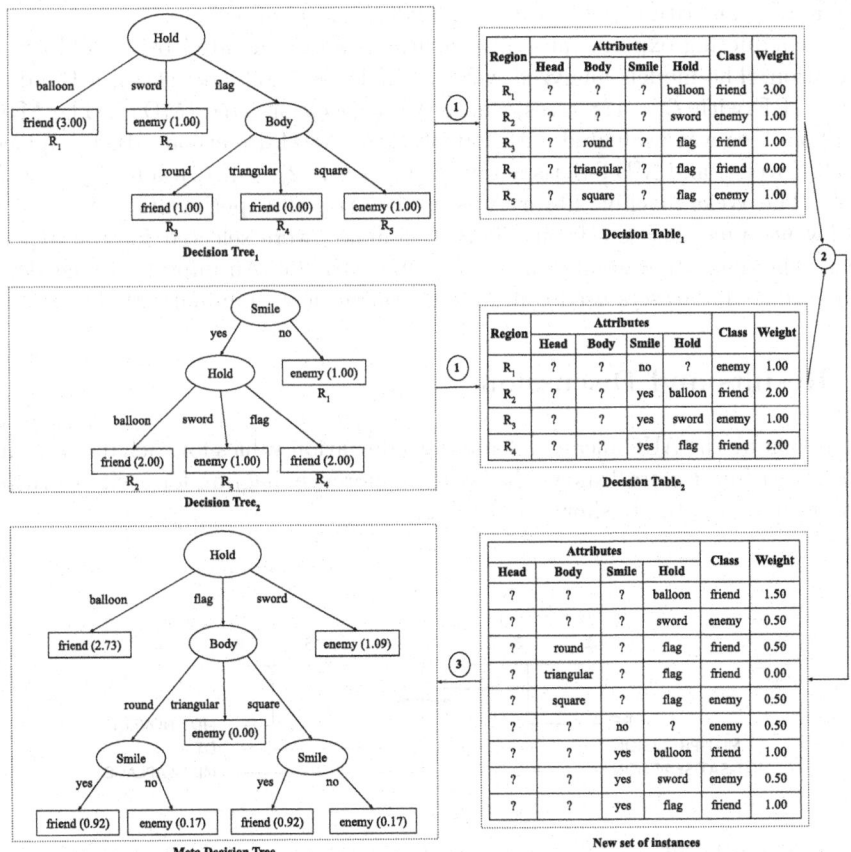

Fig. 1. Example of our meta induction tree algorithm on dataset described in Table 2. In this example, two decision trees are induced (first two trees/tables) that are then combined into a resulting Meta Decision Tree (last tree/table) in figure.

3   Experimental Setup

To analyze the efficiency of the proposed algorithm, it was evaluated through an experimental study as described below. The experimental study compared a single Decision Tree, a Random Forest and the Meta Decision Tree, considering the predictive performance criterion for evaluation.

Predictive performance was evaluated using the multiclass extension of the Area Under the Curve (AUC) measure, which aggregates the AUC values over each pair of classes [16].

Friedman's test [11] was used for pairwise multiple comparisons, which assume that the difference in the data is by chance as the null hypothesis, considering a confidence level of 95%. The null hypothesis assumes all algorithms have equal performance. The Friedman did reject the null hypothesis, and the Bonferroni-Dunn [9] post-hoc test was employed to detect any significant difference among algorithms, also using a confidence level of 95%.

In conducting experiments, all algorithms were evaluated by 10-fold cross-validation. The models analyzed were: a single Decision Tree (DT), a Random Forest (RF with $\mathcal{L} = 128$ trees) and a Meta Decision Tree (MDT). The Meta Decision Tree was evaluated with four weights: MDT-Precision, MDT-Laplace, MDT-Novelty, and MDT-Satisfaction, using Eqs. (2), (6), (4), and (5), respectively. The Weka machine library was used to run all experiments [15].

Twenty-nine datasets from different domains were selected for the experiment. The datasets were obtained from OpenML [25]. An important consideration is that all datasets used contain only categorical (nominal) attributes.

4   Results and Discussion

Table 3 shows the AUC mean and standard deviation values for each dataset and each algorithm. Figure 2 shows the critical difference diagram for each algorithm considering all datasets shown in Table 3.

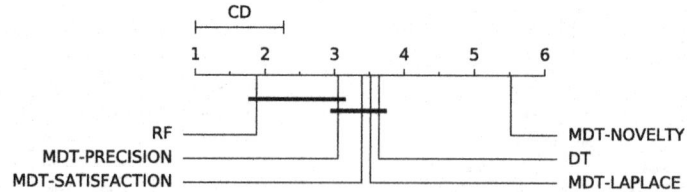

Fig. 2. Critical difference diagram for each algorithm, and all datasets using Bonferroni-Dunn post-hoc test.

Table 3. AUC Mean and standard deviation values from 10-fold cross-validation. The highest figures on a row are in boldface. Green-shaded cells correspond to values that do not have a significant difference (p-value > 0.05) when compared to the best value(s) in the row by the Bonferroni-Dunn post-hoc test.

Dataset	MDT-Prec.	MDT-Lapl.	MDT-Nov.	MDT-Satisf.	RF	DT
audiology	92.03 ± 2.94	81.74 ± 4.80	77.14 ± 0.95	92.11 ± 2.82	**97.42 ± 1.73**	93.22 ± 2.61
blogger	77.71 ± 18.46	76.76 ± 20.21	59.46 ± 20.76	74.35 ± 18.32	**90.12 ± 9.12**	69.4 ± 20.94
boxing1	84.93 ± 15.22	85.00 ± 15.03	50.00 ± 0.00	84.93 ± 15.22	**89.24 ± 8.71**	87.83 ± 12.47
boxing2	**85.69 ± 8.93**	85.66 ± 8.99	50.00 ± 0.00	**85.69 ± 8.93**	85.06 ± 10.61	84.29 ± 10.47
breast-cancer	62.29 ± 13.83	61.48 ± 14.57	50.00 ± 0.00	61.94 ± 12.10	**65.14 ± 13.89**	62.81 ± 10.02
car-df	98.96 ± 0.52	98.09 ± 0.73	50.00 ± 0.00	98.96 ± 0.52	**99.45 ± 0.23**	97.62 ± 0.64
dbworld-subjects	85.83 ± 19.61	68.19 ± 18.64	50.00 ± 0.00	85.83 ± 19.61	**95.14 ± 7.15**	75.00 ± 10.39
dmft	54.31 ± 2.69	**54.95 ± 1.86**	53.12 ± 2.18	53.84 ± 2.27	52.74 ± 2.75	54.57 ± 2.10
dna	97.39 ± 0.75	97.01 ± 1.27	82.97 ± 1.66	97.39 ± 0.75	**99.30 ± 0.20**	94.67 ± 1.51
donner	**60.00 ± 41.16**	58.33 ± 39.67	50.00 ± 0.00	58.33 ± 39.67	20.00 ± 34.96	50.00 ± 0.00
fraud	71.67 ± 24.91	73.33 ± 23.83	73.33 ± 21.08	71.67 ± 24.91	**78.33 ± 22.29**	84.23 ± 24.23
king-and-rook	91.61 ± 0.23	88.53 ± 0.29	50.00 ± 0.00	91.61 ± 0.23	**96.20 ± 0.16**	87.84 ± 0.39
kr-vs-kp	99.47 ± 0.43	99.50 ± 0.42	93.76 ± 1.16	99.47 ± 0.43	**99.93 ± 0.11**	99.88 ± 0.19
lung-cancer	52.50 ± 14.72	50.00 ± 0.00	50.00 ± 0.00	52.50 ± 14.72	**68.33 ± 28.81**	67.71 ± 22.97
marketing	52.17 ± 6.86	52.17 ± 6.86	50.00 ± 0.00	52.17 ± 6.86	**66.56 ± 5.37**	61.50 ± 10.49
monks-problems	58.99 ± 7.18	59.55 ± 8.27	50.00 ± 0.00	59.10 ± 7.34	**79.61 ± 8.05**	54.06 ± 6.89
mushroom	99.90 ± 0.09	99.84 ± 0.19	99.69 ± 0.35	99.90 ± 0.09	**100.00 ± 0.00**	**100.00 ± 0.00**
nursery	99.86 ± 0.05	99.79 ± 0.06	96.57 ± 0.44	99.86 ± 0.05	**99.97 ± 0.01**	99.54 ± 0.14
phishing	98.26 ± 0.31	98.22 ± 0.30	95.18 ± 0.39	98.22 ± 0.29	**99.59 ± 0.06**	98.43 ± 0.49
po-patient	40.06 ± 10.42	46.61 ± 16.91	**50.00 ± 0.00**	44.87 ± 11.66	44.81 ± 18.61	49.29 ± 2.26
primary-tumor	79.43 ± 3.06	72.98 ± 3.47	60.91 ± 2.00	79.24 ± 4.02	**80.17 ± 2.51**	70.38 ± 3.47
reviewer	65.33 ± 8.94	65.08 ± 7.63	50.00 ± 0.00	64.89 ± 8.95	**68.92 ± 7.54**	64.78 ± 7.54
servo	97.63 ± 3.20	97.53 ± 3.32	95.38 ± 4.73	97.63 ± 3.20	**98.91 ± 1.91**	95.38 ± 4.73
solar-flare-1	90.03 ± 3.85	**90.21 ± 2.59**	78.12 ± 2.80	89.83 ± 3.42	89.54 ± 4.46	88.93 ± 3.27
solar-flare-2	92.13 ± 1.42	**92.18 ± 1.50**	92.08 ± 1.48	92.11 ± 1.54	91.98 ± 1.47	91.96 ± 0.73
soybean	96.83 ± 0.79	94.71 ± 2.78	79.22 ± 2.17	96.84 ± 0.80	**99.70 ± 0.26**	98.42 ± 0.60
spect	78.86 ± 10.79	78.26 ± 11.36	71.21 ± 14.54	77.63 ± 10.91	79.15 ± 11.45	**80.64 ± 10.70**
splice	98.34 ± 0.50	98.02 ± 0.77	58.24 ± 13.28	98.34 ± 0.50	**99.45 ± 0.26**	96.44 ± 0.82
vote	97.79 ± 1.90	97.82 ± 1.89	96.54 ± 3.25	97.66 ± 2.13	**99.11 ± 0.96**	97.96 ± 2.24
Mean	81.37 ± 17.81	80.05 ± 17.40	67.68 ± 18.81	81.27 ± 17.60	**83.92 ± 19.35**	80.74 ± 16.88
Average Rank	3.05	3.52	5.52	3.40	1.88	3.64

The RF algorithm significantly outperformed the MDTSatisfaction, MDT-Laplace, DT, and MDT-Novelty. However, the results for both RF and MDT-Precision are not statistically significant different.

Regarding the DT algorithm, it only significantly outperformed the MDT-Novelty algorithm. For the MDT-Precision, MDT-Satisfaction and MDT-Laplace algorithms, DT obtained a lower performance, but, not significant. When compared to the RF algorithm, DT had a significantly lower performance. Regarding the performance of our algorithm and leaf weights, the ones that obtained the best performance were MDT-Precision and MDT-Satisfaction, showing an interesting result concerning precision and satisfaction metrics.

In summary, our approach MDT-Precision performs as good as a Random Forest with no statistically significant differences. Yet, its advantage is the interpretability provided by a single Decision Tree.

5 Conclusions

In this study, we have used meta-learning to transform trees from a Random Forest into a unique decision tree, a more human-interpretable model. The main contribution of our work was to show that it is possible to obtain a single tree with a performance statistically similar to that of a Random Forest using MDT-Precision. Continuing this work, we are analyzing how to handle datasets containing numeric attributes. Some initial ideas would be to represent the average value of the test performed on the attribute in the decision table; another possibility would be to represent the attribute limits with two lines in the decision table, one for the lower limit and one for the upper one.

References

1. Ampomah, E.K., Qin, Z., Nyame, G.: Evaluation of tree-based ensemble machine learning models in predicting stock price direction of movement. Information **11**(6), 332 (2020). https://doi.org/10.3390/info11060332, https://www.mdpi.com/2078-2489/11/6/332
2. Breiman, L.: The heuristics on instability in model selection. Technical report, Statistics Department, University of California (1996)
3. Burkart, N., Huber, M.F.: A survey on the explainability of supervised machine learning. J. Artif. Intell. Res. **70**, 1–74 (2021)
4. Carvalho, D.V., Pereira, E.M., Cardoso, J.S.: Machine learning interpretability: a survey on methods and metrics. Electronics **8**(8), 832 (2019)
5. Clark, P., Boswell, R.: Rule induction with CN2: some recent improvements. In: Kodratoff, Y. (ed.) EWSL 1991. LNCS, vol. 482, pp. 151–163. Springer, Heidelberg (1991). https://doi.org/10.1007/BFb0017011
6. Council of European Union: Council regulation (EU) no 279/2016 - official website of the European union (2016). https://eur-lex.europa.eu/eli/reg/2016/679/oj
7. Dietterich, T.G.: Machine learning research: four current directions, May 1997
8. Doshi-Velez, F., Kim, B.: Towards a rigorous science of interpretable machine learning. arXiv preprint arXiv:1702.08608 (2017)
9. Dunn, O.J.: Multiple comparisons among means. J. Am. Stat. Assoc. **56**(293), 52–64 (1961). https://doi.org/10.1080/01621459.1961.10482090
10. ElShawi, R., Sherif, Y., Al-Mallah, M., Sakr, S.: Interpretability in healthcare: a comparative study of local machine learning interpretability techniques. Comput. Intell. **37**(4), 1633–1650 (2021)
11. Friedman, M.: A comparison of alternative tests of significance for the problem of m rankings. Ann. Math. Stat. **11**(1), 86–92 (1940). https://doi.org/10.1214/aoms/1177731944
12. Gilpin, L.H., Bau, D., Yuan, B.Z., Bajwa, A., Specter, M., Kagal, L.: Explaining explanations: an overview of interpretability of machine learning. In: 2018 IEEE 5th International Conference on Data Science and Advanced Analytics (DSAA), pp. 80–89 (2018)
13. Guidotti, R., Monreale, A., Giannotti, F., Pedreschi, D., Ruggieri, S., Turini, F.: Factual and counterfactual explanations for black box decision making. IEEE Intell. Syst. **34**(6), 14–23 (2019)

14. Guidotti, R., Monreale, A., Ruggieri, S., Turini, F., Giannotti, F., Pedreschi, D.: A survey of methods for explaining black box models. ACM Comput. Surv. (CSUR) **51**(5), 1–42 (2018)

15. Hall, M., Frank, E., Holmes, G., Pfahringer, B., Reutemann, P., Witten, I.H.: The WEKA data mining software: an update. ACM SIGKDD Explor. Newsl. **11**(1), 10–18 (2009)

16. Hand, D.J., Till, R.J.: A simple generalisation of the area under the ROC curve for multiple class classification problems. Mach. Learn. **45**(2), 171–186 (2001). https:// doi.org/10.1023/A:1010920819831

17. Lakhani, P., et al.: Machine learning in radiology: applications beyond image interpretation. J. Am. Coll. Radiol. **15**(2), 350–359 (2018)

18. Lavrač, N., Flach, P., Zupan, B.: Rule evaluation measures: a unifying view. In: Džeroski, S., Flach, P. (eds.) ILP 1999. LNCS (LNAI), vol. 1634, pp. 174–185. Springer, Heidelberg (1999). https://doi.org/10.1007/3-540-48751-4_17

19. Linardatos, P., Papastefanopoulos, V., Kotsiantis, S.: Explainable AI: a review of machine learning interpretability methods. Entropy **23**(1), 18 (2021)

20. Lundberg, S.M., Lee, S.I.: A unified approach to interpreting model predictions. In: Proceedings of the 31st International Conference on Neural Information Processing Systems, NIPS 2017, pp. 4768–4777. Curran Associates Inc. (2017)

21. Oshiro, T.M., Perez, P.S., Baranauskas, J.A.: How many trees in a random forest? In: Perner, P. (ed.) MLDM 2012. LNCS (LNAI), vol. 7376, pp. 154–168. Springer, Heidelberg (2012). https://doi.org/10.1007/978-3-642-31537-4_13

22. Pham, K., Kim, D., Park, S., Choi, H.: Ensemble learning-based classification models for slope stability analysis. CATENA **196**, 104886 (2021). https://doi.org/ 10.1016/j.catena.2020.104886, https://www.sciencedirect.com/science/article/pii/ S0341816220304367

23. Ribeiro, M.T., Singh, S., Guestrin, C.: "Why should I trust you?" Explaining the predictions of any classifier. In: Proceedings of the 22nd ACM SIGKDD International Conference on Knowledge Discovery and Data Mining, pp. 1135–1144 (2016)

24. Todorovski, L., Flach, P., Lavrač, N.: Predictive performance of weighted relative accuracy. In: Zighed, D.A., Komorowski, J., Żytkow, J. (eds.) PKDD 2000. LNCS (LNAI), vol. 1910, pp. 255–264. Springer, Heidelberg (2000). https://doi.org/10. 1007/3-540-45372-5_25

25. Vanschoren, J., van Rijn, J.N., Bischl, B., Torgo, L.: OpenML: networked science in machine learning. SIGKDD Explor. **15**(2), 49–60 (2013). https://doi.org/10.1145/ 2641190.2641198

Hybrid (CPU/GPU) Exact Nearest Neighbors Search in High-Dimensional Spaces

David Muhr[1,2]([✉]) [iD] and Michael Affenzeller[2,3] [iD]

[1] BMW Group, Steyr, Austria
david.muhr@bmw.com
[2] Johannes Kepler University, Linz, Austria
[3] University of Applied Sciences Upper Austria, Hagenberg, Austria

Abstract. In this paper, we propose a hybrid algorithm for exact nearest neighbors queries in high-dimensional spaces. Indexing structures typically used for exact nearest neighbors search become less efficient in high-dimensional spaces, effectively requiring brute-force search. Our method uses a massively-parallel approach to brute-force search that efficiently splits the computational load between CPU and GPU. We show that the performance of our algorithm scales linearly with the dimensionality of the data, improving upon previous approaches for high-dimensional datasets. The algorithm is implemented in Julia, a high-level programming language for numerical and scientific computing. It is openly available at https://github.com/davnn/ParallelNeighbors.jl.

Keywords: Nearest neighbors · GPU · CPU · Exact · Hybrid · k-NN

1 Introduction

The k-nearest neighbors algorithm (k-NN) identifies, for a given query, the k most similar samples from a reference set. It has been applied in a broad range of applications in information retrieval and data mining, for example, in pattern classification [10], regression [33] and outlier detection [29]. k-NN is computationally intensive since every query involves the comparison to all the elements in the reference set. The computational complexity of a single nearest neighbors query with Euclidean distance is $\mathcal{O}(nd)$, where n refers to the number of examples and d to the dimensionality of the dataset [21]. When the size of the reference set is large or a large number of queries need to be solved, the execution time may become unacceptably high. In low-dimensional spaces, the complexity of exact neighbors queries can be reduced using various indexing structures, as studied in [21], for example. However, in high-dimensional spaces, index searches typically become more exhaustive, where a k-NN query for a given point needs to search through a large fraction of the points in the reference set [38]. Thus, index search largely becomes ineffective in higher dimensional spaces

© IFIP International Federation for Information Processing 2022
Published by Springer Nature Switzerland AG 2022
I. Maglogiannis et al. (Eds.): AIAI 2022, IFIP AICT 647, pp. 112–123, 2022.
https://doi.org/10.1007/978-3-031-08337-2_10

and may even degrade performance relative to a brute-force search because the index search incurs some degree of overhead. To address the challenge of nearest neighbors searches in high-dimensional spaces, we propose a massively parallel algorithm that combines the computational capabilities of a central processing unit (CPU) with that of a graphical processing unit (GPU) to enable efficient brute-force search in high-dimensional data.

The rest of this paper is organized as follows. Section 2 presents the related work and techniques used for nearest neighbors search. In Sect. 3, we describe the proposed algorithm in detail, explain the implementation, and highlight our contributions. Section 4 shows how the algorithm scales in comparison to other widely used implementations. In Sect. 5, we summarize our findings and describe possible future research directions.

2   Related Work

Various techniques have been proposed for nearest neighbors search (mostly in metric spaces) encompassing (1) hierarchical methods, (2) pivot-based methods and (3) compression-based methods. Hierarchical methods typically use some form of tree structure to partition the search space. Notable examples include the **k-d tree** and its variants and the **R-tree** and its variants. The k-d tree uses binary space partitioning to statically organize k-dimensional points [4]. R-trees, on the other hand, divide space into minimum bounding rectangles, such that regions can intersect and form a hierarchy [16]. Pivot-based approaches store pre-computed distances to a set of so-called pivot points. Using the pre-computed distances and the triangle inequality, it is possible to exclude points from further consideration. The most prominent examples of pivot-based approaches are **AESA** [36] and **LAESA** [26]. AESA uses the full pairwise distance matrix of the reference set, and LAESA uses the pairwise distances to a set of chosen pivot points. Compression-based methods use some form of quantization and lower-bounding to achieve exact nearest neighbors search in more compact spaces. An example of a compression method is the **VA-file** [37] and its variants, which uses scalar quantization to organize the search space into a grid of cells enabling filtering of points that cannot be near the query. Algorithms that combine different aspects exist as well; for example, trees that use pivot points [35], or trees that use compression ideas [5].

A problem inherent with all of the mentioned techniques is that they rapidly decline in performance once the dimensionality of the dataset increases. In fact, under some assumptions regarding the data distribution, even an optimal index structure will, as dimensionality increases, always degenerate to visiting the entire data set [38]. For example, Kibriya and Eibe [21] empirically show that the classical tree variants generally become worse than brute-force search for datasets with more than 16 dimensions. More recently proposed methods also suffer from the curse-of-dimensionality as shown, for example, in [15] or [22].

An approach to tackle the curse-of-dimensionality is to rely on a *brute-force* search of the data and use parallelization to speed up the search. A benefit of such an approach is that it can be used for non-metric spaces, as it does not rely on any assumptions about the distance function being used. Paralellization methods include shared-nothing architectures such as **MapReduce** [13] (e.g. [23]), distributed-memory architectures such as **MPI** [9] (e.g. [2]), shared-memory architectures such as **OpenMP** [11] (e.g. [39]) and massively-parallel architectures such as **GPGPU** [24]. The brute-force GPGPU methods mainly differ in the selection of the k smallest elements from every row in the distance matrix, a problem we describe as k-selection. Tang et al. [34] identify three major variants to solve the k-selection problem. A naïve approach is to sort the list and then select the k first values in the sorted list (e.g. [3]). However, this method does unnecessary work when the sorted distances are not repeatedly used. A more efficient approach is to partially sort the distances only up to the first k values (e.g. [31]). Another option is to use selection algorithms instead of sorting (e.g. [1]), which recursively divide the distances into groups.

3   Algorithm

The primary motivation for our approach is to explore the combination of CPU-based shared-memory parallelism and the GPGPU paradigm to address the curse-of-dimensionality in nearest neighbors search. We propose a generic interface to solve high-dimensional k-NN queries and split the problem into *distance computation* and *k-selection*. Using the Julia programming language [7], multiple dispatch allows us to generically implement distance computation and k-selection approaches based on abstract types, which get just-in-time compiled for the concrete, user-provided subtypes. Distance computation is performed on the GPU, which we refer to as the *device*, and k-selection is asynchronously performed on the CPU, which we refer to as the *host*. The parallelization of the distance computation on the device and the k-selection on the host is made possible through batching strategies. Batching is necessary for two reasons: (1) device memory is typically highly restricted, and not all points in the reference and query sets might fit in device memory, and (2) we can asynchronously compute the k-selection of batch n while we calculate the distances for batch $n + 1$; thus, we can overlap computations and achieve better resource utilization. Our approach enables nearest neighbors search for datasets that do not fit in memory, and work is efficiently distributed between CPU and GPU. For simplicity, we assume that the dataset initially resides in host memory, but the algorithm itself does not make assumptions about the input data location.

3.1   Distance Computation

Most of the literature on similarity search and nearest neighbors search is concerned with metric spaces. A *metric* δ is required to be non-negative $\delta(x, y) \geq 0$, identical $\delta(x, y) = 0 \Leftrightarrow x = y$, symmetric $\delta(x, y) = \delta(y, x)$ and triangular $\delta(x, y) + \delta(y, z) \geq \delta(x, z)$. However, with the increasing complexity of data entities across various domains, many distances are used that are not metrics [32].

Relaxing the last three axioms, for example, leads to the notion of a *premetric*, i.e. a distance function satisfying only the non-negative and identical axioms. Because a brute-force approach does not rely on assumptions about the used distance function, we can use any metric or non-metric distance function. Furthermore, our high-level interface allows researchers to implement such distance functions without any knowledge of the underlying GPU platform. For the purpose of evalution, we use the popular Euclidean metric given by

$$d(r_i, q_j) = \sqrt{||r_i - q_j||^2}.$$ (1)

The square of the distance metric can be written as

$$
\begin{aligned}
d^2(r_i, q_j) &= ||r_i - q_j||^2 \\
&= (r_i - q_j)^\top (r_i - q_j) \\
&= r_i^\top r_i + q_j^\top q_j - 2r_i^\top q_j \\
&= ||r_i||^2 + ||q_j||^2 - 2r_i^\top q_j.
\end{aligned}
$$ (2)

for all $i \in \{1, 2, \ldots, N\}$ and $j \in \{1, 2, \ldots, M\}$ where N is the number of reference points and M is the number of query points. If we now assume that the points in both sets are of dimensionality D and define the reference set as a matrix $R^{N \times D}$ and the query set as a matrix $Q^{M \times D}$, we can formulate the pairwise Euclidean distance matrix as

$$D = \sqrt{-2R^\top Q \underset{r}{+} ||R||^2 \underset{c}{+} ||Q||^2}.$$ (3)

where $|| \cdot ||^2$ is the row-wise squared vector norm, $+_r$ is the row-wise addition, $+_c$ is the column-wise addition and $\sqrt{\cdot}$ is the element-wise square root. For the computationally expensive dense matrix multiplication, it is common to use optimized libraries such as cuBLAS[1], clBLAS[2] or MAGMA[3]. Because our implementation is based on the Julia programming language, we can implement such a distance kernel generically based on the notion of an abstract matrix type. Depending on the user-provided matrix, for example, a CUDA-specific subtype, the computation is dispatched on that subtype and just-in-time compiled, which might, for example, invoke a cuBLAS call for the matrix multiplication. Thus, our implementation can support different devices without code specific to the device platforms through multiple dispatch, and the JuliaGPU project [6].

3.2 k-Selection

As mentioned previously, the GPU-based methods mainly differ in the k-selection process. In our case, we choose to remove the k-selection process from the GPU entirely and instead perform the computation asynchronously on the CPU. The

---

[1] https://nvidia.com.

[2] https://gpuopen.com.

[3] https://icl.cs.utk.edu/magma/.

motivation for using the GPU for distance computations and the CPU for sorting is based on the observation that dense matrix operations are much faster on the GPU than on the CPU [18, 20, 40] and that it is much more difficult to significantly outperform CPU-based sorting on the GPU [14, 30]. As with distance computations, our approach is generic enough to use arbitrary k-selection procedures, but for the purpose of evaluation, we use the popular partial quicksort algorithm. Quicksort works by selecting a pivot element from the array and partitioning the other elements into two sub-arrays depending on whether they are smaller or larger than the pivot. The sub-arrays are then sorted recursively [17]. There is no need to recursively sort partitions that only contain elements that would fall after the k-th place in the final sorted array in the partial quicksort variant. Thus, if the pivot falls in position k or later, the recursion only takes place on the left partition [25].

3.3   Batching

Recall that a k-nearest neighbors query identifies the k most similar samples from a reference set R. Of course, there can also be multiple queries, which we refer to as the query set Q. Because every point $q \in Q$ is associated with a distance to every point $r \in R$, a trivial batching approach would be to only batch the points in Q and load the entire reference set on the device. We call this approach Q-batch. Q-batch requires only a single k-selection step for each point in Q, because the distances from a single query point to all reference points are known after the distance computation for a batch is complete. The following figures show the distance computation (Fig. 1) and k-selection (Fig. 2) process using the Q-batch methodology. For simplicity, we ignore the memory transfer between host and device before each batch in the visualizations.

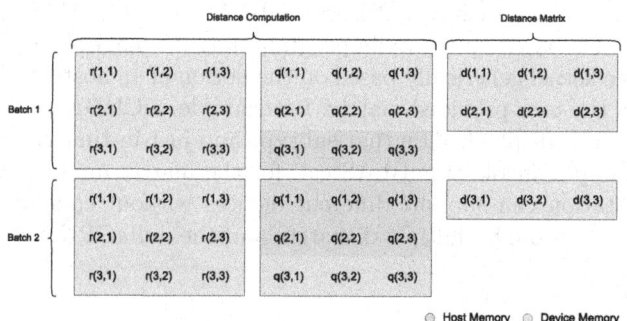

Fig. 1. Exemplary distance computation of three-dimensional points using Q-batch with a batch size of 2 where $r(i, \cdot)$ is a point in the reference set, $q(j, \cdot)$ is a point in the query set and $d(j, i)$ refers to the distance from point $q(j, \cdot)$ to $r(i, \cdot)$.

A problem with the Q-batch approach is that the full reference set must be on the device, which may not be feasible depending on the size of the reference

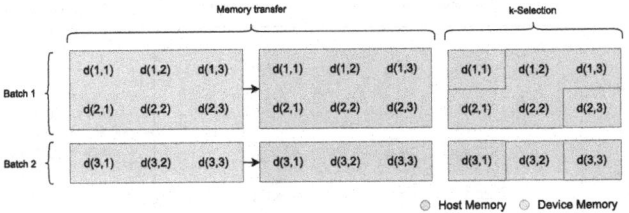

Fig. 2. Exemplary k-selection using Q-batch with a batch size of 2. Note that the selection process happens asynchronously on the host. The exemplary 1-nearest neighbors are marked with a red rectangle, thus the final nearest neighbors would be $q(1) \to r(1), q(2) \to r(3)$ and $q(3) \to r(2)$. (Color figure online)

set. A more generic approach is to batch the points in Q and R separately, given a batch size B, which yields a distance matrix that is at most of size $B \times B$. We call this approach QR-batch and conceptually show in how it differs from Q batch in distance computation (Fig. 3) and k-selection (Fig. 4).

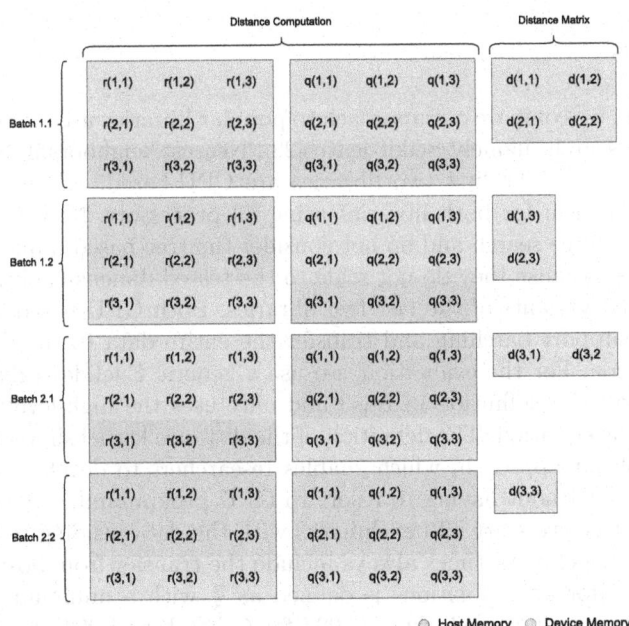

Fig. 3. Exemplary distance computation of three-dimensional points using QR-batch with a batch size of 2 where $r(i, \cdot)$ is a point in the reference set, $q(j, \cdot)$ is a point in the query set and $d(j, i)$ refers to the distance from point $q(j, \cdot)$ to $r(i, \cdot)$.

The implementation of the algorithms is open-source and available online; it can be found at https://github.com/davnn/ParallelNeighbors.jl.

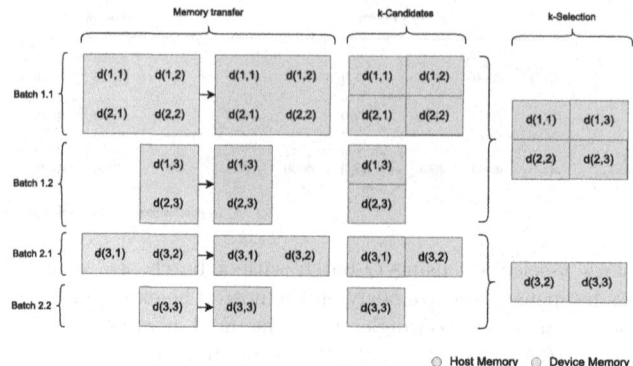

Fig. 4. Exemplary k-selection using QR-batch with a batch size of 2. Note that, in contrast to Q-batch, we have to split the k-selection process into two steps: first, we select the k possible candidates from the reference set, and then we perform k-selection on the possible candidates. Again, we mark the exemplary candidates and neighbors with a red rectangle showing that both methodologies yield the same result. (Color figure online)

4   Results

In this section, we compare our approach to popular libraries used for exact nearest neighbors search, namely Scikit-learn [28], NearestNeighbors.jl [8], PyTorch [27] and Faiss [19]. The first two libraries are CPU-based, and we use multithreaded parallelism for both libraries using all processors. Note that we only compare brute-force search and do not consider the tree-based implementations of the libraries because they do not scale to the tested dimensionalities. We use the GPU-based variants of the last two libraries. Both GPU-based variants do not natively support batching and transfer the entire data to the GPU before the computation. For the evaluation, we use a generic Euclidean distance kernel that follows the definition in Eq. 3 and only uses the high-level operations described in the equation. The definition of the distance kernel shows the generic capabilities of our approach, which enables researchers to develop custom distance functions without having to resort to GPU programming. Another point to mention is that we start all benchmarks with the data residing in host memory; thus, the benchmark times always include the transfer from host to device. The batch size for all evaluations is defined as $\frac{n}{8}$ with a minimum batch size of 256 and a maximum batch size of 1024 for Q-batch and 2048 for QR-batch. We use uniform random points in the unit hypercube for all our evaluations, and the correctness of all algorithms is ensured by comparison to a reference implementation. Our experimental environment employs an AMD Ryzen 3900X CPU and a GeForce 1080 Ti GPU with CUDA Toolkit 11.3. An initial analysis regarding different numbers of neighbors k shows that all libraries scale alike with the number of neighbors; thus, we use $k = 1$ for all further evaluations. We propose two benchmarks for the evaluation, (1) *batch prediction* and

(2) *online prediction.* The first benchmark involves an equal amount of reference and query points $n \in \{2^9, 2^{10}, \ldots, 2^{14}\}$ for varying dataset dimensionalities $d \in \{2^9, 2^{10}, \ldots, 2^{14}\}$. In Fig. 5 we show the results for benchmark (1). The CPU-based approaches deteriorate significantly with an increasing number of reference and query points for all tested dimensionalities. For dimensionalities up to $d = 2048$, the hybrid approaches incur an overhead compared to the GPU-based approaches, but starting with $d = 4096$, the hybrid approaches outperform all other approaches despite using batch-wise data transfer. For the largest number of query and reference points and $d = 16384$, using a hybrid approach results in a 30% to 40% decrease in processing time compared to the GPU libraries. Additionally, note that a one-time data transfer is more efficient than a batch-wise transfer from host to device; therefore, this benchmark favors the GPU-based libraries over our proposed approaches.

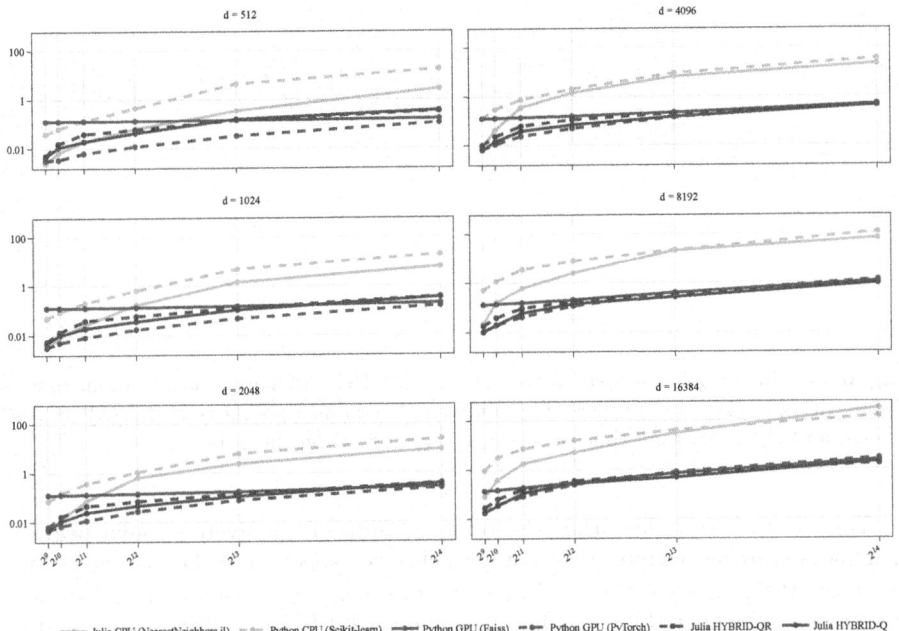

Fig. 5. Benchmark (1): Comparison of popular libraries to the proposed hybrid algorithms for $k = 1$ neighbors. The number of query and reference points is visualized on the x-axis of each plot and the processing time in seconds is visualized on the y-axis.

The second benchmark compares the GPU and hybrid approaches using a large number of reference points $n \in \{2^{14}, 2^{15}, \ldots, 2^{18}\}$ with a single query point and fixed dimensionality $d = 4096$. The dimensionality is chosen based on the observation that the compared algorithms show similar performance for that dimensionality in the first benchmark. The maximum number of reference points is the largest number of points fitting in GPU memory, enabling a comparison to libraries that do not support batch-wise data transfer. We additionally evaluate the difference between batch-wise and one-time data transfer for the hybrid approaches in this benchmark. The one-time data transfer evaluation can be interpreted as the lower bound of achievable processing time for batch-wise processing, only attainable if all data transfers can be scheduled asynchronously without impacting the rest of the computation. The result of benchmark (2) is depicted in Fig. 6. The hybrid approaches outperform the GPU-based variants when both use one-time data transfer; in this case, the processing time can be decreased by about 25% to 50%. Because there is only one query point in the second benchmark, Q-batch uses a batch size of one and shows almost no difference to one-time transfer. The performance difference between QR-batch with one-time and batch-wise data transfer hints at further optimization potential, which might be achievable through better memory allocation.

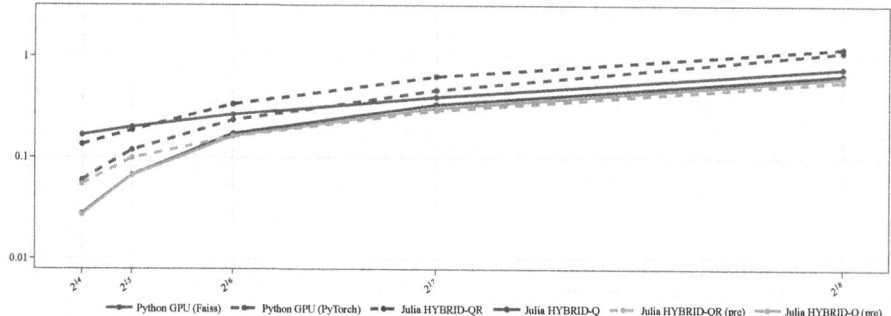

Fig. 6. Benchmark (2): Comparison of hybrid and GPU-based approaches for one query point with $k = 1$ and $d = 4096$. The number of reference points is visualized on the x-axis, and the processing time in seconds is visualized on the y-axis.

Dashti et al. [12] show that the total speedup of massively-parallel nearest neighbors searches asymptotically approaches the speedup of the distance computation. If the time required for asynchronous memory transfer and CPU-based k-selection is smaller than the time required for GPU-based distance computation, a hybrid approach should outperform a purely CPU-based or GPU-based approach.

5   Conclusions

In this paper, we set out to tackle the curse-of-dimensionality in exact nearest neighbors searches. We propose a hybrid, massively-parallel nearest neighbors algorithm that uses batching to split the computational workload efficiently between CPU and GPU. We show that a highly-generic implementation of our method significantly outperforms popular exact nearest neighbors libraries for high-dimensional data. Most notably, the performance of our proposed hybrid approach scales linearly with the dimensionality of the data. Because datasets continually increase in size and dimensionality, we believe that high-performance nearest neighbors search strategies become more relevant in future research. While the low-dimensional similarity search community has attracted a large amount of research over the last 20 years, there are many open opportunities for future research in the high-dimensional case. Future researchers should investigate existing highly-optimized distance kernels and k-selection methods and combinations thereof in the CPU, GPU, hybrid, and distributed setting.

References

1. Alabi, T., Blanchard, J.D., Gordon, B., Steinbach, R.: Fast K-selection algorithms for graphics processing units. ACM J. Exp. Algorithmics **17**, 4.2:4.1–4.2:4.29 (2012). https://doi.org/10.1145/2133803.2345676
2. Aparício, G., Blanquer, I., Hernández, V.: A parallel implementation of the K nearest neighbours classifier in three levels: threads, MPI processes and the grid. In: Daydé, M., Palma, J.M.L.M., Coutinho, Á.L.G.A., Pacitti, E., Lopes, J.C. (eds.) VECPAR 2006. LNCS, vol. 4395, pp. 225–235. Springer, Heidelberg (2007). https://doi.org/10.1007/978-3-540-71351-7_18
3. Arefin, A.S., Riveros, C., Berretta, R., Moscato, P.: GPU-FS-kNN: a software tool for fast and scalable kNN computation using GPUs. PLOS ONE **7**(8), e44000 (2012). https://doi.org/10.1371/journal.pone.0044000
4. Bentley, J.L.: Multidimensional binary search trees used for associative searching. Commun. ACM **18**(9), 509–517 (1975). https://doi.org/10.1145/361002.361007
5. Berchtold, S., Bohm, C., Jagadish, H., Kriegel, H.P., Sander, J.: Independent quantization: an index compression technique for high-dimensional data spaces. In: Proceedings of 16th International Conference on Data Engineering (Cat. No.00CB37073), pp. 577–588, February 2000. https://doi.org/10.1109/ICDE.2000.839456
6. Besard, T., Foket, C., De Sutter, B.: Effective extensible programming: unleashing Julia on GPUs. IEEE Trans. Parallel Distrib. Syst. (2018). https://doi.org/10.1109/TPDS.2018.2872064
7. Bezanson, J., Edelman, A., Karpinski, S., Shah, V.B.: Julia: a fresh approach to numerical computing. SIAM Rev. **59**(1), 65–98 (2017). https://doi.org/10.1137/141000671
8. Carlsson, K., et al.: KristofferC/NearestNeighbors.jl: V0.4.9. Zenodo, June 2021. https://doi.org/10.5281/zenodo.4943232
9. Clarke, L., Glendinning, I., Hempel, R.: The MPI message passing interface standard. In: Decker, K.M., Rehmann, R.M. (eds.) Programming Environments for Massively Parallel Distributed Systems, pp. 213–218. Monte Verità, Birkhäuser, Basel (1994). https://doi.org/10.1007/978-3-0348-8534-8_21
10. Cover, T.M., Hart, P.E.: Nearest neighbor pattern classification. IEEE Trans. Inf. Theory **13**(1), 21–27 (1967). https://doi.org/10.1109/TIT.1967.1053964
11. Dagum, L., Menon, R.: OpenMP: an industry standard API for shared-memory programming. IEEE Comput. Sci. Eng. **5**(1), 46–55 (1998). https://doi.org/10.1109/99.660313
12. Dashti, A., Komarov, I., D'Souza, R.M.: Efficient computation of k-nearest neighbour graphs for large high-dimensional data sets on GPU clusters. PLOS ONE **8**(9), e74113 (2013). https://doi.org/10.1371/journal.pone.0074113

13. Dean, J., Ghemawat, S.: MapReduce: simplified data processing on large clusters. Commun. ACM **51**(1), 107–113 (2008). https://doi.org/10.1145/1327452.1327492
14. Dominik, Z., Marcin, P., Maciej, W., Kazimierz, W.: Comparison of hybrid sorting algorithms implemented on different parallel hardware platforms. Comput. Sci. **14**(4), 679 (2013). https://doi.org/10.7494/csci.2013.14.4.679
15. Gast, E., Oerlemans, A., Lew, M.S.: Very large scale nearest neighbor search: ideas, strategies and challenges. Int. J. Multimedia Inf. Retriev. **2**(4), 229–241 (2013). https://doi.org/10.1007/s13735-013-0046-4
16. Guttman, A.: R-trees: a dynamic index structure for spatial searching. ACM SIGMOD Rec. **14**(2), 47–57 (1984). https://doi.org/10.1145/971697.602266
17. Hoare, C.A.R.: Quicksort. Comput. J. **5**(1), 10–16 (1962). https://doi.org/10.1093/comjnl/5.1.10
18. Huang, Z., Ma, N., Wang, S., Peng, Y.: GPU computing performance analysis on matrix multiplication. J. Eng. **2019**(23), 9043–9048 (2019). https://doi.org/10.1049/joe.2018.9178
19. Johnson, J., Douze, M., Jégou, H.: Billion-scale similarity search with GPUs. IEEE Trans. Big Data **7**(3), 535–547 (2021). https://doi.org/10.1109/TBDATA.2019.2921572
20. Kestur, S., Davis, J.D., Williams, O.: BLAS comparison on FPGA, CPU and GPU. In: 2010 IEEE Computer Society Annual Symposium on VLSI, pp. 288–293, July 2010. https://doi.org/10.1109/ISVLSI.2010.84
21. Kibriya, A.M., Frank, E.: An empirical comparison of exact nearest neighbour algorithms. In: Kok, J.N., Koronacki, J., Lopez de Mantaras, R., Matwin, S., Mladenič, D., Skowron, A. (eds.) PKDD 2007. LNCS (LNAI), vol. 4702, pp. 140–151. Springer, Heidelberg (2007). https://doi.org/10.1007/978-3-540-74976-9_16
22. Liu, J., Nishimura, S., Araki, T.: P-Index: a novel index based on prime factorization for similarity search. In: 2019 IEEE International Conference on Big Data and Smart Computing (BigComp), pp. 1–8, February 2019. https://doi.org/10.1109/BIGCOMP.2019.8679353
23. Lu, W., Shen, Y., Chen, S., Ooi, B.C.: Efficient processing of K nearest neighbor joins using MapReduce. Proc. VLDB Endow. **5**(10), 1016–1027 (2012). https://doi.org/10.14778/2336664.2336674
24. Luebke, D., et al.: GPGPU: general-purpose computation on graphics hardware. In: Proceedings of the 2006 ACM/IEEE Conference on Supercomputing, pp. 208-es. SC 2006. Association for Computing Machinery, New York, NY, USA, November 2006. https://doi.org/10.1145/1188455.1188672
25. Martínez, C.: Partial quicksort. In: Proceedings of the First ACM-SIAM Workshop on Analytic Algorithmics and Combinatorics, p. 5 (2004)
26. Micó, M.L., Oncina, J., Vidal, E.: A new version of the nearest-neighbour approximating and eliminating search algorithm (AESA) with linear preprocessing time and memory requirements. Pattern Recogn. Lett. **15**(1), 9–17 (1994). https://doi.org/10.1016/0167-8655(94)90095-7
27. Paszke, A., et al.: PyTorch: an imperative style, high-performance deep learning library. In: Proceedings of the 33rd International Conference on Neural Information Processing Systems, pp. 8026–8037, vol. 721. Curran Associates Inc., Red Hook, NY, USA, December 2019
28. Pedregosa, F., et al.: Scikit-learn: machine learning in Python. J. Mach. Learn. Res. **12**, 2825–2830 (2011)
29. Ramaswamy, S., Rastogi, R., Shim, K.: Efficient algorithms for mining outliers from large data sets. SIGMOD Rec. **29**(2), 427–438 (2000). https://doi.org/10.1145/335191.335437

30. Satish, N., Harris, M., Garland, M.: Designing efficient sorting algorithms for many-core GPUs. In: 2009 IEEE International Symposium on Parallel Distributed Processing, pp. 1–10, May 2009. https://doi.org/10.1109/IPDPS.2009.5161005
31. Sismanis, N., Pitsianis, N., Sun, X.: Parallel search of k-nearest neighbors with synchronous operations. In: 2012 IEEE Conference on High Performance Extreme Computing, pp. 1–6. IEEE, Waltham, MA, USA, September 2012. https://doi.org/10.1109/HPEC.2012.6408667
32. Skopal, T., Bustos, B.: On nonmetric similarity search problems in complex domains. ACM Comput. Surv. 43(4), 34:1–34:50 (2011). https://doi.org/10.1145/1978802.1978813
33. Stone, C.J.: Consistent nonparametric regression. Ann. Stat. 5(4), 595–620 (1977)
34. Tang, X., Huang, Z., Eyers, D., Mills, S., Guo, M.: Efficient selection algorithm for fast k-NN search on GPUs. In: 2015 IEEE International Parallel and Distributed Processing Symposium, pp. 397–406, May 2015. https://doi.org/10.1109/IPDPS.2015.115
35. Uhlmann, J.K.: Satisfying general proximity/similarity queries with metric trees. Inf. Process. Lett. 40(4), 175–179 (1991)
36. Vidal Ruiz, E.: An algorithm for finding nearest neighbours in (approximately) constant average time. Pattern Recogn. Lett. 4(3), 145–157 (1986). https://doi.org/10.1016/0167-8655(86)90013-9
37. Weber, R., Blott, S.: An approximation-based data structure for similarity search (1997)
38. Weber, R., Schek, H.J., Blott, S.: A quantitative analysis and performance study for similarity-search methods in high-dimensional spaces. In: Proceedings of the 24rd International Conference on Very Large Data Bases, pp. 194–205, VLDB 1998. Morgan Kaufmann Publishers Inc., San Francisco, CA, USA, August 1998
39. Xiao, B., Biros, G.: Parallel algorithms for nearest neighbor search problems in high dimensions. SIAM J. Sci. Comput. 38(5), S667–S699 (2016). https://doi.org/10.1137/15M1026377
40. Zhang, P., Gao, Y.: Matrix multiplication on high-density multi-GPU architectures: theoretical and experimental investigations. In: Kunkel, J.M., Ludwig, T. (eds.) ISC High Performance 2015. LNCS, vol. 9137, pp. 17–30. Springer, Cham (2015). https://doi.org/10.1007/978-3-319-20119-1_2

Machine Learning Approach to Detect Malicious Mobile Apps

Hassan Kazemian[✉]

Intelligent Systems Research Centre, School of Computing and Digital Media,
London Metropolitan University, London, UK
h.kazemian@londonmet.ac.uk

Abstract. Malicious developers are developing unsafe mobile apps which puts users at risk of exposing their personal data in unsafe hands. They are using techniques that change over time and their intention is to bypass the detector systems which are mostly rule-based. This paper avoids the limitations of rule-based systems by building a novel malware detector that can detect malicious apps by making use of machine learning techniques primarily focusing on deep neural networks i.e. deep multi-layer perceptron. These techniques have various properties that can adapt and identify various types of malicious applications. Simulation results on various datasets demonstrate clear superiority of this detector over other approaches, as this approach achieves 99% accuracy. Also, the detector is efficient enough to detect within 100 ms or less due to the intelligent use of autoencoder which reduces the dimensions in the feature.

Keywords: Deep neural network · Malicious mobile apps · Android

1 Introduction

The influx of range of applications in mobile environments have outpaced the desktop in the last few years. Users now seamlessly install apps with a click of a button and start using them. On average a user utilizes diverse range of apps regularly on daily basis to carry out various activities. For example, users check the timetable of their transport to plan their routes to various places. They keep track of their finances by checking their bank balances and financial transactions from their app. The most used apps are messaging based which allow sending text and multimedia messages to their friends, colleagues and families. Social apps allow users to connect to their nearest ones. Shopping apps allow users to place orders to have their items delivered to their homes. Looking at these various types of apps, they have access to messages, phone calls, data usages. Some of this information are sensitive & private and some of these provide premium services which cost the users money. Before installing an app, the apps ask for various permissions at the beginning of the installation. This allows the user to make a decision whether to allow the app to access permissions. Most users ignore them before the installation. This essentially creates a loophole. A user can install malicious

© IFIP International Federation for Information Processing 2022
Published by Springer Nature Switzerland AG 2022
I. Maglogiannis et al. (Eds.): AIAI 2022, IFIP AICT 647, pp. 124–135, 2022.
https://doi.org/10.1007/978-3-031-08337-2_11

Table 1. Android apps with various uses and permissions

Application	Use	Permissions
WhatsApp	Messaging	Photos, Contacts
Skype	Video Conference	Phone Calls, Contacts
Messenger	Messaging	Photos, Phone Calls, Contacts
HSBC	Check Bank Balance	N/A
Google Maps	Plan routes	Location
Gmail	Read Emails	Contacts, Photos

application without proper checks. Some of the example apps that have access to user per app are listed in Table 1.

Rule-based systems can detect known malware and look for traits and characteristics that exist in malicious applications. The performances of these detectors are very high and prevent applications being installed on a user's phone. Malicious developer can create a changed version with new characteristics to stop being detected. The old rules in the detector will not highlight this new app as malicious. Thus, apps which are updated regularly will avoid detection.

Traditional machine learning techniques such as naïve Bayes, decision trees, support vector machine & boosting have been used in [1] to detect malicious executables. They either look at the source code or the behavior of apps. These involve looking at consecutive bytes in executables stored on disk or in memory and creating features from these bytes which are fed into the classifiers. The work has achieved reasonable performance but faced a large feature space and had to maintain many of these features. In [2] these two issues are resolve by compressing the feature space using various hashing techniques. Surprisingly, the same level of performance was retained. Rather than reading the binaries directly, in [3–5], static flow analysis is used instead, whereas static function analysis is used in [6, 7]. Another work performs static code analysis on source code. It finds the relations between function and permissions. The work focuses on deep learning techniques which cater for more combinations and sophisticated data. Some techniques look at the behavior of apps and users. The systems look at the traces of application uses by users and monitor the usage in real time. These papers [8, 9] look at the patterns in the users.

Most of the executions take place within the mobile device where there are limits on computation, storage and battery life. Some experiments take place on remote servers, which mimic the mobile environment within hostile environments [10–12]. Although this allows for more exploits to be tested, it overlooks the limitations imposed on mobile devices.

Generative and discriminative classification techniques impact on how to solve a classification problem. Some find discriminative techniques such as support vector machine is useful in text and image categorization [13–15]. These essentially finds the boundary between the classes. On the other hand, generative techniques such as naïve Bayes are even more useful. Generative classifiers have been used in spam classification and find the distribution of each class.

Many applications request permissions from users that apps do not use at all. In [18, 19] their analysis reveals find many apps request permission that can be deemed harmful and risky to normal users. Permissions provide access to various actions and in many cases one permission give access to multiple actions [20–22]. In this scenario, the user is giving away more control to the app than necessary. For example, a particular permission gives the app access multiple API calls. Some of these calls are necessary and others can be mishandled and expose the user's private information such as messages, photos, call history, etc. which the app may not necessarily need but can exploit to carry out promotional activities.

Area Under ROC Curve (AUC) is a popular metric to verify the performance of a classifier. An area close to 1 indicates a good classifier but with a highly imbalanced dataset, this metric can be biased and may be biased to a particular class. To overcome this problem, some suggest using F1 as the metric as a more reliable metric to determine the performance of imbalanced dataset. In the paper, to avoid the problem of overfitting to a particular class, k-fold cross validation is selected where value of k is 5. This sets the training dataset to 80% and test dataset to 20% for each of the 5 iterations. This ensures that the created model is generalized and is adaptable in all conditions. The research also looks at the model error and loss as the model across various epochs is trained. AUC is a performance metric for binary classification problems. The AUC represents a model's ability to discriminate between positive and negative classes. An area of 1.0 represents a model that made all predictions perfectly. An area of 0.5 represents a model that is as good as random. ROC can be broken down into sensitivity and specificity [23, 24]. A binary classification problem is really a trade-off between sensitivity and specificity. Sensitivity is the true positive rate also called the recall. It is the number of instances from the positive (first) class that actually predicted correctly. Specificity is also called the true negative rate. It is the number of instances from the negative (second) class that were actually predicted correctly. The confusion matrix is a handy presentation of the accuracy of a model with two or more classes. The table presents predictions on the x-axis and accuracy outcomes on the y-axis. The cells of the table are the number of predictions made by a machine learning algorithm. For example, a machine learning algorithm can predict 0 or 1 and each prediction may actually have been a 0 or 1. Predictions for 0 that were actually 0 appear in the cell for prediction = 0 and actual = 0, whereas predictions for 0 that were actually 1 appear in the cell for prediction = 0 and actual = 1.

Looking at the last few years, it has been seen that with larger datasets deep learning techniques outperform traditional machine learning techniques. The research work focuses on deep learning techniques and will improve the performance while gathering more data. A Perceptron is a single neuron model that was a precursor to larger neural networks. It is a field of study that investigates how simple models of biological brains can be used to solve difficult computational tasks like the predictive modeling tasks in machine learning. The goal is not to create realistic models of the brain, but instead to develop robust algorithms and data structures that can be used to model difficult problems. The power of neural networks come from their ability to learn the representation in your training data and how to best relate it to the output variable that you want to predict. In this sense neural networks learn a mapping. Mathematically, they are capable of learning any mapping function and have been proven to be a universal approximation algorithm. The predictive capability of neural networks comes from the hierarchical or multilayered structure of the networks. The data structure can pick out (learn to represent) features at different scales or resolutions and combine them into higher-order features. For example from lines, to collections of lines to shapes.

2 Features Used in Simulation

Table 2. Top features for the top 5 families of malicious categories

Malware family	Top 5 features		
	Feature s	Feature set	Weight w_s
FakeInstaller	sendSMS	S_7 Suspicious API Call	1.12
	SEND_SMS	S_2 Requested permissions	0.84
	android.hardware.telephony	S_1 Hardware components	0.57
	sendTextMessage	S_5 Restricted API calls	0.52
	READ_PHONE_STATE	S_2 Requested permissions	0.50
DroidKungFu	SIG_STR	S_4 Filtered intents	2.02
	system/bin/su	S_7 Suspicious API calls	1.30
	BATTERY_CHANGED_ACTION	S_4 Filtered intents	1.26
	READ_PHONE_STATE	S_2 Requested permissions	0.54
	getSubscriberId	S_7 Suspicious API calls	0.49
GoldDream	sendSMS	S_7 Suspicious API calls	1.07
	lebar.gicp.net	S_8 Network addresses	0.93
	DELETE_PACKAGES	S_2 Requested permission	0.58
	android.provider.Telephony.SMS_RECEIVED	S_4 Filtered intents	0.56
	getSubscriberId	S_7 Suspicious API calls	0.53
GingerMaster	USER_PRESENT	S_4 Filtered intents	0.67
	getSubscriberId	S_7 Suspicious API calls	0.64
	READ_PHONE_STATE	S_2 Requested permissions	0.55
	system/bin/su	S_7 Suspicious API calls	0.44
	HttpPost	S_7 Suspicious API calls	0.38

The simulation uses the dataset prepared in [25] which contains 5,560 malware apps. Table 2 shows the top features in the dataset and Fig. 1 shows the categories of malware. The figure shows Detection Rates against Malware Families. As the first step, a lightweight static analysis of a given Android application is performed. Although apparently straightforward, the static extraction of features needs to run in a constrained environment and complete in a timely manner. If the analysis takes too long, the user might skip the ongoing process and refuse the overall method. Accordingly, it becomes essential to select features which can be extracted efficiently. The paper thus focuses on the manifest and the disassembled dex code of the application, which both can be obtained by a linear sweep over the application's content. To allow for a generic and extensible analysis, all extracted features are represented as sets of strings, such as permissions, intents and API calls. In particular, the following 8 sets of strings are extracted.

Every application developed for Android must include a manifest file called Android-Manifest.xml which provides data supporting the installation and later execution of the application. The information stored in this file can be efficiently retrieved on the device using the Android Asset Packaging Tool that enables us to extract the sets of data. Also, android applications are developed in Java and compiled into optimized bytecode for the dalvik virtual machine. This bytecode can be efficiently disassembled and provides DREBIN with information about API calls and data used in an application. To achieve a low run-time, a lightweight disassembler is implemented based on the dex libraries of the Android platform that can output all API calls and strings contained in an application. This information is used to construct the following feature sets.

S1 Hardware components: This first feature set contains requested hardware components. If an application requests access to the camera, touchscreen or the GPS module of the smartphone, these features need to be declared in the manifest file. Requesting access to specific hardware has clearly security implications, as the use of certain combinations of hardware often reflects harmful behavior. An application which has access to GPS and network modules is, for instance, able to collect location data and send it to an attacker over the network.

S2 Requested permissions: One of the most important security mechanisms introduced in Android is the permission system. Permissions are actively granted by the user at installation time and allow an application to access security-relevant resources. As shown by previous work [13], malicious software tends to request certain permissions more often than innocuous applications. For example, a great percentage of current malware sends premium SMS messages and thus requests the SEND SMS permission. Thus, all permissions listed in the manifest are gathered in a feature set.

S3 App components: There exist four different types of components in an application, each defining different interfaces to the system: activities, services, content providers and broadcast receivers. Every application can declare several components of each type in the manifest. The names of these components are also collected in a feature set, as the names may help to identify well known components of malware. For example, several variants of a particular family share the name of particular services in Table 3.

Table 3. Variants of families share names of particular services

Id	Family	#	Id	Family	#
A	FakeInstaller	925	K	Adrd	91
B	DroidKungFu	667	L	DroidDream	81
C	Plankton	625	M	LinuxLotoor	70
D	Opfake	613	N	GoldDream	69
E	GingerMaster	339	O	MobileTx	69
F	BaseBridge	330	P	FakeRun	61
G	Iconosys	152	Q	SendPay	59
H	Kmin	147	R	Gappusin	58
I	FakeDoc	132	S	Imlog	43
J	Geinimi	92	T	SMSreg	41

S4 Filtered intents: Inter-process and intra-process communication on Android is mainly performed through intents: passive data structures exchanged as asynchronous messages and allowing information about events to be shared between different components and applications. All intents listed in the manifest are collected as another feature set, as malware often listens to specific intents. A typical example of an intent message involved in malware is BOOT COMPLETED, which is used to trigger malicious activity directly after rebooting the smartphone.

S5 Restricted API calls: The Android permission system restricts access to a series of critical API calls. The method searches for the occurrence of these calls in the disassembled code in order to gain a deeper understanding of the functionality of an application. A particular case, revealing malicious behavior, is the use of restricted API calls for which the required permissions have not been requested. This may indicate that the malware is using root exploits in order to surpass the limitations imposed by the Android platform.

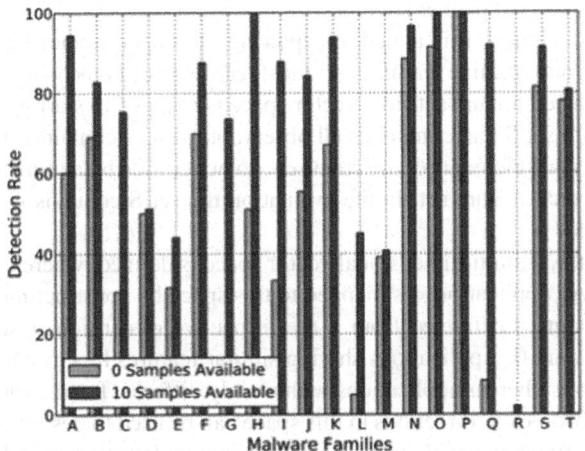

Fig. 1. Top malware families in the dataset.

S6 Used permissions: The complete set of calls extracted in S5 is used as the ground for determining the subset of permissions that are both requested and actually used. For this purpose, the method introduced by Felt et al. is implemented to match API calls and permissions. In contrast to S5, this feature set provides a more general view on the behavior of an application as multiple API calls can be protected by a single permission (e.g., sendMultipartTextMessage() and sendTextMessage() both require that the SEND SMS permission is granted to an application).

Suspicious API calls: Certain API calls allow access to sensitive data or resources of the smartphone and are frequently found in malware samples. As these calls can specially lead to malicious behavior, they are extracted and gathered in a separated feature set. In particular, the following types of API calls are collected:

• API calls for accessing sensitive data
• API calls for communicating over the network
• API calls for sending and receiving SMS messages
• API calls for execution of external commands
• API calls frequently used for obfuscation

Network addresses: Malware regularly establishes network connections to retrieve commands or data collected from the device. Therefore, all IP addresses, hostnames and URLs found in the disassembled code are included in the last set of features. Some of these addresses might be involved in botnets and thus present in several malware samples, which can help to improve the learning of detection patterns.

Malicious activity is usually reflected in specific patterns and combinations of the extracted features. For example, a malware sending premiums SMS messages might contain the permission SEND SMS in set S2, and the hardware component android.hardware.telephony in set S1. Ideally, one would like to formulate Boolean expressions that capture these dependencies between features and return true if a malware is detected. However, inferring Boolean expressions from real-world data is a hard problem and difficult to solve efficiently.

To present a solution, it is aimed at capturing the dependencies between features using concepts from machine learning. As most learning methods operate on numerical vectors, the extracted feature sets to a vector space is mapped to start with. To this end, one defines a joint set S that comprises all observable strings contained in the 8 feature sets. It is ensured that elements of different sets do not collide by adding a unique prefix to all strings in each feature set. In the evaluation the set S contains roughly 545,000 different features.

Using the set S, a multi-dimensional vector space is defined, where each dimension is either 0 or 1. An application x is mapped to this space by constructing a vector, such that for each feature s extracted from x the respective dimension is set to 1 and all other dimensions are 0. Applications sharing similar features lie close to each other in this representation, whereas applications with mainly different features are separated by large distances. Moreover, directions in this space can be used to describe combinations of features and ultimately enable us to learn explainable detection models.

Let us, as an example, consider a malicious application that sends premium SMS messages and thus needs to request certain permissions and hardware components. At a first glance, the map seems inappropriate for the lightweight analysis of applications, as it embeds data into a high-dimensional vector space. Fortunately, the number of features extracted from an application is linear in its size. That is, an application x containing m bytes of code and data contains at most m feature strings. As a consequence, only m dimensions are non-zero in the vector irrespective of the dimension of the vector space. It thus suffices to only store the features extracted from an application for sparsely representing the vector.

3   Results and Evaluations

A machine with 3.1 GHz Intel Core i7and 16 GB RAM which was powerful enough to train the deep neural nets with many hidden layers was utilized. The simplest method to evaluate the performance of a machine learning algorithm is to use different training and testing datasets. The original dataset is split into two parts. Train the algorithm on the first part, make predictions on the second part and evaluate the predictions against the expected results. The size of the split can depend on the size and specifics of the dataset, although it is common to use 67% of the data for training and the remaining 33% for testing. Ideally, you want to select a model at the sweet spot between under fitting and overfitting. This is the goal but is very difficult to do in practice. To understand this goal, one can look at the performance of a machine learning algorithm over time as it is learning a training data. We can plot both the skill on the training data and the skill on a test dataset we have held back from the training process. Over time, as the algorithm learns, the error for the model on the training data goes down and so does the error on the test dataset. If it is trained for too long, the error on the training dataset may continue to decrease because the model is overfitting and learning the irrelevant detail and noise in the training dataset. At the same time the error for the test set starts to rise again as the model's ability to generalize decreases. The sweet spot is the point just before the error on the test dataset starts to increase where the model has good skill on both the training dataset and the unseen test dataset. You can perform this experiment with one's favorite machine learning algorithms. This is often not useful technique in practice, because by choosing the stopping point for training using the skill on the test dataset it means that the test set is no longer unseen or a standalone objective measure. Some knowledge (a lot of useful knowledge) about that data has leaked into the training procedure. There are two additional techniques you can use to help find the sweet spot in practice, resampling methods and a validation dataset.

Both overfitting and under fitting can lead to poor model performance. But by far the most common problem in applied machine learning is overfitting. Overfitting is such a problem because the evaluation of machine learning algorithms on training data is different from the evaluation the research work actually cares about the most, namely how well the algorithm performs on unseen data. There are two important techniques that you can use when evaluating machine learning algorithms to limit overfitting: either use a resampling technique to estimate model accuracy or hold back a validation dataset. The most popular resampling technique is k-fold cross validation. It allows you to train and test the model k-times on different subsets of training data and build up an estimate of the performance of a machine learning model on unseen data. A validation dataset is simply a subset of training data that one holds back from your machine learning algorithms until the very end of your project. After you have selected and tuned your machine learning algorithms on your training dataset you can evaluate the learned models on the validation dataset to get a final objective idea of how the models might perform on unseen data. Using cross validation is a gold standard in applied machine learning for estimating model accuracy on unseen data. If you have the data, using a validation dataset is also an excellent practice. This algorithm evaluation technique is very fast. It is ideal for large datasets (millions of records) where there is strong evidence that both splits of the data are representative of the underlying problem. Because of the speed, it is useful to use this approach when the algorithm you are investigating is slow to train. A downside of this technique is that it can have a high variance. This means that differences in the training and test dataset can result in meaningful differences in the estimate of accuracy. In the example below the dataset is divided into 67%/33% splits for training and testing and evaluating the accuracy of a Logistic Regression model.

Cross validation is an approach that you can use to estimate the performance of a machine learning algorithm with less variance than a single train-test set split. It works by splitting the dataset into k-parts (e.g., k = 5 or k = 10). Each split of the data is called a fold. The algorithm is trained on k 1 folds with one held back and tested on the held back fold. This is repeated so that each fold of the dataset is given a chance to be the held back test set. After running cross validation, you end up with k different performance scores that you can summarize using a mean and a standard deviation. The result is a more reliable estimate of the performance of the algorithm on new data. It is more accurate because the algorithm is trained and evaluated multiple times on different data. The choice of k must allow the size of each test partition to be large enough to be a reasonable sample of the problem, whilst allowing enough repetitions of the train-test evaluation of the algorithm to provide a fair estimate of the algorithm's performance on unseen data. For modest sized datasets in the thousands or tens of thousands of records, k values of 3, 5 and 10 are common. In the example below 10-fold cross validation is used. It is a good practice to prepare the data before modeling. Neural network models are especially suitable to having consistent input values, both in scale and distribution. An effective data preparation scheme for tabular data when building neural network models is standardization. This is where the data is rescaled such that the mean value for each attribute is 0 and the standard deviation is 1. This preserves Gaussian and Gaussian-like distributions whilst normalizing the central tendencies for each attribute. When the data is comprised of attributes with varying scales, many machine learning algorithms can benefit from rescaling the attributes to all have the same scale. Often this is referred to as normalization and attributes are often rescaled into the range between 0 and 1. This is useful for optimization algorithms in used in the core of machine learning algorithms like gradient descent. It is also useful for algorithms that weight inputs like regression and neural networks. An important concern with the dataset is that the input attributes all vary in their scales because they measure different quantities. It is almost always good practice to prepare the data before modeling it using a neural network model. Continuing on from the above baseline model, one can re-evaluate the same model using a standardized version of the input dataset. A pipeline framework is used to perform the standardization during the model evaluation process, within each fold of the cross validation. This ensures that there is no data leakage from each test set cross validation fold into the training data.

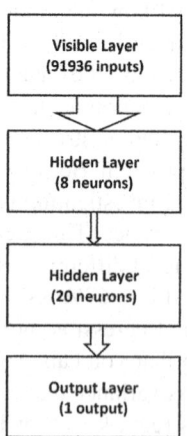

Fig. 2. Architecture of the deep neural network

One way to improve the performance of a neural network is to add more layers. This might allow the model to extract and recombine higher order features embedded in the data. In this section the effect of adding one more hidden layer to the model is evaluated. This is as easy as defining a new function that will create this deeper model, copied from the baseline model above. A new line after the first hidden layer is then inserted. In this case with about half the number of neurons. Another approach to increasing the representational capacity of the model is to create a wider network. In this section, we evaluate the effect of keeping a shallow network architecture and nearly doubling the number of neurons in the hidden layer. Again, all is needed to do is define a new function that creates the neural network model. Here, the number of neurons in the hidden layer compared to the baseline model is increased from 13 to 20.

Figure 2 shows the final architecture of the deep neural network, and it achieved an accuracy of up to 99% on a large dataset. The confusion matrix and the receiver optimistic curve is shown in Figs. 3 and 4 respectively.

		Predicted	
		Safe	Malicious
Actual	Safe	99%	1%
	Malicious	1%	99%

Fig. 3. Mean confusion matrix

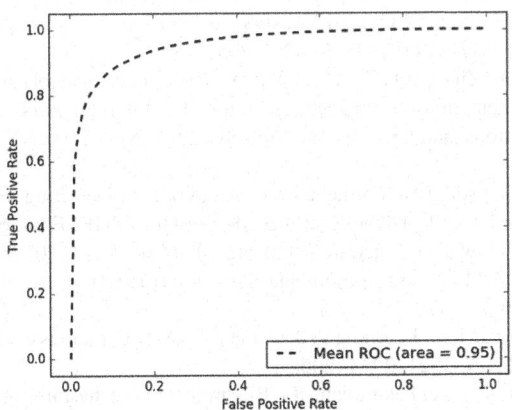

Fig. 4. Mean receiver optimistic characteristic curve

4 Conclusion

With the increase of large-scale datasets such as user behavior in minute detail, results from static code analysis of mobile applications high dimensional datasets that traditional machine learning is unable to cope. Cheap computers, storage & memory alongside new statistical modelling & data mining techniques have given us the opportunity to solve problem in range of domains, not just in security of mobile apps. Traditional machine learning techniques such as support vector machine or random forest can build accurate models for many applications but fails to achieve the same level of performance of deep neural network with larger datasets.

This research proposes to use the novel approach of deep neural network to solve the high dimensionality problem and to find more patterns at various levels. The features from various levels are gathered to represent permissions of apps in a high dimensional space. Simulation results show that the detection accuracy is over 99%, with detection time under 100 ms. In future the detector should look at using other modelling techniques such as recurrent neural network and convolutional network to take into account the time dimension and use graphical processing units to train the models even faster.

References

1. Peng, H., et al.: Using probabilistic generative models for ranking risks of android apps. In: Proceedings of the 2012 ACM Conference on Computer and Communications Security, ser. CCS 2012, New York, NY, USA, pp. 241–252. ACM (2012)
2. Felt, A.P., Chin, E., Hanna, S., Song, D., Wagner, D.: Android permissions demystified. In: Proceedings of the 18th ACM Conference on Computer and Communications Security, ser. CCS 2011, New York, NY, USA, pp. 627–638. ACM (2011)
3. Genkin, A., Lewis, D.D., Madigan, D.: Large-scale Bayesian logistic regression for text categorization. Technometrics 49, 291–304 (2007)
4. Wang, Q., Si, L., Zhang, D.: A discriminative data-dependent mixture-model approach for multiple instance learning in image classification. In: Fitzgibbon, A., Lazebnik, S., Perona, P., Sato, Y., Schmid, C. (eds.) ECCV 2012. LNCS, vol. 7575, pp. 660–673. Springer, Heidelberg (2012). https://doi.org/10.1007/978-3-642-33765-9_47
5. Grace, M., Zhou, Y., Zhang, Q., Zou, S., Jiang, X.: Riskranker: scalable and accurate zero-day android malware detection. In: Proceedings of the 10th International Conference on Mobile Systems, Applications, and Services, ser. MobiSys 2012, New York, NY, USA, pp. 281–294. ACM (2012)
6. Schmidt, A.-D., Clausen, J.H., Camtepe, S.A., Albayrak, S.: Detecting Symbian OS malware through static function call analysis. In: Proceedings of the 4th IEEE International Conference on Malicious and Unwanted Software (Malware 2009), pp. 15–22. IEEE (2009)
7. He, H., Garcia, E.A.: Learning from imbalanced data. IEEE Trans. Knowl. Data Eng. 21(9), 1263–1284 (2009)
8. Kolter, J.Z., Maloof, M.A.: Learning to detect and classify malicious executables in the wild. J. Mach. Learn. Res. 7, 2721–2744 (2006)
9. Jang, J., Brumley, D., Venkataraman, S.: Bitshred: feature hashing malware for scalable triage and semantic analysis. In: Proceedings of the 18th ACM Conference on Computer and Communications Security, ser. 1 CCS 2011, New York, NY, USA, pp. 309–320. ACM (2011)
10. Desnos, A.: Android: Static analysis using similarity distance. In: 2012 45th Hawaii International Conference on System Sciences (HICSS), pp. 5394–5403 (2012)
11. Schmidt, A.-D., et al.: Static analysis of executables for collaborative malware detection on android. In: ICC, pp. 1–5. IEEE (2009)
12. Jusoh, R., Firdaus, A., Anwar, S., Osman, M.Z., Darmawan, M.F., Ab Razak, M.F.: Malware detection using static analysis in Android: a review of FeCO (features, classification, and obfuscation). Peer J. Comput. Sci. 7, e522 (2021). https://doi.org/10.7717/peerj-cs.522

13. Aafer, Y., Du, W., Yin, H.: DroidAPIMiner: mining API-level features for robust malware detection in Android. In: Proceedings of the 9th International Conference on Security and Privacy in Communication Networks, September 2013
14. Christodorescu, M., Jha, S., Kruegel, C.: Mining specifications of malicious behavior. In: Proceedings of the 6th Joint Meeting of the European Software Engineering Conference and the ACM SIGSOFT Symposium on The Foundations of Software Engineering, ser. ESEC-FSE 2007, New York, NY, USA, pp. 5–14. ACM (2007)
15. Shanmukh, V.: Image Classification Using Machine Learning-Support Vector Machine (SVM), 3rd March 2021. https://medium.com/analytics-vidhya/image-classification-using-machine-learning-support-vector-machine-svm-dc7a0ec92e01. Accessed 25 Feb 2022
16. Bailey, M., Oberheide, J., Andersen, J., Mao, Z.M., Jahanian, F., Nazario, J.: Automated classification and analysis of internet malware. In: Kruegel, C., Lippmann, R., Clark, A. (eds.) RAID 2007. LNCS, vol. 4637, pp. 178–197. Springer, Heidelberg (2007). https://doi.org/10.1007/978-3-540-74320-0_10
17. Shabtai, A., Elovici, Y.: Applying behavioral detection on android-based devices, October 2012
18. Portokalidis, G., Homburg, P., Anagnostakis, K., Bos, H.: Paranoid android: versatile protection for smartphones. In: Proceedings of the 26th Annual Computer Security Applications Conference, ser. ACSAC 2010, New York, NY, USA, pp. 347–356. ACM (2010). https://doi.org/10.1145/1920261.1920313
19. Burguera, I., Zurutuza, U., Nadjm-Tehrani, S.: Crowdroid: behavior-based malware detection system for android. In: Proceedings of the 1st ACM Workshop on Security and Privacy in Smartphones and Mobile Devices, ser. SPSM 2011. New York, NY, USA, pp. 15–26. ACM (2011)
20. Au, K.W.Y., Zhou, Y.F., Huang, Z., Lie, D.: Pscout: analyzing the android permission specification. In: Proceedings of the 2012 ACM Conference on Computer and Communications Security, ser. CCS 2012, New York, NY, USA, pp. 217–228. ACM (2012)
21. Felt, A.P., Greenwood, K., Wagner, D.: The effectiveness of application permissions. In: Proceedings of the 2nd USENIX Conference on Web Application Development, ser. WebApps 2011, Berkeley, CA, USA, p. 7. USENIX Association (2011)
22. Davis, J., Goadrich, M.: The relationship between precision-recall and ROC curves. In: Proceedings of the 23rd International Conference on Machine Learning, ser. ICML 2006, New York, NY, USA, pp. 233–240. ACM (2006)
23. Yuan, Z., Lu, Y., Wang, Z., Xue, Y.: Droid-Sec: deep learning in an- droid malware detection. In: ACM SIGCOMM Computer Communication Review, vol. 44(4), pp. 371–372. ACM (2014)
24. Yuan, Z., Lu, Y., Xue, Y.: Droiddetector: android malware characterization and detection using deep learning. Tsinghua S. Technol. 21(1), 114–123 (2016)
25. Worldpanel, K.: Smartphone OS market share (2015)

Prediction of Wafer Map Categories Using Wafer Acceptance Test Parameters in Semiconductor Manufacturing

Martin Ying Song Lim[1,2]([✉]), Anurag Sharma[2], Cheng Siong Chin[2], Tommy Chun Ming Yip[1], and Jonathan Yoong Seang Ong[1]

[1] Globalfoundries, Singapore 738406, Singapore
martinyingsong.lim@globalfoundries.com
[2] NewRIIS, Singapore 609607, Singapore

Abstract. The semiconductor industry is always looking for new solutions to maximize yield. Recently, the focus has been on utilizing the manufacturing data to help improve operational efficiency and early detection. This paper proposes a framework to find the best combination of machine learning models and data-balancing methods to predict specific wafer map signatures using Wafer Acceptance Test (WAT). WAT is a measurement test performed at multiple locations to identify poorly manufactured wafers. However, there were instances where wafers passed every measurement test but were found to have low yield. The proposed framework will be tested on real manufacturing data to demonstrate the viability of predicting wafer map signatures.

Keyword: Semiconductor manufacturing · Machine learning · Wafer Acceptance Test

1 Introduction

As global demand for Integrated Circuit (IC) chips is increasing, semiconductor manufacturers (fab) are under pressure to improve their yield and ensure that manufacturing errors are kept to a minimum. Wafers are the material in which multiple dies are manufactured on and every die contains the circuits found in IC chips. It is crucial for semiconductor manufacturing to ensure that all wafers meet manufacturing expectations. Wafer Acceptance Test (WAT) is used by fab engineers to identify poorly manufactured wafers and determine the number of dies that are usable (yield). After passing the WAT the wafers will go for Wafer Sort (WS) testing where individual die functionality is tested. A wafer map (WM) is then produced using the WS data that indicates which die passed or failed. The WM will be sent to the fab to evaluate the yield of each wafer and look for any process improvement to perform. One of the key things fab engineers look at when performing low-yield investigation is the wafer map signature as seen in Fig. 1, which shows common low yield patterns. Identifying the WM signature is vital as it can identify possible manufacturing process failures. This is a time-consuming process

© IFIP International Federation for Information Processing 2022
Published by Springer Nature Switzerland AG 2022
I. Maglogiannis et al. (Eds.): AIAI 2022, IFIP AICT 647, pp. 136–144, 2022.
https://doi.org/10.1007/978-3-031-08337-2_12

and has generated research interest in using machine learning [1, 2] to automatically classify the signatures. However, there is a significant time gap (1–2 months) before the fab engineers get the WM from WS. Therefore, being able to predict the likelihood of the WM signature based on the yield predicted at different sections of the wafer as seen in Fig. 2 will allow faster identification of possible manufacturing process error.

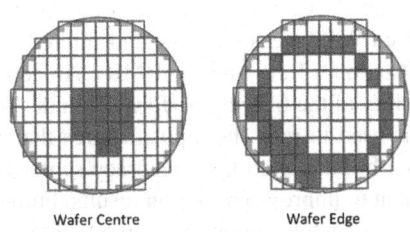

Wafer Centre   Wafer Edge

Fig. 1. Two of the most common wafer map signatures.

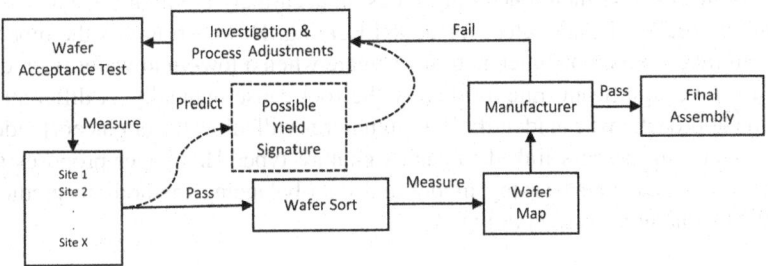

Fig. 2. Manufacturing flow after wafer fabrication stage.

In the existing literature, there has already been research on using WAT measurements to predict wafer yield. This often involves using expert inputs and feature selection methods to identify key WAT measurements that explain the predicted yield value. Chien et al. [3] made use of experts to select relevant WAT measurements to be used in modeling. The experts chose the 12 measurements that was used in a modified Partial Least Square (mPLS) model. The model aims to prove the importance of the 12 measurements chosen by adding them into the model one at a time. There is a relative increase in R squared (R^2) score with every measure added. This proves that inputs from experts can help in improving prediction accuracy. However, the improvement gained from individual measurement is relatively low, and expert inputs can be biased to experience. The relative impact of other measures should also be considered that could be missed out from expert input. Using just expert input will not give new insights into possible manufacturing issues. Chan et al. [4] use a wide combination of feature and oversampling techniques to classify every die on the wafer to either pass or fail WS test. This is a more precise prediction as it is possible to generate the actual wafer map and classify using a wafer map classification model. However, the proposed framework was only tested on two wafers from each lot which might be too small of a sample size to measure the predictive capabilities of this method. Jiang et al. [5] used WAT measurements together with descriptive data and used a one-hot encoder to create new parameters to represent the descriptive data. The data is then used to predict the yield at a final assembly where dies would have passed many tests prior, as seen in Fig. 2. The data used here is a lot wider and it is predicting past other checks that were put in place to predict just the yield at final assembly. It does not particularly explain how all the tests up to the final assembly did not catch the predicted die failures earlier. Further studies would be required to understand this in greater detail. Xu et al. [6] made use of mutual information (MI) to find the correlation between WAT measurements and filtered the measurements using minimum Redundancy Maximum Relevance (mRMR). A deep belief network (DBN) was used to test the reliability of the filtering performed on the WAT measurements and genetic algorithm (GA) is used to rank the input features that were used in the DBN model. It was tested and it has achieved high accuracy score showing that using only feature selection is sufficient to improve prediction results. Further testing on using feature selection as the only approach to achieve high prediction score will be required to test the effectiveness. It is noted that proper reduction of WAT parameters is crucial for fab engineers to narrow down the problem when low yield occurs.

All previous works mentioned only focus on accurately predicting the actual yield by shrinking the WAT parameters for model training. However, unless the model can tell fab engineers which parameters to investigate when a low-yield wafer is predicted, it will still take significant time to identify the root cause manually. A different yield prediction approach that can identify WM signatures will allow fab engineers to identify the manufacturing process linked to each signature type. This paper proposes a best combination of machine learning model and data-balancing methods to predict two major WM signatures, as seen in Fig. 3.

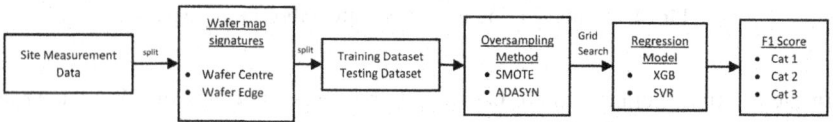

Fig. 3. Framework to predict different wafer map classes.

The remainder of the paper is organized as follows: Sect. 2 introduces the methodology that will be used to predict the respective sections of the wafer. Section 3 explains the experimental setup used on real-life manufacturing data. Section 4 concludes the findings obtained from the experiment.

2 Methodology

This section will describe how site-level yield prediction will be performed based on site-level WAT measurement data. A combination of oversampling technique and machine learning algorithm will be used to find the best combination of models to predict for the two wafer map categories (Wafer Centre & Wafer Edge) as seen in Fig. 1. These two categories are chosen as it has a high impact in terms of yield loss [1, 2] and it covers majority of the wafer. Other categories will require additional data from a wafer map classification model to accurately identify each category which will not be discussed in this paper.

2.1 Data Preprocessing

2.1.1 WAT Measurement Site

To predict Wafer Map signatures would require a different type of dataset that includes the same WAT measurements that is performed at multiple locations (sites) throughout every wafer. The dataset for each signature will only include the measurement sites that overlaps with the signature that are identified earlier in Fig. 1. The amount of measurement sites in each dataset will not be mentioned as it is confidential information. The location of the measurement sites across every wafer in a product will be the same. The chosen signatures (Wafer Center and Wafer Edge) are distinct from each other and there will be no overlapping sites in their respective dataset. The Wafer Edge signature will have significantly more measurements site as manufacturing processes are harder to control [8].

2.1.2 Wafer Yield Categories

The output used in this dataset will be the die yield that shows the number of dies that have passed all WS test. As mentioned earlier since there will be multiple sites on each wafer, the die yield will be calculated based on the Euclidean distance of the surrounding dies relative to where the location of the measurement for every wafer. As this is fundamentally a regression problem, the predicted values will show how many dies is likely to pass the WS test at every site. However, as the total number of dies at each site can be different making it difficult to determine the severity of the yield loss at each location.

To solve this, the regression output needs to have its own distinct categories to classify the severity of the yield loss at a given site. To do this a typical k-means clustering method is used to determine the threshold of yield loss at each site. There will be three category (Low, Medium & High) which will denote the amount yield loss relative to the total amount of dies associated with the site. Where the low category will represent the highest yield loss and vice versa. This will allow better distinction of how severe the yield loss at each site regardless of how many dies are associated with it.

2.2 Oversampling Algorithm

Class imbalance is a common problem when working with manufacturing data, as there is always a significantly larger quantity of good samples than bad samples. This results in most machine learning algorithms overfitting the majority class. To handle this, two over-sampling techniques are implemented to the training dataset to have the machine learning models be more sensitive to the minority class.

2.2.1 Synthetic Minority Over-Sampling Technique (SMOTE)

This is a popular oversampling method [9] that uses k-NN to create synthetic samples from the minority data by computing the distance between the vectors in the space and multiplies a random value between zero to one. It is then added back to the original vector to be a new feature. The minority data will be oversampled to the maximum value from the majority data.

2.2.2 Adaptive Synthetic Sampling (ADASYN)

It uses an improved version of the SMOTE algorithm [10]. The key difference between the two is that ADASYN will calculate the number of synthetic minority class samples based on the amount of majority class samples that is within the minority class sample space.

2.3 Machine Learning Algorithm

2.3.1 EXtreme Gradient Boost (XGB)

XGB [11] is a machine learning algorithm that has high performance and accurate ensemble model and was made as an improvement over the traditional Gradient Boost Decision Tree (GBDT) where new trees are generated to add its loss function to the previous tree, XBG main. It also with missing values which is commonly found in any manufacturing environment due to equipment failure and human error. XGB objective function is defined as:

$$obj = \sum_{i=1}^{n} [\![l(y_i, \hat{y}_i)]\!] + \sum_{k} \Omega(f_k) \tag{1}$$

where $\Omega(f_k) = \gamma T + \frac{1}{2}\lambda \|\omega\|^2$ and l defines the loss function that measures the difference between the target value y_i and the predicted value $\hat{y}_i$. The regularization term is defined as $\Omega(f_k)$ where it is used to reduce the model complexity to avoid overfitting. It achieves this by considering the number of leaves (γ) and the number of leaf nodes (T) so that the best model can be achieved with the least resources possible.

2.3.2 Support Vector Regression (SVR)

SVR [12] is effective when there are no missing data, and there is no clarity on which parameters are deemed unnecessary for the model. It has less over-fitting when data re-sampling techniques are involved as it is designed to place a new sample into the nearest class 'label'. The only disadvantage it has is the large amount of training time required when running on a high dimension dataset.

3 Experimental Studies

3.1 Experiment Setup

The experiment is conducted on an existing wafer product and all manufacturing data is provided by Globalfoundries. The dataset consists of over 3000 wafers containing all measurement information on all site with no missing values. During final WAT measurement there is a total of 89 parameters tested on each site. The measurement sites will be divided into two Wafer Map signature (Wafer Center and Wafer Edge) as explained in Sect. 2.1. For each Wafer Map signature model, 70% of the site level WAT test data and its corresponding yield value will be used as the training set for the supervised regression model, and the remainder 30% of the data will be used as the testing set for test verification.

3.2 Model Training

This subsection will introduce how the training is conducted for the experiments, as shown in Fig. 3. There will be a combination of two different class imbalance methods (ADASYN & SMOTE), and a combination of machine learning models (XGB & SVR) will be used to find the best combination of oversampling method and machine learning for the selected wafer map categories (Wafer Centre & Wafer Edge). The hyper parameters will be chosen by using K-fold cross-validation, where K = 5 and grid search to find the best sets of parameters and avoid over-fitting.

R-Squared (R^2) and Root Mean Square Error (RMSE) will be metrics used to determine how accurate the actual values predicted is. The closer the value for R^2 is to 1 the better the variance for all predicted results. However, a high R^2 will not be able to explain the actual problem on most manufacturing applications.

Therefore, a multi-class confusion matrix will indicate the category the predicted value will be classified under from the output clustering performed using k-means. The category will be classified from low yield – high yield (1 – 3). The confusion matrix will show the classification accuracy of each category with respect to the total quantity that was in each category.

3.3 Experiment Results

Both datasets for each of the Wafer Map Signature will be conducted with the experimental setup described above and the regression results can be seen in Table 1 as shown below.

Table 1. Comparison table between oversampling methods.

Regressor	Oversampling Method	R^2 (Edge)	R^2 (Center)
XGB	None	−0.05	−0.01
	SMOTE	**0.78**	**0.83**
	ADASYN	**0.78**	**0.8**
SVR	None	−0.01	−0.37
	SMOTE	0.72	0.8
	ADASYN	0.76	0.75

To compare the performance between both machine learning models used in this experiment, XGB have a higher R^2 for both models across the board with 5% higher on average of the oversampling method used. This is likely due to the oversampling performed where a decision-tree based algorithm will perform better than a cluster-based algorithm. Choosing the correct oversampling method is also important and looking at the difference in results both methods give similar accuracy. Looking at the center signature model SMOTE have a higher R^2 with an accuracy score of 0.83 and 0.8 as compared to ADASYN with an accuracy score of 0.8 and 0.75 using XGB and SVR respectively. In the edge signature prediction, both SMOTE and ADASYN have similar performances using XGB with the same R^2 of 0.78 while ADASYN have a higher accuracy with the SVR model with an R^2 of 0.76 as compared to SMOTE with an R^2 of 0.72. This shows that SMOTE would on perform better in most scenarios as compared to ADASYN. While having no sampling will result in extremely poor R^2 values where it is unable to predict anywhere close to the target yield value.

However, R^2 only shows how accurate the model predicts relative to the target yield of each site. As explained in Sect. 2.1, the number of dies associated with each measurement site is different. Therefore, to better represent the yield loss at each site, the predicted value will be classified into three different yield categories (Low, Medium, High) yield. To see prediction accuracy in each category, a multi-class confusion matrix is used to demonstrate how well the transformed predicted values is classified as seen in Table 2. Where the predicted output will be transformed and classified into the three categories

Table 2. Number of correct classifications between oversampling methods.

Regressor	Oversampling method	Yield category	Low (edge)	Medium (edge)	High (edge)	Low (center)	Medium (center)	High (center)
XGB	None	Low	**15.46%**	**84.54%**	**0%**	**25.14%**	**74.86%**	**0%**
		Medium	0%	100%	0%	0%	72.93%	27.07%
		High	0%	37.53%	62.47%	0%	0%	100%
	SMOTE	Low	**68.42%**	**31.58%**	**0%**	**70.22%**	**29.78%**	**0%**
		Medium	0%	100%	0%	0%	78.86%	21.14%
		High	0%	31.61%	68.39%	0%	0%	100%
	ADASYN	Low	**77.71%**	**22.29%**	**0%**	**82.12%**	**17.88%**	**0%**
		Medium	0%	100%	0%	0%	72.31%	27.69%
		High	0%	37.02%	62.98%	0%	0%	100%
SVR	None	Low	**1.12%**	**85.73%**	**13.15%**	**7.32%**	**66.16%**	**26.52%**
		Medium	0.38%	78.71%	20.91%	2.38%	61.25%	35.37%
		High	0.19%	76.16%	23.65%	2.23%	57.28%	40.49%
	SMOTE	Low	**76.53%**	**22.45%**	**1.02%**	**80.5%**	**17.59%**	**0.91%**
		Medium	12.85%	73.1%	14.05%	5.12%	71.95%	22.93%
		High	6.4%	72.8%	20.8%	5.22%	52.58%	42.2%
	ADASYN	Low	**68.79%**	**25.21%**	**6%**	**73.44%**	**17.57%**	**8.99%**
		Medium	3.42%	73.5%	23.08%	4.54%	61.95%	33.51%
		High	1.41%	71.51%	27.08%	2.08%	57.98%	39.94%

determined by the original yield output for each site. It also allows to see how far apart the prediction values will be.

Looking at Table 2, it is clearer in explaining how each of the R^2 score came to be. As mentioned earlier, using the original dataset with no oversampling will results in the model being unable to predict any of the target values by looking at just the R^2. However, looking closely at Table 2, the prediction inaccuracy only occurs mostly at the Low Yield and High Yield category. This will clearly indicate where the class imbalance occurs for each dataset and a more precise oversampling to target specific categories could be performed. In this experiment, only the Low Yield category is oversampled which can be seen in the increase in the classification rate by 83% on average in both XGB and SVR for both signatures while the classification rate for Medium Yield and High Yield category remains close to the unsampled dataset.

The best machine learning model and oversampling combination can also be determined using the results shown in Table 2 whereas looking at the R^2 values in Fig. 1 would not result in a clear choice. XGB performs better with ADASYN as compared to SMOTE with a classification score of 77.71% and 82.21% with ADASYN and a classification score of 68.42% and 70.22% for Wafer Edge and Wafer Center categories respectively. While SVR performs better with SMOTE with a classification score of 76.53% and 80.5% with SMOTE and a classification score of 68.79% and 73.44% for Wafer Edge and Wafer Center categories respectively.

However, XGB is the better model of the two as there are no cases in which an incorrectly predicted yield category crosses to the extreme end (i.e., Low Yield to High Yield) and is only one category apart from its intended category making it less prone to severe False Positive and False Negative classification results.

4   Conclusions

The ability to forecast potential die yield should be significant in helping fab engineers be aware of potential process issues during manufacturing earlier. This paper proposes a framework that uses WAT measurements to identify potential wafer map signature, and to compare the impact of oversampling between different types of machine learning models. It makes use of the WAT site measurement that can be used to correlate to the other kind of wafer map signatures. This is an early concept that requires more accurate data from Wafer Map classification and a better understanding of how WAT can potentially be used to predict wafer yield.

Acknowledgement. I would like to thank Globalfoundries for providing data and support for the published work.

References

1. Shim, J., Kang, S., Cho, S.: Active learning of convolutional neural network for cost-effective wafer map pattern classification. IEEE Trans. Semicond. Manuf. **33**(2), 258–266 (2020). https://doi.org/10.1109/TSM.2020.2974867

2. Chen, L.L.-Y., et al.: Semi-supervised framework for wafer defect pattern recognition with enhanced labeling. In: 2021 IEEE International Test Conference (ITC), pp. 208–212 (2021).https://doi.org/10.1109/ITC50571.2021.00029

3. Chien, C.-F., Lee, P.-C., Dou, R., Chen, Y.-J., Chen, C.-C.: Modeling collinear WATs for parametric yield enhancement in semiconductor manufacturing. In: 2017 13th IEEE Conference on Automation Science and Engineering (CASE), pp. 739–743 (2017). https://doi.org/10.1109/COASE.2017.8256192

4. Chen, X., Zhao, Y., Lü, H., Shao, X., Chen, C., Huang, Y.: A machine learning-based approach for failure prediction at cell level based on wafer acceptance test parameters. In: 2021 IEEE Microelectronics Design & Test Symposium (MDTS), pp. 1–52021https://doi.org/10.1109/MDTS52103.2021.9476151

5. Jiang, D., Lin, W., Raghavan, N.: A novel framework for semiconductor manufacturing final test yield classification using machine learning techniques. IEEE Access **8**, 197885–197895 (2020)

6. Xu, H., Zhang, J., Lv, Y., Zheng, P.: Hybrid feature selection for wafer acceptance test parameters in semiconductor manufacturing. IEEE Access **8**, 17320–17330 (2020). https://doi.org/10.1109/ACCESS.2020.2966520

7. Tin, T.C., et al.: A realizable overlay virtual metrology system in semiconductor manufacturing: proposal, challenges and future perspective. IEEE Access **9**, 65418–65439 (2021). https://doi.org/10.1109/ACCESS.2021.3076193

8. Ooi, M.P.-L., Kwang Joo Sim, E., Kuang, Y.C., Kleeman, L., Chan, C., Demidenko, S.: Automatic defect cluster extraction for semiconductor wafers. In: 2010 IEEE Instrumentation & Measurement Technology Conference Proceedings, pp. 1024–1029 (2010). https://doi.org/10.1109/IMTC.2010.5488012

9. Chawla, N.V., Bowyer, K.W., Hall, L.O., Kegelmeyer, W.P.: SMOTE: synthetic minority over-sampling technique. J. Artif. Intell. Res. **16**, 321–357 (2002)

10. He, H., Bai, Y., Garcia, E.A., Li, S.: ADASYN: adaptive synthetic sampling approach for imbalanced learning. In: 2008 IEEE International Joint Conference on Neural Networks (IEEE World Congress on Computational Intelligence), pp. 1322–1328. IEEE (2008)

11. Chen, T., et al.: Xgboost: extreme gradient boosting. R package version 0.4-2, 1(4), 1–4 (2015)

12. Awad, M., Khanna, R.: Support vector regression. In: Efficient Learning Machines. Apress, Berkeley, CA (2015). https://doi.org/10.1007/978-1-4302-5990-9_4

Machine Learning Modeling /Feature Selection

An Improved Neural Network Model for Treatment Effect Estimation

Niki Kiriakidou[(✉)] and Christos Diou

Department of Informatics and Telematics, Harokopio University of Athens, Athens, Greece
{kiriakidou,cdiou}@hua.gr

Abstract. Nowadays, in many scientific and industrial fields there is an increasing need for estimating treatment effects and answering causal questions. The key for addressing these problems is the wealth of observational data and the processes for leveraging this data. In this work, we propose a new model for predicting the potential outcomes and the propensity score, which is based on a neural network architecture. The proposed model exploits the covariates as well as the outcomes of neighboring instances in training data. Numerical experiments illustrate that the proposed model reports better treatment effect estimation performance compared to state-of-the-art models.

Keywords: Causal inference · Dragonnet · Treatment effect · Potential outcomes · Propensity score

1 Introduction

For decades, causal inference has been a crucial research topic in many scientific fields, such as healthcare [4], education [7] and economics [20]. Causal inference aims at answering questions regarding the effect of interventions, (e.g., a new drug, a new educational method or a new pricing policy) to the target outcome variables (e.g., health, learning or financial indicators, respectively).

The inference of causal effects is a challenging problem and the most effectual way to infer causality is through randomized controlled trials (RCTs). In many cases, however, it is expensive, time-consuming, unethical or even impossible to conduct an RCT. Nowadays, the abundance of observational data presents an opportunity for accurate estimation of causal effects, however, observational data contain recorded information about samples, such as actions and outcomes along with appropriate context, but there is way to directly influence the mechanism that caused the action. Furthermore, in observational data may exist confounding variables, which affect both treatment and outcome. If these are not adjusted, they could lead to incorrect and misleading results.

In this work, a neural network model is proposed for treatment effect estimation through the prediction of the conditional outcomes and the propensity score. The model extends the state-of-the-art Dragonnet architecture [18] to exploit the

I. Maglogiannis et al. (Eds.): AIAI 2022, IFIP AICT 647, pp. 147–158, 2022.
https://doi.org/10.1007/978-3-031-08337-2_13

covariates along with information from the outcomes of the instances contained in the training data. The rationale behind the proposed approach is to enrich the inputs of the model with the average outcomes of the nearest neighbors from the control and treatment group along with the covariates, in order to reduce bias and increase the prediction accuracy. To estimate treatment effects, the proposed method first trains a model for the prediction of conditional outcomes and the propensity score and then the trained model is used by a downstream estimator. Our experiments illustrate that the proposed approach maintains state of the art performance for the estimation of average treatment effect (ATE), while it leads to significant improvement in estimating the individual treatment effect (ITE).

The remainder of this paper is organised as follows: Sect. 2 presents a review of neural network based models for the estimation of treatment effects. Section 3 presents a comprehensive description of the proposed modified model and its architecture. Section 4 provides information about the data. Section 5 presents a detailed experimental analysis, focusing on the evaluation of the proposed model. Section 6 summarizes the main findings and conclusions of this research, and some interesting directions for future work.

2   Related Work

During the last decade, a lot of research has been conducted towards more accurate and reliable estimation of treatment effects. Most of this research is based on the use of neural networks, exploiting the predictive power of these machine learning models.

Johansson et al. [10] proposed a new algorithmic framework for counterfactual inference. More specifically, they formulated the causal inference problem as a domain adaptation problem and developed a new class of representation algorithms for the calculation of treatment effects. They highlighted that learning representations, which enforce similarity between control and treated groups, is able to lead to better estimations of causal effects. They compared a variant of the proposed algorithm based on a neural network approach, named Balancing Neural Network (BNN), against traditional models, which reported the best overall performance.

Shalit et al. [17] proposed a new theoretical analysis and a new framework, named Counterfactual Regression (CFR) for predicting individual treatment effects. The proposed framework aims on learning a balanced representation using a prediction model, so that the distributions of control and treated group look similar. To measure the distances between two distributions they utilized the integral probability metrics: Maximum Mean Discrepancy (MMD) [5] and Wasserstein distance (Wass) [21]. Additionaly, the major contribution of their work is the introduction of a generalization-bound for the estimation of individual treatment effect, where every individual is only identified by its features. In their experiments, they compared the performance of two proposed models, CFR (MMD) and CFR (Wass), which use MMD and Wass distances, respectively, against state-of-the-art models. Furthermore, they included a variant without balance regularization, named Treatment Agnostic Representation Network (TARNet). Based on their experimental analysis, they stated that all proposed models presented the best performance in terms of estimating treatment effects.

Another approach for estimating individual treatment effect was proposed by Yoon et al. [22], which is based on Generative Adversarial Nets (GANs). The rationale behind the proposed approach is to simulate the uncertainty in the counterfactual distributions by considering learning them using a GAN model. Along this line, they developed a novel model, named Generative Adversarial Nets for inference of Individualized Treatment Effects (GANITE), which was able to provide confidence intervals for its predictions. Their numerical experiments revealed that the proposed method exhibited promising performance.

Louizos et al. [13] highlighted the significance of handling confounders for inferring treatment effects from observational data. More specifically, they stated that there is a strong possibility of existing uncertain and noisy "proxy variables", in case there is no access to all confounders. To address the previous difficulties they proposed a new model, called CEVAE, based on variational autoencoders. A considerable advantage of their approach is that the data generating process as well as the structure of the hidden confounders requires substantially weaker assumptions. Finally, the authors presented that CEVAE exhibited more robust behaviour against hidden confounders in the case of noisy proxies.

Shi et al. [18] proposed a novel neural network model for estimating treatment effects from observational data. The proposed model, named Dragonnet, focuses on improving the estimations through the sufficiency of the propensity score. Additionally, the authors proposed targeted regularization, which constitutes a procedure to induce bias based on non-parametric estimation theory and aims to further improve the estimation of treatment effect. Finally, the authors provided experimental evidence about the superiority of Dragonnet against BNN, CEVAE, GANITE, TARNet, CFR (MMD) and CFR (Wass) using two benchmark datasets.

In this work, we propose a neural network model for predicting the potential outcomes and the propensity score. The proposed model architecture is a modification of Dragonnet's architecture. The major difference between the proposed model and Dragonnet is that the former's inputs contain information from the covariates as well as from the outputs of control and treated group.Our numerical experiments provide empirical and statistical evidence about the efficacy and efficiency of our approach.

3   Modified Dragonnet Model

In this section, we present the proposed model for the estimation of treatment effects. The rationale behind our approach is to enrich the training data with information from the outcomes, which can be exploited by the proposed model in order to obtain more accurate predictions.

3.1   Calculation of Average Outcome Vectors

We limit our discussion to the case of binary treatments. Let $\mathcal{X}$ denote the d-dimensional space of covariates and consider a joint distribution Π on $\mathcal{X} \times \{0,1\} \times \mathcal{Y}$. Suppose that $(X, T, Y) \sim \Pi$, are random variables with domains $\mathcal{X}$, $\{0,1\}$ and $\mathcal{Y}$, corresponding to the covariates, treatment and outcome for a single sample, respectively. Let also Y_0 denote the outcome for a sample when $T = 0$ and Y_1 stand for the outcome of a sample when $T = 1$.

Given a dataset (x_i, t_i, y_i), $i = 1, 2, \ldots, n$ where $x_i \in \mathcal{X}$, $t_i \in \{0,1\}$ and $y_i \in \mathcal{Y}$ our goal is to estimate the average treatment effect

$$\psi = E[Y \mid X, T = 1] - E[Y \mid X, T = 0] \tag{1}$$

For each observed sample in the dataset, either $t_i = 0$ (Y_0 is factual) or $t_i = 1$ (Y_0 is counterfactual) and $y_i = t_i Y_1 + (1 - t_i) Y_0$, based on the framework of Neyman-Rubin [16].

The main idea of our model is to reduce bias in treatment effect estimation, by utilizing the average outcomes of k nearest neighbors $\overline{y}_i^{(0)}$ of the control group and $\overline{y}_i^{(1)}$ of the treatment group for each available sample i.

Algorithm 1 presents a pseudocode for the calculation of $\overline{y}_i^{(0)}$ and $\overline{y}_i^{(1)}$. The algorithm takes as inputs the design matrix $\mathbf{X}$, whose rows correspond to the covariate vectors of samples, the binary vector of treatment values $\mathbf{t}$, the outcome vector $\mathbf{y}$ in the dataset, as well as the number of nearest neighbors k.

Initially, $\overline{\mathbf{y}}^{(0)}$ and $\overline{\mathbf{y}}^{(1)}$ are initialized to $\mathbf{0}$. (Step 1). Next, for every instance $\mathbf{x}_i$ we calculate the average outcomes for control and treated group (Steps 2–7). More specifically, we calculate the k-nearest neighbors of $\mathbf{x}_i$ in $\mathbf{X}$, contained in the control group (i.e. $T = 0$) and append their corresponding indices in the index set S_0 (Step 4). Then, we calculate the average of the outcomes of these neighbors, $\overline{y}_i^{(0)} = \frac{1}{k} \sum_{j \in S_0} y_j$ (Step 5) Similarly, we calculate the average outcome of the k-nearest neighbors of $\mathbf{x}_i$, contained in the treatment group (i.e. $T = 1$)(Step 6–7)

Algorithm 1

Inputs:
   $\mathbf{X}$: design matrix
   $\mathbf{t}$: vector of treatment values t
   $\mathbf{y}$: vector of outcome values y
   k: number of nearest neighbors

Output:
   $\overline{\mathbf{y}}^{(0)}$: vector with average of k-nearest outcomes from control group for each sample
   $\overline{\mathbf{y}}^{(1)}$: vector with average of k-nearest outcomes from treatment group for each sample

Step 1: Set $\overline{\mathbf{y}}^{(0)} = \mathbf{0}$ and $\overline{\mathbf{y}}^{(1)} = \mathbf{0}$

Step 2: for $\mathbf{x}_i, i = 1, 2, \ldots, n$ do

Step 3: $\quad \mathbf{x}_i = \mathbf{X}[i, :]$

Step 4: $\quad$ Calculate the index set $\mathcal{S}_0$ containing the indices of the k-nearest neighbors of $\mathbf{x}_i$ with $T = 0$

Step 5: $\quad \overline{y}_i^{(0)} = \dfrac{1}{k} \displaystyle\sum_{j \in \mathcal{S}_0} y_j$

Step 6: $\quad$ Calculate the index set $\mathcal{S}_1$ containing the indices of the k-nearest neighbors of $\mathbf{x}_i$ with $T = 1$

Step 7: $\quad \overline{y}_i^{(1)} = \dfrac{1}{k} \displaystyle\sum_{j \in \mathcal{S}_1} y_j$

Based on the presented iterative process the average outcome from control and treated group is obtained and stored in $\overline{\mathbf{y}}^{(0)}$ and $\overline{\mathbf{y}}^{(1)}$, respectively. Notice that these will be used by the proposed model for the prediction of the conditional outcomes $Q(t, \mathbf{x}) = E(Y \mid X = \mathbf{x}, T = t)$ and the propensity score $g(x) = P(T = 1 \mid X = \mathbf{x})$.

3.2 Modified Dragonnet Architecture

The proposed model consists of a modification of the state-of-the-art Dragonnet model [18]. The model takes as inputs the design matrix $\mathbf{X}$ and the average outcomes from control and treated group, $\overline{\mathbf{y}}^{(0)}$ and $\overline{\mathbf{y}}^{(1)}$, respectively, while its three-headed architecture produces the predictions of propensity score $\hat{g}(\cdot)$ and conditional outcomes $\hat{Q}(0, \cdot, \cdot, \cdot)$ and $\hat{Q}(1, \cdot, \cdot, \cdot)$.

Figure 1 presents a high-level architecture of the proposed modified Dragonnet model. Initially, a number of dense layers are utilized in order to produce a representation layer $Z(\mathbf{X}) \in \mathbb{R}^p$. Next, the output of $Z(\mathbf{X})$ is concatenated with $\overline{\mathbf{y}}^{(0)}$ and the combined information is further processed by dense layers for the prediction of the outcome $\hat{Q}(0, \cdot, \cdot, \cdot)$. Similarly, the output of $Z(\mathbf{X})$ is concatenated with $\overline{\mathbf{y}}^{(1)}$ and through a number of dense layers the model provides the outcome $\hat{Q}(1, \cdot, \cdot, \cdot)$. Additionally, the shared representation $Z(\mathbf{X})$ is used for predicting $\hat{g}(\cdot)$, through the use of a simple linear map followed by a sigmoid activation function.

The model is trained by minimizing the following loss function

$$\hat{\theta} = \arg \min_{\theta} \hat{R}(\theta; \mathbf{X}, \overline{\mathbf{y}}^{(0)}, \overline{\mathbf{y}}^{(1)}) \tag{2}$$

where θ is the parameter vector and $\hat{R}$ is defined by

$$\hat{R}(\theta; \mathbf{X}, \overline{\mathbf{y}}^{(0)}, \overline{\mathbf{y}}^{(1)}) = \frac{1}{n} \sum_i \left[(Q^{nn}(t_i, \mathbf{x}_i, \overline{y}_i^{(0)}, \overline{y}_i^{(1)}; \theta) - y_i)^2 + \alpha f(g^{nn}(\mathbf{x}_i; \theta), t_i) \right] \tag{3}$$

where $Q^{nn}(t_i, \mathbf{x}_i, \overline{y}_i^{(0)}, \overline{y}_i^{(1)}; \theta)$ and $g^{nn}(\mathbf{x}_i; \theta)$ are the output heads, f is the cross entropy function and $\alpha > 0$ is a hyperparameter used for weighting the two loss components.

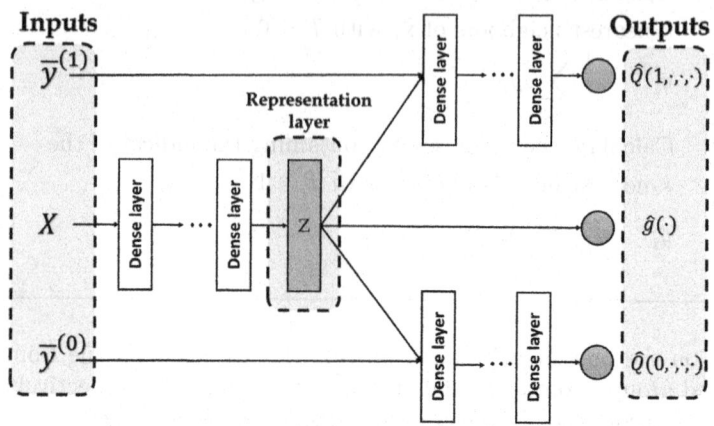

Fig. 1. Modified Dragonnet architecture

Additionally, in order to increase the performance of the proposed model we utilized *targeted regularization* [18], which constitutes a modification to the loss function (2), by introducing a regularization term and an extra parameter.

More specifically, the modified Dragonnet model is trained by minimizing the following loss

$$\hat{\theta}, \hat{\epsilon} = \arg\min_{\theta, \epsilon} \left[\hat{R}(\theta; \mathbf{X}, \overline{\mathbf{y}}^{(0)}, \overline{\mathbf{y}}^{(1)}) + \beta \frac{1}{n} \sum_i \gamma(y_i, t_i, \mathbf{x}_i, \overline{y}_i^{(0)}, \overline{y}_i^{(1)}; \theta, \epsilon) \right] \quad (4)$$

where β, ϵ are positive parameters, $\hat{R}(\theta; \mathbf{X}, \overline{\mathbf{y}}^{(0)}, \overline{\mathbf{y}}^{(1)})$ is defined by Eq. (3) and the regularization term $\gamma(y_i, t_i, \mathbf{x}_i, \overline{y}_i^{(0)}, \overline{y}_i^{(1)}; \theta, \epsilon)$ is defined by

$$\gamma(y_i, t_i, \mathbf{x}_i, \overline{y}_i^{(0)}, \overline{y}_i^{(1)}; \theta, \epsilon) = (y_i - \tilde{Q}(t_i, \mathbf{x}_i, \overline{y}_i^{(0)}, \overline{y}_i^{(1)}; \theta, \epsilon))^2$$

$$\tilde{Q}(t_i, \mathbf{x}_i, \overline{y}_i^{(0)}, \overline{y}_i^{(1)}; \theta, \epsilon) = Q^{nn}(t_i, \mathbf{x}_i, \overline{y}_i^{(0)}, \overline{y}_i^{(1)}; \theta) + \epsilon \left[\frac{t_i}{g^{nn}(\mathbf{x}_i; \theta)} - \frac{1 - t_i}{1 - g^{nn}(\mathbf{x}_i; \theta)} \right]$$

The rationale behind the loss function (4) is based on non-parametric estimation theory and consists on improving the model's estimation of treatment effects. Additionally, under conditions, the following estimator of ψ

$$\hat{\psi}^{\text{treg}} = \frac{1}{n} \sum_{i=1}^{n} [\hat{Q}^{\text{treg}}(1, \mathbf{x}_i, \overline{y}_i^{(0)}, \overline{y}_i^{(1)}) - \hat{Q}^{\text{treg}}(0, \mathbf{x}_i, \overline{y}_i^{(0)}, \overline{y}_i^{(1)})]$$

where $\hat{Q}^{\text{treg}} = \tilde{Q}(\cdot, \cdot, \cdot, \cdot; \hat{\theta}, \hat{\epsilon})$, has the following properties [11] :

1. $\hat{\psi}$ will fast converge to ψ even in case $\hat{Q}$ and $\hat{g}$ converge slowly to Q and g.
2. asymptotically $\hat{\psi}$ has the lowest variance from any other considered estimator of ψ.

4   Data

Considering that real-world data for causal inference are rarely available, we scarcely have access to the ground truth causal effects. Therefore, to overcome this problem we rely on semi-synthetic data for the empirical evaluation of causal estimation procedures.

We used the semi-synthetic IHDP dataset introduced by Hill [8]. This dataset was constructed from the Infant Health and Development Program and the outcome and treatment assignment are fully known. It comprises 25 features regarding childs and mothers and 747 units, in which 139 belong to the treatment group and the rest 608 belong to the control group. In order to have comparable results, we used 1000 realizations from the NPCI package [2] similar to Shi et al. [18].

5   Experimental Results

In this section, we evaluate the prediction performance of the proposed modified Dragonnet model against the state-of-the-art Dragonnet model. It is worth mentioning, that we selected to compare the proposed model against Dragonnet, since it outperforms all other state-of-the-art models.

The performance of each model was measured using the metrics absolute error in ATE [17] $|\epsilon_{ATE}|$ and expected Precision in Estimation of Heterogeneous Effect [8] ϵ_{PEHE}, which are respectively defined by:

$$|\epsilon_{ATE}| = \left| \frac{1}{n} \sum_{i=1}^{n} [Q(1, \mathbf{x}_i) - Q(0, \mathbf{x}_i)] - \hat{\psi}^{\text{treg}} \right|$$

and

$$\epsilon_{PEHE} = \frac{1}{n} \sum_{i=1}^{n} \left[(Q(1, \mathbf{x}_i) - Q(0, \mathbf{x}_i)) - (\hat{Q}^{\text{treg}}(1, \mathbf{x}_i, \overline{y}_i^{(0)}, \overline{y}_i^{(1)}) - \hat{Q}^{\text{treg}}(0, \mathbf{x}_i, \overline{y}_i^{(0)}, \overline{y}_i^{(1)})) \right]^2$$

It is worth noticing, that $|\epsilon_{ATE}|$ and ϵ_{PEHE} metrics are used to compare the evaluated models as estimators and predictors, respectively and have been also used in [10,13,17,22].

In our experiments, the state-of-the art model Dragonnet was used with its default optimized parameter settings [18], while the proposed model followed a similar architecture and hyper-parameter selection with Dragonnet. More specifically, we utilize three dense layers (of 200 neurons with Exponential Linear Unit (ELU) activation function) in order to produce a representation layer $Z(\mathbf{X})$. Next, the output of $Z(\mathbf{X})$ is concatenated with $\overline{\mathbf{y}}^{(0)}$ and the combined information is further processed by two dense layers (of 100 neurons each with ELU activation function and kernel regularizer of 10^{-2}) for the prediction of the outcome of the control group. A similar approach was used for providing the outcome of the treated group. The hyperperameters were set as $k = 10$, $\alpha = 1$ and $\beta = 1$ and 20% of the training data were utilized for validation as in Dragonnet. Both evaluated models were trained using stochastic gradient descent with momentum [15].

The performance of the proposed modified Dragonnet utilizing three different distance metrics i.e. Euclidean, Manhattan and Chebychev. These distances constitute the most widely used in the literature [14,19]. It is worth mentioning that these distances belong to the class of Minkowski distances, which is defined by

$$\|x - y\|_p = \left(\sum_i^d |x_i - y_i|^p \right)^{\frac{1}{p}}$$

where $x, y \in \mathbb{R}^d$ and $p \in \mathbb{N}^*$. In case, $p = 1$, $p = 2$ and $p = \infty$ the Minkowski distance is reducted to the Manhattan, Euclidean and Chebychev metric, respectively. The detailed experimental results for each model and realization of IHDP can be found in https://github.com/kiriakidou/Modified_Dragonnet.

The implementation code was written in Python 3.7 using Keras library [6] and run on a PC (3.2 GHz Quad-Core processor, 16 GB RAM) using Windows operating system.

Given into consideration that a small number of simulations tend to dominate the benchmarking process, the cumulative total for a performance metric over all simulations seem to be too uninformative and misleading. For this reason, we used Dolan and Moré's [1] performance profiles, which removes the influence of such simulations on the benchmarking process and provides us information such as probability of success, efficiency and robustness in compact form. In more detail, each profile plots the fraction P of simulations for which any given model is within a factor τ of the best model. Additionally, in order to examine and reject the hypothesis that both models perform equally and provide statistical evidence about the superiority of the proposed model, we utilize the methodology presented in [12]. More specifically, we apply the non-parametric Friedman Aligned-Ranks (FAR) test [9] in order to rank the models and the post-hoc Finner test [3] for examining the existence of significant differences. Next, we evaluate the performance of:

- "Dragonnet", which stands for Dragonnet model of Shalit et al. [18].

- "Modified Dragonnet (Euclidean)", which stands for the proposed model using Euclidean distance for the calculation of the average of the outcomes of nearest instances.

- "Modified Dragonnet (Manhattan)", which stands for the proposed model using Manhattan distance for the calculation of the average of the outcomes of nearest instances.

- "Modified Dragonnet (Chebychev)", which stands for the proposed model using Chebychev distance for the calculation of the average of the outcomes of nearest instances.

Figure 2 presents the performance profiles of the three versions of the proposed model and the Dragonnet, based on $|\epsilon_{ATE}|$ metric. Obviously, all compared models reported similar performance. More specifically, Modified Dragonnet (Euclidean) solves 30% of the simulations with the lowest error ATE, while both Dragonnet and Modified Dragonnet (Chebychev) solve 28%. Additionally, Modified Dragonnet (Manhattan) reported the worst performance solving 25% of simulations.

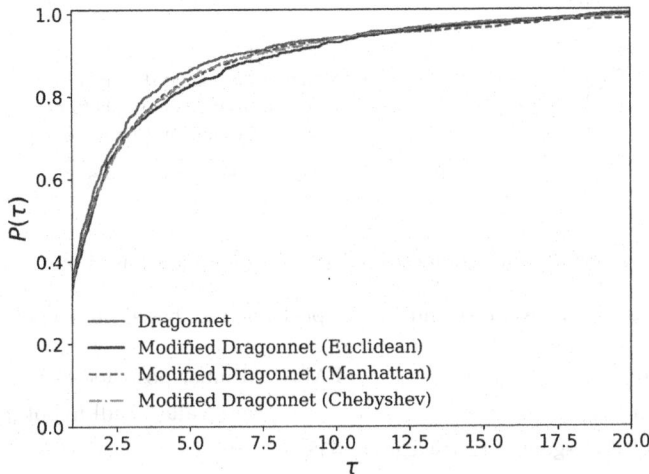

Fig. 2. Performance profiles of all evaluated models based on $|\epsilon_{ATE}|$

Figure 3 presents the performance profiles of the three versions of the proposed model and the Dragonnet, based on ϵ_{PEHE} metric. The proposed model considerably outpeformed the state-of-the-art Dragonnet with any used distance metric, in terms of ϵ_{PEHE}. All versions of Modified Dragonnet solve 34% of the simulations with the best (lowest) error PEHE, while Dragonnet solves only 8% of the simulations.

Table 1 presents the statistical comparison between the three versions of the proposed model and the Dragonnet based on $|\epsilon_{ATE}|$ metric. Clearly, Modified Dragonnet (Euclidean) reported the best performance, slightly outperforming all compared models. Additionally, it was the only version of the proposed model, which reported better FAR ranking than the state-of-the-art model Dragonnet. However, the interpretation of Finner post-hoc test illustrated that there are not considerable differences, which results that all models performed equally well.

Table 2 presents that the proposed model considerably outpeformed the Dragonnet in terms of ϵ_{PEHE} with every utilized distance metric, which is statistically confirmed by FAR and Finner tests. Modified Dragonnet (Euclidean) reported the best performance since it exhibited top ranking. However, Finner post-hoc test reveals that all versions of the model perform equally well and there are no significant statistical differences in their performances.

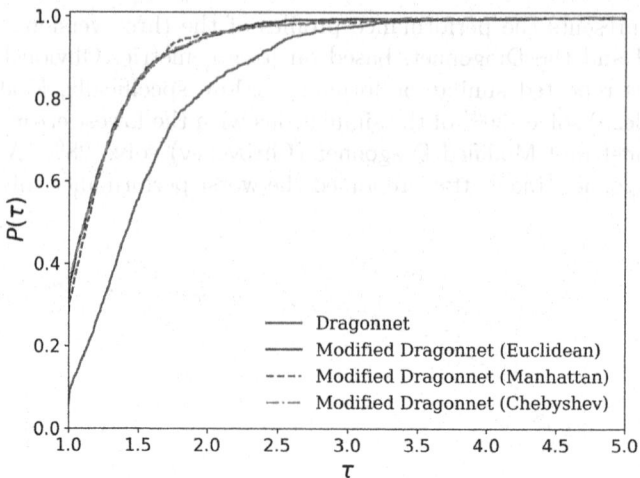

Fig. 3. Performance profiles of all evaluated models based on ϵ_{PEHE}

Table 1. FAR test and Finner post-hoc test based on $|\epsilon_{ATE}|$

Model	FAR	Finner post-hoc test	
		p_F-Value	Null hypothesis
Modified Dragonnet (Euclidean)	558.768	–	–
Dragonnet	561.822	0.911658	Fail to reject
Modified Dragonnet (Manhattan)	571.773	0.636660	Fail to reject
Modified Dragonnet (Chebychev)	581.637	0.406163	Fail to reject

Table 2. FAR test and Finner post-hoc test based on ϵ_{PEHE}

Model	FAR	Finner post-hoc test	
		p_F-Value	Null hypothesis
Modified Dragonnet (Euclidean)	485.004	–	–
Modified Dragonnet (Chebychev)	491.856	0.803454	Fail to reject
Modified Dragonnet (Manhattan)	505.099	0.465460	Fail to reject
Dragonnet	792.042	0	Reject

Based on the previous discussion, we are able to conclude, that the proposed approach estimate PEHE with higher accuracy than state-of-the-art Dragonnet, while it exhibited similar performance regarding the prediction of ATE. This suggests that although the proposed model and Dragonnet report identical performance as estimators, it considerably exhibits better performance as a predictor.

6   Conclusion

In this research, we proposed a new neural network model for the prediction of the conditional outcomes and the propensity score as well as the estimation of treatment effects. The architecture of the proposed model constitutes a modification of the state-of-the-art Dragonnet model. An advantage of the proposed model is that it exploits the covariates along with information from the outcomes of the instances contained in the training data. The motivation of our approach consists of enriching the inputs of the model with the average outcomes of the nearest neighbors from the control and treatment group along with the covariates, in order to improve the prediction performance.

The experimental analysis demonstrated that the proposed model is a better estimator than Dragonnet, while simultaneously predicts treatment effects with high accuracy. This is confirmed by the performance profiles and the statistical analysis based on a nonparametric and a post-hoc test. It is also worth mentioning that the proposed model exhibited similar performance with the utilization of all three distances.

A limitation of the proposed work is the selection of the optimal value of parameter k and the utilized metric. A study on the efficiency and sensitivity of our approach for different values of parameter k and distance metrics (such as cosine similarity, Jaccard distance and Hamming Distance [14]) is planned as future work. Finally, another interesting idea is the adoption of the proposed approach to other neural network-based models such as TARnet [17] and NedNet [18] as well as a performance evaluation using other causal modelling benchmarks.

Acknowledgements. The work leading to these results has received funding from the European Union's Horizon 2020 research and innovation programme under Grant Agreement No. 965231, project REBECCA(REsearch on BrEast Cancer induced chronic conditions supported by Causal Analysis of multi-source data).

References

1. Dolan, E.D., Moré, J.J.: Benchmarking optimization software with performance profiles. Math. Program. **91**(2), 201–213 (2002)
2. Dorie, V.: NPCI: non-parametrics for causal inference (2016). https://github.com/vdorie/npci
3. Finner, H.: On a monotonicity problem in step-down multiple test procedures. J. Am. Statist. Assoc. **88**(423), 920–923 (1993)
4. Glass, T.A., Goodman, S.N., Hernán, M.A., Samet, J.M.: Causal inference in public health. Annu. Rev. Publ. Health **34**, 61–75 (2013)
5. Gretton, A., Borgwardt, K.M., Rasch, M.J., Schölkopf, B., Smola, A.: A kernel two-sample test. J. Mach. Learn. Res. **13**(1), 723–773 (2012)
6. Gulli, A., Pal, S.: Deep Learning with Keras. Packt Publishing Ltd. (2017)
7. Gustafsson, J.E.: Causal inference in educational effectiveness research: a comparison of three methods to investigate effects of homework on student achievement. School Effectiv. School Improv. **24**(3), 275–295 (2013)

8. Hill, J.L.: Bayesian nonparametric modeling for causal inference. J. Comput. Graph. Statist. **20**(1), 217–240 (2011)

9. Hodges, J., Lehmann, E.L.: Rank methods for combination of independent experiments in analysis of variance. In: Selected Works of EL Lehmann, pp. 403–418. Springer, Boston (2012). https://doi.org/10.1007/978-1-4614-1412-4_35

10. Johansson, F., Shalit, U., Sontag, D.: Learning representations for counterfactual inference. In: International Conference on Machine Learning, pp. 3020–3029. PMLR (2016)

11. Van der Laan, M.J., Rose, S., et al.: Targeted Learning: Causal Inference for Observational and Experimental Data, vol. 4. Springer, New York (2011). https://doi.org/10.1007/978-1-4419-9782-1

12. Livieris, I.E., Kiriakidou, N., Kanavos, A., Vonitsanos, G., Tampakas, V.: Employing constrained neural networks for forecasting new product's sales increase. In: MacIntyre, J., Maglogiannis, I., Iliadis, L., Pimenidis, E. (eds.) AIAI 2019. IAICT, vol. 560, pp. 161–172. Springer, Cham (2019). https://doi.org/10.1007/978-3-030-19909-8_14

13. Louizos, C., Shalit, U., Mooij, J.M., Sontag, D., Zemel, R., Welling, M.: Causal effect inference with deep latent-variable models. Adv. Neural Inf. Process. Syst. **30** (2017)

14. Pandit, S., Gupta, S., et al.: A comparative study on distance measuring approaches for clustering. Int. J. Res. Comput. Sci. **2**(1), 29–31 (2011)

15. Qian, N.: On the momentum term in gradient descent learning algorithms. Neural Netw. **12**(1), 145–151 (1999)

16. Rubin, D.B.: Causal inference using potential outcomes: Design, modeling, decisions. J. Am. Statist. Assoc. **100**(469), 322–331 (2005)

17. Shalit, U., Johansson, F.D., Sontag, D.: Estimating individual treatment effect: generalization bounds and algorithms. In: International Conference on Machine Learning, pp. 3076–3085. PMLR (2017)

18. Shi, C., Blei, D.M., Veitch, V.: Adapting neural networks for the estimation of treatment effects. arXiv preprint arXiv:1906.02120 (2019)

19. Singh, A., Yadav, A., Rana, A.: k-means with three different distance metrics. Int. J. Comput. Appl. **67**(10) (2013)

20. Varian, H.R.: Causal inference in economics and marketing. Proc. Natl. Acad. Sci. **113**(27), 7310–7315 (2016)

21. Villani, C.: Optimal Transport: Old and New, vol. 338. Springer, Heidelberg (2009). https://doi.org/10.1007/978-3-540-71050-9

22. Yoon, J., Jordon, J., Van Der Schaar, M.: GANITE: estimation of individualized treatment effects using generative adversarial nets. In: International Conference on Learning Representations (2018)

An Industry 4.0 Intelligent Decision Support System for Analytical Laboratories

António João Silva[iD] and Paulo Cortez[(✉)][iD]

ALGORITMI Center, Department of Information Systems,
University of Minho, 4804-533 Guimarães, Portugal
id7322@alunos.uminho.pt, pcortez@dsi.uminho.pt

Abstract. This paper presents an Intelligent Decision Support System (IDSS) to enhance the management of Analytical Laboratories (AL) of a company operating in the chemical industry. This IDSS incorporates two predictive Machine Learning (ML) models, related with the prediction of the arrival of samples at the AL and the consumption of AL materials, which are then used to perform prescriptive analytics for AL instrument allocation tasks. The IDSS is also complemented with descriptive analytics of instrument similarities regarding the tests performed for better supporting the AL manager decisions. The IDSS includes interactive dashboards and it was successfully validated by the AL managers using the Technology Acceptance Model (TAM) 3 and open interviews, which resulted in a positive feedback.

Keywords: Intelligent Decision Support System · Dashboards · Machine Learning · Industry 4.0

1 Introduction

Industry 4.0 has recently emerged and with it there has been an increasing amount of digitalized data that reflects industrial processes. Within this context, Intelligent Decision Support Systems (IDSS) [2] can be very useful to extract valuable insights from the industrial data, allowing to enhance several business processes. An IDSS is a decision support system that uses Artificial Intelligence techniques (e.g., Machine Learning, Metaheuristics) to enhance managerial decisions [13]. In this work, we propose an IDSS that is based on descriptive, predictive and prescriptive analytics, aiming to assist the managerial decisions of Analytical Laboratories (AL) from a Chemical Industry that is being transformed through the Industry 4.0 concept.

In previous works, we have proposed Machine Learning (ML) solutions to assist some partial AL tasks: predict the arrival time of In-Process Control (IPC) samples at the quality testing laboratories [18]; and estimate the AL materials consumption based on weekly plans of AL sample analyses [17]. In this paper, we

© IFIP International Federation for Information Processing 2022
Published by Springer Nature Switzerland AG 2022
I. Maglogiannis et al. (Eds.): AIAI 2022, IFIP AICT 647, pp. 159–169, 2022.
https://doi.org/10.1007/978-3-031-08337-2_14

present the full IDSS that integrates both predictive analytics, supporting the allocation of AL instruments (prescriptive analytics). The IDSS is also complemented with descriptive analytics executed over AL historical records, allowing the AL managers to better identify similarities among instruments. Prior to the Industry 4.0 transformation, the relevant digital records were spread in distinct databases, located in different departments (production and the AL), making the AL manager decisions more difficult. The proposed IDSS integrates all relevant data records into a single data repository, while also providing the business analytics results in terms of an interactive visual tool based on dashboards. A IDSS prototype was deployed in the chemical company and then evaluated by the AL managers by answering a questionnaire built using the Technology Acceptance Model (TAM) 3 model [22] and by using open interviews.

2   Related Work

Within the Industry 4.0 concept, there are several studies proposing data-based interactive dashboards. For instance, our survey about the usage of Business Analytics in Industry 4.0 [19] has found several examples of dashboards used to monitoring the production process, as well as verify new insights on the shop floor [14,15]. Moreover, in the automotive industry, data-based dashboards were used to monitor the assembly processes [20]. Also in the manufacturing sector, sensors and Internet-of-Things (IoT) data were also integrated into dashboards to monitor the productive process [12]. Concerning the specific chemical industry, we have found one one dashboard example that was proposed to control and monitor the production of a chemical plant [3].

Turning to the incorporation of Artificial Intelligence techniques for decision support, there are a few studies that integrate ML results in dashboards. For instance, a few examples are: use Neural Networks to improve the energy saving in factories [11]; usage of a Random Forest algorithm and IoT sensors to improve fault diagnosis tasks [21]; and a predictive maintenance system using a Remaining Useful Life (RUL) model to estimate the health index of production machines [5]. However, regarding the application of IDSS in the AL of chemical industry the research is very scarce. This occurs because the AL are mostly managed manually, where Information Technology (IT) is mostly focused on storing the quality values and not the AL processes. Following an Industry 4.0 process transformation, we have previously developed two ML works, aiming to empower the AL of a chemical company with two data-driven models: to predict the arrival of In-Process Control (IPC) samples at the ALs [18]; and to predict the weekly consumption of AL materials [17]. In this paper, we present the full IDSS that provides interactive dashboards that integrate these two ML models and also descriptive analytics (for instruments allocation and similarities).

3   Materials and Methods

3.1   Problem Formulation

The analyzed company is from the Chemical Sector and it includes three main areas: Warehouse, Production and Analytical Laboratories (AL). The Warehouse is where the raw materials are received. It is also the destination of the products produced before being shipped to the customers. The Production area is where the chemical products are manufactured. Finally, the AL are responsible for testing all products and raw materials, checking if they meet the required quality standards. Before adopting an Industry 4.0 transformation, the entire communication process between these three areas was mainly manual and there was no real-time monitoring of the industrial processes, often leading to delays in the preparation of production materials or in the analyzes performed by the AL. These delays strongly affected deadlines for production plans.

Concerning the AL, these involve human analysts, instruments and several types of samples, namely raw materials, In-Process Control (IPC) and Final Products, that need to be analyzed, i.e., allocated into one or more analytical instruments. In particular, In Production samples are a priority because if they are not analyzed in a timely manner, the production process may stop. Each instrument allocation requires time and manual effort, to prepare and conduct the analysis and then collect the obtained results. There is an information system that records all quality test data, but such IT is mostly focused on the testing measurements and not on the AL processes. Thus, the management of the AL (e.g., human resource and instrument allocation planning, sample prioritization, prior preparation of instruments), assumes a strong manual effort, which is difficult due to the lack of a real-time data communication with the Warehouse and Production areas.

3.2   Proposed IDSS

To solve the previous mentioned AL management issues, and benefiting from the Industry 4.0 transformation performed at the company, we propose an IDSS that incorporates descriptive, predictive and prescriptive analytics. The proposed IDSS architecture is depicted in Fig. 1. It includes two main layers. The Big Data layer is responsible for extracting and processing data from the different databases used in the organization. Indeed, the IDSS consumes the data from the different areas and applications from the organization (e.g., Warehouse, Production, AL), resulting as the ground truth data repository for the AL. The processed data is then fed into the Data Analytics layer, which incorporates descriptive, predictive and prescriptive analytics for AL management.

The developed tool includes two predictive models that were previously studied. Both models are based on an Automated ML (AutoML) procedure but fed with different input attributes and training data. The adopted AutoML H2O tool (https://www.h2o.ai/) automatically selects the best regression model among 6 families of algorithms: Random Forest (RF), Extremely Randomized Trees (XRT), Generalized Linear Model (GLM), GBM, XGBoost (XG) and a Stacked

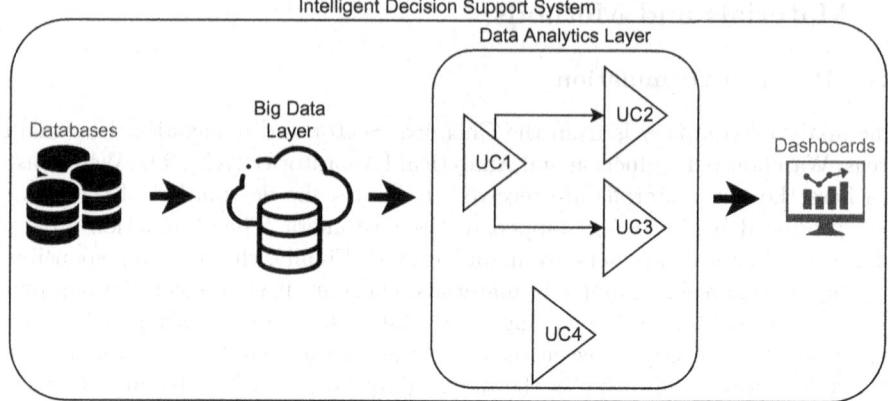

Fig. 1. Proposed Architecture

Ensemble (SE). The proposed IDSS includes an extension of the first predictive model, termed here Use Case (UC) 1 (UC1), successfully tested for estimating the arrival of IPC samples at the ALs [18]. In ths proposed IDSS, the model is adapted to perform predictions for all types of AL samples (the studied IPC and also the raw materials and final products). It should be noted that each sample arrived at the AL is associated with a fixed set of quality tests to be executed. The IDSS also integrates a second predictive model (UC2) that estimates the weekly consumption of AL materials [17]. This second predictive model requires, as input, a weekly plan of quality tests to be performed, which is built in advance by adopting the UC1 predictive model. The IDSS also includes prescriptive analytics (UC3), which is based on sample arrival estimates (UC1) and historical records regarding previous instrument allocations, allowing to provide suggestions of future instrument allocation. Finally, the IDSS also includes descriptive analytics set in terms of historical associations of instruments to quality tests (UC4), allowing to identify instrument similarities. All analytics are incorporated into friendly user dashboards.

Regarding the UC3, to issue recommendations of AL instruments allocation, we use a statistical approach that considers the UC1 predictions (tests to be executed) and that are matched with historical records of instrument allocation. For each required test, we assume as the "best" analytical instrument, the one currently available that has been mostly used for executing such test. An instrument is considered available if the its scheduled weekly allocation is lower than 70% (a value that was defined by the AL experts). Once an instrument is allocated, the IDSS is refreshed, with the allocation records being updated.

Finally, the UC4 is based on an $I \times T$ matrix computed using historical records and that measures the total number of tests ($t \in T$) executed by an instrument ($i \in I$). Then, the known Pearson correlation is used to compute the association between two rows of the matrix (i.e., two instruments). In our dashboards, the correlation matrix [8] is shown as a colored heatmap, where more similar instruments are signaled by a stronger red color.

3.3   Evaluation

The proposed IDSS was developed by a research team that included both Artificial Intelligence and Chemical company experts but not the direct AL managers. Thus, to properly evaluate the IDSS, we adopted the Technology Acceptance Model (TAM) 3 [22], allowing to define a questionnaire that contains 10 questions and that was answered by the AL managers after experimenting the proposed tool. The questionnaire assumes the following TAM 3 constructs: Perceived Usefulness (PU), Perceived Ease of Use (PEOU), Perception of External Control (PEC), Job Relevance (REL), Output Quality (OUT), and Behavioral Intention (BI). Each question included a 5-point likert scale option for each answer, ranging from 1 (extremely disagree) to 5 (extremely agree). These questionnaires were complemented by a direct feedback from the AL managers, obtained by using open interviews in which the manager freely provided their opinions about the proposed IDSS. Furthermore, we also map the capabilities of the proposed IDSS tool, which are compared with the currently available AL informational processes (denoted as "As-Is") [7].

4   Results

4.1   Developed IDSS Prototype

The designed IDSS was written using the R language, with the ML solutions being developed using specific R [16] packages, namely rminer [6], H2O AutoML [1], Forecast [9,10] and shiny [4]. The IDSS was fed with real-world data from the analyzed chemical company, collected from January 2016 to May 2019 and that results from a merge of the different databases adopted by the organization.

The user interface was developed using shiny and it includes three main dashboards to present the descriptive (UC4), predictive (UC1 and UC2) and prescriptive (UC3) analytics. The first dashboard presents: the expected arrival of samples and quality tests to be carried out in the current week (UC1); the expected raw material consumption (UC2); the history of quality analyzes carried out in the previous week; and an overview of the historical arrival of samples to the laboratory in the last year. The second dashboard shows the current allocation of AL instruments and suggestions on the best instrument to be used for each planned test (UC3). Finally, the last dashboard contains the correlation heatmaps based on the $I \times T$ association matrix (UC4).

The first dashboard is presented in Fig. 2 and it contains three components. The first one is the top bar that shows warnings about issues that could occur during the current week. This includes information about how many instruments have an expected occupation above 50%, the number of analyzes without any instrument usage history, as well as the progress of test analyzes for the current day (in Fig. 2, this value is set at 0%). The second middle component includes three tables, presenting: the daily sample arrival (UC1) predictions (left table); how many analyzes are planned to be carried out on the current day (middle table); and the predicted weekly AL material consumption (UC2, right table).

The third bottom component has two graphs. The first plot (bottom left) shows the number of samples that arrived at the laboratories every week by type (IPC, Raw Material, Final Product), while the second graph (bottom right) displays the number of analyzes performed per week by sample type.

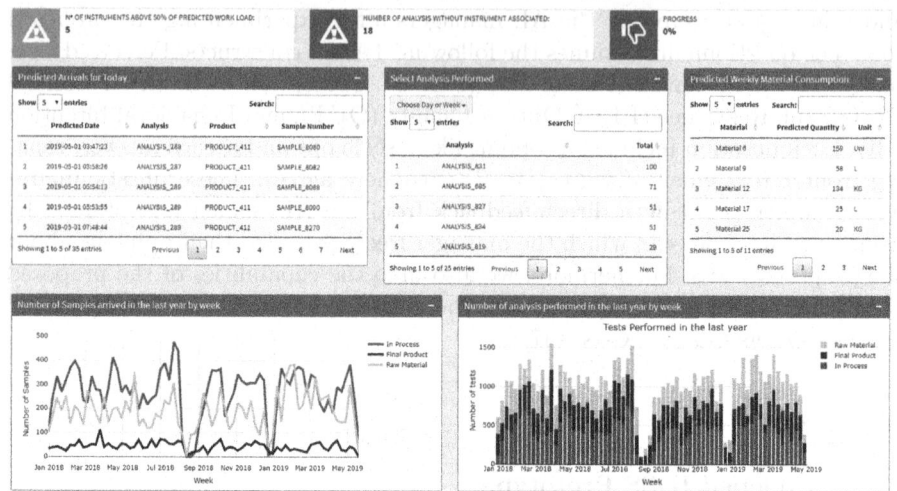

Fig. 2. Example of the first IDSS dashboard

The selection of the IDSS top menu tab allows the access to the second dashboard (Fig. 3). The top left component "Analysis to be performed in this week" allows to select a quality test, refreshing the middle barplot graphs that show the instruments that are used for that specific test and sample (left) or just for that specific test (without sample specification, right plot). At the same time, the table on the top right presents the UC3 results as the suggested instrument to be assigned to that specific test analysis, along with the load work for the same instruments for that week. Finally, the bottom left table contains the information about the tests that have no historical records of instrument usage.

The last and third dashboard is presented in two figures and it is related with the UC4 descriptive analytics. Figure 4 displays the correlation tables for a given instrument divided by two groups of instrument machines: HPLC (left table) and GC (right table). The top buttons ("Chosse HPLC/GC") allows the user to select one instrument from the displayed list. Once the instrument is selected, a table is displayed, sorting in a descending order the correlation values of most similar instruments. The third column on the tables shows the most used test analysis for each instrument. The bottom part of the third dashboard is presented in Fig. 5, which shows the instrument correlation heatmaps for each group of instruments. The heatmap provides easy visualization of the most correlated HPLC and GC instruments.

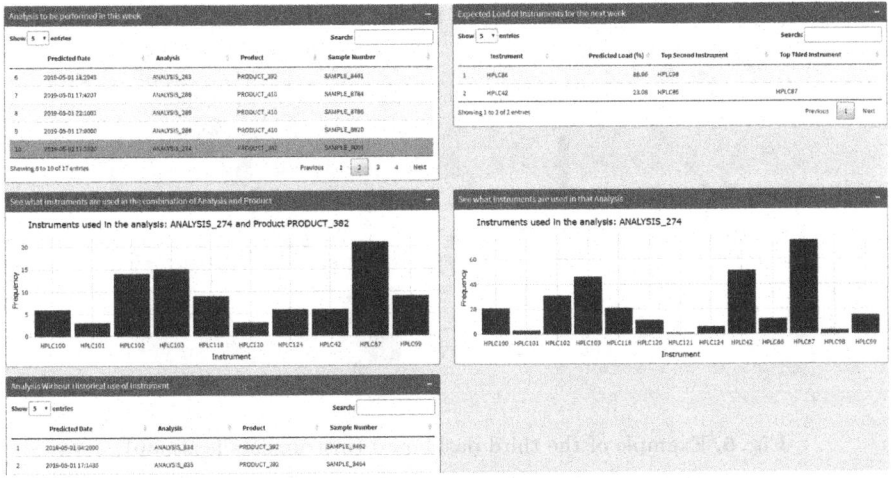

Fig. 3. Example of the second dashboard

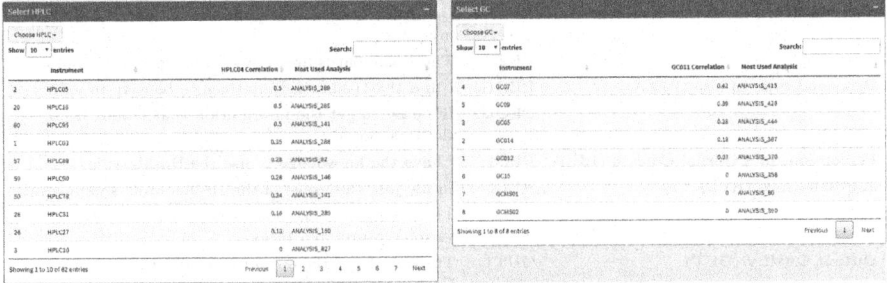

Fig. 4. Example of the third dashboard (instruments correlation)

4.2   Evaluation

The designed TAM 3 questionnaire is shown in Table 1. The obtained results are presented in Table 2, where each value corresponds to the average of two laboratory managers. We note that these managers correspond to IT AL staff from the analyzed chemical company and that were not directly involved in the presented research. The average responses are between 3.5 (70%) and 4 (80%), which means that laboratory managers had a positive acceptance of our IDSS. The most positive answers were related with the Perceived Usefulness (PU1 and PU2), Job Relevance (Rel 2) and Behavioral Intention (BI1). After obtaining the questionnaire responses, we have performed individual interviews, where the AL managers provided more specific feedback about the proposed IDSS. Regarding the first IDSS dashboard, both managers agreed that the information provided was simple and objective, being valuable to help the analysts to prepare the materials and the laboratory before the sample arrival. Turning to the second

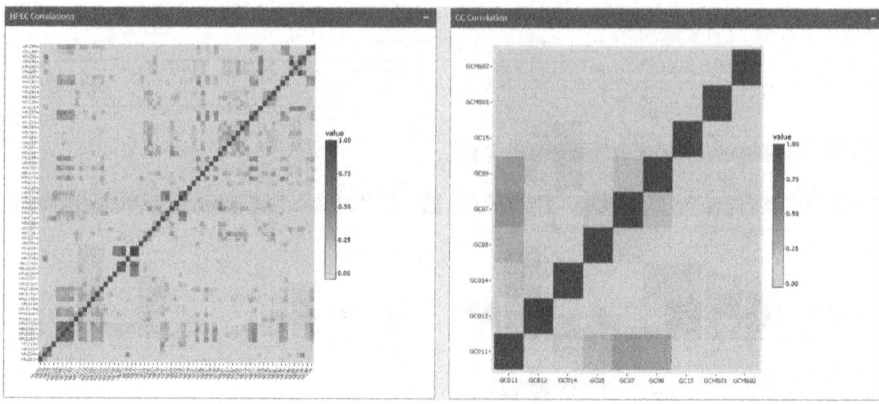

Fig. 5. Example of the third dashboard (instruments heatmap)

Table 1. The adopted TAM 3 questionnaire

Construct	Items	Question
Perceived Usefulness (PU)	PU1	Using the Dashboards improves my performance in my job
	PU2	The Dashboards are (potentially) useful in my job
Perceived Ease of Use (PEOU)	PEOU1	I find the Dashboard interface to be easy to use
	PEOU2	It's easy to get the information that I want from the Dashboards
Perceptions of External Control (PEC)	PEC1	I have the knowledge to use the Dashboards
Job Relevance (REL)	REL1	In my job, the usage of the Dashboards is important
	REL2	The use of the Dashboards is pertinent to my various job-related tasks
Output Quality (OUT)	OUT1	The quality of the output I get from the Dashboards is high
	OUT2	I have no difficulty telling others about the results ofusing the Dashboards
Behavioral Intention (BI)	BI1	Assuming I had access to the Dashboard, I intend to use it

Table 2. The TAM 3 questionnaire results (average of two responses).

PU1	PU2	PEOU1	PEOU2	PEC1	REL1	REL2	OUT1	OUT2	BI1
4	4	3.5	3.5	3.5	3.5	4	3.5	3.5	4

dashboard, related with the instruments load, they found it interesting but signaled the lack of information about new instruments and analyses. As for the third dashboard, it was considered helpful, particularly the correlation heatmap, which can be useful to identify new groups of instruments. However, such identification needs to be complemented by human domain knowledge, since there are instruments within the same group that can have different capabilities (e.g., refractive-index or infra-red). The AL managers also considered the dashboard useful to check if there a overlap between groups of instruments and if new groups of instruments could be defined. Overall, the AL managers concluded that the proposed IDSS (including its three dashboards), is valuable for planning the analyzes to be carried out on the samples, to improve the instrument allocation and to know how many analyzes will be carried out. Table 3 summarizes the main features introduced by the proposed IDSS, which substantially enhance the capabilities currently available at the AL (As-Is).

Table 3. Comparison between the current AL (As-Is) and proposed IDSS informational processes.

Capabilities	As-Is	IDSS
Historical overview of samples arrived	✓	✓
Historical overview of analysis performed	✓	✓
Sample arrival prediction		✓ (UC1)
Weekly estimates of materials consumption		✓ (UC2)
Expected instruments load		✓ (UC3)
Suggested allocation of instruments		✓ (UC3)
Information of analysis without instruments	✓	✓
Visualization of instrument similarities		✓ (UC4)

5   Conclusions

In this paper, we present an Intelligent Decision Support System (IDSS) that was developed for the Analytical Laboratories (AL) of a chemical company that is being transformed under the Industry 4.0 concept. The proposed IDSS includes two main layers: Big Data – responsible for extracting and processing data from different data sources, leading to a single and updated AL data repository; and Data Analytics – which includes descriptive, predictive and prescriptive analytics that aim to enhance the managerial decisions performed by AL managers.

Using recent data from a real-world chemical company, in previous works we have proposed two predictive analytics (IPC sample arrival prediction – UC1 and weekly AL materials consumption – UC2). The Data Analytics layer includes these analytics, extending the arrival prediction capabilities to all AL sample types (e.g., raw materials and final products). Moreover, it includes a novel prescriptive method (UC3) for suggesting instrument allocations for quality tests based on historical records and the sample arrival predictions (UC1). Finally, it includes descriptive analytics regarding laboratory instrument similarities (UC4). A IDSS prototype was developed, which integrated all proposed analytics in three main interactive dashboards and used data collected from January 2016 to May 2019. The prototype was evaluated by two AL managers that were not directly involved in the IDSS design by adopting Technology Acceptance Model (TAM) 3 questionnaires and open interviews. Overall, a very positive feedback was obtained. In particular, the proposed IDSS was considered valuable to better prepare and assign instruments to samples, as well as to better estimate the ammount of quality tests that will be carried out.

In future work, we intent to add new modules to the IDSS that are oriented to the maintenance of the instruments. The goal is to predict corrective maintenance actions and also support the scheduling of preventive maintenance operations.

Acknowledgments. This work has been supported by FCT – Fundação para a Ciência e a Tecnologia within the R&D Units Project Scope: UIDB/00319/2020. The authors also wish to thank the chemical company staff involved with this project for providing the data and also the valuable domain feedback.

References

1. Aiello, S., Eckstrand, E., Fu, A., Landry, M., Aboyoun, P.: Machine learning with r and h2o. In: H2O Booklet (2016)
2. Arnott, D., Pervan, G.: A critical analysis of decision support systems research revisited: the rise of design science. J. Inf. Technol. **29**(4), 269–293 (2014). https://doi.org/10.1057/jit.2014.16
3. Bellini, P., Cenni, D., Mitolo, N., Nesi, P., Pantaleo, G., Soderi, M.: High level control of chemical plant by industry 4.0 solutions. J. Indust. Inf. Integrat. **26**, 100276 (2022). https://doi.org/10.1016/j.jii.2021.100276
4. Chang, W., et al.: Shiny: Web Application Framework for R. r package version 1.7.1 (2021). https://CRAN.R-project.org/package=shiny
5. Chiu, Y.C., Cheng, F.T., Huang, H.C.: Developing a factory-wide intelligent predictive maintenance system based on industry 4.0. J. Chinese Inst. Eng. **40**(7), 562–571 (2017). https://doi.org/10.1080/02533839.2017.1362357
6. Cortez, P.: Modern Optimization with R. Springer, Cham (2014). https://doi.org/10.1007/978-3-319-08263-9
7. Darwish, A.: Business Process Mapping: A Guide to Best Practice. Writescope Publishers (2011)
8. Ferré, J.: 3.02 - regression diagnostics. In: Brown, S.D., Tauler, R., Walczak, B. (eds.) Comprehensive Chemometrics, pp. 33–89. Elsevier, Oxford (2009). https://doi.org/10.1016/B978-044452701-1.00076-4
9. Hyndman, R., et al.: Forecast: Forecasting Functions for Time Series and Linear Models. r package version 8.13 (2020). https://pkg.robjhyndman.com/forecast/
10. Hyndman, R.J., Khandakar, Y.: Automatic time series forecasting: the forecast package for R. J. Statist. Softw. **26**(3), 1–22 (2008)
11. Kabugo, J.C., Jämsä-Jounela, S.L., Schiemann, R., Binder, C.: Industry 4.0 based process data analytics platform: a waste-to-energy plant case study. Int. J. Electric. Power Energy Syst. **115**, 105508 (2020). https://doi.org/10.1016/j.ijepes.2019.105508
12. Mahmoodpour, M., Lobov, A., Lanz, M., Mäkelä, P., Rundas, N.: Role-based visualization of industrial iot-based systems. In: 2018 14th IEEE/ASME International Conference on Mechatronic and Embedded Systems and Applications (MESA), pp. 1–8 (2018). https://doi.org/10.1109/MESA.2018.8449183
13. Michalewicz, Z., Michalewicz, M.: Machine intelligence, adaptive business intelligence, and natural intelligence [research frontier]. IEEE Comput. Intell. Mag. **3**(1), 54–63 (2008). https://doi.org/10.1109/MCI.2007.913389

14. Neuböck, T., Schrefl, M.: Modelling knowledge about data analysis processes in manufacturing. IFAC-PapersOnLine **48**(3), 277–282 (2015). https://doi.org/10. 1016/j.ifacol.2015.06.094

15. Niño, M., Blanco, J.M., Illarramendi, A.: Business understanding, challenges and issues of big data analytics for the servitization of a capital equipment manufacturer. In: IEEE International Conference on Big Data (Big Data), pp. 1368–1377 (2015). https://doi.org/10.1109/BigData.2015.7363897

16. R Development Core Team. R: a language and environment for statistical computing. In: R Foundation for Statistical Computing, Vienna, Austria (2008). http://www.R-project.org, ISBN 3-900051-07-0

17. Silva, A.J., Cortez, P.: An automated machine learning approach for predicting chemical laboratory material consumption. In: Maglogiannis, I., Macintyre, J., Iliadis, L. (eds.) AIAI 2021. IAICT, vol. 627, pp. 105–116. Springer, Cham (2021). https://doi.org/10.1007/978-3-030-79150-6_9

18. Silva, A.J., Cortez, P., Pilastri, A.: Chemical laboratories 4.0: a two-stage machine learning system for predicting the arrival of samples. In: Maglogiannis, I., Iliadis, L., Pimenidis, E. (eds.) AIAI 2020. IAICT, vol. 584, pp. 232–243. Springer, Cham (2020). https://doi.org/10.1007/978-3-030-49186-4_20

19. Silva, A.J., Cortez, P., Pereira, C., Pilastri, A.: Business analytics in industry 4.0: a systematic review. Exp. Syst. **38**(7), e12741 (2021). https://doi.org/10.1111/exsy. 12741

20. Silva, N., et al.: Advancing logistics 4.0 with the implementation of a big data warehouse: a demonstration case for the automotive industry. Electronics **10**(18) (2021). https://doi.org/10.3390/electronics10182221

21. Tran, M.Q., Elsisi, M., Mahmoud, K., Liu, M.K., Lehtonen, M., Darwish, M.M.F.: Experimental setup for online fault diagnosis of induction machines via promising iot and machine learning: towards industry 4.0 empowerment. IEEE Access 9, 115429–115441 (2021). https://doi.org/10.1109/ACCESS.2021.3105297

22. Venkatesh, V., Bala, H.: Technology acceptance model 3 and a research agenda on interventions. Decis. Sci. **39**(2), 273–315 (2008). https://doi.org/10.1111/j.1540-5915.2008.00192.x

Combining Cox Model and Tree-Based Algorithms to Boost Performance and Preserve Interpretability for Health Outcomes

Diana Shamsutdinova[1]([✉]) [iD], Daniel Stamate[2,3] [iD], Angus Roberts[1] [iD], and Daniel Stahl[1] [iD]

[1] Biostatistics and Health Informatics Department, Institute of Psychiatry Psychology and Neuroscience, King's College London, London, UK
diana.shamsutdinova@kcl.ac.uk
[2] Data Science and Soft Computing Lab, Computing Department, Goldsmiths University of London, London, UK
[3] Division of Population Health, Health Services Research and Primary Care, School of Health Sciences, University of Manchester, Manchester, UK

Abstract. Predicting health outcomes such as a disease onset, recovery or mortality is an important part of medical research. Classical methods of survival analysis such as Cox proportionate hazards model have successfully been employed and proved robust and easy to interpret. Recent development of computational methods and digitalization of medical records brought new tools to survival analysis, which can handle large data with complex non-linear relationships. However, such methods often result in "black box" models hard to interpret. In this project we combine the Cox model with tree-based machine-learning algorithms to take advantage of both approaches' strength and to boost the overall predictive performance. Moreover, we aimed to preserve interpretability of the results, quantify the contribution of linear and non-linear and cross-term dependencies, and get insight into a potential non-linearity. The first method includes the Cox model, ensembled with the survival random forest. The second employs a survival tree algorithm to cluster the data, and then fits a separate Cox model in each cluster. The third uses the clusters obtained with a survival tree to identify interaction and non-linear terms and adds them as new terms to the Cox model. We tested the methods on simulated and real-life medical data and compared their internally validated discrimination and calibration. Our results show that classical models outperform combined methods in data with predominantly linear relationships. The proposed methods were more effective in predicting survival outcomes with strong non-linear and inter-dependent relationships and provided an insight into where the non-linearity is placed.

Keywords: Survival analysis · Health research · Cox model · Survival random forest · Machine learning · Ensemble methods

© IFIP International Federation for Information Processing 2022
Published by Springer Nature Switzerland AG 2022
I. Maglogiannis et al. (Eds.): AIAI 2022, IFIP AICT 647, pp. 170–181, 2022.
https://doi.org/10.1007/978-3-031-08337-2_15

1   Introduction

Survival analysis is one of the main methods in health research for longitudinal data. The outcome of interest can be disease onset, recovery, hospital re-admission, mortality, and others. The aims could be either explanatory or prognostic. In explanatory analysis a researcher investigates relationships of various risk factors and incidence rate of an event of interest, their statistical significance and impact size, while an overall model fit, or total variance explained may not be of primary interest. Prognostic research focuses on accurate predictions of the future incidence rate, for which the model fit is crucial, while understanding the relationship between the risk factors and the outcome can be less important. For this task machine learning (ML) algorithms have proven effective and provide alternatives to classical statistical methods. ML methods are flexible and easily adapt to data with complex dependencies. However, flexibility is often achieved by optimizing many model parameters, and the resulting logic can be difficult to interpret. For health outcomes, however, interpretability is one of the key factors: transparency can greatly facilitate model implementation into clinical practice, where clinicians and patients should sufficiently trust predictions to act on them. At the same time, black-box decisions may be avoided for legal and compliance reasons.

This project tries to merge the two approaches and intertwine linear and ML models. We aim to benefit from the interpretability of the linear model while enhancing its predictive performance with the tree-based features. Our baseline linear model is the Cox proportional hazards model (CoxPH), the machine learning algorithms are survival trees [1] and survival random forest (SRF) [2]. CoxPH is a robust model whose regression coefficients represent a multiplicative impact of a risk factor on the baseline log-hazard function, where hazard is an instantaneous event risk [3]. Proportionality assumption can be viewed as another aid for interpretability, as it ignores a potential time-dependence of the risk factor, so the coefficients estimate an integrated impact over the observation time. Nonetheless, direct input of predictors only accounts for the linear effects, while introducing non-linear and interaction terms requires adding such terms explicitly to the equation. In contrast, tree-based algorithms have a built-in ability to capture the non-linearity and cross-dependence of the predictors. However, a final prediction function that relates risk factors and the outcome may considerably with minor data alterations. Therefore, we aim to test if certain combined methods can outperform the baseline algorithms. Our first method includes the Cox model, ensembled with the survival random forest. The second employs a survival tree algorithm to cluster the data and then fits a separate Cox model in each cluster. The third uses the clusters obtained with a survival tree to identify interaction and non-linear terms and adds them to the Cox model. We test the methods on simulated and real-life medical data and compare their discrimination and calibration performance using internally validated area under receiver-operating curve (AUC-ROC) and calibration slopes.

Previously, machine learning community has been proposing to combine various methods in a similar stepwise manner [4, 5]; other papers suggested using a decision tree to automatically cluster the data or select interaction terms [6, 7]. However, we did not find papers with a similar focus on taking advantage of different approaches to enhance interpretability and performance, or recommendations on how these models can be used for these purposes.

2 Methods

We tested the following three hybrid methods to predict event incidence over a specified time. Risk factors were assumed to be constant in time and measured at the baseline. First, we provide a brief description of the baseline Cox and tree-based models, then describe those are proposed to be combined.

2.1 Models

Cox Model. Using standard notations in survival analysis, where T is a random time-to-event, its survival function $S(t) = Prob(T > t)$. Hazard function is $h(t) = \frac{-S'(t)}{S(t)}$ and represents a current rate of failure for those event-free by t. In prediction modelling the aim is to estimate survival function (or a correspondent hazard) and its dependence on predictors. That is, to estimate a conditional distribution of T, $S(t \mid x)$, or $h(t \mid x)$, given a vector of predictors $x = (x^1, \ldots, x^K)$.

Cox proportionate hazard model [3] assumes that hazard rates of observations are proportionate, and the multiplier is exponentiated linear combination of the risk factors,

$$h(t \mid x) = h_0(t) \cdot \exp(\beta_1 \cdot x_1 + \ldots + \beta_K \cdot x_K) \tag{1}$$

Here, $h_0(t)$ is a non-parametric baseline hazard function. Coefficients are estimated by maximizing the partial log-likelihood function [3] and can be maximized without estimating the baseline hazard. Coefficients represent relative change in the hazard rate to a unit of the underlying factor, $h(t \mid x_1 = 1) / h(t \mid x_1 = 0) = \exp(\beta_1)$. In the classical model, coefficients and their impact are time-invariant.

Baseline hazard function can be estimated in different ways [8, 9]. We will use the Kalbfleisch-Prentice estimator following recommendations by Xia and colleagues [10]. Kalbfleisch and Prentice introduced baseline conditional survival probabilities for each time between the failure times and expressed the likelihood function in terms of these probabilities and beta coefficients from the Cox regression. Maximizing such likelihood function by the baseline conditional probabilities, one can find the baseline function corresponding to the estimated Cox regression [9]. Finally, the individual risk of failure is estimated from the baseline survival and linear predictors, $LP = \sum_i \beta \cdot x_i$,

$$h(t \mid x) = h_0(t) \cdot \exp(L.P.), \quad S(t \mid x) = S_0(t)^{\exp(LP)} \tag{2}$$

Survival Decision Tree and Survival Random Forests. Survival tree is a type of classification and regression tree algorithm [11], in which a sample is recursively partitioned by a condition in predictors space guided by a splitting rule. All conditions are comparisons of a predictor value with a threshold. The splitting rule aims to find more homogeneous sub-populations at the two subsequent nodes (or most heterogeneous between the nodes). Definition of homogeneity is not straightforward for survival data due to the presence of censoring and time dimension [12]. Many existing packages use splitting rules based on the log-rank test statistics measuring a statistical difference of the survival curves [2, 13]. LeBlanc and Crowley suggested using the local full likelihood function under the proportional hazards assumption [1]. Purity measures for censored observations have also been proposed [14]. Shimokawa and colleagues [15] showed that different splitting rules could be preferred depending on the hazard function properties. Here we use Survival Random Forest [2] with the log-rank splitting rule from R package randomForestSRC [16] and a survival tree from the RPart package developed by Therneau and Atkinson [17]. RPart uses a rescaled Poisson process which makes the likelihood equivalent to that in the LeBlanc and Crowley's tree [17].

Any survival tree has final leaves, in which all observations are clustered depending on their risk factors and conditions at the nodes. Irrespective of the splitting rule, survival probabilities are estimated by non-parametric Kaplan-Meier curves $KM_L(t)$ in the final leaves, fitted to the observations in the training set falling into that leaf,

$$S(t \mid x) = S(t \mid \text{leaf } L : x \text{ is in } L) = KM_L(t). \tag{3}$$

Survival Random Forest. Survival random forest is an ensemble method that averages predictions over many survival trees grown on a bootstrapped version of the data [2].

Ensemble Method 1 (Cox_SRF). We develop the idea of employing the results of one model as an input to another. This approach was proposed by others [4, 5] and is similar to stacking in ML. First, we fit a standard CoxPH and compute linear predictors for the observations in the train set. Second, we add the linear predictors to the list of the risk factors and train a survival random forest. This extended SRF predicts the survival:

$$S(t \mid x) = S^{SRF}\left(t \mid x' = (x^1, \dots, x^K, \text{ Cox\_linear\_predictor}\right) \tag{4}$$

In this method, we supplied an additional predictor to SRF that aggregated "linear information" captured by CoxPH. Hence, the difference in the SRF performance and baseline CoxPH quantifies the non-linear and interaction terms contribution, and CoxPH regression coefficients describe the linear impact of the predictors.

To minimize overfitting, we split the sample into two, train the Cox model separately on either half to predict survival probability for the other half. Out-of-sample predictions are used in the consequent SRF. The ensemble method 1b explores the same idea in the reverse order, fits SRF, and adds out-of-the-bag predictions to the CoxPH model (Fig. 1).

Ensemble Method 2 (Tree_ClusterCox). The second method uses a survival tree to partition the survival data into clusters. The tree depth is limited by 4, so the number clusters is not more than 16. We then fit a separate CoxPH model in each cluster. Predictions are made by first identifying into which leaf (cluster) an observation falls, then applying the corresponding CoxPH model:

$$S(t \mid x) = \sum_L I(x \in \text{leaf } L) \cdot S_0^L(t)^\wedge \exp\left(\beta_1^L \cdot x_1 + \dots + \beta_K^L \cdot x_K\right) \tag{5}$$

where β_i^L are coefficients of the CoxPH model fitted in the leaf L, S_0^L is a corresponding baseline survival function. The method aims to enhance the Cox model in two ways. First, CoxPH assumes that there is a single baseline survival function for the entire population, and risk factors shift survival in log-hazard space. Aiming a better fit, we relax this assumption by allowing each cluster to have a separate baseline survival function.

Second, the survival tree may identify strong non-linearities or cross-dependencies in the top nodes, which could lead to an easier optimization of the linear models in the final leaves, and a better overall fit. The main challenge in this approach is the underlying tree instability in response to small data permutations. To address this problem, we select predictors with the highest variable importance index (VIMP) computed by a baseline SRF [18], then cross-validate to tune the number of predictors used in the tree.

The method results in a perfectly transparent model: one can display the tree from the 1st step and the CoxPH coefficients for each leaf. We test two versions of the method, 2A and 2B, using the packages RPart with LeBlanc and Crowley splitting rule, and randomForestSRC guided by the log-rank splitting (Fig. 1).

Ensemble Method 3 (Tree_ModifiedCox). We start by growing a tree to cluster the survival data as in Ensemble 2, using only the top VIMP variables. Then, we add cluster identifier as a categorical variable to the baseline Cox regression along with the original predictors. The underlying idea is that a survival tree can serve as a tool to identify non-linear and cross-terms, which we can add to CoxPH. For c final leaves (clusters), $L_i(x) = I(x \in$ leaf $i)$ as leaf identifiers, the final model is

$$S(t \mid x) = S_0^{Cox}(t)^{\wedge} exp(\beta_1 \cdot x_1 + \ldots + \beta_K \cdot x_K + a_1 \cdot L_1(x) + \ldots + a_c \cdot L_c(x)), \quad (6)$$

where betas are the linear impact factors, and alphas are the impact factors of the cross-terms defined by the final tree leaves, that is a product of $I(x_i < k_i)$ or $I(x_j \geq k_j)$ terms. The method is very similar to the one developed by Su and Tsai [7]. The authors developed a tree-growing algorithm that considers the linear terms already in the Cox regression while searching for the new non-linear ones, however, the advantage of our method is its straightforward implementation employing the existing software (Fig. 1).

Cox Model with Fractional Polynomial Regression (Cox_FP). Additionally, we compare the results of the combined methods to the CoxPH with fractional polynomial terms (Cox-FP) [19] using R package mfp [20]. The function selects statistically significant fractional polynomial terms that enhance the model fit once added to the CoxPH regression. We used a default version of the mfp function, in which a prediction variable x can be transformed into a linear combination

$$\xi_0 + \xi_1 x^{(P_1)} + \xi_2 x^{(P_2)}, \quad (7)$$

where $x^{(P)}$ is x^p for $p \neq 0$, and $ln(x)$ for $p = 0$; p_1, p_2 are from $\{-2, -1, -0.5, 0, 0.5, 1, 2\}$ [19, 20]. This method allows CoxPH to handle non-linearity (though not the cross-terms), so we included it as another baseline models.

Ensemble 1	Ensemble 2	Ensemble 3
1. Fit Cox model on all data 2. Fit survival random forest with Cox survival probabilities as an additional factor	1. VIMP SRF to find important predictors 2. Grow a single tree with these predictors, treat final nodes as clusters 3. Build Cox PH model in each cluster	1. -Same as in Ensemble 2- 2. -Same as in Ensemble 2- 3. Build Cox model on all data with additional risk factors – tree clusters as non-linear and interaction terms
Rationale: separate linear and non-linear steps Interpretability: Cox coefficients represent linear terms. Difference in performance (Cox and Cox+SRF) quantifies non-linear effects Challenges: individual impact factors not known	Rationale: CoxPH has single baseline survival, here baseline function by cluster Interpretability: Tree can be displayed to see the clusters. Cox coefficients are available for each cluster Challenges: overfitting, stability	Rationale: tree automatically identifies non-linear predictors Interpretability: Tree can be displayed to see leaf definitions. Cox model shows hazard ratio of added predictors Challenges: overfitting, stability
Cox → Cox lp as risk factor → SRF	SRF variable importance → Shallow tree to cluster → Cox in clusters	VIMP from SRF → Shallow tree to cluster → Clusters to Cox

Fig. 1. Summary of the methods. Each method combines the Cox proportional hazards model with tree-based machine learning algorithms (survival tree or random forest).

2.2 Samples

Simulated Samples. We tested the models using four samples, three simulated and a health-related data. Simulated samples were described by the four predictors: x_1 is uniformly distributed between -1.73 and 1.73 (so the mean is 0 and standard deviation, SD, is 1.00), x_2 is sampled from a normal distribution (mean = 0, SD = 1), x_3 is a binomial random variable, positive outcome probability p = 0.2, x_4 - binomial with p = 0.5. Such variables can typically appear in health data. For example, x_1 can represent normalized age, x_2 – normalized body mass index, x_3 – the presence of hypertension, x_4 – gender, for the outcome of cardiovascular disease.

Further, we assume an exponential time-to-event, so the survival function is $S(t \mid x) = \exp(-h(x) \cdot t)$. The hazard rate h(x) is constant in time and varies with risk factors.

We defined the hazard rate in the first sample such that it depends linearly on predictors:

$$h(x) = 0.10 \cdot \exp(0.4 \cdot x_1 + 1.0 \cdot x_2 + 0.7 \cdot x_3) \tag{8}$$

From Eq. (1), the true Cox regression coefficients are $\beta_1 = 1$, $\beta_2 = 0.7$, $\beta_3 = 0.4$, $\beta_4 = 0$, baseline hazard is 0.10. We assumed that x_4 does not impact the outcome.

In the second sample, we added non-linear dependencies:

$$h(x) = 0.08 \cdot \exp(0.2 \cdot x_1 + 1 \cdot I(x_1 \geq 1) + 1 \cdot I(1 < |x_2| \leq 1.5) + 2.0 \cdot I(|x_2| > 1.5) + 0.7 \cdot x_3) \tag{9}$$

So, one non-linearity is the jump in x_1's impact after a certain threshold. This could describe risk acceleration after a certain age. Another non-linear relationship is the impact of x_2, which is null within one standard deviation from the mean, 1 for absolute values till 1.5, 2 otherwise. It may represent an effect when the weight in a normal range does not affect disease onset, while very low or high values increase the risk.

The third sample has the same non-linearity in x_2 as the second sample, a linear x_1 impact, but non-linearity in x_1 is replaced by an interaction between x_1 and x_3, in which a combination of high x_1 and positive x_3 constitutes an elevated disease risk.

$$h(x) = 0.07 \cdot \exp(0.2 \cdot x_1 + 1.0 \cdot I(x_1 \geq 1 \ \& \ x_3 = 1) + 1.0 \cdot I(1 < |x_2| \leq 1.5) + 2.0 \cdot I(|x_2| > 1.5) + 1.0 \cdot x_3)$$
$$(10)$$

Compared to the previous sample, not all individuals experience a jump in x_1 impact for $x_1 \geq 1$, but those with $x_3 = 1$. This could be a situation when acceleration in a disease risk after a certain age only affects those with pre-existing conditions (for example, hypertension).

Baseline hazards (0.10, 0.08, and 0.07) are set such that 50% of the population experienced the event by $t = 5$, which is the time point where the models' performance for the simulated samples was assessed. In the three simulated samples, coefficients for the Eqs. 8, 9, and 10 were meant to express large non-linear or interaction effects with no linkage to a certain health data. However, the equation forms were chosen to have plausible interpretations.

ELSA Sample. The fourth sample came from the English Longitudinal Study of Ageing (ELSA). We tested our models to predict the incidence of type two diabetes over 7.5 years of observation. ELSA is an ongoing multidisciplinary study with a core cohort of 11391 individuals aged ≥ 50, representative of the older U.K. population [21]. The participants are interviewed every two years since wave 2 (2002/3), and medical examinations occur every four years from wave 2. We included participants with available blood tests, genetic information, and diabetes status for at least one wave after the baseline. Diabetes was established by a self-reported medical diagnosis of diabetes, or HbA1C ≥ 48 mmol/mol (6.5%). The analytical sample had 5957 participants, mean observation time 8.9 years, mean time before diabetes incidence 4.9 years; 398(7%) developed diabetes before 7.5y. Risk factors were age, gender, body mass index, hypertension history, accumulated wealth (low/medium/high), level of education, exercise regime, smoking, depression, and blood cholesterol. As type 2 diabetes has a considerable genetic component [22], we included a polygenic risk score for type 2 diabetes into the analysis, which sums common genetic variants associated with the disease weighted by their impact size [23].

2.3 Performance Assessment

Performance Measures. The performance of a survival model varies in time, so we compare the models for the task of predicting an outcome by a pre-defined time. Examples in health research could be predicting 1-year mortality after a surgery or risk of heart failure in the next 5 years. We assessed model performance in three domains: discrimination, calibration, and interpretability. Discrimination is an ability to separate high-risk and low-risk individuals, which we measure with AUC-ROC. Censored observations should be accounted for while computing AUC-ROC, and we use timeROC function developed for survival data [24]. Calibration is how well an estimated event probability corresponds to the observed share of individuals with similar risk factors experiencing the event. It is measured by the calibration slope and intercept. Intercept, or calibration-in-the-large, is the difference between the mean observed and predicted rates, so the ideal value is 0. Calibration slope is the correspondence of the predicted values to the observed across the probability scale. The ideal value is 1, a lower number means predictions are too extreme (too low for low-risk and too high for high-risk observations), and a sign of over-fitting; a slope > 1 may indicate underfitting. To qualitatively assess interpretability, we question whether predictions are easy to explain and if they give an insight into the underlying relationships.

Internal Validation. We used 5-fold cross-validation to assess model performance. Further, an internal loop of the 3-fold cross-validation was used to tune model parameters: tree depth and a number of risk factors for a node split for SRF; minimum node size, maximum tree depth (2, 3 or 4), and the number of risk factors for tree clustering tree in Ensemble 2 and 3 (the factors were sorted by variable importance and method tuned for using the top 3, ..., or 10). Combinations with the highest AUC-ROC at the selected time defined the final models.

3   Results

Tables 1, 2, 3 and 4 contain internally validated performance statistics of the described methods. The first table is for the sample with linear dependencies, the second for the sample with non-linear terms, the third with interaction terms, and the fourth is for the diabetes data from the ELSA study. Baseline methods were Cox model, Cox model with fractional polynomials, survival random forest, ensemble methods 1A (training Cox regression, then using probabilities to SRF), 1B (training SRF, then using probabilities in Cox), 2A and 2B (building a shallow tree for data clustering, then fitting Cox models in each cluster) and 3 (with clusters as additional parameters in the Cox model).

All methods performed well in the linear sample with similar performance metrics (Table 1). AUCs were between 0.809 (SD 0.011) and 0.816 (SD 0.011).

For the non-linear sample, AUC was considerably better in the ensemble methods compared to the baseline Cox regression results (Table 2). AUC-ROC was 0.715 (SD 0.023) for baseline Cox, and 0.769 (SD 0.010) for Ensemble 3. Worth noting that the Cox model with fractional polynomials performed as well as the ensembled methods, AUC 0.757 (SD 0.013).

The outperformance of the ensembled methods was even higher when cross-terms were present (Table 3). Baseline Cox had AUC-ROC 0.648 (SD 0.027), adding fractional polynomials got it to 0.694 (SD 0.022), Ensemble 1A reached AUC 0.715 (SD 0.017), Ensemble 2A 0.719 (SD 0.016), Ensemble 3 0.721 (SD 0.016).

However, in the real-life health data from the ELSA study, all the methods displayed similar results (Table 4). Figure 2 displays the RPart tree from methods 2 and 3, which captured non-linear dependencies.

Table 1. Internally validated performance of the methods in the first sample

Linear sample	Cox	SRF	CoxMFP	1A	1B	2A	2B	3
AUC-ROC at t = 5	0.815	0.815	0.809	0.811	0.816	0.814	0.813	0.815
AUC-ROC std	0.011	0.014	0.011	0.012	0.011	0.012	0.002	0.011
AUC diff to Cox	**0.000**	**0.000**	**−0.007**	**−0.005**	**0.000**	**−0.001**	**−0.002**	**0.000**
Slope	0.991	0.991	1.007	0.989	0.994	0.990	0.979	0.990
Alpha	−0.012	−0.013	0.008	0.000	−0.014	0.001	0.004	0.007

Table 2. Internally validated performance of the methods in the second sample

Non Linear	Cox	SRF	CoxMFP	1A	1B	2A	2B	3
AUC-ROC	0.715	0.773	0.757	0.767	0.758	0.762	0.755	0.769
AUC-ROC std	0.023	0.006	0.013	0.009	0.015	0.013	0.012	0.010
AUC diff to Cox	**0.000**	**0.059**	**0.042**	**0.053**	**0.044**	**0.048**	**0.040**	**0.054**
Slope	1.051	1.017	1.119	0.956	0.998	0.943	0.956	0.948
Alpha	−0.024	0.000	−0.006	−0.002	−0.003	0.007	0.006	0.006

Table 3. Internally validated performance of the methods in the third sample

Cross-terms	Cox	SRF	CoxMFP	1A	1B	2A	2B	3
AUC-ROC at t = 5	0.648	0.715	0.694	0.715	0.705	0.719	0.720	0.721
AUC-ROC std	0.027	0.014	0.022	0.017	0.017	0.016	0.008	0.016
AUC diff to Cox	**0.000**	**0.067**	**0.047**	**0.067**	**0.058**	**0.071**	**0.072**	**0.073**
Slope	0.958	0.964	1.027	0.972	0.942	0.969	0.972	0.995
Alpha	−0.012	0.018	−0.005	0.018	−0.014	0.002	0.003	0.001

Table 4. Internally validated performance of the methods in the fourth sample

Cross-terms	Cox	SRF	CoxMFP	1A	1B	2A	2B	3
AUC-ROC at t = 5	0.750	0.753	0.753	0.758	0.750	0.731	0.722	0.752
AUC-ROC std	0.011	0.014	0.011	0.012	0.011	0.021	0.023	0.011
AUC diff to Cox	**0.000**	**0.003**	**0.003**	**0.008**	**−0.001**	**−0.019**	**−0.028**	**0.001**
Slope	0.977	0.948	1.229	1.087	0.999	0.755	0.758	0.850
Alpha	0.101	0.098	0.145	0.149	0.182	0.156	0.239	0.158

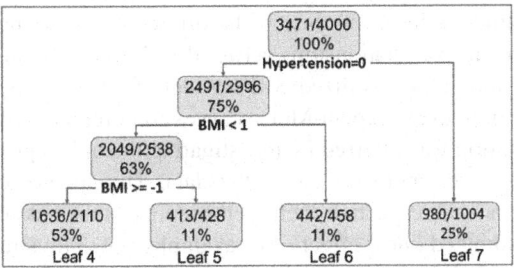

Fig. 2. Example of the RPart survival tree used as the first step for the Ensemble methods 2 and 3 for the simulated sample 3 with non-linear and interaction terms.

	coef	exp(coef)	se(coef)	Pr(>|z|)	
age	0.2851	1.3298	0.0182	<0.001	***
BMI	-0.0046	0.9964	0.0278	0.867	
hypertension	1.4731	4.3626	0.0439	<0.001	***
gender	0.0212	1.0214	0.0340	0.534	
as.factor(Leaf)5	0.8663	2.3781	0.0696	<0.001	***
as.factor(Leaf)6	0.9127	2.4910	0.0692	<0.001	***
as.factor(Leaf)7	na	na	0.0000	na	

Fig. 3. Example of the modified Cox regression model which uses clusters of a survival tree as additional risk factors for simulated sample 3. The clusters are the final leaves of the tree in Fig. 2 (number 4–7, left to right): Cluster 4 (baseline) is (hypertension = 0) and (BMI < 1) and (BMI > −1), Cluster 5 is (hypertension = 0) and (BMI < −1), Cluster 6 is (hypertension = 0) and (BMI > 1), Cluster 7 is (hypertension = 1). Cluster 7 coincided with hypertension, so not estimated.

4   Discussion

We have proposed several methods to embed the survival tree algorithms and classical Cox regression into each other to explore their advantages and overcome their limitations. We aimed to employ Cox model interpretability and enhance it with the CART ability to capture non-linear and interaction relationships. The methods performed at par with the Cox model in linear data and outperformed complex data.

Ensemble 1 stacks two algorithms in a different order (first Cox, then SRF in Ensemble 1A, reverse in 1B). This is not a novel approach [4], but we reiterate its utility for health research, where classical regression models are often preferred. For example, one could train Ensemble 1a or 1b, and if a similar performance is achieved compared to the baseline Cox model, this could justify using a Cox regression.

Moreover, if the difference is considerable, it may represent the marginal contribution of the non-linear terms in the predictive performance. Indeed, AUC-ROC difference for the simulated samples 2 and 3 was 0.04–0.07 with a standard deviation of 0.02 (Table 2 and 3). Had we not known the underlying distribution, this would be a sign of non-linearity. Similarly, a comparison of the fractional polynomial model and ensemble methods results for sample 3 indicates cross-dependencies (Table 3).

Ensembles 2 and 3 can give an insight into where non-linearity lies. A clustering tree structure is the first source of such information. For example, the tree in Fig. 2 has "guessed" hypertension and BMI non-linearity. Further, Ensemble 2 results contain estimated Cox parameters for each cluster; the difference in coefficients could reveal structural differences in the relationships across the clusters. A similar algorithm was used in [6], where the authors utilized SRF to identify clusters of different survival patterns. However, they used Kaplan-Meier curves to compute survival probabilities, and model interpretation was inferred by investigating the object properties by cluster.

Ensemble 3 gives yet another view of the data. The augmented Cox model has clusters as risk factors, and respective coefficients represent the risk of being in a cluster, in addition to the estimated linear effects. For example, Fig. 3 illustrates how Ensemble 3 has correctly identified that the linear BMI impact is negligible, while absolute BMI values above 1 (clusters 6 and 7) possess an elevated risk.

There are several ways to develop the methods further. First, combined methods 2 and 3 rely on a clustering tree. Methods behind the tree construction may affect predictive accuracy, and we may test other splitting rules. For example, an optimal tree proposed by Dunn and colleagues [25] may perform well, in which splitting minimizes the loss of the entire tree instead of optimizing a current node. Customizing the splitting criteria to the proposed methods may also enhance their performance: a partition maximizing Cox fit in the daughter leaves would realign how the tree is grown, and the predictions are made. An integrated Brier score [26] can be used as an alternative assessment measure, aggregating performance over time.

The strength of this work is a focus on targeting specific strengths and weaknesses of the classical Cox model and employing machine learning algorithms not to compete but enhance its performance. However, we acknowledge several weaknesses. First, qualitative insight into non-linearity still requires assessing the tree structures and differences between the Cox regressions in the Ensemble methods. The underlying tree instability is a challenge; further work to increase stability could be done. Second, we did not test our models on non-exponential time distribution. Finally, we primarily tested the models on the simulated data; future work to focus on real-life health data.

Conclusion. The proposed ensemble methods combining classical Cox proportionate hazard rate model and non-linear machine-learning algorithms can effectively build high-performing and interpretable prognostic models for health research, especially for the data where strong interaction dependencies are suspected.

References

1. LeBlanc, M., Crowley, J.: Relative risk trees for censored survival data. Biometrics **48**, 411–425 (1992)
2. Ishwaran, H., Kogalur, U.B., Blackstone, E.H., Lauer, M.S.: Random survival forests. Ann. Appl. Stat. **2**, 841–860 (2008)
3. Cox, D.R.: Regression models and life-tables. J. Roy. Stat. Soc.: Ser. B (Methodol.) **34**, 187–202 (1972)
4. Amunategui, M.: Data Exploration & Machine Learning, Hands-on. https://amunategui.git hub.io/survival-ensembles/index.html
5. Marmerola, G.D.: Calibration of probabilities for tree-based models | Guilherme's Blog. https://gdmarmerola.github.io/probability-calibration/

6. Shi, T., Seligson, D., Belldegrun, A.S., Palotie, A., Horvath, S.: Tumor classification by tissue microarray profiling: random forest clustering applied to renal cell carcinoma. Mod. Pathol. **18**, 547–557 (2005)

7. Su, X., Tsai, C.-L.: Tree-augmented Cox proportional hazards models. Biostatistics **6**, 486–499 (2005)

8. Breslow, N.E.: Discussion of Professor Cox's paper. J. Roy. Stat. Soc. Ser. B (Methodol.) **34**, 202–220 (1972)

9. Kalbfleisch, J.D., Prentice, R.L.: The Statistical Analysis of Failure time Data. Wiley, Hoboken (2002)

10. Xia, F., Ning, J., Huang, X.: Empirical comparison of the Breslow estimator and the Kalbfleisch prentice estimator for survival functions. J. Biom. Biostat. **9**, 392 (2018)

11. Breiman, L., Friedman, J.H., Olshen, R.A., Stone, C.J.: Classification and Regression Trees. Wadsworth & Brooks/Cole Advanced Books & Software, Monterey, CA (1984)

12. Zhou, Y., McArdle, J.J.: Rationale and applications of survival tree and survival ensemble methods. Psychometrika **80**, 811–833 (2015)

13. Segal, M.R.: Regression trees for censored data. Biometrics **44**, 35 (1988)

14. Molinaro, A.M., Dudoit, S., van der Laan, M.J.: Tree-based multivariate regression and density estimation with right-censored data. J. Multivar. Anal. **90**, 154–177 (2004)

15. Shimokawa, A., Kawasaki, Y., Miyaoka, E.: Comparison of splitting methods on survival tree. Int. J. Biostat. **11**, 175–188 (2015)

16. Ishwaran, H., Lauer, M.S., Blackstone, E.H., Lu, M.: randomForestSRC: Random Survival Forests Vignette (2021)

17. Therneau, T., Atkinson, E.: An introduction to recursive partitioning using the RPART routines (2019)

18. Ishwaran, H.: Variable importance in binary regression trees and forests. Electron. J. Stat. **1**, 519–537 (2007)

19. Royston, P., Altman, D.G.: Regression using fractional polynomials of continuous covariates: parsimonious parametric modelling. Appl. Stat. **43**, 429 (1994)

20. Heinze, G., Ambler, G., Benner, A.: Package 'mfp.' CRAN (2022)

21. Steptoe, A., Breeze, E., Banks, J., Nazroo, J.: Cohort profile: the English longitudinal study of ageing. Int. J. Epidemiol. **42**, 1640–1648 (2013)

22. Hackinger, S., et al.: Evidence for genetic contribution to the increased risk of type 2 diabetes in schizophrenia. Transl. Psychiatry. **8**, 252 (2018)

23. Wray, N.R., Lee, S.H., Mehta, D., Vinkhuyzen, A.A.E., Dudbridge, F., Middeldorp, C.M.: Research review: polygenic methods and their application to psychiatric traits. J. Child Psychol. Psychiatry **55**, 1068–1087 (2014)

24. Blanche, P., Latouche, A., Viallon, V.: Time-dependent AUC with right-censored data: a survey. In: Lee, M.-L., Gail, M., Pfeiffer, R., Satten, G., Cai, T., Gandy, A. (eds.) Risk Assessment and Evaluation of Predictions. LNS, vol. 210, pp. 239–251. Springer, New York (2013). https://doi.org/10.1007/978-1-4614-8981-8_11

25. Dunn, J., Gibson, E., Orfanoudaki, A.: Optimal survival trees. arXiv preprint (2020)

26. Graf, E., Schmoor, C., Sauerbrei, W., Schumacher, M.: Assessment and comparison of prognostic classification schemes for survival data. Stat. Med. **18**, 2529–2545 (1999)

Distribution Guided Neural Disaggregation of PM₁₀ and O₃ Hourly Concentrations from Daily Statistics and Low-Cost Sensors

Evangelos Bagkis$^{(\boxtimes)}$ ⓘ, Theodosios Kassandros ⓘ, and Kostas Karatzas ⓘ

Environmental Informatics Research Group, School of Mechanical Engineering, Aristotle University of Thessaloniki, 54124 Thessaloniki, Greece
mpagkise@meng.auth.gr

Abstract. It is common for state-of-the-art research to demand higher granularity data to effectively model the atmospheric composition and personal exposure to air pollution. With the advent of Low-Cost Sensors (LCS) technology, the potential of increased spatiotemporal monitoring resolution arises, however, low cost comes with reduced measurement quality. On-site calibration via supervised machine learning (ML) is the most promising technique for the operational calibration of such devices. This study aims (a) to introduce the distribution guided neural disaggregation (DGND) method to increase the temporal resolution of air quality (AQ) low frequency data based on LCS high frequency readings and (b) simultaneously learn a calibration function with the ability to infer over the hourly resolution but with daily supervision. Towards this two-fold objective we propose an indirect training loss based on the first and second distribution moments errors to optimize a multi-layer perceptron (MLP). DGNDs generalization performance is compared against a traditionally trained MLP with the same architecture on a withheld test set in terms of errors and linearity. Furthermore, using the same metrics, the disaggregation results are evaluated on the original time series from which the reference moments originated. Results suggest that modeling the disaggregated (hourly) resolution of PM₁₀ and O₃ concentrations is feasible from aggregated (daily) information indicated by modest to high linearity with coefficient of determination R^2 between 0.57–0.69 on the test set (except Sindos PM₁₀ where R^2 < 0), and 0.49–0.83 on the original time series accompanied by moderate to low errors.

Keywords: Multi-layer perceptron · Disaggregation · Nowcasting · Low-cost sensors · On-site calibration · Air quality

1 Introduction

1.1 Air Quality Monitoring

Spatially and temporally representative monitoring of air quality (AQ) is especially relevant for the urban atmospheric environment because 1) most pollution sources such

I. Maglogiannis et al. (Eds.): AIAI 2022, IFIP AICT 647, pp. 182–193, 2022.
https://doi.org/10.1007/978-3-031-08337-2_16

as traffic and domestic heating are present and 2) most anthropogenic activities take place. Currently, the AQ in Europe is monitored with high precision reference analyzers on the basis of procedures and methods detailed in the EU Directive on Ambient Air (2008/50/EC) [1] however, the high costs related with this kind of instrumentation results in sparse monitoring networks. In practice, these instruments are operated by experts under strict protocols, are calibrated regularly and therefore provide the most reliable measurements of pollutant concentrations. During the last decade, the low-cost sensor (LCS) technology has developed rapidly, and several solutions have entered the market concerning ambient air quality monitoring, for a fraction of the cost of a reference analyzer. LCS is a compelling technology as it reduces the expenses of obtaining and maintaining a reference AQ monitoring instrument, and thus offers the opportunity to establish dense AQ networks in urban areas [2, 3]. Commercially available LCS can be operated by companies, citizen science projects and interested individuals. Research, however, has shown that LCS responses are subject to aging, drifts and cross sensitivity degradation effects among others, and operation requires identification of such problems and careful calibration before and after deployment [4]. To address the high costs associated with reliable data and the reduced accuracy of the LCS simultaneously, a combined AQ network can be achieved where the reference analyzers facilitate a reference network against whose measurements, a complementary LCS network is calibrated, on-site, and in real time. Several studies [5] continue to confirm that this approach can help increase the accuracy of LCS to comply with the data quality objective of the relevant EU Directive [6]. Furthermore, the resolution increases 10-fold, potentially 100-fold with allegedly minimal maintenance costs.

1.2 LCS Calibration as Time Series Nowcasting

On-site LCS calibration can be viewed through the prism of nowcasting. According to the World Meteorological Organization (WMO) nowcasting is defined on the basis of meteorological systems, as the estimation of a continuous variable in the present and up to six hours in the future [7]. Supervised ML nowcasting of an AQ time series depends on the temporal resolution of official high-quality data provided mainly by local officials and the European Environmental Agency (EEA). We will refer to those measurements as ground truth concentrations (GTC) onwards. As the interest for AQ information moves from sparse and regionally representative to personal exposure assessments aided via fixed and mobile LCS, the need for higher quality LCS data arises. As a demonstrative example, there are reference methods (like the gravimetric method for PM) which by definition provides only with daily PM mean concentration estimates, and therefore equivalent automatic methods are employed capable of delivering hourly concentrations. In addition, there are cases where LCS AQ measurements are available in a finer time scale in comparison to the GTC. In all those situations, a sub-timescale calibration model is required when the standard ML supervision (each instance has one ground truth value) is insufficient.

Temporal disaggregation can be achieved either by modeling the univariate time series or through multivariate modeling assisted by higher resolution time series [8]. The former approach applies the autoregressive integrated moving average (ARIMA) model to the univariate time series and relies on modeling the autocorrelation. The latter approach has the benefit of still including temporal information but can also be assisted with feature engineering techniques to include moving statistics from a multivariate feature space. When correlations between the low frequency target and the high frequency covariates exist then it is possible to accurately reconstruct the temporal patterns [9]. Commonly, pollutant concentrations follow 24-h diurnal patterns depending on human activities, the weather, solar radiation, cloud coverage, and land-use. In the LCS calibration setting, temperature (T) and relative humidity (RH) are among the main factors that affect the sensors performance [10] and thus, including those into the modeling procedure can drive the model response. Additionally, other pollutant species measurements can lead to further improvement. The aforementioned observables can be considered as the high frequency covariates holding information to guide the disaggregation of the low frequency target.

1.3 Aim of the Study

This investigation is a proof-of-concept study to determine the ability of a neural network to learn an hourly model indirectly from the daily GTC probability distribution instead of the hourly GTC. This formulation is interesting because 1) when combined with LCS it opens up the opportunity to temporally disaggregate low to high frequency AQ measurements and 2) learn a high-frequency model for deployment without explicitly having access to low enough granular information.

2   Materials and Methods

2.1   Experimental Set-Up

Aiming to establish a LCS network for AQ monitoring, the KASTOM project [11] operates 33 multi-sensor devices spread throughout the Greater Thessaloniki Area (GTA). Three LoRaWAN transmitters help to collect the data in a local database. All the devices measure the temperature, relative humidity, the pressure (P) and estimate coarse (PM_{10}), fine ($PM_{2.5}$) and ultra-fine (PM_1) particulate matter levels via optical particle counters operating under the orthogonal laser scattering principle [12] (Manufacturer: Plantower PMS5003). Additionally, 20 of the devices also include electrochemical gas sensors (Alphasense) to monitor concentration levels of carbon monoxide (CO), ground level ozone (O_3) and nitrogen dioxide (NO_2) [13]. PM_{10} GTC levels are measured by an analyzer (Eberline FH 62 I-R, reference equivalence with European Standard EN 12341) that uses β-attenuation, while reference O_3 concentration levels are measured with the aid of UV photometry according to European Standard EN 14625. Three devices (including PM as well as gaseous sensors) are collocated with three reference stations. Data obtained from the LCS are collected every minute and are aggregated by their median value into hourly values. The reference data are accessed from the EEA API that exports the latest observations on an hourly basis. For the purposes of this study, the daily mean and std of the GTC are calculated and the hourly measurements are discarded from the training and are only used as test data to validate the proposed method.

2.2   Preprocessing and Temporal Feature Engineering

Only days with a full 24 cycle of observations were identified and included in the modeling thus, the missing values were dropped along with incomplete days. For each pollutant and each station, different time periods are evaluated (Table 1). As the focus is concentrated on the algorithm presentation and evaluation, a subset of all the measurements was selected to demonstrate the method. This analysis is not concerned with the evaluation of the LCS network and the identification of the fittest calibration methods as these results are already published in [11]. As nowcasting is an inherently time dependent task, several feature identification techniques are employed to engineer an input vector that includes temporal patterns and moving distribution properties as well as interactions between the covariates. Initially, the interactions are represented by fractions between the covariates (the LCS readings) and supplement the input vector. Specifically, the following fractions are included: PM_{10}/RH, NO_2/O_3, NO_2/T, O_3/T, RH/PM_{10}, T/P, T/RH, P/RH. To inject the temporal pattern first, 12 lags are extracted from each covariate (original and fraction) to complement the input vector. This technique lets the model infer the short-term evolution. Furthermore, for each of the original variables, the statistical properties (mean, median, std, min, max, and the difference between the min and max) in the last 24-h and 48-h range represent the long-term behavior of the system. To elaborate further, for example the fraction PM_{10}/RH can potentially provide information about the relationship between particulate matter and relative humidity, which is a known factor affecting the performance of optical particle counters [14]. The following features are extracted: $(PM_{10}/RH)_{t-1}$ ... $(PM_{10}/RH)_{t-12}$, mean $(PM_{10}/RH, 24\ h)$, mean $(PM_{10}/RH, 48\ h)$, median $(PM_{10}/RH, 24\ h)$, median $(PM_{10}/RH, 48\ h)$, ... min_max_difference $(PM_{10}/RH, 24\ h)$, min_max_difference $(PM_{10}/RH, 48\ h)$. In this way a total of 320 features were constructed.

Table 1. The measurement periods included in the study.

Pollutant/station	Start (dd/mm/yyyy)	End (dd/mm/yyyy)	Training days
PM_{10} Agia Sofia	06/11/2019	30/4/2020	70
PM_{10} Kordelio	06/11/2019	17/11/2021	500
PM_{10} Sindos	06/11/2019	30/4/2020	250
O_3 Agia Sofia	06/11/2019	30/05/2020	100
O_3 Kordelio	06/11/2019	30/09/2020	300
O_3 Sindos	06/11/2019	30/10/2020	150

2.3 Distribution Guided Neural Disaggregation

Apart from the state-of-the-art performance in a multitude of tasks [15, 16], artificial neural networks (ANN) are particularly interesting for their flexibility in processing high dimensional or/and unstructured data (e.g., text, medical imaging data). On the one hand, architectures like MLP do not understand temporal relationships by design in contrast to other architectures such as the long-short term memory (LSTM) ANNs [17]. On the other hand, feature identification/engineering techniques have been established for time series that can summarize and present the temporal dimension to simpler architectures. Although the LSTM and its successor, the transformer architecture have proven very useful in modeling language from colossal amounts of text, in time series problems it struggles to surpass simpler approaches with expert feature engineering input [18]. This is partly because most time series of interest are non-stationary in contrast to language which is complex and high dimensional but static (the words and syntax do not change with time). Taking advantage of the flexibility we design a simple MLP and modify the training procedure as follows:

Let $X \in \mathbb{R}^N$, where N is the dimension (number of columns) of the dataset, be a sample of the input space and $y \in \mathbb{R}$ the GTC time series. Suppose that an underlying generating mechanism produces (X, y) pairs in discrete time steps. The pairs obey the identically and independently distributed (iid) assumption [19] and the joint distribution probability P(X, y) represents the unknown generating function. The goal is to approximate the true generating function with the MLP function $F_w: X \rightarrow y$, where w are the weights (parameters) of the network. MLP is a directed graph of perceptrons [20] ordered in layers, with each layer interacting with the previous and the next layer via the weights w and the bias b. Forward propagation from a n-layer MLP translates into the following equation.

$$F_w(X) = f_n\left(w^{(n)}f_{n-1}\left(\ldots f_2\left(w^{(2)}f_1\left(w^{(1)}X^T + b^{(1)}\right) + b^{(2)}\right)\ldots + b^{(n-1)}\right) + b^{(n)}\right) \tag{1}$$

Suppose that M1, M2,..., Mn are the successive hidden layer sizes with the output layer comprised of one neuron (with linear activation for regression settings). The weight matrix $w^{(1)}$ with dimensions $M1 \times N$ between the input dataset X with N features, called input layer, and the first hidden layer with M1 nodes, is multiplied with X^T and the bias vector of length M1 is added. A non-linear activation function f_1 is applied resulting in the first layer output. The first layer is connected with the second layer via the $w^{(2)}$ weight matrix with dimensions $M2 \times M1$; following the same steps the result passes through the activation function f_2 and so on. Weights are initialized either pseudo-randomly from a known distribution or with more sophisticated approaches such as the Glorot [21] initialization. Training refers to the optimization of a loss function calculated between the estimations the MLP produces and the GTC and is usually achieved via the gradient descent algorithm.

There are three main approaches to implementing the gradient descent algorithm. In stochastic gradient descent, backpropagation of the loss is applied for every instance and has the ability to find global minima for a specific dataset but with increased time requirements during training. In batch gradient descent the full training dataset is processed at once by the neural network but this leads to slow convergence, possibly to local minima [22] and high memory requirements. To compensate, commonly the third approach is followed namely, the mini-batch gradient descent, where the dataset is partitioned randomly and processed into batches leading to faster training times and introduces enough stochasticity to effectively avoid local minima. In this setting, we assign temporal meaning to each batch by including a fixed number (24) of hourly LCS measurements (high frequency time series) of complete days. By representing the time dimension of the problem with the batch size we can effortlessly train an hourly model with daily (low frequency time series) supervision. Therefore, forward propagation of each batch produces a vector $\hat{y}$ of 24 estimations for every hour of the day. We incorporate the MAE or L1 loss function to construct the full loss (Loss) as follows.

$$Loss1 = \lambda \left(\frac{1}{m} \sum_{i=1}^{m} \left| mean\left(\hat{y}_{00:00:00}, \ldots, \hat{y}_{23:00:00}\right) - \mu_i \right| \right) \tag{2}$$

$$Loss2 = \lambda \left(\frac{1}{m} \sum_{i=1}^{m} \left| std\left(\hat{y}_{00:00:00}, \ldots, \hat{y}_{23:00:00}\right) - \sigma_i \right| \right) \tag{3}$$

$$Loss = Loss1 + Loss2 \tag{4}$$

where i represents the day, μ_i is the true mean, σ_i the true std of the day, m is the total number of training days and λ is the learning rate. It is therefore evident that the full loss we apply, takes into account deviations both in terms of mean and std values. After manual hyperparameter tuning the MLP is chosen with 4 layers, 20 nodes at each layer, $\lambda = 0.0001$ (a typically low learning rate), and the leaky rectified linear unit (Leaky ReLu), an activation function not suffering from the "vanishing gradient" or the "dying neuron" problem, [23] for all the studied cases. Finally, the Adam [24] optimizer is employed to implement the backpropagation of the loss.

Algorithm 1: Distribution Guided Neural Disaggregation
Input: Training tensors X_{MxN} , $\mu_{M/24}$, $\sigma_{M/24}$, N features, M hourly steps
Step 1: Construct MLP graph with n layers
Step 2: Initialize weights from the uniform distribution $U(-\sqrt{1/N}, \sqrt{1/N})$
Step 3: For epoch until max_epochs:
For each complete day i:
$x_i \leftarrow X^i_{(00:00:00,\ 23:00:00)xN}$
$\hat{y}_i \leftarrow F_w(x_i)$ calculated with eq. (1)
$\hat{\mu}_i \leftarrow mean(\hat{y}_i)$
$\hat{\sigma}_i \leftarrow std(\hat{y}_i)$
$loss \leftarrow Loss(\hat{\mu}_i, \hat{\sigma}_i, \mu_i, \sigma_i)$ calculated with eqs (2), (3), (4)
$w_{i+1} \leftarrow Adam(w_i, loss)$
Output: $\hat{y}_M \leftarrow F_w(X_{MxN})$

2.4   Evaluation

ML models are usually validated with train-validation-test splits or with various forms of cross-validation [25]. In the former approach, the model is trained on the training subset and continuously evaluated on the validation subset after every epoch. The validation subset serves as a test proxy for the metrics to be compared against the training metrics aiming to find an equilibrium to the bias-variance tradeoff. The generalization error is then calculated on the test subset to provide a more robust evaluation on data that are completely new for the model. In cross-validation (CV), the dataset splits into k randomly separated subsets; the first $k-1$ subsets provide the fitting set and the last subset the validation set. Once the metrics are obtained from the first run, the procedure repeats another $k-1$ times until every instance has been validated as a test instance once. This technique is used either for validation or for hyperparameter tuning. Several extensions exist such as time-block CV, spatial CV and forward CV. Forward CV is indicated as the more appropriate method for time series problems [26]. In this setting however, all of the aforementioned methods are not directly applicable because disaggregation is applied to historical data. Therefore, the evaluation metrics are calculated on the hourly time series from which the daily statistics were calculated. Addressing the second research objective, a direct comparison responding to generalization performance between the traditional MLP and the DGND approach must be made on a withheld test set thus we split the original dataset into training and test; the disaggregation performance is evaluated on the training subset and the generalization performance on the test set. Moreover, the daily and the hourly loss are calculated during the DGND training to investigate and compare their behavior. The evaluation metrics are presented in Table 2.

Table 2. Evaluation metrics.

Metric	Symbol	Formula
Pearson correlation	R	$\dfrac{\sum_{i=1}^{n} y_i \hat{y}_i - n\mu_i \hat{\mu}_i}{\sqrt{(\sum_{i=1}^{n} y_i^2 - n\mu_i^2)(\sum_{i=1}^{n} \hat{y}_i^2 - n\hat{\mu}_i^2)}}$
Coefficient of determination	R^2	$1 - \dfrac{\sum_{i=1}^{n}(y_i - \hat{y}_i)^2}{\sum_{i=1}^{n}(y_i - \bar{y})^2}$
Root mean squared error	RMSE	$\sqrt{\dfrac{\sum_{i=1}^{n}(y_i - \hat{y}_i)^2}{n}}$
Mean absolute error	MAE	$\dfrac{1}{n}\sum_{i=1}^{n}|y_i - \hat{y}_i|$

3 Results

The evaluation results of the DGND approach are presented in Table 3 and for the standard MLP in Table 4. Regarding the former approach, we observe that in all stations and for both pollutants, the disaggregated time series show high linearity as the R^2 and R indicate. When compared against the training metrics the errors increase substantially which is expected considering that one approach "sees" the GTC directly while the other indirectly. Therefore, to provide a more representative comparison on performance degradation, we employ a test set to calculate the metrics. The errors slightly increase for the DGND method which indicates that even though some information is lost in aggregation, a larger part can be reconstructed through this method. Overall, the Ozone GTC is modeled with higher precision than PM$_{10}$ in all cases. This is explained partly because Ozone follows a clear diurnal (daily) pattern due to the photochemistry production mechanism that is catalyzed by ultraviolet radiation. On the contrary, PM$_{10}$ diurnal pattern at the city center is strongly correlated with human activities and in Thessaloniki, shows two peaks usually at 10:00 and at 24:00 local time [27], directly related with traffic and commercial activities in the area [28]. This is a more complex pattern to model as it evolves according to human irregular schedules (reduced traffic on weekends, holidays, daily peaks shifted according to season, etc.). Moreover, focusing on Sindos PM$_{10}$ metrics, we observe that in the test set of both approaches the linearity is lost in terms of R^2. Interestingly, the disaggregation still works as well as for the other two stations. This indicates that if a time series can be modeled, even when the extrapolation errors are high on the test set, the disaggregation can work in case the metrics are adequate in the training set. One caveat that we didn't address here is that when the actual hourly measurements are unknown, then the model can't be validated in this resolution.

Table 3. The evaluation metrics of the DGND approach. Abbreviations: Kord stands for Kordelio, Sind for Sindos and Agia stands for Agia Sofia.

Disaggregation metrics (training set)				Generalization metrics (test set)			
	RMSE	MAE	R^2	R	RMSE	MAE	R^2	R
O_3								
Kord	14.93	11.00	0.76	0.88	15.65	12.19	0.70	0.86
Agia	11.10	7.96	0.83	0.91	15.50	11.94	0.69	0.84
Sind	15.44	11.23	0.71	0.85	15.95	12.26	0.67	0.83
PM_{10}								
Kord	15.25	10.54	0.49	0.73	13.43	9.76	0.58	0.77
Agia	14.44	9.94	0.75	0.87	13.94	8.85	0.57	0.87
Sind	13.78	8.27	0.59	0.79	18.72	15.52	-3.52	0.45

Table 4. The evaluation metrics of the traditional MLP approach. Abbreviations: Kord stands for Kordelio, Sind for Sindos and Agia stands for Agia Sofia.

Training metrics (training set)				Generalization metrics (test set)			
	RMSE	MAE	R^2	R	RMSE	MAE	R^2	R
O_3								
Kord	9.28	6.45	0.91	0.95	14.55	10.94	0.74	0.88
Agia	7.76	5.07	0.92	0.96	14.64	11.62	0.72	0.86
Sind	10.12	7.46	0.88	0.94	11.77	8.88	0.82	0.91
PM_{10}								
Kord	10.79	6.77	0.74	0.87	11.65	8.01	0.69	0.83
Agia	11.00	6.87	0.86	0.93	12.13	7.81	0.68	0.83
Sind	11.99	6.39	0.69	0.84	12.76	10.77	-1.10	0.59

In Fig. 1 we present the evaluation of the DGND method for O_3 in Agia Sofia. The slope of the regression analysis represents the accuracy in the LCS calibration setting; therefore, the disaggregated time series accuracy is 92%. The shape of the predicted distribution resembles the observed distribution, and the peaks are accurately estimated; however, in the lower concentration range (0–10 $\mu g/m^3$) predictions are noisier. More importantly, it can be observed that the hourly loss (calculated only for comparison) is driven by the daily loss. This is evident as the daily loss decreases slowly and remains high (>10 $\mu g/m^3$) but the hourly loss continues its decreasing trajectory. Given that the DGND method outputs a trained MLP, the generalization performance is depicted in Fig. 2; the accuracy is 88% and the distributions match as well. Interestingly, the training and the testing GTC distributions differ visibly but nonetheless the diurnal pattern is present in both datasets and the model discovers it from the LCS measurements. It should be mentioned that the DGND approach needs approximately twice the number of epochs to converge compared with the traditional MLP training. This is expected considering that in the former approach the MLP learns with 12 times less supervision because for every 24 h only the mean and std are available.

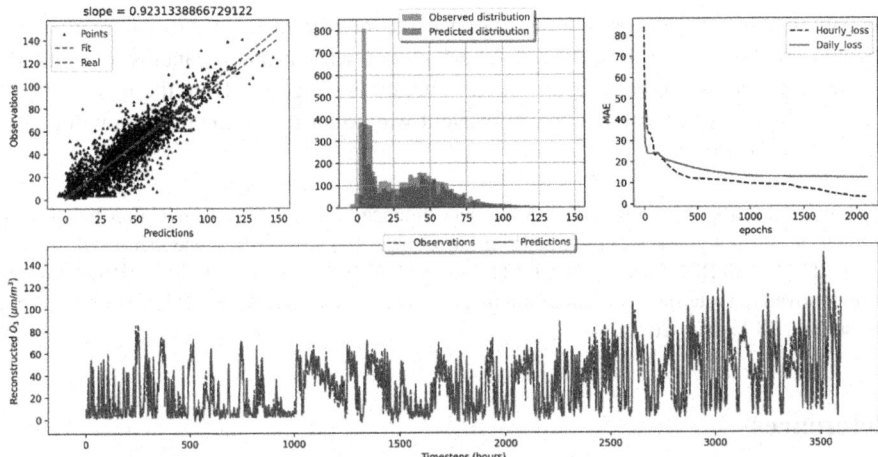

Fig. 1. Disaggregation results for O$_3$ in Agia Sofia station. Upper left panel: scatter plot, upper center panel: comparison between the real and predicted distributions, upper right panel: loss progression against epochs calculated for both resolutions, bottom panel: the reconstructed O$_3$ time series against the reference time series (hourly).

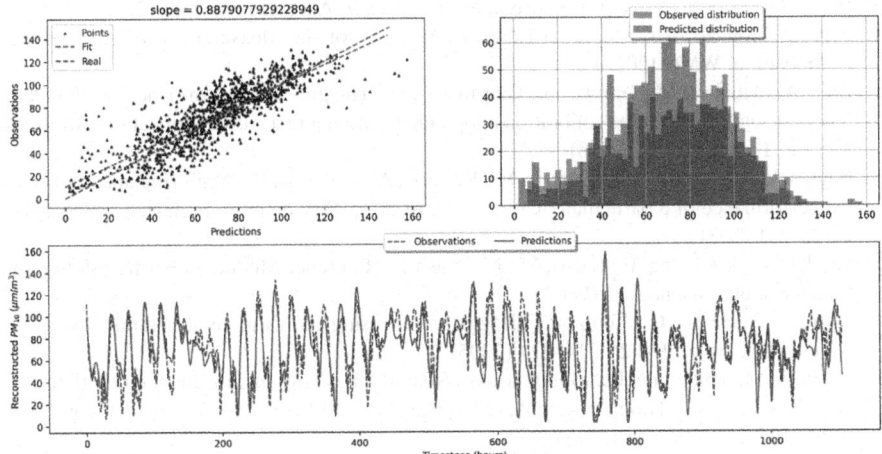

Fig. 2. Generalization results for O$_3$ in Agia Sofia station. Upper left panel: scatter plot, upper right panel: comparison between the real and predicted distributions, bottom panel: the reconstructed O$_3$ time series against the reference time series (hourly).

4 Conclusions

The AQ modeling community focuses on increasing the spatiotemporal monitoring resolution to accurately describe the atmospheric composition of urban environments. Towards this goal, we demonstrated the DGND method, capable of increasing the temporal resolution of highly sought reference GTC. Overall, incorporating LCS to guide the disaggregation procedure based on the flexibility of neural networks shows a promising path in increasing the granularity of expensive measurements. Furthermore, the constructed MLP model has the potential to be deployed without significant loss of accuracy and serve as an on-site calibration function which is suggested from the metrics in all but one cases. Further insights on a consistent way to terminate the training will be the focus of future studies.

Acknowledgments. This research has been co-financed by the European Union and Greek national funds through the Operational Program Competitiveness, Entrepreneurship and Innovation, under the call RESEARCH—CREATE—INNOVATE. Project code T1EDK-01697; project name Innovative system for air quality monitoring and forecasting (KASTOM, www.air4me.eu, accessed on 28 January 2022).

References

1. EUD (European Union Directive). Directive 2008/50/EC of the European Parliament and of the Council of 21 May 2008 on ambient air quality and cleaner air for Europe. Off. J. Eur. Union **2008**, L152 (2008)
2. Castell, N.: Low-cost sensors and networks-Overview of current status by the Norwegian Reference Laboratory for Air Quality. NILU report 15/2020 (2020)
3. RIVM Data Portal. https://sensors.rivm.nl/dataportaal/. Accessed 05 Mar 2022
4. Peltier, R., et al.: An Update on Low-cost Sensors for the Measurement of Atmospheric Composition. WMO (2021)
5. Bigi, A., Mueller, M., Grange, S., Ghermandi, G., Hueglin, C.: Performance of NO, NO2 low cost sensors and three calibration approaches within a real world application. Atmosph. Measur. Techniq. **11**(6) (2018)
6. Bagkis, E., Kassandros, T., Karteris, M., Karteris, A., Karatzas, K.: Analyzing and improving the performance of a particulate matter low cost air quality monitoring device. Atmosphere **12**(2), 251 (2021)
7. Wapler, K., de Coning, E., Buzzi, M.: Nowcasting. Reference Module In Earth Systems And Environmental Sciences (2019)
8. Moauro, F., Savio, G.: Temporal disaggregation using multivariate structural time series models. Economet. J. **8**(2), 214–234 (2005)
9. Banbura, M., Giannone, D., Modugno, M., Reichlin, L.: Now-casting and the real-time data flow. In: Elliott, G., Timmermann, A. (eds.) Handbook of Economic Forecasting, vol. 2 Part A, pp. 195–237. Elsevier (2013)
10. Samad, A., Obando Nuñez, D., Solis Castillo, G., Laquai, B., Vogt, U.: Effect of relative humidity and air temperature on the results obtained from low-cost gas sensors for ambient air quality measurements. Sensors **20**(18), 5175 (2020)
11. Bagkis, E., Kassandros, T., Karatzas, K.: Learning calibration functions on the fly: hybrid batch online stacking ensembles for the calibration of low-cost air quality sensor networks in the presence of concept drift. Atmosphere **13**(3), 416 (2022)

12. Yu, X., Shi, Y., Wang, T., Sun, X.: Dust-concentration measurement based on Mie scattering of a laser beam. PLoS ONE **12**(8), e0181575 (2017)
13. Park, C., Fergus, J., Miura, N., Park, J., Choi, A.: Solid-state electrochemical gas sensors. Ionics **15**(3), 261–284 (2009)
14. Di Antonio, A., Popoola, O., Ouyang, B., Saffell, J., Jones, R.: Developing a relative humidity correction for low-cost sensors measuring ambient particulate matter. Sensors **18**(9), 2790 (2018)
15. Perone, C., Calabrese, E., Cohen-Adad, J.: Spinal cord gray matter segmentation using deep dilated convolutions. Sci. Rep. **8**(1) (2018)
16. Han, J., Liu, H., Xiong, H., Yang, J.: Semi-supervised air quality forecasting via self-supervised hierarchical graph neural network. In: IEEE Transactions on Knowledge and Data Engineering, vol. 5966 (2022)
17. Jiang, X., Luo, Y., Zhang, B.: Prediction of PM2.5 concentration based on the LSTM-TSLightGBM variable weight combination model. Atmosphere, **12**(9), 1211 (2021)
18. Elsayed, S., Thyssens, D., Rashed, A., Jomaa, H.S., Schmidt-Thieme, L.: Do We Really Need Deep Learning Models for Time Series Forecasting? https://arxiv.org/abs/2101.02118. Accessed 05 Mar 2022
19. Stats Exchange. https://stats.stackexchange.com/questions/213464/on-the-importance-of-the-i-i-d-assumption-in-statistical-learning. Accessed 05 Mar 2022
20. Hounmenou, C., Gneyou, K., Glele Kakaï, R: A Formalism of the General Mathematical Expression of Multilayer Perceptron Neural Networks. Preprint (2021)
21. Glorot, X., Bengio, Y.: Understanding the difficulty of training deep feedforward neural networks. In: Proceedings of the Thirteenth International Conference on Artificial Intelligence and Statistics, PMLR, vol. 9, pp. 249–256 (2010)
22. Ge, R., Huang, F., Jin, C., Yuan, Y.: Escaping From Saddle Points --- Online Stochastic Gradient for Tensor Decomposition. https://arxiv.org/abs/1503.02101. Accessed 05 Mar 2022
23. Maas, A.L.: Rectifier Nonlinearities Improve Neural Network Acoustic Models (2013)
24. Kingma, D.P., Ba, J.: Adam: A Method for Stochastic Optimization. https://arxiv.org/abs/1412.6980. Accessed 05 Mar 2022
25. Maleki, F., Muthukrishnan, N., Ovens, K., Reinhold, C., Forghani, R.: Machine learning algorithm validation. Neuroimag. Clin. N. Am. **30**(4), 433–445 (2020)
26. Fan, K., Dhammapala, R., Harrington, K., Lamastro, R., Lamb, B., Lee, Y.: Development of a Machine Learning Approach for Local-Scale Ozone Forecasting: Application to Kennewick, WA. Frontiers In Big Data, vol. 5 (2022)
27. Giannakidou, P.A.: Study on aerosols PM10 concentrations in the region of Thessaloniki, M.Sc. Thesis, in Greek (2021). https://doi.org/10.26262/heal.auth.ir.335294
28. Athanasakis, E., Kassandros, Th., Karatzas, K.: Investigation of traffic and air pollution in Thessaloniki, Greece, under ordinary and COVID-19 pandemic conditions. In: Kamilaris, A., Wohlgemuth, V., Karatzas, K., Athanasiadis, I. (eds.) Environmental Informatics. New perspectives in Environmental Information Systems: Transport, Sensors, Recycling. Adjunct Proceedings of the 34th Edition of the EnviroInfo, Shaker Verlang, Kassel, Germany, pp. 84–92 (2020). ISBN:978-3-8440-7628-8

Experimental Comparison of Metaheuristics for Feature Selection in Machine Learning in the Medical Context

Thibault Anani[2]([✉]), François Delbot[1,2], and Jean-François Pradat-Peyre[1,2]

[1] Université Paris Nanterre, Nanterre, France
[2] LIP6, Sorbonne Université, Paris, France
{thibault.anani-agondja,francois.delbot,
jean-francois.pradat-peyre}@lip6.fr

Abstract. We explore in this paper the use of metaheuristics to select features from a dataset in order to improve the prediction performance of models build with different machine learning methods. To this end, we compare the performances of 5 learning methods: Logistic Regression (LR), K-Nearest Neighbors (KNN), Gaussian Naive Bayes (GNB), Support Vector Machine (SVM) and Random Forest (RF) on 4 heterogeneous datasets in the number of data and features, for different feature selection methods (metaheuristics or statistical filters).

The results obtained show that feature selection by improving a metaheuristic derived from the genetic algorithm leads to much better performances no matter the learning method used compared to without feature selection on the same dataset.

Keywords: Machine learning · Features selection · Optimization

1 Introduction

The implementation of a recommendation algorithm based on a learning method is confronted with various concerns, including the dimension of the data (the number of features) versus the number of available and usable data. It is frequent in real contexts that the data set is relatively small in size but faces a large dimension. This is mainly the case in many problems coming from the medical world. In this case, the risks of overfitting are frequent and the solutions of recommendations found generalize poorly to a real population. One of the solutions adopted consists in reducing the dimension of the data.

Dimension reduction is characterized by the projection of data described in N dimensions to a reduced space of dimension $K < N$. The main objective is to preserve the initial profile of the data by proposing a more relevant and compact representation. Moreover, reducing the dimensionality makes visible the underlying structure generally not very readable in high dimension; one

© IFIP International Federation for Information Processing 2022
Published by Springer Nature Switzerland AG 2022
I. Maglogiannis et al. (Eds.): AIAI 2022, IFIP AICT 647, pp. 194–205, 2022.
https://doi.org/10.1007/978-3-031-08337-2_17

thus avoids the problems related to the concept of 'the curse of dimensionality' introduced by Bellman in 1961.

Several approaches exist [1] to reduce the dimension: feature selection which consists in keeping only a subset of the initial features or feature extraction which relies on a global transformation of the data thanks to an application that induces a change of coordinates [2], as in the case of the Fourier transform in signal processing.

Confronted with this high dimensionality problem in previous work on medical data analysis to improve the management of patients suffering from Amyotrophic Lateral Sclerosis (ALS) [3], we have developed a robust method based on 1) manual selection (with the help of ALS experts) of patient characteristics 2) followed by a dimension reduction phase using the Uniform Manifold Approximation and Projection (UMAP) method which is based on the assumption that the data belong to a Riemannian variety, a particular form of regular variety [4].

We are interested here in dimension reduction by feature selection and more precisely in dimension reduction with the envelope approach [5]. This approach is associated with learning and compares the different subsets of possible features with the performance of the learning model used.

More precisely, we show empirically that the use of metaheuristics and in particular a variant of the population-based metaheuristic called 'differential evolution' gives excellent results no matter the learning method used by selecting a relevant subset of features from the data of the problem studied.

These results are obtained by considering multiple datasets from the medical field one from Pro-Act on ALS and several benchmarks regularly used in comparisons of learning methods.

2 Methodology Used

The data used in the medical context (for classification or prediction) present a particular profile: we frequently observe quite few complete data but the features associated with these data are often numerous (or even very numerous) due to the fear of underfitting by neglecting important parameters. This means that, without precaution, the models obtained by learning (supervised or not) generalize rather poorly. Reducing the number of features used during the learning phases has several benefits: on the one hand, it avoids overfitting and reduces the noise produced by the data, which improves the performance of the model and its ability to generalize. On the other hand, it induces a simplification of the hypotheses necessary for the use of the model, thus facilitating the treatments and improving the calculation time. Finally, it is easier to produce complete datasets because the amount of information to be collected is less.

In order to select the 'best' subset of features. We need to define how one subset is better than another and how to obtain this subset in an efficient and relevant way and how to validate this choice.

2.1 Evaluation Criteria

The evaluation criteria we use are the most frequently used criteria in this context; let $D = \{x\}$ be a data set. $V(x)$ a classification function that defines whether x is 1 or 0 and $f(x)$ a prediction function (that associates a boolean to x); We first define TP as the true positive (i.e. $\{x|f(x) = V(x) = 1\}$), FP as the false positive (i.e. $\{x|f(x) = 1 \wedge V(x) = 0\}$), TN as the true negative (i.e. $\{x|f(x) = V(x) = 0\}$), and FN as the false negative (i.e. $\{x|f(x) = 0 \wedge V(x) = 1\}$).

- The **sensitivity** or **recall** measures the true positive rate (i.e. $\frac{|TP|}{|TP|+|FN|}$). In medicine: the proportion of people correctly tested positive for a disease among those who have this disease.
- The **specificity** measures the true negative rate (i.e. $\frac{|TN|}{|TN|+|FP|}$). In medicine: the proportion of people tested negative for a disease among those who do not have that disease.
- The **accuracy** measures the proportion of correct predictions (i.e. $\frac{|TP|+|TN|}{|D|}$). In medicine: the proportion of people correctly diagnosed for a disease among the whole population.

We use either the accuracy (for datasets that have a balance between positive and negative cases) or the average of the sensitivity and the specificity (for unbalanced datasets) to measure performance.

2.2 Obtaining and Validating an 'Optimal' Subset

The objective of the experiments is to find the optimal subset of features i.e. the subset that will allow us to obtain the most performing model (w.r.t. accuracy, recall or specificity) with the data we have. A potential subset called solution is represented as a vector of booleans of the size of the number of features we have (see Fig. 1). Depending on the value of a boolean, a feature is taken into account or not to perform a learning: 0 the feature is not taken into account and 1 it is taken into account for learning. To carry out a learning, at least one explanatory feature is needed, therefore a vector cannot be composed only of 0.

	v_0	v_1	v_2	v_3	v_4	v_5
i_1	0	1	0	1	0	1
i_2	0	1	1	0	1	0
i_3	1	1	0	1	1	1

Fig. 1. Example of 3 solutions represented as a vector of booleans with a number of Features equal to 6

In order to validate the relevance of a solution for a learning method, we use cross-validation which consists in decomposing the dataset into k subsets and then using $k - 1$ subsets for learning and the kth subset for validation. More precisely, we do k experiments by choosing at each experiment a different subset for the validation. We use $k = 5$ in our experiments.

The machine learning methods we use are the Logistic Regression (LR), the Support Vector Machine (SVM), the K-Nearest Neighbors (KNN), the Random Forest (RF) and the Gaussian Naive Bayes (GNB). See [6] for a complete description of these methods.

3   Feature Selection with the Use of Metaheuristics

Feature selection consists of selecting a portion of our features that are most relevant to the construction of the model to improve its performance. Ideally, we should test and evaluate all combinations of features to find the most efficient one. However, when the number of features is high, it is simply impossible to test and evaluate all possible combinations. which leads to a combinatorial explosion e.g. with 180 features, we have $2^{180} - 1$ subsets to explore, which is impossible to achieve in a reasonable time. We will therefore use methods from operational research, called metaheuristics, to find the best possible subset of features.

Metaheuristics are computational methods for solving complex optimization problems and finding the optimal solution or at least an approximate solution. These methods are divided into 2 branches. Solution based metaheuristics try to improve one solution at a time by searching in its neighborhood whereas Population-based metaheuristics improve several solutions at the same time and merge them together to obtain better solutions. In a previous study we used 7 metaheuristics: 4 are solution-based (Tabu search, Simulated annealing, Random search and Hill climbing) and 3 are population-based (Genetic algorithm, Differential evolution and Particle swarm optimization). Here we focus on the ones that gave the best results: 3 population-based (Population-Based Incremental Learning, Differential evolution and Particle swarm optimization) and 2 solution-based (Tabu search and Simulated annealing). For all metaheuristiscs the number of individuals/neighbors at each generation is set to 50 and the number of generations is set to 500.

3.1   Solution-Based Metaheuristics

Tabu Search (TS) performs a local search to solve complex or large optimization problems [7]. The concept is to use a memory system to deny for a given period of time to revisit a previously visited solution and to allow moves that do not necessarily improve it, thus allowing the search to continue even when a local optimum is found. The size of the tabu list is set to 1000.

Simulated Annealing (SA) is an algorithm based on the annealing process used in metallurgy to achieve thermal equilibrium at each temperature. The initial solution is used as a candidate feature subset, and the feature subset is updated according to its neighborhood and according to the temperature-dependent probabilities of selecting better or worse solutions [8]. The temperature is set to 500 and decrease by 1 at each generation.

3.2   Population-Based Metaheuristics

Population-Base Incremental Learning (PBIL) is an improvement of the well-known genetic algorithm. It converges toward the optimal solution of a problem using a probability vector as large as the number of features [9]. This vector is used to generate the individuals of a population and is updated at each generation. The learning rate is set to 0.1, the mutation probability to 0.2 and the mutation shift to 0.05.

Particle Swarm Optimization (PSO) relies on population collaboration. Individuals called particles move in the search space, each representing a features subset. The particles will evolve by following the influence of the best performing ones and their own previous movements in the search space [10]. The inertia weight coefficient and both the acceleration factors are set to 0.5.

Differential Evolution (DE) uses the diversity present between individuals of a population to explore the different areas of the search space using mutation operations [11]. The population is composed of N Individuals denoted $P_G = \{X_1^G, X_2^G, ..., X_N^G\}$ at the generation G (where $G \in [1, G_{max}]$ and $X_{i,j}^G$ denoting the j-th, $j \in [1, D]$, component of the vector X_i^G). By performing mutation, crossover and selection operations the population improves over the generations until the stopping criterion is reached. For the initial generation, these individuals are generated randomly.

At each generation the algorithm performs first a mutation step using a mutation strategy which can be expressed as 'DE/x/y' where DE stands for differential evolution, x refers to how a vector (individual) in the mutation operation is chosen and $y \in \mathbb{N}$ specifies the number of differential vectors in the mutation strategy. Then the algorithm performs a crossover operation.

The most common and widely used strategy for the mutation is 'DE/rand/1' as depicted below (V_i^G is the mutant obtained by the mutation):

$$V_i^G = X_{r1}^G + F \times (X_{r2}^G - X_{r3}^G) \tag{1}$$

with $i = \{1, 2, ..., N\}$, $r1, r2, r3$ are random numbers belonging to $\{1, 2, ..., N\}$ s.t. $r1 \neq r2 \neq r3 \neq i$ and where $F \in [0, 2]$ is a constant probability factor that controls the amplification of the differential variation. There are other mutation strategies like 'DE/best/1' which uses the best performing vector of the generation instead of a randomly chosen one for X_{r1}^G.

In this paper the strategy 'DE/best/1' is the one used for better convergence in a limited number of generations.

The crossover is performed in order to generate a new vector U_i^G which is the cross between the original vector X_i^G and the mutant V_i^G. There are two types of crossover: binomial and exponential. In this paper the binomial crossover is used. The new vector U_i^G is generated as follows:

$$U_{i,j}^G = \begin{cases} V_{i,j}^G, & \text{if rand}(0,\ 1) \leq CR \text{ or } j = j_{rand} \\ X_{i,j}^G, & \text{otherwise} \end{cases} \tag{2}$$

where $j_{rand} \in [1, D]$ is a number chosen at random to reduce the chances that the vector U_i^G is composed only of the elements of X_i^G and $CR \in [0, 1]$ is the crossover probability. CR has a great influence on the diversity of the population build by the algorithm, since depending on its value, the number of elements that will change will be different: the higher the value, the greater the variation.

The last step is to select the best performing individuals. To know if the vectors generated by the crossover step will be kept, their score is compared to the score of the current vectors.

$$X_i^{G+1} = \begin{cases} U_i^G, & f(U_i^G) \geq f(X_i^G) \\ X_i^G, & \text{otherwise} \end{cases} \tag{3}$$

where $f()$ represents the fitness function of an individual. If a vector U_i^G has a better score than the vector X_i^G then we keep this vector for the next generation otherwise we reject it and we keep the previous one. The parameter F is set to 1 and CR is set to 0.5 in our experiments.

3.3   A New Population-Based Metaheuristics

We propose in this paper a new enhanced binary differential evolution algorithm: the binary progressive learning differential evolution (BPLDE). This one is based on an improved mutation strategy: we propose to use directly the binary strings of the different individuals for the mutation strategy. The only possible values for a bit are 1 or 0 to indicate that a feature is selected for learning or not respectively. From this observation it is possible to calculate the result of all combinations of the initial mutation strategy 'DE/best/1' as follows:

$$V_{i,j}^G = \begin{cases} X_{best,j}^G, & \text{if } X_{r1,j}^G = X_{r2,j}^G \\ X_{r1,j}^G, & \text{otherwise} \end{cases} \tag{4}$$

Performing this transformation removes the F factor from the equation. Besides, this approach allows to use the bits present in a vector directly without having to perform a conversion operation which can take time when the size and number of the vectors are relatively important.

The choice of the mutation strategy is crucial to achieve good convergence. 'DE/rand/1' strategy takes a single random individual of the population as reference which allows to have a good exploration in the search space and to keep a good diversity in the population. However, performing a learning can be time consuming depending on the structure of the data and the learning algorithm used, thus the number of possible iterations for the algorithm is also limited. 'DE/best/1' strategy takes the best individual as a reference which allows to favour the exploitation and a faster convergence at the risk of reducing quickly the diversity between the individuals of the population and to remain blocked on a local optimum.

Therefore we can conclude that determining the reference individual has an important place in the proper running of the strategy. We propose a mutation strategy that offers a compromise between the two by emphasizing the exploration by using $\frac{N}{2}$ random individuals of the population ($P'_G \subset P_G$) with a wide range of possibilities to select the reference individual at early stage while towards the end we only use the best individual for the whole population to favor the exploitation. Based on these assumptions we propose the same equation as Eq. 4 except that instead of using $X^G_{best,j}$ we use $X^G_{pbest,j}$ which stands for one of the $p \in \mathbb{N}$ best performing individuals. If $X^G_i \notin P'_G$ then the best solution is chosen like 'DE/best/1' mutation strategy. Furthermore, $X^G_{r2',j}$ is now a solution randomly chosen from the union of the current population and the archive $P \cup A$. Indeed, at each generation the individuals that have been rejected are kept for a certain amount of time in a separate population A called archive. Having an archive provides information about the progress direction and is also capable of improving the diversity of the population [12]. If the size of A exceeds that of P then randomly selected solutions are removed from A to keep its size at most N. As the algorithm progresses the value of p is gradually reduced until it reaches 1 by using this method:

$$p = Max(1, N \times (1 - (\sqrt{\frac{G}{G_{max}}} \times \alpha)))$$

where α is a parameter that determines the speed of reduction of p. The smaller α is, the slower p will decrease and more the exploration will be privileged over the exploitation.

Some values of CR generate individuals that are more likely to survive and these values should be kept for the following generations. This is the reason why having CR that can adapt itself according to population evolution at each generation is important. The operation is to record successful crossover probabilities (SCR) and use them to guide the new generation of new crossover rate for each individual X^G_i according to a normal distribution ($\mathcal{N}$) of mean μ_{CR} and standard deviation 0.1 which are described in [12].

$$CR^G_i = \mathcal{N}(\mu_{CR}, 0.1) \tag{5}$$

CR^G_i is the crossover probability of the individual X^G_i. The value of μ_{CR} is set to 0.5 at the beginning and is updated at each generation as follow:

$$\mu_{CR} = \mu_{CR} \times (1 - LR) + LR \times (\frac{1}{n} \sum_{i=1}^{n} SCR^G_i) \tag{6}$$

where $LR \in [0.1]$ is the learning rate which is a constant value that will impact the speed at which the value of μCR increase or decrease.

In our study, μ_{CR} is set to 0.05 and the α parameter to 1.5.

Algorithm 1: Binary progressive learning differential evolution

---

Set $\mu CR := 0.5$; $A := \emptyset$;
for $G := 1$ to G_{max} **do**

   $SCR^G := \emptyset$;

   $p := Max(1, N \times (1 - (\sqrt{\frac{G}{G_{max}} \times \alpha})))$;

   $P'_G :=$ Randomly choose $\frac{N}{2}$ individuals from P;

   for $i := 1$ to N **do**

      $CR_i := \mathcal{N}(\mu_{CR}, 0.1)$;

      if $i \in P'_G$ **then**

         | $X^G_{pbest} :=$ Randomly choose one of the p best individuals from P;

      else

         | $X^G_{pbest} :=$ Best individual from P;

      end

      do

         | Randomly Choose X^G_{r1} from P and $X^G_{r2'}$ from $P \cup A$;

      while $r1 \neq r2 \neq i$;

      for $j := 1$ to D **do**

         if $X^G_{r1,j} = X^G_{r2',j}$ **then**

            | $V^G_{i,j} := X^G_{pbest,j}$;

         else

            | $V^G_{i,j} := X^G_{r1,j}$;

         end

      end

      $j_{rand} := randint(1, D)$;

      for $j := 1$ to D **do**

         if $rand(0, 1) \leq CR_i$ *or* $j = j_{rand}$ **then**

            | $U^G_{i,j} := V^G_{i,j}$;

         else

            | $U^G_{i,j} := X^G_{i,j}$;

         end

      end

      if $f(U^G_i) > f(X^G_i)$ **then**

         | $A \leftarrow X^G_i$; $X^G_i := U^G_i$; $SCR^G \leftarrow CR_i$;

      end

   end

   $\mu_{CR} := \mu_{CR} \times (1 - LR) + LR \times (\frac{1}{n} \sum_{i:=1}^{n} SCR^G_i)$;

   Randomly removes solutions from A so $size(A) \leq N$;

end

---

4 Datasets

4.1 ALS Database

ALS is a rare neurodegenerative disease that induces a progressive degeneration of the neurons that innervate the muscles of the body, the motor neurons. Although studied since 1824 [13]. It was not until 1864 that Charcot, on the basis of his anatomical work carried out at the Pitié Salpêtrière Hospital (Paris, French), proposed the current name of the pathology and synthesized the work of his European colleagues. He established the link between the damage to the corticospinal bundle on post-mortem examination and the symptoms of the disease. ALS leads to a gradual loss of motor skills and dysfunctions in the bulbar sphere. There are no treatments to date to cure the disease. Survival from the onset of the first symptoms is, on average, between 3 and 5 years. Death often occurs as a result of respiratory failure. High clinical variability and heterogeneity of disease progression complicate reliable prognostication. The incidence of ALS is approximately 2.5 per 100,000 population per year and the prevalence is approximately 8 per 100,000 population (ARSLA 2020)[1].

The ALS Therapy Development Institute (ALS TDI) estimates that approximately 450,000 people worldwide have ALS (ALS TDI 2020)[2]. Only two treatments have been approved by the U.S. Food and Drug Administration (FDA) to slow disease progression: riluzole (Bensimon et al. 1994) and edaravone (Takei et al. 2017). However, their effect on survival is limited, providing only a relative slowing of progression (Dharmadasa et al. 2018; Fang et al. 2018).

In our work on the prognosis of 1 year survival of patients with ALS[3], we primarily used the PRO-ACT database, an acronym for Pooled Resources Open-Access ALS Clinical Trials [4]. It includes twenty-two clinical trials and one observational study, conducted between 1990 and 2010. Funded in 2012 by the ALS Treatment Alliance, it was made available through the "DREAM Phil Bower ALS prediction Prize4Life" research competition. The PRO-ACT data has a sample to feature ratio of 765 when considering the seventeen features from the database. The size of the overall set, while significant for the domain, is not sufficient for complex model development.

Due to an imbalance in the number of patients in the different classes the score used for this specific dataset is $\frac{recall + specificity}{2}$. This metric takes this information into account, unlike accuracy, which is biased towards the largest class.

4.2   Benchmarks

In the study presented here we use also the following data sets :

- **Scene:** Scene recognition dataset from OpenML. It contains characteristics about images and their classes. The current dataset is a binary classification problem [5] (Instances: 2407; Features: 299)
- **Gravier:** Gravier et al. (2010) have considered small, invasive ductal carcinoma without axillary lymph node involvement (T1T2N0) to predict metastasis of small node-negative breast carcinoma. [16]. (Instances: 168; Features: 2 905)
- **Tian:** Tian et al. (2003) investigated the purified plasma cells from the bone marrow of control patients along with patients with newly diagnosed multiple myeloma. [17] (Instances: 173; Features: 12 625)

For these datasets we use accuracy for the scoring since the distribution between the classes is balanced.

---

[1] https://www.arsla.org/la-sla-en-chiffres.

[2] https://www.als.net/als-resources/faq/.

5   Results

We compare now the performance of different machine learning method presented above completed by 5 state-of-the-art filter-based methods Chi-squared (Chi2) test, Anova test, Mutual Information (MI) [18], ReliefF [19] and Maximum Relevance Minimum Redundancy algorithm (MRMR) [20] - applied to the different mentioned datasets without and with feature selection. The results obtained with these methods presented below are those with the best $k \in [1, D]$ number of features.

Table 1. The classification performance (%) between the algorithms

Dataset	Algorithm	LR	SVM	KNN	RF	GNB	Avg. score	Max. score	Rank
ALS	w/o FS	77.03	73.14	57.04	57.18	73.36	67.55	77.03	12
	ReliefF	77.78	76.12	65.44	78.94	77.30	75.12	78.94	10
	MRMR	78.60	78.63	63.31	79.98	78.34	75.77	79.98	7
	MI	78.73	77.02	65.43	79.67	76.86	75.54	79.67	9
	Chi2	77.71	76.42	64.01	70.24	76.54	72.98	77.71	11
	Anova	78.17	77.24	65.43	79.98	76.46	75.46	79.98	7
	TS	81.93	79.84	64.78	62.83	79.75	73.83	81.93	6
	SA	82.59	79.41	66.02	63.21	79.65	74.18	82.59	5
	PBIL	83.38	81.04 (+7.9)	67.90	66.60	81.30	76.04	83.38	3
	PSO	83.30	80.33	67.07	66.36	80.87	75.59	83.30	4
	DE	84.26	80.53	69.88	86.60	82.03	80.66	86.60	2
	BPLDE	**84.42** (+7.39)	80.26	**71.06** (+14.02)	**86.67** (+29.49)	**82.20** (+8.84)	**80.92** (+13.37)	**86.67** (+9.64)	**1**
Scene	w/o FS	97.22	96.14	91.65	92.15	85.67	92.34	97.22	12
	ReliefF	97.47	97.55	92.52	93.69	85.75	93.40	97.55	11
	MRMR	97.47	97.71	95.68	94.97	87.08	94.58	97.71	10
	MI	97.80	98.13	96.51	94.68	85.67	94.56	98.13	9
	Chi2	98.92	98.92	98.92	**98.92** (+6.77)	86.95	96.53	98.92	7
	Anova	97.47	98.30	95.89	94.64	86.12	94.48	98.30	8
	TS	98.92	98.63	99.00	95.35	93.85	97.15	99.00	5
	SA	98.96	98.63	98.59	95.35	94.02	97.11	98.96	6
	PBIL	98.96	98.92	99.04	96.43	94.27	97.52	99.04	4
	PSO	99.09	98.84	99.04	96.55	93.73	97.45	99.09	3
	DE	99.09	98.88	99.13	96.51	**95.39** (+10.84)	97.80	99.13	2
	BPLDE	**99.17** (+1.95)	**99.84** (+8.19)	**99.21** (+7.06)	96.43	95.26	**97.98** (+5.64)	**99.84** (+2.62)	**1**
Gravier	w/o FS	72.62	73.21	67.86	68.45	70.24	70.48	73.21	12
	ReliefF	80.36	82.74	73.81	82.74	79.76	79.88	82.74	7
	MRMR	86.90	**86.90** (+13.69)	**84.52** (+16.66)	**84.52** (+16.07)	**83.33** (+13.09)	**85.23** (+14.75)	86.90	3
	MI	80.95	80.36	75.00	80.36	77.98	78.93	80.95	11
	Chi2	82.14	81.55	75.60	80.36	80.95	80.12	82.14	10
	Anova	82.14	83.33	77.98	82.14	80.36	81.19	83.33	6
	TS	79.76	82.74	71.43	80.95	75.60	78.10	82.74	7
	SA	77.98	82.74	71.43	79.76	75.60	77.50	82.74	7
	PBIL	86.31	85.12	75.60	77.98	78.57	80.72	86.31	4
	PSO	84.52	83.93	75.60	78.57	78.57	80.24	84.52	5
	DE	88.10	83.33	76.79	77.38	80.36	81.19	88.10	2
	BPLDE	**89.29** (+16.67)	84.52	77.38	77.98	79.76	81.79	**89.29** (+16.08)	**1**
Tian	w/o FS	73.41	77.46	78.61	79.19	80.35	77.80	80.35	12
	ReliefF	80.92	81.50	84.39	85.55	87.28	83.93	87.28	6
	MRMR	91.33	84.39	83.82	**86.71** (+7.52)	90.17	87.28	91.33	3
	MI	82.08	84.97	82.66	85.55	86.71	84.39	86.71	7
	Chi2	78.61	83.92	84.39	84.39	84.97	83.26	84.97	11
	Anova	80.92	84.97	83.24	86.71	86.13	84.39	86.71	7
	TS	79.77	84.97	83.24	83.24	86.13	83.47	86.13	10
	SA	79.19	86.13	82.66	82.66	86.71	83.47	86.71	7
	PBIL	91.33	**89.02** (+11.56)	86.71	81.50	90.17	87.75	91.33	3
	PSO	90.17	87.86	86.71	82.08	89.60	87.28	90.17	5
	DE	**94.22** (+20.81)	87.86	**87.28** (+18.67)	81.50	**90.75** (+10.4)	**88.32** (+10.52)	**94.22** (+13.87)	**1**
	BPLDE	93.64	88.44	86.71	82.08	**90.75** (+10.4)	**88.32** (+10.52)	93.64	2

The bold numbers in this Table 1 indicate the best score obtained for each of the statistical learning or filtering methods used for a given data set (ALS, Scene, Gravel, Tian) with in parenthesis the performance delta between the feature selection method and the performance when no feature selection is performed (w/o FS: first lines in the table).

These results show that using metaheuristics to select part of data feature leads to a better performance for all machine learning methods used.

6   Conclusion

We have shown in this paper that feature selection by metaheuristics improve significantly the performance of learning methods commonly used to build predictive models when the number of data is low and the number of characteristics is high (as in the medical field).

The extra cost related to feature selection comes mainly from the cost of cross-validation which leads to evaluate several times the performance of the model on parts of the initial dataset (up to $k = 5$ times longer than without feature selection). Nevertheless, the quality of the obtained model is much better in terms of performance (accuracy, recall or specificity) as our experiments show.

So, in view of this study, we recommend to systematically proceed to a feature selection by the DE or BPLDE metaheuristic whatever the method chosen to build a prediction model for a given dataset.

In our future works on this topic, we plan to use a statistical filter (e.g. MRMR) to initialize the first population of the DE or BPLDE metaheuristics in order to improve their efficiency or to study if smaller values of k for the cross-validation (which has an impact on the learning time) allow to keep as good results.

References

1. Motoda, H., Liu, H.: Feature Selection Extraction and Construction (2002)
2. Chipperfield, A.J., et al.: A. Carreira-perpiñán. A Review of Dimension Reduction Techniques. Technical
3. Grollemund, V., et al.: Development and validation of a 1-year survival prognosis estimation model for amyotrophic lateral sclerosis using manifold learning algorithm UMAP. Sci. Rep. **10**(1), 13378 (2020). https://doi.org/10.1038/s41598-020-70125-8
4. Grollemund, V., Chat, G.L., Pradat-Peyre, J.-F., Delbot, F.: Manifold learning for innovation funding: identification of potential funding recipients. In: Maglogiannis, I., Iliadis, L., Pimenidis, E. (eds.) AIAI 2020. IAICT, vol. 583, pp. 119–127. Springer, Cham (2020). https://doi.org/10.1007/978-3-030-49161-1_11
5. Kohavi, R., John, G.H.: Wrappers for feature subset selection. Artif. Intell. Relev. **97**(1), 273–324 (1997)
6. Grollemund, V., et al.: Machine learning in amyotrophic lateral sclerosis: achievements, pitfalls, and future directions. Front. Neurosci. **13**, 135 (2019). https://doi.org/10.3389/fnins.2019.00135

7. Zhang, H., Sun, G.: Feature selection using tabu search method. Pattern Recognit. **35**, 701–711 (2002)

8. Mafarja, M.M., Mirjalili, S.M.: Hybrid whale optimization algorithm with simulated annealing for feature selection. Neurocomputing **260**, 302–312 (2017)

9. Baluja, S.: Population-Based Incremental Learning: A Method for Integrating Genetic Search Based Function Optimization and Competitive Learning. Tech. rep. CMU-CS-94-163. Carnegie Mellon University, Pittsburgh (1994)

10. Marandi, A., et al.: Boolean Particle Swarm Optimization and Its Application to the Design of a Dual-Band Dual-Polarized Planar Antenna, Jan 2006, pp. 3212–3218 (2006). https://doi.org/10.1109/CEC.2006.1688716

11. Chakravarty, K., et al.: Feature selection by differential evolution algorithm - a case study in personnel identification. In: 2013 IEEE Congress on Evolutionary Computation, pp. 892–899 (2013)

12. Zhang, J., Sanderson, A.C.: JADE: adaptive differential evolution with optional external archive. IEEE Trans. Evolution. Comput. **13**(5), 945–958 (2009)

13. Rowland, L.P.: How amyotrophic lateral sclerosis got its name: the clinicalpathologic genius of Jean-Martin Charcot. Archiv. Neurol. **58**(3), 512–515 (2001)

14. Atassi, N., et al.: The PRO-ACT database. Neurology **83**, 1719–1725 (2014)

15. Boutell, M.R., et al.: Learning Multi-label Scene Classification (2004)

16. Gravier, E., et al.: A prognostic DNA signature for T1T2 nodenegative breast cancer patients. Genes Chromos. Cancer **49**(12), 1125–1125 (2010)

17. Tian, E., et al.: The role of the wnt-signaling antagonist DKK1 in the development of osteolytic lesions in multiple myeloma. New Engl. J. Med. **349**(26), 2483–2494 (2003)

18. Bommert, A., et al.: Benchmark for filter methods for feature selection in highdimensional classification data. Comput. Statist. Data Anal. **143**, 106839 (2020). https://doi.org/10.1016/j.csda.2019.106839

19. Robnik-Sikonja, M., Kononenko, I.: Theoretical and empirical analysis of ReliefF and RReliefF. Mach. Learn. **53**(1), 23–69 (2003). https://doi.org/10.1023/A:1025667309714

20. Peng, H., Long, F., Ding, C.: Feature selection based on mutual information criteria of max-dependency, max-relevance, and minredundancy. IEEE Trans. Pattern Anal. Mach. Intell. **27**(8), 1226–1238 (2005). https://doi.org/10.1109/TPAMI.2005.159

Exploring the Pertinence of Distance Functions for Nominal Multi-label Data

Payel Sadhukhan$^{(\boxtimes)}$ (iD)

Institute for Advancing Intelligence, TCG CREST, Kolkata, India
payel0410@gmail.com

Abstract. Data with nominal features constitute a good fraction of multi-label datasets. Dealing with high-dimensional, nominal data is different from the handling of data with numeric features. The key reason being – the distance functions which work good on numeric datasets may not function optimally (without returning the true separations of the points) in a nominal feature space. We have further observed that, in a multi-label dataset, an imbalance exists in the distribution nominal features which further aggravates the learning. In this work, we focus to find the suitability of four different distance functions –*euclidean, hamming, jaccard and kulsinski* in a binary-nominal context. Additionally, we also propose and explore an ensemble of two classifiers where one classifier is modelled using jaccard distance and the other is modelled on kulsinski distance. An empirical study involving five binary-nominal datasets, four evaluation metrics and three multi-label classifiers is used to evaluate the pertinence of each distance function and the ensemble. We find that the proposed ensemble gives the best outcome across all but one case.

Keywords: Nominal features · Multi-label · Distance functions · Ensemble · Jaccard · Kulsinski

1 Introduction

Distance function is one of the key aspects for learning any dataset. A distance function should be able to capture the true separations of the feature vectors of a dataset. The quantitative and qualitative structures of a dataset has to be kept into account while choosing a distance function for the same. In most cases, we are biased towards using the euclidean distance, possibly due to its familiarity in our daily lives. But, it may not be the best choice always. To obtain a fruitful learning, we need to look at aspects like dimensionality of features, density, nature of the features and sparsity of the features before choosing the distance function. Multi-label datasets are obtained from several real-world domain. Quite a number of these domain deals with features which are nominal in nature, namely text [1], medical [18] and object detection [20]. Besides the abundance of binary (0 or 1) nominal features, the presence of multiple-way nominal features

© IFIP International Federation for Information Processing 2022
Published by Springer Nature Switzerland AG 2022
I. Maglogiannis et al. (Eds.): AIAI 2022, IFIP AICT 647, pp. 206–216, 2022.
https://doi.org/10.1007/978-3-031-08337-2_18

(with more than two possible feature values) is also seen. In order to accomplish a proper learning from these data, it is necessary to have a distance function which will aptly capture the dissimilarities and similarities of the nominal feature vectors. In this work, we are particularly interested to explore the pertinence of different distance functions in context of multi-label datasets with binary nominal features. We denote a multi-label as $\mathcal{D} = \{(\mathbf{x}_i, \mathcal{Y}_i), i = 1, 2, \ldots, n\}$ and the label set cardinality as $\mathcal{L}$. Here, $\mathbf{x}_i$ is the ith instance and $\mathcal{Y}_i = \{y_{i1}, y_{i2}, \ldots, y_{i\mathcal{L}}\}$ is the corresponding label assignment for $\mathbf{x}_i$. y_{ik} indicates the kth label membership for the ith instance. If $y_{ik} = 1$ signifies that the kth label is relevant (positive) for $\mathbf{x}_i$ while $y_{ik} = 0$ denotes that the kth label is irrelevant (negative) for $\mathbf{x}_i$. Let the feature space be d-dimensional and $\mathbf{x}_i = \{x_{i1}, x_{i2}, \ldots, x_{id}\}$ denotes an instance. In a nominal, multi-label dataset, $x_{ij} = 0$ or 1 $\forall i, j$. It is further seen that for each feature, the 0 count often outnumbers the 1 count. Sometimes, we may notice the opposite also, 1 count outnumbers the 0 count. To be precise, there is often a feature-imbalance which gives rise to a sparsity in the feature vector matrix.

We could find one work which explores the suitability of different distance functions for generic multi-label data (numeric as well as nominal) [6]. We have found the usage of hamming distance function to capture the dissimilarities of the labels (but not features) in a number of works [16]. Apart from a couple of works, we could not really find any significant work which has discussed the occurrence and consequences of these distinctive aspects of nominal multi-label feature vectors [10]. There remains a lot to be done to efficiently tackle the nominal features of the multi-label datasets which is the focus of our work. In this work, we analyze the suitability of each distance function and the proposed ensemble in the nominal, multi-label context. We run three sets of classifiers —i] Binary Relevance (BR) classifier with k-nearest neighbor classifier as the base classifier, ii] Classifier Chain Scheme with k-nearest neighbor classifier as the base classifier and iii] Rakel-D with k-nearest neighbor classifier—to test the efficacy of each function in being able to rightfully deal with the nominal feature vectors. Our goal is to study the intrinsic effect of the distance functions. Hence, we have chosen k-nearest neighbor classifier as the base classifier (as it does not involve any other parameters other than separation of the points) in all three cases. We discuss the extant works in the field of multi-label learning in the next section.

2   Related Works

The study of multi-label learning has gained momentum in the past few decades. The primary reason is the availability of this class of data from several real-world domain. Accordingly, the need for a dedicated learning of such datasets was established. The sincere efforts of the research community has resulted in the formulation of diversified techniques which can be principally classified into i] Problem transformation (PT) approaches and ii] Algorithm Adaptation (AA) approaches [5]. In PT approaches, a certain number of base classifiers are used to tackle the multi-label classification. A base classifier can be a traditional classifier in its innate form or a tweaked form which can facilitate multi-label learning better. PT approaches can be further classifier into – i) *first-order*, ii) *second-order* or iii) *higher-order* approaches on the basis of the number of labels that are considered together to train the models. In First order approach, a classifier is learned for a label independently of all other labels [18]. In second order methods, the pair-wise correlations of labels are explored by packing the learning of two labels in one classifier [21]. The cumulative learning of all pairs of labels are taken together to ddliver the final output. Capturing the association of three or more labels is the primary focus of higher order approaches [12]. A number of diversified techniques have facilitated higher order label associations through interesting schemes including classifier chains [3], RAkEL [19], random graph ensembles [2] and IBLR-ML+. In a recent work by [11], zero-shot learning is used to facilitate the learning in images. In AA approaches, an existing learning scheme is transformed to learn the multi-label datasets. Several approaches have been made and techniques like k-nearest neighborhood [7], bayesian learning [22], neural network [8] to name a few. In addition to the above described class of methods, researchers have also resorted to the methods of data transformation via feature extraction and selection [17] for enhanced learning of multi-label datasets. Class-imbalance is an important characteristic of multi-label datasets and in recent years a number of schemes have been developed to address this issue via data preprocessing [9], label-correlation [23], cost-sensitive learning [14] and Helinger forests [4]. However, we could not find any specific study on nominal multi-label datasets. In all the works (barring a few) [16] that we have described in the previous paragraphs of this section, we have seen that nominal multi-label datasets are treated in the same way as that of the numeric multi-label datasets. This work seems to be the first one which is carrying out a study focused on this aspect. We explain the motivation of our work using a toy example in the next section.

3   A Toy Example and the Motivation of This Work

Let us consider three pairs of nominal features a) x_1, x_2, b) y_1 and y_2 and c) z_1 and z_2. All six feature points are in the binary domain.

- Case 1: $x_1 = \{0, 1, 1, 0\}$ and $x_2 = \{1, 0, 1, 0\}$. We can see that x_1 and x_2 varies at exactly two positions and if we were to compute their Euclidean distances, the value would be $\sqrt{2}$.
- Case 2: $y_1 = \{0, 1, 1, 0, 0, 0, 0\}$ and $y_2 = \{1, 0, 1, 0, 0, 0, 0\}$. A simple inspection like in the previous case will tell us that y_1 and y_2 also vary at exactly two locations and their euclidean distance is $\sqrt{2}$.
- Case 3: $z_1 = \{0, 1, 1, 0, 1, 1, 1\}$ and $z_2 = \{1, 0, 1, 0, 1, 1, 1\}$. A similar computation like the previous two cases will tell us that z_1 and z_2 also vary at exactly two locations and their euclidean distance is $\sqrt{2}$.

Feature vector length of a vector is the number of components present in it. Percentage of positive features of a vector denotes the fraction of feature

Vectors	Dimensionality of features	Percentage of positive features
x_1, x_2	4	0.500
y_1, y_2	7	0.286
z_1, z_2	7	0.714

components which are positive among all the components. In the following table, we show the values of these two parameters of the pair of feature vectors.

Euclidean distance returned $\sqrt{2}$ value in each of the three cases as the vector components varied at exactly two positions in each. And this very popular distance function (widely used in multi-label learning) seems to be thoroughly unaware of two basic properties of the binary-nominal, multi-label datasets. In two of three cases (Case 1 vs Case 2, Case 3), the feature vector lengths varied, but the number of differences were same. Euclidean metric, being unaware of this aspect, gave us the same distance. But we can presume that, given a shorter vector length in Case 1, the difference would be much more significant in Case 1 than that of Case 2 and Case 3. When we inspect Case 2 and Case 3 (where the feature vector lengths are same), there is a significant difference in the percentage of positive features between the two cases. Given that, the implication of the two-vector difference is more in Case 2 than that of Case 3. We need to explore some more distance functions or metrics which will have a higher suitability to capture the true dissimilarities and similarities of the multi-label, binary-nominal feature vectors (in the two given contexts). We will use this example in later parts of this example, wherever we require it.

4   Exploration

We explore the pertinence of each of four distance functions in three contexts. In our first study, we use a state-of-the-art multi-label learner, Classifier Chain [13] where a k-nearest neighborhood classifier is used as the base classifier. We run four different instances of it. A different distance function (described in the previous section) is used in each of these four instances. In a similar fashion, in our second study, we employ Binary Relevance classifier [15] with k-nearest neighborhood classifier as the base classifier. In our third study, we perform the experiments on another state-of-the art approach, RAKEL-d (without overlap) [19] with k-nearest neighborhood classifier as the base classifier.

Classifier Chain (CC) is a higher order approach of multi-label learning where the label correlations are also taken into account. On the contrary, Binary Relevance (BR) classifier is a first-order learning approach, which is unaware of the learning of the remaining labels. The working principle of RAKEL-d is to learn a set of multiclass classifiers obtained through powersets of non-overlapping subsets of labels). Classifier Chain incorporates label correlation by packing the input space of succeeding labels with the outputs of the preceding ones. The competence of these three methods is well established in multi-label domain [24]. The modus operandi of each is significantly different from each other. We select these three distinct and non-overlapping approaches to find the suitability of the distance functions diversified multi-label contexts. We have used k-nearest neighborhood classifier (as a base classifier) in all three cases as its working protocol is based on distance between the points only. In the following paragraph, we briefly describe our thoughts for selecting these four distance functions.

- *Euclidean distance*: The most widely used distance function and is indicative of the disagreements of the feature vector components. It is used as a baseline.
- *Hamming distance*: It uses a scaling with respect to the number of features. Hence it is aware of the disagreements of the features values as well as the total number of features.
- *Jaccard distance*: It gives zero weightage the zero matches and ignores them in distance computation. It can be employed to tackle the sparsity of the features (class-imbalance of features). Jaccard distance is particularly helpful, when the number of zero matches are considerably high.
- *Kulsinski distance*: This distance function is also useful in tackling class-imbalance of feature, specially when the number of 1's outnumbers the number of zeros. The all-one matches are ignored in kulsinski distance computation.

4.1   The Proposed Ensemble

We construct an ensemble of classifiers where we consider two classifiers
- i]$Classifier_j$ -*jaccard* distance is used for modelling the classifier and prediction of the test points and ii] $Classifier_k$-*kulsinski* distance is used for modelling the classifier and prediction of the test points. We integrate the predictions and scores from these two classifiers to obtain the final classification results.

We compute the pairwise distances of the points using jaccard and kulsinski separately and compute the overall variance in the distances (for each function). If the variance obtained (using a specific distance function) is high, we can say that the function is able to capture the dispersion (as well as separation) of the data in a given space. Hence, for a dataset we are motivated to assign more weightage to the classifier which is trained using a distance function that returned more variance. We assign weights to the predictions from $Classifier_j$ and $Classifier_k$ in accordance with the variances of *jaccard* distances values and *kulsinski* distance values respectively. We integrate the two of them to obtain the final prediction from the ensemble. Let D_j and D_k denote the population mean of the pair-wise distances for a given set of points with respect to jaccard and kulsinski functions respectively. Let $d_j(\cdot, \cdot)$ and $d_k(\cdot, \cdot)$ be the jaccard and kulsinski distance functions. Let $\mathbf{x}_1, \mathbf{x}_2, \ldots, \mathbf{x}_n$ be the points in the dataset.

$$D_j = \frac{1}{\binom{n}{2}} \sum_{j=1,\ i \neq j}^{n} \sum_{i=1}^{n} d_j(\mathbf{x}_i, \mathbf{x}_j) \tag{1}$$

Similarly, we obtain D_k.

$$D_k = \frac{1}{\binom{n}{2}} \sum_{j=1,\ i \neq j}^{n} \sum_{i=1}^{n} d_k(\mathbf{x}_i, \mathbf{x}_j) \tag{2}$$

We compute the weights w_j and w_k for $Classifier_j$ and $Classifier_k$ from D_j and D_k. We may note that $w_j + w_k = 1$.

$$w_j = \frac{D_j}{D_k + D_j} \tag{3}$$

$$w_k = \frac{D_k}{D_k + D_j} \tag{4}$$

Let y^l_{ij} and y^l_{ik} be the predictions for instance $\mathbf{x}_i$ for some label l from $Classifier_j$ and $Classifier_k$ respectively. Let $scores^l_{ij}$ and $scores^l_{ik}$ be the prediction probabilities of $\mathbf{x}_i$ with respect to the positive class of l from $Classifier_j$ and $Classifier_k$ respectively. Let y^l_i and $scores^l_i$ the final prediction and prediction probability with respect to the positive class of label l for instance $\mathbf{x}_i$.

$$y^l_i = \begin{cases} 1, & \text{if} (y^l_{ij} \times w_j + y^l_{ik} \times w_k) > 0 \\ 0, & \text{otherwise} \end{cases} \tag{5}$$

$$scores^l_i = scores^l_{ij} \times w_l + scores^l_{ik} \times w_k \tag{6}$$

We empirically evaluate the suitability of the distance functions and the proposed ensemble by evaluating their performance scores in an experimental study, which is described in the next section.

5 Experimental Study

The empirical study is devoted to evaluate the effectiveness of different distance functions for binary-nominal, multi-label datasets. This section describes the datasets, experimental setup and evaluating metrics involved in the study. We have taken five binary-nominal, multi-label datasets in our study and their statistics are given in Table 1. The datasets are obtained from MULAN[1] and MEKA[2]. In Table 1, *instances*, *inputs* and *labels* indicate the total number of instances, features, and the number of labels respectively. *Type* indicates if the input space is numeric or nominal. *Cardinality* calculates the average number of labels per instance, and Cardinality scaled with respect to the number of labels is reported as *Density*. All the datasets have binary, nominal features. Two multi-label classifiers, Binary Relevance classifier and Classifier Chain are used in our experimental study. In each case, the base classifer is k-nearest neighbor classifier with $k = 5$. We have used *four* metrics *micro F_1*, *macro F_1*, *hamming loss* and *average precision* to evaluate the performance of the classifiers.

We discuss the results and analysis of our experiment in the next section.

---

[1] http://mulan.sourceforge.net/datasets-mlc.html.
[2] http://meka.sourceforge.net/.

Table 1. Description of datasets

Dataset	Instances	Inputs	Labels	Type	Cardinality	Density
Medical	978	144	14	Nominal	1.075	0.077
Enron	1702	50	24	Nominal	3.113	0.130
Llog	1460	100	18	Nominal	0.851	0.047
Corel5k	5000	499	44	Nominal	2.241	0.050
Slashdot	3782	53	14	Nominal	1.134	0.081

6 Results and Analysis

We have randomly partitioned each dataset into a training set and a test set. We have performed our experiment in the Hold-out settings where i] the training set and the test set are mutually exclusive and exhaustive ii] the training set and the test set comprises of 50% data instances. The training set is used to model the classifier and the test set is used for prediction. We conduct three studies – each one is devoted to a particular classifier (Binary Relevance, Classifier Chain and Rakel-d). Five sets of outputs are obtained in each study, where the first four sets are dedicated to the use of four distance functions (*euclidean*, *hamming*, *jaccard* and *kulsinski*)and the fifth set corresponds to the output from the *ensemble*. The process is repeated 10 times in each case for each dataset. The mean values obtained on *micro* F_1, *macro* F_1, *hamming loss* and *average precision* are reported in Tables 2, 3, and 4. Firstly, we analyze the outcomes of the four distance metrics. The scores obtained from Tables 2, 3, and 4 are in congruence with each other. All the tables indicate that *jaccard* distance function (which is focused on handling the sparsity of features and ignores the zero-zero matchings) is most effective for learning binary-nominal, multi-label datasets. In 49 out of 60 cases ($> 80\%$), the use of *jaccard* distance has given the best results among the four distance metrics *excluding the ensemble*. In most of the cases (27 out of 60), the use of *jaccard* has given more than 50% improvement in performance over *euclidean* and *hamming* distances. In the remaining 11 cases (excluding the ensemble), the best scores are obtained with the use of *kulsinski* distance function which is aware of the one-one abundances (thereby ignores them in distance computation). It is worth noting that the difference in performance between *jaccard* and *kulsinski* is not as high as that of the previous case (*jaccard* versus *euclidean* and *hamming*). *kulsinski* distance function is also focused on handling sparsity of the features (where positive-positive feature matchings outnumber the remaining combination of features). The use of *kulsinski* distance function has given the least perfect scores in case of *Llog* dataset. Overall, *jaccard* distance function has served as the most consistent distance function for learning the binary-nominal multi-label datasets. Usually, in a binary-nominal, multi-label dataset, zeros are in abundance (compared to ones) as features which results in higher number of zero-zero matchings. The zero-zero matchings (ZE) are ignored in computation of *jaccard* distance between two points and that is the likely explanation of its efficiency in binary-nominal, multi-label context. Secondly, we make a comparative study of the multi-label performance delivered by the *four* distance functions and the *ensemble*. The proposed *ensemble* has achieved the best scores in 58 out of 60 cases (> 96%). The only two remaining best cases are obtained by the use of *jaccard* distance on *Enron* dataset in *Classifier Chain* classifier. The ensemble comprises of a *jaccard* distance based classifier and a *kulsinski* distance based classifier. Each one caters to a specific component of feature imbalance – i] zero-zero matchings (ZEs) are ignored in the computation of the *jaccard* distance between the points (thereby taking care of the zero abundance), while ii] one-one matchings are ignored in the computation of the *kulsinski* distance between the points (which takes care of the one-one abundance). The complementary nature of the ensemble components contributes to the betterment of the multi-label performance across all datasets.

Table 2. Micro F_1 and Macro F_1 results for Binary Relevance based on k-nearest neighbor classifier. On *hamming loss*, a lower score is desirable, but on *micro F_1*, *macro F_1 and average precision* a higher score is desirable.

	Micro F_1 ↑					Macro F_1 ↑				
Datasets	Euclidean	Hamming	Jaccard	Kulsinski	Ensemble	Euclidean	Hamming	Jaccard	Kulsinski	Ensemble
Enron	0.3495	0.3514	0.5494	0.3897	**0.5176**	0.1973	0.1972	0.2891	0.1789	**0.2615**
Medical	0.6474	0.6402	0.6942	0.6722	**0.7129**	0.4556	0.4650	0.5346	0.5299	**0.5873**
Slashdot	0.1845	0.1774	0.4264	0.4235	**0.4504**	0.0524	0.0522	0.3119	0.3244	**0.3356**
Llog	0.1017	0.1012	0.1266	0.0421	**0.1774**	0.0582	0.0570	**0.0949**	0.0398	0.1264
Corel5k	0.0651	0.0646	0.1519	0.1509	**0.1774**	0.0397	0.0406	0.1232	0.1202	**0.1268**

	Hamming loss ↓					Average precision ↑				
Datasets	Euclidean	Hamming	Jaccard	Kulsinski	Ensemble	Euclidean	Hamming	Jaccard	Kulsinski	Ensemble
Enron	0.3598	0.3606	0.2349	0.3780	**0.1880**	0.2487	0.2500	0.2500	0.2098	**0.3247**
Medical	0.1060	0.1034	0.0906	0.0917	**0.0778**	0.5788	0.5773	0.6174	0.6053	**0.6434**
Slashdot	0.6570	0.6481	0.3203	0.3227	**0.2983**	0.1365	0.1377	0.3279	0.3303	**0.3458**
Llog	0.4670	0.4672	0.3914	0.4525	**0.3129**	0.1043	0.1049	0.1373	0.0903	**0.1654**
Corel5k	0.6149	0.6152	0.4818	0.4834	**0.4789**	0.0923	0.0921	0.0987	0.1230	**0.1421**

Table 3. Micro F_1,Macro F_1, *hamming loss* and *averaage precision* results for Classifier Chain based on k-nearest neighbor classifier. On *hamming loss*, a lower score is desirable, but on *micro F_1, macro F_1 and average precision* a higher score is desirable.

	Micro F_1 ↑					Macro F_1 ↑				
Datasets	Euclidean	Hamming	Jaccard	Kulsinski	Ensemble	Euclidean	Hamming	Jaccard	Kulsinski	Ensemble
Enron	0.3327	0.3351	**0.5462**	0.4047	0.5132	0.1753	0.1765	**0.2896**	0.1784	0.2608
Medical	0.6610	0.6612	0.6974	0.6778	**0.7097**	0.0521	0.0527	0.3389	0.3392	**0.3474**
Slashdot	0.1756	0.1757	0.4406	0.4304	**0.4558**	0.0535	0.0536	0.1090	0.0437	**0.1193**
Llog	0.1065	0.1036	0.1333	0.0444	**0.1732**	0.0464	0.0501	0.1452	0.1383	**0.1484**
Corel5k	0.0702	0.0721	0.1783	0.1745	**0.1792**	0.0885	0.0897	0.1403	0.1388	**0.1436**

	Hamming loss ↓					Average precision ↑				
Datasets	Euclidean	Hamming	Jaccard	Kulsinski	Ensemble	Euclidean	Hamming	Jaccard	Kulsinski	Ensemble
Enron	0.3830	0.3806	0.2451	0.3740	**0.1929**	0.2451	0.2450	0.3019	0.2052	**0.3262**
Medical	0.1242	0.1264	0.1085	0.1227	**0.0829**	0.5609	0.5570	0.5947	0.5539	**0.6456**
Slashdot	0.6559	0.6586	0.3194	0.3223	**0.2949**	0.1276	0.1260	0.3311	0.3332	**0.3503**
Llog	0.4588	0.4585	0.3853	0.4501	**0.3039**	0.1015	0.1014	0.1328	0.0904	**0.1616**
Corel5k	0.6438	0.6425	0.4892	0.4909	**0.4821**	0.0885	0.0897	0.1403	0.1388	**0.1436**

Table 4. Micro F_1, Macro F_1, *average precision* and *haming loss* results for RAKEL-D classifier based on k-nearest neighbor classifier. On *hamming loss*, a lower score is desirable, but on *micro F_1*, *macro F_1 and average precision* a higher score is desirable.

	Micro F_1 ↑					Macro F_1 ↑				
Datasets	Euclidean	Hamming	Jaccard	Kulsinski	Ensemble	Euclidean	Hamming	Jaccard	Kulsinski	Ensemble
Enron	0.6505	0.6494	0.6852	0.6740	**0.7011**	0.4339	0.4503	0.5336	0.5193	**0.5821**
Medical	0.6413	0.6396	0.6865	0.6889	**0.7093**	0.4321	0.4512	0.5318	0.5674	**0.5884**
Slashdot	0.1778	0.1811	0.4331	0.4332	**0.4589**	0.0501	0.0530	0.3144	0.3255	**0.3447**
Llog	0.1083	0.1065	0.1553	0.0746	**0.1863**	0.0548	0.0544	0.1113	0.0535	**0.1329**
Corel5k	0.0718	0.0671	0.1596	0.1537	**0.1715**	0.0418	0.0416	0.1226	0.1191	**0.1301**
	Hamming loss ↓					Average precision ↑				
Datasets	Euclidean	Hamming	Jaccard	Kulsinski	Ensemble	Euclidean	Hamming	Jaccard	Kulsinski	Ensemble
Enron	0.1236	0.1261	0.1000	0.1110	**0.0760**	0.5729	0.5570	0.5972	0.5821	**0.6518**
Medical	0.1173	0.1201	0.0942	0.0912	**0.0678**	0.5593	0.5459	0.5923	0.5894	**0.6565**
Slashdot	0.6561	0.6446	0.3219	0.3196	**0.2990**	0.1391	0.1384	0.3284	0.3345	**0.3472**
Llog	0.4684	0.4670	0.3939	0.4506	**0.3113**	0.1015	0.1024	0.1360	0.0911	**0.1631**
Corel5k	0.6188	0.6160	0.4830	0.4839	**0.4801**	0.0926	0.0942	0.1427	0.1406	**0.1438**

7   Conclusion

In this work, we have explored the use of different distance functions in binary-nominal context (features) of multi-label datasets. Four different distance functions have been used to address the specific characteristics of such datasets, namely – feature imbalance, zero-zero abundance and one-one abundance. The outcomes of the study indicate that the feature imbalances do play some role in aggravating the performance of such datasets. The use of *jaccard* and *kulsinski* distance function helps in tackling the feature imbalances. The simulation of the classifiers using these two distance functions is shown to improve the macro F_1 and micro F_1 scores over the others. Our study indicates *jaccard* distance is most effective among the chosen distance function in learning the binary-nominal, multi-label datasets. The results from the empirical study further establishes that the use an ensemble of classifiers – one of which is modelled on *jaccard* and the other is modelled on *kulsinski* improves the learning of such datasets to a significant extent (over the four chosen distance functions). In our future work, we would like to carry out this investigation in nominal, multi-label features with more than two values and also mixed feature space containing both nominal and numeric features.

References

1. Chen, W., Yan, J., Zhang, B., Chen, Z., Yang, Q.: Document transformation for multi-label feature selection in text categorization. In: Seventh IEEE International Conference on Data Mining (ICDM 2007), pp. 451–456. IEEE (2007)
2. Cheng, W., Hüllermeier, E.: Combining instance-based learning and logistic regression for multilabel classification. Mach. Learn. **76**(2–3), 211–225 (2009)

3. Cheng, W., Hüllermeier, E., Dembczynski, K.J.: Bayes optimal multilabel classification via probabilistic classifier chains. In: Proceedings of the 27th International Conference on Machine Learning (ICML-10), pp. 279–286 (2010)
4. Daniels, Z., Metaxas, D.: Addressing imbalance in multi-label classification using structured hellinger forests. In: Proceedings of the AAAI Conference on Artificial Intelligence, vol. 31 (2017)
5. Gibaja, E., Ventura, S.: Multi-label learning: a review of the state of the art and ongoing research. Wiley Interdiscip. Rev. Data Mining Knowl. Discov. 4(6), 411–444 (2014)
6. Gjorgjioski, V., Kocev, D., Džeroski, S.: Comparison of distances for multi-label classification with PCTs. In: Proceedings of the Slovenian KDD Conference on Data Mining and Data Warehouses (SiKDD'11), vol. 8 (2011)
7. Kanj, S., Abdallah, F., Denoeux, T., Tout, K.: Editing training data for multi-label classification with the k-nearest neighbor rule. Pattern Anal. Appl. 19(1), 145–161 (2016)
8. Kurata, G., Xiang, B., Zhou, B.: Improved neural network-based multi-label classification with better initialization leveraging label co-occurrence. In: Proceedings of the 2016 Conference of the North American Chapter of the Association for Computational Linguistics: Human Language Technologies, pp. 521–526 (2016)
9. Liu, B., Tsoumakas, G.: Synthetic oversampling of multi-label data based on local label distribution. arXiv preprint arXiv:1905.00609 (2019)
10. Moyano, J.M., Gibaja, E.L., Cios, K.J., Ventura, S.: Review of ensembles of multi-label classifiers: models, experimental study and prospects. Inf. Fusion 44, 33–45 (2018)
11. Narayan, S., Gupta, A., Khan, S., Khan, F.S., Shao, L., Shah, M.: Discriminative region-based multi-label zero-shot learning. arXiv preprint arXiv:2108.09301 (2021)
12. Nazmi, S., Yan, X., Homaifar, A., Doucette, E.: Evolving multi-label classification rules by exploiting high-order label correlations. Neurocomputing 417, 176–186 (2020)
13. Read, J., Pfahringer, B., Holmes, G., Frank, E.: Classifier chains for multi-label classification. Mach. Learn. 85(3), 333 (2011)
14. Sadhukhan, P., Palit, S.: Reverse-nearest neighborhood based oversampling for imbalanced, multi-label datasets. Pattern Recognit. Lett. 125, 813–820 (2019)
15. Sorower, M.S.: A literature survey on algorithms for multi-label learning. Oregon State University, Corvallis (2010)
16. Spolaôr, N., Cherman, E.A., Monard, M.C., Lee, H.D.: Relieff for multi-label feature selection. In: 2013 Brazilian Conference on Intelligent Systems, pp. 6–11. IEEE (2013)
17. Spolaôr, N., Monard, M.C., Tsoumakas, G., Lee, H.D.: A systematic review of multi-label feature selection and a new method based on label construction. Neurocomputing 180, 3–15 (2016)
18. Tanaka, E.A., Nozawa, S.R., Macedo, A.A., Baranauskas, J.A.: A multi-label approach using binary relevance and decision trees applied to functional genomics. J. Biomed. Inf. 54, 85–95 (2015)
19. Tsoumakas, G., Katakis, I., Vlahavas, I.: Random k-labelsets for multilabel classification. IEEE Trans. Knowl. Data Eng. 23(7), 1079–1089 (2011)
20. Wang, D., Zhang, S.: Unsupervised person re-identification via multi-label classification. In: Proceedings of the IEEE/CVF Conference on Computer Vision and Pattern Recognition, pp. 10981–10990 (2020)

21. Weng, W., Lin, Y., Wu, S., Li, Y., Kang, Y.: Multi-label learning based on label-specific features and local pairwise label correlation. Neurocomputing **273**, 385–394 (2018)
22. Yan, X., Wu, Q., Sheng, V.S.: A double weighted Naive Bayes with niching cultural algorithm for multi-label classification. Int. J. Pattern Recogn. Artif. Intell. **30**(06), 1650013 (2016)
23. Zhang, M.L., Li, Y.K., Yang, H., Liu, X.Y.: Towards class-imbalance aware multi-label learning. IEEE Trans. Cybern. (2020)
24. Zhang, M.L., Zhou, Z.H.: A review on multi-label learning algorithms. IEEE Trans. Knowl. Data Eng. **26**(8), 1819–1837 (2013)

Feature Selection Methods for Uplift Modeling and Heterogeneous Treatment Effect

Zhenyu Zhao[1(✉)], Yumin Zhang[2], Totte Harinen[3(✉)], and Mike Yung[4]

[1] Tencent, Palo Alto, USA
zzy287@gmail.com
[2] Purdue University, West Lafayette, USA
zhan2013@purdue.edu
[3] Toyota Research Institute, Los Altos, USA
th.harinen@gmail.com
[4] Spotify, San Franciso, USA

Abstract. Uplift modeling is a causal learning technique that estimates subgroup-level treatment effects. It is commonly used in industry and elsewhere for tasks such as targeting ads. In a typical setting, uplift models can take thousands of features as inputs, which is costly and results in problems such as overfitting and poor model interpretability. Consequently, there is a need to select a subset of the most important features for modeling. However, traditional methods for doing feature selection are not fit for the task because they are designed for standard machine learning models whose target is importantly different from uplift models. To address this, this paper introduces a set of feature selection methods explicitly designed for uplift modeling, drawing inspiration from statistics and information theory. Empirical evaluations are conducted on the proposed methods on publicly available datasets, demonstrating the advantages of the proposed methods compared to traditional feature selection. We make the proposed methods publicly available as a part of the *CausalML* open-source package.

Keywords: Feature selection · Uplift modeling · Causal learning

1 Introduction

Uplift modeling [8,10,12,13,18,21,24,29,31,33–36,38], also known as heterogeneous treatment effect estimation or incremental modeling, is a technique designed to estimate the individual treatment effect (ITE) or the conditional average treatment effect (CATE) of an intervention. It is often used for user targeting, budget allocation, and personalization applications.

In practice, there is often a rich set of features that can be used to build an uplift model. However, using all of the available features in the model can lead to computational inefficiency, over-fitting, high maintenance workload, and

© IFIP International Federation for Information Processing 2022
Published by Springer Nature Switzerland AG 2022
I. Maglogiannis et al. (Eds.): AIAI 2022, IFIP AICT 647, pp. 217–230, 2022.
https://doi.org/10.1007/978-3-031-08337-2_19

model interpretation challenges. A feature selection method screens the large feature space and picks the important features for the model, and then the uplift model can be built based on the most important features. As Radcliffe and Surry [26] noted, feature selection is actually of greater importance to improve model quality and stability in uplift modeling than in conventional modeling because uplift models estimate the difference between two outcomes, which is often small relative to the direct outcomes (which conventional models estimate), increasing the risk of over-fitting markedly.

This work contributes to the feature selection of uplift modeling from both methodological and empirical perspectives, specifically:

- Five filter methods and two types of embedded methods are proposed as feature selection methods for uplift modeling.
- These feature selection methods are empirically evaluated and compared with ordinary feature selection methods on two data sets. One synthetic dataset is generated for this study and made available online [37], and the other dataset is from Megafon Uplift Competition training data [1].
- This study demonstrates that the ordinary feature selection methods for conventional machine learning models are sub-optimal in the uplift modeling context.
- To make these feature selection methods easily accessible for broad applications, the proposed methods are implemented in the *CausalML* [7] open-source package.

To simplify the discussion, the rest of this paper assumes the outcome variable to be binary, covering most common use cases such as advertisement click-through, new user conversion, and existing user retention.

The structure of the paper is as follows. Section 2 discusses existing work on feature selection methods for uplift modeling, and the difference from feature selection for conventional models and observational causal inference. Section 3 reviews the critical concepts of uplift modeling. Section 4 introduces five filter methods and three embedded methods for uplift modeling. Section 5 evaluates these methods with benchmark methods on two data sets. Finally, Sect. 7 summarizes the findings and makes recommendations for choosing and using the proper feature selection methods for uplift modeling applications.

2   Related Work

Feature selection methods for conventional machine learning problems have been well studied [4–6,32]. Nevertheless, as this paper will show, these methods are ineffective for solving feature selection problems for uplift modeling. The main reason is that such methods try to select predictive features of the outcome variable, which may not be the features related with treatment effect variability.

This paper assumes the data for uplift modeling is collected from a randomized experiment (a.k.a A/B testing [17]), which is often the case in practice. It is essential to differentiate the feature selection methods for uplift modeling based on data from randomized experiments and the feature selection methods developed for observational causal inference. Feature selection algorithms for observational causal inference, such as the lasso-based approach proposed by [30], are designed to help models whose goal is to reduce confounding. These methods are out of scope for discussion in this paper as the framework and goals are different.

Several feature selection methods for uplift modeling purposes have been discussed in the literature. A filter method named net information value (NIV) [19] is built based on the net weight of evidence (NWOE), where NWOE is the difference between the weight of evidence (WOE) of treatment and WOE of control, and NIV is a weighted average of NWOE. Radcliffe [26] introduced the pessimistic qini estimate that uses one feature to train an uplift model at a time, and the resulting model accuracy measure (qini) is taken as the feature importance score. Certain regularizations are added to this method to improve stability. The pessimistic qini method can be more computationally costly as it involves training and potentially tuning an uplift model.

3   Uplift Models

Uplift modeling can be viewed as a way to estimate ITE using machine learning models. Following the commonly used Neyman-Rubin causal model [15,22,27, 28], the ITE for unit $i \in \{1, 2, ..., N\}$ can be expressed as:

$$Y_i(1) - Y_i(0) \tag{1}$$

where $Y_i(1)$ and $Y_i(0)$ denotes the outcome variable for individual i under treatment condition and control condition respectively.

A closely related concept is the conditional average treatment effect (CATE). Let $X = (X_1, X_2, ..., X_M)$ denote M covariates (also called features) and $x_i = (x_{i1}, x_{i2}, ..., x_{iM})$ denote the observed realisation of X for unit i. The conditional average treatment effect (CATE) is the expected treatment effect within groups of units that have a similar realisations of X:

$$\tau(x) := E[Y(1) - Y(0) \mid X = x] \tag{2}$$

In practice, many uplift modeling approaches train on CATEs. [13]

There are two main categories of uplift models. The first category is known as meta-learners ([18,23]). The models in this category are built based on conventional machine learning models as base learners in such a way that they can estimate CATEs, such as the "*TwoModel*" approach (a.k.a. *T-Learner* [14]), *X-Learner* [18], and *R-Learner* [23]. The other category of uplift models is known as uplift trees or causal trees. These models are based on modifying the loss functions within the classification or regression trees, such that the split is optimized for estimating the heterogeneous treatment effect [2,3,11,12,29,34]. In this paper, feature selection methods are evaluated with models from both uplift modeling categories to test the generality of the proposed feature selection methods.

4 Feature Selection Methods for Uplift Modeling

To identify the important features for uplift modeling, we propose both filter methods, which are easy and fast to use as a screening step for the data, and embedded methods, which are a by-product from training an uplift model.

4.1 Filter Methods

As discussed above, a feature's importance in an uplift modeling task depends on how well it predicts the CATE. A filter method calculates the importance score for each feature based on the marginal relationship between the treatment effect and the feature. It can be used for quickly screening the feature space and selecting important features for downstream modeling tasks.

F Filter. The F filter method is named after the F statistic for testing the significance of the interaction between the treatment indicator and a feature in linear regression. To capture possible nonlinear associations between features and the treatment effect, we extend this method by including higher-order terms of the features in the regression. For a given feature X_j ($j \in \{1, ..., M\}$), the heterogeneous treatment effect of X_j can be studied in the following regression:

$$Y = \alpha + \delta I + \sum_{r=1}^{R} \beta_r X_j^r + \sum_{r=1}^{R} \theta_r I X_j^r + \epsilon \tag{3}$$

where Y stands for the response variable, I is the treatment indicator (1 for treatment, and 0 for control), R is a hyperparameter controlling the order to be studied (X_j^r is X_j to the power of r), ϵ represents the error term, and α, δ, β, θ are the coefficients, where the significance of θ indicates the strength of the heterogeneous treatment effect in the dimension of X_j.

The significance of θ can be studied by contrasting the model above with the following reduced model:

$$Y = \alpha' + \delta' I + \sum_{r=1}^{R} \beta_r' X_j^r + \epsilon' \tag{4}$$

The feature importance score by F filter method is defined as the F-statistic for the coefficient of the interaction term:

$$F = \frac{(RSS - RSS')/R}{RSS'/(N - R - 2)} \tag{5}$$

with

$$RSS = \sum_{i=1}^{N} (y_i - \hat{\alpha} - \hat{\delta} I_i - \sum_{r=1}^{R} \hat{\beta}_r x_{ij}^r - \sum_{r=1}^{R} \hat{\theta}_r I x_{ij}^r)$$

$$RSS' = \sum_{i=1}^{N} (y_i - \hat{\alpha}' - \hat{\delta}' I_i - \sum_{r=1}^{R} \hat{\beta}_r' x_{ij}^r)$$

where N is the total number of observations, RSS is the Residual Sum of Squares for fitted model 3 and RSS' is the Residual Sum of Squares for fitted model 4, that are calculated by plugging in the sample data and fitted coefficients.

This F statistic follows an F distribution with $(R, N - R - 2)$ degrees of freedom assuming that the true value of θ equals 0. A byproduct of the F filter method is a p-value for the correlation between the feature and the treatment effect, which can be used to deem whether heterogeneity in a given feature dimension counts as statistically significant.

Setting the hyperparameter $R > 1$ will enable the F filter to capture the nonlinear relationship between feature and HTE. As empirical results show in Sect. 5, F filter with $R = 2$ outperforms F filter with $R = 1$ remarkably.

The F filter method works for both the regression uplift modeling problem where Y is continuous and the classification uplift modeling problem where Y is binary. Both continuous and binary features can be evaluated by the F filter. A multi-class categorical feature can fit in this method with one-hot-encoding approach (transforming one multi-class feature to multiple binary features).

LR Filter. The LR (Likelihood Ratio) filter defines the feature importance score as the likelihood ratio test statistic for the interaction coefficient in a logistic regression model. Similar to the F filter, the LR filter for any feature X_j is constructed by contrasting two logistic regression models:

$$logit(p(X_j, I; \alpha, \delta, \beta_1, ..., \beta_R, \theta_1, ..., \theta_R)) = \alpha + \delta I + \sum_{r=1}^{R} \beta_r X_j^r + \sum_{r=1}^{R} \theta_r I X_j^r \quad (6)$$

$$logit(p(X_j, I; \alpha', \delta', \beta'_1, ..., \beta'_R)) = \alpha' + \delta' I + \sum_{r=1}^{R} \beta'_r X_j^r \quad (7)$$

where $p(X_j, I; \alpha, \delta, \beta_1, ..., \beta_R, \theta_1, ..., \theta_R)$ and $p(X_j, I; \alpha', \delta', \beta'_1, ..., \beta'_R)$ are probability representations of $Pr(Y = 1|X_j, I)$ under two functions, and R is a hyperparameter.

The significance of interaction coefficient θ can be tested through a likelihood ratio test. Let $\hat{\alpha}, \hat{\delta}, \hat{\beta}_1, ..., \hat{\beta}_R, \hat{\theta}_1, ..., \hat{\theta}_R, \hat{\alpha}', \hat{\delta}', \hat{\beta}'_1, ..., \hat{\beta}'_R$ denote the fitted coefficient estimates for the logistic regression models. The likelihood ratio statistic can be calculated by plugging in the sample data and fitted coefficients:

$$LR = -2 \sum_{i=1}^{N} [y_i log(p(x_{ij}, I_i; \hat{\alpha}, \hat{\delta}, \hat{\beta}_1, ..., \hat{\beta}_R, \hat{\theta}_1, ..., \hat{\theta}_R)) \quad (8)$$

$$+ (1 - y_i) log(p(x_{ij}, I_i; \hat{\alpha}, \hat{\delta}, \hat{\beta}_1, ..., \hat{\beta}_R, \hat{\theta}_1, ..., \hat{\theta}_R)) \quad (9)$$

$$- y_i log(p(x_{ij}, I_i; \hat{\alpha}', \hat{\delta}', \hat{\beta}'_1, ..., \hat{\beta}'_R)) \quad (10)$$

$$- (1 - y_i) log(p(x_{ij}, I_i; \hat{\alpha}', \hat{\delta}', \hat{\beta}'_1, ..., \hat{\beta}'_R)] \quad (11)$$

The LR statistic is taken as the feature importance score by the LR filter. Assuming that the true value of θ is 0, then the LR statistic follows a χ_R^2 distribution. This LR filter method can also produce a p-value for feature importance.

Similar to the F filter, setting $R > 1$ for the LR filter extends its capability for capturing the nonlinear importance of features.

The LR filter method can be used for categorical (binary and multi-class) outcome, as well as continuous and binary features. Similar to the F filter, the LR filter can be applied to a multi-class categorical feature with one-hot-encoding approach.

Bin-Based Divergence Filter (KL Filter, ED Filter, Chi Filter). The section introduces three variants of the bin-based divergence filter method, which are direct applications from the split criteria for uplift trees proposed by [29]. Similar to the NIV method [19], for a given feature, the bin-based method first divides the samples into S (preferably equally sized) bins, where S is a hyper-parameter. The importance score is defined as the divergence measure of the treatment effect over these S bins.

Formally, let p_k and q_k denote the sample proportion of class $Y = 1$ in the kth ($k = 1, \ldots, K$) bin for the treatment group and control group respectively. The KL (Kullback-Leibler divergence) filter, ED (squared Euclidean Distance), and Chi (chi-squared divergence) filter feature importance scores are defined as follows:

$$\Delta_{KL} := \sum_{k=1}^{K} \frac{N_k}{N} KL(p_k, q_k) = \sum_{k=1}^{K} \frac{N_k}{N} [p_k \log \frac{p_k}{q_k} + (1 - p_k) \log \frac{1 - p_k}{1 - q_k}] \quad (12)$$

$$\Delta_{ED} := \sum_{k=1}^{K} \frac{N_k}{N} ED(p_k, q_k) = 2 \sum_{k=1}^{K} \frac{N_k}{N} (p_k - q_k)^2 \quad (13)$$

$$\Delta_{Chi} := \sum_{k=1}^{K} \frac{N_k}{N} \chi^2(p_k, q_k) = \sum_{k=1}^{K} \frac{N_k}{N} [\frac{(p_k - q_k)^2}{q_k} + \frac{(p_k - q_k)^2}{1 - q_k}] \quad (14)$$

where N_k is the sample size in the kth bin.

Even though these bin-based filter methods share the same divergence measures as an uplift tree, they are simpler to implement and compute than training an uplift model. For data with M features, the time complexity of the bin-based filter methods is linear with sample size, $O(M \cdot N)$, while the time complexity of building a single complete uplift tree is $O(M \cdot N \log(N))$.

The bin-based divergence filter method can be directly applied to categorical outcome and continuous features. For discrete features, the divergence measure can be applied without the binning step.

4.2   Embedded Methods

The final category of methods that we propose, the embedded methods, obtain feature importance as a byproduct of training an uplift model. The way in which the importance scores are calculated differs depending on whether the target model is a meta-learner or an uplift tree. The embedded methods can be used for continuous and categorical outcomes, as well as continuous and discrete features.

Embedded Methods by Meta-learners. For meta-learners, feature importance can be obtained from the base-learners, which are the composite models making up a meta-learner.

The simplest meta-learner, the *OneModel* or *S-Learner* [20], is based on just one base-learner and predicts treatment effects as the difference between $E[Y \mid X = x, I = 1]$ and $E[Y \mid X = x, I = 0]$ where I is the treatment indicator. Because the importance scores from the single base-learner in *S-Learner* tend to be similar to an outcome based model (the only difference between the two is that the base-learner in *S-Learner* has a treatment indicator as an additional feature), we will not differentiate these two embedded methods and let *Outcome* embedded represent these two methods in the following discussion.

The *TwoModel* embedded feature selection method is derived from the *TwoModel* uplift model, which feature importance score is defined as the sum of its embedded importance scores produced by the two base-learners. As the embedded methods derived from Meta-learners are based on ordinary feature selection methods in base learners (conventional model), the feature selection performance for uplift modeling is expected to be poor as it does not consider HTE during the process.

Embedded Methods by Uplift Trees. For uplift trees, the importance score for a feature can be defined as the cumulative contribution to the loss function during the tree node splits in the trees. This is similar to the well-known embedded feature importance for standard classification trees, except the score is obtained from an uplift tree with a special splitting criterion. At each split, we calculate the gain in the distribution divergence:

$$\Delta = \sum_{k \in \{\text{left, right}\}} \frac{n_k}{n} D\left(p_k, q_k\right) - D(p, q), \tag{15}$$

where n is the sample size in the parent node, n_k is the sample size in the child node, $D()$ is divergence measure defined as $KL(), ED(), \chi^2()$ in Eq. (12), p and q denote the proportion of $Y = 1$ for the treatment group and control group separately in the parent node, and p_k, q_k are corresponding proportions in the child notes. The feature importance score is calculated by summing over all the Δ from the tree node splits where the feature is used.

The time complexity for embedded methods depend on the learners used. For random forest algorithms, it is at order of $O(t_{tree} \cdot m_s \cdot N \cdot \log(N))$ where t_{tree} is the number of trees and m_s is the maximum features considered in each split.

5   Empirical Evaluation

This section compares different feature selection methods empirically, and evaluate their performance consistency with different uplift models.

5.1   Experiment 1: Evaluation with Synthetic Data

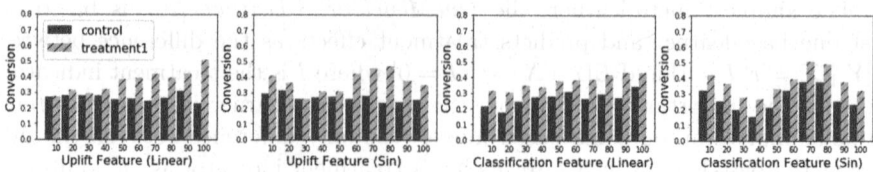

Fig. 1. Feature association pattern with outcome by experiment group in Experiment 1. The first two plots demonstrate a heterogeneous treatment effect associated with uplift features in a linear and sine pattern respectively. The last two plots illustrate classification features are correlated with outcome, but not treatment effect.

For evaluating the feature selection methods, a specific synthetic data generation process is designed, such that the data contains three types of features: (1) uplift features influencing the treatment effect on the conversion probability; (2) classification features affecting the conversion probability but independent of the treatment effect; and (3) irrelevant features that are independent of both conversion probability and the treatment effect.

The binary response variable is generated based on the probability $Pr(Y = 1|X, I)$, where X denotes the feature vector and I is the treatment indicator. Assuming there are m_1 classification features and m_2 uplift features, the probability $Pr(Y = 1|X, I)$ itself is modeled as:

$$logit(Pr(Y = 1|X, I)) = a_1 + \sum_{j=1}^{m_1} f_j(X_j)\beta_j + I \cdot (a_2 + \sum_{j=m_1+1}^{m_1+m_2} f_j(X_j)\beta_j) + \epsilon$$

where $a_1, a_2, \{\beta_j\}_1^{m1+m2}$ are coefficient parameters, ϵ is a random noise added, $\{f_j(\cdot)\}_1^{m1+m2}$ is transformation function for the features, such that features have six types of association with the outcome: linear, quadratic, cubic, ReLU (Rectified Linear Unit [9]), trigonometric function sine, and cosine. Example feature patterns are plotted in Fig. 1.

In this study, there are 36 features in total, including $m_1 = 10$ classification features, $m_2 = 6$ uplift features, and $m_3 = 20$ irrelevant features. The values for the coefficients are set such that the average control conversion probability is around 0.2 and the average treatment effect is around 0.1. The generated synthetic data is published online [37].

Eleven feature selection methods are evaluated, including six uplift filter methods (F filter, LR filter, KL filter, Chi filter, ED filter, NIV filter), two uplift embedded methods (*TwoModel* embedded and KL embedded), two ordinary filter methods (ordinary Mutual Information and ordinary F Score [25]), and one ordinary embedded method *Outcome embedded* as a benchmark [25]. For F filter and LR filter, variants (F, F2, F3, LR, LR2, LR3) are created based on $R =$

$1, 2, 3$. For the bin-based filter methods, the number of bins is set at 10 as default. Four uplift models are used to evaluate the performance of the feature selection methods: *TwoModel, X-Learner, R-Learner*, and uplift random forest (with KL criterion), given the results are similar in the order of feature selection method performance, only *TwoModel* results are presented in the paper. A random forest classifier ($n\_estimators = 10, max\_depth = 10, min\_child\_samples = 100$) [25] is used as the base learner.

Each simulation trial consists of four steps. First, the data generator simulates the data with a new random seed and randomly splits the data into training and testing (with $50\% : 50\%$ ratio). Second, each feature selection method is applied to the training data and ranks the features by importance score. Third, for each feature selection method, the top m^* (for $m^* \in \{2, 4, 6, 8, 10\}$) features are used to build uplift models using training data. Fourth, the testing data is used to evaluate the accuracy of the uplift models based on the top features selected by each feature selection method. Each trial generates $20,000$ samples ($10,000$ for control and $10,000$ for treatment) and the simulation study consists of $t = 50$ trials.

Table 1. RMSE (and Standard Deviation of RMSE) for estimating ITE using *TwoModel* as evaluating model based on Synthetic Data (RMSE lower the better).

Top features	2	4	6	8	10
F filter	0.183(0.005)	0.174(0.005)	0.174(0.006)	0.174(0.006)	0.174(0.007)
F2 filter	0.184(0.004)	0.163(0.003)	0.165(0.005)	0.166(0.006)	0.168(0.005)
F3 filter	0.185(0.004)	0.163(0.003)	0.163(0.005)	0.165(0.006)	0.167(0.005)
LR filter	0.184(0.005)	0.175(0.006)	0.174(0.006)	0.176(0.006)	0.175(0.006)
LR2 filter	0.184(0.004)	0.163(0.003)	0.166(0.005)	0.168(0.006)	0.170(0.005)
LR3 filter	0.186(0.004)	0.163(0.003)	0.165(0.005)	0.167(0.005)	0.168(0.005)
KL filter	0.184(0.004)	0.163(0.005)	0.153(0.006)	0.162(0.006)	0.165(0.005)
ED filter	0.184(0.003)	0.162(0.004)	0.151(0.004)	0.157(0.006)	0.160(0.005)
Chi filter	0.184(0.004)	0.163(0.005)	0.154(0.007)	0.162(0.006)	0.165(0.005)
NIV filter	0.184(0.004)	0.163(0.005)	0.152(0.006)	0.158(0.005)	0.162(0.005)
KL embedded	0.187(0.005)	0.171(0.011)	0.165(0.009)	0.165(0.008)	0.167(0.007)
TwoModel embedded	0.210(0.007)	0.198(0.010)	0.191(0.008)	0.184(0.007)	0.181(0.006)
Outcome embedded	0.212(0.006)	0.207(0.009)	0.199(0.009)	0.190(0.009)	0.185(0.008)
Ordinary FScore	0.208(0.008)	0.195(0.011)	0.185(0.008)	0.181(0.003)	0.181(0.006)
Ordinary MutualInfo	0.211(0.006)	0.207(0.009)	0.202(0.010)	0.198(0.010)	0.196(0.010)

A preferred feature selection method is expected to provide important features that lead to accurate ITE estimation by the downstream uplift model based on the features selected. Table 1 summarizes the RMSE (Root Mean Square Error) of ITE estimation and its standard deviation over synthetic data trials. As a benchmark, if all 36 features are used in an uplift model, then the RMSE by *TwoModel* is 0.186 (with standard deviation 0.003).

Table 2. Proportion of uplift features selected in top 6 positions by method (Feature Recall). The table is ranked by the 'All Uplift' column, that indicates proportion of all uplift features (6 in total) being captured in the top 6 features ranked by each method. A breakdown of feature recall score by different uplift feature pattern is presented.

Method	All uplift	Linear	Quadratic	Cubic	ReLU	Sin	Cos
F filter	55%	100%	12%	100%	100%	6%	12%
F2 filter	69.3%	100%	100%	100%	100%	4%	12%
F3 filter	70.3%	100%	100%	100%	100%	10%	12%
LR filter	55%	100%	10%	100%	100%	6%	14%
LR2 filter	69.3%	100%	100%	100%	100%	6%	10%
LR3 filter	69.3%	100%	100%	100%	100%	6%	10%
KL filter	97.7%	100%	100%	90%	100%	98%	98%
ED filter	99.7%	100%	100%	98%	100%	100%	100%
Chi filter	95.3%	100%	100%	80%	98%	98%	96%
NIV filter	98.3%	100%	100%	90%	100%	100%	100%
KL embedded	75.7%	94%	88%	82%	86%	42%	62%
TwoModel embedded	32.7%	66%	8%	22%	92%	6%	2%
Outcome embedded	23%	66%	20%	8%	42%	0%	2%
Ordinary FScore	38.7%	96%	0%	46%	88%	2%	0%
Ordinary MutualInfo	20%	24%	22%	14%	20%	12%	28%

The results show that 1) the ordinary feature selection methods (ordinary F Score and ordinary Mutual Information) have poor performance and are not suitable for selecting top features for uplift modeling; 2) the bin-based divergence filter methods (KL filter, ED filter, Chi filter, NIV filter) have consistent top performance in all scenarios, followed by KL embedded, and F2, F3, LR2, LR3 filters; 3) adding higher-order terms in F filter and LR filter ($R > 1$) improved the performance; 4) the outcome embedded method and the *TwoModel* embedded method have essentially similar logic as ordinary feature selection methods, thus failing in the tasks.

To better understand what features are selected by each method, we report the proportion of uplift features selected in top 6 positions in Table 2. The proportion is averaged across the 100 trials. The detailed breakdown by uplift feature type explains why some methods are not performing well. F filter and LR filter fail to capture quadratic features, Sin features, and Cos features. Setting $R > 1$ for these two methods improved the capability for capturing quadratic features. The ordinary filter methods and *Outcome* embedded and *TwoModel* embedded methods fail to capture uplift features in general.

5.2 Experiment 2: Evaluation with MegaFon Uplift Competition Data

This example uses a data set that is publicly available for an online competition [1], that contains $600,000$ observations and 50 features.

AUUC based on Top 20 Features

Feature Selection Method	KL-RF	TwoModel-LR	TwoModel-RF	TwoModel-LGBM	TwoModel-NN	XLearner-LR	XLearner-RF	XLearner-LGBM	XLearner-NN	RLearner-LR	RLearner-RF	RLearner-LGBM	RLearner-NN
All Features	103.1%	57.8%	115.8%	138.9%	142.9%	61.7%	131.2%	137.4%	144.5%	64.0%	123.4%	137.0%	123.9%
F1 filter	77.2%	59.5%	83.6%	92.9%	109.3%	59.0%	87.9%	94.4%	109.8%	60.7%	78.4%	91.5%	67.4%
F2 filter	107.5%	65.4%	114.5%	134.7%	141.0%	64.2%	128.6%	133.7%	138.5%	64.1%	121.8%	133.4%	136.8%
F3 filter	104.5%	65.4%	113.7%	134.7%	140.9%	64.2%	128.3%	133.7%	138.7%	64.1%	122.4%	133.6%	136.9%
LR1 filter	77.9%	57.0%	86.4%	95.2%	112.1%	57.8%	90.1%	96.1%	111.7%	61.0%	82.1%	93.6%	96.5%
LR2 filter	104.8%	58.3%	112.7%	132.4%	135.5%	58.0%	126.5%	131.6%	135.4%	62.9%	119.5%	131.1%	131.0%
LR3 filter	104.5%	58.3%	112.4%	132.4%	134.9%	58.0%	126.6%	131.6%	134.3%	63.0%	119.0%	131.2%	133.4%
KL filter	104.6%	56.1%	112.6%	132.8%	137.3%	57.6%	126.7%	131.6%	134.1%	62.2%	119.7%	131.3%	132.9%
ED filter	106.5%	63.4%	112.9%	134.0%	139.5%	62.4%	127.3%	132.8%	136.7%	62.4%	121.6%	132.2%	138.7%
Chi filter	102.3%	56.1%	112.1%	132.8%	136.8%	57.6%	126.6%	131.6%	138.1%	62.2%	120.0%	131.2%	125.6%
NIV filter	106.0%	56.1%	112.7%	132.8%	136.4%	57.7%	126.7%	131.6%	136.4%	62.2%	119.6%	131.4%	125.3%
KL embedded	107.3%	55.1%	115.3%	136.2%	143.1%	59.5%	129.9%	134.6%	142.9%	63.7%	123.5%	134.3%	142.1%
TwoModel embedded	100.2%	60.7%	109.1%	125.3%	128.3%	59.0%	119.7%	124.7%	129.9%	60.6%	112.1%	124.0%	126.0%
Outcome embedded	84.4%	56.5%	90.0%	94.3%	107.5%	54.6%	92.8%	95.9%	103.4%	56.7%	83.8%	94.5%	96.8%
Ordinary FScore	78.7%	59.2%	88.0%	99.1%	118.5%	57.3%	94.1%	99.8%	119.0%	61.5%	85.7%	97.1%	90.5%
Ordinary MutualInfo	91.0%	57.1%	97.6%	110.2%	121.1%	57.3%	103.4%	109.8%	122.4%	58.2%	94.6%	108.6%	96.5%

Uplift Model

Fig. 2. AUUC of uplift models using the top 20 selected features by different feature selection methods in the MegaFon data experiment with $300,000$ training data and $300,000$ testing data (AUUC larger the better). The Y-axis shows the feature selection method and the X-axis shows the uplift model (in a {uplift model - base learner} format) used for producing the AUUC score. The first row represents the AUUC using all 50 features as reference.

To test the generality of the feature selection methods for different uplift models, the uplift models considered include: (1) *TwoModel-LR, X-Learner-LR, R-Learner-LR* using {Logistic Regression Classifier & Linear Regression Regressor} as base learners; (2) *TwoModel-LGBM, X-Learner-LGBM, R-Learner-LGBM* using {Gradient Boosting Classifier & Gradient Boosting Regressor} from *LightGBM* implementation [16] as base learners, with hyperparameter values ($n\_estimators = 100, max\_depth = 10, min\_child\_samples = 100$); (3) *TwoModel-RF, X-Learner-RF, R-Learner-RF* using {Random Forest Classifier & Random Forest Regressor} as base learners, with hyper-parameter values ($n\_estimators = 100, max\_depth = 10, min\_samples\_leaf = 100$); (4) *TwoModel-NN, X-Learner-NN, R-Learner-NN* using {Neural Network (Multilayer Perceptron) Classifier & Neural Network Regressor} from scikit-learn [25] implementation as base learners: each contains two layers with 100 neurons on the first layer and 10 neurons on the second layer; (5) *KL-RF* as the uplift random forest using KL divergence criterion with hyper-parameter values ($n\_estimators = 20, max\_depth = 10, min\_samples\_leaf = 100$).

The evaluation with this data is conducted by equally splitting the data into training data and testing data, each with $300,000$ observations, where training data is used for feature selection and uplift modeling training, and testing data is used for evaluating the accuracy of uplift modeling. The results are summarized in Fig. 2, reporting the AUUC (area under the uplift curve) scores [13,29,31,36] from the uplift models using the top 20 features selected by each feature selection method. The relative performance of different feature selection methods can be compared within each column given the same uplift model. The results are roughly aligned with the synthetic data results, except the performance of F2, F3, LR2, LR3 filters become comparable with other bin-based divergence methods. A possible reason is that this dataset does not have extreme nonlinear feature patterns like the sine or cosine forms in the previous synthetic data. Despite the differences in uplift models, the relative order of feature selection method performance is quite consistent across different uplift models. Models using all 50 features still perform better than models using 20 features. One reason is that the sample size is large compared with the feature space, in which case over-fitting is unlikely to occur.

6   Discussion

Our experiments demonstrate that the proposed methods can select important features based on their association with heterogeneous treatment effects and outperform ordinary feature selection methods for uplift modeling tasks. The F filter and LR filter can enhance performance by adding nonlinear terms, and such methods can perform well in noisy data settings. The bin-based divergence filter methods also show good performance, although their performance is expected to suffer if the feature space makes it hard to create equal-sized bins. The embedded method with uplift random forest also perform competitively because the split criterion for such trees directly models HTE in child nodes. This approach, however, is more time-consuming compared to the other variable selection methods because it involves uplift model training. Additionally, its performance depends on the uplift model's hyperparameters.

7   Conclusion

We started by hypothesizing that traditional variable selection methods are not suitable for uplift models. We developed a number of alternative approaches that took into account the unique character of uplift models, namely the fact that the target in such models is the treatment effect. We then tested our proposed methods in a number of experiments, establishing that they conclusively outperform traditional variable selection approaches. We further highlighted different strengths and weaknesses of the proposed methods.

Given the increasing use of uplift model in industry applications and elsewhere, we believe the proposed methods to prove practically relevant for several purposes, including accuracy, efficiency and interpretability. For this reason, we have made the proposed methods publicly available in the *Causal ML* open source library. Promising areas for future development include covering more of the ever-increasing group of uplift models, applying the methods to observational in addition to experimental data, and integrating the methods with emerging model interpretability approaches.

The future work may include a detailed empirical study of feature selection methods for continuous outcome, as well as discussing feature selection methods for selecting the best set of features (collaboratively instead of individually).

References

1. Megafon Uplift Competition (2021). https://ods.ai/tracks/df21-megafon/competitions/megafon-df21-comp/data
2. Athey, S., Imbens, G.: Recursive partitioning for heterogeneous causal effects, April 2015
3. Athey, S., Tibshirani, J., Wager, S.: Generalized random forests, October 2016
4. Bolón-Canedo, V., Sánchez-Maroño, N., Alonso-Betanzos, A.: A review of feature selection methods on synthetic data. Knowl. Inf. Syst. **34**(3), 483–519 (2013)
5. Bommert, A., Sun, X., Bischl, B., Rahnenführer, J., Lang, M.: Benchmark for filter methods for feature selection in high-dimensional classification data. Comput. Stat. Data Anal. **143**, 106839 (2020)
6. Chandrashekar, G., Sahin, F.: A survey on feature selection methods. Comput. Electr. Eng. **40**(1), 16–28 (2014)
7. Chen, H., Harinen, T., Lee, J.Y., Yung, M., Zhao, Z.: CausalML: Python package for causal machine learning. arXiv preprint arXiv:2002.11631 (2020)
8. Chen, X., et al.: Imbalance-aware uplift modeling for observational data (2022)
9. Dahl, G.E., Sainath, T.N., Hinton, G.E.: Improving deep neural networks for LVCSR using rectified linear units and dropout. In: 2013 IEEE International Conference on Acoustics, Speech and Signal Processing, pp. 8609–8613. IEEE (2013)
10. Grimmer, J., Messing, S., Westwood, S.J.: Estimating heterogeneous treatment effects and the effects of heterogeneous treatments with ensemble methods. Polit. Anal. **25**(4), 413–434 (2017)
11. Guelman, L., Guillén, M., Pérez-Marín, A.M.: Random forests for uplift modeling: an insurance customer retention case. In: Engemann, K.J., Gil-Lafuente, A.M., Merigó, J.M. (eds.) MS 2012. LNBIP, vol. 115, pp. 123–133. Springer, Heidelberg (2012). https://doi.org/10.1007/978-3-642-30433-0_13
12. Guelman, L., Guillén, M., Pérez-Marín, A.M.: Uplift random forests. Cybern. Syst. **46**(3–4), 230–248 (2015)
13. Gutierrez, P., Gerardy, J.Y.: Causal inference and uplift modeling a review of the literature. In: JMLR: Workshop and Conference Proceedings, vol. 67 (2016)
14. Hansotia, B., Rukstales, B.: Incremental value modeling. Res. Council J. **16**, 35–46 (2001)
15. Holland, P.W.: Statistics and causal inference. J. Am. Stat. Assoc. **81**(396), 945–960 (1986)
16. Ke, G., et al.: LightGBM: a highly efficient gradient boosting decision tree. In: Advances in Neural Information Processing Systems, pp. 3146–3154 (2017)
17. Kohavi, R., Tang, D., Xu, Y.: Trustworthy Online Controlled Experiments: A Practical Guide to A/B Testing. Cambridge University Press, Cambridge (2020)
18. Künzel, S.R., Sekhon, J.S., Bickel, P.J., Yu, B.: Meta-learners for estimating heterogeneous treatment effects using machine learning, June 2017
19. Larsen, K.: Data exploration with weight of evidence and information value in R (2015)
20. Lo, V.S.: The true lift model: a novel data mining approach to response modeling in database marketing. ACM SIGKDD Explor. Newsl. **4**(2), 78–86 (2002)

21. Mouloud, B., Olivier, G., Ghaith, K.: Adapting neural networks for uplift models. arXiv preprint arXiv:2011.00041 (2020)
22. Neyman, J.: Sur les applications de la théorie des probabilités aux experiences agricoles: Essai des principes. Roczniki Nauk Rolniczych **10**, 1–51 (1923)
23. Nie, X., Wager, S.: Quasi-Oracle estimation of heterogeneous treatment effects, December 2017
24. Olaya, D., Coussement, K., Verbeke, W.: A survey and benchmarking study of multitreatment uplift modeling. Data Mining Knowl. Discov. **34**(2), 273–308 (2020). https://doi.org/10.1007/s10618-019-00670-y
25. Pedregosa, F., et al.: Scikit-learn: machine learning in Python. J. Mach. Learn. Res. **12**, 2825–2830 (2011)
26. Radcliffe, N.J., Surry, P.D.: Real-world uplift modelling with significance-based uplift trees. In: White Paper TR-2011-1, Stochastic Solutions, pp. 1–33 (2011)
27. Rubin, D.B.: Estimating causal effects of treatments in randomized and nonrandomized studies. J. Educ. Psychol. **66**(5), 688–701 (1974)
28. Rubin, D.B.: Causal inference using potential outcomes: design, modeling, decisions. J. Am. Stat. Assoc. **100**(469), 322–331 (2005)
29. Rzepakowski, P., Jaroszewicz, S.: Decision trees for uplift modeling with single and multiple treatments. Knowl. Inf. Syst. **32**(2), 303–327 (2012)
30. Shortreed, S.M., Ertefaie, A.: Outcome-adaptive lasso: variable selection for causal inference. Biometrics **73**(4), 1111–1122 (2017)
31. Sołtys, M., Jaroszewicz, S., Rzepakowski, P.: Ensemble methods for uplift modeling. Data Mining Knowl. Discov. **29**(6), 1531–1559 (2014). https://doi.org/10.1007/s10618-014-0383-9
32. Tang, J., Alelyani, S., Liu, H.: Feature selection for classification: a review. Data Classif. Algorithms Appl. 37 (2014)
33. Teinemaa, I., Albert, J., Goldenberg, D.: Uplift modeling: from causal inference to personalization (2021)
34. Wager, S., Athey, S.: Estimation and inference of heterogeneous treatment effects using random forests, October 2015
35. Zaniewicz, L., Jaroszewicz, S.: Support vector machines for uplift modeling. In: 2013 IEEE 13th International Conference on Data Mining Workshops, pp. 131–138, December 2013
36. Zhao, Y., Fang, X., Simchi-Levi, D.: Uplift modeling with multiple treatments and general response types, May 2017
37. Zhao, Z.: Synthetic data for uplift modeling and heterogenous treatment effect with known counterfactuals and ITE, March 2022. https://doi.org/10.5281/zenodo.6342553
38. Zhao, Z., Harinen, T.: Uplift modeling for multiple treatments with cost optimization. arXiv preprint arXiv:1908.05372 (2019)

Machine Learning Applications in Real Estate: Critical Review of Recent Development

Jamal Al-Qawasmi[(✉)] [iD]

Architecture Department, King Fahd University for Petroleum and Minerals,
Dhahran 31261, Saudi Arabia
jamalq@kfupm.edu.sa

Abstract. Machine learning (ML) and deep learning (DL) methods have recently become a hot topic in the real estate discipline. They have contributed to the advancement of various domains in real estate sector. This paper provides a critical review of recent trends in applying machine learning and deep learning (ML/DL) techniques in various domains of real estate and investigate their potential for the real estate sector. Recent advances in model development, testing and areas of application in real estate in the past 4 years (2017–2020) are presented. Findings reveal that 20 different ML and DL algorithms were utilized to examine various aspects of real estate development and valuation, and that the most commonly used algorithms are neural networks, regression models, random forest, booting, support vector machine and cubist/pruned model tree.

Keywords: Machine learning · Deep learning · Real estate · Properties

1 Introduction

Real estate is the arena of human activities. During the past two decades or so, machine learning (ML) and deep learning (DL) algorithms and methods have moved into real estate research, thus there is enormous opportunities for future research in order to enhance several areas in the field. ML/DL algorithms and models have been applied in a wide range of activities and processes in real estate development and valuation such as valuation of land, mass appraisal for taxation purposes, renting value, and market value of real estate properties. However, the application of ML and DL in this field still new and more growth is expected in the future [1].

Valuation is one of the major application areas of ML/DL in real estate. Real estate valuation is the process of developing an opinion of value for real estate property. Real estate valuation and estimations are needed for purposes such as selling, buying, renting, real estate development, secure bank loans, taxation, amongst others. In all these cases, stakeholders are interested in getting the most accurate estimation of the value of the real estate property. Traditionally, the valuation of real estate properties is based on the expertise of the valuators/appraisers. This process suffers from inaccuracy in estimating the value of proprieties due to the differences in the perception of valuators. As

© IFIP International Federation for Information Processing 2022
Published by Springer Nature Switzerland AG 2022
I. Maglogiannis et al. (Eds.): AIAI 2022, IFIP AICT 647, pp. 231–249, 2022.
https://doi.org/10.1007/978-3-031-08337-2_20

such, the conventional valuation process is often supported by computer systems called Automated Valuation Models (AVM) and Computer Assisted Mass Appraisal (CAMA) which employ various statistical methods and models to estimate the value of a single or a mass of properties [2, 3]. The ML/DL methods have entered the field as new addition to these conventional practices.

This paper aims to identify the main ML and DL techniques used in the real estate field. The paper provides an extensive survey of recent developments and achievements in applying ML/DL algorithms and techniques to advance real estate field. Extensive literature review showed that there is no similar systematic survey on the topic in the past decade or so [4].

This survey paper is organized as follows: Sect. 2 summarizes the paper methodology. Section 3 examines and analyzes the ML and DL algorithms and techniques applied in real estate literature and outlines the relevant studies, Sect. 4 provides a discussion of results, and Sect. 5 provides conclusion of findings.

2   Materials and Methodology

To identify relevant literature in the area of applying ML/DL algorithms and techniques in real estate development and valuation, the author explored Google Scholar, Web of Science (WoS), and Scopus databases with the following search keywords: "real estate", "property" or "mass appraisal" along with "machine learning", "deep learning" in addition to names of a wide range of ML and DL algorithms. The search in these databases showed that there is high increase in using ML and DL algorithms in real estate development and valuation during the past decade or so. However, the application of ML and DL in this field still new and more growth is expected in the future. Our search was focused on recent research studies that have been published in the past four years (i.e. between 2017 and 2020). After removing duplicates, the search resulted in a total number of 36 papers. Based on reading the abstract of each paper, a total of 16 papers have been excluded as they are unrelated to the topic. We also excluded most of conference papers as our research is focused on journal papers. Only 20 papers were remained for analysis, for of them are conference papers. The final list of papers selected for analysis is presented in Table 1.

Table 1. Descriptive analysis of the 22 examined research papers.

Study	Pub. year	Study area	ML/Dl methods	Objective of the study
Abidoye and Chan [5]	2017	Lagos, Nigeria	Artificial Neural Network	Examine accuracy and feasibility of using ANN technique to predict the prices of properties

(continued)

Table 1. (*continued*)

Study	Pub. year	Study area	ML/Dl methods	Objective of the study
Guo et al. [6]	2019	Beijing, and other 5 cities, China	Artificial Neural Network	Optimize ANN to work for cities with insufficient real estate data without compromising accuracy
Alexandridis et al. [7]	2019	Several cities, Greece	Artificial Neural Network	Assess performance and accuracy of ANN models with 2 traditional real estate valuation methods (i.e. MRA and SMV)
Abidoye and Chan [8]	2018	Lagos metropolis, Nigeria	Artificial Neural Network	Evaluate the predictive accuracy of ANN model with the hedonic pricing model (HPM) in residential property valuation
Yu et al. [9]	2018	Beijing, China	Convolution Neural Network (CNN), Recurrent Neural Network (RNN), Logical regression model	Comparative analysis of prediction power of 3 ML models of the market value of second-hand housing
Poursaeed et al. [10]	2018	(House photos from) USA	Convolutional neural network	Predict the impact of (quality of) appearance on the value of residential properties using CNN
Bin et al. [11]	2017	NA	Recurrent Neural Network (RNN)	Apply RNN in a model to predict property value and compare its accuracy/performance with other non-ML appraisal models
Petkov [12]	2020	Lisbon, Portugal	Self-organizing Map (SOM), and Support Vector Machine (SVM)	Compare performance of SOM with SVM, and hedonic price model (HPM) in predicting rental prices

(*continued*)

Table 1. (*continued*)

Study	Pub. year	Study area	ML/Dl methods	Objective of the study
Ceh et al. [13]	2018	Ljubljana, Slovenia	Random Forest	Empirically evaluate the predictive power of the random forest technique compared with the hedonic pricing model (HPM) in predicting of prices apartments
Aydinoglu et al. [14]	2020	Istanbul, Turkey	Random Forest	Propose a land valuation model for residential properties as an extension of the national geographic data infrastructure (GDI) and assess its accuracy in estimating market value of land
Dimopoulos et al. [15]	2018	Nicosia, Cyprus	Random Forest, Linear (Multivariate) Regression	Compare the performance of random forest method with linear multivariate regression in predicting apartments values
Alfaro-Navarro et al. [16]	2020	48 provinces in Spain	Boosting, Random forest, and Bagging	Automate the selection of best ML/DL model for each city of a country, and compare the prediction power of 3 ML/DL models of the market value of properties, and identify variables that impact value
Kok et al. [17]	2017	California, Florida, and Texas, USA	Decision tree	Evaluate the accuracy of decision tree models compared to the hedonic pricing model (HPM) in predicting value and net operation oncome (NOI) of multi-family properties

(*continued*)

Table 1. (*continued*)

Study	Pub. year	Study area	ML/Dl methods	Objective of the study
Dimopoulos and Bakas [18]	2019	Nicosia, Cyprus	Gradient Boosting, Random Forests, Linear Regression, and Non-Linear Regression	empirically investigate how the four ML/DL models work to predict apartment prices, and how it takes various variables (property characteristics) into consideration
Vargas-Calderón and Camargo [19]	2019	Bogota, Colombia	XGBoost (gradient boosting)	Investigate the ability of XGBoost, a gradient boosting algorithm, to predict property prices based on data published in real estate market websites
Gružauskas et al. [20]	2020	Tauragė, Lithuania	Boosted Decision Tree	Develop and test a model based on the boosted decision tree algorithm as a supplement to traditional "comparative method" when similar historical data is unavailable or limited
Bogdan et al. [21]	2017	Poland	Pruned Model Tree (M5P), Multilayer Perceptron, Linear Regression	Evaluate the accuracy of predicting sales prices of residential building using 3 ML/DL models (M5P, MLP and linear regression) compared with 2 expert algorithms used in real state valuation
Trawiński et al. [22]	2017	Wrocław, Poland	Pruned Model Tree (M5P), Multilayer Perceptron	Evaluate the accuracy of predicting sales prices of apartments by Pruned Model Tree (M5P), and Multilayer Perceptron (MLP) algorithms compared with 3 expert algorithms used in real state valuation
Clark and Lomax [23]	2018	England (whole country)	Cubist, Gradient Boost, Multivariate adaptive regression splines (MARS), Support Vector Machine (SVM)	Assess performance and accuracy of 4 ML/DL algorithms (Cubist, gradient boosting, MARS, and SVM) and one hedonic price model (GLM)

(*continued*)

Table 1. (*continued*)

Study	Pub. year	Study area	ML/Dl methods	Objective of the study
Derdouri and Murayama [24]	2020	Fukushima, Japan	Generalized linear model (GLM), Generalized additive model using splines (GAMS), Multivariate adaptive regression spline (MARS), k-nearest neighbors (kNN), SVMRadial, Cubist, Stochastic gradient boosting (GBM), Random forest	compare and evaluate the performance of 9 ML/DL algorithms and one non-ML algorithm in predicting land prices

3   ML/DL Algorithms and Their Applications in Rea Estate

The analyzed 20 research papers have proposed and tested several ML/DL algorithms for application in the real estate field. A total of 20 different ML/DL algorithms have been examined in the 20 papers. The number of ML/DL algorithms examined in each paper ranged between one to nine. The following is a detailed analysis of each paper, the ML/DL algorithms examined, and the major findings.

3.1   Neural Networks (NN)

Neural networks have a wide range of applications in real estate. They are the most used ML/DL methods in real estate. As shown in Table 1, ten research papers (out of 20 papers) have addressed the use of 11 neural network models in the context of real estate development and valuation. Five types of neural network algorithms were examined: artificial neural network (ANN), convolutional neural network (CNN), recurrent neural network (RNN), multilayer perceptron (MLP) and self-organizing map (SOM).

Artificial Neural Network (ANN). Abidoye and Chan [5], for instance, investigated the accuracy and feasibility of using ANN technique to predict the prices of properties in Lagos, Nigeria. The study examined the impact of 11 property attributes on the value of property. Results showed that ANN provided suitable and reliable predictions of values of properties. The model also able to assess the impact of each attribute on the property value.

Guo et al. [6] developed a framework to predict prices of properties across several cities in china using semi-supervised ANN. This is done by separating homogeneous attributes from heterogeneous attributes of properties and dealing with each separately.

Alexandridis et al. [7], on the other hand, proposed an ANN model to forecast the value of properties in Greece and compared its performance and accuracy with traditional real estate valuation methods; the multiple regression analysis (MRA) and similarity measure valuation (SMV) models. After examining the strengths and the performance of each method, authors applied a combined forecasting rule to improve forecasting accuracy. They also identified the property characteristics that lead to large forecasting errors. Results showed that the proposed ANN model provides an accurate tool for property valuation in non-homogeneous, newly developed markets, and constantly outperform traditional valuation methods (i.e. MRA and SMV).

Abidoye and Chan [8] evaluated the predictive accuracy of hedonic pricing model (HPM) in comparison with the artificial neural network (ANN) technique in property valuation. Residential property transaction data were collected from registered real estate firms operating in the Lagos metropolis, Nigeria, and were fitted into the ANN and HPM models. The results showed that the ANN technique outperformed the HPM approach in terms of accuracy in predicting property values with higher r2 and lower accuracy error (MAPE, RMSE, MAPE).

Convolutional Neural Network (CNN) and Recurrent Neural Network (RNN). Yu et al. [9] built three ML/DL models, namely Convolution Neural Network (CNN), Recurrent Neural Network (RNN) and logistic regression model, to predict housing prices in a city according to range of characteristics such as building age, location, surrounding facilities and so on. They found that the accuracy of the prediction of a model is directly affected by the characteristic and attributes used. For example, they found that CNN is more accurate in predicting when using the dataset based on characteristic factors obtained by deep crawling, while the RNN is more accurate in predicting when using the time series data.

Poursaeed et al. [10] have used convolutional neural network (CNN) in a novel application to evaluate the impact of visual characteristics of residential properties (i.e. their interior and exterior appearance) on their market value. They develop a method that used deep convolutional neural networks on a large dataset of photos of home interiors and exteriors for estimating the luxury level of real estate photos and estimate their value. They found that the approach is more accurate and provide better value estimation compared to existing methods that do not consider visual aspects of residential buildings.

Bin et al. [11] proposed a boosting tree model facilitated with a recurrent neural network (RNN) to forecast the average price of real estate in a city. The model uses properties attributes such as qualities of houses, location, and trend of market price to estimate property value. However, the model doesn't take spatial and temporal aspects of properties into account. The results indicate that the proposed RNN model outperforms the existing non-ML models used in the real estate appraisal industry.

Self-Organizing Map (SOM). For example, Petkov [12] used self-organizing map (SOM), a type of ANN, and support vector machine (SVM) to predict mid-term rental prices based on various spatial variables.

Multilayer Perceptron (MLP). MLP is a special type of feedforward artificial neural network. Each of Bogdan et al. [21] and Trawiński et al. [22] conducted a comparative study in which they examined the performance of MLP method compared to other ML algorithms. These two papers are discussed in Sect. 3.4 below.

Table 2. Applications of neural networks in real estate and major findings.[a]

Study	Highlighted finding	Domain of application
Abidoye and Chan [5]	Price predictions of ANN technique are feasible, highly accurate and reliable	Property valuation, mass appraisal, predict property value
Guo et al. [6]	The developed semi-supervised ANN model achieved similar or even superior performance compared to a fully supervised ANN in property evaluation	Property valuation, mass appraisal, predict property value
Alexandridis et al. [7]	The proposed ANN method is an accurate prediction tool and constantly outperform traditional valuation methods (i.e. MRA and SMV)	Property valuation in non-homogeneous, newly developed markets
Abidoye and Chan [8]	The proposed ANN method outperformed the HPM approach in prediction of market value for residential properties	Property valuation of residential properties, mass appraisal
Yu et al. [9]	Accuracy of ML/DL methods (CNN, RNN and LRM) depends on type of attributes/variables used. CNN is more accurate when using housing characteristic data, while RNN is more accurate when using time series data	Market value of second-hand housing
Poursaeed et al. [10]	The approach (CNN and novel algorithm) is more accurate and provide better value estimation compared to existing methods that do not consider visual aspects of residential buildings	Valuation of various types of residential buildings based on quality/luxury level of property
Bin et al. [11]	The proposed RNN model outperformed the existing non-ML models used in the real estate appraisal industry	Property valuation, property appraisal
Petkov [12]	ML methods (SVM and SOM) outperformed the non-ML methods (i.e. hedonic price model). Accuracy of ML methods depends on type of attributes/variables used	Mid-term rental prices

[a]See also papers [21, 22] that address these algorithms

3.2   Random Forest, Bagging and Decision Tree

Six papers have investigated the application of random forest algorithm, while one paper has examined each of bagging and decision tree algorithms, as shown in Table 3. For instance, Ceh et al. [13] examined the predictive performance of the random forest algorithm in comparison to commonly used hedonic pricing models (HPM) in predicting prices of apartments in Slovenia. Results revealed that prediction results of the random forest model are significantly better than the results obtained through HPM model according all performance measures (R2 values, sales ratios, mean average percentage error (MAPE), coefficient of dispersion (COD)). Ten of the most important predicting variables identified by random forest models are also supported by Principal Component Analysis (PCA).

Aydinoglu et al. [14] proposed an interoperable land valuation model using random forest method and evaluated its accuracy in estimating market value of residential urban land. The model is developed as an extension of the national geographic data infrastructure (GDI) of Turkey. Experimental results showed that the random forest algorithm accurately predicted the value of residential land in the light of all related performance measures (i.e. median ratio, COD and PRD) and standards International Association of Assessing Officers (IAAO).

Dimopoulos et al. [15] conducted a comparative study to assess the performance and accuracy of random forest and linear multivariate regression methods in predicting market values of apartments (multifamily residences). The result revealed that the random forest method outperformed the linear multivariate regression in predicting market value of apartments, and that the difference in the accuracy measure (the root mean squared error -RMSE) between the two models ranged between 7.87% and 11.17%. The set of most important variables affected the value of apartments were identified.

Alfaro-Navarro et al. [16] developed an application that automates the selection of best ML model for each city/district in Spain. Real estate property prices in 433 municipalities are estimated from a sample of 790,631 dwellings, using three ensemble methods (bagging, random forest and boosting) based on decision trees. Results showed that the ability of the three ensemble methods (bagging, random forest and boosting) in estimating the price of dwellings is clearly outperformed individual regression trees, with the best results being achieved using the techniques of bagging and random forest, as reflected in the measures of prediction error.

Kok et al. [17] examined the accuracy of decision tree (i.e. regression tree) model in comparison with the traditional hedonic pricing model (HPM) in predicting value and net operation oncome (NOI) of multi-family properties in several states in USA. They tested the two models using large datasets of over 28,145 unique properties. Results revealed the superiority of the decision tree model compared to HPM technique. The absolute error (MdAPE) between property value as predicted by the model and the actual transaction price is 9.3% for multifamily assets. Results showed that only 48% or less of property value is explained by property characteristics, whereas local amenities, census data, and local market dynamics contributed to the remaining 52%.

Dimopoulos and Bakas [18] used sensitivity analysis to investigate how random forest algorithm performed compared to other three algorithms (i.e. gradient boosting, linear regression, and non-linear regression) regarding predicting apartment prices. They found major similarity across the four methods as discussed in Sect. 3.3 below.

Table 3. Applications of random forest and bagging algorithms in real estate.[a]

Study	Major findings	Domain of application
Ceh et al. [13]	The developed random forest model provided accurate prediction and significantly outperform traditional HPM approach, according to actual sales price and all performance measures	Valuation of apartments and multi-family properties
Aydinoglu et al. [14]	The random forest algorithm accurately predicted the value of residential land as evaluated by performance measure and IAAO standards	Valuation of urban land (residential land)
Dimopoulos et al. [15]	The random forest random forest outperformed the linear regression models in predicting apartment's market value	Valuation of apartments/multi-family properties
Alfaro-Navarro et al. [16]	Bagging and random forest performed better than boosting technique. Feasibility of applying the method to many cities through automating selecting best ML/DL model for particular city/district	Value of apartments, automate the selection of best ML/DL model for each city of a country
Kok et al. [17]	The developed decision tree model outperformed the HPM approach in predicting market value net operating income (NOI) of multi-family properties	Valuation of multi-family properties, and the net operating income (NOI) of these properties

[a]See also papers [18, 24] that address these algorithms

3.3 Boosting and Gradient Boosting

Three papers have investigated gradient boosting algorithm, while another three papers have examined boosting algorithm as shown in Table 4 and discussed below. Dimopoulos and Bakas [18] empirically investigated the capabilities of four ML/DL algorithms (i.e. gradient boosting, random forests, linear regression, and non-linear regression) and how they can be used for the mass appraisal of real estate properties. They used sensitivity analysis to examine how each algorithm perform regarding predicting apartment prices, and what property variables (property characteristics) are taken into account in predicting apartment price. Results demonstrated major similarity patterns across the four methods, in addition to some differences. The aim of the approach is to make the models more transparent for professional working in real estate field.

Vargas-Calderón and Camargo [19] investigated the ability of XGBoost, a gradient boosting model, to predict property prices based on data published by sellers on real estate market websites. The model which predicts whether a property has higher or lower price than the average price of its similar properties was evaluated based on a data set of 57,516 records. The experiment results demonstrated that the accuracy of a classifier that involves property descriptions by sellers is slightly higher than a classifier that only uses the features of the property. The authors recommend to add this model to features-based models to improve the accuracy of predicting property prices.

Gružauskas et al. [20] explored how to integrate ML algorithms for practicing real estate professionals where regulations require reasoning for value thus it is not allowed to mass valuation models to provide the final value of a real estate property. The authors proposed a model that uses the boosted decision tree algorithm as a supplement to the sales comparison method, a traditional real estate valuation method, when historical real estate transaction data is limited. The model predicts the average price of real estate in a region which can be used as correction coefficients in the sales comparison method where historical data is limited or unavailable.

As discussed in Sect. 3.2, Alfaro-Navarro et al. [16] compared the performance of boosting algorithm with other two ensemble algorithms (bagging, random forest) and

Table 4. Applications of boosting algorithms in real estate and major findings.[a]

Study	Major findings	Domain of application
Dimopoulos and Bakas [18]	Major similarity patterns, in addition to some differences, between across the 4 ML/DL methods (gradient boosting, random forests, linear and non-linear regression)	Property valuation, mass appraisal
Vargas-Calderón and Camargo [19]	That the accuracy of XGBoost algorithm working on property descriptions by sellers is slightly higher than a classifier that only uses the features of the property	Property valuation, Predict property value
Gružauskas et al. [20]	The proposed approached based on boosted decision tree is highly accurate, feasible and highly needed for practicing real estate professionals	Single (object) property valuation

[a]See also papers [16, 23, 24] that address those algorithms

found that the bagging and random forest outperformed the boosting method. Gradient Boosting is also examined by Clark and Lomax [23] and Derdouri and Murayama [24] as detailed in Sect. 3.6.

3.4 M5 Model Tree and Cubist

The Cubist model, which was developed by J.R Quinlan in 1992, is also referred to as M5 of which M5P is a special type. The M5 Model Tree/Cubist model is examined in 4 papers as shown in Table 5 and discussed below. Bogdan et al. [21] conducted a comparative study using data of actual sales transactions to examine the performance and accuracy of three ML algorithms with two real estate expert algorithms in predicting the prices of residential buildings in urban areas in Poland. The ML algorithms are Pruned Model Tree (M5P), Multilayer Perceptron (MLP), and Linear Regression (LR), while the expert algorithms are: N-Nearest Similar Properties (NSP), N-Latest Transactions in an Area (LTA). Empirical results showed that ML algorithms surpassed the expert algorithms in accuracy. When comparing ML algorithms, the M5P revealed the best performance and linear regression showed the least accuracy. On the other hand, the LTA expert algorithm outperformed the NSP. Although the ML models performed better than the expert systems, the accuracy among them were not high: the median of MAPE, as a measure of accuracy in prediction, ranged from 10% to 13.4%.

Trawiński et al. [22] conducted an experimental study to evaluate the accuracy of predicting the prices of residential apartments by two ML algorithms (i.e. Pruned Model Tree -M5P, and Multilayer Perceptron -MLP) compared with three expert algorithms used in real state valuation (N-Nearest Similar Transactions -NST, N-Latest Transactions in an Area -LTA, N-Random Similar Transactions -RST) using real-world data of actual real estate transactions. Each of M5P and MLP algorithms is applied as a base learner three times differently: single model, bagging ensemble, and additive regression. Empirical results revealed that bagging ensembles of both M5P decision trees and MLP gave better accuracy than single models and boosting ensembles. The ML also performed better than the expert systems. Nevertheless, all analyzed models and algorithms, but RST, could be employed in an automated system to support professional valuators in real estate appraisal.

Cubist algorithm is examined by Clark and Lomax [23] and Derdouri and Murayama [24] as detailed in Sect. 3.6. In these two papers the cubist algorithm and its accuracy in predicting land and property value is investigated.

Table 5. Applications of M5 model tree/Cubist in real estate and major findings.[a]

Study	Major finding	Domain of application
Bogdan et al. [21]	ML/DL algorithms surpassed the expert algorithms in accuracy, though the difference is not high. For ML/DL models: M5P showed best performance while linear regression showed the least accuracy. The LTA expert algorithm outperformed the NSP	Valuation of sales prices of residential buildings
Trawiński et al. [22]	Bagging ensembles of both M5P and MLP gave better accuracy than single models and boosting ensembles, and also outperformed the expert systems	Valuation of apartment prices

[a]See also papers [23, 24] that address these algorithms

3.5 Support Vector Machine (SVM)

Four papers have studied the application of support vector machine (SVM) in real estate. Petkov [12] developed an application based on support vector machine (SVM) and self-organizing map (SOM) to predict mid-term rental prices based on various spatial variables in Lisbon city. He found that the ML methods (SVM and SOM) outperformed the non-ML methods (i.e. hedonic price model) and that the performance of ML methods depends on the type of variables used in the model.

Support vector machine (SVM) method is also examined by papers [23, 24], as detailed in Sect. 3.6 below. Derdouri and Murayama [24] conducted a comparative study to examine the accuracy of predicting land prices of 10 algorithms: 9 ML algorithms and 1 statistical method (the universal kriging regression). Two of those algorithms are SVM: support vector machines with linear kernel (SVMLinear) and Support vector machines with radial basis function kernel (SVMRadial) as detailed in Sect. 3.6 below.

3.6 Linear and Non-linear Regression Model

Regression models are the second most used ML methods in real estate, after the neural networks. As shown in Table 1 and Figs. 1 and 2, seven research papers (out of 20 papers) have examined the application of 7 regression models in the context of real estate development and valuation. The regression algorithms and the papers that examined them are as follows: the generalized additive model using splines (paper [24]), generalized linear model (paper [24]), k-nearest neighbors (paper [24]), linear regression (papers [15, 18, 21]), logical regression model (paper [9]), and multivariate adaptive regression splines (paper [23, 24]), and non-linear regression (paper [18]).

Clark and Lomax [23] investigated the accuracy of predicting rental prices of properties using four ML algorithms: Cubist, gradient boosting, multivariate adaptive regression splines (MARS), and Support Vector Machine (SVM), in addition to one hedonic

Table 6. Applications of SVM in real estate and major findings.[a]

Study	Major findings	Domain of application
Petkov [12]	ML methods (SVM and SOM) outperformed the non-ML methods (i.e. hedonic price model) in predicting rental prices. Performance of ML methods depends on type of used variables	Mid-term rental prices
Derdouri and Murayama [24]	Tree-based models (cubist, random forest and gradient boosting) performed the best in estimating land prices, while linear regression models were the worst models. Random forest ranked the best. The universal kriging regression model ranked better than several ML models examined	Valuation of land

[a]See also papers [23, 24] that address these algorithms

model traditionally used in valuating real estate proprieties which is generalized linear model (GLM). The study used large dataset of rental prices extracted from property listings web site that covers whole England. The data set include a wide range of residential properties types including bungalow, detached, semi-detached, terraced, apartment among others. Experimental results showed that ML algorithms outperformed the GLM. In addition, the two tree-based methods (Gradient Boost and Cubist) outperformed the regression-based approaches of SVM, MARS and GLM. The cubist performed the best.

Derdouri and Murayama [24] conducted a comparative study to examine the accuracy of predicting land prices of ten algorithms: 9 ML algorithms and 1 statistical method (the universal kriging regression). The 9 ML methods are 3 linear regression models generalized linear model (GLM), generalized additive model using splines (GAMS), support vector machines with linear kernel (SVMLinear); 3 non-linear regression models multivariate adaptive regression spline (MARS), k-nearest neighbors (kNN), support vector machines with radial basis function kernel (SVMRadial); and 3 tree-based models Cubist, stochastic gradient boosting, random forest. The results revealed the superiority of the tree-based models (Cubist, random forest and gradient boosting) in estimating land prices accurately, while linear regression models were the worst models. Random forest was the most robust method among all methods in estimating land prices reliably. The universal kriging regression model ranked better than other ML models examined.

Table 7. Applications of regression models in real estate and major findings.[a]

Study	Major findings	Domain of application
Clark and Lomax [23]	The two tree-based methods (gradient boost and cubist) outperformed the regression-based approaches of SVM, MARS and GLM	Valuation of rental prices of wide range of properties
Derdouri and Murayama [24]	Tree-based models (cubist, random forest and gradient boosting) performed the best in estimating land prices, while linear regression models were the worst models. Random forest ranked the best. The universal kriging regression model ranked better than several ML models examined	Valuation of land

[a]See also papers [9, 15, 18, 21], that address these algorithms

4 Results and Discussion

The results show that the analyzed research papers examined the use of 20 different types of ML/Dl algorithms, as summarized in Fig. 1. As illustrated in Fig. 1, the analyzed 20 research papers have examined a total of 43 ML/DL algorithms, of which only 20 algorithms are unique ones, as listed in the left-side column of Fig. 1. The number of ML/DL algorithms examined in each paper ranged between one to nine.

For further analysis, the 20 ML/DL algorithms/models are grouped in six thematic groups/categories (see Fig. 2). Figure 2 shows the frequency of use of ML/DL algorithms across the six main groups of ML/DL algorithms. As shown in Fig. 1, the neural network is the most used algorithm (examined 11 times in 10 papers), followed by regression models (examined 10 times in 6 papers). Tables 2, 3, 4, 5, 6, and 7 shows that the main application of ML/DL models is oriented toward valuation and the estimation of market value and prices of various types of real estate such as land, apartments, single family house, villas and semi-detached villas as well as rental prices.

The scope of the analyzed papers falls under four categories: 1) compare the performance of ML with non-ML algorithms traditionally used in the real estate field, 2) compare the performance of different ML algorithms, 2) optimize ML algorithms for real estate through novel applications, and 4) general utilization and exploration of the use of ML/DL models in real estate field. Figure 3 provides an outline of the scope of the analyzed papers as related to these four categories. As shown in Fig. 3, most of the papers (10 out of 20) are focused on comparing the performance of ML/DL algorithms with other ML/DL algorithms or with non-ML algorithms (category 1 and 2), while 7 papers investigated optimizing ML/DL algorithms for real estate use through novel applications

Group	Used ML/DL algorithm	5	6	7	8	9	10	11	12	13	14	15	16	17	18	19	20	21	22	23	24
Neural Network	Artificial neural network	√	√	√	√																
	Convolution Neural Network					√	√														
	Recurrent neural network					√		√													
	Multilayer perceptron																	√	√		
	Self-organizing map								√												
RF, B, DT	Bagging												√								
	Random forest									√	√	√	√		√						√
	Decision tree													√							
Boost	Boosting												√				√				
	Gradient boosting														√	√				√	√
Cub, M5	Cubist																			√	√
	Pruned model tree																	√	√		
	Support vector machine								√											√	√2
Regression models	Linear regression											√			√			√			
	Generalized linear model																				√
	Generalized additive model using splines																				√
	Non-linear regression														√						
	Multivariate adaptive regression spline																			√	√
	K-nearest neighbors																				√
	Logical regression model					√															
	Total # of used ML/DL algorithms	1	1	1	1	3	1	1	2	1	1	2	3	1	4	1	1	3	2	4	9

Fig. 1. The ML/DL algorithms used in the 20 analyzed papers.

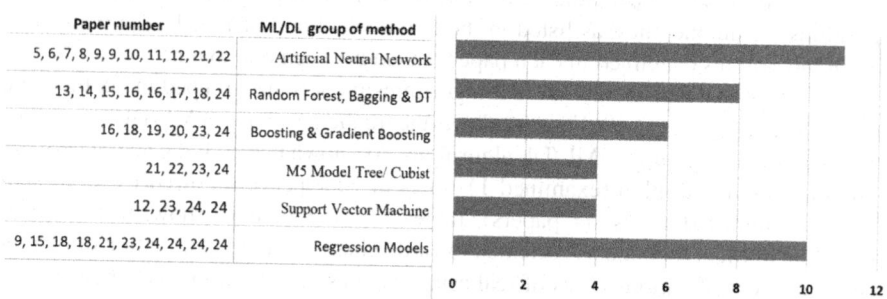

Paper number	ML/DL group of method
5, 6, 7, 8, 9, 9, 10, 11, 12, 21, 22	Artificial Neural Network
13, 14, 15, 16, 16, 17, 18, 24	Random Forest, Bagging & DT
16, 18, 19, 20, 23, 24	Boosting & Gradient Boosting
21, 22, 23, 24	M5 Model Tree/ Cubist
12, 23, 24, 24	Support Vector Machine
9, 15, 18, 18, 21, 23, 24, 24, 24	Regression Models

Fig. 2. Frequency of use of ML/DL algorithms in the examined research studies.

(category 3), while 3 papers explored the general utilization and applicability of ML/DL in real estate (category 4).

Scope of the study	Paper/study																			
	5	6	7	8	9	10	11	12	13	14	15	16	17	18	19	20	21	22	23	24
Compare performance of ML with non-ML algorithms			√	√			√	√	√				√				√	√	√	√
Compare performance across ML Algorithms				√			√			√	√		√				√	√	√	√
Optimize ML algorithms for real estate /novel application	√	√		√	√			√		√	√									
General utilization & exploration of ML applicability in RE	√														√	√				

Fig. 3. The scope of the examined research papers as related to utilizing ML/DL algorithms in real estate.

5 Conclusions and Future Prospects

This paper provides a systematic survey of the application of ML and DL algorithms in real estate development and valuation. It provided a comprehensive analysis of ML and DL methods that have been applied and examined in real estate research in the past four years (2017–2020) as investigated in 20 empirical studies. It systematically described and characterized the ML/DL techniques used in the real estate field and their potential to advance and improve a wide range of activities and processes in real estate development and valuation.

The results show that there is high increase in using ML and DL algorithms in real estate valuation and appraisal during the past decade or so. The ML and DL methods have been deployed in several domains in real estate such as valuation of land, renting and market value of real estate properties. However, the application of ML and DL in this field still new and more growth is expected in the future.

Several types of classification were used to identify the most frequently used ML/DL models and the domains of application of these models in the real estate field. The results showed that the most used ML/DL algorithms in real estate were neural networks (5 variations of the algorithm, examined in 11 studies), regression models (7 variations of the model, examined in 7 studies), random forest (used in 6 studies), booting (2 variations of the algorithm, examined in 6 studies), cubist/M5P (used in 4 studies), support vector machine (2 variations of the model, used in 3 studies). These studies have examined the prediction power and accuracy of the ML/DL models particularly in property and land valuation, and their potential to improve data quality and interpretability and advance work in the real estate field. They also highlighted the challenging problems encountered and presented possible solutions to these challenges.

Acknowledgment. The author acknowledges the support of the King Fahd University of Petroleum and Minerals for the research project.

References

1. Rizun, A., Baj-rogowska, A.: Can web search queries predict prices change on the real estate market. IEEE Access **9**, 70095–70117 (2021)

2. Jahanshiri, E., Buyong, T., Shariff, A.R.M.: A review of property mass valuation models. Pertanika J. Sci. Technol. **19**(1), 23–30 (2011)
3. d'Amato, M., Kauko, T. (eds.): Advances in Automated Valuation Modeling. SSDC, vol. 86. Springer, Cham (2017). https://doi.org/10.1007/978-3-319-49746-4
4. Zhou, G., Ji, Y., Chen, X., Zhang, F.: Artificial neural networks and the mass appraisal of real estate. Int. J. Onl. Biomed. Eng. (iJOE) **14**(3), 180–187 (2018)
5. Abidoye, R.B., Chan, A.P.C.: Modelling property values in Nigeria using artificial neural network. J. Prop. Res. **34**(1), 36–53 (2017)
6. Guo, Y., Lin, S., Ma, X., Bal, J., Li, C.-T.: Homogeneous feature transfer and heterogeneous location fine-tuning for cross-city property appraisal framework. In: Islam, R., et al. (eds.) AusDM 2018. CCIS, vol. 996, pp. 161–174. Springer, Singapore (2019). https://doi.org/10.1007/978-981-13-6661-1_13
7. Alexandridis, A.K., Karlis, D., Papastamos, D., Andritsos, D.: Real estate valuation and forecasting in non-homogeneous markets: a case study in Greece during the financial crisis. J. Oper. Res. Soc. **70**(10), 1769–1783 (2019)
8. Abidoye, R.B., Chan, A.P.C.: Improving property valuation accuracy: a comparison of hedonic pricing model and artificial neural network. Pac. Rim Prop. Res. J. **24**(1), 71–83 (2018)
9. Yu, L., Jiao, C., Xin, H., Wang, Y., Wang, K.: Prediction on housing price based on deep learning. Int. J. Comput. Inf. Eng. **12**(2), 90–99 (2018)
10. Poursaeed, O., Matera, T., Belongie, S.: Vision-based real estate price estimation. Mach. Vis. Appl. **29**(4), 667–676 (2018)
11. Bin, J., et al.: Regression model for appraisal of real estate using recurrent neural network and boosting tree. In The 2017 2nd IEEE International Conference on Computational Intelligence and Applications (ICCIA), pp. 209–213. IEEE, Beijing (2017)
12. Petkov, M.: Evaluation of Spatial Data's Impact in Mid-Term Room Rent Price Through Application of Spatial Econometrics and Machine Learning: Lisbon. MS thesis, Geospatial Technologies, University NOVA de Lisboa, Lisbon (2020)
13. Ceh, M., Kilibarda, M., Lisec, A., Bajat, B.: Estimating the performance of random forest versus multiple regression for predicting prices of apartments. ISPRS Int. J. Geo Inf. **7**(5), 168 (2018)
14. Aydinoglu, A.C., Bovkir, R., Colkesen, I.: Implementing a mass valuation application on interoperable land valuation data model designed as an extension of the national GDI. Surv. Rev. **53**(375), 349–365 (2020)
15. Dimopoulos, T., Tyralis, H., Bakas, N.P., Hadjimitsis, D.: Accuracy measurement of random forests and linear regression for mass appraisal models that estimate the prices of residential apartments in Nicosia, Cyprus. Adv. Geosci. **45**, 377–382 (2018)
16. Alfaro-Navarro, J., Cano, E.L., Alfaro-Cortés, E., García, N., Alfaro-Cortés, M., Larraz, B.: A fully automated adjustment of ensemble methods in machine learning for modeling complex real estate systems. Complexity **2020**, 1–12 (2020)
17. Kok, N., Koponen, E., Martínez-Barbosa, C.A.: Big data in real estate? From manual appraisal to automated valuation. J. Portfolio Manag. **43**(6), 202–211 (2017)
18. Dimopoulos, T., Bakas, N.: Sensitivity analysis of machine learning models for the mass appraisal of real estate: case study of residential units in Nicosia, Cyprus. Remote Sens. **11**, 3047 (2019)
19. Vargas-Calderón, V., Camargo, J.E.: A model for predicting price polarity of real estate properties using information of real estate market websites (2019)
20. Gružauskas, V., Kriščiūnas, A., Čalnerytė, D., Navickas, V.: Analytical method for correction coefficient determination for applying comparative method for real estate valuation. Real Estate Manag. Valuat. **28**(2), 52–62 (2020)

21. Trawiński, B., et al.: Comparison of expert algorithms with machine learning models for real estate appraisal. In: Jędrzejowicz, P., Yildirim, T., Czarnowski, I. (eds.) IEEE International Conference on Innovations in Intelligent Systems and Applications Inista 2017, pp. 51–54. IEEE, Gdynia (2017)
22. Trawiński, B., Lasota, T., Kempa, O., Telec, Z., Kutrzyński, M.: Comparison of ensemble learning models with expert algorithms designed for a property valuation system. In: Nguyen, N.T., Papadopoulos, G.A., Jędrzejowicz, P., Trawiński, B., Vossen, G. (eds.) ICCCI 2017. LNCS (LNAI), vol. 10448, pp. 317–327. Springer, Cham (2017). https://doi.org/10.1007/978-3-319-67074-4_31
23. Clark, S.D., Lomax, N.: A mass-market appraisal of the English housing rental market using a diverse range of modelling techniques. J. Big Data 5(1), 1–21 (2018)
24. Derdouri, A., Murayama, Y.: A comparative study of land price estimation and mapping using regression kriging and machine learning algorithms across Fukushima prefecture, Japan. J. Geogr. Sci. 30, 794–822 (2020)

Predictive Maintenance Based on Machine Learning Model

Bassem Hichri[1]([✉]) [ID], Anass Driate[1] [ID], Andrea Borghesi[2] [ID],
and Francesco Giovannini[1] [ID]

[1] GCL International, Guala Closures Group, Foetz, Luxembourg
bhichri@gclinternational.com
[2] University of Bologna, Bologna, Italy
https://www.gualaclosures.com/

Abstract. This paper addresses the problem of predictive maintenance in industry 4.0. Industry 4.0 revolutionized companies in the way they produce, manufacture, improve and distribute products. Industries are competing to implement and develop digital technologies driving Industry 4.0 which leads to increased automation (integration of advanced sensors, embedded software and robotics that collect and analyse data and allow for better decision making), predictive maintenance, self-optimization of process improvements and, above all, a new level of efficiencies and responsiveness to customers not previously possible. From this context the goal of the proposed work is to provide an industrial use case of machine smartifying to predict its Remaining Useful Life based on internal and external data collection and analysis using a Machine Learning algorithms. A digital Twin dashboard for real time monitoring of the machine and the result of the Machine Learning model prediction will be presented.

Keywords: Predictive maintenance · Digital technologies · Remaining useful life · Machine learning algorithms

1 Introduction

Industrial facilities and the machinery composing them are extremely complex systems which are a fundamental parts of nowadays world. The quest for improving their management and functioning has crucial importance, with huge impacts on economy and society. Predictive maintenance is one of the key innovations enabled by the intensive exploitation of big data in Industry 4.0. Starting from real-time data harvested by embedded sensors on machineries in industrial plants, and properly gluing and fusing these data, predictive maintenance makes it possible to forecast the time to fault or the probability of fault in specific machinery components on the basis of features extracted from data. The forecasting is based on simulation and machine learning techniques that identify the

Supported by the EU Commission for IoTwins project number 857191.

most salient features of sensor data to enable the prediction and extraction of models of machinery functioning [10].

Maintenance is a core aspect of every manufacturing process. At its most naive, it simply consists in substituting a component when it breaks (reactive maintenance), which could lead to enormous costs. A slightly better approach is to schedule maintenance regularly, according to the characteristics of the asset and related mathematical models. An increasingly popular alternative is to make use of rich historical data and Machine Learning (ML) techniques to create digital models of the industrial systems. Thanks to such models it is possible to characterize the target system's behaviour in detailed way, allowing to forecast its behaviour, to plan in advance maintenance operations and to optimize its management (i.e., with proactive workload balancing); broadly speaking, the methods combining Big Data and ML approaches fall under the umbrella of *predictive maintenance* [9].

Among the many aspects covered by predictive maintenance approaches, the Remaining Useful Life (RUL) of an asset or system is defined as the length from the current time to the end of the useful life [8]. Being able to predict this metric with sufficient reliability is among the chief research question in the domain of predictive maintenance. If the end of useful life of a component is predicted to be before the scheduled maintenance, an unexpected failure can be handled; if the scheduled maintenance is near, but the metric tells us the component is still healthy enough, more value can be extracted out of it before substitution. In recent years, Deep Learning data-driven approaches for RUL predictions have been introduced in literature and applied in practice in different contexts.

The proposed work will present online data collection from industrial plant for a selected injection moulding machine to train a Machine Learning (ML), model capable of accurately approximating the machine behavior, in particular focusing on the RUL estimation. The main contribution of this work is the creation of a *digital twin* for the industrial moulding machine using a holistic approach which integrates data from the IoT and Edge layers and uses it to train ML models for predictive maintenance, exploiting High Performance Computing resources for the computation-intensive training. The proposed approach has been implemented and deployed on a real industrial testbed.

This paper is organized as follow: Sect. 2 provides a brief overview of related works, then Sect. 3 states the treated problem. Section 4 details the overall proposed architecture to estimate the RUL and the technical setup of the injection moulding machine. Section 5 discusses the experimental results.

2   Related Works

Industrial **fault identification** and **diagnosis** have gained a lot of interest in the last decade and with industry 4.0 revolution, many industries and research institution focused on statistical learning methods (*e.g.* probabilistic models, Bayesian networks, etc.) to develop solutions applied to diverse production areas, from electrical motors [1] to complex systems [2].

Fully supervised approaches for anomaly detection based on neural networks (NNs) have been widely discussed in recent years. Wang et al. [3] propose an approach for fault diagnosis on power systems based on sparse stacked autoencoder (SSAE) NNs. SSAE are composed by a set of sparse autoencoders disposed in a chain-like structure, where the output of the previous autoencoder is fed as input to the following one. Siegel et al. [5] propose a supervised approach for arc-fault detection in electronic circuits for the Internet-of-Things, based on a deep NN acting as a classifier and trained on real data. In the data center context Borghesi et al. [6] proposed the usage of a semi-supervised method for anomaly detection in data centres which require only normal data and is based on an autoencoder deep NN: the NN learns the behaviour of the normal system state and is then capable to recognize it from faulty conditions due to their implicit difference (normal points are projected in different areas of the latent space w.r.t. anomalous examples). This capability of not requiring explicit labels can be a key strength in that context where labelled data are very costly to obtain and where the anomalous events are extremely rare [7].

In recent years, many Deep Learning (DL) algorithms tailored for dealing with time-series data have been applied to industrial contexts. In particular, the most widespread DL models for time-series forecasting are Recurrent Neural Networks (RNN) and Convolutional Neural Networks (CNN). RNNs are endowed with a memory component which allows them to remember previous states, in contrast with standard feed-forward networks which have a combinatorial nature. In RNNs the neuron has a state which depends on the state generated in the previous time step. RNNs can be fed with sequences of variable length and can be applied in different ways, according to the relationship between the input and output RNNs have been widely used for RUL estimation in industrial settings as well [13,15]. CNNs were originally devised for dealing with images, by working on the implicit spatial *locality* of images (pixels close to each other are likely to be correlated); 1-dimensional CNNs have been shown to effectively exploit the *temporal locality* underlying time-series data. 1D CNNs have been used in many industrial applications as well [11,12]. More recently, a variant of CNNs called Temporal CNNs (TCNNs) [14] has emerged and used in industrial contexts, especially for dealing with multi-variate time-series data [16,17].

3   Problem Statement

The proposed use-case of Guala Closures Group (GCL) in this paper is a showcase and an application of the concept of **IoTwins** European project in the manufacturing sector. IoTwins aims at enabling SMEs in the manufacturing and facility management/service sectors to access edge enabled and cloud based big-data analysis services to create hybrid digital companions to improve their production process and optimize the management of their facilities. A production plant of GCL Group contains up to 200 machines with different purposes, brands, and type of use. With the support of the maintenance team and department managers, monitoring activities have been introduced to identify all possible unexpected events that should occur during the production life cycle and its possible related causes. Among the various hypothetical failure events examined, it was decided to move towards a dedicated event of breakage which cyclically, but unpredictably, occurs on a defined plastic injection moulding machine. The anomaly that has been decided to prevent is an abnormal wear of the spindle bearing coating (worm screw that allows the mobile table to close by acting on the brace of the toggle). The material that comes off the bearing settles on the crests of the worm screw, damaging it.

The goal of the proposed work is to predict the occurrence of the "alarm" status during normal production runs. This will be done by developing, with the help of our project partners from University of Bologna, validating and testing a machine learning model, based on deep learning, capable of predicting the **Remaining Useful Life RUL** of the ball bearing. The model outputs the RUL in the form of a survival probability (cf. Fig. 1), with values ranging from 0 to 1, where 1 indicates that no failure will occur within now and a given time window, and 0 indicating the certainty that a failure will occur within now and a given time window.

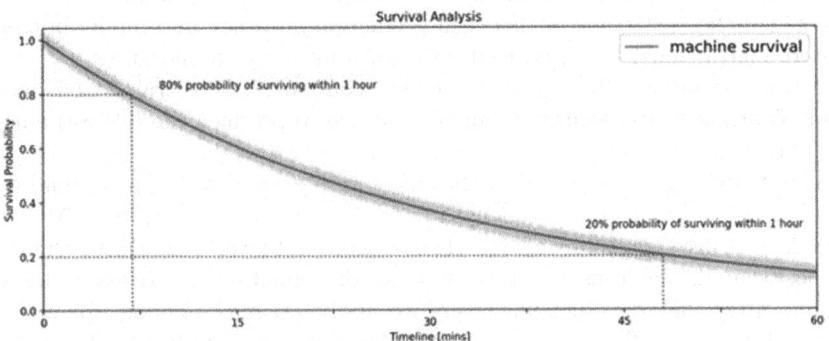

Fig. 1. Survival probability model outputs

4   Overall Proposed Architecture

In this section we provide details on the ML model used forecast the RUL of the target industrial component to and on the overall architecture of the proposed methodology.

4.1   Machine Learning Model

The data from the sensors has the shape of a multi-variate time-series; the sampling rate is 5 min. We start by pre-processing it to remove clearly useless values (e.g., constant values for all the monitored period) and by normalizing it in the [0, 1] range. Then we prepare the data for the actual task of RUL estimation; the key aspect is building the RUL label. We adopt the classical method of segmenting the time-series in runs-to-failure[18], i.e., periods of time where a component starts as perfectly healthy and goes towards the end of its useful life (where RUL is 0). This can be done as we have information describing the state of the component at every time step. The next step is to create multiple sequences from the historical data (the); we chose a sequence length equal to 512 time steps (each time step is 5 min), corresponding to more or less 43 h.

The RUL estimation ML model is a supervised one: it relies on the presence of a label associated with the data (time-series) collected from the target system. To effectively train the ML model the training data (the data used to teach the DL models) must contain some run-to-failure events, that is periods of time where a failure/a problem/an anomaly happened; there must be at least one run-to-failure, but a larger amount is welcomed and could greatly improve the accuracy of the service. In the absence of critical events (e.g., the target system has a lifespan of several years and no failure has yet happened), simulated or synthetic run-to-failure data could be generated. We implemented and performed experiments with several types of neural network for handling the time series and predicting the RUL (after the data have been pre-processed): RNNs, CNNs, and TCNs. After an empirical preliminary evaluation we opted for the 1D CNN as it provided the best trade-off between prediction accuracy and model inference time. In fact, it must be noted that we both want accurate measures but at the same time we prefer DL models not overly complex, as the trained DL model should continuously executed on an edge device to produce the live estimate of the RUL.

The model take as input a batches of sequences, and so 3-dimensional data (number of batches × sequence length in steps × number of features). After the input layer, there is a series of five 1D convolutional layers, each with the same composition: 128 neurons, stride and kernel size equal to 2, and batch normalization. After the convolutional layers we apply 1D max pooling, followed by a dense layer with 32 neurons. All activation functions are ReLU. The output layer has a single neuron with a linear activation function, which is common practice for regression models; the model is trained to minimize the Mean Squared Error of the predicted RUL. We used 100 training epochs and a batch size of 256; Adam optimizer has been used. The model was developed using the TensorFlow[1] Python package (v2.2).

4.2   Architecture

On-line data and off-line historical data from industrial plant and machinery are used to generate an upstream flow of data to feed the machine learning models. To realize the required upstream of data, industrial control technology and IT solutions are implemented to the manufacturing testbed.

The chosen IT architecture (cf. Fig. 2) decided to approach this project was Edge-Cloud distributed architecture, in our case and to facilitate the comprehension of this document, we divided it in 3 different levels: IoT/Premises, Edge

---

[1] https://www.tensorflow.org/.

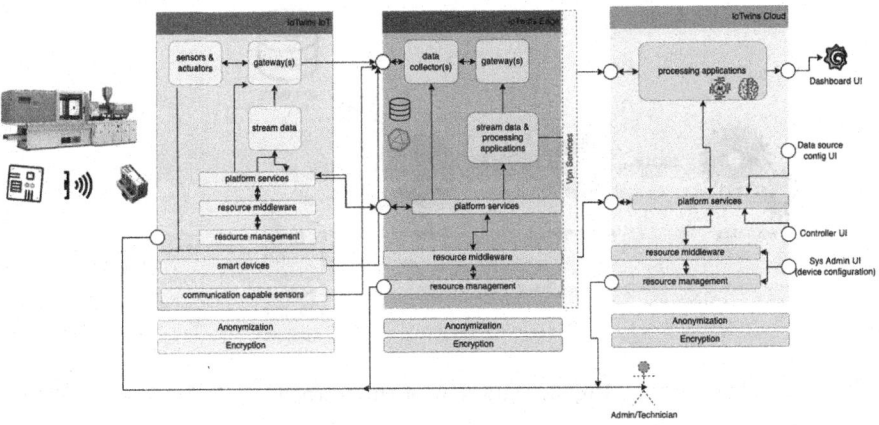

Fig. 2. Architecture overview

and Cloud. the first level consists of devices that are equipped with different kinds of sensors that capture and send information using different industrial protocols. Within the scope of this project, it has been added some critical ball bearings sensors on the injection moulding machines, measuring its vibration speed, acceleration and temperature. Between all variables, it has been identified which ones are the most responsible for indicating the overall health of the machine. Then, following the ISO 10816-3 regulation, it has been defined thresholds for these measured values, where each threshold corresponds to one of four bearing statuses - normal, pre-warning, warning, alarm. Due to the heterogeneity of the communication methodologies, emerged the necessity of a middleware communicator, that would be capable of integrating the information exposed by the machines and analysing the data. The first middleware chosen for the edge server (second level) was KepServerEX, a platform of PTC, a world leader in the world of the Internet of Things. This tool incorporates hundreds of different communication drivers and can connect directly to the machine, exposing the normalized data to the outside. We also employ an additional middleware called ThingWorx, as it is capable of processing the information received and storing it in any type of database; the database chosen for the project was InfluxDb, which is an open-source time series database (TSDB) developed by InfluxData. It is optimized for fast, high-availability storage and retrieval of time series data in fields such as operations monitoring, application metrics and Internet of Things sensor data. Figure 3 shows the data flow of the proposed use case.

After data is processed by the edge middleware (KepServerEX, ThingWorx) and stored in InfluxDB, it is visualized in a comprehensible way using Grafana tool. Grafana is a multi-platform open source analytics and interactive visualization web application. It provides charts, graphs, and alerts for the web when connected to supported data sources. Using docker (Docker is a set of platform as a service products that use OS-level virtualization to deliver software in packages called containers. The service has both free and premium tiers. The software

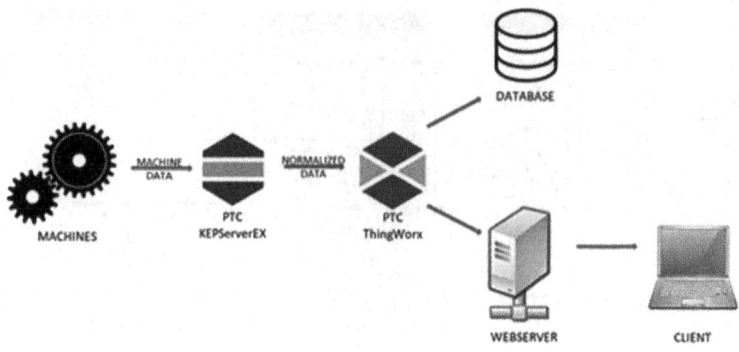

Fig. 3. Data flow of the testbed

that hosts the containers is called Docker Engine) many services are running as containers to link between the edge level and cloud level. Every 15 min data is retrieved from the InfluxDB using a specific service and reshaped to a the cloud required format using another service. Every 1 h 4 csv files are sent to the cloud to run the ML model. For training the model we use the CINECA supercomputer. The HPC system chosen for this case, uses these information to train the model exploiting CINECA computing resources. Results of this activity are neural network models that are used to calculate RUL estimation of the injection machine component object of this use case. Every 2 months it is scheduled a re-train activity with the up-to-date information in order to provide a more efficient and reliable model. CINECA HPC also provides a specific REST API used to obtain in real time the information of the RUL expressed in hours.

4.3 Technical Set up

The machine identified (cf. Fig. 4) was, at its state of the art, not connectable to any platform because of the lack of technical equipment (hardware and software). With the support of the machine supplier the machine has been equipped with the interfaces to expose externally its process data and the plant was predisposed with an appropriate networking structure in order to connect our plant machines with the edge server.

Moreover, PTC KEPServerEX[2] has been installed on the edge server, this software provides a series of drivers and plugin that allow the machine to communicate with our platform. KEPServerEX is an industry connectivity platform that provides a single source of industrial automation data to all the applications. The platform design allows users to connect, manage, monitor and control different automation devices and software applications through one intuitive user interface. Connected to KEPServerEX, an instance of another software, PTC ThingWorx[3], is responsible elaborating the normalized information returned,

---

[2] https://www.kepware.com/en-us/products/kepserverex/.
[3] https://www.ptc.com/en/products/iiot/thingworx-platform.

(a) Moulding machine.

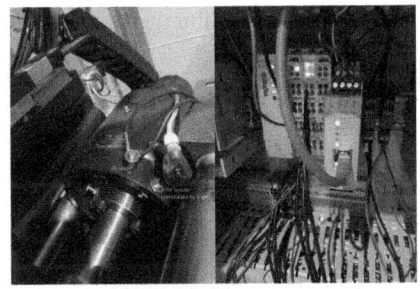

(b) Integrated sensors.

Fig. 4. TestBed set up.

store and manipulate them into an historical database and send them to the webserver displaying human readable information to the end-user. The moulding machine chosen (see Fig. 4) for the pilot natively provides about 2000 information tags, but just some of them are sensible information about the process. To identify the correct breakdown event, it was necessary to find out the best way to obtain this information in real time. The solution adopted was to mount on the molding machine a series of new sensors to obtain real time information. In particular:

– PLC Wago[4] this tool allows the platform to retrieve information about the electric consumption.
– Pruftechnik VIBGUARD COMPACT[5] Sensors: on Injection and Closing side. These sensors have been placed to monitor rotation, temperature, and vibration of the bearings. For the injection bearing two warning thresholds has been set to detect the breakage event to prevent. These threshold were defined based on ISO 10816-3 norm of bearing constructors.

5   Results and Discussion

The validation aspect is done in one specific plant in Italy. Input data for the model is a multivariate time-series sampled every 500 ms with 49 input features. Data is then grouped in batches of 15 min for model training. The features include:

– the electric current consumption of the machine,
– the temperature in each of the cavities of the mould,
– the velocity of the vibration of the bearing
– the acceleration of the vibration of the bearing.

---

[4] https://www.wago.com/us/discover-plcs.
[5] https://www.pruftechnik.com/com/Products-and-Services/Condition-Monitoring-Systems/Online-Condition-Monitoring/Online-Condition-Monitoring-Systems/VIBGUARD-compact/.

Figure 5 below illustrates the sample input data and an abnormal event (red line).

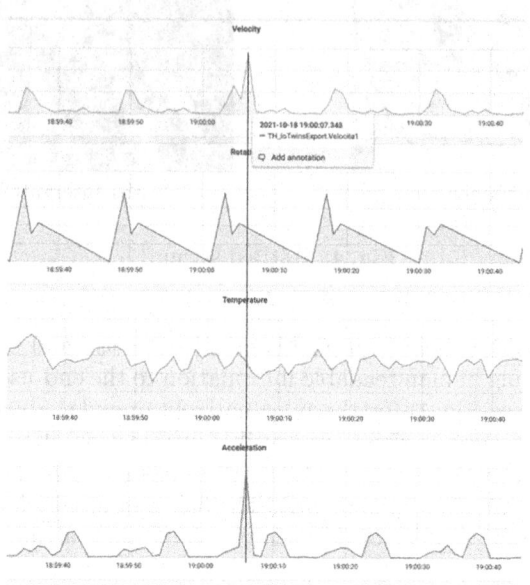

Fig. 5. Multivariate features by time (Color figure online)

Preliminary results, illustrated in Fig. 6, indicate that the model predictions are in accord with the real data. Given a day in which the machine had one critical alarm at around 14:15, the model correctly begins predicting this failure at 13:30. This is illustrated in Fig. 6, showing a gradual decrease in model output value p from 13:30 (p = 0.8642) until 14:30 (p = 0.0353). Once the failure is resolved and the machine status goes back to Normal, the output value computed by the model increases and stabilises itself around approximately 1.

Using the machine data, the machine learning model described in Sect. 4.1 was developed by a corresponding service in the IotWins project and sent to a demonstration/validation dashboard that has been developed in order to capture singularities that can help to improve the performance. A screenshot of this dashboard is shown in Fig. 7(a).

The Dashboard was built using JAVA and JavaScript as languages and Spring and Express Js as its respective framework. There is one specific microservice in charge of handling the requests from our front-end and our edge server that will manage and redirect all of them to the respective microservice, it will also control the authorization and authentication for each request. Once the request of login is made, the application will validate that user, an access token (Json Web Token) will be created and used within every single further request.

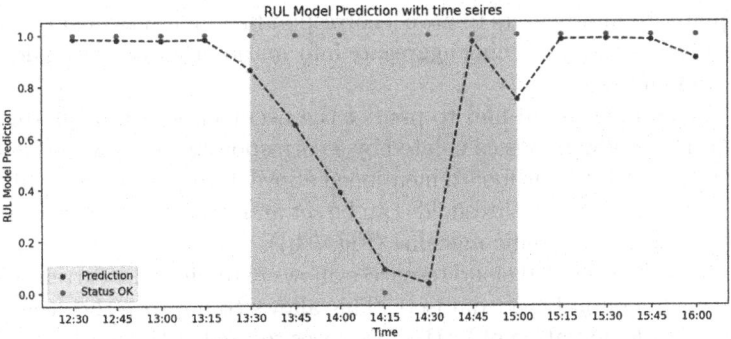

Fig. 6. Model prediction following bearing status

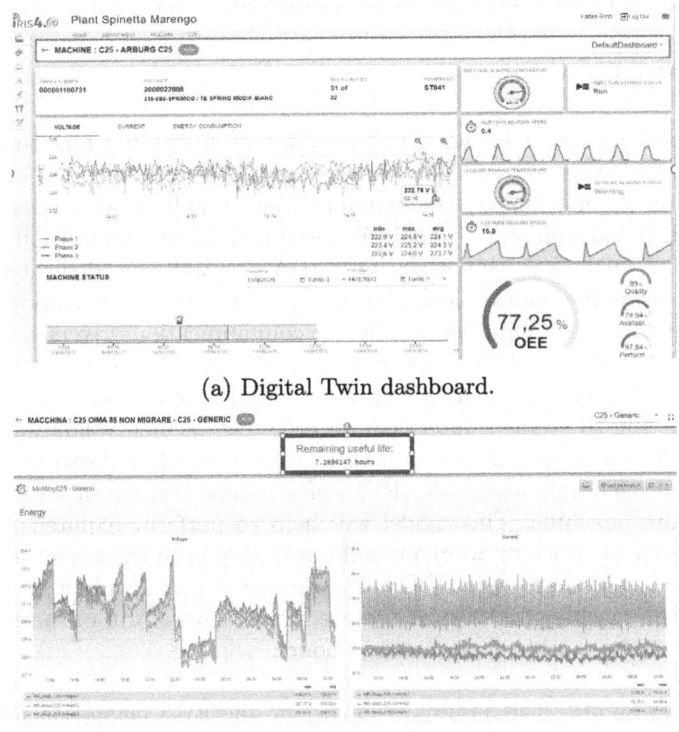

(a) Digital Twin dashboard.

(b) RUL reporting dashboard

Fig. 7. Digital twin and validation dashboards

The technology used by the front-end to render all data visualisable is Angular Framework that will make requests to the server side using a representational state transfer application programming interface (REST API), it is therefore possible for the user to view information from the machines, both real time and historical data.

The platform allows users to have a corresponding digital twin of the machine with the advantage of obtaining aggregate information that can give added value to the data collected.

RUL (remaining useful life) to predict the occurrence of the "alarm" status during normal production is calculated by a corresponding service in the IotWins project and sent to the dashboard mentioned above. Using the integrated alerting features in the dashboard, thresholds can be set and defined to generate an alarm about the RUL for a specific machine (Fig. 7(b)).

The use of the provided cloud resources allows extending the current model by training the model on bigger datasets. This allows to improve the accuracy and enables the implementation of further use cases to predict the machine behavior. Furthermore, as with more diverse data, it is expected that also the model will become more complex, and more parameters have to be tuned. Therefore, an optimization of the ML models will be considered.

6   Conclusion

In the proposed work we connected an injection moulding machine to a custom-made data-gathering system. The collected data sources include both sensors embedded on the machine by the manufacturer, as well as other sensing equipment installed and validated by GCL. We used various communication standards - OPC/UA, CODESYS, MODBUS, OPC/DA - as well as a dedicated middleware to integrate the information exposed by the machines and analyse the data. This tool incorporates hundreds of different communication drivers and can connect directly to the machine, exposing the normalized data to the outside. In addition, we devised a SaaS architecture to handle the complete data pipeline, from acquisition to storage. Intermediate processes include validation and pretreatment. The collected data was used to train a Machine Learning model to estimate the remaining useful life (RUL) of a critical bearing in a Plastic injection moulding machine. This model will help to perform required preventing maintenance in advance to avoid any failures during production on the machine. The model runs on the Cineca HPC infrastructure. Every 15 min it receives fresh data from the machine and returns its prediction in the form of the Remaining Useful Life of the machine, expressed in hours.

Acknowledgements. This project is funded by the EU Commission for IoTwins project number 857191.

References

1. Cai, B., Liu, Y., Xie, M.: A dynamic-Bayesian-network-based fault diagnosis methodology considering transient and intermittent faults. IEEE Trans. Autom. Sci. Eng. **14**(1), 276–285 (2017)
2. Cai, B., Liu, H., Xie, M.: A real-time fault diagnosis methodology of complex systems using object-oriented Bayesian networks. Mech. Syst. Sig. Process. **80**, 31–44 (2016)

3. Wang, Y., Liu, M., Bao, Z., Zhang, S.: Stacked sparse autoencoder with PCA and SVM for data-based line trip fault diagnosis in power systems. Neural Comput. Appl. **31**(10), 6719–6731 (2019)
4. Shen, C., Qi, Y., Wang, J., Cai, G., Zhu, Z.: An automatic and robust features learning method for rotating machinery fault diagnosis based on contractive autoencoder. Eng. Appl. Artif. Intell. **76**, 170–184 (2018)
5. Siegel, J.E., Pratt, S., Sun, Y., Sarma, S.E.: Real-time Deep Neural Networks for internet-enabled arc-fault detection. Eng. Appl. Artif. Intell. **74**, 35–42 (2018)
6. Borghesi, A., Bartolini, A., Lombardi, M., Milano, M., Benini, L.: A semisupervised autoencoder-based approach for anomaly detection in high performance computing systems. Eng. Appl. Artif. Intell. **85**, 634–644 (2019)
7. Borghesi, A., Bartolini, A., Lombardi, M., et al.: Anomaly detection using autoencoders in high performance computing systems. In: Proceedings of the AAAI Conference on Artificial Intelligence, pp. 9428–9433 (2019)
8. Si, X.-S., Wang, W., Hu, C.-H., Zhou, D.-H.: Remaining useful life estimation – a review on the statistical data driven approaches. Eur. J. Oper. Res. **213**(1), 1–14 (2011)
9. Zhang, S., Zhang, S., Wang, B., Habetler, T.G.: Deep learning algorithms for bearing fault diagnostics—a comprehensive review. IEEE Access **8**, 29857–29881 (2020)
10. Borghesi, A., et al.: IoTwins: design and implementation of a platform for the management of digital twins in industrial scenarios. In: 2021 IEEE/ACM 21st International Symposium on Cluster, Cloud and Internet Computing (CCGrid). IEEE (2021)
11. Ince, T., Kiranyaz, S., Eren, L., Askar, M., Gabbouj, M.: Real-time motor fault detection by 1-D convolutional neural networks. IEEE Trans. Ind. Electron. **63**(11), 7067–7075 (2016)
12. Zhang, W., Peng, G., Li, C., Chen, Y., Zhang, Z.: A new deep learning model for fault diagnosis with good anti-noise and domain adaptation ability on raw vibration signals. Sensors **17**(2), 425 (2017)
13. Bai, S., Zico Kolter, J., Koltun, V.: An empirical evaluation of generic convolutional and recurrent networks for sequence modeling. arXiv preprint arXiv:1803.01271 (2018)
14. van den Oord, A., et al.: WaveNet: a generative model for raw audio. arXiv preprint arXiv:1609.03499 (2016)
15. Guo, L., Li, N., Jia, F., Lei, Y., Lin, J.: A recurrent neural network based health indicator for remaining useful life prediction of bearings. Neurocomputing **240**, 98–109 (2017)
16. Cao, Y., Ding, Y., Jia, M., Tian, R.: A novel temporal convolutional network with residual self-attention mechanism for remaining useful life prediction of rolling bearings. Reliab. Eng. Syst. Saf. **215**, 107813 (2021)
17. Wang, Y., Deng, L., Zheng, L., Gao, R.X.: Temporal convolutional network with soft thresholding and attention mechanism for machinery prognostics. J. Manuf. Syst. **60**, 512–526 (2021)
18. Spiegel, S., et al.: Pattern recognition and classification for multivariate time series. In: Proceedings of the 5th International Workshop on Knowledge Discovery from Sensor Data (2011)

Production Time Prediction for Contract Manufacturing Industries Using Automated Machine Learning

Afonso Sousa[1,3], Luís Ferreira[1,3(✉)], Rui Ribeiro[1,3], João Xavier[2], André Pilastri[3], and Paulo Cortez[1]

[1] ALGORITMI R&D Centre, Department of Information Systems, University of Minho, 4804-533 Guimarães, Portugal
pcortez@dsi.uminho.pt
[2] Colep Packaging, 3730-423 Vale de Cambra, Portugal
joao.xavier@colep-pk.com
[3] EPMQ - IT CCG ZGDV Institute, 4804-533 Guimarães, Portugal
{afonso.sousa,luis.ferreira,rui.ribeiro,andre.pilastri}@ccg.pt

Abstract. The estimation of production time is an essential part of the manufacturing domain, allowing companies to optimize their production plan and meet the dates required by the customers. In the last years, there have been several approaches that use Machine Learning (ML) to predict the time needed to finish production orders. In this paper, we use the CRISP-DM methodology and Automated Machine Learning (AutoML) to address production time prediction for a Portuguese contract manufacturing company that produces metal containers. We performed three CRISP-DM iterations using real data provided by the company related to production orders and production operations. We compared four open-source modern AutoML technologies to predict production time across the three iterations: AutoGluon, H2O AutoML, rminer, and TPOT. Overall, the best results were achieved in the third CRISP-DM iteration by the H2O AutoML tool, which obtained an average error of 3.03 days. The obtained results suggest that the inclusion of data about individual manufacturing operations is useful for improving production time for the entire production order.

Keywords: Contract manufacturing · Automated Machine Learning · Regression

1 Introduction

Under the current highly competitive market, manufacturing companies are constantly being challenged by growing demands for individualized products that present a higher quality and simultaneously a lower production cost. In particular, modern logistics methods, such as high on-time or short delivery and lead times, are a way to differentiate the companies from their competitors [16]. In

© IFIP International Federation for Information Processing 2022
Published by Springer Nature Switzerland AG 2022
I. Maglogiannis et al. (Eds.): AIAI 2022, IFIP AICT 647, pp. 262–273, 2022.
https://doi.org/10.1007/978-3-031-08337-2_22

general, the manufacturing process consists of the transformation of raw materials into components or final products, through a sequence of operations [13]. Since a production plan can contain several production orders with different operations, the exact prediction of the production time for an order plays a determining role in improving the efficiency of the plan, allowing to meet the dates required by the customer [11].

This paper presents an implementation of the CRISP-DM methodology [17] and Automated Machine Learning (AutoML) [6] to predict production time in the manufacturing domain. We used real-world data collected from a Portuguese contract manufacturing company that produces metal containers, such as cans and aerosols. The prediction of production time is essential for the company, in order to optimize the production plan.

Our approach consisted of using several CRISP-DM iterations to provide predictions of the time needed to conclude a production order. We used four recent open-source AutoML tools for the CRISP-DM modeling phase, to automate algorithm selection and hyperparameter tuning: AutoGluon, H2O AutoML, rminer, and TPOT. The usage of AutoML allowed us to focus on the data preparation phase. We executed a total of three CRISP-DM iterations, in which we tested different data preprocessing and feature engineering techniques.

The paper is structured as follows. Section 2 presents the background work. Section 3 describes the CRISP-DM methodology and the AutoML tools. Section 4 details the three CRISP-DM iterations we performed. Then, Sect. 5 presents the overall results and discussion. Finally, Sect. 6 presents the main conclusions and future work directions.

2   Background

The lithography process of the company begins with cutting the coil. Given the diversity of containers that the company produces, there are numerous metal and cutting specifications to meet the product requirements. The next step is the varnishing process. In this process, varnish or enamel is applied to the metal sheet, to protect the can from the erosion caused by its contents. Next, the sheet goes through a printing process. This stage consists of applying ink to a certain area of the sheet, translating the color and illustration according to the client's request. Finally, the sheet goes through a secondary cutting process, transforming it into several bodies or strips.

Each step of the lithography factory process has a set of associated operations that influence production time. Through a predictive modeling approach, we can increase the accuracy of forecasts for the production times of an order, which is a key indicator for the development of a successful production plan [8]. Although there are research works on the use of Data Mining techniques for the forecasting of manufacturing order delivery times, within our knowledge the research concerning data-driven modeling of lithography process is scarce.

In [1], the authors estimated the weekly lead times of a producer of heavy electric motors by using Artificial Neural Networks (ANN), fuzzy regression, and a traditional regression. The obtained results showed that ANN is superior to both regression and fuzzy regression, obtaining lower Mean Absolute Percentage Error (MAPE) values. ANN were also used by [9]. The authors used technical specifications demanded by the customer to predict the flow time of a wide range of products, obtaining an accuracy superior to 90% when comparing the results of ANN and factorial design with check data. [8] compared a traditional Operations Research (OR) approach with ML approaches and concluded that ML provides more precise results than OR when predicting the production lead time of optical lenses for eyeglasses.

3   Materials and Methods

3.1   CRISP-DM

CRISP-DM (CRoss Industry Standard Process for Data Mining) is a framework that allows translating a business problem into a Data Mining project, providing a holistic view of the life cycle of a Data Mining project, beyond the application of ML models. It is divided into six different phases, that cover further general tasks [17]. First, in the business understanding phase it is necessary to understand what the goals are from a business point of view and to fit these requirements into a Data Mining problem. In the data understanding phase, it is essential to analyze the collected data in order to draw insights and identify possible problems. The data preparation phase processes all relevant data to generate the final dataset. In the modeling phase, various techniques and algorithms are applied to extract knowledge from the processed data. In the evaluation phase, the generated model is typically tested with real data, to ensure the quality of the model. Finally, the deployment phase can vary depending on the project requirements. It can be a final report or the implementation of a repeatable Data Mining process [2].

3.2   AutoML

The modeling phase of CRISP-DM is mainly related to the choice of a modeling technique, usually involving ML algorithms (e.g., Linear Regression, Decision Trees) and their hyperparameters. Typically, this is a very iterative phase, that might require trial and error approaches, domain knowledge, or heuristics [7]. Given the iterative nature of this step, this can become a time-consuming process. Automated Machine Learning (AutoML) helps reduce the time needed for the modeling phase of CRISP-DM by choosing the best algorithm and hyperparameters for a given dataset, without the need for human input [6].

In this work, we use AutoML to automate algorithm selection and hyperparameter tuning for the modeling phase of CRISP-DM. The usage of AutoML intends to reduce the time needed for the modeling phase and allowed us to focus on other key phases, such as data understanding and data preparation [15].

For our experiments, we used four open-source AutoML tools: AutoGluon, H2O AutoML, rminer, and TPOT. AutoGluon is the AutoML module for the Gluon framework [4]. For our experiments, we used the tabular prediction component of AutoGluon. H2O AutoML is the open-source AutoML module from the H2O framework [10]. Rminer is a package for the R language that facilitates the usage of ML algorithms and also includes flexible AutoML functions [3]. For rminer, we used the "automl3" template[1]. Lastly, TPOT is an AutoML library based on the Scikit-Learn framework that uses Genetic Programming [14]. Table 1 summarizes the characteristics of the four used AutoML technologies (**Framework, API** language, number of **Algorithm Families** used by each tool, and **Version** used in this work).

Table 1. Description of the adopted AutoML tools.

Tool	Framework	API	Algorithm families	Version
AutoGluon [4]	Gluon	Python	7	0.3.1
H2O AutoML [10]	H2O	Java, Python, R	6	3.36.0.3
rminer [3]	rminer	R	6	1.4.6
TPOT [14]	Scikit-Learn	Python	5	0.11.7

4 CRISP-DM Methodology

4.1 First CRISP-DM Iteration

In the first iteration, we performed the first five phases of CRISP-DM (from Business Understanding to Evaluation). Our goal was to predict production time, in other words, the time needed to conclude a production order.

Business Understanding. In this phase, the company identified the need to predict when a production order will be finished, given a defined starting date. We identified a regression task, in which we aim to predict the number of days needed to finish a production order after it starts.

Data Understanding. For this phase, we analyzed the first data source provided by the company: Production Orders. This dataset is composed of 14,614 records, gathered from December 2018 to December 2020. Each record is related to a finished production order. Table 2 summarizes the attributes of the dataset.

---

[1] https://CRAN.R-project.org/package=rminer.

Table 2. Description of the Production Orders dataset attributes.

Attribute	Description	Type	Levels	Example
Order_ID	ID of the production order	Categorical	14438	1000234997
Material	Material of the final product	Categorical	4490	51-49012
Order_quantity	Produced quantity of order	Numerical	–	423
Start_order	Starting date of production order	Date	394	28/03/2019
End_order	Ending date of production order	Date	341	06/01/2020

Data Preparation. First, we created the target variable: the number of days needed to finish each production order, which we named Delta. This new column resulted from the subtraction of the columns End_order and Start_order (in total days since the company also works at the weekends). For the data preprocessing, we deleted records with missing values (e.g., records without a registered material or with missing dates). There were instances of records with duplicate Order_ID (around 175 records). In these cases, we deleted the duplicate records and only considered the first record with a distinct ID. Then, we removed the column Order_ID since it has no predictive value (every record has a distinct ID). Additionally, we removed the target column outliers. The company experts suggested that records with production time higher than 150 days should be considered outliers, so we removed any record with a Delta over 150. We noticed some records had negative Delta and we also remove these records.

Finally, we applied a standardization technique to the only numeric column (Order_quantity), which transformed the values into a new scale with a mean equal to 0 and a standard deviation equal to 1. For the column Material, we used the Inverse Document Frequency (IDF) technique, which converts a categorical column into a numerical column of positive values, based on the frequency of each level of the attribute [12]. The resulting preprocessed data resulted in a reduction of records from 14,614 to 14,101 production orders.

Modeling. For the modeling phase, we selected four open-source AutoML tools detailed in Sect. 3.2: AutoGluon, H2O AutoML, rminer, and TPOT. The validation method we used was based on a recent AutoML benchmark [5], adopting a 10-fold external cross-validation to evaluate the test set predictions. Additionally, for each AutoML training, we used an internal 5-fold cross-validation to select the best algorithm and hyperparameters, a task that is performed automatically by these tools. The test set predictions for each of the external 10 folds were evaluated using the Mean Absolute Error (MAE) ($\in [0.0, \infty[$, where the lower the value, the better are the predictions). In addition, we computed the Normalized MAE (NMAE), which is equal to the MAE divided by the range of the target column (in percentage). For the internal validation (performed by the AutoML tools), we used the MAE. To keep the comparison fair between the AutoML tools, we defined a maximum training of one hour when available (only unavailable on rminer).

Evaluation. To evaluate the predictive results we computed the average metrics of the external 10 folds. We also added a confidence interval based on the t-distribution with 95% confidence, to ensure the statistical significance of the experiments. Table 3 shows the average results for the first CRISP-DM iteration. For each tool, the table shows the algorithm that was most often the leader during training across the 10 folds (**Best Algorithm**). The results also show the average test scores of the external 10 folds and confidence intervals (**MAE** and **NMAE**), with the best scores in bold.

Table 3. Average results obtained on the first CRISP-DM iteration on test data (best values in **bold**).

AutoML Tool	Best algorithm	MAE	NMAE
AutoGluon	Ensemble	4.00 ± 0.15	3.46 ± 0.26
H2O AutoML	Stacked Ensemble	$\mathbf{3.70 \pm 0.10}$	$\mathbf{3.21 \pm 0.24}$
rminer	Stacked Ensemble	3.98 ± 0.12	3.45 ± 0.27
TPOT	Gradient Boosting	3.77 ± 0.12	3.26 ± 0.25

The results show that H2O AutoML obtained the best results with an average error of 3.70 days, corresponding to an average NMAE of 3.21%. Nevertheless, the four tools obtained close results (average MAE ranging from 3.70 to 4.00 and average NMAE ranging from 3.21% to 3.46%). After this iteration, the company provided an additional dataset related to the individual operations of a production order, which were addressed in the second CRISP-DM iteration.

4.2 Second CRISP-DM Iteration

Business Understanding. During a new phase of business understanding, the company provided new insights about the manufacturing process. Each production order is composed of a series of operations (e.g., cut, paint). Each one of these operations is carried out in a specific work center and might involve different types of raw materials. Also, every production operation is associated with a production order ID and has a defined start and end timestamp. In this CRISP-DM iteration, we attempt to improve the previous iteration results by predicting the time needed to carry out production operations (instead of production orders). By predicting this attribute, we can estimate the total time needed to conclude the associated production order.

Data Understanding. For this phase, a new data source was analyzed (Operations), related to production operations associated with a specific production order. The dataset has 40,610 records and 8 attributes. Each production order has between one and nine operations. The most common number of operations is three, while the average value is 2.83. Table 4 summarizes the attributes of the operations dataset.

Table 4. Description of the Production Operations dataset attributes.

Attribute	Description	Type	Levels	Example
Order_ID	ID of the production order	Categorical	14438	1000234997
Operation_ID	ID of the operation type (e.g., cut)	Categorical	36	25
Work_Center	Work center that performed the operation	Categorical	21	1LE02
Operation_quantity	Quantity associated to the operation	Numerical	–	44587
Start_date_op	Starting date of operation	Date	385	16/09/2020
End_date_op	Ending date of operation	Date	390	04/11/2020
Start_time_op	Starting time of operation	Time	29362	10:54:27
End_time_op	Ending time of operation	Time	29369	14:26:02

Data Preparation. The creation of the target attribute followed an approach similar to the first iteration. We created a target column that specifies the number of days that an operation takes to finish. In this case, since the operations dataset has start and end times, we computed the difference between the starting timestamp and the ending timestamp. The result is that the values of target variable were converted to decimals (e.g., 1.25 days). For the data preprocessing we also used similar transformations. First, we deleted rows with missing values. Then, we used the same threshold to remove outliers from the target, so that operations that took more than 150 days were removed from the dataset (only 12 records were discarded).

Given that several production operations are associated with the same production order, we did not need to remove duplicate Order IDs. However, we removed operations associated with Order IDs that were not on the Orders dataset (used on the first CRISP-DM iteration). Contrary to the first iteration, we did not remove the column Order_ID because in this approach the ID is not unique to every record. Finally, we standardized the Operation_quantity column and applied IDF to the columns Order_ID, Operation_ID, and Work_Center. The Data Preparation phase reduced the number of records from 40,610 to 39,225.

Modeling. The modeling phase was similar to the first iteration, detailed in Sect. 4.1. It used the same four AutoML tools (AutoGluon, H2O AutoML, rminer, and TPOT), the same validation (10-fold external cross-validation and 5-fold internal cross-validation), as well as the same predictive metrics (MAE and NMAE).

Evaluation. Given that in this iteration we predict the operation time instead of the total production time, we aggregate the Operations dataset after the predictions. We group the dataset by Order_ID and sum the time for all individual operations, resulting in a predicted production time. Then, we compare the obtained production time with the real values from the Orders dataset. Thus, instead of measuring the MAE and NMAE for the individual operations, we aggregate the results to maintain a meaningful comparison between CRISP-DM iterations. Also, the main problem identified by the company is related to the total production time instead of operations time. Table 5 shows the average results for the second CRISP-DM iteration.

Table 5. Average results obtained on the second CRISP-DM iteration on test data (best values in **bold**).

AutoML tool	Best algorithm	MAE	NMAE
AutoGluon	Ensemble	6.00 ± 0.10	4.46 ± 0.35
H2O AutoML	Deep Learning	$\mathbf{5.83 \pm 0.68}$	$\mathbf{4.35 \pm 0.76}$
rminer	Support Vector Machine (SVM)	6.51 ± 0.11	4.82 ± 0.38
TPOT	Gradient Boosting	6.64 ± 0.11	4.92 ± 0.40

The second iteration results show that, in general, this approach obtained worse results, when compared to the first iteration. Even though the best AutoML tool for this iteration (H2O AutoML) obtained an average error of 5.83 days, this is still worse than all the results from the first iteration (which had an average MAE ranging from 3.70 to 4.00 days).

These results suggest that, in this case, predicting production time by predicting each operation time is less effective than using the ML models to directly predict the total production time. After analyzing the results of this iteration with the company experts, we concluded that the degradation of the results was caused by two factors: first some operations may be executed simultaneously in two or more production lines, and the second was that different operations have different machine setup times, which the company does not store. Instead, it uses the average time for all operations. To check if we could improve the results, we decided to perform a third CRISP-DM iteration, using both the Orders and Operations dataset together.

4.3   Third CRISP-DM Iteration

On this iteration, we used the two datasets from the previous iterations (Orders and Operations). We merged the two datasets so that we remain with one record for each Order ID, but with additional columns regarding which operations are performed for each order. Since we used the same datasets, the business understanding and data understanding phases were skipped for this iteration.

Data Preparation. In order to merge the two datasets (Orders and Operations), we first removed the records that had missing values from each dataset. Then, we pivoted the Operations dataset, such that each different operation became a new column. Since this dataset has 36 different operations (as shown on Table 4), this created 36 new columns for the Operations dataset. After the pivot, we changed the values with 1 and 0 (1, if the order includes the operation;

0, otherwise). Next, we performed a left join between the Orders and Operations. This join added 36 new columns to the Orders dataset (those created by the Operations pivot). Then, we created the target column by subtracting the end date from the initial date. Figure 1 exemplifies the merging process.

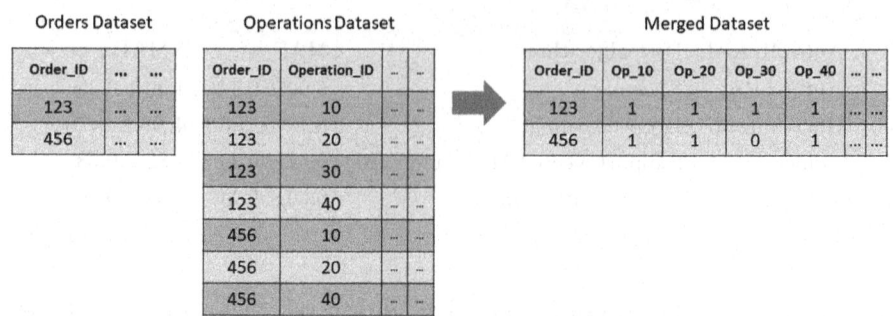

Fig. 1. Representation of the merging process.

Finally, similarly to the first iteration, we standardized the Order quantity column and applied IDF to the Material column. This resulted in a dataset with 14,106 rows and 39 features (excluding the target column).

Modeling. The modeling phase was similar to the previous two CRISP-DM iterations, using AutoML (Sect. 4.1).

Evaluation. Table 6 shows the average results for the third CRISP-DM iteration, including, for each AutoML tool, the algorithm that was most often the leader, the average predictive scores (MAE and NMAE), and confidence intervals (t-distribution with 95% confidence).

Table 6. Average results obtained on the third CRISP-DM iteration on test data (best values in **bold**).

AutoML Tool	Best algorithm	MAE	NMAE
AutoGluon	Ensemble	3.38 ± 0.07	2.81 ± 0.31
H2O AutoML	Stacked Ensemble	$\mathbf{3.03 \pm 0.04}$	$\mathbf{2.53 \pm 0.29}$
rminer	Stacked Ensemble	3.42 ± 0.08	2.85 ± 0.31
TPOT	Gradient Boosting	3.17 ± 0.08	2.64 ± 0.29

The results from the third iteration show that for the third time H2O AutoML obtained the best results, with an average error of 3.03 days, corresponding to 2.53% of the target range. Similar to the first iteration, all tools obtained close results, with a maximum difference of 0.39 for MAE and 0.32% points for NMAE. Overall, this was the iteration that achieved the best predictions.

5 Discussion

Table 7 presents a summary of the predictive results for the three CRISP-DM iterations. For each **Iteration**, we detail the used datasets (**Datasets**). For each **AutoML Tool**, we also include the algorithm that was most often the leader during training across the 10 folds (**Best Algorithm**). The results show the average test scores of the external 10 folds (**MAE** and **NMAE**), with the best values for each iteration in bold.

Table 7. Average results obtained on each CRISP-DM iteration on test data (best values in **bold**).

Iteration	Datasets	AutoML Tool	Best algorithm	MAE	NMAE
1st	Orders	AutoGluon	Ensemble	4.00 ± 0.15	3.46 ± 0.26
		H2O AutoML	Stacked Ensemble	**3.70 ± 0.10**	**3.21 ± 0.24**
		rminer	Stacked Ensemble	3.98 ± 0.12	3.45 ± 0.27
		TPOT	Gradient Boosting	3.77 ± 0.12	3.26 ± 0.25
2nd	Operations	AutoGluon	Ensemble	6.00 ± 0.10	4.46 ± 0.35
		H2O AutoML	Deep Learning	**5.83 ± 0.68**	**4.35 ± 0.76**
		rminer	SVM	6.51 ± 0.11	4.82 ± 0.38
		TPOT	Gradient Boosting	6.64 ± 0.11	4.92 ± 0.40
3rd	Orders and Operations	AutoGluon	Ensemble	3.38 ± 0.07	2.81 ± 0.31
		H2O AutoML	Stacked Ensemble	**3.03 ± 0.04**	**2.53 ± 0.29**
		rminer	Stacked Ensemble	3.42 ± 0.08	2.85 ± 0.31
		TPOT	Gradient Boosting	3.17 ± 0.08	2.64 ± 0.29

The results became worse between the first and second iterations, when we tried to predict the production time using only data from operations. While in the first iteration the best AutoML tool (H2O AutoML) obtained an average MAE of 3.70 days, the best results in the second iteration were almost doubled (MAE of 5.83 days, also by H2O AutoML). As mentioned in Sect. 4.2, the degradation of results obtained during the second iteration can be related to the absence of information about setup time and parallel operations.

On the third iteration, when we merged the Orders and Operation datasets, the predictive results presented an improvement from both the first and second iterations. In effect, the third iteration obtained the best predictive results, with the best MAE of 3.03 days and NMAE of 2.53%, by H2O AutoML. Nevertheless, on the third iteration, all tools achieved average results better than all the other results from the first and second iterations. This suggests that using data about individual operations might be useful for improving production time for the whole order.

It is worth mentioning that, on all three CRISP-DM iterations, the AutoML results were close: maximum MAE difference of 0.30 for 1st iteration; 0.81 - 2nd iteration; 0.39 - 3rd iteration. For the NMAE, the maximum predictive differences were: 0.25 *percentage points (pp)* for the 1st iteration; 0.57 *pp* - 2nd iteration; 0.32 *pp* - 3rd iteration. Regarding the best performing AutoML tools, H2O AutoML achieved the best results on all three iterations. TPOT was the second-best tool on iterations 1 and 3. AutoGluon was the second-best tool on the 2nd iteration.

6   Conclusion

In this paper, we applied the CRISP-DM methodology to predict production time for the lithography process of a Portuguese manufacturing company. This company produces metal cans for several sectors (e.g., food, cosmetics, pharmaceutical) and each type of can might involve different types of operations (e.g., cutting, applying varnish, printing). The prediction of the production time is essential for the company, in order to further optimize the production plan.

We executed a total of three CRISP-DM executions, using data provided by the company, between December 2018 to December 2020. The company provided two datasets: the first one (Orders) included data about production orders; the second one (Operations) provided information about individual operations associated with production orders. For the modeling phase of CRISP-DM, we used AutoML to automatically select the best ML algorithms and hyperparameters. We used four recent open-source AutoML tools: AutoGluon, H2O AutoML, rminer, and TPOT. During the first CRISP-DM iteration, we only used data from the Orders dataset. For the second iteration, we predicted production time using only the Operations dataset. In the third and final iteration, we merged the Orders and Operations datasets. The best predictive results were achieved on the third CRISP-DM iteration (average MAE of 3.03 days, by H2O AutoML).

In future work, we intend to explore more AutoML technologies to automate the Modeling phase of CRISP-DM. Moreover, we intend to address issues related to the second iteration, namely the setup time and usage of parallel operations. Lastly, we wish to use more datasets from the analyzed manufacturing domain to predict production time, aiming to check if there is further consistency in the results obtained in this paper.

Acknowledgements. This work has been supported by the European Regional Development Fund (FEDER) through a grant of the Operational Programme for Competitivity and Internationalization of Portugal 2020 Partnership Agreement (POCI-01-0247-FEDER-046102, PRODUTECH4S&C).

References

1. Asadzadeh, S., Azadeh, A., Ziaeifar, A.: A neuro-fuzzy-regression algorithm for improved prediction of manufacturing lead time with machine breakdowns. Concurr. Eng. **19**(4), 269–281 (2011)

2. Chapman, P., Clinton, J., Kerber, R., Khabaza, T., Reinartz, T., Shearer, C., et al.: CRISP-DM 1.0: step-by-step data mining guide. SPSS Inc. 9, 13 (2000)
3. Cortez, P.: Data mining with neural networks and support vector machines using the R/rminer tool. In: Perner, P. (ed.) ICDM 2010. LNCS (LNAI), vol. 6171, pp. 572–583. Springer, Heidelberg (2010). https://doi.org/10.1007/978-3-642-14400-4_44
4. Erickson, N., et al.: AutoGluon-Tabular: robust and accurate AutoML for structured data. arXiv preprint arXiv:2003.06505 (2020)
5. Ferreira, L., Pilastri, A.L., Martins, C.M., Pires, P.M., Cortez, P.: A comparison of AutoML tools for machine learning, deep learning and XGBoost. In: International Joint Conference on Neural Networks, IJCNN 2021, pp. 1–8. IEEE (2021). https://doi.org/10.1109/IJCNN52387.2021.9534091
6. Feurer, M., Klein, A., Eggensperger, K., Springenberg, J., Blum, M., Hutter, F.: Efficient and robust automated machine learning. In: Advances in Neural Information Processing Systems, vol. 28 (2015)
7. Gibert, K., Izquierdo, J., Sànchez-Marrè, M., Hamilton, S.H., Rodríguez-Roda, I., Holmes, G.: Which method to use? An assessment of data mining methods in environmental data science. Environ. Model. Softw. 110, 3–27 (2018). https://doi.org/10.1016/j.envsoft.2018.09.021
8. Gyulai, D., Pfeiffer, A., Nick, G., Gallina, V., Sihn, W., Monostori, L.: Lead time prediction in a flow-shop environment with analytical and machine learning approaches. IFAC-PapersOnLine 51(11), 1029–1034 (2018). https://doi.org/10.1016/j.ifacol.2018.08.472
9. Karaoglan, A.D., Karademir, O.: Flow time and product cost estimation by using an artificial neural network (ANN): a case study for transformer orders. Eng. Econ. 62(3), 272–292 (2017)
10. LeDell, E., Poirier, S.: H2O AutoML: scalable automatic machine learning. In: 7th ICML Workshop on Automated Machine Learning (AutoML) (2020)
11. Lingitz, L., et al.: Lead time prediction using machine learning algorithms: a case study by a semiconductor manufacturer. Procedia CIRP 72, 1051–1056 (2018). https://doi.org/10.1016/j.procir.2018.03.148
12. Matos, L.M., Cortez, P., Mendes, R., Moreau, A.: A comparison of data-driven approaches for mobile marketing user conversion prediction. In: 9th IEEE International Conference on Intelligent Systems, IS 2018, pp. 140–146. IEEE (2018). https://doi.org/10.1109/IS.2018.8710472
13. Okoshi, C.Y., Pinheiro de Lima, E., Gouvea Da Costa, S.E.: Performance cause and effect studies: analyzing high performance manufacturing companies. Int. J. Prod. Econ. 210, 27–41 (2019). https://doi.org/10.1016/j.ijpe.2019.01.003
14. Olson, R.S., Moore, J.H.: TPOT: a tree-based pipeline optimization tool for automating machine learning. In: Proceedings of the 2016 Workshop on Automatic Machine Learning, vol. 64, pp. 66–74. JMLR.org (2016)
15. Purbasari, A., Rinawan, F.R., Zulianto, A., Susanti, A.I., Komara, H.: CRISP-DM for data quality improvement to support machine learning of stunting prediction in infants and toddlers. In: ICAICTA 2021, pp. 1–6 (2021)
16. Reuter, C., Brambring, F.: Improving data consistency in production control. Procedia CIRP 41, 51–56 (2016)
17. Wirth, R., Hipp, J.: CRISP-DM: towards a standard process model for data mining. In: Proceedings of the 4th International Conference on the Practical Applications of Knowledge Discovery and Data Mining, Manchester, vol. 1, pp. 29–40 (2000)

Social Media, Sentiment Analysis/Natural Language - Text Mining

A Multi-Objective Optimization Algorithm for Out-of-Home Advertising

Nader Nader, Rafael Alexandrou, Iasonas Iasonos, Andreas Pamboris,
Harris Papadopoulos[(✉)], and Andreas Konstantinidis

Department of Electrical Engineering, Computer Engineering and Informatics,
Frederick University, Nicosia, Cyprus
n.nader@stud.frederick.ac.cy,
{res.ar,com.ii,res.ap,com.ph,com.ca}@frederick.ac.cy

Abstract. This paper presents a Multi-Objective Optimization (MOO) approach for Out-of-Home (OOH) advertising campaign billboard selection. In particular, it exploits a large variety of features from different sources, such as Geographic Information Systems (GIS) and demographics data, for the construction of billboard profiles that take into account all factors that affect the attractiveness of each billboard both in general and for different types of customers. These profiles are utilized by a Multi-Objective Evolutionary Algorithm based on Decomposition (MOEA/D) hybridized with two problem specific techniques to provide a set of non-dominated solutions, each corresponding to a different allocation of billboards to a given campaign. The experimental results enable exploration of the trade-offs between multiple conflicting objectives (e.g., cost vs. coverage) as well as demonstrate that the two problem specific techniques have improved the conventional MOEA/D performance with respect to both convergence and diversity.

Keywords: Billboards advertising · Out-of-Home advertising · Multi-Objective Optimization · Evolutionary computation · GIS

1 Introduction

Out-of-Home (OOH) advertising [8] is one of the oldest, yet among the most popular, forms of advertising. This is testified by the fact that, amid the COVID-19 crisis, the global market for OOH advertising was estimated at $27Bn (2020) and is projected to grow to $33Bn by 2026 [7]. In OOH advertising, selecting the "right" billboards for a given customer campaign (with implications on corresponding impressions, conversions, footfall, and ROI) remains an open challenge [9]. The optimal selection of billboards needs to consider multiple, often conflicting, objectives and constraints, such as the campaign cost, the area covered by the selected billboards and the similarity between the billboard and customer profiles. Consequently, this needs to be tackled as a Multi-Objective Optimization Problem (MOOP), providing a set of near-optimal solutions, as opposed to other studies [5] that treat multiple objectives as a single weighted function.

© IFIP International Federation for Information Processing 2022
Published by Springer Nature Switzerland AG 2022
I. Maglogiannis et al. (Eds.): AIAI 2022, IFIP AICT 647, pp. 277–288, 2022.
https://doi.org/10.1007/978-3-031-08337-2_23

A MOOP [1] can be mathematically formulated as:

$$\text{minimize } F(X) = (f_1(X), ..., f_k(X)), \text{ subject to } X \in \Omega$$

where Ω is the decision space and $X \in \Omega$ is the decision vector. $F(X)$ consists of k objective functions $f_i : \Omega \to R$, $i = 1, ..., k$, where R^k is the decision space. Objectives often conflict with each other and improving one objective may lead to the deterioration of another. Thus, no single solution exists that can optimize all objectives simultaneously. In such a case, the decision maker often requires the means for exploring the trade-offs between multiple alternative solutions, called the set of Pareto optimal (or non-dominated) solutions. The Pareto optimality concept is formally defined as follows:

Definition 1. A vector $u = (u_1, ..., u_k)$ is said to dominate another vector $v = (v_1, ..., v_k)$, denoted as $u \prec v$, iff $\forall i \in \{1, ..., k\}$, $u_i \leq v_i$ and $u \neq v$.

Definition 2. A feasible solution $X^* \in \Omega$ is called *Pareto optimal solution* iff $Y \in \Omega$ such that $F(Y) \prec F(X^*)$. The set of all Pareto optimal solutions is called the Pareto Set (PS) in the decision space, denoted as:

$$PS = \{X \in \Omega | \exists Y \in \Omega, F(Y) \prec F(X)\}$$

The image of the PS in the objective space is called Pareto Front (PF)

$$PF = \{F(X)|X \in PS\}$$

Multi-objective Evolutionary Algorithms (MOEAs) [2] can obtain an approximate PF in a single run by accommodating different forms of operators to iteratively generate a population of such solutions. A major goal of MOEAs when dealing with a MOOP is to produce a diverse set of non-dominated solutions that is as close as possible to the real PF.

In our previous work [6], we have introduced and demonstrated the Smart OOH Advertising web platform, focusing on its Graphical User Interface and main functionalities. In this paper, the main focus and contribution is on the Multi-Objective Optimization Problem for OOH Advertising (MOOP for OOHA) definition and formulation, as well as on the extended MOEA/D approach. Specifically, we have mathematically formulated the MOOP for OOH advertising billboard selection using a variety of data features constructed from data sources such as demographics and GIS data. Based on this formulation, the proposed approach mitigates much of the hurdles involved with OOH advertising through the use of advanced AI techniques. Specifically, the presented approach uses (i) *Feature Engineering* - cleaning, preparing and extracting knowledge from raw data; and (ii) *Multi-Objective Optimization* - obtaining a set of Pareto optimal solutions for exploring the trade-offs between multiple conflicting objectives in a single run, thus providing the decision maker (customer) with a set of near-optimal choices (based on their specific objectives/constraints).

The rest of this paper starts with an overview of the data used in this study and the feature engineering process performed in Sect. 2. Section 3 gives the mathematical formulation of the OOH advertising MOOP, while Sect. 4 describes the Multi-Objective Evolutionary Algorithm Based on Decomposition (MOEA/D) as well as two problem specific heuristics used in this work. Section 5 presents three experimental studies and discusses their results. Finally, Sect. 6 gives the conclusions and future directions of this work.

2 Data and Feature Engineering

In order to achieve more accurate profiling of both billboards and customers, it is required to identify, collect and analyze the most appropriate data related to OOH advertising. This data is not limited to billboard specs and locations, but also includes geo-spatial and demographics data. Geographical data was provided by *Geomatic Ltd*, a local cartography company in Cyprus, and was enriched with billboard locations from *Adboard Media Ltd*, one of the largest media firms in Cyprus.

2.1 GIS Data

The digital geographical database of *Geomatic Ltd*, i.e. Geomatic Maps^{TM}, covers the entire island of Cyprus and includes data on the National, Urban and Provincial Road Network of Cyprus (>23,785 Km), providing detailed navigation to 522 Municipalities and Communities. The incorporated GIS data are described in more detail below:

Road Network Data. The effectiveness of OOH advertising (via billboards) is greatly affected by the road network surrounding the billboards. The database used contains data about the national and local road network of Cyprus (accounting for a total of 98% island coverage). The road network's hierarchy, which categorizes roads according to their functions and capacities, as well as the traffic load, are a few of the characteristics that have a significant impact on OOH advertising. In particular, the following types of data are considered:

- Network hierarchy (freeways/highways, arterials, collectors, residential roads, and pedestrian roads)
- Street Names as defined by the Cyprus Post Office, the responsible authority for naming streets in Cyprus.
- House numbering.
- One-way or two-way roads.
- Distance of roads from billboard locations.

Points of Interest (POI) Data. Factors affecting how people are attracted to POIs include their preferences and needs, but also the "importance/role" of a given POI. The level of attraction reflects the number of people who are likely to view a billboard located close to certain POI. 15 main POI categories are identified (e.g., Accommodation, Culture, Education, Shopping), which are divided into 74 subcategories (e.g., Hotels 5 stars, Museums, Universities, Supermarkets). The POI data consists of the list of POIs with information regarding their type as well as their distance from billboards.

Public Transport Network Data. If the location of a billboard is traversed by the Public Transportation Network, it is more likely to be viewed by more people. Our presented approach combines data regarding the location of billboards and the relevant geographical data on the Public Transportation Network (within a radius of 60 m around the billboards). The corresponding features used in our study include: bus stops, bus routes, and bus lines, which corresponds to the number of times a given route is performed.

Building Footprints Data. The spatial characteristics of buildings such as their footprint, covered area, total volume, height and floor count.

Planning Zones Data. Zoning is a method of urban planning in which all tiers of government divide land into areas called zones. Each zone has a set of regulations for new development that differs from other zones. For planning purposes, Cyprus is divided into various planning zones. These mainly include residential, industrial, agricultural and tourist zones. The type of each planning zone surrounding a billboard is considered.

2.2 Demographics Dataset

The demographics data used are based on the Statistical Service of Cyprus (CYSTAT) 2011 decennial census survey. The data is provided at different granularities, namely at the postal code, quarter, municipality, and district levels. The demographic data includes 196 different statistical variables regarding the population, employment, education, and living conditions. In particular, the features used in our study are: total population by postal code, gender, age ranges, living quarters, employed persons by place of work and employed persons per NACE Rev.2 sectors (primary, secondary and tertiary).

2.3 Billboards Dataset

This data were provided by *Adboard Media Ltd* and includes data for 202 static billboards. The exact considered features include: billboard types, face count, frame dimensions, height from ground, illumination option, address, location, and monthly rental price. Additionally, further features regarding over than 1800

Fig. 1. Visibility analysis, Billboards & POI locations

customers are considered, including features such as the company name, type of industry and location, as well as data on campaigns, including historical records of customers, billboards per campaign and budget.

2.4   Feature Engineering

Feature engineering refers to the process of using domain knowledge to select and transform the most relevant features from raw data. This may lead to combining, deleting, aggregating and transforming features into new ones. The data concerning a particular billboard is defined based on the billboard's location and its corresponding viewing distance. A billboard's viewing distance depends on its size and image resolution. After consulting our media partner, a 500-m range has been adopted in this work.

The demographics-related data concerning a certain billboard are inherited from the billboards' postal code. However, since the billboard's viewing area may fall across multiple postal codes, the visible portions of all surrounding areas (i.e., within the 500-m radius) are considered and the corresponding demographics-related data are adjusted accordingly.

Additionally, important new features are generated through *Visibility Analysis*, which takes into consideration what is visible by an observer from a given location. Key terrain, observation posts, and other locations are used to assess capabilities (what is visible) and vulnerabilities (blocked view). The visibility analysis tools use elevation data and observer information to produce linear line of sight (LLOS) and radial line of sight (RLOS) information. The visibility analysis (illustrated in Fig. 1) has been conducted based on features such as: (i) the coordinates and height from ground of the billboards, (ii) the Digital Elevation Model, and (iii) the buildings surrounding the billboards within a 500-m range.

For simplicity, the billboard's orientation and viewing angle were not considered. The outcomes of this analysis include the visibility pixel count and the visibility percentage of an area covered by a certain road that can view a given billboard. This data was provided by *Geomatic Ltd* based on LiDAR data processed by the ArcGIS software.

3   Problem Formulation

Various objective functions for optimizing OOH advertising from the perspective of both advertising companies and customers have been identified:

Maximize Visibility/Attractiveness. The visibility is calculated for each billboard based on a weighted sum function. For a billboard $B_j \in \{B_0, ..., B_n\}$:

$$\max visibility(B_j) = \sum_{i=0}^{k} w_i B_j(a_i), \text{where} \sum_{i}^{k} w_i = 1,$$

$B_j(a_i)$ is the value of visibility variable i for B_j and w_i is its weight. The included visibility variables in the aforementioned weighted sum function are the following: visibility pixel count, visibility percentage per road type based on road type importance and speed, population, POI count, living quarters, employment count by place of work, road length, urbanization degree, building footprints volume and count, and bus lines for each billboard location within the predefined 500 m range.

Minimize Cost. Let c_j be the rental cost for the billboard B_j in solution X_i. The objective is to minimize the total cost (billboards rental costs for one month):

$$\min \sum_{B_j \in X_i} c_j.$$

A primary goal of advertising customers is to minimize spending and not exceed the planed advertising budget.

Maximize Similarity – Customer to Billboard Matching. Similarity refers to how well a billboard matches customer preferences based on the corresponding billboard and customer profiles. The traditional cosine measure [3] is used to determine the similarity between customers and billboards, which are both represented as vectors of attributes. These include the targeted age ranges, educational level, and related POIs, which are captured through appropriate online questionnaires incorporated into the platform.

$$similarity(x, y) = \frac{x.y}{\parallel x \parallel \cdot \parallel y \parallel},$$

where $\parallel x \parallel$ is the Euclidean norm of vector $x = (x_1, x_2, ..., x_p)$, defined as:

$$\parallel x \parallel = \sqrt{x_1^2 + x_2^2 + ... + x_p^2}.$$

In our case, x is the vector of customer profile data and y is the vector of billboard profile data.

Maximize Coverage. Coverage represents the distribution of billboards on the map. To maximize coverage, one needs to select billboards that have a higher visibility rate, while at the same time aiming for a wide geographically-dispersed configuration, which is represented by a spread function as in [4]. Given any two billboards B_i and B_j in $\{B_0, ..., B_n\}$, let $D(B_i, B_j)$ denote the length of the shortest path between them, i.e., the distance between B_i and B_j. Let $maxD$ denote the maximum such length of the shortest path between any pair of billboards in $\{B_0, ..., B_n\}$. The spread of the selected billboards in solution X is expressed as the normalized average distance between all possible pairs of billboards and is denoted by:

$$Spread(X) = \frac{\overline{D_x}}{maxD}, \text{ where } \overline{D_x} = \frac{\sum_{B_i \neq B_j \in X} D(B_i, B_j)}{n(n-1)}.$$

The Haversine distance method is applied in order to compute the shortest distance between any pair of billboards based on their geo-location.

Budget Constraint: Is a customer predefined budget for a specific marketing campaign, denoted as:

$$\sum_{B_j \in X_i} c_j <= C,$$

where C is the predefined budget and c_j is the cost billboard B_j in solution X_i.

4 Multi-Objective Evolutionary Algorithm Based on Decomposition (MOEA/D)

Initially, MOEA/D needs to decompose a MOOP into a set of sub-problems. Any decompositional technique can be used for this purpose [10]. In this paper, the Weighted Sum approach is used, as follows. The multi-objective problem is decomposed into m scalar optimization sub-problems considering two objectives from the problem set of objectives. The ith scalar optimization sub-problem can be defined as: $g^i(X, \lambda^i) = \lambda^i F_a(X) + (1 - \lambda^i) F_b(X)$, where λ^i is the weight

---

Algorithm 1. The MOEA/D general framework

Input:

- m: population size and number of subproblems;
- T: neighborhood size;
- uniform spread of weight vectors
  $(\lambda^1, 1 - \lambda^1), ..., (\lambda^m, 1 - \lambda^m)$
- gen_{max}: maximum number of generations;

Output: the external population, EP;
Step 0 – Setup: Set $EP := \phi$; $gen := IP_{gen} := \phi$;
Step 1 – Initialization: Generate an initial internal population
  $IP_0 = \{X^1, ..., X^m\}$
Step 2: For $i = 1, ..., m$ **do**
Step 2.1 – Genetic Operators: Generate a new solution Y using the genetic operators.
Step 2.2 – Repair heuristic: Apply a problem-specific repair heuristic on Y to produce Z.
Step 2.3 – Update Populations: Use Z to update IP_{gen}, EP and the T closest neighbour solutions of Z.
Step 3 – Stopping criterion: If stopping criterion is satisfied, i.e.
  $gen = gen_{max}$, **then** stop and output EP, **otherwise** $gen = gen + 1$, go to step 2.

---

coefficient of sub-problem $i = 1, ..., m$. For the remainder of this paper, we consider a uniform spread of the weights λ^i, which remain fixed for each i for the whole evolution and are determined as follows: $\lambda^i = 1 - (i/m)$, for $i = 2, ..., m$ and $\lambda^1 = 1$. Hence, the λ^i coefficient is mainly utilized for decomposing a MOOP into a set of scalar sub-problems by adding different weights to the objectives.

A general MOEA/D approach proceeds as in Algorithm 1:

- The internal population IP_{gen} of size m keeps the best solution found so far for each sub-problem. The initial solutions of IP_0 are generated either randomly as in [3] or deterministically using a problem-specific heuristic.
- Then at each iteration, a random selection operator chooses two parent solutions from the IP_{gen}, e.g., Pr_1, Pr_2. A one-point (1X) crossover operator produces an offspring solution O from Pr_1, Pr_2 and a random mutation operator modifies O to generate a new solution Y.
- Solution Z is finally produced by using a repair method on Y in case of any infeasibility (e.g., violation of the budget constraint).

4.1 Problem-Specific Heuristics

For further improving the convergence and diversity of the MOEA/D approach, two enhancements have been developed.

Population Initialization: in the case of a min-max objective functions in Sect. 3 (e.g., cost and coverage objectives), the initial population has been

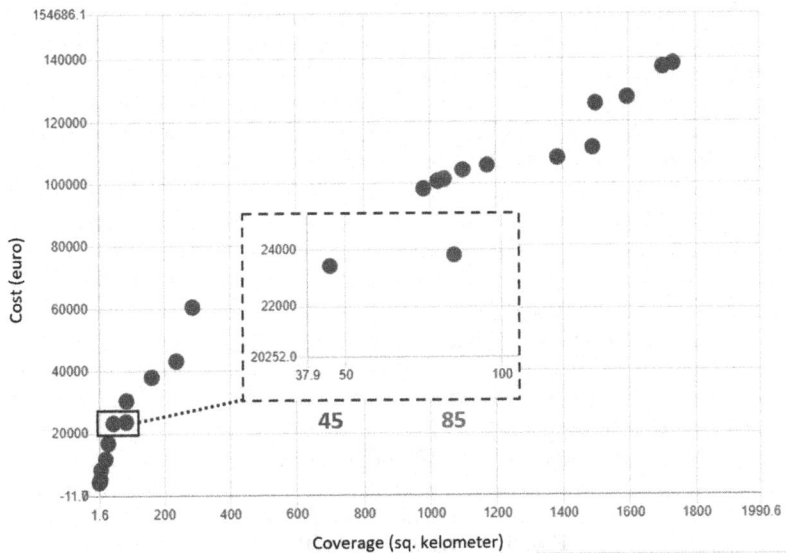

Fig. 2. Cost vs. Coverage

injected with the extreme solutions each satisfying one objective. The first extreme solution includes all billboards and therefore benefits the maximization objective function and the second extreme solution includes only one billboard and therefore benefits the minimization objective function. By including the two extreme solutions in the initial population it is expected to enhance the diversity and convergence of the MOEA.

Repair Heuristic: for handling the infeasible solutions there are several techniques that can be adopted. For example, one can be just dropping the infeasible solutions or repairing them. In this paper, a repair heuristic has also been implemented that removes one billboard iteratively until satisfying the budget constraint, as defined in Sect. 3.

5 Experimental Setup and Results

In this section, the algorithmic parameters used during the experimental studies are initially introduced followed by the experimental results.

5.1 Experimental Setup

For all experimental studies, the following algorithmic parameters are used: maximum number of generations $gen_{max} = 250$, population size $m = 100$, one-point (1X) crossover rate $r_c = 0.5$, random mutation rate $r_m = 0.2$ and neighborhood size $T = 2$. The contribution of the proposed problem-specific heuristics

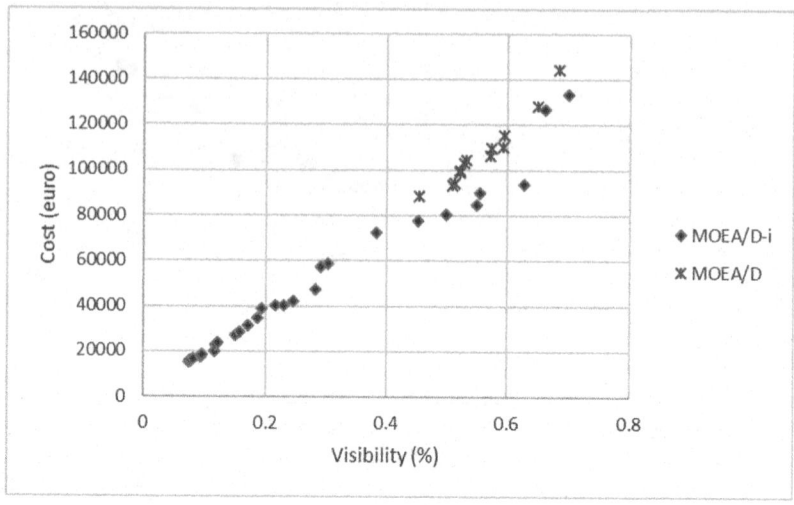

Fig. 3. MOEA/D vs MOEA/D-i

has been also demonstrated with individual experimental studies. That is the conventional MOEA/D has been compared with MOEA/D-i that includes the proposed population initialization as well as with MOEA/D-r that includes the proposed repair heuristic.

5.2   Experimental Study 1: MOO for OOH Advertising

In the first experimental study, the MOEA/D approach with both the population initialization and the repair heuristic is used for tackling the two conflicting objective functions namely maximizing coverage and minimizing cost (price). A thorough discussion follows for explaining the contradiction between the objective function as well as the benefit that a decision maker can have tackling OOH advertising in the context of MOO.

The Pareto front in Fig. 2 shows the trade-off between maximizing coverage and minimizing cost, where optimizing one deteriorates the other. Each feasible solution provides a certain level of coverage which could be desired in term of the solution cost depending on the customer budget. A decision maker can obtain further marketing insights by comparing Pareto front solutions. For example, Fig. 2 shows a comparison between two consecutive solutions. The first solution has a coverage of $45\,km^2$ while the next one has almost double the coverage ($84\,km^2$) for an additional cost of 380 EUR. Therefore, a customer could opt to spend 1.5% more in order to gain twice as much coverage.

5.3   Experimental Study 2: MOEA/D Versus MOEA/D-i

In this subsection, we examine the contribution of the proposed population initialization technique by comparing the conventional MOEA/D with random

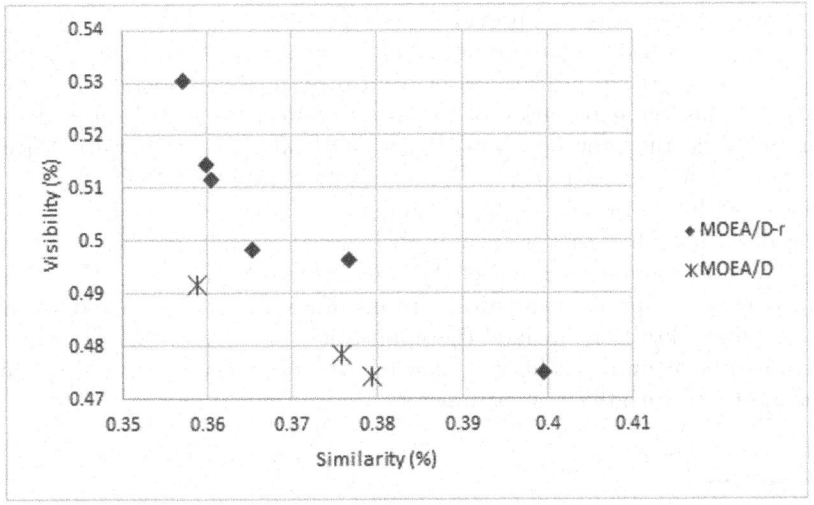

Fig. 4. MOEA/D vs MOEA/D-r

population initialization against the MOEA/D-i that injects the initial population with the extreme solutions as explained in Subsect. 4.1 in a min Cost - max Visibility MOOP. The results of Fig. 3 show that the proposed technique significantly improves the performance of the conventional MOEA/D by obtaining a higher quality and more diverse Pareto Front. In particular, MOEA/D-i offers the decision maker about three times more non-dominated solutions, which cover the objective space much better, while all of its solutions clearly dominate the solutions obtained by the conventional MOEA/D.

5.4   Experimental Study 3: MOEA/D Versus MOEA/D-r

In this subsection, we examine the contribution of the proposed repair heuristic by comparing the conventional MOEA/D that drops solutions in case of infeasibility against the MOEA/D-r that repairs infeasible solutions as explained in Subsect. 4.1 in a max Visibility - max Similarity MOOP. The results of Fig. 4 demonstrate the effectiveness of the repair heuristic compared to its counterpart. Similarly to the results of experimental study 2, the Pareto Front obtained by MOEA/D-r improves the performance of the conventional MOEA/D with respect to both convergence and diversity. Particularly, MOEA/D-r offers to the decision maker two times more non-dominated solutions, covering the objective space better and again all of its solutions clearly dominate the non-dominated solutions obtained by the conventional MOEA/D.

6   Conclusions

In this work, a Multi-Objective Optimization Problem (MOOP) for optimizing the selection of billboards for OOH advertising campaigns is initially defined and formulated. In the literature, previous studies treat the optimization of multiple objectives as a single weighted function and therefore provide a single solution, the proposed approach provides a set of near-optimal solutions (i.e., a Pareto Front) enabling the exploration of trade-offs between conflicting objectives. In order to tackle the proposed MOOP for OOH advertising a Multi-Objective Evolutionary Algorithm based on Decomposition (MOEA/D) is adopted and enhanced with two problem-specific heuristics. The experimental results show the benefits of tackling this problem in the context of Multi-objective Optimization, as well as the improvement of the conventional MOEA/D when combined with the problem specific heuristics in terms of both convergence and diversity.

Our future directions include the application of the proposed approach on data from other countries. This will allow further experimentation and evaluation of the approach with different parameters.

References

1. Coello, C.A.C., Lamont, G.B., Van Veldhuizen, D.A., et al.: Evolutionary Algorithms for Solving Multi-objective Problems, vol. 5. Springer, New York (2007). https://doi.org/10.1007/978-0-387-36797-2
2. Deb, K.: Multi-Objective Optimization Using Evolutionary Algorithms. Wiley, Hoboken (2002). S. Ross and R. Weber (eds.)
3. Han, J., Kamber, M., Pei, J., et al.: Getting to know your data. In: Data Mining, vol. 2, pp. 39–82. Elsevier, Amsterdam, Netherlands (2012)
4. Konstantinidis, A., Demetriades, A., Pericleous, S.: A multi-objective indoor localization service for smartphones. In: Proceedings of the 34th ACM/SIGAPP Symposium on Applied Computing, pp. 1174–1181 (2019)
5. Lotfi, R., Mehrjerdi, Y.Z., Mardani, N.: A multi-objective and multi-product advertising billboard location model with attraction factor mathematical modeling and solutions. Int. J. Appl. Logist. (IJAL) 7(1), 64–86 (2017)
6. Nader, N., Alexandrou, R., Iasonos, I., Pamboris, A., Papadopoulos, H., Konstantinidis, A.: Smart out-of-home advertising using artifcial intelligence and GIS data. In: Proceedings of the AAAI Conference on Artificial Intelligence (2022)
7. Randall, N.: Out of home advertising up (2.0% in q1 2018, tech, digital brands driving growth (2018). https://bit.ly/3kjcVwr. Accessed 28 Apr 2022
8. Taylor, C.R., Franke, G.R., Bang, H.K.: Use and effectiveness of billboards: perspectives from selective-perception theory and retail-gravity models. J. Advert. 35(4), 21–34 (2006)
9. Webb, A.: Google's targeted ads are coming to a billboard near you - bloomberg opinion (2018). https://bloom.bg/3komKJL. Accessed 28 Apr 2022
10. Zhang, Q., Li, H.: MOEA/D: a multiobjective evolutionary algorithm based on decomposition. IEEE Trans. Evol. Comput. 11(6), 712–731 (2007)

AutoMC: Learning Regular Expressions for Automated Management Change Event Extraction from News Articles

Murat Kalender$^{(\boxtimes)}$ (iD)

IgniteTech, Austin, TX, USA
murat.kalender@ignitetech.com
https://ignitetech.com

Abstract. Event extraction is one of the challenges to be tackled in order to extract valuable insight from unstructured text. The process of automatically identifying events in a corpus of text and extracting comprehensive information about them is called event extraction. Although a number of systems have been proposed for event extraction, there is currently no publicly available system specific to management changes. This paper presents a novel event extraction system - AutoMC - that identifies management change events from business news articles. Specifically, we propose a novel regular expressions based management change event extraction algorithm. The effectiveness of AutoMC is validated empirically over generated data sets. The experimental results show that our system performs competitively in comparison to management change event detection studies in the literature. High event detection performance (78.72% accuracy score) is achieved by the proposed event extraction rule learning method.

Keywords: Event extraction · Information extraction · Natural language processing

1 Introduction

In the new era of internet news publishing, hundreds of business articles are being published every day by popular news organizations. Business decision makers require an intuitive understanding of the health of their market, which is typically particularly sensitive to breaking news about economic events like acquisitions, management changes, stock splits, and dividend announcements [11].

It is a difficult task for business decision makers to process a continuous flow of news articles through various internet sources. Therefore, automated solutions that can analyze internet news articles in natural language are becoming increasingly valuable in today's information-driven business ecosystem [2]. Automating information extraction and knowledge acquisition processes can help decision-makers to save time and assist them to make better decisions by providing valuable input.

© IFIP International Federation for Information Processing 2022
Published by Springer Nature Switzerland AG 2022
I. Maglogiannis et al. (Eds.): AIAI 2022, IFIP AICT 647, pp. 289–300, 2022.
https://doi.org/10.1007/978-3-031-08337-2_24

In this context, the identification of events can guide decision making processes, as these events provide means of structuring information using concepts, with which knowledge can be generated by applying inference. Automating information extraction and knowledge acquisition processes can facilitate or support decision makers in fulfilling their cumbersome tasks, as faster processing of aggregated data from various sources enables one to make better informed decisions [3].

Formally, event extraction is defined as the process of automatically identifying events in a corpus of text and extracting comprehensive information about them [7]. In this study, we introduce AutoMC, a system that identifies the management change events from business news articles using natural language processing (NLP) and machine learning based techniques.

There are two main aspects of an event detection system: the detection of the event and the extraction of the entities associated with the respective event. We address the first part with a supervised text classifier to detect business news articles that contain a management change event. The second part is addressed with a named entity recognizer and auto generated regular expressions. Figure 1 shows an example of a management change event that can be detected automatically using an event detection system.

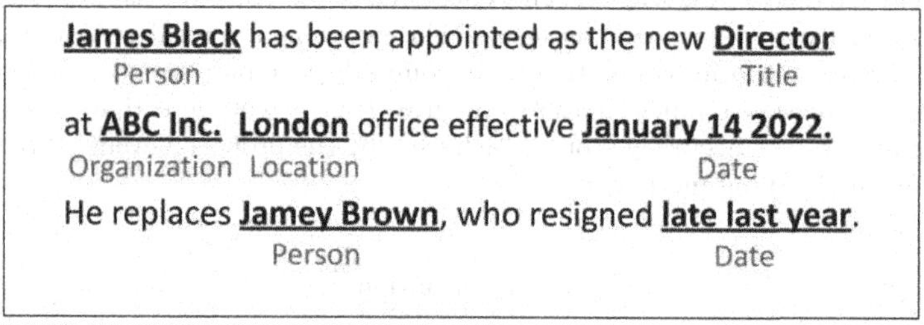

Event Type	Person	Organization	Title	Location	Date
Hire	James Black	ABC Inc.	Director	London	Jan 2022
Departure	Jamey Brown	ABC Inc.	Director	London	Dec 2021

Fig. 1. An example extraction of the management change event and its linking of a piece of textual content to event entities.

The effectiveness of AutoMC is validated empirically by using evaluations over generated data sets. The experimental results show that AutoMC performs competitively in comparison to the previous methods in the literature. The main contributions of this paper are summarized as follows.

– A novel event detection system is proposed to extract management change events from unstructured text. AutoMC relies on the automated extraction

of management change rules compared to manually constructed rules-based event detection studies in the literature.
- A new data set was created to evaluate the performance of the proposed system.

The remainder of this paper is organized as follows. Section 2 reviews related work. Section 3 presents a detailed model of the AutoMC system. Experimental results are shown in Sect. 4 and we conclude in Sect. 5.

2 Related Work

Many researchers have made extensive efforts to develop a variety of methods [5,9,18,20] for extracting events from news articles. In this section, we review related work on business event extraction and analysis. The differences between existing work and our approach are then presented.

In recent years, most event extraction studies use deep learning methods to extract general events [6,14,19]. Specifically, Wang et al. [19] propose a document-level joint event extraction model, TDJEE, to extract financial events from numerous financial announcements. TDJEE uses BERT and CRF methods for event argument extraction and role labeling. To capture the semantic information of the document-level context, a relation-aware Transformer and attention network are used.

A large-scale training corpus is essential for deep learning models. Since it is challenging to create a large-scale training corpus many approaches to the detection of business events are template-based and rule-based methods [1,7, 15]. These studies use rule-sets or ontology knowledge-bases that are largely or entirely constructed by hand, rather than fully relying on manually annotated supervised datasets [8].

Arendarenko et al. [1] proposed BEECON, an information and event extraction system for business intelligence. It is an ontology-based system for business documents analysis that can detect 41 different types of business events from unstructured documents using NLP techniques, pattern recognition algorithms, and hand-written detection rules.

Hogenboom et al. [7] proposed SPEED that identifies the concepts defined in a semantic lexicon (WordNet [13]) related to economic events and applies rule based algorithms to detect economic events, which are defined in a domain ontology. In order to maximize recall of their proposed system, the authors match lexical representations of concepts retrieved from the text with event-related concepts that are available in WordNet.

Sahnoun et al. [15] presented an ontology-based system for management change event extraction. The authors defined a management change event ontology and a set of event rules manually and then consumed it using regular expressions, named entity recognition, and reasoning methods to extract management change events.

The creation of rules is a complicated process that requires a significant degree of domain knowledge, which makes rule based information extraction approaches less desirable. We propose a novel approach for automated extraction of management change rules using a human-annotated ground-truth data and n-gram technique. The annotated ground truth data is created manually by the business experts over years in the scope of IgniteTech's Business Intelligence (BI) solution named FirstRain[1]. AutoMC utilizes this annotated dataset to learn the event extraction rules in the form of regular expressions. Then our rule based algorithm uses those rules in the event extraction process.

3   AutoMC

AutoMC is an event extraction tool designed for detecting management changes from business news articles. AutoMC can identify 4 types of management change events:

- Internal Move: Change in position of an individual within the same organization.
- Move: A person switches from one organization to another one.
- Hire: Organization announces a new hire event and the story does not mention the previous organization.
- Departure: A person leaves an organization and no information is available about his/her new position.

AutoMC has been realized through the design and implementation of two major modules: AutoMC Workbench and Management Change Extraction Pipeline.

The AutoMC Workbench is used for presenting the identified events and allowing domain experts to fix if there are incorrect or missing event extractions. The AutoMC Workbench is a web application where users can also input text content and view the event extraction results. Figure 2 shows an example of extracted events from a news article[2]. In the workbench, the news article content is presented with highlighted person entities. Then all the extracted event related entities are listed. At the bottom, all the extracted events are listed in text fields so that the operator can update them when it is needed.

Management Change Extraction Pipeline is the core module that extracts management change events from a given input text. This module is composed of three submodules: Regex Learner, News Classifier, and Management Change Extractor. In the following sections, these sub-modules will be analyzed comprehensively.

3.1   Regex Learner

The Regex Learner module generates a list of regular expression rules for a given annotated dataset. Specifically, this task consists of; (i) entity annotation step where management change event named entities are annotated; (ii)

---

[1] https://ignitetech.com/softwarelibrary/firstrain.

[2] https://theproducenews.com/people/walmart-produce-exec-named-ceo-farm-fresh-direct.

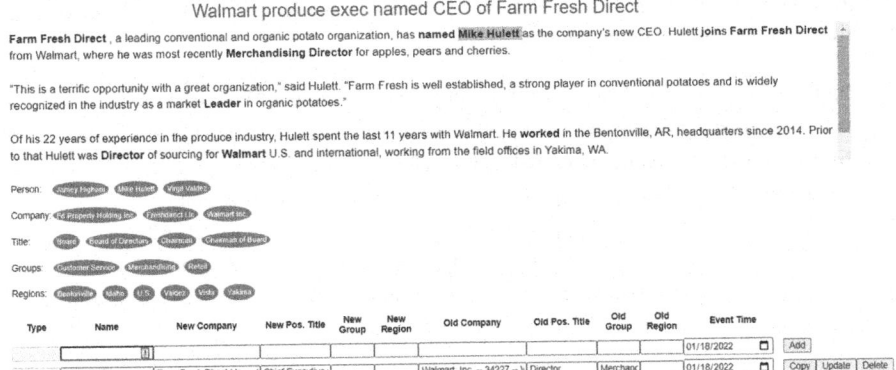

Fig. 2. The event extraction result of a news article is shown through the AutoMC Workbench.

natural language processing step where the input text is split into sentences, stop and infrequent words are removed; (iii) rule generation step where possible rules are generated using n-grams; (iv) rule filtering step where too generic and infrequently matching rules are filtered out.

In the entity annotation step, the event entities are replaced with special tokens of organization, title, and person. Management change events contain 6 different entity types (person, organization, title, group, region, and date) and the move event type has two instances of event entities; previous and new. In order to reduce the complexity of generated rules and to increase the detection rate, Regex Learner module is designed to generate rules which can detect the core entity types of person, title, and organization.

In the NLP step, we split documents into sentences and tokenize each sentence using Stanford's CoreNLP [12]. Regex Learner only retains words appearing more than 100 times in the dataset and removes the words that appear less. Regex Learner also removes stop words along with special words (as, to, of, new, etc.) that are observed frequently in management change events.

In the rule generation step, Regex Learner filters out the sentences if it does not contain all the event tokens of organization, title, and person. Then for each remaining sentence, Regex Learner generates all possible rule combinations using the n-gram technique with the restriction of retaining all entity tokens, a sentence verb, and at least one word between entity tokens. Regex Learner also adds the matches any number of characters regular expression token between each word in order to learn more generic rules. For example, Table 1 shows the generated rules for a given example sentence from a document annotated with a hire type of event. The event rule learning algorithm is applied for each management change event type and distinct rules are learned. In order to detect the previous position entities of move or internal move events, Regex Learner also learns rules using the same approach.

Table 1. An illustration of the Regex Learner Module on a sample sentence that contains management change events.

Input text	James Black has been appointed as the new Director at ABC Inc
Annotated text	_Person_ has been appointed as the new _Title_ at _Organization_
Processed text	_Person_ appointed as new _Title_ at _Organization_
Extracted rules	_Person_ .* appointed .* _Title_ .* at .* _Organization_
	Person .* appointed .* as .* _Title_ .* at .* _Organization_
	Person .* appointed .* new .* _Title_ .* at .* _Organization_
	Person .* appointed .* as .* new .* _Title_ .* at .* _Organization_

In the rule filtering step, Regex Learner filters out too generic and infrequently matching rules. If a rule is generated less than 100 times in the whole dataset, then it is considered infrequent and discarded. A rule is also discarded if it is too generic that it might cause false event detection. We label rules as too generic unless it is not generated 2 times more than the summation of its extracted subset rules. For example, the firstly listed extracted rule in Table 1 is a generic rule that would cover all the possible event extractions of the other three subset rules.

The proposed rule learning method is one of the key contributions of this study. We have utilized our method on the annotated data, which is created manually by the business experts of IgniteTech to learn the management change event rules. The annotated dataset contains 30,106 published news articles in 2021 about management change events. Table 2 shows the number of news articles and the number of distinct event types in our final training dataset.

Table 2. Regex Learner training dataset characteristics.

# Article	# Event	# Move	# Departure	# I_Move	# Hire
30,106	47,387	5,947	8,532	9,878	23,030

Regex Learner is able to learn three types of rules; new, previous, and departure. New rules help us to extract new positions, new organizations, and person entities for the hire and move event types. Previous rules help us to extract previous positions, previous organization, and person entities for the move event types. Similarly, departure rules help us to extract previous position, previous organization, and person entities for the departure event types. Table 3 shows the total number of auto generated rules along with 3 sample rules for each rule type as a result of the rule learning step using our training dataset.

Table 3. Auto generated management change event rules statistics along with sample ones.

Type	Size	Samples
New	207	_Organization_ .* announce .* promotion .* _Person_ .* to .* _Title_
		Person .* is appointed .* to .* _Title_ .* of .* _Organization_
		Organization .* replaced .* _Title_ .* with .* _Person_
Previous	164	_Person_ .* prior .* joining .* , .* _Title_ .* at .* _Organization_
		Person .* served as .* _Title_ .* of .* _Organization_
		Person .* was .* _Title_ .* at .* _Organization_
Departure	45	_Organization_ .* announces .* _Person_ .* resigned .* _Title_
		Organization. * of .* _Person_ .* resigned .* as .* _Title_
		Organization .* retire .* _Person_ .* from .* _Title_

3.2 News Classifier

The News Classifier module aims to solve a binary classification problem by detecting news articles about management change events. This module is realized in two steps: the creation of training data and the development of a fast and accurate supervised text classification algorithm.

The first step, creating a training set is achieved by combining the articles about management change events used in the rule learning step and other business news articles, which are collected using the FirstRain solution for the same period of 2021. We have created a balanced dataset, where each target class is represented by the equal number of input samples. The dataset contains totally 60, 000 published news articles.

In the second step, we have used FastText [10] as a linear text classifier on the created dataset. FastText considers distributed word representation and word order using a variety of methods while utilizing computationally efficient algorithms. It converts documents to vectors by averaging the word embeddings that correspond to their words and is used as the input to train linear classifiers with a hierarchical softmax function [10]. In recent studies [16,17], it is reported that FastText outperforms the traditional machine learning algorithms such as Logistic Regression, Support Vector Machines (SVM), Random Forests, and it is frequently used for text classification [4]. For that reason, FastText is used in this study as the text classifier to detect news articles about management change events.

3.3 Management Change Extractor

Management Change Extractor module is used for extracting the events from news articles by utilizing a rule based approach. Specifically, our approach consists of three main steps that are described in Algorithm 1.

In the first step, the input text is processed with Stanford's CoreNLP tool [12] to extract named entities, sentences, and words. Then the extracted entities are

```
events = [];
sentences, entities = stanford_corenlp_service(document);
for sentence in sentences do
    annotated_sentence = annotate_entities(sentence, entities);
    new_matchings = match_rules(annotated_sentence, new_rules);
    previous_matchings = match_rules(annotated_sentence, previous_rules);
    departure_matchings = match_rules(annotated_sentence, departure_rules);
end
events.add(new_matchings);
for new_match in new_matchings do
    for previous_match in previous_matchings do
        if new_match.person = previous_match.person then
            unified_event = unify(new_match, previous_match);
            events.remove(new_match);
            events.add(unified_event);
            break;

    end
end
events.add(departure_matchings);
for departure_match in departure_matchings do
    for new_match in new_matchings do
        if new_match.person = departure_match.person then
            unified_event = unify(new_match, departure_match);
            events.remove(departure_match);
            events.add(unified_event);
            break;

    end
end
return events;
```

Algorithm 1: The algorithm for a rule based management change event extraction for an input document.

replaced with special tokens of organization, title, and person. In the second step, event extraction rules are applied to each sentence in the order of new, previous, and departure. In the final step, the matching rules are unified and interpreted to find the management change events that would be presented in the AutoMC Workbench. The possible event unification cases per event type are listed below:

- Hire: If there is only a new rule matching for a person entity then it is classified as a hire event type.
- Internal Move: When the same person entity is matched with a new and previous rule and organization names are identical for the new and previous matchings then an internal move event is created by combining the extracted entities.

– Move: When the same person entity is matched with a new and previous rule and organization names are different for the new and previous matchings then a move type of event is created by combining the extracted entities.
– Departure: If there is only a departure rule matching for a person entity then it is classified as a departure event type.

4 Evaluations and Experiments

The primary goal of this work is to create a system for extracting management change events from texts automatically. To evaluate the performance of the proposed system, a corpus is formed as described below.

News articles about the management change event has been collected using the FirstRain product in January 2022. FirstRain collects hundreds of articles published every day by popular news agencies like CNN, BBC, etc. Then, 500 different English news articles about a management change event are selected randomly and annotated manually by business experts to create the final testing dataset. The characteristics of the generated dataset are described in Table 4.

Table 4. AutoMC management change event dataset characteristics.

Total event	Hire	Move	I_Move	Departure	
578	335	55	100	88	
Total entity	Person	New_Org	New_Title	Prev_Org	Prev_Title
2003	578	490	490	243	202

To evaluate the performances of the proposed AutoMC system, accuracy metric is used as in the following formula:

$$Accuracy = \frac{\# \text{ correct predictions}}{\# \text{ total events or entities}} \tag{1}$$

The results of the overall performance on the test dataset are illustrated in Tables 5 and 6. As Table 5 shows AutoMC has achieved 78.22% accuracy. The highest performance 90.75% accuracy is measured with the detection of the hire event type. We also observed the lowest performance of 54.55% accuracy with the detection of the move event type.

Table 5. Comparison of the performance values of AutoMC event extraction with varying event types.

Hire	Departure	I_Move	Move	Total
90.75%	65.91%	63.00%	54.55%	78.72%

Table 6 shows the performance values of AutoMC entity detection with varying entity types. The highest performance 93.25% accuracy is observed with the detection of the person entity, which can be also be interpreted as event detection performance of AutoMC. We observed the lowest performance of 44.55% accuracy with the detection of the previous title entity. Similarly, low performance (59.26%) is observed for the previous organization entity too.

Table 6. Comparison of the performance values of AutoMC entity detection with varying entity types.

Person	New_Org	New_Title	Prev_Org	Prev_Title	Total
93.25%	84.90%	79.80%	59.26%	44.55%	78.88%

Low performance on detection of the previous entities has caused AutoMC to perform worse compared to hire event type as we see in Table 5. The main reason for this low performance is that previous position information is mostly given partially in a sentence of management change article and it can be extracted by interpreting the whole document content. Since the AutoMC system extracts events at the sentence level, it doesn't perform well to extract previous entity types for certain cases.

For example, for the passage below, AutoMC recognizes that this passage contains a management change event. It would identify "John Black" as the person entity, "ABC Inc." as the new organization entity, and "Chief Executive Officer" as the new title entity of the event. However, AutoMC fails to detect the previous organization entity since there is no sentence that contains the previous organization and previous title entities. Therefore, AutoMC classifies the event as a hire event type rather than an internal move event, which can be interpreted only from the second sentence.

"ABC Inc. announces the appointment of John Black as the Company's Chief Executive Officer. Jim Nolan, Chairman of ABC Inc., commented, We are excited to welcome John as the CEO of Diamond Wipes, who has been with the company for several years."

One of the management change event detection studies in the literature is proposed by Sahnoun et al. [15], which is also a rule based system. Our work differs from this study in the aspect of rule creation, which is automated in our proposed study. The authors have evaluated their system on a manually annotated dataset of 40 news articles. They reported a 79.34% F1 score in their evaluation results and closer performances for new and previous organization and title entity types. Even though our performance results are closer to this study, we can deduce that we arrived at an acceptable rate for a fully automated system to extract management change events from unstructured text.

5   Conclusion

This study presents - AutoMC - a management change event detection system that can extract management change event entities for a given unstructured text by using NLP and machine learning based techniques. The creation of the extraction rules is one of the key challenges addressed in the proposed system. To address this problem, a rule based algorithm is proposed, which leverages NLP methods. Moreover, a series of experiments are conducted to evaluate the performance of the system. Evaluations show that the proposed system has a satisfactory performance (78.72% accuracy score) for the task and it performed competitively in comparison to the previous methods in the literature.

In future work, the proposed management change event detection system could be improved by learning rules at the document level rather than the sentence level by incorporating the state of the art document level event extraction algorithms.

References

1. Arendarenko, E., Kakkonen, T.: Ontology-based information and event extraction for business intelligence. In: Ramsay, A., Agre, G. (eds.) AIMSA 2012. LNCS (LNAI), vol. 7557, pp. 89–102. Springer, Heidelberg (2012). https://doi.org/10.1007/978-3-642-33185-5_10
2. Cao, L., Yang, Q., Yu, P.S.: Data science and AI in fintech: an overview. Int. J. Data Sci. Analyt. **12**(2), 81–99 (2021)
3. Chaturvedi, N., Dubey, J.: Study of state of arts methods for event extraction. In: Kiran Mai, C., Kiranmayee, B.V., Favorskaya, M.N., Chandra Satapathy, S., Raju, K.S. (eds.) Proceedings of International Conference on Advances in Computer Engineering and Communication Systems. LAIS, vol. 20, pp. 117–126. Springer, Singapore (2021). https://doi.org/10.1007/978-981-15-9293-5_10
4. Collobert, R., Weston, J., Bottou, L., Karlen, M., Kavukcuoglu, K., Kuksa, P.: Natural language processing (almost) from scratch. J. Mach. Learn. Res. **12**, 2493–2537 (2011)
5. Elloumi, S., et al.: General learning approach for event extraction: case of management change event. J. Inf. Sci. **39**(2), 211–224 (2013)
6. Han, Z., Jiang, J., Qiao, L., Dou, Y., Xu, J., Kan, Z.: Accelerating event detection with DGCNN and FPGAS. Electronics **9**(10), 1666 (2020)
7. Hogenboom, A., Hogenboom, F., Frasincar, F., Schouten, K., Van Der Meer, O.: Semantics-based information extraction for detecting economic events. Multim. Tools Appl. **64**(1), 27–52 (2013)
8. Jacobs, G., Hoste, V.: Extracting fine-grained economic events from business news. In: Proceedings of the 1st Joint Workshop on Financial Narrative Processing and MultiLing Financial Summarisation, pp. 235–245 (2020)
9. Jacobs, G., Lefever, E., Hoste, V.: Economic event detection in company-specific news text. In: Proceedings of the First Workshop on Economics and Natural Language Processing, pp. 1–10 (2018)
10. Joulin, A., Grave, E., Bojanowski, P., Mikolov, T.: Bag of tricks for efficient text classification. In: Proceedings of the 15th Conference of the European Chapter of the Association for Computational Linguistics, vol. 2, Short Papers, pp. 427–431. Association for Computational Linguistics (2017)

11. Konchitchki, Y., O'Leary, D.E.: Event study methodologies in information systems research. Int. J. Account. Inf. Syst. **12**(2), 99–115 (2011)
12. Manning, C.D., Surdeanu, M., Bauer, J., Finkel, J.R., Bethard, S., McClosky, D.: The stanford corenlp natural language processing toolkit. In: Proceedings of 52nd Annual Meeting of the Association for Computational Linguistics: System Demonstrations, pp. 55–60 (2014)
13. Miller, G.A.: WordNet: An Electronic Lexical Database. MIT Press (1998)
14. Peng, G., Chen, X.: Entity-relation extraction-a novel and lightweight method based on a gate linear mechanism. Electronics **9**(10), 1637 (2020)
15. Sahnoun, S., Elloumi, S., Ben Yahia, S.: Event detection based on open information extraction and ontology. J. Inf. Telecommun. **4**(3), 383–403 (2020)
16. Salur, M.U., Aydin, I.: A novel hybrid deep learning model for sentiment classification. IEEE Access **8**, 58080–58093 (2020)
17. Stein, R.A., Jaques, P.A., Valiati, J.F.: An analysis of hierarchical text classification using word embeddings. Inf. Sci. **471**, 216–232 (2019)
18. Tong, M., et al.: Image enhanced event detection in news articles. Proc. AAAI Conf. Artif. Intell. **34**(05), 9040–9047 (2020)
19. Wang, P., Deng, Z., Cui, R.: Tdjee: a document-level joint model for financial event extraction. Electronics **10**(7), 824 (2021)
20. Yang, H., Sui, D., Chen, Y., Liu, K., Zhao, J., Wang, T.: Document-level event extraction via parallel prediction networks. In: Proceedings of the 59th Annual Meeting of the Association for Computational Linguistics and the 11th International Joint Conference on Natural Language Processing (vol. 1: Long Papers), pp. 6298–6308 (2021)

How Dimensionality Reduction Affects Sentiment Analysis NLP Tasks: An Experimental Study

Leonidas Akritidis$^{(\boxtimes)}$ and Panayiotis Bozanis

School of Science and Technology, International Hellenic University, 14th km Thessaloniki, Nea Moudania, Thessaloniki 570 01, Greece
{lakritidis,pbozanis}@ihu.gr

Abstract. Dimensionality reduction is a well-known technique for limiting the size of the feature space and for discovering latent meaningful variables in the input data. It is particularly valuable when the raw data is sparse and its processing by machine learning algorithms becomes computationally very expensive. On the other hand, sentiment analysis refers to a collection of text classification methods that identify the polarity of the user opinions in blog posts, reviews, tweets, etc. However, since text is naturally very sparse, training classification models is often intractable, rendering the importance of dimensionality reduction even greater. In this paper we study the impact of dimensionality reduction in sentiment analysis classification tasks. Through extensive experimentation with traditional algorithms and benchmark datasets, we verify the general intuition that the dimensionality reduction methods significantly improve the data preprocessing times and the model training durations, while they sacrifice only small amounts of accuracy. Simultaneously, we highlight several exceptions to this rule, where the training times actually increase and the accuracy losses are significant.

Keywords: Sentiment analysis · Sentiment classification · Text classification · Dimensionality reduction · PCA · SVD

1 Introduction

Sentiment analysis refers to the popular problem of recognizing the polarity of user opinions in standard, usually unstructured excerpts of text. The opinion polarities may be binary (positive or negative), ternary (e.g., neutral), or fall into a specific range (for example, ratings within 1–5 or 1–10 scale). Nowadays, sentiment analysis techniques are widely applied in numerous applications, with the aim of automatically evaluating the submitted user opinions. Indicative examples include blog communities [2,4], customer reviews [13,16], social networks [6,18], microblogs [22,23], forums, messengers, and so on.

From the perspective of machine learning, the sentiment analysis algorithms fall into the broader category of text classifiers. Text classification is one of the

© IFIP International Federation for Information Processing 2022
Published by Springer Nature Switzerland AG 2022
I. Maglogiannis et al. (Eds.): AIAI 2022, IFIP AICT 647, pp. 301–312, 2022.
https://doi.org/10.1007/978-3-031-08337-2_25

most well studied machine learning problems, and a vast amount of research is presently conducted towards the improvement of the existing models [1, 3, 10]. The most common approaches train either binary, or multi-class text classifiers by utilizing manually, or artificially labeled training sets. The learned models are subsequently employed to determine the polarity of user opinions in previously unseen text corpora.

The most recent advances in the area include sophisticated NLP methods based on deep learning architectures such as the LSTM [5, 12], Convolutional Neural Networks [19], attention-based Transformers [24], etc. These methods have been proved effective at capturing the text semantics either at word level [14, 20], or at sentence level [9, 24]. Despite their success in pure NLP tasks (e.g., in machine translation), the traditional classification algorithms are still of great usefulness because they combine simplicity, effectiveness, and fast training rates.

Since the vast majority of machine learning algorithms work with numerical vectors, the typical raw text representation is not applicable, and the input documents must be appropriately transformed (namely, *vectorized*) to satisfy this requirement. Nevertheless, the traditional text vectorization methods such as tf-idf, convert each word (or n-gram) of the corpus to a distinct feature with its own weight. Hence, they lead to representations of very long and sparse vectors, with hundreds of thousands, or even millions of features, that negatively affect both the model training durations and memory consumption. These side effects are broadly known in the literature as the *curse of dimensionality*.

To limit its consequences, the dimensionality reduction methods construct latent spaces of lower dimensionality, and project the original feature vectors onto that space. This is primarily performed by applying matrix decomposition (or factorization) techniques, so that the least significant features are discarded, and the most significant ones are used to build another space of lower dimensionality. In this way, they partially confront the problems of the curse of dimensionality, usually with a small sacrifice in the generated model accuracy.

This paper presents an extensive study of the effectiveness of dimensionality reduction in sentiment analysis NLP tasks. Our motivations derive from i) the importance of sentiment analysis and its wide adoption by numerous systems, and ii) the limited number of similar studies in the relevant literature. In general, our experimental evaluation confirmed that the dimensionality reduction methods greatly improve the model training durations, while they introduce small accuracy losses. Nonetheless, the main contribution of this work lies in the detection of several cases where this observation does not hold. In these cases, the training durations on lower dimensional spaces were actually increased, whereas the accuracy losses were significantly larger than normal. This indicates that an in-depth research is required to accurately evaluate the impact of dimensionality reduction in sentiment analysis classification.

The rest of this paper is organized as follows: Sect. 2 presents the current advances in the fields of text classification, sentiment analysis, and dimensionality reduction algorithms. Subsequently, Sects. 3 and 4 present the results of our experimental study and discuss the significance of our findings, respectively. Finally, Sect. 5 summarizes the conclusions of this research and outlines the most important elements of our future work.

2   Related Work

The rapid growth of the (micro)blogging communities, social networks and commercial platforms has rendered sentiment analysis one of the hottest topics in the Natural Language Processing (NLP) research field. As a result, the relevant literature includes numerous works that deal with this interesting problem. The earliest articles tested the performance of several text classifiers, such as Naive Bayes, SVMs, Neural Networks, etc., in small datasets containing user reviews for products and events [11,15]. A survey on multiple sentiment analysis algorithms and applications was conducted in [13].

During the past few years, the deep learning methods have been proved very successful in numerous classification tasks. Therefore, a significant amount of research has focused on the exploitation of these methods in the problem of sentiment analysis. More specifically, [19] proposed a framework based on the Convolutional Neural Networks (CNN) and the Word2Vec model [14] to improve the accuracy and generalizability of their approach.

In addition, the Long Short-Term Memory (LSTM) networks are presently among the most effective deep learning methods for modeling sequential data. They have been applied extensively in numerous text classification problems, including sentiment analysis. For instance, in [25], the authors introduced an attention-based network for aspect-level sentiment classification, whereas [12] augmented the LSTM framework with a stacked attention mechanism consisting of attention models for both the target and sentence levels. Furthermore, in [5], the LSTM Recurrent Neural Network (RNN) has been utilized to perform sentiment classification and topic discovery in COVID-19 online discussions.

The transformers constitute another recent, yet powerful deep learning architecture for NLP tasks. Similarly to RNNs, they also process sequential data, but not necessarily in the provided order. In contrast, they implement an attention mechanism that identifies the context at any position in the input sequence [24]. The work of [17] introduced DICET, a transformer-based method for Twitter sentiment analysis. DICET encodes the transformer representations, and applies a contextual embedding technique to enhance the quality of tweets. Moreover, [26] presented an experimental comparison between 5 sentiment analysis tools and 4 pre-trained Transformer-based models on six datasets, demonstrating that the 4 fine-tuned models were superior to the 5 tools by a margin of 6.5–35.6%.

On the other hand, dimensionality reduction is a well-established technique for reducing the size of the input space and limiting the side effects of the curse of dimensionality. In the context of sentiment analysis, it has been applied to project the initial feature vectors onto a lower dimensional space that retains the most important input variables. Indicatively, [8] introduced a semi-supervised Laplacian eigenmap, called SS-LE, that discards the redundant features by decreasing the detection errors of the sentiments. In [21], the authors employed the traditional Singular Value Decomposition (SVD) to perform dimensionality reduction in sentiment classification. Finally, the method of [7] considered the label and structural information of text by adopting a semi-supervised approach for feature weighting and extraction.

Although the effectiveness of the deep learning architectures in sentiment classification is unquestionable, the traditional machine learning algorithms are still of great usefulness, mainly because they are able to quickly train simple, yet powerful models. In the following experiments, we demonstrate multiple cases where simple algorithms, such as Logistic Regression, combine both decent classification quality and fast training procedures.

This preliminary work is among the first to consider the implications of dimensionality reduction in the performance of these algorithms in sentiment analysis tasks. In future versions, we intend to further extend this study with the aim of covering the majority of the aforementioned deep learning architectures.

3   Sentiment Analysis and Dimensionality Reduction

This section presents the experimental evaluation of the effectiveness of various machine learning algorithms in sentiment analysis NLP tasks, against the dimensionality of the underlying feature space. The analysis is organized in four subsections: i) Sect. 3.1 describes the characteristics of the utilized datasets, ii) Sect. 3.2 briefly presents the six classification algorithms that participated in our tests along with the selected values of their hyper parameters, iii) Sect. 3.3 outlines our text preprocessing methodology, and iv) Sect. 3.4 discusses the accuracy results of the classifiers and the model training durations.

All the experiments were conducted on a single workstation equipped with 32 GB of RAM, and an Intel Core i7-7700 processor running at 3.6 GHz. The code was developed by using several Python libraries, whereas all the algorithms were executed without CPU or GPU parallelization. To facilitate the reproducibility of the presented results, we released the code on Github[1].

3.1   Datasets

Four popular sentiment analysis datasets were used in this study. All of them are publicly available, and have been utilized extensively in the relevant literature for evaluating NLP algorithms. In particular, IMDb[2] consists of 50,000 movie reviews for binary sentiment classification. The second dataset, Twitter US Airline[3], includes more than 14 thousand tweets with ternary user opinions (namely, positive, negative, and neutral) on five major US airlines.

The third dataset also originates from Twitter, and includes a collection of roughly 28 thousand tweets[4]. The tweets have been authored by a set of influential users, and contain positive, negative, and neutral opinions on publicly traded companies. The dimensionality of the input vector space of this dataset, after text cleaning and data preprocessing (full details are provided in Sect. 3.4), was approximately 12 thousand features.

---

[1] https://github.com/lakritidis/SADR.

[2] https://www.kaggle.com/lakshmi25npathi/imdb-dataset-of-50k-movie-reviews.

[3] https://www.kaggle.com/crowdflower/twitter-airline-sentiment.

[4] https://www.kaggle.com/vivekrathi055/sentiment-analysis-on-financial-tweets.

Table 1. Datasets for sentiment analysis accompanied by their characteristics

Dataset	Instances	Dimensionality	Classes
IMDb Movie Reviews	50,000	77,026	2
Twitter US Airline Sentiment	14,640	9,849	3
Financial Tweets Sentiment	28,437	12,138	3
Amazon Reviews (office products)	53,258	35,229	5

A subset of the Amazon Reviews[5] collection was also included in our analysis. This dataset contains about 53 thousand reviews on office products, accompanied by user ratings in a 1–5 scale. In this case, the dimensionality of the input space, after cleaning and preprocessing, was considerably lower than that of IMDb; specifically, 35,229. The most important characteristics of these four datasets are summarized in Table 1.

3.2 Text Classifiers

Six classification methods were used in this work: k-Nearest Neighbors (kNN), Logistic Regression (LR), Decision Tree (DT), Random Forest (RF), Support Vector Machines (SVM), and the feed-forward Artificial Neural Network (ANN). Each classifier may be parameterized by fine-tuning several hyper parameters. Nevertheless, notice that a head-to-head comparison between these classifiers is out of the scope of this article. In contrast, we are primarily interested in evaluating the impact of dimensionality reduction in the performance of these algorithms. For this reason, we did not attempt to individually fine-tune the hyper parameters to improve the performances in terms of both effectiveness and efficiency; rather, we used typical values that yielded decent classification accuracy values.

In Table 2 we refer to these 6 algorithms, and we report some indicative values for their respective hyper parameters. In brief, the nearest neighbor queries of kNN were executed with $k = 10$, whereas the distances were measured by using the Minkowski metric. Regarding Logistic Regression, the optimization of the cost function was performed by using the Limited-memory BFGS algorithm, and the maximum number of iterations was set to 300. The Decision Trees that we trained were programmed to expand until all their leaves are pure. The same setting was also applied to the 100 estimators that were included in our Random Forest classifier. Concerning SVM, we employed the RBF kernel, since, in general, it performed better than the linear kernel on our data. Similarly to Logistic Regression, we also applied L2 regularization in the SVM classifier. The architecture of the ANN included two hidden layers, with 50 and 300 neurons, respectively, whereas ReLU was used as the network activation function.

Finally, for all binary classifiers that do not natively support multi-label classification, the well-established One-vs-Rest (OvR) technique was applied.

---

[5] https://jmcauley.ucsd.edu/data/amazon/.

Table 2. Classifiers and hyper-parameters

Classifier	Hyper-parameters
k-Nearest Neighbors	$k = 10$, Minkowski distance
Logistic Regression	LBGFS, L2 regularization, Max iterations: 300
Decision Tree	Expand the tree until all leaves are pure
Random Forest	Estimators: 100, Expand the trees until all leaves are pure
SVM	RBF kernel, L2 regularization
Feed-Forward Neural Net	Architecture: (50,300), Activation function: ReLU

3.3   Text Preprocessing and Dimensionality Reduction

Before we proceed to the presentation of the results of our experimental study, we briefly describe the text preprocessing methodology. Initially, the input raw text was converted to lowercase, and a simple word-level tokenization process was executed to split each input document to a bag of words. In the sequel, the stop words were removed, and the WordNet lemmatizer was employed to convert each word to its meaningful base form. The collection was subsequently split to training and test sets by applying a constant ratio of 70%/30% and stratification by class. Finally, the two sets were transformed to numerical vectors by applying tf-idf vectorization, a well-established technique that leads to sparse, high-dimensional vectors.

Eventually, the dimensionality of both the training and test sets was reduced by applying a variant of Principal Component Analysis (PCA), called Truncated Singular Value Decomposition (TSVD). Notice that, although PCA identifies the principal components by maximizing the variance of the projected data, it is not feasible to sparse matrices. In contrast, TSVD does not center the data before computing the singular value decomposition; therefore, it operates efficiently on sparse matrices. In this context, TSVD is often known as Latent Semantic Analysis (LSA).

3.4   Results

Figures 1 and 2 illustrate the accuracy values (left diagrams) and the training durations (right diagrams) of the six classifiers on the 4 datasets of Table 1. In both types of diagrams, the horizontal axes are in logarithmic scale, and denote the various dimensionalities of the respective input vector spaces. Since the measured time differences among the different algorithms were frequently large (i.e., many orders of magnitude), we also adopted the logarithmic scale for the vertical axes of the right diagrams of all figures. Furthermore, notice that, in all figures, the rightmost markers represent the performances of the algorithms in the original feature space. That is, without applying dimensionality reduction.

Regarding the IMDb dataset, SVM and Logistic Regression were the most effective classifiers, since they respectively achieved accuracy values of 0.9 and 0.89 in the original feature space of the 77 thousand features. Nevertheless, the

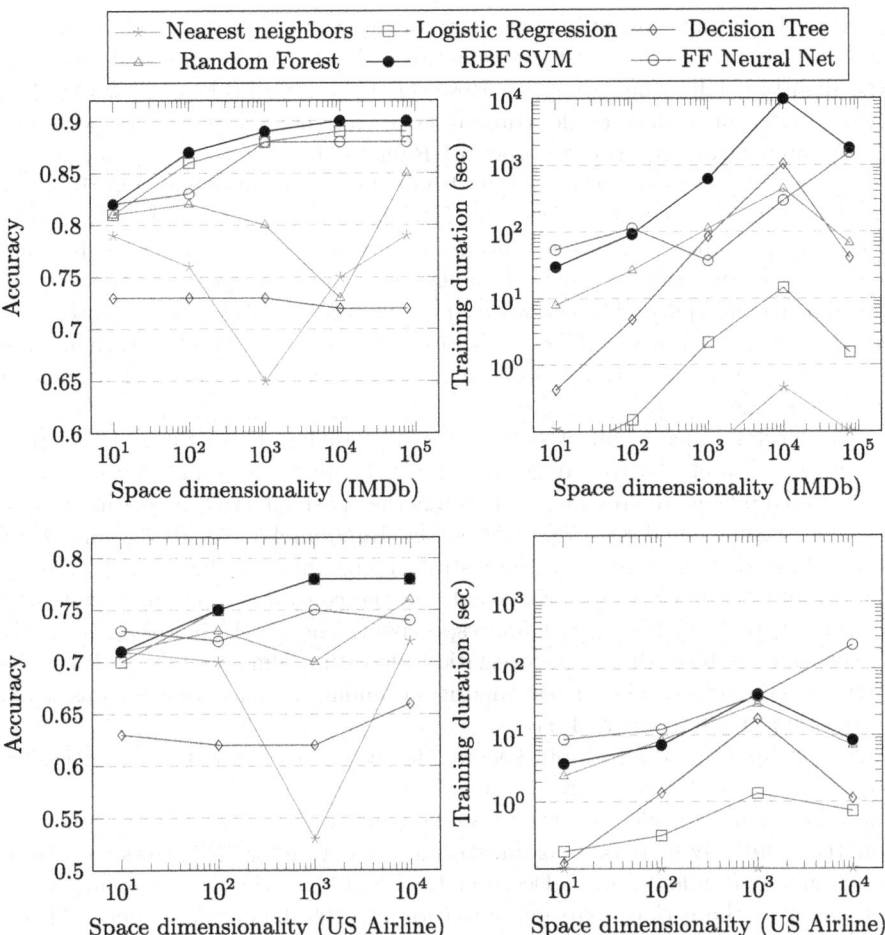

Fig. 1. Accuracy values (left) and training durations (right) of the six classifiers of Table 2 for the IMDb (top) and the Twitter US Airline (bottom) datasets. The horizontal axes are plotted in logarithmic scale, and represent various input spaces of different dimensionalities. In all diagrams, the rightmost markers denote the performance of the algorithms in the original feature spaces; namely, without dimensionality reduction.

latter was much faster than the former, since its training duration was smaller than 2 s, compared to the roughly 30 min of SVM. The performance of ANN was competitive, since it achieved an accuracy of 0.88, by consuming about 25 min to learn the required weights and biases.

Next, we applied TSVD to project the data into vector spaces of 10, 10^2, 10^3, and 10^4 dimensions. Remarkably, the accuracy losses for the smallest vector space (i.e., with 10 dimensions) were not very large. More specifically, the performances of SVM and ANN have dropped to 0.82 from 0.9 and 0.88, respectively, whereas the training durations were drastically reduced to 30 and 54 s, respectively. LR and RF were almost equivalent to SVM and ANN, since their accuracy was slightly smaller; namely, 0.81. However, they were both much faster than their counterparts, since model training lasted for just 8 and 0.1 s, respectively.

Counter-intuitively, the accuracy of Random Forests was dropping as the input vector space was growing larger, from 10 to 10^4 components. On the other hand, the performance of the Decision Tree was almost unchanged and independent of the number of features. Another interesting conclusion derives by comparing the model training times of all classifiers in the original and the reduced 10^4-dimensional space. The model training was faster in the former case, with one exception for ANN. This is the second counter-intuitive observation, since one would expect that the utilization of shorter vectors would led to smaller execution times.

The performance of all classifiers was degraded in the Twitter US Airline Sentiment dataset (bottom diagrams of Fig. 1). In the original feature space, SVM and Logistic Regression were again the most effective algorithms, with accuracy values equal to 0.78, followed by Random Forests (0.76) and ANN (0.74). Logistic Regression was the fastest among these methods, with training times that were lower than one second. On the contrary, Random Forests and SVM consumed roughly 7 and 8.5 s, respectively, whereas ANN was significantly slower, since it took the backpropagation algorithm almost 4 min to learn the network parameters. The fastest algorithm among all six classifiers was kNN, with a rapid training time of 0.07 s.

Regarding the reduced input spaces, one may observe a pattern that is similar to the one of IMDb. More specifically, when the dimensions are reduced by one order of magnitude, i.e., they become equal to 10^3, the training times are counter-intuitively increased, again, with an exception for ANN. In some classifiers, namely, Random Forest, Decision Tree, and kNN, the accuracies are worse compared to those that were measured for the 100-dimensional space. Therefore, dimensionality reduction is actually meaningless in this case. In contrast, a reduction by two orders of magnitude (e.g., the vector space includes 100 components) leads to improved model training durations, accompanied by a tolerable decrease in the effectiveness.

ANN and the two tree classifiers were the most effective methods in the Financial Tweets dataset, since, in the original input space, all of them scored a very high accuracy of 0.97. LR and SVM were slightly outperformed in this case, with their accuracy values measured at 0.92 and 0.94, respectively. In terms of efficiency, kNN was the fastest method, followed by LR: they both consumed less than 1 s to train their models. Decision Tree and Random Forest were significantly slower, with roughly 3 and 9 s, respectively.

Similarly to the two previous datasets, the reduction of the dimensionality of the input vector space by one order magnitude rendered the algorithms slower, except for ANN. Indicatively, the model training procedure for SVM consumed 68 s in the original vector space with the 12 thousand dimensions, and 228 s in the reduced space of the 1000 dimensions. At this point, it is becoming solid

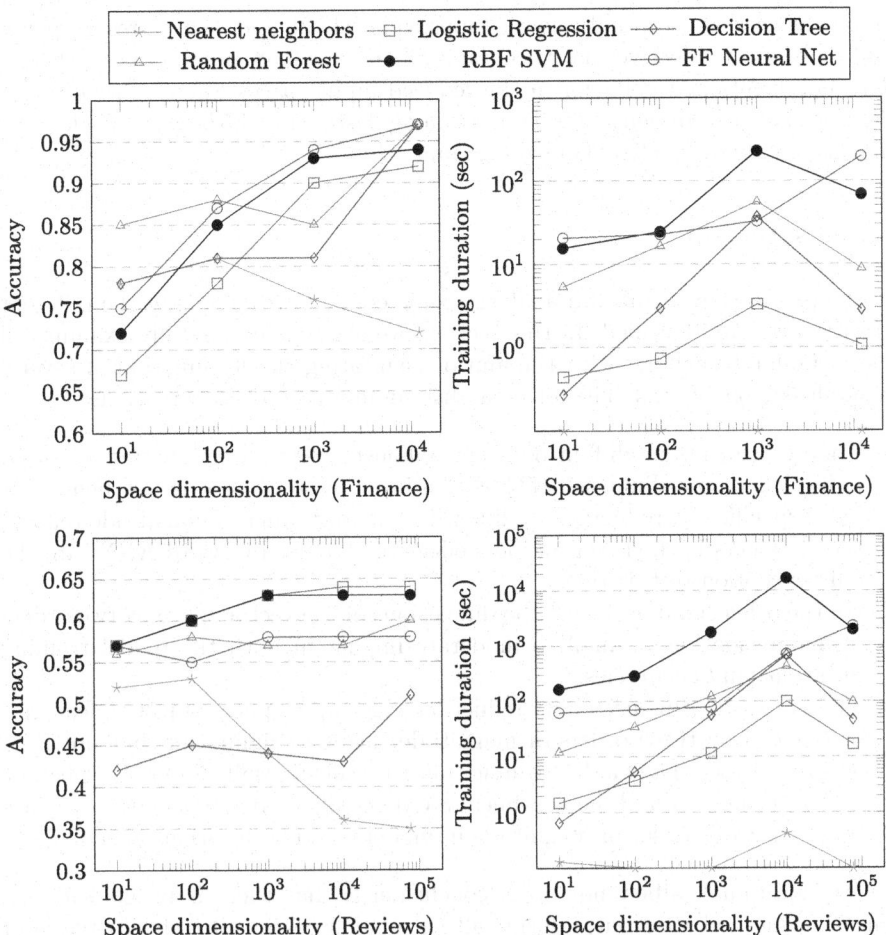

Fig. 2. Accuracy values (left) and training durations (right) of the six classifiers of Table 2 for Financial Tweets (top) and Amazon Product Reviews (bottom). The horizontal axes are plotted in logarithmic scale, and represent various input spaces of different dimensionalities. In all diagrams, the rightmost markers denote the performance of the algorithms in the original feature spaces; namely, without dimensionality reduction.

that a limited reduction by one order of magnitude is only beneficial for Neural Networks, since the rest of the classifiers are rendered both slower and less accurate. The genuine gains in execution speeds are obtained by performing a more aggressive reduction, namely, by at least two orders of magnitude.

Finally, in the fourth dataset with the 53 thousand Amazon product reviews (bottom diagrams of Fig. 2), Logistic Regression was again the most accurate and the second fastest algorithm. In the original feature space, its accuracy was equal to 0.64, whereas model training consumed roughly 17 s. On the other hand, ANN and SVM were substantially slower (approximately 38 and 33 min, respectively) and slightly less effective; their accuracy values were 0.58 and 0.63, respectively. The aforementioned behavior in the reduced input spaces was repeated in this dataset. For 10^4 dimensions, SVM training lasted for 4.5 h, whereas for 10^3 dimensions the respective time was 28 min.

4   Discussion

In the previous experimental analysis, some common behaviors of the different algorithms were identified. In this section, we attempt to carefully examine all these similar behaviors, with the aim of facilitating the formulation of several generalized conclusions. The following list summarizes our observations:

1. The experiments in all four datasets demonstrated that conducting a limited reduction in the dimensionality of the input vector space is not beneficial. More specifically, reducing the dimensions by one order of magnitude renders the classifiers both slower and less effective. The feed-forward ANNs are the only exception to this rule.
2. On the other hand, reducing the dimensions of the vector space by two orders of magnitude has a small to moderate impact in both the model training durations and accuracies.
3. The aggressive dimensionality reduction (e.g., input spaces of just 10 features, or reduced by three orders of magnitude) leads to significant, but not fatal accuracy losses. The model training times are substantially lowered, especially for the deep ANN and the non-linear SVM classifiers. In particular, a decrease by at least one order of magnitude in model training durations is achieved.

An additional, albeit not novel conclusion is that there is no golden classification method that outperforms all its adversaries in all tests. In terms of accuracy, the experimentation with four different data sets revealed five winning methods: SVM (IMDb and US Airline), Logistic Regression (US Airline and Amazon Reviews), and Decision Tree, Random Forest and ANN (in the Twitter Finance Sentiment dataset). On the other hand, in terms of model training durations, kNN and Logistic Regression were clearly the most efficient sentiment classification methods.

5   Conclusions and Future Work

This paper investigated the impact of dimensionality reduction in the performance of sentiment classification methods. Sentiment analysis is presently one of the hottest topics in NLP research, due to the explosive growth rates of social networks, blogging communities, commercial platforms, and so on. For this reason, a huge amount of research is conducted today with the aim of improving the performance of the current state-of-the-art models.

Nevertheless, text is a particularly sparse and high-dimensional form of data that occasionally triggers the notorious curse of dimensionality. This a condition where the majority of algorithms are rendered both inefficient and memory demanding. Consequently, dimensionality reduction plays a crucial role in the feasibility of the applied machine learning models, especially in NLP tasks such as sentiment analysis.

The experimental study that we conducted on four popular datasets with six major classification algorithms yielded several interesting conclusions. Firstly, reducing the dimensional space by one order of magnitude is rather meaningless, since it may be harmful for both model training durations and achieved accuracies. Secondly, reducing by two orders of magnitude leads to only small accuracy losses, but with small improvements in training times. The results of our study showed that significant benefits in the efficiency derive by reductions of three orders of magnitude, or more. Remarkably, the effectiveness degradation ranges from small to significant, albeit, not fatal.

We intend to further extend this research in the future with the aim of studying the implications of dimensionality reduction in the performance of the deep learning models. The current dominant NLP techniques, such as the RNNs, the LSTMs and the Transformers, are the objectives of our future work. We also intend to conduct experiments with additional state-of-the-art dimensionality reduction algorithms by employing large-scale training sets, with the aim of strengthening our conclusions.

References

1. Akritidis, L., Bozanis, P.: A supervised machine learning classification algorithm for research articles. In: Proceedings of the 28th ACM Symposium on Applied Computing, pp. 115–120 (2013)
2. Akritidis, L., Bozanis, P.: Improving opinionated blog retrieval effectiveness with quality measures and temporal features. World Wide Web **17**(4), 777–798 (2013). https://doi.org/10.1007/s11280-013-0237-1
3. Akritidis, L., Fevgas, A., Bozanis, P.: Effective products categorization with importance scores and morphological analysis of the titles. In: Proceedings of the 30th IEEE International Conference on Tools with Artificial Intelligence, pp. 213–220 (2018)
4. Boldrini, E., Balahur, A., Martínez-Barco, P., Montoyo, A.: Using EmotiBlog to annotate and analyse subjectivity in the new textual genres. Data Mining Knowl. Discov. **25**(3), 603–634 (2012)
5. Jelodar, H., Wang, Y., Orji, R., Huang, S.: Deep sentiment classification and topic discovery on novel coronavirus or COVID-19 online discussions: NLP using LSTM Recurrent Neural Network approach. IEEE J. Biomed. Health Inf. **24**(10), 2733–2742 (2020)
6. Kaya, T., Bicen, H.: The effects of social media on students' behaviors; Facebook as a case study. Comput. Human Behav. **59**, 374–379 (2016)
7. Kim, K.: An improved semi-supervised dimensionality reduction using feature weighting: application to sentiment analysis. Exp. Syst. Appl. **109**, 49–65 (2018)
8. Kim, K., Lee, J.: Sentiment visualization and classification via semi-supervised nonlinear dimensionality reduction. Pattern Recogn. **47**(2), 758–768 (2014)

9. Kusner, M., Sun, Y., Kolkin, N., Weinberger, K.: From word embeddings to document distances. In: Proceedings of the 2015 International Conference on Machine Learning, pp. 957–966 (2015)

10. Lai, S., Xu, L., Liu, K., Zhao, J.: Recurrent convolutional neural networks for text classification. In: Proceedings of the 29th AAAI Conference on Artificial Intelligence, pp. 2267–2273 (2015)

11. Lane, P.C., Clarke, D., Hender, P.: On developing robust models for favourability analysis: model choice, feature sets and imbalanced data. Decis. Supp. Syst. **53**(4), 712–718 (2012)

12. Ma, Y., Peng, H., Khan, T., Cambria, E., Hussain, A.: Sentic LSTM: a hybrid network for targeted aspect-based sentiment analysis. Cognit. Comput. **10**(4), 639–650 (2018)

13. Medhat, W., Hassan, A., Korashy, H.: Sentiment analysis algorithms and applications: a survey. Ain Shams Eng. J. **5**(4), 1093–1113 (2014)

14. Mikolov, T., Chen, K., Corrado, G., Dean, J.: Efficient estimation of word representations in vector space. arXiv preprint arXiv:1301.3781 (2013)

15. Moraes, R., Valiati, J.F., Neto, W.P.G.: Document-level sentiment classification: an empirical comparison between SVM and ANN. Exp. Syst. Appl. **40**(2), 621–633 (2013)

16. Mukherjee, S., Bhattacharyya, P.: Feature specific sentiment analysis for product reviews. In: Proceedings of the 13th International Conference on Intelligent Text Processing and Computational Linguistics, pp. 475–487 (2012)

17. Naseem, U., Razzak, I., Musial, K., Imran, M.: Transformer based deep intelligent contextual embedding for twitter sentiment analysis. Future Gen. Comput. Syst. **113**, 58–69 (2020)

18. Ortigosa, A., Martín, J.M., Carro, R.M.: Sentiment analysis in Facebook and its application to e-learning. Comput. Human Behav. **31**, 527–541 (2014)

19. Ouyang, X., Zhou, P., Li, C.H., Liu, L.: Sentiment analysis using convolutional neural network. In: Proceedings of the 2015 IEEE International Conference on Computer and Information Technology, pp. 2359–2364 (2015)

20. Pennington, J., Socher, R., Manning, C.D.: Glove: global vectors for word representation. In: Proceedings of the 2014 Conference on Empirical Methods in Natural Language Processing, pp. 1532–1543 (2014)

21. Shyamasundar, L., Rani, P.J.: Twitter sentiment analysis with different feature extractors and dimensionality reduction using supervised learning algorithms. In: Proceedings of the 2016 IEEE Annual India Conference, pp. 1–6 (2016)

22. Stieglitz, S., Dang-Xuan, L.: Emotions and information diffusion in social media-sentiment of microblogs and sharing behavior. J. Manag. Inf. Syst. **29**(4), 217–248 (2013)

23. Thelwall, M., Buckley, K., Paltoglou, G.: Sentiment in Twitter events. J. Am. Soc. Inf. Sci. Technol. **62**(2), 406–418 (2011)

24. Vaswani, A., et al.: Attention is all you need. Adv. Neural Inf. Process. Syst. **30** (2017)

25. Wang, Y., Huang, M., Zhu, X., Zhao, L.: Attention-based lSTM for aspect-level sentiment classification. In: Proceedings of the 2016 Conference on Empirical Methods in Natural Language Processing, pp. 606–615 (2016)

26. Zhang, T., Xu, B., Thung, F., Haryono, S.A., Lo, D., Jiang, L.: Sentiment analysis for software engineering: how far can pre-trained transformer models go? In: Proceedings of the 2020 IEEE International Conference on Software Maintenance and Evolution, pp. 70–80 (2020)

Invention Concept Latent Spaces for Analogical Ideation

Nicholas Walker[(✉)]

Iprova SA, Building I, EPFL Innovation Park, 1015 Lausanne, Switzerland
nwalker@iprova.com

Abstract. Analogy is a powerful form of ideation and therefore an automated or semiautomated analogical method is a potentially useful way to develop, or at least inspire, new and possibly patentable ideas.

The last few years have shown significant developments in the training and use of latent spaces for text generation using Variational Autoencoders (VAE), though many problems remain including preventing 'collapse' of the latent space during its training and successfully disentangling the latent variables, including the syntax from the semantics.

A hierarchical sentence and document variational denoising autoencoder architecture is presented, in which the encoded sentence vectors are first generated and then an encoding and decoding is performed of the sequence (in the document) of these sentence vectors. The latent vectors for both sentences and documents are structured into 'syntactic' and 'semantic' subsections based on their use in auxiliary training tasks. A large dataset of patent titles and abstracts, along with their IPC6 codes, is used to train the VAE networks.

The resulting document latent space is used to perform analogy transforms to seek to generate/inspire useful and potentially novel patent concepts.

Keywords: Patent analysis · Ideation · Analogy · Latent space · Text VAE

1 Introduction

There is a need to enable innovation and automation in the process of invention, by providing for the human inventor powerful data-driven tools for uncovering novel and patentable concepts. One method is using analogies, where we find a meaningful existing analogy and apply this to a concept to generate a new, derived concept.

A variety of concept generation by analogy methods have been applied to patents (e.g. [1]), but here we seek a primarily data-driven approach.

1.1 Analogy in Latent Spaces

Suppose we can describe a large set of 'concepts' using the values of many underlying generative variables. Each concept is then a location in the multidimensional space of

© IFIP International Federation for Information Processing 2022
Published by Springer Nature Switzerland AG 2022
I. Maglogiannis et al. (Eds.): AIAI 2022, IFIP AICT 647, pp. 313–324, 2022.
https://doi.org/10.1007/978-3-031-08337-2_26

these variables. Then suppose we find that a common transform of one concept into another is to change the values of these generative variables in some consistent way. We can then find all the concepts within our area of interest that meet the conditions for this transform, apply it, and then check the space near the generated concept's 'location' to ensure that no existing concept lies there. If not, we have a promising new concept and can examine it to determine its merits.

The classic example of this kind of approach is using word embeddings [2, 3] where we ask:

$$A \text{ is to } B \text{ as } X \text{ is to } Y. \text{ What is } B?$$

For example:

$$King \text{ is to } B \text{ as } Man \text{ is to } Woman. Answer \ B \ = \ Queen.$$
$$Paris \text{ is to } B \text{ as } Madrid \text{ is to } Spain. Answer: B \ = \ France.$$

Using Glove embeddings [4] and the equation: $B \ = \ A \ + \ (Y \ - \ X)$, we can get something like these results. We perform the vector arithmetic on the embeddings and find the best matching word as the one with the largest Cosine Similarity of existing word embeddings to the resulting vector.

Such word embeddings have no generative function – we cannot take an arbitrary embedding (latent) vector and generate a new word. For our purposes we need an encoder, which converts a concept into its latent vector, but also a decoder which can convert an arbitrary latent vector to a comprehensible concept. Finally, the analogical vector arithmetic will presumably only work successfully if the underlying latent variables are sufficiently disentangled.

Large collections of concept text descriptions are available in the patent literature. Therefore, if it is possible to derive well-structured latent spaces for these texts, and we can determine the subset of the latent variables which are important for describing the underlying concept, rather than superficial features of the text, and finally have a decoder which generates a comprehensible description of any vector sampled from that latent space, we should be able to perform our desired analogical transformations on short patent texts using such vector arithmetic [5].

1.2 Creativity Using Latent Spaces

Generation of novel works from both continuous and categorical latent spaces is of increasing interest but has to date been mainly restricted to continuous data such as images or sound, predominantly using Generative Adversarial Networks (GAN). In [6] the authors use iterative guided exploration of an image latent space to design logos for companies. In [7], novelty in design images is identified and the GAN fine-tuned to increase its production of such novel features. The exploration of latent spaces for musical synthesis has been undertaken, including loudness-invariant musical timbre [8] and images (piano-rolls) of musical excerpts [9]. However, text latent spaces using GANs [10] remains difficult, since the discriminator gradient cannot easily backpropagate through the hard selection of text tokens and therefore training must use reinforcement learning or approximations such as the Gumbel-Softmax [11].

2 Text Autoencoders

In a text autoencoder, we train a network consisting of an encoder and decoder to reconstruct its input text via a latent vector. Text decoders are normally autoregressive - the text is generated a token at a time, starting at the beginning of the text and moving forward, and the decoder has access to the latent vector and the previous tokens. They are generally implemented using either recurrent neural networks such as LSTM [12], or transformers [13]. At inference, tokens are selected using a greedy or stochastic algorithm or using beam search. Additional methods prevent repetitive text.

2.1 The Denoising Autoencoder (DAE)

With a simple autoencoder latent vectors for every different sequence of text in the training set could theoretically be placed in unique disjoint points in the latent space, with no 'structure' between them, such as similar sentences being encoded to similar latent vectors. By adding suitable 'noise' to the text, and reconstructing against the original text without noise, the encoder is encouraged to map a (set of small variations of) text to some compact volume of the latent space [14, 15]. If the extent of the latent space is constrained, the latent vector volumes will overlap and there is pressure on the autoencoder to map between similar latent vectors and similar sentences.

In [14], Shen et al. added noise to the text by randomly replacing/removing words during training. They demonstrated that such noising encourages similar sentences to map to similar latent representations.

2.2 The Variational Autoencoder (VAE)

Another important method for structuring the latent space is to constrain it by forcing the latent variables to match a prior, such as a zero mean, unit variance Gaussian. The Variational Autoencoder [16, 17] has been one of the most popular generative models. A VAE encodes the input data samples into a latent variable from the distribution of representations from a probabilistic encoder, which is parameterized by a neural network outputting a value of the mean and variance of the encoded distribution. One or more samples are taken from this distribution by generating a random Gaussian vector and scaling it with the estimated mean and variance before passing to the decoder (at inference, the mean vector only is used).

A VAE aims to maximize the marginal likelihood of the reconstructed data, but this involves intractable posterior inference. Thus, this is approximated by training it to minimize a loss, which consists of a reconstruction term, generally the cross-entropy loss on the logits from the decoder, and a Kullback-Leibler (KL) loss on the divergence of the distribution of each latent variable from the prior.

2.3 β-VAE

β-VAE [17, 19, 20] is an extension to the basic VAE framework used for learning a more disentangled representation of the generative variables. A disentangled representation can be considered as one where single variables are sensitive to changes in single generative factors, while being relatively invariant to changes in other factors. Compared to the original VAE, β-VAE adds an extra hyperparameter β ($\beta > 1$) as a weight of the KL divergence in the original VAE objective. The drawback of β-VAE is that the improved disentangling is offset by a poorer reconstruction.

3   Problems with Latent Vectors in Text VAEs

3.1   Latent Space Collapse

Text VAEs are quite difficult to successfully train. Basic VAE models cannot explicitly control the KL divergence and the KL term can progressively dominate the loss. They then suffer from KL vanishing [21, 22], which means the KL divergence can become zero during optimization – the latent variables collapse their means to 0.0 and contribute no information to the decoder.

The underlying reason is that the text decoders are autoregressive and can therefore operate moderately well as a pure language model, generating the text solely from the previous tokens and ignoring the latent vector.

Preventing collapse has been explored using a variety of approaches:

1. Text generation with a more limited decoder [23] or without using an autoregressive decoder [24].
2. Masking or corrupting some of the tokens used in the autoregression decoder to force greater use of the latent vector (noisy decoder) [25].
3. Providing additional tasks for the latent vector to ensure it retains information content, such as:

    a. Predicting a text class or topic label
    b. Predicting the bag of words in the text
    c. Predicting entailment between texts, for example:

        i. Entailment between sentences from the same document
        ii. Entailment between immediately previous or subsequent sentences

4. Controlling the KL loss by scaling it with a factor (similar to β) which is:

    a. Annealed from a low value to a high value using a sigmoid time course [20] or cyclically changed over the course of training [22].
    b. Have a value scaled such that the KL loss for a minibatch is proportional to the reconstruction loss for that same minibatch [26].
    c. Have a slowly modified factor controlling the average KL loss to a specific target value over the training set [27].
    d. Gradually decreased from a starting high value to slowly increase the size of the informational bottleneck during training [20].

3.2 'Prompt Only' Text Generation from Latent Vector

An unfortunate additional problem for autoregressive decoders is that, even when actively using the latent vector, the latent, rather than coding the entire sentence, need only memorize the first few tokens in a text to produce a near unique 'prompt' which the language model aspect of the decoder can then use to reconstruct the rest of the sentence [27]. Two approaches that can be adopted to help overcome this issue are:

- Independent masking 'noise' is added to the tokens used in the decoder [25].
- Use two autoregressive decoders - one going forward through the text and a second going backward, with the second, backward, decoder being dropped for inference [29].

4   Hierarchical VAE for Text

Given we have a set of sentences, which are themselves sequentially organized within documents, and there are limits to the length of word sequence sensibly mapped to a single sentence latent vector, a hierarchical text VAE can be implemented in the manner of [30] to generate an encoding of the whole document. Therefore, in this work we created a 2 level autoencoder:

1. First each sentence's tokenized text, plus special tokens <SOS>, <MASK>, <EOS> and <PAD>, is converted to a sentence latent vector.
2. Then the document sequence of variational samples of its sentence latent vectors plus concatenated 1-hot tokens <SOS>, <SEQ_N>*, <EOS>, <PAD> are converted by the document encoder into a single document latent vector, where <SEQ_N> are numbered sequence tokens for sentence vectors
3. A variational sample is generated and using this, the sentence vector sequence (and token logits) is reconstructed by the document decoder.
4. Finally, these reconstructed sentence latent vectors are in turn reconstructed as text by the sentence decoder.

The total set of losses (not including any auxiliary tasks) are then: the sentence KL divergence loss; the document KL divergence loss; the document sentence vector reconstruction loss (Mean Squared Error from the original un-noised sentence vectors to the decoded sentence vectors and cross entropy of the tokens); and the final sentence text reconstruction loss (cross entropy on the un-noised original text tokens). The document decoder also generates (from its syntax vector – see Sect. 5) an estimate of the total number of sentences to be reconstructed. A transformer encoder and decoder were used for the sentence VAE and a transformer encoder and causal convolutional decoder for the document VAE.

5   Syntax and Semantics

In the desired conceptual representations, our interest is the inherent content - its semantics, rather than the way the author has specifically written the sentences - its syntax. Ideally, the latent space should be disentangled by these parts [31].

To seek to achieve this disentanglement, we can assume that close sentences (those from the same document, or specifically adjacent sentences in the same document) are most semantically similar to each other and that a topic label, such as the patent IPC code, again captures the semantics and not the syntax. Document syntax is more related to the number of sentences in a document.

Using these assumptions, auxiliary tasks were added for the latent spaces during training:

- The semantic part of the sentence latent vector samples was used in a two-vector input MLP binary classifier to discriminate between the sentences from the same document and sentences from other documents.
- The semantic part of both the sentence and the document latent vector samples were used (separately) in one vector input MLP classifiers to determine the main patent IPC class (in a one of N classification using cross entropy).
- The document syntactic vector sample was used in an MLP to predict the number of sentences in the document (one of N using cross entropy).

To preserve the syntax/semantics split in the sentence latent vectors, the document encoder and decoder were both split into two: one taking the sentence syntactic latent vectors and one the sentence semantic latent vectors.

For 50,000 documents, both latent spaces (sentence and document) were set as 312 dimensional, of which 32 dimensions were assigned as the syntactic part and 280 dimensions as the semantic part.

6   Implementation

6.1   Data

The BigPatent dataset [32] 'abstract' section was used. Patents were selected whose tokenized sentence length did not exceed 96 and with 7 or fewer sentences. IPC codes and citation links were downloaded from the USPTO datasets and matched to the patent abstracts. Abstracts were split into sentences using the NLTK sentence tokenizer and sentence text was word tokenized using the BERT lowercase tokenizer. A training set of 50,000 patents (178,787 sentences, 10,127,981 tokens) was made by selecting 25 patents from each of 2,000 IPC6 patent classes.

6.2   Network Architecture

The sentence encoder consisted of a 4 layer, 8 head transformer using sinusoidal positional encodings. An initial whole sentence embedding vector was formed by concatenating the first two transformer top layer (<SOS> and first token) token embeddings along with the maximum and mean top layer token embeddings. This vector was then processed by a 3-layer MLP and then two linear heads to generate the latent vector means and log variances. The variational sample from these was passed to a 4-layer MLP which generated a fixed length (9) sequence with same embedding dimension as the decoder. This 'pseudo-sequence' was used as the final latent description for the sentence decoders. The dual directional decoders consisted of 3-layer 4 head transformers with (per token) 3-layer MLP heads yielding the token logits.

The document encoder consisted of dual transformers, each with 5 layers and 8 heads, taking the sentence syntactic and semantic sentence subvector samples. Again, the first and second tokens plus max and means of the transformer top embedding layers produced, via MLP heads, the mean and log variance vectors. A sample from these was again transformed into a multichannel 'pseudo-sequence' of length 9. The document decoder was a dual causal convolutional network [33] followed by a (per vector) 3-layer MLP yielding the sentence vectors and the added token logits (from the syntactic document decoder only). The document syntactic vector was also projected through a 3-layer MLP to yield the total number of sentences in the document, which was used to truncate the document decoder output at inference.

Auxiliary MLP heads were provided in the sentence encoder for the sentence semantic vector - one is a 1 of N classifier for the main IPC6 class, the other takes two vectors and returns a binary classification for the sentences coming from the same document or not. A similar main IPC6 class classifier was used for the document semantic vector.

6.3 Training

The sentence VAE was first trained alone, then its weights frozen and the document VAE trained. Both VAEs were then trained together. The Adam optimizer and a slow linear warm up followed by an exponential learning rate decay was used.

Noise was added to the sentence text for the sentence encoder to effect the benefits of a denoising autoencoder by a combination of masking (9% probability) and replacing words with similar words pre-generated by a large masked language model (6% probability). Different masked (only) sequences were used for the sentence decoder (15% masking). For sentence vectors supplied to the document encoder (only), masking was applied with only a low probability (1%) replacement of a sentence vector with a vector of zeros and a <MASK> rather than a <SEQ_N> token, since the sentence vectors are already 'noised' by the sentence noising and variational sampling.

The KL loss (both sentence and document) was structured as a proportion of the reconstruction loss for each minibatch. This proportion was increased during the start of their individual training using a sigmoid function from 0.0001 to 0.4 (sentence) and from 0.005 to 0.1 (document) and then fixed at the final value.

7 Results

Three approaches for concept generation from the resulting patent document latent space were investigated:

1. **Concept Fusion**
2. **Latent White Space**
3. **Citation Analogy**

50 examples of each approach were generated, their order randomized and presented blind to origin to five invention engineers at Iprova to assess the utility of the concepts for novel ideation on the basis of: Clarity and Coherence; Novelty/Patentability; and Utility for Ideation. Concepts were rated 0–5 for these 3 metrics and the average concept results obtained.

7.1 Concept Fusion

Two patents of interest are selected, and vectors formed as interpolations between their document latent vectors. Figure 1 shows an example of this approach.

Patent 1	**A locking preset mechanism for a fishing reel is provided by interlocking balls in the preset knob face and the depressions in the mating face of an axially moveable force transmitting means in the mechanism. In free spool, the knob can be rotated. In drag, the knob is locked against rotation.**
0.6 P1 0.4 P2	A surgical knife for use in a medical procedure comprises a handpiece capable of axial movement and a drive mechanism which controls the position of the movable member from its proximal end. The cutting board permits axial movement of a driving element into the opposed shank end. The clinician action is thereby effected into multiple positions.
0.5 P1 0.5 P2	According to embodiments a method and apparatus for controlling the flexure of a patient's limb are provided with which an operator can apply pressure to a field. The instrument features a guide assembly which permits placement of the pin in a substantially static and radial position. Additionally, the cutting element may be fitted with a guidewire. According to this disclosure there is variation and different mechanical characteristics are incorporated into the handle of the instrument with each other.
0.4 P1 0.6 P2	Specifically, a device and method for insertion of a valve for widening living tissue such as the human body and veins of a patient are provided. In particular a radiolucent structure is used at a distal end of the optical system and allows for numerous applications. In an alternate embodiment the sheath may be movable with respect to the distal portion. Additionally, the flexible assembly includes magnets which connect and protects the flaps in an opposed manner during operation of the device.
0.3 P1 0.7 P2	This invention provides a system and method for installing a stent made of a material such as a material that includes the radius of conical objects. In particular a pneumatic coupling device is formed across each of its plates providing for ease thereof. The catheter tip can carry the two modular elements into a body lumen upon insertion into a body lumen. The tip further comprises a working section suited for insertion into and along the isolated tissues
Patent 2	**The present invention provides methods and devices for closing two overlapping layers of tissue in a mammalian heart, for example a patent foramen ovale. The closure devices may take a number of different forms and may be retrievable. In some embodiments, a device is sized and shaped to extend from septum secundum, into the left atrium, through septum primum, and into the right atrium, such that the first and second ends cooperate to provide a compressive force to the overlapping layers of tissue. In some embodiments, the closure devices may be delivered with a catheter capable of puncturing mammalian tissue.**

Fig. 1. Concept fusion interpolated vector texts.

7.2   Latent White Space

A subset of relevant patents is selected and their mean latent vector determined. Random Gaussian distributed vectors are found around this mean. Vectors whose semantic Cosine Similarity to existing patents exceed 0.75 are removed and the resulting latent vectors decoded into text (Fig. 2).

Raw decoded text	Interpretation
An implant for forming a substance into a living body of a patient such as the method comprising the steps of providing a stent having a plurality of chambers and being insertable together into a root canal of a subject and methods of using the same are provided. The applicator further includes a filter element disposed within the cavity and is adapted to be placed in a substantially rigid state. One phase composition includes a polymer film impregnated with a dispersion of magnetic material and a polymeric material attached to the surface of the substrate and to the shell chain adhesive component.	A stent-like tooth implant which forms the tooth by depositing within it a dispersion of a magnetic material and a powerful adhesive which adheres to the internal filter to form the synthetically grown tooth. Magnets used for moving material (?) or heating material (?).
A coating comprising a deformable base for insertion into a body cavity, a cell surface capable of absorbing bone growth and passage and a hydrating solution material for making a dental prosthesis to be positioned on the tooth outer surface of the dental implant. The patch is more specifically to a solid cement and the structural shell comprising a fibrous resin which is more from the rest of the coating. An applicator for use in a dental implant the method including the steps of forming a tooth and or a rubber material so that the solid portion of the implant can be used to make the implant to be applied.	A similar concept to the above but using biological (?) tooth growth within a resinous cement and it is placed on a tooth (rather than replacing the tooth) as a patch. Tooth material is grown within the patch on top of the old tooth or an implant.
An invasive vascular diagnostic device designed to be inserted into human tissue and capable of administering the delivery of carbon dioxide which is used as a means of both filling and obtaining results from the same tissue. Such electrode units penetrate the tissue with rods which allow the gas to be applied at a variety of discrete locations along the path through the living tissue. Thus, the delivery system of the present invention can be applied to a tumor site and the patent describes methods for making and using such devices in a variety of therapeutic and diagnostic applications.	A rod delivering CO_2 gas with electrodes on it, which is inserted into the body for cancer diagnosis and treatment. The gas expands the tissue to enable biopsy (?) and possibly is therapeutic (?). Electrodes measure the pH (?).

Fig. 2. Examples of concepts from 'Latent White Space' and their interpretation by an inventor.

7.3   Citation Analogy

Two relevant and relatively similar patents are found. The forward citations (inverted normal citations) of one of these patents are used to determine the vector difference between that patent and its forward cited patents. These difference vectors are applied to the other selected patent and a set of possible concept vectors (one for each forward citation) generated. These again are checked to reject those too close (semantic Cosine Similarity > 0.75) to existing patents and the remaining vectors decoded into text (Fig. 3).

Analogy start actual patent: A card dispensing system for dispensing cards along a conveying surface which conveys sliced products downstream of a slicer for packaging the sliced products. A hopper contains a stack of cards which are withdrawn from the hopper by a suction force provided via at least one suction cup, The suction cup is moveable vertically to retrieve and remove the card from the hopper. The suction cup is moveable laterally to move the card into a receiving position where a card clamp on a damp carriage arrives to receive the card, Suction force on the card is released when the card damp damps down on the card the clamp carriage moves the card from the receiving position to the staging position where a nip engages with the card to feed the card through a junction in the conveyor line just as a food product passes over the junction.

New Concept: A method of dispensing a web of bags having first and second conveying paths, the method including translational movement which accomplishes sequentially advancing the web of bags from the first conveying path to the second conveying path such that the web of bags is unwound from the first conveying path. The procedure is repeated until the product is exhausted through a nip by dispensing the web, whereupon it is then removed from the nip by suction. This ensures that the second portion of the web is able to be exhausted from the second portion through the nip of the reserve roll, while the reserve roll is dispensed from the first portion of the web and thence through the nip of the reserve roll to the second portion of the reserve roll for discharge. When the spool of the bale is being displaceable along the path of travel of the first knife and the suction line, thus preventing jams, are made by moving the first knife past the dispensing line until it reaches an edge of the path of travel of the second knife.

New Concept: A plurality of paper dispensing cells for dispensing paper webs, each of the cells having a predetermined spacing that is skewed in relation to a direction perpendicular to the direction of conveyance of the paper webs and a predetermined spacing that is perpendicular to the direction of conveyance of the paper webs. The measuring device is positioned within the gap between the two rollers for measuring the distance between the first rollers and the spacing between the first rollers. The sensing element is then moved towards the exit conveyor, the sensing element is blocking the exit conveyor when the sensing element is moved from a first position to a second position. The sensor is activated when the receiving element is received by the first conveyor and the card feeding means and the receiver cooperating with the first conveyor.

Fig. 3. Analogical start patent and new concepts using Citation Analogy.

7.4 Evaluation

The following table gives the average concept evaluation results by five Iprova invention engineers all given the same sets of 50 concept texts per approach (total 150) (Table 1).

Table 1. Results of inventor evaluations.

Analogical process	Clarity and coherence	Novelty/Patentability	Ideation potential
Concept fusion	2.7	1.4	2.15
Latent white space	**3.3**	**2.4**	**3.2**
Citation analogy	2.2	1.65	2.1

8 Summary

The unsupervised learning of well-structured document latent spaces enables a variety of approaches for generating new concepts from existing concepts. The work reported here demonstrates a method of generating a document latent space for short patent abstracts, including addressing the problems associated with the training process. The resulting patent latent space was used for novel concept ideation. An evaluation of the generated concept text descriptions by Iprova invention engineers indicates that the 'Latent White Space' approach proved to be superior to the other two approaches evaluated.

Further work is required on better structuring and disentangling of the latent spaces, training significantly larger latent spaces on the entire patent corpus, along with automated screening and scoring of the resulting generated concepts.

References

1. Jia, L.-Z., Wu, C.-L., Zhu, X.-H., Tan, R.-H.: Design by analogy: achieving more patentable ideas from one creative design. Chin. J. Mech. Eng. **31**, Article no. 37 (2018)
2. Allen, C., Hospedales, T.: Analogies explained: towards understanding word embeddings. In: Proceedings of the 36th International Conference on Machine, Learning, Long Beach, California, PMLR 97 (2019)
3. Chen, D., Peterson, J.C., Griffiths, T.L.: Evaluating vector-space models of analogy. In: Proceedings of the 39th Annual Conference of the Cognitive Science Society (2017)
4. Pennington, J., Socher, R., Manning, C.D.: GloVe: global vectors for word representation. In: Proceedings of the 2014 Conference on Empirical Methods in Natural Language Processing (EMNLP) (2014)
5. Bengio, Y., Courville, A., Vincent, P.: Representation learning: a review and new perspectives. IEEE Trans. Pattern Anal. Mach. Intell. **35**(8), 1798–1828 (2014)
6. Jain, P., Mathema, N., Skaggs, J., Ventura, D.: Ideation via critic-based exploration of generator latent space. In: Proceedings of the 12th International Conference on Computational Creativity (ICCC 2021) (2021)
7. Nobari, A.H., Rashad, M.F., Ahmed, F.: CreativeGAN: editing generative adversarial networks for creative design synthesis. In: Proceedings of the ASME 2021 International Design Engineering Technical Conferences and Computers and Information in Engineering Conference IDETC/CIE 2021, 17–20 August 2021 (2021)
8. Caillon, A., Bitton, A., Gatinet, B., Esling, P.: Timbre latent space: exploration and creative aspects. In: Proceedings of the 2nd International Conference on Timbre (Timbre 2020), Thessaloniki, Greece, 3–4 September 2020 (2020)
9. Cádiz, R.F., Macaya, A., Cartagena, M., Parra, D.: Creativity in generative musical networks: evidence from two case studies. Front. Robot. AI **8**, 680586 (2021)
10. de Rosa, G.H., Papa, J.P.: A survey on text generation using generative adversarial networks. Pattern Recognit. **119**, 108098 (2021)
11. Jang, E., Gu, S., Poole, B.: Categorical reparameterization with gumbel-softmax. In: 5th International Conference on Learning Representations (ICLR 2017) Toulon, France (2017)
12. Hochreiter, S., Schmidhuber, J.: Long short-term memory. Neural Comput. **9**(8), 1735–1780 (1997)
13. Vaswani, A., et al.: Attention is all you need. In: 31st Conference on Neural Information Processing Systems (NIPS), Long Beach, CA, USA (2017)
14. Shen, T., Mueller, J., Barzilay, R., Jaakkola, T.: educating text autoencoders: latent representation guidance via denoising. In: Proceedings of the 37th International Conference on Machine Learning, Vienna, Austria, PMLR 119 (2020)
15. Freitag, M., Roy, S.: Unsupervised natural language generation with denoising autoencoders. In: Proceedings of the 2018 Conference on Empirical Methods in Natural Language Processing, pp. 3922–3929 (2018)
16. Rezende, D.J., Mohamed, S., Wierstra, D.: Stochastic backpropagation and approximate inference in deep generative models. In: Proceedings of the 31st International Conference on Machine Learning, Beijing, China, 2014 (2014)

17. Kingma, D.P., Welling, M.: Auto-encoding variational Bayes. In: ICLR 2014 (2014)
18. Higgins, I., et al.: beta-VAE: learning basic visual concepts with a constrained variational framework. In: ICLR April 2017 (2017)
19. Chen, R.T.Q., Li, X., Grosse, R., Duvenaud, D.: Isolating sources of disentanglement in VAEs. In: 32nd Conference on Neural Information Processing Systems (NeurIPS 2018), Montréal, Canada (2018)
20. Burgess, C.P., et al.: Understanding disentangling in B-VAE. In: 31st Conference on Neural Information Processing Systems (NIPS 2017), Long Beach, CA, USA (2017)
21. Bowman, S.R., Vilnis, L., Vinyals, O., Dai, A., Jozefowicz, R., Bengio, S.: Generating sentences from a continuous space. In: Proceedings of The 20th SIGNLL Conference on Computational Natural Language Learning, Berlin, Germany 2016 (2016)
22. Fu, H., Li, C., Liu, X., Gao, J., Celikyilmaz, A., Carin, L.: Cyclical annealing schedule: "a simple approach to mitigating KL vanishing. In: Proceedings of the 2019 Conference of the North American Chapter of the Association for Computational Linguistics: Human Language Technologies, Volume 1 (2019)
23. Yang, Z., Hu, Z., Salakhutdinov, R., Berg-Kirkpatrick, T.: Improved variational autoencoders for text modeling using dilated convolutions. In: Proceedings of the 34th International Conference on Machine Learning, Sydney, Australia, PMLR 70 (2017)
24. Huang, F., Guan, J., Ke, P., Guo, Q., Zhu, X., Huang, M.: A text GAN for language generation with non-autoregressive generator. In: Under Review as a Conference Paper at ICLR 2021 (2020)
25. Song, K., Tan, X., Qin, T., Lu, J., Liu, T.-Y.: MASS: masked sequence to sequence pre-training for language generation. In: Proceedings of the 36th International Conference on Machine Learning, Long Beach, California, PMLR 97 (2019)
26. Asperti, A., Trentin, M.: Balancing reconstruction error and Kullback-Leibler divergence in variational autoencoders. IEEE Access **8**, 199440–199448 (2020)
27. Shao, H., et al.: ControlVAE: controllable variational autoencoder. In: Proceedings of the 37th International Conference on Machine Learning, Vienna, Austria, PMLR 108 (2020)
28. Bosc, T., Vincent, P.: Do sequence-to-sequence VAEs learn global features of sentences? In: Proceedings of the 2020 Conference on Empirical Methods in Natural Language Processing, 16–20 November 2020, pp. 4296–4318 (2020)
29. Watzel, T., Kürzinger, L., Li, L., Rigoll, G.: Regularized forward-backward decoder for attention models. In: Karpov, A., Potapova, R. (eds.) SPECOM 2021. LNCS (LNAI), vol. 12997, pp. 786–794. Springer, Cham (2021). https://doi.org/10.1007/978-3-030-87802-3_70
30. Zhao, K., Ding, H., Ye, K., Cui, X.: A transformer-based hierarchical variational autoencoder combined hidden Markov model for long text generation. Entropy **23**(10), 1277 (2021)
31. Bao, Y., et al.: Generating sentences from disentangled syntactic and semantic spaces. In: Proceedings of the 57th Annual Meeting of the Association for Computational Linguistics, pp. 6008–6019 (2019)
32. Sharma, E., Li, C., Wang, L.: BIGPATENT: a large-scale dataset for abstractive and coherent summarization. In: Proceedings of the 57th Annual Meeting of the Association for Computational Linguistics, Florence, Italy, 2019, pp. 2204–2213 (2019)
33. Javaloy, A., García-Mateos, G.: Text normalization using encoder–decoder networks based on the causal feature extractor. Appl. Sci. **10**(13), 4551 (2020)

Multilingual Sentiment Analysis on Twitter Data Towards Enhanced Policy Making

George Manias$^{(\boxtimes)}$, Athanasios Kiourtis , Argyro Mavrogiorgou ,
and Dimosthenis Kyriazis

University of Piraeus, Piraeus, Greece
{gmanias,kiourtis,margy,dimos}@unipi.gr

Abstract. The great expansion in the usage and popularity of social media platforms during the last decades has led to the production of an enormous real-time
volume of social texts and posts, including tweets, that are being produced by
users. These collections of social data can be potentially useful and provide useful
insights to policymakers to adjust new user-centric policies and regulations. However, extracting and analyzing valuable information and knowledge out of these
data is a challenging task as concerns the high multilingualism that describes
these data. Thus, both the research and the business communities focus on the
utilization of multilingual approaches and solutions to enhance the policy making
procedures. To investigate a portion of these challenges this research work performs a comparative analysis of two multilingual sentiment analysis approaches.
In this context, three multilingual deep learning classifiers and a zero-shot classification approach were utilized and compared. Their comparison has unveiled
insightful outcomes and has a two-fold interpretation. Multilingual deep learning
classifiers that have pre-trained and evaluated in monolingual data achieve high
performances and transfer inference when applied afterwards in multilingual data.
However, the zero-shot classification approach fails to achieve high accuracies in
monolingual data as in contrary to when applied on multilingual data.

Keywords: Multilingual sentiment analysis · Transformers · Multilingual
classifiers · Transfer learning · Zero-shot classification

1 Introduction

During the last decade, social networks have shown a tremendous growth in their usage
and popularity. It is worth to mention that in January 2022 the number of people around
the world using the social media has been 4.62 billion, 59.5% of the global population,
with an increase of 10.1% (+424 million) compared to the same period on 2021 [1]. Especially during the COVID-19 pandemic outbreak social media increasingly assumed a key
role in information provision, news spreading and advertising [2] and became one of the
most effective digital marketing tools, with more companies embracing the potency of
the analysis of social medial [3]. As the number of social media users continues to soar,

I. Maglogiannis et al. (Eds.): AIAI 2022, IFIP AICT 647, pp. 325–337, 2022.
https://doi.org/10.1007/978-3-031-08337-2_27

their sentiment is increasingly impacted by tweets and posts. Thus, marketers and policymakers vividly leverage these networks' emerging power for promoting their products and influencing users' opinions. In fact, social media ad spends stood at approximately 132 billion U.S. dollars in 2021, with spending expected to surpass the 200-billion-dollar mark by 2024 [4]. One of the most popular social media platforms is Twitter, as it is considered one of the main micro-blogging and news sharing platforms [5], while Twitter's potential advertising has greatly increased within the same period [6]. The latter has a two-fold interpretation. In one hand it indicates the increasing need for modern stakeholders to leverage this enormous amount of information to further enhance their policies and advertising strategies for their own products or services. However, as it has been highlighted in recent research works, only a small amount of this large portion of data gives added value, making the retrieval of valuable knowledge out of these data a challenging task [7, 8].

What is more, concerning the agricultural and food technology domains a recent survey highlights that only few research works have been conducted with specific focus on the utilization of sentiment analysis in these two domains [9]. More specifically, this research work [9] performs a bibliometric analysis based on Web of Science (WoS) database examining the relationship between sentiment analysis and advertising in several different domains indicating that from a total of 919 examined research works only 26 (2.8%) out of them are related to the agricultural and food technology domains. On top of this, another issue that modern social analysis tools face is highlighted by the aspect of multilingualism that designates these data. While English is the most used language, however relevant brand, product, or service information can be provided in a variety of languages especially when the examined item is of worldwide interest and consumption. The latter limits the use of supervised machine learning models as well as of monolingual sentiment analysis tools to extract and analyze information due to the lack of high-quality annotated and labelled data and corpora in languages other than English to train these specific models. Thus, in recent years, the implementation of multilingual sentiment analysis tools has steadily increased through the utilization of approaches from the domain of Artificial Intelligence (AI) and more specifically from the domain of Deep Learning (DL). To achieve multilingual sentiment analysis one of the most common approaches is based on the translation of the original text to English. Afterwards, a neural sentiment analysis model is applied on the translated data. However, this approach has revealed a significant loss in the sentiment of the examined data [10]. Another approach is to use sentiment lexicon translated into multiple languages. The main drawbacks of this approach are that it requires the involvement of humans in the process of text analysis, as well as that several lexical objects lack of domain interoperability, thus lexicon-based analysis does not have high accuracy yet and its optimization is still an ongoing research topic [11]. In recent years, the performance of multilingual sentiment analysis tools has improved and enhanced through the utilization of approaches and techniques that are mainly based on the implementation of Neural Networks (NNs) and Transformers [12].

To this end, this paper leverages the potentials that these emerging technologies pose to implement a comparative analysis for achieving multilingual sentiment analysis on collected data related to multilingual reviews of wine products. The analysis seeks to highlight the value of the utilization of multilingual sentiment analysis on tweets related to food and agricultural brands and products as a great tool for the modern policy makers. In this context different NNs were exploited coupled with the utilization of pre-trained multilingual sentence embeddings to be used as inputs on the first layers of these NNs. The exploitation and evaluation of pre-trained multilingual sentence embeddings is a key aspect as they have shown remarkable results in the task of multilingual sentiment analysis [13]. What is more, a zero-shot classification approach is also implemented in the context of this paper to further evaluate the application of a model that has not been trained before on data belonging to the same language. The overall evaluation and comparison of the first approach is performed through the training of the proposed NN models to open labelled data and reviews related to wines and then applied to raw unlabeled tweets written in different languages, thus achieving zero-shot and transfer inference in terms of model accuracy. While the zero-shot classification approach is utilized without pretraining on both the labelled data and on the unlabeled multilingual tweets.

The remainder of this paper is structured as follows. Section 2 describes the related work from the domains of multilingual sentiment classifiers and zero-shot classification. The dataset as well as the methodology implementation and the approaches that are followed are being presented in Sect. 3. Afterwards, Sect. 4 presents the achieved performances and the experimental results of the utilization of the proposed approaches. Finally, Sect. 5 concludes the paper and outlines some directions for future works and further enhancements on the proposed methodology.

2   Related Work

One of the main challenges facing the modern field of Natural Language Processing (NLP) is the need for the implementation of sophisticated, holistic, and multilingual approaches in modern multilingual and multicultural societies. Therefore, researchers are constantly trying to develop the most comprehensive multilingual systems. To this end, several AI research teams from major pioneers, such as Google AI and Facebook AI Research, have introduced multilingual tools, corpora and sentence encoding models that are able to cover any language, thus overcoming the limitations imposed by the lack of labelled data in all languages [14, 15]. The utilization of transfer learning techniques leverages the development of multilingual models [16]. On top of this, recent research works have been applied on a specific form of transfer learning, the zero-shot learning [17]. The latter is utilized when no training data are available for a model that is used for prediction and with the ultimate objective to minimize the overall latency while maintaining robust classification performances. The main idea is to learn a mapping from classes to a vector in such a way that an unseen class in the future can be mapped to the same space and specific information can be retrieved for this unseen class. To this end, several research works take advantage of this approach and apply to several NLP tasks achieving great results [18, 19].

Moreover, one of the latest milestones in the NLP field is the introduction of BERT that enables transfer learning with large language models reaching the state-of-the-art for a great number of NLP tasks and applications [20]. In this context several research works have proposed multilingual models based on the utilization of BERT for a wide range of cross-lingual transfer tasks. More specifically, XLM-RoBERTa (XLM-R) is trained on a multi-lingual language modeling objective using only monolingual data [12], while XLM-T framework has based its implementation on an XLM-R model pretrained specifically on millions of tweets in over thirty languages with the scope for using and evaluating multilingual language models in Twitter [21]. On top of this, XLM-T features a set of unified sentiment analysis Twitter datasets in eight different languages. In the same context, several research works have introduced multilingual BERT-based models specifically pre-trained on tweet corpora, thus have focused their implementation on the task of sentiment analysis on tweets [22–24]. A cornerstone in the task of multilingual sentiment analysis [25] is the release of the Multilingual Universal Sentence Encoder (MUSE) from the Google AI team [26], which is a sentence encoding model simultaneously trained on multiple tasks and languages and creates a single embedding space common for all languages on which it has been trained on. The alignment in the same latent space provided by such embeddings allows to apply a transfer learning approach, thus the learned knowledge from a single training language can be transferred to other languages. Moreover, authors in [14] introduce a new evaluation framework for multilingual document classification in eight languages and provide the baselines for all language transfer directions using multilingual word and sentence embeddings.

In this paper is implemented a comparative analysis of two different approaches to indicate the maturity and accuracy of these approaches in the task of multilingual sentiment analysis. At first, the approach of Multilingual Sentence Classification (MSC) is analyzed and presented as a tool for retrieving semantically similar text in multiple languages. This approach has a two-fold interpretation, as it also utilizes and evaluates the use of multilingual sentence embeddings coupled with different NNs models. Thanks to the ability of multilingual sentence embeddings to represent meanings of words from different languages in the same vector space, the proposed multilingual sentiment analysis models become almost independent from the input language. Moreover, exploiting the vector alignment of multilingual sentence embeddings, a language-agnostic pipeline is defined that can be trained with any initial labeled data set, and then applied to Tweets written in different languages. Finally, a zero-shot classification approach is followed, and its outcomes are also evaluated and compared with those of the different NNs models of the MSC approach, thus a comprehensive analysis and comparison between these two approaches is.

3 Multilingual Sentiment Analysis

The proposed methodology to evaluate multilingual sentiment analysis involves two key approaches, the Multilingual Sentence Classification (MSC) and a zero-shot classification approach. Concerning the first approach, the first step is based on the computation of sentence embeddings. Afterwards, NN models were implemented and compared for performing the multilingual sentiment analysis task. Hence, a DL approach is followed and depicted as an activity pipeline in "Fig. 1". Moreover, a zero-shot classification approach is also introduced and followed as presented in "Fig. 2", and its outcomes were evaluated and compared with the ones of the MSC approach.

3.1   Multilingual Sentence Classification (MSC)

The Google Universal Sentence Encoder Multilingual (GUSEM) module is an extension of the MUSE [26] and was introduced for retrieving semantically similar text. Moreover, this tool is specifically optimized for increased semantic retrieval performance as it is designed to be used for tasks such as text classification and cross-lingual text retrieval, among others. Thus, before utilizing the NNs, the sentence embedding representation leveraging the functionalities of the GUSEM module was being created, as it was also used as input in the first layers of the proposed NN models. Under the scopes of this approach three different types of Neural Networks (NNs) were also utilized and more specifically a Vanilla NN (VNN), a Convolutional NN (CNN) and a Long-Short Term Memory (LSTM). The Vanilla NN (MSC-VNN) consisted of 4 layers fully connected. At first an input dense layer was initialized with input the sentence embeddings that have been previously generated. The second layer has a Dropout function of 0.3 to avoid overfitting, and the third layer and the last layer were also Dense layers. Most importantly the last layer has 5 neurons, as the total number of the classes in which the data are classified, and it utilizes a "*softmax*" activation classifier, as a multiclass classification task was performed in the context of this research work [27]. On top of this, the second NN that was implemented is a Convolutional NN (MSC-CNN) as it has proven that they perform well in text classification tasks [28]. Moreover, an Embedding layer was used as a first layer on this model to leverage the sentence embeddings from the previous step. Though text data are one-dimensional, since they are represented in sentence vectors, 1D convolutional NNs used to extract features from these data. In addition, by adding a GlobalMaxPooling1D layer it extracts the maximum value from each filter, and the output dimension is just a 1-dimensional vector with length as same as the number of filters that were applied. What is more, Recurrent NNs (RNNs) are a type of NNs that is proven to work well with sequence data [29]. Long Short-Term Memory Networks (LSTMs), a variant of RNNs, are used widely to address the sentiment analysis problems, thus it is also implemented in the context of this paper [30]. All layers except the LSTM layer and the pooling layer, that is not necessary in this model, were the same with those created in the previous MSC-CNN model.

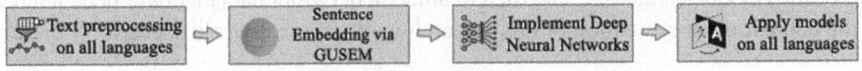

Fig. 1. Multilingual sentence classification (MSC) pipeline

3.2 Zero-Shot Sentiment Classification (ZSSC)

Recently, zero-shot text classification attracted a huge interest as it is an approach that facilitates the prediction of the target class of a text without having trained on any of the candidate classes/labels [31]. To this end, zero-shot classification is a revolution for unsupervised text classification as it provides more flexibility and demonstrates all the power of transfer learning for more general and unlabeled data. In this context, a zero-shot classification pipeline from Hugging Face library was utilized [32]. More specifically, after the initial text preprocessing the pipeline module and the multilingual model were defined. Hence, the *xlm-roberta-large-xnli* model was selected as the appropriate one to be utilized and evaluated [33], as it is fine-tuned on 100 different languages on the multilingual XNLI dataset [34]. Moreover, as the problem in this research work is a multi-class classification, the *"multi_label"* parameter was placed on *True* during its training phase, thus the scores are independent for each class, but for each of them its probability is computed between 0 and 1. Zero-shot approach was selected as it refers to a problem setup in which a model performs classification on labels it has never seen before, hence it can classify newly fetched and unlabeled twitter data as in the real-world scenario that is examined in the context of this research work. The latter facilitates the training of a model using a limited amount of labeled data that is scarce and not available in many languages, and then the knowledge gained from it to be applied to a wider range of languages and domains.

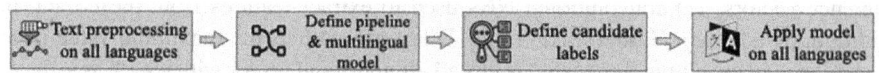

Fig. 2. Zero-shot sentiment classification (ZSSC) pipeline

4 Experimental Results

This section presents the experimental results of the utilization of the above presented approaches in labeled datasets and then in unlabeled Twitter data that have been fetched in the context of an evaluation of this research work in a real-world scenario.

4.1 Datasets Description

For the purposes of this research work two different datasets have been used and two different sets of experiments were performed. Under the scopes of the training and an initial evaluation of the examined MSC models, a Kaggle dataset has been used and training and testing iterations performed on English-only data [35]. This dataset contains two files with wine reviews, the rating of the wine (measured in points) and other relevant information for wine products. Finally, the trained models were applied in unlabeled multilingual twitter data to evaluate these models on a real-world scenario. Thus, their transfer inference level was evaluated through testing the accuracy of them on multilingual data that are seen first time. These twitter data have been fetched based on specific wine products as keywords and more specifically based on the *"merlot"*, *"cabernet"* and *"carinena"* keywords. With regards to the ZSSC approach the selected pre-trained model (i.e., *xlm-roberta-large-xnli*) was applied in all set of experiments and datasets without prior training on the data to evaluate its accuracy and performance on monolingual and multilingual data that are seen for first time.

4.2 Evaluation Setup and Measures

Experiments presented in this paper were based on implementing the multilingual senti-ment analysis task and the presented approaches with the Python programming language and the utilization of TensorFlow 2.0 [36] and Keras libraries [37]. Moreover, the imple-mentation of the code, for both MSC and ZSSC approaches, was performed on Google Colab [38] online platform to facilitate the overall running time through the usage of the GPU option that is available. Moreover, several tools and libraries were utilized to perform several tasks, such as the *sklearn* that was utilized for the computation of the performances of the implemented models, as well as for the splitting of the initial examined dataset to train and test set. Moreover, measures of evaluating the efficiency of NLP systems go beyond the concepts of Precision, Accuracy, Recall and F1-Score. F1-Score has proven to be a better measure to be used and examined, as it provides a balance between Precision and Recall and there is an uneven class distribution (large number of Actual Negatives).

4.3 Pre-processing

The initial reviews of the wine products in the Kaggle datasets are provided via a 100-point scale. However, under the scopes of this research work and as the task that is performed is a sentiment analysis problem, thus a transformation should be applied in the rating to also reducing the dimensionality of the problem. The overall range of the review points was ranged from 80–100, thus under the scopes of this research work the Table 1 was created with the corresponding mapping ratings to also include 5 different classes to express the sentiment and the classification of the wines. Hence, text reviews were analyzed to predict whether a wine is *"Mediocre"*, *"Good"*, *"Very Good"*, *"Outstanding"*, and *"Classic"* based also on the wine rating information that collected from official wine-related sources [39] and the needed transformations to fit to the examined datasets. One hot encoding approach also utilized to further encode the identified classes for each sentence.

Moreover, it was observed that many records occur in classes 1 and 2, while only a few can be observed in class 4. Hence, class weights were used to give more emphasis on the minority classes and manage this imbalance, thus higher weights were attached to less occurred classes (e.g., *class No4: 7*, while *class No1: 1*) to have a higher impact on the training of the NNs. Finally, the preprocessing of raw texts is a crucial and mandatory step as they can contain a high portion of unwanted elements, from plain text, mentions, links, and punctuations, to many other html tags. Hence, all these "noisy data" need to be removed before proceeding to the further processing and analysis of the texts. In the context of this research work, filtering, and removal of punctuations, links, mentions and stopwords were performed in all examined datasets. Following the abovementioned steps

Table 1. Description and mapping of ratings

100-point scale	Rating	Number of reviews	No of class
96–100	Classic	1266	4
92–95	Outstanding	20436	3
88–91	Very good	57301	2
84–87	Good	59437	1
80–83	Mediocre	12491	0

of pre-processing results in cleaned texts and tweets, which can be further processed and analyzed to implement the multilingual sentiment analysis task on them.

4.4 Results and Discussion

As analyzed in previous sections two different sets of experiments were implemented to evaluate the proposed approaches and models. At first, the dataset that was used from the Kaggle contains two files, the *winemag-data_first150k.csv* and the *winemag-data-130k-v2.csv*. The first of these files was used as the training dataset for the evaluation of the MSC approach. Initially, it was separated at 70% as the training and 30% as the test set and then the two different approaches were utilized. The ZSSC approach is utilized without any prior training in the data. The results in Table 2 indicate that the three models of the MSC approach achieve good performances in the monolingual multilabel classification task. Of course, further fine-tuning and different settings in the selected layers and the activation functions can be performed to enhance their performances. On the other hand, the ZSSC approach fails to generalize well and performs pure in this task. Utilizing a multilingually pretrained model in a single source-language leads to poor accuracy as forgetting of its multilingual knowledge and underperforming of its functionalities. Moreover, the performance of the ZSSC approach is rather poor due to high similarity between the predicted classes. It is a very hard task to make distinction between *Outstanding*, *Very Good* and *Good* without any prior data. Afterwards, the same MSC trained models were utilized in the second file (*winemag-data-130k-v2.csv*). Table 3 indicates that all three models of the MSC approach can generalize very well and achieve high performance rates and high transfer learning rate. However, the ZSSC approach also fails to achieve high performances in this experiment, which is in align with the prior results.

Table 2. Experimental results for the training dataset

Model	Precision	Accuracy	Recall	F1-Score
MSC-VNN	0.7520	0.7513	0.7493	0.7504
MSC-CNN	0.7654	0.7702	0.7689	0.7775
MSC-LSTM	0.8103	0.8079	0.8032	0.8142
ZSSC	0.5105	0.5086	0.5041	0.5003

Table 3. Experimental results for the evaluation dataset

Model	Precision	Accuracy	Recall	F1-Score
MSC-VNN	0.8351	0.8431	0.8484	0.8534
MSC-CNN	0.8296	0.8312	0.8343	0.8394
MSC-LSTM	0.8678	0.8756	0.8631	0.8732
ZSSC	0.5203	0.5352	0.5261	0.5215

Finally, the already implemented models were evaluated in real-world multilingual twitter data that have been fetched based on specific keywords related with wine products and more specifically the keywords "*merlot*", "*cabernet*" and "*carinena*". The outcomes of the utilization of these models in multilingual tweets have shown remarkable results and have indicated that the implemented models generalize very well in other languages than the initial in which they were trained (English), thus achieving high transfer inference in terms of model accuracy. Table 4 depicts five sample tweets from the overall 2000 collected that represent a good performance and classification from the application of these models. In this experiment it is worth to mention that the ZSSC approach has resulted in close or same classification outcomes as the NNs in the MSC approach, and especially as the MSC-VNN. The latter indicates that the ZSSC approach outperforms compared to when utilized in large monolingual sentences, as in the first set of experiments, as it generalizes better via self-training in multilingual data. The latter indicates the need for specific fine-tuning and pretraining of this model in monolingual data and the introducing of weights in the candidate classes.

Table 4. Sample classifications for the multilingual tweets

Description	Language	Model	Predicted Class
Anbefaler en tur til Mendoza for grillet bloddopet bøff og merlot	Danish	MSC-VNN	Outstanding
		MSC-CNN	Outstanding
		MSC-LSTM	Classic
		ZSSC	Outstanding
Little Merlot Meatball Marinara Murder the perfect evening	English	MSC-VNN	Very Good
		MSC-CNN	Very Good
		MSC-LSTM	Outstanding
		ZSSC	Very Good
de boassa aqui tomando meu merlot e chega leon e lança dindo eu vomitei no seu computador	Portuguese	MSC-VNN	Good
		MSC-CNN	Good
		MSC-LSTM	Good
		ZSSC	Mediocre
Para empezar la Semana Tranquilo y Mimando a mi Pequeño Diamante,Salió Sushi 🍣 al estilo Cadiboni, obvio acompañado de una buena Copa de Vino 🍷 hoy Un Rosado Merlot Disfrutando de una cena con mi Pequeño Diamante	Spanish	MSC-VNN	Outstanding
		MSC-CNN	Classic
		MSC-LSTM	Classic
		ZSSC	Very Good
Merrez'ca เบอร์02 Merlot สีสวยไม่ไหว โทนส้มอิฐ ก่ำๆ เกาหลีเกาใจ เนื้อครีมแต่พอเกลียแล้วจะเป็นเนื้อมูสนิดๆ พิกเม้นต์แน่น ท	Thai	MSC-VNN	Outstanding
		MSC-CNN	Outstanding
		MSC-LSTM	Outstanding
		ZSSC	Outstanding

5 Conclusion

In this paper, a comparative analysis and evaluation of two different experimentation sets in multilingual sentiment analysis task are presented and examined to specify and indicate the increasing need of utilizing multilingual tasks of NLP. Both approaches were utilized in labeled as well as in unlabeled data that have been fetched based on a real-world scenario in the context of PolicyCLOUD project [40]. The latter provides actionable knowledge to interested stakeholders to further enhance their policies based on the multilingual sentiment analysis task on specific wine products. On top of this, the challenges of performing multilingual sentiment analysis have been examined with emphasis on the evaluation of the role and the impact that pre-trained sentence embeddings and zero-shot classification can have. What is more, the fundamental characteristics of transfer learning approaches are analyzed, as well as the utilization of pre-trained sentence embeddings.

The outcomes of the proposed approaches have a twofold interpretation. The comparison on using the same trained NNs, and more specifically the MSC-LSTM model, in source and target languages by using also a pre-trained sentence embedding model reveals that great achievements have been accomplished and that these models capture semantic information in multiple languages and in high performance. Their utilization in different languages than in the initial language in which they were trained on, enhances the multilingualism and interoperability of these NN models with almost zero losses. Hence, their transfer inference and their application in other languages can be accomplished without significant losses. On the other hand, the overall outcomes and performance rates of zero-shot classification pipeline leads to a conclusion that utilizing a multilingually pretrained model in a single source-language leads to poor accuracy and its pretraining on monolingual data may lead to better results. Moreover, further fine-tuning on this model should be implemented especially in the cases where the texts need to be classified in more than one classes/labels.

To this end, there is a lot of additional work to perform according to the utilization of zero-shot classification, as it is a comparatively new topic and its adaptation in many domain fields needs to be further examined. On top of this, the initial manually labeling of a large portion of examples may enhance its performance and finally achieve higher accuracy than supervised models that have been trained on hundreds of labeled training items. The latter, as also both the proposed approaches in this paper, will be further evaluated and applied in the context of a holistic environment for data-driven policy making as realized by the PolicyCLOUD project [40], where data from four different languages (Bulgarian, Italian, Spanish, and English) will be utilized and processed.

Acknowledgement. The research leading to the results presented in this paper has received funding from the European Union's funded Project PolicyCLOUD under grant agreement no 870675.

References

1. Global Social Media Stats | DataReportal – Global Digital Insights. https://datareportal.com/social-media-users. Accessed 27 Feb 2022
2. Wiederhold, B.K.: Social media use during social distancing. Cyberpsychol. Behav. Soc. Netw. **23**(5), 275–276 (2020)
3. Alalwan, A.A.: Investigating the impact of social media advertising features on customer purchase intention. Int. J. Inf. Manag. **42**, 65–77 (2018)
4. Social media marketing - statistics & facts. https://www.statista.com/topics/1538/social-media-marketing/#dossierKeyfigures. Accessed 26 Feb 2022
5. Social Media Statistics For 2022 [+Infographic] | Statusbrew. https://statusbrew.com/insights/social-media-statistics. Accessed 25 Feb 2022
6. The Latest Twitter Stats: Everything You Need to Know | DataReportal – Global Digital Insights. https://datareportal.com/essential-twitter-stats. Accessed 26 Feb 2022
7. Păvăloaia, V.D., et al.: Opinion mining on social media data: sentiment analysis of user preferences. Sustainability **11**(16), 4459 (2019)
8. Tao, D., Yang, P., Feng, H.: Utilization of text mining as a big da-ta analysis tool for food science and nutrition. Compr. Rev. Food Sci. Food Safety **19**(2), 875–894 (2020)
9. Sánchez-Núñez, P., et al.: Opinion mining, sentiment analysis and emotion understanding in advertising: a bibliometric analysis. IEEE Access **8**, 134563–134576 (2020)
10. Manias, G., et al.: An evaluation of neural machine translation and pre-trained word embeddings in multilingual neural sentiment analysis. In: 2020 IEEE International Conference on PIC, pp. 274–283. IEEE (2020)

11. Sadia, A., Khan, F., Bashir, F.: An overview of lexicon-based approach for sentiment analysis. In: IEEC 2018, pp. 1–6 (2018)
12. Conneau, A., et al.: unsupervised cross-lingual representation learning at scale. In: Proceedings of the 58th Annual Meeting of the Association for Computational Linguistics, pp. 8440–8451. Association for Computational Linguistics (2020)
13. Aydoğan, M., Karci, A.: Improving the accuracy using pre-trained word embeddings on deep neural networks for Turkish text classification. Physica A **541**, 123288 (2020)
14. Schwenk, H., Li, X.: A corpus for multilingual document classification in eight languages. arXiv preprint arXiv:1805.09821 (2018)
15. Eriguchi, A., et al.: Zero-shot cross-lingual classification using multilingual neural machine translation. arXiv preprint arXiv:1809.04686 (2018)
16. Tan, C., Sun, F., Kong, T., Zhang, W., Yang, C., Liu, C.: A survey on deep transfer learning. In: Kůrková, V., Manolopoulos, Y., Hammer, B., Iliadis, L., Maglogiannis, I. (eds.) ICANN 2018. LNCS, vol. 11141, pp. 270–279. Springer, Cham (2018). https://doi.org/10.1007/978-3-030-01424-7_27
17. Xian, Y., et al.: Zero-shot learning—a comprehensive evaluation of the good, the bad and the ugly. IEEE Trans. Pattern Anal. Mach. Intell. **41**(9), 2251–2265 (2018)
18. Artetxe, M., Schwenk, H.: Massively multilingual sentence embeddings for zero-shot cross-lingual transfer and beyond. TACL **7**, 597–610 (2019)
19. Sarkar, A., Reddy, S., Iyengar, R.S.: Zero-shot multilingual sentiment analysis using hierarchical attentive network and BERT. In: Proceedings of the 2019 3rd International Conference on Natural Language Processing and Information Retrieval, pp. 49–56 (2019)
20. Devlin, J., Chang, M., Lee, K., Toutanova, K.: BERT: pre-training of deep bidirectional transformers for language understanding. In: Conference of the NAACL-HLT 2019, pp. 4171–4186 (2019)
21. Barbieri, F., Anke, L.E., Camacho-Collados, J.: XLM-T: A multilingual language model toolkit for twitter. arXiv preprint arXiv:2104.12250 (2021)
22. Gonzalez, J.A., Hurtado, L.F., Pla, F.: TWilBert: pre-trained deep bidirectional transformers for Spanish Twitter. Neurocomputing **426**, 58–69 (2021)
23. Pota, M., Ventura, M., Catelli, R., Esposito, M.: An effective BERT-based pipeline for Twitter sentiment analysis: a case study in Italian. Sensors **21**(1), 133 (2021)
24. Polignano, M., et al.: Alberto: Italian BERT language understanding model for NLP challenging tasks based on tweets. In: 6th Italian Conference on Computational Linguistics, CLiC-it 2019, vol. 2481, pp. 1–6. CEUR (2019)
25. Wehrmann, J., Becker, W.E., Barros, R.C.: A multi-task neural network for multilingual sentiment classification and language detection on twitter. In: Proceedings of the 33rd Annual ACM Symposium on Applied Computing, pp. 1805–1812 (2018)
26. Yang, Y., et al.: Multilingual universal sentence encoder for semantic retrieval. In: Proceedings of the 58th Annual Meeting of the Association for Computational Linguistics: System Demonstrations, pp. 87–94 (2020)
27. Janocha, K., Czarnecki, W.M.: On Loss functions for deep neural networks in classification. Schedae Informaticae **25** (2017)
28. Afridi, M.J., Ross, A., Shapiro, E.M.: On automated source selection for transfer learning in convolutional neural networks. Pattern Recognit. **73**, 65–75 (2018)
29. Manaswi, N.K.: RNN and LSTM. In: Deep Learning with Applications Using Python, pp. 115–126. Apress, Berkeley (2018)
30. Muhammad, P.F., Kusumaningrum, R., Wibowo, A.: Sentiment analysis using Word2vec and long short-term memory (LSTM) for Indonesian hotel reviews. Procedia Comput. Sci. **179**, 728–735 (2021)

31. Kumar, A., Albuquerque, V.H.C.: Sentiment analysis using XLM-R transformer and zero-shot transfer learning on resource-poor Indian language. Trans. Asian Low Resour. Lang. Inf. Process. **20**(5), 1–13 (2021)
32. Hugging Face. https://huggingface.co. Accessed 26 Feb 2022
33. joeddav/xlm-roberta-large-xnli-Hugging Face. https://huggingface.co/joeddav/xlm-roberta-large-xnli. Accessed 02 Mar 2022
34. Conneau, A., et al.: XNLI: evaluating cross-lingual sentence representations. In: Proceedings of the EMNLP 2018, pp. 2475–2485 (2020)
35. Wine Reviews | Kaggle. https://www.kaggle.com/zynicide/wine-reviews/home. Accessed 05 Mar 2022
36. TensorFlow. https://www.tensorflow.org/. Accessed 27 Feb 2022
37. Keras: the Python deep learning API. https://keras.io/. Accessed 27 Feb 2022
38. Google Colaboratory. https://colab.research.google.com/. Accessed 09 Mar 2022
39. Wine-Searcher. https://www.wine-searcher.com/wine-scores. Accessed 28 Mar 2022
40. Kyriazis, D., et al.: PolicyCLOUD: analytics as a service facilitating efficient data-driven public policy management. In: Maglogiannis, I., Iliadis, L., Pimenidis, E. (eds.) AIAI 2020. IAICT, vol. 583, pp. 141–150. Springer, Cham (2020). https://doi.org/10.1007/978-3-030-49161-1_13

On the Evaluation of the Plausibility and Faithfulness of Sentiment Analysis Explanations

Julia El Zini, Mohamad Mansour, Basel Mousi, and Mariette Awad$^{(\boxtimes)}$

Electrical and Computer Engineering Department,
American University of Beirut, Beirut, Lebanon
{jwe04,mgm35,bam20}@mail.aub.edu, mariette.awad@aub.edu.lb

Abstract. With the pervasive use of Sentiment Analysis (SA) models in financial and social settings, performance is no longer the sole concern for reliable and
accountable deployment. SA models are expected to explain their behavior and
highlight textual evidence of their predictions. Recently, Explainable AI (ExAI)
is enabling the "third AI wave" by providing explanations for the highly non-
linear black-box deep AI models. Nonetheless, current ExAI methods, especially
in the NLP field, are conducted on various datasets by employing different metrics to evaluate several aspects. The lack of a common evaluation framework is
hindering the progress tracking of such methods and their wider adoption.

In this work, inspired by offline information retrieval, we propose different
metrics and techniques to evaluate the explainability of SA models from two
angles. First, we evaluate the strength of the extracted "rationales" in *faithfully*
explaining the predicted outcome. Second, we measure the agreement between
ExAI methods and human judgment on a homegrown dataset (Dataset and code
available at https://gitlab.com/awadailab/exai-nlp-eval) to reflect on the rationales
plausibility. Our conducted experiments comprise four dimensions: (1) the underlying architectures of SA models, (2) the approach followed by the ExAI method,
(3) the reasoning difficulty, and (4) the homogeneity of the ground-truth rationales.

We empirically demonstrate that *anchors* explanations are more aligned with
the human judgment and can be more confident in extracting supporting rationales. As can be foreseen, the reasoning complexity of sentiment is shown to
thwart ExAI methods from extracting supporting evidence. Moreover, a remarkable discrepancy is discerned between the results of different explainability methods on the various architectures suggesting the need for consolidation to observe
enhanced performance. Predominantly, transformers are shown to exhibit better
explainability than convolutional and recurrent architectures. Our work paves the
way towards designing more interpretable NLP models and enabling a common
evaluation ground for their relative strengths and robustness.

1 Introduction

Sentiment Analysis (SA) is instrumental to the financial services industry [28, 29] as it
develops techniques to interpret customer feedback, monitor product reputations, understand the customers' needs, and conduct market research. Harnessing the power of Deep

© IFIP International Federation for Information Processing 2022
Published by Springer Nature Switzerland AG 2022
I. Maglogiannis et al. (Eds.): AIAI 2022, IFIP AICT 647, pp. 338–349, 2022.
https://doi.org/10.1007/978-3-031-08337-2_28

Learning (DL) in understanding general contexts, the performance of SA models is considerably boosted [11,12,23]. However, the non-linearity and the black-box nature of such models hinder the interpretation of the predictions [20,32]. Besides providing guarantees on reliability, generalization, robustness, and fairness, the interpretability of the SA models can be of service to behavioral marketing and personalized advertisement.

Recently, Explainable Artificial Intelligence (ExAI) algorithms are breathing a new flexibility in general AI applications by developing methods to explain model's prediction [5,30,41]. Numerical data frameworks and computer vision applications have witnessed an explosive growth of ExAI nurtured by the ease of expression of features as interpretable components [10,22,26]. However, only a few ExAI methods are applied to textual classifiers, embeddings, and language models [7]. In the SA framework, researchers integrated data augmentation techniques to improve the interpretability of SA models [6], studied attention mechanisms in SA through an explainability lens [3] and applied ExAI on aspect-based SA models [37]. To date, ExAI methods on Natural Language Processing (NLP) tasks are not evaluated on standardized benchmarking datasets through common metrics which hinders the progress and adoption of such methods in the NLP field. Evaluating explainability methods is two-fold. First, it helps assess the extent to which a deep model can be made explainable. Second, it provides a common ground to measure the contrast between explanations produced by diverse ExAI approaches.

In this work, we inspect two human aspects of explainability methods: (1) faithfulness to the model being explained and (2) plausibility from a human lens. For this purpose, we select eight state-of-the-art SA models with underlying architectures of recurrent, convolutional, and attention layers. We generate explanations of the predictions of these models on three ExAI methods that can be applied in NLP; mainly LIME [30], *anchors* [31] and SHAP [18]. The generated explanations are then evaluated through two procedures. First, *faithfulness*[1] is evaluated by examining the degradation in the model's performance when only extracted rationales are fed to the model. Second, the *plausibility*[1] of extracted rationales is evaluated via comparison to the human judgment of what a sufficient explanation is. This experiment entails a homegrown dataset of manually labeled explanations on SA data aggregated through conjunction and disjunction means. The comparison is achieved on six proposed metrics, inspired by information retrieval, to evaluate the precision and fallout of exAI methods on the SA models. Hence, our evaluation is carried out over four different dimensions: (1) SA model, (2) ExAI method, (3) reasoning complexity, and (4) human judgment homogeneity.

The contributions of this work are: (1) a dataset for SA explainability labeled on different dimensions (2) the first faithfulness and plausibility evaluation inspired from information retrieval (3) a thorough four-dimensional ExAI evaluation on SA models.

Our empirical analysis allows us to draw conclusions on the faithfulness of LIME rationales and the plausibility of the anchors model which is found to be more confident in extracting supporting evidence. Moreover, we highlight the consistency of different attention architectures in deriving relatively more plausible explanations.

Next, we provide a general background on the sentiment analysis and ExAI models used in this work in Sect. 2. Then, we present our evaluation dataset and framework in

---

[1] Refers to the metric hereafter.

Sects. 3 and 4. We report our comparative analysis in Sect. 5 before concluding with final remarks in Sect. 6.

2 Background

Little has been done on the evaluation of ExAI in NLP settings. Recently, a framework to evaluate rationalized explanations is introduced in ERASER [9]. ERASER provides benchmarking data for 7 NLP tasks and suggests sufficiency and comprehensiveness as evaluation metrics. While ERASER considers a wider range of NLP tasks; it is narrow in terms of the deep architectures and angles that it considers. In contrast, we study the explainability of SA from four different perspectives. Prior to ERASER, the work of [1] evaluates the explainability of SVMs compared to CNNs to find that the latter models yield more interpretable decisions. Other attempts only consider the attention mechanism and the debate concerning its inherent interpretability [14,21,34]. Additionally, the concept of explanation faithfulness has been introduced before [13,30] with no explicit evaluation of textual classifiers.

Next, we provide the background on sentiment analysis and explainability methods.

2.1 Sentiment Analysis Models

SA models currently exploit deep architectures, word embeddings, transfer learning, and attention mechanisms [35]. In this work, we experiment with eight state-of-the-art SA models with different architectures that vary between convolution, recurrent, and attention networks. The models are chosen with a diversity of word embeddings and some of the models leverage transfer learning techniques during training.

First, *CNN-MC*, a CNN for sentiment classification [15], consists of a simple CNN trained on top of static *word2vec* word embeddings. To experiment with different embedding models, the Universal Sentence Encoder (USE) [4], is used to train additional convolution layers. USE obtains sentence embeddings through a deep averaging network. The recurrent architecture is tested on the Byte-multiplicative LSTMs (*bmL-STM*), used in [27] to generate reviews and discover sentiments.

The attention architecture [39] is studied in five transformer models. We first study the parent transformer, *BERT* [8] which pre-trains deep bidirectional representations by jointly conditioning on the left as well as the right context extracted by each layer on unlabeled data. Then, we study an optimized version of BERT, *RoBERTa* [17], which is trained longer and on prolonged sequences. We further study a different optimization of BERT, *ALBERT* [16], that factorizes the embedding matrix into smaller matrices, separating thus the size of vocabulary from the size of the hidden layers. Moreover, we consider *DistilBERT* [33], a distilled version of BERT trained on very large batches while leveraging the computation of the gradients through dynamic masking. Finally, a non-BERT transformer, *XLNET* [40], introduces the auto-regressive formulation to transformers and considers all permutations of the factorization order of the context while learning of bidirectional contexts.

A comparison of the performance of the studied models on the IMDB movie review dataset is reported under *accuracy* in Table 3.

2.2   Explainability Models

Explainability entails various realizations such as visualization, attention interpretation and alignment [5,25,38,41] as surveyed in [42]. We focus on *rationale* extraction that supports a particular decision by highlighting causal input segments. Hence, we consider three explainability methods: Local Interpretable Model-agnostic Explanations (LIME) [30], high-precision model-agnostic explanations (anchors) [31] and SHapley Additive exPlanations (SHAP) [18]. All these explainability models are black-box algorithms with a profound theoretical ground and a sound practical implementation.

LIME [30] approximates *any* model locally in a model-agnostic fashion. In NLP settings, LIME presents the interpretation in terms of bag-of-words regardless of what the NLP model originally accepts. This is achieved by approximating the classifier with a locally-more-explainable, potentially linear, model which is then trained on perturbed inputs in a local neighborhood.

Later, [31] define "anchors" as if-then rules to generate model agnostic explanations. These rules are a set of predicates, A, that are defined on interpretable representations in such a way that $A(x)$ returns 1 if all its feature predicates are satisfied on x. Consequently, a rule is an anchor if $A(x) = 1$ and A is a sufficient condition for the prediction $f(x)$. Then, random words, having the same Part-of-Speech (POS) TAG as "absent" tokens, are sampled and the "absent" tokens are then replaced by the random words to apply input perturbations and study their effect on the model prediction.

Inspired by game theoretical concepts, [18] developed a unified approach to interpret model predictions. Analogous to the Shapley value computation, SHAP values are proposed as a unified measure that different explainability models, such as LIME [30], Deep LIFT [36] and layer-wise relevance propagation [2], approximate. SHAP is theoretically proven to satisfy *local accuracy*, *missingness* and *consistency* as defined in [18].

3   Evaluation Dataset

We anticipate the support of a group of ten data scientists who contributed to providing ground truth rationales. The labelers are between 21 and 26 years old balanced across gender. We consider the Rotten Tomatoes dataset [24] with binary labels and we complement it with two additional labels: *reasoning difficulty*, and *extracted rationales*[2].

First, the *reasoning difficulty* reflects the complexity of reasoning about the sentiment and takes three values: 1, 2, and 3 with 3 being the most difficult. A special tag 4 for *reasoning difficulty* is used when a sentence requires additional context understanding. For example, the following review is labeled as 4: *"not even the hanson brothers can save it"*. Explaining this sentence would require a higher-level knowledge of what the reviewer meant by *hanson brothers* in a different context. It is noteworthy that the *reasoning difficulty* does not reflect the readability nor the semantic complexity. It rather shows the difficulty of extracting evidence of a particular sentiment.

Second, the *extracted rationales* are a list of particular words in the sentence that contributed to the sentiment prediction. In curating the dataset, we alleviate human bias and subjectivity by asking more than one labeler to extract the rationales of each sentence.

---

[2] Instructions to labelers are provided in the supplementary material.

The aggregation of these explanations is done using the conjunction and disjunction operations. An additional correction step was applied to the aggregated explanations.

Table 1 shows samples from our dataset and Table 2 represents the dataset description aggregated by reasoning difficulty. Specifically, we have 1973 sentences with 20.9 words per sentence on average. Rationales consist of 3.1 words on average when merging (union) across labelers. When considering rationales that different labelers agree on (intersection), the sentences have 0.9 words on average. 934 sentences yield an empty set of rationale intersections. The latter statistic is important to show the degree of agreement between the labelers. A high number of empty intersections reflects diversity in the human thinking in the group of labelers.

Table 1. Dataset sample. Rationales are individual words separated by a space.

Sentence	Label	Reasoning diff.	Rationales (union)	Rationales (intersection)
Beautiful to watch and holds a certain charm	1	1	Beautiful charm	Beautiful charm
It turns out to be smarter and more diabolical than you could have guessed at the beginning	1	1	Smarter more diabolical	Smarter diabolical
None of this is very original, and it isn't particularly funny	0	1	None original is n't funny	None is n't funny
The film tunes into a grief that could lead a man across centuries	1	2	Grief	Grief
The film is about the relationships rather than about the outcome and it sees those relationships, including that between the son and his wife, and the wife and the father, and between the two brothers, with incredible subtlety and acumen	1	3	Incredible subtlety acumen	Incredible subtlety
Hard as this may be to believe, here on earth, a surprisingly similar teen drama, was a better film	0	3	Better	Better
Not even the hanson brothers can save it	0	4	–	–
More than simply a portrait of early extreme sports, this peek into the 1970s skateboard revolution is a skateboard film as social anthropology	1	4	–	–

4 Methodology

In what follows, we describe the design of our evaluation of faithfulness and plausibility and the formulation of our information retrieval-based metrics for *plausibility* evaluation.

4.1 Experimental Design

Once the explanations are derived, two evaluation methods are adopted.

Table 2. Dataset description

Difficulty	1	2	3	4	**Total**
Number of sentences	1535	208	148	82	**1973**
Words per sentence	20.1	24.2	23.7	23.2	**20.9**
Words per explanation (union)	3.4	2.9	2.6	0.0	**3.1**
Words per explanation (intersection)	1.07	0.7	0.45	0.0	**0.9**
Number of empty intersections	629	121	102	82	**934**

Faithfulness. To evaluate the significance of the words in E to the sentiment classification task objectively, we feed E as an input to $\mathcal{M}$ and we compute the prediction accuracy. This experiment does not require a comparison to ground-truth data; it rather studies the validity of the explanations through prediction. In this experiment, we investigate the effect of the ExAI model and its confidence on the explanation accuracy.

Plausibility. After getting the explanations E and their corresponding contributions W, a comparison with the ground truth labels L allows us to compute our proposed metrics as in Sect. 4.2. Figure 1 summarizes the experimental design.

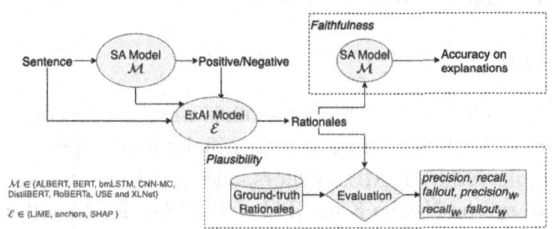

Fig. 1. Experimental design

4.2 Plausibility Evaluation Metrics

In what follows we assume the following: an explanation model $\mathcal{E} \in \{$ SHAP, anchors, LIME $\}$ is outputting a set of words $E = \{e_1, e_2, \ldots, e_{N_1}\}$ with their corresponding contributions $W = \{w_1, w_2, \ldots, w_{N_1}\}$ when explaining a machine learning model $\mathcal{M}$, where $\mathcal{M} \in \{$ ALBERT, BERT, bmLSTM, CNN-MC, DistilBERT, RoBERTa, USE, XLNet$\}$, on an input sentence $S = \{s_1, s_2, \ldots, s_n\}$. To evaluate *plausibility*, we compare E to a sequence of ground truth words provided by human labelers $L = \{l_1, l_2, \ldots, l_{N_2}\}$. Consequently, we propose three metrics inspired from information retrieval: *precision, recall* and *fallout*. The *precision* computes the fraction of the words retrieved by $\mathcal{E}$ that are relevant from a human perspective. The *recall* computes the fraction of words that are relevant from a human perspective and that are retrieved by $\mathcal{E}$. The *fallout* computes the fraction of non-relevant explanations that are retrieved from all the non-relevant words.

$$precision = |L \cap E|/|E| \tag{1}$$
$$recall = |L \cap E|/|L| \tag{2}$$
$$fallout = |(S - L) \cap E|/|S - L| \tag{3}$$

where $|.|$, $\cap$, and $-$ are the set cardinality, intersection, and set difference respectively.

A plausible rationale extraction is reflected in explanations that match human judgment, hence high precision and recall and low fallout rates. A high precision suggests that it is unlikely that the model will provide the word s_i in the explanation if s_i is not provided in the annotations. A high recall reflects that it is unlikely for the model to miss a word if it is in the annotations. We integrate the contribution scores W to generate the weighted version of our metrics as follows:

$$precision_w = |L \cap E|_W \ / \ |E|_W \tag{4}$$
$$recall_w = |L \cap E|_W \ / \ |L| \tag{5}$$
$$fallout_w = |(S - L) \cap E|_W \ / \ |S - L| \tag{6}$$

where $|.|_W$ is the weighted set cardinality computed as $|s_1, s_2, s_M|_W = w_1 + w_2 + w_M$, with $w_i \in W$ is the weight assigned to the word s_i by the explainability method.

5   Results and Discussion

5.1   Back-end Setup

Before generating the explanations, the SA models were re-trained on the same dataset, IMDB movie reviews [19], according to their official code repositories. The obtained models are then explained by LIME, anchors, and SHAP on our provided dataset. All the experiments are run on Nvidia K80 GPU with 12 GB RAM and 0.82 GHz memory clock rate. Following their official repositories, the considered back-end of the SA models varies between *keras*, *torch* and *tensorflow*. Repositories implemented on Python 2.x were translated to Python 3.x and models were retrained accordingly.

5.2   Evaluation of Faithfulness

Table 3 shows the initial model validation accuracy and its reduction when only the explanations are fed to the model $\mathcal{M}$ with different confidences ϵ. The parameters ϵ are tailored to the confidences that each explainer $\mathcal{E}$ produces. Anchors models produce explanations with confidence ≈ 1 and thus no thresholds are considered. One can see that the explanations provided by LIME consistently outperform those provided by *anchors* and SHAP on all SA models. This consistency is also maintained with different thresholds per model. Predominantly, *anchors* produces the least *faithful* explanations yielding significant degradation of SA accuracy. Furthermore, the most interpretable models are predominantly transformers as bmLSTM, RoBERTa and ALBERT scored the highest according to LIME, anchors, and SHAP respectively. The consistency is not maintained on different SA models $\mathcal{M}$. For instance, bmLSTM is more explainable than BERT when LIME is used to explain but less explainable when SHAP is used.

More strikingly, LIME generally enhances the SA accuracy. This can suggest that the sentiment is highly concentrated in the rationales derived by LIME. SHAP, on the other, hand reduces this accuracy and the anchors model further significantly deteriorates it. This can be explained by two factors. First, the models are all trained on full sentences; discontinuous chunks might mislead the model. Second, in some cases, the ExAI models fail to correctly label the negation in their provided explanations which might lead to misclassification. These results suggest that LIME's explanations are more absolute, hence useful, and can serve as standalone representations of the original sentences.

Table 3. Accuracy of $\mathcal{M}$ on explanations of $\mathcal{E}$. Highest accuracies per explanation model are highlighted in bold. Highest accuracies per SA model are underlined.

Model	Accuracy	LIME $\epsilon = 0.1$	$\epsilon = 0.2$	$\epsilon = 0.3$	Anchors	SHAP $\epsilon = 0.1$	$\epsilon = 0.2$	$\epsilon = 0.3$	$\epsilon = 0.5$
ALBERT	89.55	93.15	<u>93.20</u>	93.16	68.30	**88.54**	**88.34**	**88.54**	**88.54**
BERT	89.86	92.60	<u>92.65</u>	92.44	67.28	87.63	87.53	87.20	86.56
bmLSTM	82.61	**93.93**	**93.93**	93.83	77.38	76.84	76.28	75.87	75.22
CNN-MC	71.36	88.35	88.89	<u>88.90</u>	55.40	69.08	68.52	68.02	68.12
DistilBERT	88.77	<u>91.05</u>	90.84	90.70	63.91	88.40	88.10	88.35	87.97
RoBERTa	**90.26**	88.34	<u>88.39</u>	<u>88.39</u>	**82.32**	88.25	88.24	88.21	88.19
USE	83.05	92.74	92.78	<u>92.87</u>	80.43	75.45	74.65	74.48	74.48
XLNet	90.11	92.61	<u>92.65</u>	92.60	71.50	87.83	86.87	86.87	85.85

5.3 Plausibility Evaluation on Ground Truth Data

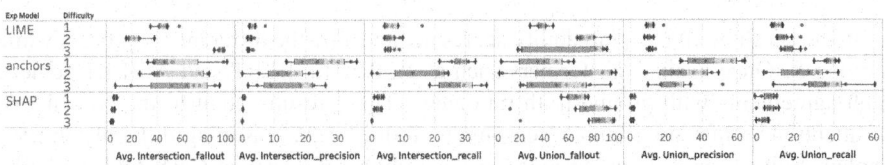

Fig. 2. Explainability scores achieved by ExAIs (for different SA models)

Figure 2 shows the distribution *precision*, *recall* and *fallout* computed on the SA models explained by LIME, anchors and SHAP. Regardless of the reasoning difficulty, the anchors model consistently achieves higher scores on all models $\mathcal{M}$ with the union and intersection operations. This observation can be explained by the fact that anchors' explanations are in harmony with human rationales, especially since anchors are defined as "if-then" rules. However, the anchors model exhibits higher variability and a consistent improvement is seen with the union operation giving the explanation a higher chance to be matched in the ground truth dataset. Finally, the reasoning difficulty level has an effect on the plausibility of explanations but the effect is not significant when aggregating across different SA and ExAI models.

As in the previous experiment, the explanation consistency is not maintained by $\mathcal{E}$. For instance, the most explainable model according to anchors is XLNet followed by RoBERTa (as in the previous experiment), where CNN-MC and RoBERTa are the most explainable according to LIME and SHAP respectively. However, similar to the previous findings, the majority of transformer models disclose higher explainability scores compared to convolutional and recurrent ones. These results are consistent with the weighted metrics which further accentuate the outperformance of anchors' explanations over those of LIME and SHAP. Besides exhibiting better explainability, the anchors model is demonstrated to be more confident in generating its explanations.

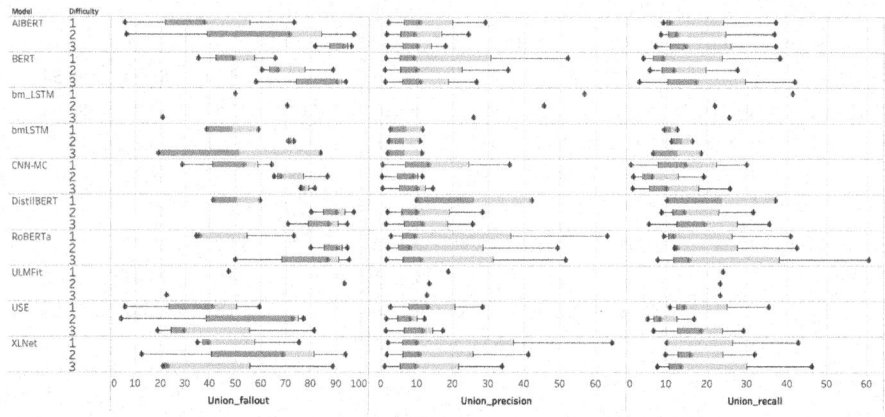

Fig. 3. (Unweighted) explainability scores of SA models when varying the ExAI model

Figure 3 shows the explainability scores achieved by the different SA models while varying $\mathcal{E}$. Once again, transformers such as RoBERTa, BERT, and AlBERT achieve high agreements with ground-truth rationales. These results point to the crucial role of attention in matching human reasoning. Additionally, reasoning difficulty thwarts explainability, especially in non-transformer architectures such as CNN-MC and USE.

5.4 Qualitative Evaluation

Inherently, instances with reasoning difficulty 4 are missing ground-truth explanations. We conduct a qualitative assessment of their explanations. For the sentence: *"watching queen of the damned is like reading a research paper, with special effects tossed in"*, LIME produces *tossed, paper, in, like, is, effects* and *damned* as explanations with confidences < 0.3 on RoBERTa. Clearly, the provided explanation is of low confidence and requires context knowledge such as boredom from reading a research paper. For sentences with a difficulty of 4, SHAP also provides an explanation with negligible weights (order of 10^{-3}–10^{-7}).

5.5 Take-Away Messages

All dimensions have been considered, our evaluation allows us to conclude with the following speculations. LIME produces rationales with high "sentiment concentration" leading to more faithful explanations and *useful* interpretations from a human perspective. The anchors model extracts supporting evidence that is more aligned with human judgment with higher confidence. On the level of the SA architecture, transformers can be, generally, deemed more faithful in deriving explanations. To a significant extent, attention can emulate human reasoning at the back of sentiment extraction. Nonetheless, no single tailor-made deep architecture is highly interpretable when changing the explainability lenses which motivates the ensembling of ExAI results. Finally, high confidence in the evidence extraction can be linked to reasoning simplicity rather than complexity.

6   Conclusion

In this work, we set the grounds for a rigorous evaluation framework for ExAI methods on SA models. We develop metrics to evaluate the explainability of SA models for their faithfulness and plausibility on our annotated rationales. We study the explainability of the SA methods from different angles: reasoning difficulty level, degree of agreement in the annotated data, ExAI model and its confidence level, and the underlying architecture of the SA model. Our empirical study derives important insights concerning the explainability of NLP models, SA specifically. Mainly the plausibility of anchors' explanations and faithfulness of LIME is demonstrated in our set of experiments. More importantly, we highlight the potential that attention mechanisms have in matching human reasoning.

This work paves the way for a sound explainability evaluation framework that would engender user trust in NLP models and support behavioral marketing and market analysis systems. An immediate step in this line of work would be the extension to multi-target and multi-aspect sentiment analysis tasks and general NLP models.

Acknowledgment. This work was supported by the University Research Board (URB) and the Maroun Semaan Faculty of Engineering and Architecture (MSFEA) at the American University of Beirut.

References

1. Arras, L., Horn, F., Montavon, G., Müller, K., Samek, W.: What is relevant in a text document?: an interpretable machine learning approach. arXiv preprint arXiv:1612.07843 (2016)
2. Bach, S., Binder, A., Montavon, G., Klauschen, F., Müller, K.R., Samek, W.: On pixel-wise explanations for non-linear classifier decisions by layer-wise relevance propagation. PloS One **10**(7), e0130140 (2015)
3. Bodria, F., Panisson, A., Perotti, A., Piaggesi, S.: Explainability methods for natural language processing: applications to sentiment analysis (discussion paper) (2020)
4. Cer, D.E.A.: Universal sentence encoder for English. In: Proceedings of the 2018 Conference on Empirical Methods in Natural Language Processing, pp. 169–174. Association for Computational Linguistics, Brussels (2018)

5. Chattopadhay, A., Sarkar, A., Howlader, P., Balasubramanian, V.N.: Grad-cam++: generalized gradient-based visual explanations for deep convolutional networks. In: 2018 IEEE Winter Conference on Applications of Computer Vision (WACV) (2018)
6. Chen, H., Ji, Y.: Improving the explainability of neural sentiment classifiers via data augmentation. arXiv preprint arXiv:1909.04225 (2019)
7. Danilevsky, M., Qian, K., Aharonov, R., Katsis, Y., Kawas, B., Sen, P.: A survey of the state of explainable AI for natural language processing (2020)
8. Devlin, J., Chang, M.W., Lee, K., Toutanova, K.: Bert: pre-training of deep bidirectional transformers for language understanding. arXiv preprint arXiv:1810.04805 (2018)
9. DeYoung, J., et al.: Eraser: a benchmark to evaluate rationalized NLP models. In: Proceedings of the 58th Annual Meeting of the Association for Computational Linguistics, pp. 4443–4458 (2020)
10. Guidotti, R., Monreale, A., Ruggieri, S., Turini, F., Giannotti, F., Pedreschi, D.: A survey of methods for explaining black box models. ACM Comput. Surv. **51**(5), 1–42 (2018)
11. Habimana, O., Li, Y., Li, R., Gu, X., Yu, G.: Sentiment analysis using deep learning approaches: an overview. Sci. China Inf. Sci. **63**(1), 1–36 (2019). https://doi.org/10.1007/s11432-018-9941-6
12. Hassan, A., Mahmood, A.: Deep learning approach for sentiment analysis of short texts. In: 2017 3rd International Conference on Control, Automation and Robotics (ICCAR), pp. 705–710. IEEE (2017)
13. Jacovi, A., Goldberg, Y.: Towards faithfully interpretable NLP systems: how should we define and evaluate faithfulness? In: Proceedings of the 58th Annual Meeting of the Association for Computational Linguistics, pp. 4198–4205 (2020)
14. Jain, S., Wallace, B.C.: Attention is not explanation. In: Proceedings of the 2019 Conference of the North American Chapter of the Association for Computational Linguistics: Human Language Technologies, vol. 1 (Long and Short Papers), pp. 3543–3556 (2019)
15. Kim, Y.: Convolutional neural networks for sentence classification. arXiv preprint arXiv:1408.5882 (2014)
16. Lan, Z., Chen, M., Goodman, S., Gimpel, K., Sharma, P., Soricut, R.: Albert: a lite bert for self-supervised learning of language representations (2020)
17. Liu, Y., et al.: Roberta: a robustly optimized Bert pretraining approach (2019)
18. Lundberg, S.M., Lee, S.I.: A unified approach to interpreting model predictions. Adv. Neural Inf. Process. Syst. 4765–4774 (2017)
19. Maas, A.L., Daly, R.E., Pham, P.T., Huang, D., Ng, A.Y., Potts, C.: Learning word vectors for sentiment analysis. In: Proceedings of the 49th Annual Meeting of the Association for Computational Linguistics: Human Language Technologies, Portland, June 2011, pp. 142–150 (2011)
20. Mishra, P.: Explainability for Non-Linear Models, pp. 93–127. Apress, Berkeley (2022). https://doi.org/10.1007/978-1-4842-7158-2_4
21. Mullenbach, J., Wiegreffe, S., Duke, J., Sun, J., Eisenstein, J.: Explainable prediction of medical codes from clinical text. In: Proceedings of the 2018 Conference of the North American Chapter of the Association for Computational Linguistics: Human Language Technologies, Vol. 1 (Long Papers), pp. 1101–1111 (2018)
22. Nguyen, A., Yosinski, J., Clune, J.: Understanding neural networks via feature visualization: a survey. In: Samek, W., Montavon, G., Vedaldi, A., Hansen, L.K., Müller, K.-R. (eds.) Explainable AI: Interpreting, Explaining and Visualizing Deep Learning. LNCS (LNAI), vol. 11700, pp. 55–76. Springer, Cham (2019). https://doi.org/10.1007/978-3-030-28954-6_4
23. Onan, A.: Sentiment analysis on massive open online course evaluations: a text mining and deep learning approach. Comput. Appl. Eng. Educ. **29**(3), 572–589 (2021)
24. Pang, B., Lee, L.: Seeing stars: exploiting class relationships for sentiment categorization with respect to rating scales. In: Proceedings of the ACL (2005)

25. Patro, B.N., Lunayach, M., Patel, S., Namboodiri, V.P.: U-cam: visual explanation using uncertainty based class activation maps. In: Proceedings of the IEEE International Conference on Computer Vision, pp. 7444–7453 (2019)
26. Qin, Z., Yu, F., Liu, C., Chen, X.: How convolutional neural network see the world - a survey of convolutional neural network visualization methods (2018)
27. Radford, A., Jozefowicz, R., Sutskever, I.: Learning to generate reviews and discovering sentiment. arXiv preprint arXiv:1704.01444 (2017)
28. Rambocas, M., Gama, J., et al.: Marketing Research: The Role of Sentiment Analysis. Universidade do Porto, Faculdade de Economia do Porto, Tech. Rep. (2013)
29. Rambocas, M., Pacheco, B.G.: Online sentiment analysis in marketing research: a review. J. Res. Interact. Market. (2018)
30. Ribeiro, M.T., Singh, S., Guestrin, C.: Why should i trust you?: explaining the predictions of any classifier (2016)
31. Ribeiro, M.T., Singh, S., Guestrin, C.: Anchors: high-precision model-agnostic explanations. In: Proceedings of the AAAI Conference on Artificial Intelligence, vol. 32 (2018)
32. Samek, W., Müller, K.-R.: Towards explainable artificial intelligence. In: Samek, W., Montavon, G., Vedaldi, A., Hansen, L.K., Müller, K.-R. (eds.) Explainable AI: Interpreting, Explaining and Visualizing Deep Learning. LNCS (LNAI), vol. 11700, pp. 5–22. Springer, Cham (2019). https://doi.org/10.1007/978-3-030-28954-6_1
33. Sanh, V., Debut, L., Chaumond, J., Wolf, T.: Distilbert, a distilled version of Bert: smaller, faster, cheaper and lighter (2020)
34. Serrano, S., Smith, N.A.: Is attention interpretable? In: Proceedings of the 57th Annual Meeting of the Association for Computational Linguistics, pp. 2931–2951 (2019)
35. Shi, Y., Zhu, L., Li, W., Guo, K., Zheng, Y.: Survey on classic and latest textual sentiment analysis articles and techniques. Int. J. Inf. Technol. Decis. Making 18(04), 1243–1287 (2019)
36. Shrikumar, A., Greenside, P., Kundaje, A.: Learning important features through propagating activation differences (2019)
37. De Sousa Silveira, T., Uszkoreit, H., Ai, R.: Using aspect-based analysis for explainable sentiment predictions. In: Tang, J., Kan, M.-Y., Zhao, D., Li, S., Zan, H. (eds.) NLPCC 2019. LNCS (LNAI), vol. 11839, pp. 617–627. Springer, Cham (2019). https://doi.org/10.1007/978-3-030-32236-6_56
38. Sundararajan, M., Taly, A., Yan, Q.: Axiomatic attribution for deep networks. arXiv preprint arXiv:1703.01365 (2017)
39. Vaswani, A., et al.: Attention is all you need. In: Advances in Neural Information Processing Systems, pp. 5998–6008 (2017)
40. Yang, Z., Dai, Z., Yang, Y., Carbonell, J., Salakhutdinov, R., Le, Q.V.: Xlnet: generalized autoregressive pretraining for language understanding (2020)
41. Zeiler, M.D., Fergus, R.: Visualizing and understanding convolutional networks. arXiv preprint arXiv:1311.2901 (2013)
42. Zini, J.E., Awad, M.: On the Explainability of Natural Language Processing Deep Models. ACM Computing Surveys (2022)

Sentiment Analysis on COVID-19 Twitter Data: A Sentiment Timeline

Makrina Karagkiozidou, Paraskevas Koukaras⬤, and Christos Tjortjis⁽✉⁾⬤

The Data Mining and Research Analytics Group, School of Science and Technology,
International Hellenic University, 57001 Thessaloniki, Greece
{mkaragkiozidou,p.koukaras,c.tjortjis}@ihu.edu.gr

Abstract. COVID-19 has been one of the most dominant discussion topics on Twitter since 2019. Users express their opinions representing public sentiment on the topic. This paper presents a sentiment timeline of Twitter users, regarding COVID-19 vaccines. This work raises concerns about the extracted information with regards to sentiment analysis, the dominance of each sentiment and its influential power. During the implementation of the analysis, several datasets were examined for the creation of the model. Various algorithms were employed with Random Forest performing best and therefore selected for training the model, achieving an accuracy of 91.5%. Our findings indicate that the majority of Twitter users are positive regarding COVID-19 vaccines and support WHO's recommendations. Negative tweets comprising the minority of the tweets, appear to have a higher influential power with their retweet rates, outperforming positive and neutral sentiments.

Keywords: Sentiment analysis · Text mining · Social media · Vaccination · COVID-19

1 Introduction

Since the creation and wide spread of Social Media (SM) their users have been offered a platform to post and publish opinions in public. That has led companies and organizations to gather and benefit from the information published. Therefore, SM have been widely used for a variety of analytics [12] also including predictions [23] that may integrate sentiment as an extra feature [14]. In microblogs users can share their opinion on any matter, even serious social and political affairs. Such is the COVID-19 virus, a coronavirus that first appeared in December of 2019 in Wuhan, China [24].

Aiming to stop the spread of the virus, each country has taken various measures, including mandatory mask use, local and nationwide lockdowns and more. The citizens of each community have developed increased anxiety levels and insecurity about their future [2]. Even with the creation and production of vaccines, it occurred that a part of each country's community was unwilling or against it, expressing their negative opinion on various types of SM platforms [13].

© IFIP International Federation for Information Processing 2022
Published by Springer Nature Switzerland AG 2022
I. Maglogiannis et al. (Eds.): AIAI 2022, IFIP AICT 647, pp. 350–359, 2022.
https://doi.org/10.1007/978-3-031-08337-2_29

In this study, sentiment analysis on Twitter data has been conducted, regarding COVID-19 vaccines. The aim is to identify patterns and changes in users' public opinion throughout time (during the past year, 2021) and based on milestone events and important announcements of the World Health Organization (WHO) but also actions from authorities. The remaining of the paper is structured as follows. Section 2 reviews related work. Section 3 elaborates on the methodology, while Sect. 4 presents the results of the experimentation we conducted. The paper concludes with Sect. 5 discussing research accomplishments and future work.

2 Related Work

This section presents and analyses recent related work. The aim is to provide a concrete background knowledge regarding sentiment analysis using SM data.

Nemes and Kiss [20] conducted COVID-19 related sentiment analysis on data gathered from Twitter. They focused on comparing the utilized methods. In their training model they verified their findings with an external open-source dataset. Overall, a positive sentiment was identified in the posts, that was maintained over time. An increase in negative sentiment was also observed, leading to a diversity in sentiment polarisation.

Manguri et al. [16] conducted sentiment analysis based on posts published on Twitter during the week of 09-04-2020 to 15-04-2020 related to the keywords 'Covid19' and 'coronavirus'. The findings showed a high percentage of polarisation among users. Furthermore, they related daily opinion changes, depending on government and media actions, broadcasts and new guidelines. To further support their findings they identified higher sample quality on Twitter compared to other SM.

Kruspe et al. [15], conducted cross-language sentiment analysis. The research time frame expanded from December 2019 to April 2020, including countries such as the UK, Spain, Germany, Italy, France and Netherlands. Their findings show that until February 2020, there was little reference to COVID-19 related keywords and topics. Additionally, with the announcement of a lockdown, the sentiments were mostly negative, but improved over time.

Garcia and Berton [10] focused on Brazil and the USA. In their research, they detected and ranked 10 topics, ranging from economic impacts, politics and case reports to anti-racism protests, online events and sports. The dataset includes tweets within a four-month time span, between April and August 2021. Their analysis showed that negative emotions were dominant, especially for the topics of case studies, 'proliferation care' and 'statistics'.

Boon-Itt and Skunkan [5] completed a sentiment analysis study aiming to provide insights on the public perception of COVID-19 using Twitter data. Data were collected during the period from the 13th of December 2019 up to the 9th of March 2020, establishing this research as one of the first on the topic. They created a timeline of the frequency of each symptom mentioned in the posts. Meanwhile, the results indicated that there was in general a negative sentiment for COVID-19.

The analysed literature focuses on specific time periods, topics and Twitter sentiment without considering the total sentiment changes throughout the last year. Therefore, in this study, open-source Twitter datasets are combined with twitter data collected during the period expanding from 15-09-2021 up to 10-12-2021 to identify the sentiment of users after public announcements of governments, WHO, and various FDA vaccination approvals.

3   Methodology

The main purpose of this research is to identify and elaborate the sentiment of Twitter users with regards to the topic of COVID-19 vaccines. Therefore, a clear and well-defined methodology was structured. To identify the response of Twitter users on important COVID-19 vaccine events and announcements, published tweets on the topic were collected in combination with external datasets. RapidMiner was employed for partial data gathering (for some periods) but mainly for data processing. The research model was developed with the use of the Python programming language. The environment in which the code was developed, was Jupyter Notebook. The external dataset was trained with the use of the Random Forest classifier. The main dataset was pre-processed, leading to the prediction of each tweet's sentiment. Finally, the results of the analysis were extracted and visualized using word clouds.

3.1   Dataset

The utilized data in the analysis were collected using Twitter API v2. For the collection of tweets, a workflow on RapidMiner was implemented. Then 10 'Twitter Search' nodes were implemented for each one of the researched keywords. These were: 'covid19 vaccines', 'coronavirus', 'pandemic', 'Pfizer Vaccine', 'Delta Variant', 'Vaccine Certificate', 'Covidiots', 'Covidscam', 'PCR test', 'Rapid test'. For each search, the most recent English tweets were selected.

For integrating more data in the sentiment analysis approach we also employed an existing coronavirus dataset [7]. It contains more than 165,000 tweets with their sentiment annotation. The tweets were notated as positive, neutral and negative. 55% of the tweets were labelled as neutral, 23% as positive and 22% as negative. The downside of this dataset is that there is no data description, therefore, we could only assume the process followed for the annotation of each tweet. To establish the validity of that work, we conducted manual data evaluation.

Dataset Structure
With the use of Twitter API v2 and RapidMiner for the collection of the tweets, there was a specific number of features extracted for every tweet. The main tweet information that is required for the analysis contains the text of the tweet, the date and time of its creation, its retweet count, and the name of the author. Therefore, since there was a combination of self-gathered and external datasets, they both needed to contain the same information.

Pre-processing

The pre-processing of the dataset was implemented using the Python programming language and was divided into two parts. Firstly, the dataset was pre-processed, cleaning the 'text' field from elements that reduce the accuracy of the model based on the research of Beleveslis et al. [4]. The implemented pre-processing function aimed at the removal of the retweet feature, the '@user-names' mentioned in the main part, the '#' symbol, the possible link that might accompany the text and the numbers. Since the final data used in the analysis originated from various sources, their interoperability characteristics were important. Therefore, actions to eliminate duplicate records were implemented. Then, we executed a function for cleansing every tweet text.

3.2 Sentiment Model Development

The libraries that were used throughout the analysis were 'Pandas', 'NumPy', 'Re', 'Seaborn' and 'Sklearn'. It occurred from the examination of the dataset, that tweets characterised as neutral were dominant totalling 98,844 records while positive and negative followed with counts of 40,693 and 40,322, respectively. It appeared that the selected dataset was imbalanced in favour of neutral tweets. For that reason, the overall dataset was divided into three subsets using under-sampling and according to their sentiment. Under-sampling is a method for balancing unequal datasets that involves maintaining all of the data in the minority class while reducing the size of the majority class. This operation caused the most dominant sentiments, neutral and positive to become equal to the number of negative tweets. Positive tweets were represented by the numerical annotation '3', neutral by '2' and negative by '1'.

The next action was to split data into the training and test sets. 80% for training set and 20% for testing was chosen after running multiple variations of these percentage thresholds and checking the output results. For the vectorization of the tweets we used TF-IDF (Term Frequency - Inverse Document Frequency) vectorizer [11].

In the final part of the model, Random Forest Classifier was employed. The model was trained to fit the training set and finally, it predicted the label of the test set, indicating the final accuracy of the model. The accuracy percentage achieved was 91.58%. Other classifiers including Support Vector Machine (SVM), Naïve Bayes and kNN were also tested, but they achieved lower accuracy rates.

3.3 Sentiment Analysis

After successfully training the model, the prediction of the gathered dataset's sentiment took place along with the data pre-processing. Only English tweets and unique tweets were maintained. Next, feature selection was conducted using the 'Optimize Selection' operator[1] from RapidMiner, eliminating features that did not include valuable to the research information. The second external dataset was

---

[1] https://docs.rapidminer.com/latest/studio/operators/.

imported and pre-processed in the same way as the first one. Furthermore, the sentiment of each tweet was calculated and stored using the TF-IDF vectorizer. Tweets were split into tokens of words for the generation of the general, negative and positive word clouds. The findings and results of this analysis are presented and discussed in the next section.

4   Results

4.1   Overview

The gathered tweets, cover a one-year time frame, from 12 Dec 2020 to 10 Dec 2021. During this year, the first COVID-19 vaccine was produced and shared but also mass vaccination became available. At the same time, objections against the vaccines by part of the public were also made. The word clouds presented are indicators of the discussion topics of Twitter.

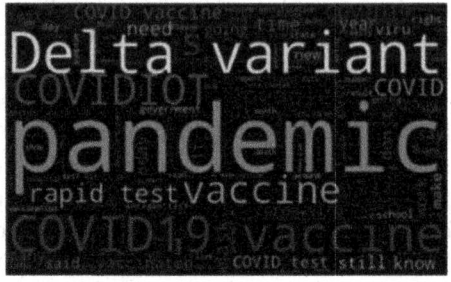

Fig. 1. General word cloud.

In the general word cloud (Fig. 1) the most dominant topic is 'pandemic', showing that most people were discussing the pandemic in general, not only 'vaccines' which follow, and 'Delta variant', which is one of the topics that gained attention in the last five months. Other words that appear to dominate in the word cloud are 'COVID19' and 'COVIDIOT', indicating polarity among the sentiments.

In the positive word cloud (Fig. 2), users tweet about 'vaccines', the new variant, but apart from the topic words, there are noted some smaller very indicative words. Namely, 'still', 'need', 'good', 'work', 'well', 'right', are proof that supporters of the vaccine, try to convince the rest of users of the vaccine's necessity. It is also noticed, that the term 'COVIDIOT' appears in this word cloud indicating polarity among the sentiments.

On the contrary, the negative word cloud (Fig. 3) contains fewer terms, indicating that most users were focusing on a smaller variety of topics. Respectively, for this sentiment, the most dominant terms are 'pandemic', 'vaccine'. Twitter users of this sentiment, appear to use the term 'COVIDIOT'. Other less dominant terms include 'mask', 'work', 'sick','which indicate their focus on more

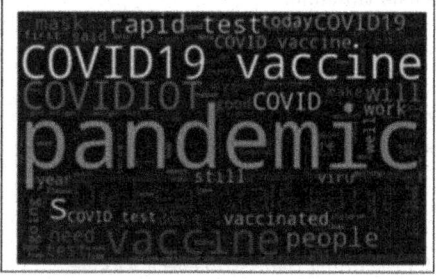 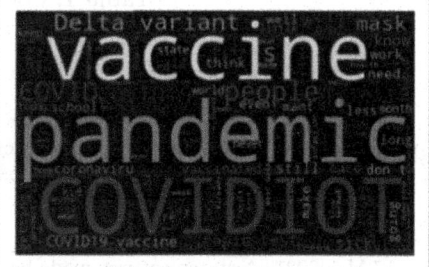

Fig. 2. Positive word cloud.   **Fig. 3.** Negative word cloud.

practical aspects of the topic. Researchers in [6] claim that most negatively driven users, use the 'mask' topic to express their opposition to political or ideological beliefs rather than to the actual effects of masks on health and COVID-19 spread prevention.

4.2 Twitter Timeline

Based on the information of authorised announcements about the virus and WHO's response in their COVID-19 pandemic website [25], a timeline of the expansion and WHO's response is presented starting in December 2020 (Table 1).

Isolation and strict measurements has led to shifts in sentiment on Twitter, such as increments in observed anger for every new wave of the pandemic [1]. Therefore, this work is implemented to monitor Twitter user sentiment on the announcement of each event from WHO and the authorities.

4.3 Sentiment Overview

The dataset used in the analysis initially consisted of 611,022 Tweets in total. After data pre-processing and cleansing, the total number of records was decreased to 388,220. With the prediction of the label per tweet, it appears that the majority of tweets are positive. This observation shows that Twitter users are positive and support COVID-19 vaccines. In detail, positive tweets that are labelled with '3' comprise 67.8% of the records, showing the support and belief of users for the vaccines released. 23% were labelled as Neutral, while only 9.2% of the tweets were labelled as Negative, indicating disbelief, anger and disapproval of the vaccines.

4.4 Sentiment Timeline

We found that the average sentiment during the past year, ranges from 2.25 to 2.8 indicating a neutral to positive sentiment (Fig. 4). The lowest sentiment was noted in the week between 17 Jun 2021 and 24 Jun 2021, while the highest was almost a month later between 07 Aug 2021 and 14 Aug 2021. Based on the plot

Table 1. Coronavirus timeline.

Date	Event
14 Dec 2020	The first vaccination shot took place in the United States [22]. United Kingdom reported a SARS-CoV-2 variant to WHO
31 Dec 2020	WHO issued the emergency use validation for a COVID-19 vaccine, focusing on equitable global access
29 Jan 2021	WHO publishes their recommended COVID-19 tests (PCR and Antigen)
17 Mar 2021	A statement was made by WHO regarding the AstraZeneca vaccine safety. The reason was reports of rare blood coagulation disorders in people that had recently received the vaccine
14 Jun 2021	Lockdown extended in England by four weeks due to Delta Variant [18]
18 Aug 2021	US government announces the initiation of booster doses from September [21]
23 Aug 2021	The Pfizer 2-dose COVID-19 vaccine receives full FDA approval [8]
19 Nov 2021	FDA Authorizes boosters of the Pfizer and Moderna COVID-19 vaccines for adults [9]
22 Nov 2021	Austria is the first country in Europe to impose a 'lockdown' both for vaccinated and not [3]
26 Nov 2021	The latest variant called Omicron is detected in South Africa and Botswana [26,27]

presented, it is obvious that sentiment has shifted daily. One of the most intense decreases was noted at the end of Jan 2021, where the sentiment average reached approximately 2.42. Considering the timeline with the most important events, on 25 Jan WHO released recommendations for use of the Moderna vaccine, while on 29 Jan they publish a list of recommended COVID-19 tests. The most intense general drop in sentiment average over the past year was at the beginning of summer, especially in the week between 12 Jun 2021 and 19 Jun 2021.

Further researching on the information published about COVID-19, it appears that on 14 Jun 2021, the UK announced the extension of the lockdown for four more weeks, based on the threat of the Delta Variant. Since the selected tweets were written in English, it is expected that many users were located in the UK and the US. Therefore, the sentiment could partly reflect their discomfort. The higher sentiment average was noted in the middle of August reaching almost 2.8 with 3 representing a purely positive dataset. Moreover, booster doses were announced in the US on 18 Aug 2021 and the FDA approval of the Pfizer vaccine, on 28 Aug 2021 allowing people to feel more certain that the vaccine is safe and effective. Until 10 Dec 2021, the sentiment was maintained at high levels, with a small drop on 12 Nov 2021. At that period, once again cases started to increase, restrictions to non-vaccinated people were applied in Europe.

4.5   Influential Power

The influence of a tweet is described by several metrics, including 'replies', 'if exists', 'link clicks', 'mentions' and 'retweets' [19]. Based on the findings of a

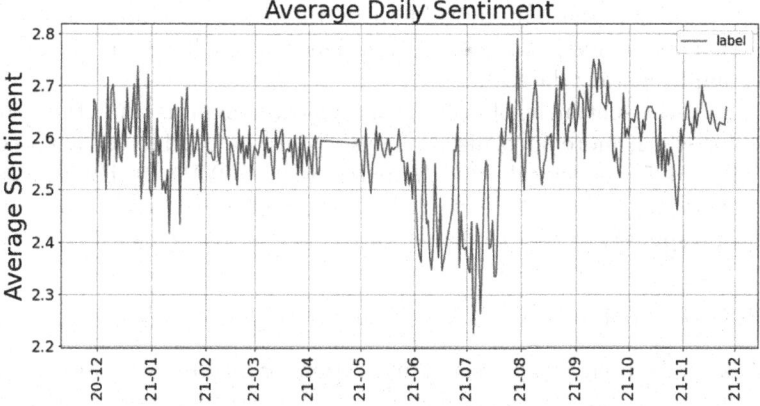

Fig. 4. Average daily sentiment.

similar approach from Medford et al. [17], the tweets with the most retweets were those with a negative context. In this research, their finding can be also be verified. Regarding the retweets per sentiment, some controversial findings occurred. It was found that the number of retweets, compared to the actual number of each sentiment tweets show a different dynamic at each label. It shows that negative tweets tend to have a higher influence and retweet rate per tweet reaching 47.1% with positive having 31.8% and neutral 21.1% respectively. Daily analysis of the sentiments is difficult to be implemented as retweets can happen over several days.

5   Conclusion

5.1   Discussion

During COVID-19, SM were a means for people to express their opinion publicly. It was found that the majority of the users were positive for the course of the pandemic, supporting the work of scientists, governments and WHO. On the contrary, the negative sentiment tends to have a higher engagement rate. The novelty of this work can be attributed to the fact that it investigates the trajectory of the COVID-19 Twitter sentiment over a year and associates it with important events. It also integrates a machine learning approach to evaluate sentiment data from SM. A sentiment timeline is generated to validate certain social behaviors, based on the same features, yet from multiple data sources, i.e. different Twitter datasets. Such an multi-source approach may be employed by officials or researchers, leading to useful knowledge extraction, considering switches in sentiment polarity in SMinitiated by or associated with real-world events.

Moreover, according to our findings, it was observed that people being against the vaccination prefer to share already published thoughts. It can also be concluded that researchers, that base their findings on the work of external datasets are prone to bias potentially introduced by the original dataset curators. This may happen due to missing dataset descriptions and small volume of daily tweets from a complementary dataset.

All in all, the sentiment of every geographical domain is a multidimensional feature, for which more specialized analysis could be conducted. Each country reacted in a different way during the battle with COVID-19. For that reason, a customised analysis per country could be more effective, while rendering governmental responses to the pandemic waves more easily manageable.

5.2   Future Work

This work can be used as a basis and inspiration for future work. Researchers can focus either on a specific geographic location or extend it targeting additional vaccine related keywords. Since the pandemic and its relationship with people is affected by various aspects, such as social, health, political and financial factors, researchers could attempt to extract knowledge based on this research and also considering such parameters. Furthermore, the analyzed dataset might be expanded by incorporating other COVID-19 related search results from Twitter, such as 'Moderna', 'AstraZeneca' vaccines and others. Scientists may also use this work as a point of reference to enhance or doubt their findings on similar attempts. Finally, this work can be imitated or utilized for the extraction of information in any domain of interest, apart from the case of coronavirus.

References

1. Aiello, L.M., Quercia, D., Zhou, K., Constantinides, M., Šćepanović, S., Joglekar, S.: How epidemic psychology works on twitter: evolution of responses to the covid-19 pandemic in the us. Human. Soc. Sci. Commun. **8**(1), 1–15 (2021)
2. Atalan, A.: Is the lockdown important to prevent the covid-19 pandemic? effects on psychology, environment and economy-perspective. Ann. Med. Surg. **56**, 38–42 (2020)
3. BBC. Austria to go into full lockdown as Covid surges (2021). https://www.bbc.com/news/world-europe-59343650
4. Beleveslis, D., Tjortjis, C., Psaradelis, D., Nikoglou, D.: A hybrid method for sentiment analysis of election related tweets. In: 2019 4th South-East Europe Design Automation, Computer Engineering, Computer Networks and Social Media Conference (SEEDA-CECNSM), pp. 1–6. IEEE (2019)
5. Boon-Itt, S., Skunkan, Y., et al.: Public perception of the covid-19 pandemic on twitter: sentiment analysis and topic modeling study. JMIR Publ. Health Surveil. **6**(4), e21978 (2020)
6. Cerbin, L., DeJesus, J., Warnken, J., Gokhale, S.S.: Understanding the anti-mask debate on social media using machine learning techniques. Int. J. Comput. Their Appl. **28**(3), 150–161 (2021)
7. Dhawan. Sentimental analysis of covid-19 tweets — Kaggle. https://www.kaggle.com/dhruvdhawan/sentimental-analysis-of-covid19-tweets/version/1
8. FDA. FDA Approves First COVID-19 Vaccine — FDA. https://www.fda.gov/news-events/press-announcements/fda-approves-first-covid-19-vaccine

9. FDA. Coronavirus (COVID-19) Update: FDA Expands Eligibility for COVID-19 Vaccine Boosters (2021). https://www.fda.gov/news-events/press-announcements/coronavirus-covid-19-update-fda-expands-eligibility-covid-19-vaccine-boosters

10. Garcia, K., Berton, L.: Topic detection and sentiment analysis in twitter content related to covid-19 from brazil and the USA. Appl. Soft Comput. **101**, 107057 (2021)

11. Gupta, D.K., Ekbal, A.: Iitp: supervised machine learning for aspect based sentiment analysis. In: SemEval@ COLING, pp. 319–323 (2014)

12. Koukaras, P., Tjortjis, C.: Social media analytics, types and methodology. In: Tsihrintzis, G.A., Virvou, M., Sakkopoulos, E., Jain, L.C. (eds.) Machine Learning Paradigms. LAIS, vol. 1, pp. 401–427. Springer, Cham (2019). https://doi.org/10.1007/978-3-030-15628-2_12

13. Koukaras, P., Tjortjis, C., Rousidis, D.: Social media types: introducing a data driven taxonomy. Computing **102**(1), 295–340 (2020)

14. Koukaras, P., Tsichli, V., Tjortjis, C.: Predicting stock market movements with social media and machine learning. In: Proceedings of the 17th International Conference on Web Information Systems and Technologies - vol. 1: WEBIST, pp. 436–443. INSTICC, SciTePress (2021). https://doi.org/10.5220/0010712600003058

15. Kruspe, A., Häberle, M., Kuhn, I., Zhu, X.X.: Cross-language sentiment analysis of European twitter messages during the covid-19 pandemic. arXiv preprint arXiv:2008.12172 (2020)

16. Manguri, K.H., Ramadhan, R.N., Amin, P.R.M.: Twitter sentiment analysis on worldwide covid-19 outbreaks. Kurdistan J. Appl. Res. 54–65 (2020)

17. Medford, R.J., Saleh, S.N., Sumarsono, A., Perl, T.M., Lehmann, C.U.: An "info-demic": leveraging high-volume twitter data to understand early public sentiment for the coronavirus disease 2019 outbreak. In: Open Forum Infectious Diseases, vol. 7, p. ofaa258. Oxford University Press, New York (2020)

18. Morton, B., Lee, J.: Covid: lockdown easing in England to be delayed by four weeks (2021). https://www.bbc.com/news/uk-57464097

19. Muñoz-Expósito, M., Oviedo-García, M.Á., Castellanos-Verdugo, M.: How to measure engagement in twitter: advancing a metric. Internet Res. **27**(5), 1122–1148 (2017)

20. Nemes, L., Kiss, A.: Social media sentiment analysis based on covid-19. J. Inf. Telecommun. **5**(1), 1–15 (2021)

21. O'donnell, C., Aboulenein, A.: U.S. to begin offering COVID-19 vaccine booster shots in September (2021). https://www.reuters.com/world/us/us-start-offering-covid-19-vaccine-booster-doses-september-2021-08-18/

22. Ritchie, H., et al.: Coronavirus pandemic (covid-19). Our World in Data (2020)

23. Rousidis, D., Koukaras, P., Tjortjis, C.: Social media prediction: a literature review. Multim. Tools Appl. **79**, 6279–6311 (2019). https://doi.org/10.1007/s11042-019-08291-9

24. Singhal, T.: A review of coronavirus disease-2019 (covid-19). Indian J. Pediatrics **87**(4), 281–286 (2020)

25. World Health Organisation. Timeline of WHO's Response to COVID-19. https://www.who.int/news-room/detail/29-06-2020-covidtimeline

26. World Health Orgainisation. Tracking SARS-CoV-2 Variants (2021). https://www.who.int/en/activities/tracking-SARS-CoV-2-variants/

27. World Health Organisation. Update on Omicron (2021). https://www.who.int/news/item/28-11-2021-update-on-omicron

Social Media Sentiment Analysis Related to COVID-19 Vaccines: Case Studies in English and Greek Language

Evridiki Kapoteli, Paraskevas Koukaras[ID], and Christos Tjortjis[(✉)][ID]

The Data Mining and Research Analytics Group, School of Science and Technology, International Hellenic University, 57001 Thessaloniki, Greece
{ekapoteli,p.koukaras,c.tjortjis}@ihu.edu.gr

Abstract. SARS-CoV-2 and its mutations are spreading around the world, threatening the human population with millions of infections and deaths. Vaccines are considered the main available weapon at hand to mitigate the spread. As a result, the development of efficient systems to understand and supervise the information dissemination, as well as the evolution of sentiments towards vaccines is critical. The goal of this research was to build and apply a supervised learning approach to monitor the dynamics of public opinion on COVID-19 vaccines using Twitter data. 1,394,535 and 61,077 tweets about COVID-19 vaccines, respectively in English and Greek, were collected, classified based on sentiment polarity and analyzed over time to gain insights into sentiment trends. Our findings reveal that overall negative, neutral, and positive sentiments were at 36.5%, 39.9%, and 23.6% in the English language dataset, respectively, whereas overall negative and non-negative sentiments were at 60.1% and 39.9% in the Greek language dataset. Policymakers and health experts could take into consideration social media sentiment analysis alongside other ways of evaluating public sentiment. Social media users are actively seeking and sharing information about pandemic-related topics, allowing governments to use social media to develop effective crisis management strategies, better inform the public with accurate and reliable news, and alleviate disease-specific concerns.

Keywords: Sentiment analysis · COVID-19 vaccines · Machine learning

1 Introduction

The first coronavirus cases emerged in mid-December 2019, but it was not until WHO declared a global pandemic in mid-March 2020 [22] that concern escalated around the world. Initially, social distance, masks, and lockdowns were the only preventive measures available to combat the pandemic, but vaccines were developed soon thereafter, and the pandemic's long-term containment depended solely

I. Maglogiannis et al. (Eds.): AIAI 2022, IFIP AICT 647, pp. 360–372, 2022.
https://doi.org/10.1007/978-3-031-08337-2_30

on their uptake. Nevertheless, the novelty of the disease and worries regarding efficacy, safety, and vaccine development speed, as well as poor or insufficient communication, all contributed to the population's unwillingness to receiving the COVID-19 vaccine. The continuing spread of coronavirus and its variants necessitates the development of efficient systems to understand and monitor the flow of information and the evolution of sentiment about vaccines.

This research is motivated by the extensive use of Twitter during the COVID-19 outbreak and intends to analyze Twitter data for monitoring public opinion regarding COVID-19 vaccines. We consider the seven-month period between May 19, 2021, and November 19, 2021, to collect Twitter messages written in English and Greek. The sentiment analysis performance of various models was evaluated for each language, using an annotated dataset, and the best performing one was chosen and applied to the entire dataset. For Greek language text the sentiment analysis task was addressed as a binary task of classifying sentiment into negative and non-negative classes, and for English language text, as a three-way classification problem with negative, neutral, and positive classes.

Key contributions of our work include: i) A collection and annotation of two COVID-19 vaccination datasets, one in English and one in Modern Greek. To our knowledge, this is the first Modern Greek Twitter dataset about COVID-19 vaccines. ii) A comparative evaluation of how sentiment analysis methods work on Modern Greek, an under-resourced language for Natural Language Processing (NLP) tasks where sentiment analysis is rare, and English, the language on which most research in this area is conducted. iii) A comparison between classic machine learning models and pre-trained language models for sentiment classification. iv) An analysis of social media opinions and sentiments towards the COVID-19 vaccination among Greek individuals and the global community.

The following is an outline of the remaining paper. Section 2 provides an overview of sentiment analysis literature, with a focus on vaccines. Section 3 elaborates on the proposed research design, while Sect. 4 analyzes the experimental results and the trend of sentiments expressed on Twitter. The paper concludes by summarizing accomplishments, presenting limitations and future directions.

2 Background

2.1 Sentiment Analysis

Sentiment analysis focuses on emotion recognition and may employ different types of social media analytics [10], data mining and NLP methods to identify and collect information and opinions from the massive textual content available online [3]. Sentiment analysis can be applied at the document, sentence, and aspect level depending on how the text is viewed and can be classified as being machine learning-based, lexicon-based, or hybrid, depending on the techniques used. Sentiment analysis allows for real-time monitoring on all types of social media platforms [11], and thus its applications exist in nearly every field, including various types social media predictions [19] such as stock movement prediction

[12,17], election results prediction [18] and even depression detection [21]. Next we review some recent studies with an emphasis on Twitter sentiment analysis related to vaccinations.

2.2 Sentiment Analysis for Multilingual Documents

Vaccination has always been an emotionally charged topic for societies, and as a result, a substantial amount of research has been conducted on the subject. Yuan and Crooks [23] for example, used sentiment analysis to investigate how anti- and pro-vaccination Twitter users interacted about the MMR vaccine, while Du et al. [6] suggested a hierarchical machine learning-based methodology to analyze public sentiment on HPV vaccine-related tweets. Twitter sentiment analysis related to vaccinations is a study area that has received a lot of interest, the more so because of the emergency imposed by COVID-19.

Cotfas et al. [4] compared classic Machine Learning (ML) and deep-learning algorithms to determine which one best captured public perception of the new coronavirus vaccines. The authors gathered a dataset of tweets written in English. In order to train the models, they randomly sampled a portion of the data and manually classified it as: in favor, against, or neutral to vaccination. According to their findings, classic classifiers outperformed deep-learning classifiers, with the Bidirectional Encoder Representations from Transformers (BERT) language model achieving the highest accuracy of 78.94%. When the BERT model was applied to the entire dataset, it was found that the predominant stance, either daily or entirely was neutral, whereas in favor tweets, outnumbered against tweets.

Marcec and Likic [16] performed a lexicon-based sentiment analysis and identified potential events and news that may have caused the sentiment regarding different available COVID-19 vaccines to change. During the four-month study period, the sentiment towards the Pfizer/BioNTech and Moderna vaccines has been positive and stable, while the sentiment towards the AstraZeneca/Oxford vaccine appeared to be decreasing. Another study [9] employed an open-source dataset comprising COVID-19 vaccine tweets, to determine the public stance about vaccination. The sentiment polarity of each tweet was extracted using TextBlob, and the sentiment analysis task was performed using Multinomial Naïve Bayes (MNB), Support Vector Machine (SVM), and Logistic Regression (LR) classifiers. When only positive and negative tweets were considered, the LR model performed the best, with an accuracy of 97.3%, followed by SVM and MNB, which had accuracy values of 96.26% and 88%, respectively.

Even though sentiment analysis of English-language corpora has evolved into a prominent research topic in recent years, published work on sentiment analysis of Greek-language text collections has been limited. Giatsoglou et al. [7] employed ML algorithms and deep feed-forward neural networks to classify the sentiment of online user reviews. For text representation, they trained a new model directly on a large social media corpus written in Greek, and then trained an existing language model, GreekBERT, on the same data. It was found that pre-trained language models performed better than traditional representation models, and that they performed even better when a proper language model was trained on a smaller yet domain and task-relevant corpus. The approach of Athanasiou and Maragoudakis [1] on sentiment analysis of Greek text, incorporated each Greek token's translation into account as an extra input feature in the training data's feature set, and employed the Gradient Boosting Machines algorithm. A study focusing on Twitter Sentiment Analysis applications on Greek, employed a combination of Greek lexicons and classification methods to determine how various political events influenced the emotions of Greek Twitter users in the days before the elections [2]. A corpus of annotated tweets was pre-processed to create features, and each tweet was classified using a probabilistic classifier and a hashtag-based filter.

In the context of sentiment analysis using COVID-19 data, Kydros et al. [15] collected Twitter data and used an existing lexicon enriched with specific coronavirus-related words, to assess Greek citizens' feelings during the pandemic's first wave in Greece. The authors found that sentiment fluctuated over time, fear dominated other emotions, and positive feelings declined while negative ones increased. The only related work in Greek on COVID-19 vaccines is the cross-sectional survey that Kourlaba et al. conducted [13], which revealed that two out of five Greek citizens were not willing or sure about getting a SARS-CoV-2 vaccine, with only 57.7% indicating they would. When the findings were compared to those of other researchers, it was found that Greeks were more hesitant to get vaccinated against COVID-19 than other Europeans.

3   Research Design

The goal of the proposed methodology is to create a model capable of predicting the sentiment of vaccine-related tweets of unknown polarity. We started by collecting two COVID-19 vaccination datasets, one with English language tweets and one with Greek language tweets, and manually annotating a subset of tweets from each dataset, that will be used to train the sentiment analysis models. The next step was to pre-process the collected tweets and determine the best representation and classification techniques. We examined Bag-of-Words and word embeddings representations with classic ML and BERT. The performance of various classifiers has been assessed using metrics such as Accuracy, Precision, Recall, and F-score, and the best-performing algorithm has been used to predict and assign a class label to each tweet. Finally, we analyzed the labeled tweets to investigate how public sentiment on Twitter has changed over time. All of the aforementioned steps are detailed in the following subsections.

3.1   Dataset Collection and Annotation

We retrieved Twitter data using several COVID-19 vaccine-related hashtags. Table 1 contains the list of hashtags that were used to collect English-language tweets. When searching for tweets in Greek, this list was modified by replacing the three first hashtags with the Greek equivalents for vaccination and vaccines.

The two distinct Twitter datasets, one for each language, were compiled between May 19, 2021, and November 19, 2021. A total of 1,394,535 English language and a total of 61,077 Greek language tweets were identified, which were reduced to 1,257,944 and 50,796 respectively after removing duplicates.

Table 1. Hashtags list for tweet search.

COVID-19 vaccination topic	#vaccinessaveslives, #vaccinesafety, #vaccinesdontwork,
	#vaccine, #GetVaccinated, #CovidVaccine,
	#vaccinated, #vaccination, #VaccinesWork,
	#COVID19Vaccination, #vaxxed, #antivaxx,
	#vaccinationdone, #Vaccine-Deaths

We then manually annotated the tweets, because we either could not identify a labeled dataset for sentiment analysis regarding COVID-19 vaccines, like in the case of Modern Greek, or identified domain-specific datasets that did not perform sufficiently well. The annotation procedure was carried out as follows.

A positive label was assigned to tweets containing expressions of support, positive attitude or emotion, and tweets describing positive situations and events. Accordingly, a negative label was assigned to tweets containing expressions of judgment, negative attitude, or emotions, as well as tweets describing negative situations and events. Tweets that did not express an emotional state were assigned a neutral label. Consequently, tweets were assigned categorical values "2", "1" or "0" indicating a positive, neutral or negative sentiment towards vaccination. However, given the low number of positive tweets present in the Greek dataset, the positive and neutral classes were merged into the non-negative one, and Greek tweets were labeled as "0" for negative and "1" for non-negative. We selected and manually annotated 2403 English and 1424 Greek language tweets, equally distributed across the classes under consideration in each case.

3.2 Data Pre-processing

The data pre-processing step follows data collection and prepares data for further analysis, whilst ensuring its quality. In this context, tweet texts were first converted to lowercase. The most frequently used emoticons were then replaced with the corresponding words, while many popular contractions, slang, and informal abbreviations were also replaced with their original forms. Elements like URLs, username mentions, numbers, and special characters were discarded since they did not contribute to our analysis. Regarding hashtags, we deleted the hashtag symbol ("#") while keeping the content because they are frequently used instead of normal words and contain valuable information. For Greek language tweets, we considered an additional step at the start of the cleaning process that includes replacing accented vowels with unaccented ones.

In addition, we eliminated stopwords depending on the classification model being tested, and conducted lemmatization of the remaining words. Lemmatization is the process of eliminating a word's inflectional endings and returning it to its base form. Stopwords are words that appear frequently in a corpus, but do not provide additional meaning in an analysis, and need to be eliminated. In our case, negative terms like "no" and "don't", which are commonly found in stopwords lists express sentiment, and eliminating them would completely change the stance of the text. As a result, we used a stopwords list provided by the Natural Language Toolkit (NLTK) library [20] and a list of Greek stopwords [8] after eliminating negative keywords.

3.3   Text Representation and Classification

Using the annotated dataset as training data, the performance of the following prominent classifiers was reviewed in our research: Support Vector Machine (SVM), Logistic Regression (LR), Random Forest (RF), and Extreme Gradient Boosting (XGBoost). However, before using any classification algorithm, text data needs to be translated into a numerical feature vector. The simplest method is known as Term Frequency - Inverse Document Frequency (TF-IDF) and weights each term and assigns it a TF and IDF score, where the former determines the number a term appears in a document, and the latter indicates how common or rare a term is across the entire collection of documents. The second most common method is word embeddings. This study employs the Word2Vec algorithm, which builds a vocabulary by considering the words that occur in a collection of sentences more times than a numeric threshold specified by the user. It then implements the continuous bag-of-words model or the skip-gram model to learn a D-dimensional vector representation of each word from the input documents. In addition to learning individual word representations, using Word2Vec there is the option of learning word context representations with BERT. BERT is a transformer-based language model, that can be fine-tuned to a user's specifications using its pre-training as a base layer. In this research, we selected $BERT_{BASE}$[1] as described by the research team [5] and $GreekBERT$[2], the Greek equivalent of $BERT_{BASE}$ [14].

4   Results

First, we used a TF-IDF Vectorizer with its n-gram parameter set to (1, 2), referring to unigrams and bigrams. Then, we trained a Word2Vec model on our collected training data to obtain vector representations for all the unique words present in the corpus, using the skip-gram training algorithm and setting the dimensionality of its word vectors equal to 100. Lastly, we further trained $BERT_{BASE}$ and GreekBERT language models, on our collected English

---

[1] https://huggingface.co/bert-base-uncased.
[2] https://huggingface.co/nlpaueb/bert-base-greek-uncased-v1.

and Greek language social media corpus respectively, fine-tuning them using a batch size of 16, a learning rate of 2e−5 and four epochs.

As already mentioned, we evaluated the selected models by considering if the elimination of stopwords and the implementation of lemmatization improved their performance. We present the findings of the scenario that most classifiers perform best in. For the TF-IDF scheme, this entails performing both stopwords elimination and lemmatization in each tweet. For the English language Word2Vec model, we only performed stopwords removal, while for the Greek language Word2Vec model we did not apply stopwords removal or lemmatization. Figure 1 lists the hyperparameters optimized for each tunable algorithm using the grid search technique, as well as their optimal values in the best models.

		SVM	LR	RF	XGBoost
English	TF-IDF	'C': 2, 'gamma': 'scale', 'kernel': 'linear'	'C': 10, 'max_iter': 100	'max_features': 'log2', 'min_samples_split': 4, 'n_estimators': 200	'gamma': 0.1, 'max_depth': 3, 'n_estimators': 200
	Word2Vec	'C': 10, 'gamma': 0.1, 'kernel': 'rbf'	'C': 5, 'max_iter': 500	'max_features': 'auto', 'min_samples_split': 2, 'n_estimators': 300	'gamma': 0.01, 'max_depth': 9, 'n_estimators': 200
Greek	TF-IDF	'C': 1, 'gamma': 'scale', 'kernel': 'linear'	'C': 10, 'max_iter': 100	'max_features': 'log2', 'min_samples_split': 2, 'n_estimators': 500	'gamma': 0.1, 'max_depth': 3, 'n_estimators': 100
	Word2Vec	'C': 5, 'gamma': 0.5, 'kernel': 'rbf'	'C': 10, 'max_iter': 500	'max_features': 'auto', 'min_samples_split': 5, 'n_estimators': 500	'gamma': 0.1, 'max_depth': 9, 'n_estimators': 100

Fig. 1. Hyperparameters and their optimal values in each case.

Next, Fig. 2 shows the accuracy score achieved by BERT and each ML algorithm. When employing the TF-IDF technique for representing text in English, we can see that Logistic Regression was the best performing classifier, followed by SVM, with 85% and 84% accuracy scores, respectively. The results indicate that the use of word embeddings improved the performance of all algorithms except LR for which the accuracy score did not change. The RF and XGBoost classifiers showed the greatest improvement in accuracy, whereas SVM outperformed all models, and was the best classifier when word embeddings representations were used. Having an accuracy of 91% the BERT$_{BASE}$ model exceeded the performance of all the aforementioned classifiers. We also observed that for both weighting schemes, TF-IDF and word embeddings, the considered algorithms performed worse in terms of precision, recall, and f-score, for the neutral class, which did not hold for the BERT language model.

When examining the classification performance results for the Greek language dataset, we observe that SVM was the best performing classifier for the TF-IDF weighting method, with an accuracy of 86%, followed by LR. The other two algorithms performed relatively poorly with accuracy rates of 78% and 76%. When it comes to word embeddings, the performance of RF and XGBoost classifiers improved by 4% and 3% respectively, whilst the accuracy rates of the SVM and LR models were slightly reduced. Despite the decrease in its accuracy, the SVM model still outperformed the other classifiers. However, the best performance among the explored approaches was achieved when fine-tuning the GreekBERT language model with an accuracy of 93%. This model also outperformed the others in terms of precision, recall, and f-score across all classes, negative and non-negative.

Representation Technique & Classifier	TF-IDF				Word2Vec				BERT
	SVM	LR	RF	XGBoost	SVM	LR	RF	XGBoost	
English	0.84	0.85	0.79	0.77	0.86	0.85	0.82	0.83	0.91
Greek	0.86	0.85	0.78	0.76	0.83	0.81	0.82	0.79	0.93

Fig. 2. Classification Accuracy scores for English and Greek language models.

To summarize, most of the trained classifiers performed well, however, the two fine-tuned BERT models had the highest accuracy scores. Consequently, after discarding the training tweets we applied the fine-tuned $BERT_{BASE}$ model to all 1,255,554 tweets in the English language corpus, and the fine-tuned GreekBERT model to all 49,375 tweets in the Greek language corpus. The objective of this process was to determine the polarity of each tweet, so we could analyze the classified tweets over time and identify sentiment changes towards the vaccination topic, which could occur in response to vaccine-related news or events.

4.1 Trend Analysis

Figure 3 shows the percentage of tweets distributed across the different sentiment categories in both languages. Based on the distribution of English language tweets, the "Neutral" category had the highest percentage of tweets, reaching almost 40%, while the "Positive" category with 23.6% was outnumbered by the "Negative" category with 36.5%. On the other hand, the overwhelming majority of Greek language tweets (60.1%) fell into the "Negative" category, with the remaining 39.9% falling into the "Non-negative" category.

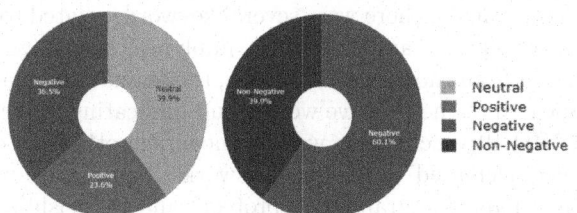

Fig. 3. Tweets percentage distribution by sentiment category collectively for English (left) and Greek (right).

Since these are aggregated results and may conceal fluctuations that occurred within the time range, we further plotted the daily timeline showing the evolution of vaccine-related tweets based on sentiment, for the study period. The daily progression of negative and non-negative sentiments on the left side of Fig. 4 shows that the dominant sentiment was negative, but its trend is closely followed by the non-negative trend. The time series for the English language dataset, presented on the right side of Fig. 4, shows that the prevailing sentiment remained neutral until July 15, 2021, when negative sentiment started to dominate, with a few exceptions. The number of positive tweets did not exhibit dramatic fluctuations except for September 17, 2021, and October 21, 2021, when it peaked.

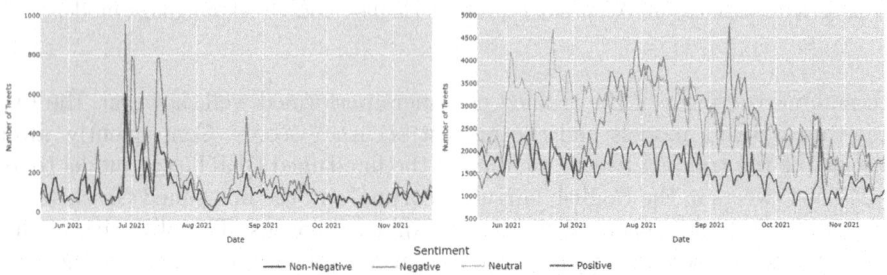

Fig. 4. Time series between May 19, 2021 and November 19, 2021, for the collected tweets on a daily basis based on sentiment for Greek (left) and English (right).

Next, we studied word clouds displaying the one hundred most frequently occurring words for each sentiment class, that were generated using the log-likelihood values. According to Fig. 5, the words "death", "unvaccinated", "covidiot" and "antivaxxer" appeared frequently in negative English language tweets, indicating that many Twitter users expressed their displeasure with people who refused to receive the vaccine. People were still concerned about the mask mandates and the coronavirus repercussions, as evidenced by terms like "mask", "mandate", "sick" and "risk." Words that appeared often in neutral tweets such as "vaccine", "dose", "available", and "date", indicate a need for information on the vaccination program. Interestingly, there were several keywords related to India, such as "indiafightscorona", "pune" and "covaxin", implying that a significant number of tweets originated from Indian users. Finally, terms like "vaccinated", "thank", and "great" appeared in the positive word cloud, indicating that people support and receive COVID-19 vaccines, as well as encourage others to do so by using hashtags like "getvaccinated" and "vaccineswork". Some more words shown in a smaller size are "happy", "grateful", "protect" and the hashtag "staysafe".

Moreover, according to Fig. 5 and in the case of Greek language word clouds, the most interesting conclusions can be drawn from the negative one. It is evident that it was dominated by references to Greece's prime minister and the government in general, the mass media, as well as rude and inelegant characterizations of them. Other negative words refer to vaccine deniers, vaccine side-effects, coronavirus variants and deaths, whereas some of the most popular keywords associated with non-negative sentiment referred to the pandemic, covid cases, and mutations, vaccines, dose, children, and hashtags like "covidgreece", and "rollingupsleeves".

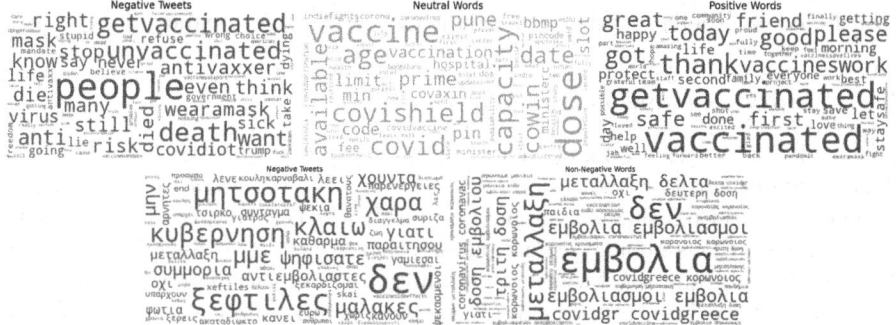

Fig. 5. Word clouds for the English (top) and Greek (bottom) datasets, showing the most frequent appearing words in vaccine-related tweets for each sentiment category.

5 Conclusion

This paper follows the evolution of sentiment towards COVID-19 vaccines between May 19, 2021, and November 19, 2021, by creating a ML based sentiment analysis model using pre-annotated tweets, that is capable of classifying Twitter posts written in English or Greek. Several established classifiers and language models were examined for both languages, with their accuracy rates ranging from 76% to 93%. The proposed framework classifies English language tweets into positive, neutral, and negative categories employing BERT with 91% accuracy. Greek language tweets are classified as negative and non-negative, employing GreekBERT with an accuracy of 93%.

When the English dataset was studied collectively, the prevailing sentiment was neutral, but daily, neutral was only dominant during the first months, as the sentiment shifted to negative in the months that followed, with the exception of a few days. When we compare the percentage of tweets belonging into each sentiment category on the beginning and end dates of the study period, we find that negative sentiment increased by nearly 12%, positive sentiment decreased by 11%, and the percentage of neutral sentiment remained almost stable. Except for a few days negative sentiment dominated the Greek dataset both overall and daily. When the percentage of tweets on May 19 and November 19 were compared, it was found that negative tweets grew by 17% while non-negative tweets declined by 17%.

As the vaccination process is still hampered by several barriers, and new cases and deaths are growing worryingly, our work demonstrates that social media sentiment analysis can yield useful insights, which governments and health experts can use to develop effective crisis management strategies, better inform the public and plan ahead of time to prevent disease-specific concerns. Quick responses and actions facilitated by social media analysis, aimed at minimizing and preventing negative emotional and psychological impacts will enhance global health and well-being amid crises such as the SARS-CoV-2 pandemic.

5.1 Limitations and Future Work

Although Twitter is a valuable data source for studying real-time social media content about coronavirus vaccines, its users are not representative of the general Greek- and English-speaking public, and their tweets simply reflect netizens' views and emotions about vaccination. Another limitation is linked to data collection, since we queried Twitter using limited sets of vaccine-related hashtags, which may have been incomplete. Next, determining the class to which each tweet belongs introduces subjectivity, since each opinion may have different interpretations. We should also keep in mind that social media data contains a lot of noise, which is difficult to completely eliminate, and that the selection of data processing techniques is subjective and may significantly impact the research's outcomes. Additional limitations stem from the use of ML, which can process large amounts of data considerably faster than human approaches, but still struggles to detect irony and sarcasm in tweets.

For that reason, the primary focus of future research should be on building better-performing sentiment classification models and conducting the analysis with a larger dataset, acquired from multiple social network sites or sources other than social media. It would be also interesting to detect and classify emotions in tweets, such as happiness, fear, trust, which has the potential to improve citizens' and society's understanding. Another future direction involves studying the geographic distribution of tweets and their sentiment, comparing how sentiment changes across different countries around the world.

Acknowledgements. The authors would like to thank the Hellenic Artificial Intelligence Society (EETN) for covering part of their expenses to participate in AIAI 2022.

References

1. Athanasiou, V., Maragoudakis, M.: A novel, gradient boosting framework for sentiment analysis in languages where NLP resources are not plentiful: a case study for modern Greek. Algorithms **10** (2017). https://doi.org/10.3390/A10010034
2. Beleveslis, D., Tjortjis, C., Psaradelis, D., Nikoglou, D.: A hybrid method for sentiment analysis of election related tweets. In: 2019 4th South-East Europe Design Automation, Computer Engineering, Computer Networks and Social Media Conference (SEEDA-CECNSM), pp. 1–6 (2019). https://doi.org/10.1109/SEEDA-CECNSM.2019.8908289

3. Cambria, E., Schuller, B., Xia, Y., Havasi, C.: New avenues in opinion mining and sentiment analysis. IEEE Intell. Syst. **28**, 15–21 (2013). https://doi.org/10.1109/MIS.2013.30

4. Cotfas, L.A., Delcea, C., Roxin, I., Ioanăş, C., Gherai, D.S., Tajariol, F.: The longest month: analyzing COVID-19 vaccination opinions dynamics from tweets in the month following the first vaccine announcement. IEEE Access **9**, 33203–33223 (2021). https://doi.org/10.1109/ACCESS.2021.3059821. https://ieeexplore.ieee.org/document/9354776

5. Devlin, J., Chang, M., Lee, K., Toutanova, K.: BERT: pre-training of deep bidirectional transformers for language understanding. CoRR abs/1810.04805 (2018). http://arxiv.org/abs/1810.04805

6. Du, J., Xu, J., Song, H., Liu, X., Tao, C.: Optimization on machine learning based approaches for sentiment analysis on HPV vaccines related tweets. J. Biomed. Semant. **8**, 9 (2017). https://doi.org/10.1186/s13326-017-0120-6

7. Giatsoglou, M., Vozalis, M.G., Diamantaras, K., Vakali, A., Sarigiannidis, G., Chatzisavvas, K.C.: Sentiment analysis leveraging emotions and word embeddings. Expert Syst. Appl. **69**, 214–224 (2017). https://doi.org/10.1016/J.ESWA.2016.10.043

8. Greek stopwords collection. https://github.com/stopwords-iso/stopwords-el. Accessed 23 Feb 2022

9. Khakharia, A., Shah, V., Gupta, P.: Sentiment analysis of COVID-19 vaccine tweets using machine learning. SSRN Electron. J. (2021). https://doi.org/10.2139/ssrn.3869531

10. Koukaras, P., Tjortjis, C.: Social media analytics, types and methodology. In: Tsihrintzis, G.A., Virvou, M., Sakkopoulos, E., Jain, L.C. (eds.) Machine Learning Paradigms. LAIS, vol. 1, pp. 401–427. Springer, Cham (2019). https://doi.org/10.1007/978-3-030-15628-2_12

11. Koukaras, P., Tjortjis, C., Rousidis, D.: Social media types: introducing a data driven taxonomy. Computing **102**(1), 295–340 (2020)

12. Koukaras, P., Tsichli, V., Tjortjis, C.: Predicting stock market movements with social media and machine learning. In: Proceedings of the 17th International Conference on Web Information Systems and Technologies - Volume 1: WEBIST, pp. 436–443. INSTICC, SciTePress (2021). https://doi.org/10.5220/0010712600003058

13. Kourlaba, G., et al.: Willingness of Greek general population to get a COVID-19 vaccine. Glob. Health Res. Policy **6** (2021). https://doi.org/10.1186/s41256-021-00188-1

14. Koutsikakis, J., Chalkidis, I., Malakasiotis, P., Androutsopoulos, I.: GREEK-BERT: the Greeks visiting sesame street. CoRR abs/2008.12014 (2020). https://arxiv.org/abs/2008.12014

15. Kydros, D., Argyropoulou, M., Vrana, V.: A content and sentiment analysis of Greek tweets during the pandemic. Sustainability **13**(11) (2021). https://doi.org/10.3390/su13116150. https://www.mdpi.com/2071-1050/13/11/6150

16. Marcec, R., Likic, R.: Using Twitter for sentiment analysis towards AstraZeneca/Oxford, Pfizer/Biontech and Moderna COVID-19 vaccines. Postgrad. Med. J. (2021). https://doi.org/10.1136/postgradmedj-2021-140685

17. Nousi, C., Tjortjis, C.: A methodology for stock movement prediction using sentiment analysis on Twitter and stocktwits data. In: 2021 6th South-East Europe Design Automation, Computer Engineering, Computer Networks and Social Media Conference (SEEDA-CECNSM), pp. 1–7 (2021). https://doi.org/10.1109/SEEDA-CECNSM53056.2021.9566242

18. Oikonomou, L., Tjortjis, C.: A method for predicting the winner of the USA presidential elections using data extracted from Twitter. In: 2018 South-Eastern European Design Automation, Computer Engineering, Computer Networks and Society Media Conference (SEEDA-CECNSM), pp. 1–8 (2018). https://doi.org/10.23919/SEEDA-CECNSM.2018.8544919

19. Rousidis, D., Koukaras, P., Tjortjis, C.: Social media prediction: a literature review. Multimedia Tools Appl. **79**(9), 6279–6311 (2020)

20. Steven, B., Ewan, K., LoperEdward: Natural Language Processing With Python. O'Reilly, Sebastopol (2009)

21. Wang, X., Zhang, C., Ji, Y., Sun, L., Wu, L., Bao, Z.: A depression detection model based on sentiment analysis in micro-blog social network. In: Li, J., et al. (eds.) Trends and Applications in Knowledge Discovery and Data Mining, pp. 201–213. Springer, Heidelberg (2013)

22. Timeline: Who's COVID-19 response. https://www.who.int/emergencies/diseases/novel-coronavirus-2019/interactive-timeline#event-72. Accessed 23 Feb 2022

23. Yuan, X., Crooks, A.T.: Examining online vaccination discussion and communities in Twitter. In: ACM International Conference Proceeding Series, pp. 197–206, July 2018. https://doi.org/10.1145/3217804.3217912

Time Series Modeling/Transfer Learning

Comparing Boosting and Deep Learning Methods on Multivariate Time Series for Retail Demand Forecasting

Georgios Theodoridis and Athanasios Tsadiras[(✉)]

Aristotle University of Thessaloniki, Thessaloniki, Greece
{ttgeorgios,tsadiras}@econ.auth.gr

Abstract. Retail demand forecasting is an inherently complex problem as many different time-related factors as well as the correlation of demands in between each and every retail product have to be taken into account. In technical terms, retail demand forecasting is a multivariate timeseries forecasting problem where every single timeseries has to be not only analyzed but also predicted. Hence, added complexity is introduced necessitating the use of advanced methods with machine/deep learning backgrounds. Boosting models, such as XGBoost and LightGBM, are perfect choices with extensive bibliographic background and have been widely used to tackle multivariate timeseries forecasts. Simultaneously, recent advancements in deep neural networks have introduced new promising architectures that are yet to be applied on many different scenarios. Therefore, within this paper, two of those architectures with different core components are introduced, analyzed and applied. The Temporal Convolutional Network based on Convolution and the Temporal Fusion Transformer based on the Transformer architecture, which uses self-attention, are compared to boosting methods as well as standard statistical approaches, namely Exponential Smoothing and Seasonal ARIMA. The results indicate that the deep learning networks are the better choices contributing to the notion that deep learning has extraordinary capabilities in relation to large scale, complex and noisy data and that the aforementioned newly adopted designs are excellent choices for multivariate timeseries forecasting.

Keywords: Time Series Forecasting · Multivariate forecasting · Retail demand forecasting · Boosting models · Deep neural networks

1 Introduction

Demand forecasting is a major challenge for retailers as it is the input for many operational decisions, especially for perishable goods with a high deterioration rate [11]. Retailers offer a vast variety of products via many different stores. Consequently, numerous forecasts are necessary daily to predict the demand of every item in every store. Therefore, it is of great importance to introduce methods that, regardless of scale and complexity, perform accurate forecasts.

© IFIP International Federation for Information Processing 2022
Published by Springer Nature Switzerland AG 2022
I. Maglogiannis et al. (Eds.): AIAI 2022, IFIP AICT 647, pp. 375–386, 2022.
https://doi.org/10.1007/978-3-031-08337-2_31

Time Series Forecasting (TSF) is the fundamental process of predicting future values after analyzing chronologically ordered past values and is applied in many different fields such as energy consumption [3], financial analysis [16], sales forecasting [17], anomaly detection [18], database optimization [5] etc. TSF problems are inherently complex as there are time-related factors that must be taken into account; trend, seasonality and correlation of values based on time-distance [19].

Classical statistic models focus on univariate TSF, meaning the prediction of the future values of a single variable by observing the past values of that variable alone. But in today's reality of big data and especially in relation to retail demand, multivariate predictions are nothing sort of a necessity, hence the usage of complex machine learning models and, recently, deep learning techniques is required. Multivariate TSF may also be categorized in two main classes:

1. The usage of multiple past variables to predict one future variable, for example the prediction of electricity prices based on past electricity prices as well as past temperatures, past gas prices etc. We can define this category as many-to-one.
2. The usage of multiple past variables to predict multiple future variables, for example predicting the future sales of 5 products based on the past sales of all 5 products interchangeably. We can define this category as many-to-many.

The focus of this paper are multivariate TSFs of the latter category as retail demand forecasting is a many-to-many multivariate TSF. The contributions offered by the current paper are the following:

- Bibliographic enrichment of recently proposed DNNs with promising architectures.
- A comparison of the aforementioned DNNs with well established Boosting methods that are often considered the golden standard in machine learning practices.
- A benchmark comparison using popular statistical methods (ETS, ARIMA) that have, historically, been the default approaches in many different scenarios, including retail demand forecasting.

2 Background

Multivariate TSF is characterized by nonlinearity and difficulties in detecting overall trends and seasonality [27]. Therefore, many specialized models of different mathematical background have been developed to tackle the complexity of multivariate problems.

An initial and intuitive approach is to treat TSF as a generic regression problem whilst converting "time" into input features and using well known machine learning models as predictors such as Support Vector Regression (SVR) [21], Random Forest [9] and Gradient Boosting models like LightGBM [24]. The inherent advantage of this approach is the preestablished research and bibliographic robustness of said regression models. On the contrary, large multivariate datasets may include complex nonlinear correlations that are tedious to detect by equating TSF to general regression and simply applying generic regression models without tweaking their architecture.

Meanwhile, deep neural network approaches that were initially designed to solve image and/or language recognition problems have now gained popularity in general TSF problems. Convolutional Neural Networks (CNN) and Recurrent Neural Networks (RNN) are mathematically great choices offering models such as Long-Short Term Memory (LSTM) [10] and Convolutional LSTM (ConvLSTM) [23]. These models are able to detect complex dependencies as they are designed to learn from both short- and long-term time correlations. A potential disadvantage is handling aperiodic and noisy data as these models depend on the existence of seasonality. Recently, to resolve the aforementioned issues, a new network architecture has been proposed, the Temporal Convolutional Network (TCN) [2]. It is described as straightforward in its convolution architecture and has the ability to create both deep and wide networks that are more resilient to aperiodic inputs.

Current advancements in hardware technology, mainly GPUs, reveal the capability and benefits of running deep learning processes in parallel. RNN's are unable to parallelize their internal calculations as they, by design, read and produce predictions in sequence. Hence, the Transformer model [26] was proposed that depends on multi-head self-attention which can easily be parallelized. Since then, many different novel designs based on self-attention have surfaced including the Temporal Fusion Transformer (TFT) [15] which improves the original concept by allowing the use of known past and future covariates as inputs and focusing on predicting multiple outputs.

3 Model Analysis

In the following paragraphs an overview of every model studied within this paper will be presented, focusing more on Deep Neural Networks (DNNs) and their architecture.

3.1 Multivariate Boosting

XGBoost (eXtreme Gradient Boosting) is an optimized distributed gradient boosting library designed to be highly efficient, flexible and portable [4]. It implements parallel tree boosting (also known as GBDT, GBM) under the Gradient Boosting ensemble learning framework. LightGBM is another boosting framework that uses tree-based learning algorithms. It is considered a predecessor to the XGBoost framework that achieves faster training speed and higher efficiency [14]. LightGBM uses histogram-based algorithms [13] which bucket continuous feature values into discrete bins and grows trees leaf-wise (best-first) [22]. It is currently considered one of the standard machine learning frameworks and has been heavily analyzed [1, 12].

In terms of multivariate TSF, both boosting algorithms use time dependent covariates such as numerical values representing the day of the week, month, year etc. or boolean values revealing if the current day is a weekday, holiday etc. to explain the time axis as well as the values of each series as input. By design, the output of the regressor is one dependent variable, therefore this approach can only solve a many-to-one multivariate TSF. To forecast many-to-many time series, n number of separate predictors need to be implemented where n equals the number of time series in the current problem. Simply put, instead of solving the initial problem directly, this method solves numerous many-to-one problems. In fact, via this process, every general regression machine learning model may be used to solve many-to-many multivariate TSFs.

A seemingly obvious disadvantage is the huge number of predictors necessary for larger scale TSFs but, in reality, both the execution time is faster and the size in memory is lower compared to complex DNNs that solve the problem directly.

3.2 TCN

A Temporal Convolutional Network (TCN) [2] addresses TSF problems with the usage of convolution. At its core, TCN applies multiple dilated, causal 1D convolutions on its input to create an equally sized output. A convolution is causal when an.

output at time t is convolved only with elements from time t and earlier. For univariate TSF, 1D (one dimensional) convolutions are straightforward to explain; the only dimension is time with every timestep being assigned a single value. One would assume that multivariate TSF problems would require 2D convolutional layers and technically they are equivalent to a 2D convolution with kernel size (k, n), where n is static and equal to the number of timeseries, but they are still 1D in the sense that the window only moves along a single axis, the time axis, and the kernel size is essentially just k.

The dilated convolution of a 1D sequence $x \in R^n$ and a filter $f : \{0, \ldots, k-1\} \to R$ is defined as the operation F on element s of the sequence so that:

$$F(s) = (x *_d f)(s) = \sum_{i=0}^{k-1} f(i) \cdot x_{s-d \cdot i} \tag{1}$$

where d is the dilation factor, k is the kernel size and $s - d \cdot i$ is the direction in the past. Essentially, dilation adds a fixed step in between every two consecutive filter taps.

To actually train and forecast via convolution, as the output has to be equal to the input, the network will equate its output to the values of the timeseries shifted forward by the forecast window, hence the tail of said output is the forecast.

The architecture of the current TCN follows that of [2] and shall be broken down in three levels as visualized in Fig. 1:

1. The network consists of sequential Residual blocks that contain a branch leading out to a series of transformations $\mathcal{F}$, whose outputs are added to the input x of the block:

$$o = Activation(x + \mathcal{F}(x)) \tag{2}$$

Every block has a dilation factor that increases exponentially (base b) per block. The number of blocks m is decided automatically so that full history coverage can be achieved, meaning that every output value has been affected by every input value.

2. Every Residual block consists of 2 Convolutional layers that are followed by a potential weight normalization, a ReLU activation to achieve non-linearity and a spatial dropout layer. Assuming input x with n timeseries (meaning depth of n), the number of filters f, used during convolution on it, will change the depth of the output to f. More specifically, the first layer of the first block will have an input depth n and

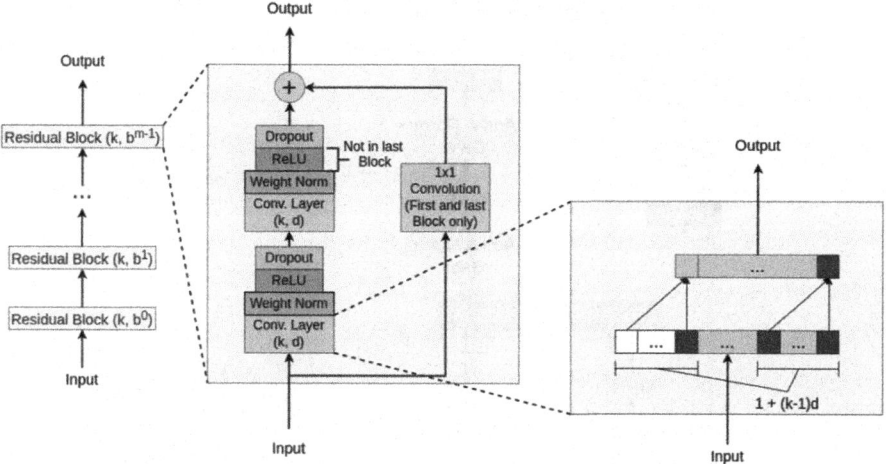

Fig. 1. The TCN architecture in three levels with kernel size as k, dilation exponent base b, Residual block number m and dilation factor d.

an output depth f. During the element-wise addition as defined in (2) the shapes of x and $\mathcal{F}(x)$ will be incompatible. For that reason, a 1×1 Convolution is applied on x to adjust its dimensions accordingly. Similarly, the last convolution layer of the last block will receive an input of depth f and it has to output the forecast, therefore a tensor of depth n. The ReLU activation is skipped during that last output as the forecast is allowed to contain negative values.

3. The Convolutional layers of every block apply filters with kernel size k dilated by d.

3.3 TFT

The Temporal Fusion Transformer [15] is a DNN designed to learn both long- and short-term relationships from time-varying inputs. It employs a sequence-to-sequence layer of LSTMs to learn short-term correlations and a multi-head attention block for long-term dependencies. Gating mechanisms are also present to skip potentially useless parts of the network, as well as variable selection networks that, for multivariate inputs, assign weights to each timeseries for a given timestep. The input accepted by TFT is not only past values with potential covariates but also future known values - future covariates. The prediction performed by TFT is probabilistic, using a quantile forecast to asses best-worst case scenarios which are extremely practical in application. If such analysis is not desired, as within this study, the 50% quantile is outputted. Figure 2 visualizes the TSF architecture based on [15] but with the lack of Static Encoders as Static Metadata are not examined.

The Gated Residual Network (GRN) of the TFT gives the model the flexibility to apply non-linear processing only where needed. Given input a:

$$GRN_{\omega}(a) = LayerNorm(a + GLU_{\omega}(\eta)) \qquad (3)$$

where GLU is the gate, ω denotes weight sharing as weight is shared throughout the GRN and $\eta \in R^{d_{model}}$ (d_{model} is the hidden state size which is common across TSF) is the

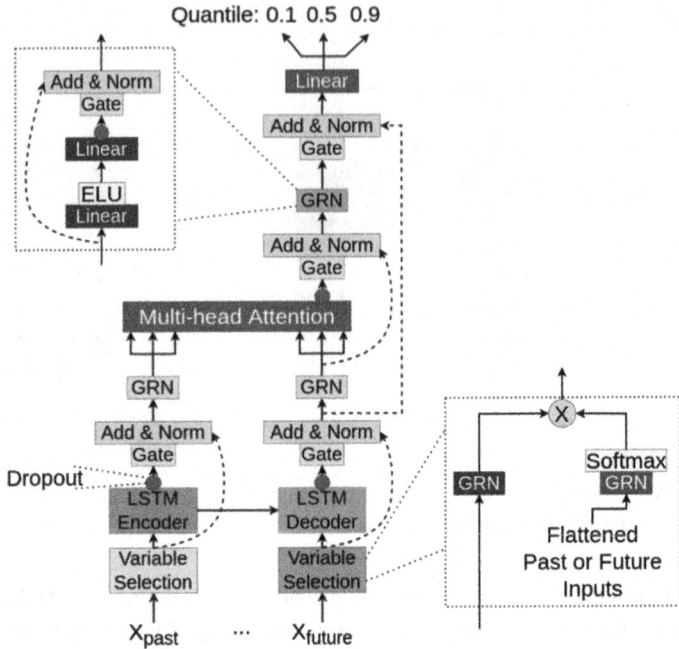

Fig. 2. The TFT architecture.

end result of two Linear transformations with an ELU [6] activation function in between. The GLU is then defined as:

$$GLU_\omega(\eta) = \sigma\left(W_{3,\omega}\eta + b_{3,\omega}\right) \odot (W_{4,\omega}\eta + b_{4,\omega}) \qquad (4)$$

where the weights and biases are indexed starting with 3 as 1 and 2 are used in the Linear transformation, $\odot$ is element-wise Hadamard product. This gate acts as a cutoff as it may output values close to 0 and based on (3) only the initial input will move on.

Within the variable selection network, the weights are calculated based on the flattened vector of all the past or future inputs (depending on encoding/decoding), meaning all the values of every timeseries for every past/future timestep.

Attention, in general, is defined as the scaling of values $V \in R^{N \times d_V}$ based on relationships between keys $K \in R^{N \times d_{attn}}$ and queries $Q \in R^{N \times d_{attn}}$. The scaled dot-product attention, which is a common choice [26], is:

$$Attention(Q, K, V) = Softmax(QK^T / \sqrt{d_{attn}}) \times V \qquad (5)$$

In multi-head attention, multiple copies of the attention module are used in parallel. Each head captures different relationships between the input values. To be able to extract feature importance and interpret the predictions, TFT uses a modified multi-head attention that shares values in each head, and employs additive aggregation of all heads [15].

4   Performance Evaluations

4.1   The Dataset

To evaluate the aforementioned TFS methods within the retail demand forecasting field, a sales dataset is sourced from [25]. It contains the daily sales of 50 items in 10 different stores over the timespan of 5 years. Therefore, in terms of timeseries analysis, the dataset can be deconstructed as a multivariate set of 500 timeseries, the sales of every item for every store. The forecasting problem is predicting future sales based on the historical sales of every item, hence a many-to-many multivariate forecast. To properly stress test the models and investigate their ability to withhold long term correlations, a relatively large history window is provided to every model, a year, so as to forecast 30 timesteps (days) in the future. The sales statistics for every timeseries is displayed in Table 1. It's important to note that the values have been 0–1 scaled and the timeseries are split in train, validation and test sets so that the train timespan is 3 years and both the validation and the test set are 1 year.

Table 1. Basic statistic values for every sale in every store.

Metric	Values
Mean	0.23
Std	0.12
25% quantile	0.13
Median	0.20
75% quantile	0.30

The 75% percentile is just 0.3 while the max is by design 1. This might indicate the existence of numerous outliers or the fact that some items in some stores might sell in way bigger quantities which does make logical sense, for example milk vs bicycles. To investigate this, the boxplot of the mean sales of every item-store combination (the 500 timeseries) is graphed in Fig. 3. It seems that, even though more popular items do exist, on average the sales are consistent throughout without outlier mean values. Subsequently, we can conclude that the timeseries do have sale spikes individually. Moreover, a reasonable thought is that those spikes might happen during specific days or months. Figure 4 displays the boxplots per weekday (a) and month (b). The results indicate that sale spikes aren't weekday or month dependent ergo they are possibly outliers that will be challenging to detect. This adds an extra layer of difficulty to our forecasts as it will test the resiliency of each method to noise. To assist each model in its endeavor to handle said noise, a single covariate timeseries is added that explicitly states, for every day within the timespan, the weekday, the month, the year and if the current day is some form of holiday based on the US holiday calendar as the dataset originates from there.

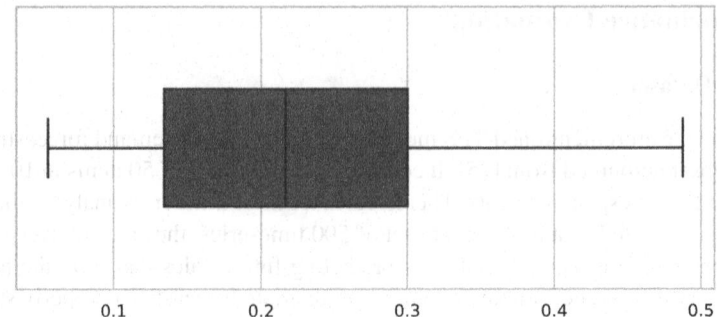

Fig. 3. Boxplot of mean values of every timeseries.

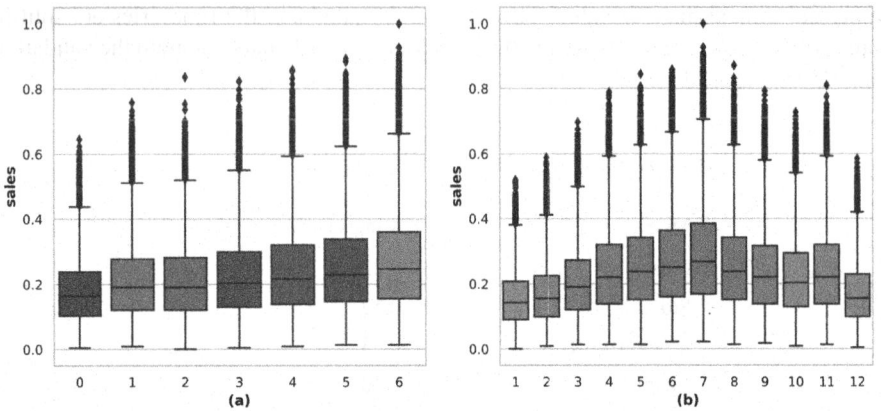

Fig. 4. Boxplot of sales per weekday (a) and month (b) for every item in every store.

4.2 Model Fine-Tuning and Training

Each model previously introduced has a list of potential hyperparameters that can be fine-tuned to optimize a forecasting score. Fine-tuning is performed via repeated train-validation.

At this point it's important to note some computational costs. Whilst the LightGBM and XGBoost models compute quite fast, the same cannot be said for the TCN and TFT models. To yield results within reasonable timespans on a single Nvidia Tesla P100 GPU some maximums need to be set and they have to be applied on every model so as to preserve fairness of comparison. Ideally, every model is trained and validated on the entirety of the training and validation set accordingly. To reduce these exhaustive training/validation iterations, a maximum number of 50 iterations is set. The algorithm will pick a random valid starting point (same seed for all models) within the timespans and start training/validating from that point on. Then this process is repeated 49 more times. Another limitation is the usage of random search within the hyperparameter space, which is limited to 100 iterations. The maximum number of estimators for boosting algorithms and epochs for neural networks is set to be 400 and early stopping is applied every 50 rounds to return the best performing model.

Table 2. Hyperparameters used and selected (**bold**) during fine-tuning.

XGBoost	LightGBM
The dropout rate: 0, **0.1**, 0.3	The dropout rate: 0, **0.1**, 0.3
The learning rate: 0.001, **0.01**, 0.1	The learning rate: 0.001, 0.01, **0.1**
The hessian: 0.5, **1**, 2	The hessian: **0.5**, 1, 2
The gamma: 0.01, 0.1, **1**	The number of leaves: 100, **200**, 300
The maximum depth: 5, 10, 20, **None**	The maximum depth: 5, 10, 20, **None**

TCN	TFT
The dropout rate: **0**, 0.1, 0.3	The dropout rate: **0**, 0.1, 0.3
The learning rate: **0.001**, 0.01, 0.1	The learning rate: **0.001**, 0.01, 0.1
The kernel size: 2, **3**, 4	The size of the state: **8**, 16, 32
The number of filters: 2, 3, **4**	The number of LSTM layers: 1, **2**, 3
The dilation base: **2**, 3, 4	The number of attention heads: 2, **4**, 8
The use of weight norm.: True, **False**	Multi-head attention on both encoder and decoder: **True**, False

The hyperparameters of each model are presented in Table 2 with optimal in bold. The search minimizes the MSE loss. The optimizers used during training are not part of the hyperparameters; DART [20] is used for boosting and Adam [8] for the neural networks. The batch size is also kept static and equal to 64.

4.3 Results

After fine-tuning each model, they are tested on the test set. In addition to every method used, an Exponential Smoothing (ETS) as well as a Seasonal ARIMA (SARIMA – via the Auto-ARIMA method [7]) are also performed in a univariate way; for every single timeseries the models are fine-tuned and then tested. This process sets a more advanced benchmark compared to possible naïve methods such as a typical moving average as well as portraying how effective classical statistical models, that are heavily used to this day, really are in a multivariate scenario. Table 3 presents the results using multiple metrics and for each metric the mean score (top) as well as the median score (bottom) are displayed as the models forecast multiple times for all 500 timeseries.

After inspecting the results, it is clear that both boosting and DNN methods are superior to the standard statistical methods. It should be noted that multivariate versions of ARIMA do exist but, as an attempt was made to apply them on the current TSF problem, it was quickly revealed that they were extremely inefficient for the large number of timeseries present. Consequently, the usage of more advanced algorithms for bigger scale multivariate TSF is nothing sort of warranted. By comparing boosting methods to DNNs, the results are in favor of the neural networks. With TFT having the best results and TCN being a close second, the future of these architectures but also DNNs in general seems bright for multivariate TSF problems. As per their design, the neural network approaches are able to extract dependencies and correlations even in extremely large, complex and noisy timeseries. That said, their training and, more importantly, fine-tuning is marginally slower and resource heavier than the boosting counterparts. Using a single Nvidia Tesla P100 GPU, the boosting methods were able to be fine-tuned in under two hours whilst the DNNs needed more than six. Nonetheless, both TFT and TCN are excellent predictors and the better approach for the current retail demand forecasting problem.

Table 3. Forecasting results of each method based on different metrics (mean on top, median on bottom).

Method (rank) metrics	ETS (6)	SARIMA (5)	XGBoost (4)	LightGBM (3)	TCN (2)	TFT (1)
MAE	0.031	0.028	0.024	0.022	0.021	**0.021**
	0.030	0.026	0.023	0.022	0.021	**0.021**
sMAPE	20.16	18.36	16.26	15.48	14.67	**14.38**
	19.38	17.35	15.37	14.06	13.60	**13.41**
MSE ($\times 10^{-4}$)	17	13	9	8	7	**7**
	14	11	8	7	6	**6**
RMSE	0.039	0.034	0.030	0.027	0.026	**0.026**
	0.038	0.033	0.029	0.026	0.026	**0.025**
R^2	−0.423	−0.232	0.101	0.210	0.289	**0.320**
	−0.402	−0.071	0.140	0.276	0.339	**0.349**

5   Conclusions

Throughout this paper, the retail demand forecasting problem is addressed. Retail demand forecasting is essentially a multivariate timeseries forecasting problem that introduces large numbers of timeseries that are mutually dependent.

Within this scope, newly suggested DNN architectures have been introduced, analyzed, tuned, trained and tested. At the same time, highly praised and frequently used machine learning regressors based on boosting methods are also tuned, trained and tested.

The results indicate that neural networks and deep learning is an excellent approach to multivariate TSF and by extension retail demand forecasting. Both the Temporal Fusion Transformer and the Temporal Convolutional Network surpass XGBoost and LightGBM as well as staple statistical methods, namely Exponential Smoothing and Seasonal ARIMA.

The main conclusion is that deep learning techniques are exceptionally accurate even under the complexity of multiple noisy timeseries. New and improved designs, such as TFT and TCN, are able to overthrow the current machine learning standards in multivariate TSF. Secondly, the boosting algorithms are a great alternative when resources are limited yielding great overall results. Lastly, statistical methods seem to fall behind and, as the number of data increases worldwide, their usage might seem obsolete. They are a great tool for quickly analyzing any given timeseries but as soon as more variables are introduced with increased complexity, more advanced models should be considered instead.

As for future work, new DDN preprocessing methods may be introduced to denoise the data, potentially perform timesries classification to inspect which items are highly correlated and consequently tweak the architecture of the neural networks so as to process said information to yield better results.

Acknowledgements. The authors would like to acknowledge the support provided by the IT Center of the Aristotle University of Thessaloniki (AUTh) throughout the progress of this research work. This work has been co-financed by the European Regional Development Fund of the European Union and Greek national funds through the Operational Program Competitiveness, Entrepreneurship, and Innovation, under the call "Investment Plans Innovation" in the Region of Central Macedonia in the framework of the Operational Program "Central Macedonia 2014–2020"(project code: KMP6-0107776). All data were processed within the project "TI4ΔOMO, 72001, Industry 4.0 Technologies for production planning and management of the supply chain of Construction and Insulating Materials".

References

1. Al Daoud, E.: Comparison between XGBoost, LightGBM and CatBoost using a home credit dataset. Int. J. Comput. Inf. Eng. **13**(1), 6–10 (2019)
2. Bai, S., Kolter, J.Z., Koltun, V.: An empirical evaluation of generic convolutional and recurrent networks for sequence modeling. arXiv preprint arXiv:1803.01271 (2018)
3. Deb, C., Zhang, F., Yang, F., Lee, S.E., Shah, K.W.: A review on time series forecasting techniques for building energy consumption. Renew. Sust. Energy Rev. **74**, 902–924 (2017)
4. Chen, T., Guestrin, C.: XGBoost: a scalable tree boosting system. In: Proceedings of the 22nd ACM SIGKDD International Conference on Knowledge Discovery and Data Mining, pp. 785–794 (2016)
5. Van Aken, D., Pavlo, D., Gordon, G.J., Zhang, B.: Automatic database management system tuning through large-scale machine learning. In: Proceedings of the 2017 ACM International Conference on Management of Data, pp. 1009–1024. ACM (2017)
6. Clevert, D.-A., Unterthiner, T., Hochreiter, S.: Fast and accurate deep network learning by exponential linear units (ELUs). In: ICLR (2016)
7. Dhamo, E., Puka, L.: Using the R-package to forecast time series: ARIMA models and application. In: International Conference Economic & Social Challenges and Problems (2010)
8. Kingma, D.P., Ba, J.L.: ADAM: a method for stochastic optimization. Published as a Conference Paper at ICLR 2015 (2015)
9. Hamidi, O., Tapak, L., Abbasi, H., Maryanaji, Z.: Application of random forest time series, support vector regression and multivariate adaptive regression splines models in prediction of snowfall (a case study of Alvand in the middle Zagros, Iran). Theoret. Appl. Climatol. **134**(3–4), 769–776 (2017). https://doi.org/10.1007/s00704-017-2300-9
10. Hochreiter, S., Schmidhuber, J.: Long short-term memory. Neural Comput. **9**, 1735–1780 (1997)
11. Huber, J., Stuckenschmidt, H.: Daily retail demand forecasting using machine learning with emphasis on calendric special days. Int. J. Forecast. **36**(4), 1420–1438 (2020)

12. Ke, G., et al.: LightGBM: a highly efficient gradient boosting decision tree. In: Advances in Neural Information Processing Systems, vol. 30 (2017)
13. Li, P., Wu, Q., Burges, C.J.: Mcrank: learning to rank using multiple classification and gradient boosting. In: Advances in Neural Information Processing Systems, vol. 20 (2008)
14. LightGBM's documentation. https://lightgbm.readthedocs.io/. Accessed 1 Feb 2022
15. Lim, B., Arık, S.Ö., Loeff, N., Pfister, T.: Temporal fusion transformers for interpretable multi-horizon time series forecasting. Int. J. Forecast. 37(4), 1748–1764 (2021)
16. Chen, M., Chen, B.: A hybrid fuzzy time series model based on granular computing for stock price forecasting. Inf. Sci. 294, 227–241 (2015)
17. Rafiei, M.H., Adeli, H.: A novel machine learning model for estimation of sale prices of real estate units. J. Constr. Eng. Manag. 142, 04015066 (2015)
18. Paolanti, M., Liciotti, D., Pietrini, R., Mancini, A., Frontoni, E.: Online detection of stealthy false data injection attacks in power system state estimation. IEEE Trans. on Smart Grid 9(3), 1636–1646 (2018)
19. Lara-Benítez, P., Carranza-García, M., Riquelme, J.C.: An experimental review on deep learning architectures for time series forecasting. Int. J. Neural Syst. 31(03), 2130001 (2021)
20. Rashmi, K.V., Gilad-Bachrach, R.: DART: dropouts meet multiple additive regression trees. http://arxiv.org/abs/1505.01866 (2015)
21. Sapankevych, N., Sankar, R.: Time series prediction using support vector machines: a survey. IEEE Comput. Intell. Mag. 4, 24–38 (2009)
22. Shi, H.: Best-first decision tree learning. The University of Waikato (2007)
23. Shi, X., Chen, Z., Wang, H., Yeung, DY., Wong, W.K., Woo, W.C.: Convolutional LSTM network: a machine learning approach for precipitation nowcasting. In: Proceedings of the Neural Information Processing Systems Conference, Montreal, QC, Canada, pp. 802–810 (2015)
24. Sun, X., Liu, M., Sima, Z.: A novel cryptocurrency price trend forecasting model based on LightGBM. Finan. Res. Lett. 32, 101084 (2020)
25. The Item Demand Forecasting Dataset on Kaggle. https://www.kaggle.com/c/demand-foreca sting-kernels-only/data. . Accessed 1 Feb 2022
26. Vaswani, A., et al.: Attention is all you need. In: Advances in Neural Information Processing Systems, vol. 30 (2017)
27. Wan, R., Mei, S., Wang, J., Liu, M., Yang, F.: Multivariate temporal convolutional network: a deep neural networks approach for multivariate time series forecasting. Electronics 8(8), 876 (2019)

Equilibrium Resolution for Epoch Partitioning

Wojciech Wisniewski[1]([✉]) [ID], Yuri Kalnishkan[1]([✉]) [ID], David Lindsay[2] [ID],
and Siân Lindsay[2] [ID]

[1] Department of Computer Science, Royal Holloway,
University of London, Egham, UK
wojciech.wisniewski.2019@live.rhul.ac.uk, yuri.kalnishkan@rhul.ac.uk
[2] Algorithmic Laboratories Ltd., Ocean House, Bracknell, Berkshire RG12 1AX, UK
{david,sian}@algolabs.com

Abstract. This paper proposes a method for determining the resolution
for the processing of irregularly-sampled time series data to provide a
balanced perspective of agents' behaviour. The behaviour is described as
a collection of prolonged events, which are characterised by start/open
and end/close times in addition to other useful attributes. We propose
the definition of an equilibrium resolution and carry out its analysis based
on probabilistic assumptions. The resulting methods of determining the
equilibrium resolution are tested on real-life time series data sets from
the Financial and Travel problem domains.

Keywords: Time series resolution · Time series partitioning ·
Database management · Big data

1 Introduction

Dealing with a number of time series that have been monitored by an infrastructure recording only the beginning and the end of every one of them can be
problematic if insight into what happened in between those times is required. A
detailed data flow derived from a collection of agents acting within some interval of interest could be storage intensive, yet there remains the need to gain
insight into agent behaviour. In this study we focus on two distinct data flows
pertaining to the behaviours of 1) clients trading with financial market makers,
and 2) taxis making journeys in New York City. The agents in both case studies
present complex challenges which relate to their choice of action (i.e. buy or
sell a particular financial instrument and geographic locations of a taxi pick-
up and drop off), as well as the frequency and duration of their actions. Many
hundreds of clients may trade with a financial market maker, with each client
trading many different instruments and holding positions for different periods
of time - seconds, days or months. Likewise with taxi journeys, customers may
take trips throughout New York that can take minutes or hours. Studies such

© IFIP International Federation for Information Processing 2022
Published by Springer Nature Switzerland AG 2022
I. Maglogiannis et al. (Eds.): AIAI 2022, IFIP AICT 647, pp. 387–401, 2022.
https://doi.org/10.1007/978-3-031-08337-2_32

as [1] have introduced methods to help manage this complexity by aggregating related time series together, thereby gleaning further information about agent behaviour, epoch-by-epoch and in a way that is practical to store and access. The choice of partition-size, or resolution, at the aggregation step is important for inferring best-possible insights into agent behaviour: too large and information is missed; too small and aggregation is no longer meaningful.

In this study we propose a method for determining a so called "equilibrium resolution" for agents' data flow using time series from the aforementioned case studies. First, we present a definition solely dependent on the duration of an agents action behaviour which is based on probabilistic assumptions. We then give an empirical extension of the this, introducing the concept of a "monitoring function" which binds the duration of agents behaviour with a feature that one wishes to infer insight into. For example, in the financial trading dataset we may want to track the profit and loss (PnL) as an attribute of client trading activity.

This paper is organised as follows: in Sect. 2 we provide a literature review, in Sect. 3 we describe a framework for efficient monitoring/information retrieval and in Sect. 4 we propose a definition of the equilibrium resolution based on the equilibrium between different types of events. In Sect. 5 we carry out the theoretical study based on probabilistic assumptions. Corollary 1 shows that under natural assumptions the equilibrium is achieved when the resolution equals to the average duration of the event. This provides an important intuition and gives us a method for calculating the equilibrium resolution. In Sect. 6 we apply the method to real-life datasets and analyse the performance. Section 7 discusses an extension of our approach based on monitoring functions.

2   Literature Review

In the literature we can find many studies which deal with similar topics relating to the study of time series resolution. In [13], the optimal resolution of time series is proposed based on wavelet transform and structural similarity measure. Studies such as [8] look at methods of using variable width intervals that increase sampling during more active regions in the time series. Elsewhere, work by [2–4], and [12] chooses a resolution which results in the lowest forecast error.

Since agents' behaviour can be modelled via complex networks, several papers have addressed the issue of selecting the best time intervals for meaningful analysis and insights. The structural features of networks emerging from aggregating empirical data over different time intervals is studied in [6], focusing on networks derived from time-stamped, anonymized mobile telephone call records. In [9], the authors focus on identifying meaningful resolution levels that best reveal critical changes in the network structure, by balancing the reduction of noise with the loss of information. Whilst these studies tackled time series resolution, their methods were not able to completely satisfy the needs of our particular problem. For example, if we consider the approach by [9] - which involves the construction of a dynamic network at time intervals of the form $[t, t + w)$ (where w is the resolution) to produce a time series of labeled graphs. The optimal window of aggregation is determined to balance between the loss of temporal structural information and fluctuations that obscure what is relevant in a structural change. We applied Statistically Validated Networks (see in [5,10]) to build dynamic networks from the financial trading dataset. However in order to obtain reasonably large and stable networks the time window needed to be set to a time resolution of roughly a month, which is far too large to track meaningful trading behaviour such as profit and loss.

In [13] only a general idea is presented without a precise description. In studies by [2–4] and [12] the authors determine the best resolution for forecasting purposes. In our financial trading case study, predicting PnL is a hard task as it is based on the underlying dynamics of noisy trade data in addition to the randomness of price movements, making a meaningful comparison with such techniques infeasible. To best of the authors' knowledge no other study provided a suitable candidate method for tackling our problem. We could argue that our proposed method should be considered as an ad hoc approach for monitoring a desired feature in a complex system.

3   Preliminaries

3.1   Prolonged Events

Consider an environment where prolonged events occur in continuous time. We identify an *event* with a triple $\langle OT_j, CT_j, a_j \rangle$, where $OT_j \in \mathbb{R}_+$ is the *opening time*, $CT_j \in \mathbb{R}_+$ is the *closing time*, and a_j is the array of event attributes (such as id, the list of agents associated with it, certain discrete or continuous characteristics) which will be referred as *exogenous* variables that are deemed useful in helping to explain agent behaviour. We assume that $CT_j > OT_j$.

In this paper we consider two main examples (discussed in more detail in Sect. 6). The first is *trading*. Here an event consists of opening, holding, and closing a position. The starting time describes when the position was opened, the closing time shows when it was closed, and the attributes include the id of the trader who opened the position, the assets involved, the size of the position, and whether the position is long or short. We study a publicly available dataset by [7] as exemplifying this environment.

In the second example the events are *taxi rides*. The opening time describes when the ride started, the closing time shows when it ended, and the attributes include the ids of the driver and passenger and the coordinates of the starting and finishing points. A dataset of taxi rides by [11] is based on data from the NYC Taxi and Limousine Commission (TLC).

3.2   Epoch Partitioning

We would like to apply the following transformation called *epoch partitioning* to the original set of events. It may render the set more suitable for further processing, reduce its size and so forth. Take a resolution $\delta > 0$ and consider the partitioning of the time line $\mathbb{R}$ into a union of disjoint *epochs* $\mathbb{R}_+ = \bigcup_{i=0}^{+\infty}[i\delta, (i+1)\delta)$. We will refer to the interval $[i\delta, (i+1)\delta)$ as *epoch i*. A natural choice of resolution, which is problem specific, includes a second, a minute, an hour and so on. For an epoch i consider all events $\langle OT_j, CT_j, a_j \rangle$ intersecting with this epoch, i.e., such that $[OT_j, CT_j) \cap [i\delta, (i+1)\delta) \neq \varnothing$. Intersecting events can be classified into the following disjoint groups:

- *float*: the event has started in a previous epoch and is still open at the end of the current epoch, i.e. $OT_j < i\delta < (i+1)\delta \leq CT_j$
- *open*: the event opened but has not closed in the current epoch, i.e. $i\delta \leq OT_j < (i+1)\delta \leq CT_j$
- *closed*: the event closed in the current epoch, but opened before it started, i.e. $OT_j < i\delta \leq CT_j < (i+1)\delta$
- *locked*: the event opened and closed in the current epoch i.e., $i\delta \leq OT_j < CT_j < (i+1)\delta$

We will refer to the *epoch type* $\tau_{i,j} \in \mathcal{T} = \{\text{float, open, close, locked}\}$ of an epoch $[OT_j, CT_j)$ w.r.t. an overlapping event $\langle OT_j, CT_j, a_j \rangle$. This concept describes agents behaviour w.r.t. the epoch partitioning (see Fig. 1).

Epoch type partitionning

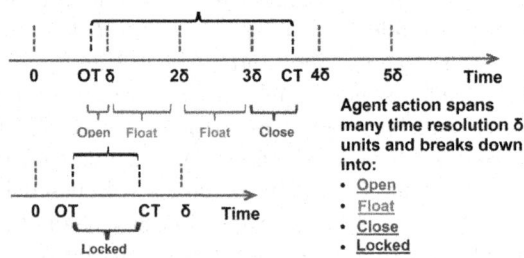

Fig. 1. Visual explanation of epoch types

The epoch partitioning transforms the original set of events $\mathcal{D}$ to a set of tuples $E_i = \langle f_i, o_i, c_i, l_i \rangle$, where i is the epoch number, f_i, o_i, c_i, and l_i are the numbers of floating, open, closed, and locked events, respectively, overlapping with this epoch. In this paper we are only considering partitioning which is time based. In Sect. 7 we present an extension to the time based approach.

The values f_i, o_i, c_i, and l_i can be represented in the following manner:

$$f_i := \sum_j \mathbb{1}_{\{\tau_{i,j} = \text{float}\}}, \qquad o_i := \sum_j \mathbb{1}_{\{\tau_{i,j} = \text{open}\}},$$

$$c_i := \sum_j \mathbb{1}_{\{\tau_{i,j} = \text{close}\}}, \qquad l_i := \sum_j \mathbb{1}_{\{\tau_{i,j} = \text{locked}\}}.$$

The following variables will be needed below:

$$T_\delta^{(j)} := \frac{CT_j - OT_j}{\delta}, \quad S_\delta^{(j)} := \frac{OT_j}{\delta} - \left\lfloor \frac{OT_j}{\delta} \right\rfloor.$$

They represent the duration of an event i and its starting time within its epoch in the units of δ.

We can define the aggregate quantities $L_\delta, O_\delta, C_\delta$, and F_δ as follows:

$$L_\delta := \sum_{i=0}^{+\infty} l_i = \sum_j \mathbb{1}_{\{T_\delta^{(j)} + S_\delta^{(j)} < 1\}}, \quad O_\delta := \sum_{i=0}^{+\infty} o_i = \sum_j \mathbb{1}_{\{1 \le T_\delta^{(j)} + S_\delta^{(j)}\}}, \quad C_\delta := \sum_{i=0}^{+\infty} c_i$$

$$F_\delta := \sum_{i=0}^{+\infty} f_i = \sum_j \sum_{i \ge 1} i \mathbb{1}_{\{i+1 \le T_\delta^{(j)} + S_\delta^{(j)} < i+2\}} = \sum_j \sum_{i \ge 1} \mathbb{1}_{\{i+1 \le T_\delta^{(j)} + S_\delta^{(j)}\}}$$

The choice of resolution δ should provide a trade-off making the epoch representation concise but still meaningful and retaining as much useful information as possible about the original set of events.

In what follows, we define an equilibrium resolution δ^* based on these numbers and study its properties.

4 Equilibrium Resolution: A Numerical Example

In this section, we apply epoch partitioning to the example datasets. Table 1 shows the total numbers of floating and locked events at various resolutions.

One can observe that as resolution increases, the number of locked events L_δ increases, while the number of floating events F_δ drops. At some point they become approximately equal (see the rows in bold). This motivates the following definition.

Definition 1. *A resolution δ is called an* empirically equilibrium resolution *for a dataset $\mathcal{D}$ if*

$$L_\delta = F_\delta.$$

It will be denoted as $\delta^*(\mathcal{D})$.

The equilibrium resolution provides an equilibrium between Locked and Float epoch types. If there is a significant imbalance of either epoch type, the choice of δ must be very small (a lot of floats) or very big (a lot of locked).

Table 1. Number of epoch types at various resolutions

Case study	Resolution	Float	Locked	Locked/Float
Case study 1: trade data	1 day	$3.2 \cdot 10^6$	$3.7 \cdot 10^6$	1.16
	0.91 day	$\mathbf{3.61 \cdot 10^6}$	$\mathbf{3.61 \cdot 10^6}$	**1.00**
	0.5 day	$7.3 \cdot 10^6$	$3.2 \cdot 10^6$	0.44
Case study 2: taxi data	15 min	$1.7 \cdot 10^6$	$5.0 \cdot 10^6$	2.9
	11.5 min	$\mathbf{3.7 \cdot 10^6}$	$\mathbf{3.7 \cdot 10^6}$	**1.00**
	10 min	$5 \cdot 10^6$	$3.0 \cdot 10^6$	0.6

Remark 1. An equilibrium resolution for a given sample dataset $\mathcal{D}$ can be expressed as

$$\delta^*(\mathcal{D}) = \arg_\delta \{ N = \sum_j \sum_{i \geq 1} \mathbb{1}_{\{T_\delta^{(j)} + S_\delta^{(j)} \geq i\}} \}$$

5   Probabilistic Modelling

5.1   The Probabilistic Approach to Equilibrium Resolution

We will develop an analytic approach to finding the equilibrium resolution. It is based on probabilistic modelling.

Let the opening and closing times OT_j and CT_j be random variables, $i = 1, 2, \ldots, N$, where N is the total number of events. Then L_δ and F_δ become random variables. In this framework, one can use the following working definition.

Definition 2. *Let $T_\delta^{(j)} \in \mathbb{L}^1$ for all $j = 1, \ldots, N$. Then a resolution δ^* is average equilibrium if $\mathbb{E}L_{\delta^*} = \mathbb{E}F_{\delta^*}$.*

For further analysis we will assume that all $T_\delta^{(j)}$ and $S_\delta^{(j)}$ are independent and identically distributed, $j = 1, 2, \ldots, N$. One can think of the values of $T_\delta^{(j)}$ and $S_\delta^{(j)}$ as of independent realisations of the same variables T_δ and S_δ.

Theorem 1. *A resolution δ is average equilibrium if and only if $\mathbb{E}\lfloor T_\delta + S_\delta \rfloor = 1$.*

Proof.

$$\delta^* = \arg_\delta \left\{ \mathbb{E}\left(\sum_j \mathbb{1}_{\{T_\delta^{(j)} + S_\delta^{(j)} < 1\}} \right) = \mathbb{E}\left(\sum_j \sum_{i \geq 1} \mathbb{1}_{\{i+1 \leq T_\delta^{(j)} + S_\delta^{(j)}\}} \right) \right\}$$

$$= \arg_\delta \left\{ N = N \cdot \mathbb{E}\left(\sum_{i \geq 1} \mathbb{1}_{\{i \leq T_\delta + S_\delta\}} \right) \right\} = \arg_\delta \left\{ 1 = \mathbb{E}\lfloor T_\delta + S_\delta \rfloor \right\}$$

We will now make an assumption on the behaviour of S_δ. It is natural to assume that the starting time of an event is not coordinated with the epochs and therefore S_δ is uniformly distributed on $[0,1]$, i.e., $S_\delta \sim U(0,1)$.

Theorem 2. Let $S_\delta \sim U(0,1)$. Then

$$\frac{\mathbb{E}L_\delta}{\mathbb{E}F_\delta} = \frac{\mathbb{E}(1 - T_\delta)_+}{\mathbb{E}(1 - T_\delta)_+ + \mathbb{E}T_\delta - 1}$$

We use the notation $x_+ = \max(x, 0)$.

Proof. For a positive random variable X, let $\lfloor X \rfloor$ be the integer part of X. The expected number of Float epochs can be expressed in the following manner:

$$\mathbb{E}(F_\delta) = \mathbb{E}\left(\sum_j \sum_{i \geq 1} \mathbb{1}_{\{i+1 \leq T_\delta^{(j)} + S_\delta^{(j)}\}}\right) = \sum_j \sum_{i \geq 1} \mathbb{P}(i + 1 \leq T_\delta^{(j)} + S_\delta^{(j)})$$

$$= N \cdot \sum_{i \geq 1} \mathbb{P}(S_\delta + T_\delta \geq i + 1) = N \cdot \sum_{i \geq 1} \mathbb{E}[\mathbb{1}_{S_\delta \geq (i+1) - T_\delta} \cdot \mathbb{1}_{T_\delta \in [i, i+1)} + \mathbb{1}_{T_\delta \geq i+1}]$$

$$= N \cdot \sum_{i \geq 1} \mathbb{E}[(T_\delta - i) \cdot \mathbb{1}_{T_\delta \in [i, i+1)} + \mathbb{1}_{T_\delta \geq i+1}] = N \cdot \left(\mathbb{E}T_\delta + \mathbb{E}(1 - T_\delta)_+ - 1\right)$$

The expected number of Locked epochs can be expressed in the following manner:

$$\mathbb{E}(L_\delta) = \mathbb{E}\left(\sum_j \mathbb{1}_{\{T_\delta^{(j)} + S_\delta^{(j)} < 1\}}\right) = N \cdot \mathbb{P}(S_\delta + T_\delta < 1) = N \cdot \mathbb{E}[\mathbb{1}_{S_\delta < 1 - T_\delta} \mathbb{1}_{T_\delta < 1}]$$

$$= N \cdot \mathbb{E}[(1 - T_\delta)\mathbb{1}_{T_\delta < 1}] = N \cdot \mathbb{E}(1 - T_\delta)_+$$

Corollary 1. If $S_\delta \sim U(0,1)$ then

$$\delta^* = \mathbb{E}T_1 .$$

Proof. From the definition of δ^*:

$$1 = \frac{\mathbb{E}L_{\delta^*}}{\mathbb{E}F_{\delta^*}} = \frac{\mathbb{E}(1 - T_{\delta^*})_+}{\mathbb{E}(1 - T_{\delta^*})_+ + \mathbb{E}T_{\delta^*} - 1} .$$

This is equivalent to: $0 = \mathbb{E}T_{\delta^*} - 1$. Since $T_{\delta^*} = \frac{T_1}{\delta^*}$ therefore $\delta^* = \mathbb{E}T_1$.

Recall that $T_1^{(j)} = CT_j - OT_j$ and thus $\mathbb{E}T_1$ is the expected duration of an event. The corollary implies that our definition of the equilibrium resolution has a natural intuitive interpretation. Corollary 1 provides an easy way for calculating the equilibrium resolution. While calculating $\delta^*(D)$ from the definition would require a solver, calculating the average is simple and straightforward. In the case studies we fit distributions to better understand the nature of the processes, but this is clearly not necessary to find the equilibrium resolution.

Instead of 1, one could be interested in a ratio $c > 0$, hence the following generalisations of the empirical and average equilibrium resolution.

Definition 3.

$$^c\delta^*(\mathcal{D}) := \arg_\delta \left\{ \frac{L_\delta}{F_\delta} = c \right\}, \quad {}^c\delta^* := \arg_\delta \left\{ \frac{\mathbb{E}L_\delta}{\mathbb{E}F_\delta} = c \right\}$$

Using this notation one can write $\delta^*(\mathcal{D}) = {}^1\delta^*(\mathcal{D})$ and $\delta^* = {}^1\delta^*$.

Corollary 1 does not generalise to an arbitrary $^c\delta^*$ straightforwardly, but one can find the equilibrium value numerically using the ratio from Theorem 2.

5.2   Approximating Equilibrium Resolution

For practical reasons one may be interested in the resolution to be equilibrium up to some error ϵ. This motivates the following definition.

Definition 4. *A resolution δ is* approximately c-equilibrium up to ε, *if*

$$\left| \frac{\mathbb{E}L_\delta}{\mathbb{E}F_\delta} - c \right| \le \varepsilon.$$

Hence two handy approximations $_\epsilon\delta_*^+$ and $_\epsilon\delta_*^-$ are such that

$$^c_\epsilon\delta^*_- = \arg_\delta \left\{ \frac{\mathbb{E}L_\delta}{\mathbb{E}F_\delta} = c(1 - \epsilon) \right\}, \quad {}^c_\epsilon\delta^*_+ = \arg_\delta \left\{ \frac{\mathbb{E}L_\delta}{\mathbb{E}F_\delta} = c(1 + \epsilon) \right\}$$

and thus the resolutions $_\epsilon\delta_+^*$ and $_\epsilon\delta_-^*$ are approximately equilibrium up to ϵ since

$$^c_\epsilon\delta^*_- \le {}^c\delta^* \le {}^c_\epsilon\delta^*_+$$

5.3   Equilibrium Resolution for Lognormaly Distributed Agents Action Duration

The analysis of case studies (see Sect. 6 and [1]) suggests the duration of agent's action is often lognomal. We derive formulas for this distribution and its truncated counterpart.

Let $T_1 \sim \text{LogNormal}(\mu, \sigma)$. Then we have $T_\delta = \frac{T_1}{\delta} \sim \text{LogNormal}(\mu - \ln \delta, \sigma) = \text{LogNormal}(\mu_\delta, \sigma)$, where $\mu_\sigma = \mu - \ln \sigma$. With use of properties of this law the equilibrium resolution estimators are

$$\delta^* = e^{\mu + \frac{\sigma^2}{2}}, \quad {}_\epsilon\delta^*_\pm = \arg_\delta \left\{ \frac{A^\delta}{A^\delta + B^\delta - 1} = 1 \pm \epsilon \right\}.$$

where

$$A^\delta = \Phi\left[\beta_{1,\delta}\right] - e^{\mu_\delta + \frac{\sigma^2}{2}} \cdot \Phi\left[-\alpha_{1,\delta,1}\right], \quad B^\delta = e^{\mu_\delta + \frac{\sigma^2}{2}}.$$

Φ is the normal cumulative distribution function and

$$\alpha_{n,\delta,k} = \frac{\mu_\delta + k\sigma^2 - \ln n}{\sigma}, \quad \beta_{n,\delta} = \frac{\ln n - \mu_\delta}{\sigma}.$$

5.4   Equilibrium Resolution for Truncated Lognormal Distributed Agents Action Duration

If $T_\delta = \frac{T_1}{\delta} \sim$ TruncatedLogNormal$(\mu_\delta, \sigma, \frac{l}{\delta}, \frac{u}{\delta})$. Using the properties of this distribution, we can write the equilibrium resolution estimators as

$$\delta^* = \arg_\delta \left\{ B^\delta - C^\delta = 0 \right\}, \quad {}_\epsilon\delta^*_\pm = \arg_\delta \left\{ \frac{A^\delta}{A^\delta + B^\delta - C^\delta} = 1 \pm \epsilon \right\}$$

where

$$A^\delta = \Phi\left[\beta_{1,\delta}\right] - \Phi\left[\beta_{\frac{l}{\delta},\delta}\right] - e^{\mu_\delta + \frac{\sigma^2}{2}} \left\{ \Phi\left[-\alpha_{1,\delta,1}\right] - \Phi\left[-\alpha_{\frac{l}{\delta},\delta,1}\right] \right\}$$

$$B^\delta = e^{\mu_\delta + \frac{\sigma^2}{2}} \cdot \left\{ \Phi\left[-\alpha_{\frac{u}{\delta},\delta,1}\right] - \Phi\left[-\alpha_{\frac{l}{\delta},\delta,1}\right] \right\} C^\delta = \Phi\left[\beta_{\frac{u}{\delta},\delta}\right] - \Phi\left[\beta_{\frac{l}{\delta},\delta}\right]$$

6   Application on Case Study Data

6.1   Case Study: Trading Data

The first case study considers financial data gathered from the client trades of a retail foreign exchange broker. The data comprises irregular time series data pertaining to opening and closing trade times of client trades. The exogenous data stream in this case describes the price of the underlying currency pair which is then converted in USD dollars.

The FX broker is the "middleman" – it links to the best liquidity providers (or LPs), such as investment banks, and the LP's stream "tradeable" currency prices to the broker. The FX broker then passes these prices on to its thousands of clients worldwide all of whom can trade from their mobile phones or personal computers at the click of a button. A typical retail broker will provide their clients with online trading platform software such as MetaTrader 4 where clients may place trades, monitor positions, track both historic and live movements in prices, and access the latest world economic news.

Table 2. Example of client order data

OpenTime	Client	Amount	Sign	Symbol	OpenPrice	CloseTime	ClosePrice
03/01/2017 03:24	82	8232	1	EUR/CAD	1.40524	03/01/2017 03:48	1.40548
03/01/2017 03:24	82	11000	−1	EUR/CHF	1.07079	03/01/2017 05:16	1.07096

The publicly available dataset [7] consists of order data (Table 2) and quote data (Table 3) (exogenous) for the foreign exchange broker data.

Table 3. Example of price quote data

Datetime	Symbol	OpenUsdMult	ContraUsdMult	Price
01/03/2017 03:30	AUD/JPY	0.72239	0.00852	84.11
01/03/2017 03:30	EUR/CHF	0.04713	0.97813	1.0705

In order to find and analyse the equilibrium resolutions for different values of c, a modelling stage has to be done. For that purpose we tried to fit 85 distributions from `scipy.stats` library. By ranking the fit by the smallest Akaike Information Criterion (AIC) we identified that the truncated lognormal distribution seems to fit reasonably well. A comparison between complementary cumulative distribution functions of lognormal fit and empirical data justified the choice of the truncation. Standard maximum likelihood estimators were calculated on the truncated data returning $\mu = 4.583$, $\sigma = 2.55$, $l = 0$, and $u \approx 6 \cdot 10^4$.

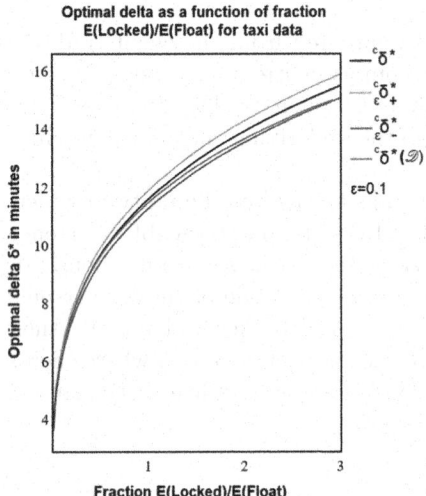

Fig. 2. The relationship between $\frac{\mathbb{E}L_\delta}{\mathbb{E}F_\delta}$ and $^c\delta^*$ for the taxi data.

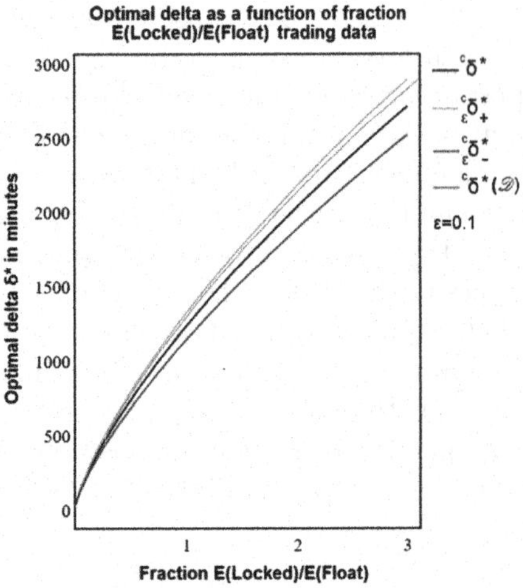

Fig. 3. The relationship between $\frac{\mathbb{E}L_\delta}{\mathbb{E}F_\delta}$ and $^c\delta^*$ for the trading data.

In Fig. 3 the equilibrium resolution is calculated, which is around 0.86 days. This is close to the sample-wise equilibrium resolution (0.91 days). Again we note that the empirical equilibrium resolution $\delta^*(\mathcal{D})$ is within the approximation bounds, $^c_\epsilon\delta_-$ and $^c_\epsilon\delta_+$, of ϵ equal 0.1.

Once applied with equilibrium resolution to the source data, the resulting target data was used in the analysis of [1].

6.2 Case Study: NYC Taxi Journey Data

For the second case study, which is about taxi journeys around NYC, we obtained similar results. The dataset [11] comprises irregular time series data pertaining to the pick-up and drop-off time stamps of taxi journeys undertaken by individual taxis. For the taxi ride duration the lognormal fit appeared to be satisfactory and MLE estimators are $\hat{\mu} = 6.31$ and $\hat{\sigma} = 0.69$. In Fig. 2 one can see that for different values of parameter c, the resolution $^c\delta^*$ stays close to the empirical equilibrium resolution $^c\delta^*(\mathcal{D})$.

7 Partitioning Based on Monitoring Functions

In this section we extend the notion of epoch partitioning. So far we have only considered the time-based approach. It is natural to partition the dataset with respect to the duration of events as well as the attributes. For instance a market maker may want to efficiently partition a dataset in order to gain insight into the evolution of their profit and loss through time.

If we calculated the PnL over the whole order period we would have no insight into what happened during the order. Indeed the longer the lifetime of a trade, the more likely that its PnL will fluctuate due to other exogenous factors such as price movement, economic news releases and related temporal events. Figure 4 illustrates this point, showing quite a stark contrast in client trading PnL profile when all price data is used (full resolution - pink line), to the profile shown when PnL is calculated using only the price data available at the open and close of a trade (no resolution - purple line). Neither profile is ideal; a simplistic approach would be to use resolution that derives from periods such as hours or minutes, but one would need a rule of thumb.

Client trading PnL profile for different price data resolutions

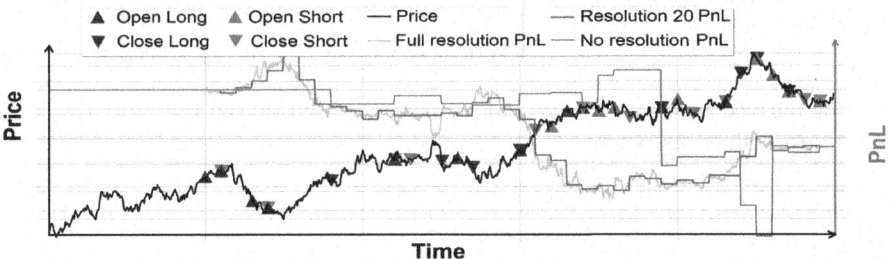

Fig. 4. Client trading PnL profiles when all price data used (full resolution - pink line); when price data only at the open and close of a trade is used (no resolution - purple line); and when a resolution of 20 units of time according to the method proposed in this study is used (blue line). The example is based on 30 randomly selected trades with random positions (Long/Short) over 1000 units of time. (Color figure online)

Let the epoch partitioning reduce the original set of events $\mathcal{D}$ to a set of tuples $E_i = \langle f_i, o_i, c_i, l_i, d_i^{(1)}, , ..., d_i^{(K)} \rangle$, where i is the epoch number, f_i, o_i, c_i, and l_i are the numbers of floating, open, closed, and locked events, respectively, overlapping with this epoch, and $d_i^{(k)}$ are derived fields, i.e., functions of attributes calculated on the basis of the events intersecting with the epoch (see Fig. 5). Every $d_i^{(k)}$ will be an output of what we will refer to from now on as a *monitoring function*.

Process of deriving a monitoring function

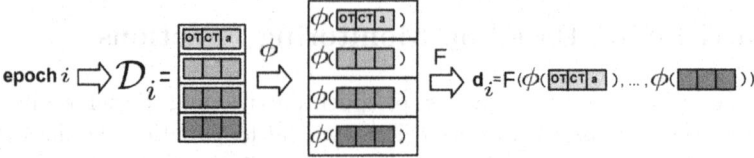

Fig. 5. The process of deriving a monitoring function in epoch partitioning. A function ϕ is applied to every prolonged events in the considered dataset and then an aggregation function F transforms the latter data into an element of E_i.

For $k = 1, 2, \ldots, K$ let

$$d_i^{(k)} = F_k(\phi_{k,i}(\langle OT_{j_1}, CT_{j_1}, a_{j_1} \rangle), ..., \phi_{k,i}(\langle OT_{j_I}, CT_{j_I}, a_{j_I} \rangle)).$$

where $j_1, j_2, \ldots, j_I$ are the events overlapping with $[\delta i, \delta(i+1))$, F_k is an aggregation function and $\phi_{k,i}$ is given by

$$\phi_{k,i}(\langle OT_j, CT_j, a_j \rangle) := \begin{cases} \phi_k(a_j, i\delta, (i+1)\delta) & \text{if } \tau_{i,j} = \text{float} \\ \phi_k(a_j, i\delta, CT_j) & \text{if } \tau_{i,j} = \text{close} \\ \phi_k(a_j, OT_j, (i+1)\delta) & \text{if } \tau_{i,j} = \text{open} \\ \phi_k(a_j, OT_j, CT_j) & \text{if } \tau_{i,j} = \text{locked} \end{cases}$$

The derived field monitoring functions are defined by the user and f_i, o_i, c_i, and l_i are defined as before.

Table 4. Illustration of epoch Epoch type partitioning procedure on raw data.

ID	OT	CT	OP	CP
1	2.5	6.5	10	20
2	6.2	6.7	4	8

ϕ
↓

Epoch	ID	Open	Float	Locked	Close	OpenPnL	FloatPnL	LockedPnL	ClosePnL
2	1	1	0	0	0	1.25	0	0	0
3	1	0	1	0	0	0	2.5	0	0
4	1	0	1	0	0	0	2.5	0	0
5	1	0	1	0	0	0	2.5	0	0
6	1	0	0	0	1	0	0	0	1.25
6	2	0	0	1	0	0	0	4	0

F
↓

Epoch	Open	Float	Locked	Close	OpenPnL	FloatPnL	LockedPnL	ClosePnL
2	1	0	0	0	1.25	0	0	0
3	0	1	0	0	0	2.5	0	0
4	0	1	0	0	0	2.5	0	0
5	0	1	0	0	0	2.5	0	0
6	0	0	1	1	1	0	4	1.25

To be precise, a USD normalised profit and loss for each order is required. Therefore, the PnL monitoring function is calculated over interval $[\delta i, \delta(i+1))$ for a currency s as follows:

$$\mathrm{PnL}_i^{(s)} := \sum_{l=1}^{I} \phi_{s,i}(\langle OT_{j_l}, CT_{j_l}, a_{j_l}\rangle)$$

where F_s is a simple sum, $\phi_{s,i}(\langle OT_j, CT_j, a_j\rangle)$ depends on the $\tau_{i,j}$ and ϕ_s is given by

$$\phi_s(a_j, t_1, t_2) := (P_{t_1}(s) - P_{t_2}(s)) \cdot CM_{t_2}(s) \cdot SD_j \cdot AM_j,$$

where notation $P_t(s)$ represents the price of the symbol s at time t, AM_j refers to the number of units for the underlying the order was for and SD_j refers to whether the order was either long or short, $+1$ or -1 respectively.

However, all PnL made as a result of trading currencies will be paid in the contra currency of the symbol pair traded. This is often not the most useful figure when trying to conduct financial analysis of a collection of trades. It is standard practice to normalise the PnL's by calculating the value in some common currency which is typically USD. This is achieved by multiplying the PnL with the exchange rate between the contra currency and USD at the close time of the order. We will refer to this as the contra multiplier using the notation, $CM_t(s)$ to be the contra multiplier at time t of symbol s.

An example of the epoch partitioning process is visible in Table 4, where the monitoring function is the Profit and Loss (PnL). The raw data consists of only two rows of data with resolution equal to 1 unit where ID is the identification number, OP and CP are opening and closing prices. For the sake of simplicity the price is supposed here to evolve linearly.

Until now the equilibrium resolution exclusively took into account the time dependency of agents behaviour, however it may be of interest to define a binding function merging the latter with a target monitoring function (or functions). Taking the example of the broker we propose an analogical definition of equilibrium resolution which makes the mean of the PnL to be equal for Locked an Float epoch events.

Definition 5. *The equilibrium resolution for a PnL monitoring function is:*

$$\delta^*_{PnL} = \arg_\delta \left\{ \mathbb{E}\left[PnL \mathbb{1}_{\{T_\delta + S_\delta < 1\}} \right] = \mathbb{E}\left[\sum_{i \geq 1} PnL \mathbb{1}_{\{i+1 \leq T_\delta + S_\delta < i+2\}} \right] \right\}$$

Deriving the explicit formula is not that simple but we will use estimated values and we assume trading duration is identically distributed. The empirical results are shown in Fig. 6. We obtain a set of possible equilibrium resolutions and observe that a good candidate for equilibrium resolution is around 10 min (since the expected PnL is less noisy in this time-neighbourhood) which is more insightful for a broker than equilibrium time resolution obtained with respect to agent event duration (1200 min).

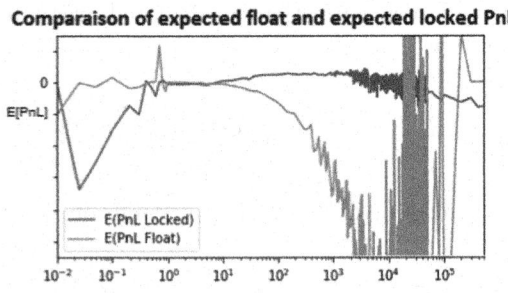

Fig. 6. $\mathbb{E}[PnL_\delta^{\text{Locked}}]$ vs. $\mathbb{E}[PnL_\delta^{\text{Float}}]$

8   Conclusion

We proposed definitions of equilibrium resolution for epoch partitioning of a dataset of prolonged events based on the equilibrium of locked and float events and carried out theoretical analysis using probabilistic assumptions. The study of two real-life datasets showed that the theoretical results are in agreement with empirical observations. We have thus developed a novel method for determining the equilibrium resolution based on events duration and on a monitoring function, which can be considered as an ad hoc approach for finding a meaningful partitioning of irregularly-sampled time series data.

References

1. Al-baghdadi, N., Wisniewski, W., Lindsay, D., Lindsay, S., Kalnishkan, Y., Watkins, C.: Structuring time series data to gain insight into agent behaviour. In: 2019 IEEE International Conference on Big Data, pp. 5480–5490 (2019)
2. Al-Hmouz, R., Pedrycz, W., Balamash, A., Morfeq, A.: Granular representation schemes of time series: a study in an optimal allocation of information granularity. In: 2013 IEEE Symposium on Foundations of Computational Intelligence (FOCI), pp. 44–51 (2013)
3. Arandia, E., Eck, B., McKenna, S.: The effect of temporal resolution on the accuracy of forecasting models for total system demand. Procedia Eng. **89**, 916–925 (2014). 16th Water Distribution System Analysis Conference, WDSA2014
4. Athanasopoulos, G., Hyndman, R.J., Kourentzes, N., Petropoulos, F.: Forecasting with temporal hierarchies. Eur. J. Oper. Res. **262**(1), 60–74 (2017)
5. Challet, D., Chicheportiche, R., Lallouache, M., Kassibrakis, S.: Statistically validated leadlag networks and inventory prediction in the foreign exchange market. Adv. Complex Syst. 22 p. (2018)
6. Krings, G., Karsai, M., Bernhardsson, S., Blondel, V.D., Saramäki, J.: Effects of time window size and placement on the structure of an aggregated communication network. EPJ Data Sci. **1**(1), 1–16 (2012). https://doi.org/10.1140/epjds4
7. Lindsay, D.: Fxclienttrades. https://www.kaggle.com/davidlindsay1979/toptradingclientdata/kernels
8. Nason, G.P., Powell, B., Elliott, D., Smith, P.A.: Should we sample a time series more frequently?: decision support via multirate spectrum estimation. J. R. Stat. Soc. Ser. A (Stat. Soc.) **180**(2), 353–407 (2017)
9. Sulo, R., Berger-Wolf, T., Grossman, R.: Meaningful selection of temporal resolution for dynamic networks. In: Proceedings of the Eighth Workshop on Mining and Learning with Graphs, MLG 2010, pp. 127–136. Association for Computing Machinery, New York (2010)
10. Tumminello, M., Miccichè, S., Lillo, F., Piilo, J., Mantegna, R.N.: Statistically validated networks in bipartite complex systems. PLoS ONE **6**(3), e17994 (2011)
11. Wong, C.: Nyc taxi trips. http://www.andresmh.com/nyctaxitrips/
12. Wu, X., Shi, B., Dong, Y., Huang, C., Faust, L., Chawla, N.: Restful: resolution-aware forecasting of behavioral time series data, pp. 1073–1082 (2018)
13. Xue-dong, G., Chen, H.: The method of time granularity determination on time series based on structural similarity measure algorithm. In: The International Symposium on the Analytic Hierarchy Process (ISAHP) (2016)

Topological Data Analysis of Time-Series as an Input Embedding for Deep Learning Models

Morgan Byers[1]([⊠]) [ID], Lee B. Hinkle[2] [ID], and Vangelis Metsis[2] [ID]

[1] Department of Computer Science, University of Colorado Boulder,
Boulder, CO 80309, USA
morgan.byers@colorado.edu
[2] Department of Computer Science, Texas State University, San Marcos,
TX 78666, USA
{leebhinkle,vmetsis}@txstate.edu

Abstract. An appreciable portion of medical data exist in the form of a time-series, e.g. electroencephalogram (EEG) and electrocardiogram (ECG) readings of the biopotentials related to the head and heart. Scarcity of labeled data and class imbalance pose challenges when training deep learning models. Topological data analysis (TDA) is an emerging area of research that can be applied to time-series data. In this paper we show that using TDA as a time-series embedding methodology for input to deep learning models offers advantages compared to direct training of such models on the raw data. In our work TDA acts as a generic, low-level feature extractor that is able to capture common signal patterns and thus improve performance with limited training data. Our experimental results on publicly available human physiological biosignal datasets show an improvement in accuracy, especially for imbalanced classes with only a few training instances compared to the full dataset.

Keywords: Topological data analysis · Time-series data · Embedding · Physiological signals

1 Introduction

Medical data is very often represented as a time-series, e.g. when recording the progression of symptoms over time. Additionally, when data is collected for medical research it is not uncommon to have a deficit of instances of rare conditions or scenarios. For example, in the case of human activity recognition (HAR), datasets may be largely comprised of instances of activities with a long duration such as walking and have only a few instances of events such as falling. As a result, those interested in researching the applications of machine learning to time-series medical data must work to overcome class imbalance that can interfere with training.

© IFIP International Federation for Information Processing 2022
Published by Springer Nature Switzerland AG 2022
I. Maglogiannis et al. (Eds.): AIAI 2022, IFIP AICT 647, pp. 402–413, 2022.
https://doi.org/10.1007/978-3-031-08337-2_33

Topological data analysis (TDA) is an nascent area of interest to the data science community. Persistent homology is a tool used by TDA that has recently been applied to time-series analysis with much success [7]. Since TDA is still in its inception there is much room for exploring the ways this tool can be applied to deep learning. In this paper, we provide a data pipeline that takes advantage of the powerful tools of TDA in order to improve the per-class precision, recall and f1-scores of time-series data with underrepresented classes.

We use TDA as an embedding method to transform the raw time-series data before input to the deep learning model for training or prediction. The hypothesis is that similar signal patterns formed by time-series data will form similar topological representations, which can be learned more easily by deep learning models. The idea of input embedding is not new to the deep learning research community. For example, word embeddings are a common way of representing text as a vector for input to LSTM and Transformer models [4, 13]. Similar approaches have been used for image embeddings [26]. Although the general idea of time-series embeddings has been introduced in a few previous research works [14, 22], the use of TDA as an input embedding for deep learning models has so far been explored minimally. One example is the impact of TDA coupled with machine learning and the benefits for chaotic time-series data [24]. The deep learning pipeline described in this paper not only provides another tool to improve prediction scores for imbalanced data, but also demonstrates another application of the robust tools provided by TDA.

The rest of this paper is organized as follows. Section 2 provides background information on embeddings and topological data analysis. Section 3 describes the datasets and libraries used, as well as the overall methodology. Section 4 summarizes the results of our experiments. We conclude and suggest future work in Sect. 5.

2 Background

2.1 Time-Series Embeddings

Embeddings improve a machine learning algorithm's ability to model high-dimensional inputs such as sparse vectors representing sequential data in the form of time-series. A sequence of time-series data represents a set of measurements over time. Each data point (i.e. time-step) in the sequence carries very little information on its own, and it only creates a meaningful pattern when associated with multiple data points from neighboring time-steps. Furthermore, even for the same types of events, no two sequences are exactly the same, and added artifacts, such as measurement noise, push the data points farther apart in the vector space.

When large amounts of training data are available, as is usually the case with image datasets, deep neural networks perform well by learning the low-level features in the first few layers of the network and then combine the low-level features in deeper layers to form more complex patterns. However, in the medical domain the size of the available datasets are often not large enough to allow a deep neural network to be trained effectively. In such applications a more shallow network can benefit from an embedding layer which can capture similarities between signal patterns. Ideally, an embedding captures some of the semantics of the input by placing semantically similar inputs close together in the embedding space. The wave2vec [27] library is a notable previous effort toward the creation of time-series embeddings.

2.2 Takens' Embedding

Performing TDA requires data in the form of a multidimensional time-series, so we must first perform an embedding to bring our data into higher dimensions. A Takens' embedding, also referred to as a time-delay embedding, is a method for embedding a time-series $x \in \mathbb{R}$ into a higher dimensional space. Performing such an embedding necessitates the choice of two parameters:

1. The window size, which will become the embedding dimension
2. The stride, which specifies how far along we move the window at each step

Choosing a stride that is too small will result in data that is highly overlapped and prone to over-fitting. Conversely, a stride which it too large with little to no overlap will result in a training set that may lose critical information near the window boundary. Thus, the choice of window size and stride must be tuned to each data set individually, as proper values for these parameters are crucial. Takens' theorem [19] explains that this embedding is topologically significant, given the correct choice of embedding parameters.

2.3 Topological Data Analysis (TDA)

The principle idea behind TDA is that discrete data are samples of an underlying continuous shape [7]. If we can properly reconstruct the features of this underlying continuous shape, then we can leverage those features as input for our deep learning models. Persistent homology is the field of mathematics that provides us with the very tools needed to perform this reconstruction. The particular mathematical feature that we look for with persistent homology is the number of holes present in our data. Because this idea is robust to outliers, it is very attractive for use in situations where data are particularly noisy [5].

The groundwork for our pipeline was laid by prior research in the field of TDA. Many applications of TDA to both time-series [7,23] and other types of data [5,8] have been explored. The use of Takens' embedding [19] for time-series data was shown to be effective in preparing data for TDA [18,23]. However, much of what has been discovered with regards to TDA has been applied to traditional machine learning methods [6,15]. One notable work is the previously mentioned application of TDA to volatile time-series data as input to a convolutional neural network [24].

2.4   Persistence Diagrams

After using a delay embedding on a time-series, we are left with a collection of vectors on which we can employ TDA. We do this by constructing simplicial complexes from our data. A simplicial complex is a collection of simplices, which are the generalized definition of a triangle. Simplices exist in all dimensions; a 0-simplex is a singular point, a 1-simplex consists of two points joined by a line segment, and a 3-simplex is what we know as a traditional triangle. More generally, a k-simplex consists of a collection of k+1 vertices residing in $\mathbb{R}^{k+1}$ [6].

As mentioned above, we begin with each instance consisting of a discrete set of vectors in $\mathbb{R}^d$. This is sometimes referred to as a data cloud. With this data cloud, we can construct a simplicial complex. Specifically, we create a Vietoris-Rips complex, often abbreviated as a Rips complex. The act of creating this complex is known as Rips filtration. More information about the construction of these complexes can be found in [8].

Of interest to us is the number of holes, called a Betti number, that appear in our data as we perform this Rips filtration. Formally, the ith Betti number, β_i is the rank of the ith homology group of a topological space. Informally, the ith Betti number is the number of (i+1)-dimensional holes in our data. We are primarily interested in the number of loops, or 2-dimensional holes, β_1, present in our data cloud.

However, the Betti numbers of a single Rips complex constructed in isolation reveals little about the data. We must determine which of these holes persist in the Rips complexes that are constructed at different values of ϵ [8]. This requires the construction of a persistence diagram (Fig. 1).

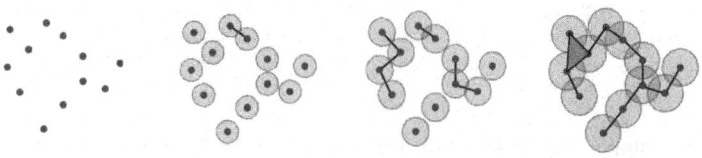

Fig. 1. An example of Rips filtration.

A persistence diagram is a graph that provides information about the components and loops that appear in the data as ϵ increases in value. Imagine a set of discrete points that constitute an incomplete set of connect-the-dots. Rather than playing the game traditionally, where the dots would be connected according to a predefined order, a different approach is used. This begins with drawing an arbitrarily small circle around each point in the connect-the-dot game. Incrementally larger and larger circles are drawn around each point until two or more of those circles intersect. When two dots' circles intersect, they are connected. As more and more dots are connected, loops will start to appear (and eventually disappear) in the data and individual components will start to disappear. For each component or loop, a point (x, y) is plotted in the persistence diagram so that x represents the radius of the circles when the component or loop first appeared (called its "birth") and y represents the radius of the circles when the component or loop disappeared (its "death"). The persistence diagram gives us insight into the true structure of our data set - the loops and holes which persist throughout many values of ϵ are true features of our data, which the machine learning models can then utilize when making predictions.

After constructing a persistence diagram, it is likely that many points in the diagram will be clustered around the line $y = x$. The points that are further away from the line $y = x$ are considered persistent. An example of one of our persistence diagrams is shown in Fig. 2.

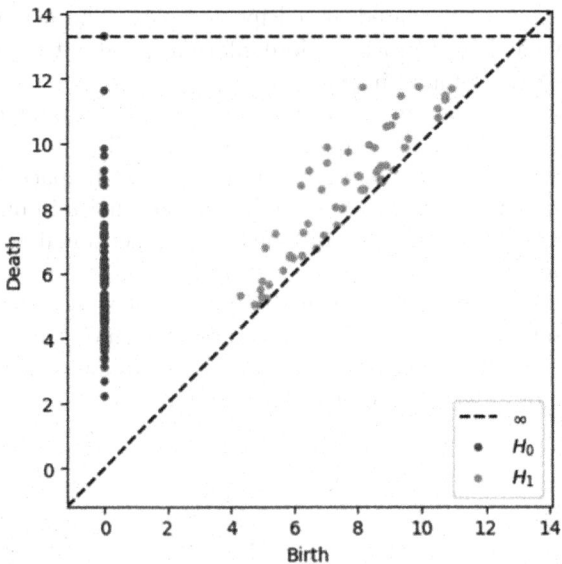

Fig. 2. An example of a persistence diagram. Note that 'Birth' refers to the radius at which the feature appeared and 'Death' refers to the radius at which the feature disappeared. New components are not created after a radius of 0. Instead, when two components' balls intersect, one component dies and the other lives on.

Although persistence diagrams are powerful, they are not suitable as input for many popular machine learning algorithms. This is where a persistence image becomes useful. Persistence images offer a stable, vector-based representation of persistence diagrams that work as input for many machine learning algorithms. As described in [1], to create a persistence image, we begin by mapping a persistence diagram PD to an integrable function $\rho_{PD} : \mathbb{R}^2 \to \mathbb{R}$ that's defined as a weighted sum of probability density functions (one centered at each point in PD). Then a grid is defined by taking a discretization of a subdomain of ρ_{PD}. Finally, a persistence image is yielded by taking an integral of the function on each grid box (Fig. 3).

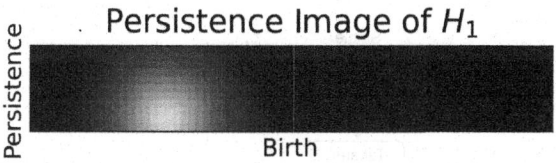

Fig. 3. An example of a persistence image

3 Methodology

3.1 Datasets

Multiple datasets were used in this work, including three human activity recognition (HAR) datasets and one Electroencephalogram (EEG) dataset. The UniMiB SHAR [12] dataset contains acceleration data captured using a smartphone on 30 subjects and includes nine types of activities and seven types of falls. The Mobi-Act [25] dataset includes both accelerometer and gyroscope (rotation) data also recorded on a smartphone with 50 subjects. It includes nine activities and four types of falls. The third activity dataset is UCI HAR [2] which contains smartphone accelerometer and gyroscope data for 30 subjects performing six physical activities. The final dataset used was the EEG Motor Movement/Imagery [9,17] dataset. For this dataset we worked with Task 3.

3.2 Tools and Libraries

The models were implemented using Python. The NumPy [10] and Sci-kit Learn [16] libraries were used to preparing the data and the deep learning models were built using Tensorflow Keras [3]. The Takens' Embedding was performed with the Giotto-tda library [20]. We used Ripser [21] and Persim [1] to perform the topological data analysis.

3.3 Data Pipeline

Since applying TDA necessitates that each instance consists of a collection of vectors, in the case of a single channel time-series, we must first embed the data from $\mathbb{R}$ into $\mathbb{R}^d$, where $d \in \mathbb{N}$ is the embedding dimension, by using a Takens' embedding with a stride of one. In the case of a multi-channel time-series, we consider each variable to be already embedded in $\mathbb{R}^t$, where t is the number of time steps. For each of the human activity recognition data sets the quadratic mean (RMS) of the acceleration in the x, y, and z axes is used as a single channel time-series. Takens' embedding is performed on the data before continuing with the pipeline. In the case of EEG classification we do not use Takens' embedding and instead use each channel of the EEG data as-is, because our EEG data is already highly dimensional (see Fig. 4). After the data has been prepared, a baseline deep learning estimator is trained solely on the data without performing

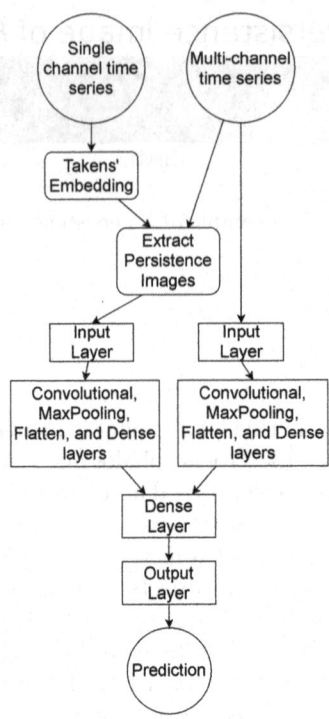

Fig. 4. The setup of our data pipeline and our baseline comparison.

topological data analysis. The architecture of our baseline model consists of the same layers that the non-TDA side of our final model uses (see Fig. 4), followed by additional dense layers for output prediction.

In the case of single channel data, the baseline classifier is trained on the data after Takens' embedding has been applied. The architecture of this baseline estimator is variable and can be changed to suit the particulars of the specific data type. For instance, when creating the baseline model for classifying EEG data, the model described in [11] was used. After the initial model has been trained, the probabilities output by the model's predictions are used with the test set for evaluation.

At the same time, we use the embedded data to extract topological features from our time-series. A Rips filtration [21] yields persistence diagrams (Fig. 2) from each instance. Persim [1] is used to convert the persistence diagrams into persistence images, which are stable vector representations of persistence diagrams. These persistence images will be used as input to our final model. The particular pixel size and dimensions of each persistence image are hyperparameters that are tuned to fit each time-series individually. In our case, these hyperparameters were determined by using five-fold cross-validation of the training set with the final pipeline.

The persistence images are used as input data to one side of our final model (see our pipeline in Fig. 4). The basic architecture of this side of our model will remain the same for any data, and consists of 1D convolutional layers, dropout, maxPooling, flatten, and dense layers. However, hyperparameters like kernel and batch size must be tuned to achieve the best performance on each set of data. The deep learning model is completed by concatenating the outputs of last layers of our two networks: the network trained on traditional features and the network trained on the topological features. This is passed through a dense layer and then to a final output layer.

To evaluate our pipeline, the classification reports yielded by both the baseline and final models were compared. Group based five-fold cross validation was used to evaluate the models' performance. Since all of our datasets are segmented by subject, we delineated each fold by subject. For instance, all of subject one's data would be included in the test set for one fold, and then subject one's data would be in the training set for the four remaining folds. In the case of the UCI HAR data set, the data is already segmented into a training and testing sets. As a result, in order to avoid overfitting, we perform only one trial with this model, training on the provided training set and evaluating on the provided test set.

4   Results

In Tables 2 through 5, results are formatted similarly to a classification report. In these tables, 'Base' refers to the metrics obtained by our baseline classifier, while 'TDA' refers to the metrics obtained by our final deep learning model. Our TDA deep learning approach yielded a statistically significant improvement over the baseline in almost every case of data that we tried (Table 1). The best results were obtained on the MobiAct dataset, which is perhaps because of the severity of class imbalance present in the data set. In fact, just two classes comprise roughly 70% of instances in the data set. Although the f1-score has improved for a majority of the classes in each data set, due to the imbalanced nature of most of these data sets, the overall prediction accuracy rarely changed by a significant amount. As mentioned previously, the most significant improvement in accuracy came from the MobiAct data. In particular, our TDA pipeline improved the f1-score of every class and improved the recall of five of the six classes (Table 2).

Table 1. Hypothesis test for difference in mean recall and f1-score ($H_0 : \mu_d \leq 0$)

DataSet	p-value (recall)	p-value (f1-score)
MobiAct	0.013	0.009
UniMiB	0.018	<0.001
UCI HAR	0.336	0.051
EEG	0.255	0.025

Table 2. MobiAct classification report

Class	Precision		Recall		f1-score		Support
	Base	TDA	Base	TDA	Base	TDA	
0	0.84	**0.96**	0.98	0.98	0.90	**0.97**	697
1	0.83	**0.96**	0.75	**0.96**	0.79	**0.96**	677
2	0.90	**1.00**	0.98	**1.00**	0.94	**1.00**	2086
3	0.50	**0.81**	0.26	**0.80**	0.34	**0.81**	287
4	0.59	**0.77**	0.67	**0.89**	0.63	**0.82**	286
5	0.99	0.99	0.93	**0.98**	0.96	**0.98**	2675

The TDA pipeline also showed an increase in recall and f1-score for the UniMiB data. The per-class f1-score improved in each of the nine classes, and eight classes also showed an improvement in recall (Fig. 5).

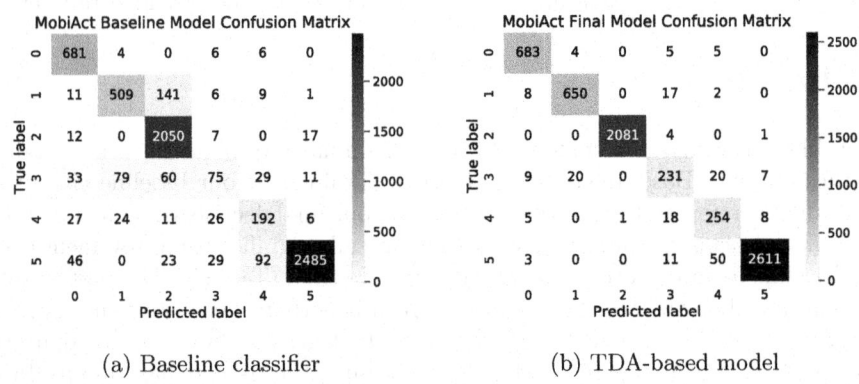

(a) Baseline classifier   (b) TDA-based model

Fig. 5. Confusion matrices comparing the performance of the baseline classifier against our TDA-based model.

Similarly, on the UCI HAR data our pipeline improved the f1-score for five of the six classes; the overall classification accuracy increased from 58% to 60%.

The EEG dataset consists of only two classes. In this case our pipeline improved the f1-score for both classes; the overall accuracy increased by 2%. Typically, the classes that showed improvement in f1-score consisted of fewer instances than that of the classes which showed no improvement.

Table 3. UniMiB classification report

Class	Precision		Recall		f1-score		Support
	Base	TDA	Base	TDA	Base	TDA	
0	0.73	**0.80**	0.63	0.63	0.68	**0.70**	153
1	0.53	**0.54**	0.37	**0.51**	0.44	**0.53**	216
2	0.89	**0.93**	**0.90**	0.89	0.90	**0.91**	1738
3	0.96	0.96	0.94	**0.97**	0.95	**0.96**	1985
4	**0.85**	0.83	0.77	**0.82**	0.81	**0.82**	921
5	0.90	**0.96**	0.95	**0.96**	0.93	**0.96**	746
6	0.79	**0.83**	0.88	0.88	0.83	**0.85**	1324
7	0.52	**0.54**	0.55	**0.60**	0.53	**0.57**	296
8	0.64	**0.72**	0.58	**0.67**	0.61	**0.69**	200

Table 4. UCI HAR classification report

Class	Precision		Recall		f1-score		Support
	Base	TDA	Base	TDA	Base	TDA	
0	0.75	**0.82**	**0.90**	0.88	0.82	**0.85**	496
1	**0.84**	0.81	0.60	**0.75**	0.70	**0.78**	471
2	0.83	**0.87**	**0.90**	0.87	0.86	**0.87**	420
3	0.35	**0.37**	**0.50**	0.37	**0.41**	0.37	491
4	**0.40**	0.38	0.36	**0.38**	0.37	**0.38**	532
5	**0.42**	0.41	0.30	**0.41**	0.35	**0.41**	537

Table 5. EEG classification report

Class	Precision		Recall		f1-score		Support
	Base	TDA	Base	TDA	Base	TDA	
0	0.58	**0.61**	**0.59**	0.58	0.59	0.59	445
1	0.59	**0.61**	0.58	**0.63**	0.59	**0.62**	455

5   Conclusion

The experiments detailed in this paper provide a novel deep neural network embedding method utilizing Topological Data Analysis. The presented data pipeline and results show increased per-class recall and f1-scores for underrepresented classes that may be applicable to a variety of time-series data. Since medical research is typically interested in identifying rare occurrences (e.g. seizure detection), it is expected that much medical data is imbalanced, with many more normal instances than those experiencing an anomaly. Finding a methodology to represent persistence diagrams in such a way that transformers are capable of learning from these representations remains an open question.

Acknowledgements. This material is based upon work supported by the National Science Foundation under REU Site Grant No. 1757893. The research work was conducted while Morgan Byers was an undergraduate student at Texas State University. Any opinions, findings, and conclusions or recommendations expressed in this material are those of the author(s) and do not necessarily reflect the views of the National Science Foundation.

References

1. Adams, H., et al.: Persistence images: a stable vector representation of persistent homology. J. Mach. Learn. Res. **18**, 1–35 (2017). http://jmlr.org/papers/v18/16-337.html
2. Anguita, D., Ghio, A., Oneto, L., Parra, X., Reyes-Ortiz, J.: A public domain dataset for human activity recognition using smartphones. In: 21th European Symposium on Artificial Neural Networks, Computational Intelligence and Machine Learning (April 2013)
3. Chollet, F., et al.: Keras (2015). https://keras.io
4. Devlin, J., Chang, M.W., Lee, K., Toutanova, K.: Bert: pre-training of deep bidirectional transformers for language understanding. arXiv preprint arXiv:1810.04805 (2018)
5. Edelsbrunner, H., Harer, J., et al.: Persistent homology - a survey. Contem. Math. **453**, 257–282 (2008)
6. Gholizadeh, S., Seyeditabari, A., Zadrozny, W.: Topological signature of 19th century novelists: persistent homology in text mining. Big Data Cogn. Comput. **2**, 1–10 (2018). https://doi.org/10.3390/bdcc2040033
7. Gholizadeh, S., Zadrozny, W.: A short survey of topological data analysis in time series and systems analysis. arXiv (October 2018). http://arxiv.org/abs/1809.10745
8. Ghrist, R.: Barcodes: the persistent topology of data. Bull. Am. Math. Soc. **45**(1), 61–75 (2008)
9. Goldberger, A.L., et al.: Physiobank, physiotoolkit, and physionet: components of a new research resource for complex physiologic signals. Circulation **101**, E215–E220 (2000). https://doi.org/10.1161/01.cir.101.23.e215. https://pubmed.ncbi.nlm.nih.gov/10851218/
10. Harris, C.R., et al.: Array programming with NumPy. Nature **585**(7825), 357–362 (2020). https://doi.org/10.1038/s41586-020-2649-2
11. Lawhern, V.J., Solon, A.J., Waytowich, N.R., Gordon, S.M., Hung, C.P., Lance, B.J.: EEGNet: a compact convolutional neural network for EEG-based brain-computer interfaces. J. Neural Eng. **15**, 056013 (2018). https://doi.org/10.1088/1741-2552/aace8c. https://iopscience.iop.org/article/10.1088/1741-2552/aace8c
12. Micucci, D., Mobilio, M., Napoletano, P.: UniMiB SHAR: a dataset for human activity recognition using acceleration data from smartphones. Appl. Sci. **7**(10) (2017). https://doi.org/10.3390/app7101101. http://www.mdpi.com/2076-3417/7/10/1101
13. Mikolov, T., Sutskever, I., Chen, K., Corrado, G.S., Dean, J.: Distributed representations of words and phrases and their compositionality. In: Advances in Neural Information Processing Systems, pp. 3111–3119 (2013)

14. Nalmpantis, C., Vrakas, D.: Signal2Vec: time series embedding representation. In: Macintyre, J., Iliadis, L., Maglogiannis, I., Jayne, C. (eds.) Engineering Applications of Neural Networks: 20th International Conference, EANN 2019, Xersonisos, Crete, Greece, May 24-26, 2019, Proceedings, pp. 80–90. Springer, Cham (2019). https://doi.org/10.1007/978-3-030-20257-6_7
15. Obayashi, I., Hiraoka, Y.: Persistence diagrams with linear machine learning models. arXiv (June 2017). http://arxiv.org/abs/1706.10082
16. Pedregosa, F., et al.: Scikit-learn: machine learning in Python. J. Mach. Learn. Res. **12**, 2825–2830 (2011)
17. Schalk, G., McFarland, D.J., Hinterberger, T., Birbaumer, N., Wolpaw, J.R.: BCI 2000: a general-purpose brain-computer interface (BCI) system. IEEE Trans. Biomed. Eng. **51**, 1034–1043 (2004). https://doi.org/10.1109/TBME.2004.827072. https://pubmed.ncbi.nlm.nih.gov/15188875/
18. Seversky, L.M., Davis, S., Berger, M.: On time-series topological data analysis: new data and opportunities. In: Proceedings of the IEEE Conference on Computer Vision and Pattern Recognition Workshops, pp. 59–67 (2016)
19. Takens, F.: Detecting strange attractors in turbulence. In: Rand, D., Young, L.-S. (eds.) Dynamical Systems and Turbulence, Warwick 1980, pp. 366–381. Springer, Heidelberg (1981). https://doi.org/10.1007/BFb0091924
20. Tauzin, G., et al.: giotto-tda: a topological data analysis toolkit for machine learning and data exploration (2020)
21. Tralie, C., Saul, N., Bar-On, R.: Ripser.py: a lean persistent homology library for Python. J. Open Source Softw. **3**(29), 925 (2018). https://doi.org/10.21105/joss.00925
22. Tran, Q.H., Hasegawa, Y.: Topological time-series analysis with delay-variant embedding. Phys. Rev. E **99**(3), 032209 (2019)
23. Ty, A.J., Fang, Z., Gonzalez, R.A., Rozdeba, P.J., Abarbanel, H.D.: Machine learning of time series using time-delay embedding and precision annealing. Neural Comput. **31**(10), 2004–2024 (2019)
24. Umeda, Y.: Time series classification via topological data analysis. Inf. Media Technol. **12**, 228–239 (2017). https://doi.org/10.11185/imt.12.228
25. Vavoulas, G., Chatzaki, C., Malliotakis, T., Pediaditis, M., Tsiknakis, M.: The MobiAct dataset: recognition of activities of daily living using smartphones. In: International Conference on Information and Communication Technologies for Ageing Well and e-Health, vol. 2, pp. 143–151. SciTePress (2016)
26. Wang, J., et al.: Learning fine-grained image similarity with deep ranking. In: Proceedings of the IEEE Conference on Computer Vision and Pattern Recognition, pp. 1386–1393 (2014)
27. Yuan, Y., Xun, G., Suo, Q., Jia, K., Zhang, A.: Wave2Vec: learning deep representations for biosignals. In: 2017 IEEE International Conference on Data Mining (ICDM), pp. 1159–1164. IEEE (2017)

Transfer Learning for Predicting Gene Regulatory Effects of Chemicals

Bahattin Can Maral[iD] and Mehmet Tan[(⊠)][iD]

TOBB University of Economics and Technology, Sogutozu, Ankara, Turkey
{bahattincanmaral,mtan}@etu.edu.tr

Abstract. Among the recent developments in bioinformatics and chemogenomics, various deep learning methods have been the most prevalent [4,5,9]. This resulted in an over-saturation of powerful models that easily pushed the limits of existing datasets. Subsequently, many novel advancements have been done with improvements to the datasets. Amidst these advancements, researchers of Deep Compound Profiler (DeepCOP) [10] set themselves apart with a novel method of introducing new features whilst keeping the deep learning model relatively basic. In this study, we propose to take this novel method one step further by applying transfer learning between cell lines. In order to better evaluate the benefits of transfer learning, we've introduced 2 drug-based data splits. The transfer learning method, as its core, utilizes the learned knowledge of "source" cell lines to give a head start to "target" cell lines. Taking advantage of prior knowledge from source cell lines not only boosts existing compounds' effect prediction, but it can also be used as a premonition for the compounds' (explicit to the source), effects on target cell lines before they are tested in real life. Our experiments showed improvements up to 22.81% improvement on area under ROC curve (AUC) on the split closest to a wet lab experiment.

Keywords: Transfer learning · Chemogenomics · Domain adaptation

1 Introduction

Chemogenomics [1] studies chemical compounds and their genomic/proteomic effects on biological systems.

Since machine learning, chemogenomics has been advancing rapidly, the ability to simulate chemical effects on different cell lines with almost no cost also helped the drug-discovery process by identifying potential side effects of the candidate drugs early.

DeepCOP is a recently proposed deep learning model that is trained on the LINCS L1000 [8] transcriptomics dataset to predict differential gene expression effects of chemicals. In the study, researchers train two deep learning models in the form of a multilayer perceptron (MLP) for each selected cell line.

The study distinguishes itself with the heavy focus on feature generation and uncomplicated model structure.

© IFIP International Federation for Information Processing 2022
Published by Springer Nature Switzerland AG 2022
I. Maglogiannis et al. (Eds.): AIAI 2022, IFIP AICT 647, pp. 414–425, 2022.
https://doi.org/10.1007/978-3-031-08337-2_34

In this study, we aim to take the work done by DeepCOP researchers one step further by introducing transfer learning to utilize the knowledge of different cell lines.

In machine learning, transfer learning is defined as the use of previously acquired knowledge gained while solving one problem on a different but related problem. For this study, different problems correspond to different cell lines. Utilizing the data from other cell lines also comes with the advantage of training a more general model due to there being experiments with chemical compounds unique to some cell lines. In addition to transfer learning, we have introduced 2 splitting methods that we think better represents the high-throughput screening process and 17 previously discarded cell lines.

This paper includes 3 key sections: Materials and methods, discussion, and conclusion. In the first of which, we briefly explain preparation of the dataset, clarify the key differences between the splitting methods, and give average improvements for each method. The discussion section mainly focuses on splitting complications, what can be done to counter them, and what we did in this study. In the conclusion section, we wrap up the paper, and give a short summary for the planned studies moving forward.

2 Materials and Methods

We aim to prove the usefulness of transfer learning for the prediction of chemical induced differential gene expression. To produce comparable results to DeepCOP, the data production and preparation steps have been replicated, and the novel ideas repeated with the original methodology.

2.1 Datasets

L1000 dataset provides the data in the form of levels. In this study, we utilize the Level 5 dataset. Level 5 data comprise the gene profiles of 978 landmark genes' drug-gene interaction experiments on distinct cell lines. To get to the Level 5 of the L1000 dataset, the same method of genex measurement, namely flow cytometry, is used throughout levels 1 to 5. At Level 5 these values are reformed into standardized z-scores. Further information about this dataset can be found in [8].

For data preparation, we've closely followed DeepCOP; with the only difference being the removal of the 10% threshold, for the sake of space limitations.

In DeepCOP, from the processed dataset, researchers selected the top six cell lines that had the largest number of drug-gene interaction experiments i.e., VCAP, A549, A375, PC3, MCF7, and HT29. For this study, we expanded this selection to every cell line that had more than 10 samples, which resulted in 17 additional cell lines compared to [10]. These additional cell lines are as follows: BT20, HA1E, HCC515, HEK293T, HEPG2, HL60, HS578T, HUH7, JURKAT, MCF10A, MDAMB231, NKDBA, NOMO1, SKBR3, THP1, U266, and U937 where details are given in Table 1.

Table 1. The details of the cell line id's that are included in this study.

Cell line	Primary site	Sample type	Subtype
A375	Skin	Tumor	Malignant melanoma
A549	Lung	Tumor	Non small cell lung cancer carcinoma
BT20	Breast	Tumor	Carcinoma
HA1E	Kidney	Normal	Normal kidney
HCC515	Lung	Normal	Carcinoma
HEK293T	Kidney	Normal	Embryonal kidney
HEPG2	Liver	Tumor	Hepatocellular carcinoma
HL60	Haematopoietic, lymphoid tissue	Tumor	Acute myelogenous leukemia, promyelocytic
HS578T	Breast	Tumor	Carcinoma
HT29	Large intestine	Tumor	Colorectal adenocarcinoma
HUH7	Liver	Tumor	Hepatocellular carcinoma
JURKAT	Haematopoietic, lymphoid tissue	Tumor	Acute lymphoblastic leukemia, T-cell
MCF10A	Breast	Normal	Epithelial
MCF7	Breast	Tumor	Adenocarcinoma
MDAMB231	Breast	Tumor	Adenocarcinoma
NKDBA	Kidney	Normal	Kidney epithelial
NOMO1	Haematopoietic, lymphoid tissue	tumor	Acute myeloid leukemia
PC3	Prostate	Tumor	Adenocarcinoma
SKBR3	Breast	Tumor	Adenocarcinoma ·
THP1	Haematopoietic, lymphoid tissue	tumor	Acute myelogenous leukemia, monocytic
U266	Blood	Tumor	Myeloman, haematopoietic, lymphoid
U937	Haematopoietic, lymphoid tissue	tumor	Lymphoma, B-cell, non-hodgkin's, histiocytic
VCAP	Prostate	Tumor	Carcinoma

2.2   Feature Generation

Similar to the well-known Extended-connectivity fingerprints (ECFPs) or Functional-class fingerprints (FCFPs), Morgan fingerprints are used to represent chemical structures as binary arrays. From the first time, it was introduced [3], to the modernized implementation in [7], Morgan fingerprints have been one of the most prevalent fingerprinting methods to this day. In this study, Morgan descriptors were generated using the RDKIT Open-source cheminformatics toolkit [6] to correlate the chemical structure to gene perturbation. The descriptors on the conventional SMILES form were computed with a radius of 2 to generate a one-hot vector of 2048 features for 19 811 compounds.

While there are no widely acknowledged techniques for describing a gene, the gene ontology (GO) consortium [2], with 40 thousand GO terms and over 200 000 qualitative annotations for Homo sapiens, is the most prominent. DeepCOP proposes a novel way to utilize the GO descriptors along with the 978 landmark genes. Using the OntologyX R package, GO terms that correlated with at least 3 landmark genes were extracted. Then each gene was described using the appropriate GO terms. One-hot encoding of these GO descriptors resulted in a binary array of size 1107 that can be used as features alongside the Morgan fingerprints.

2.3   Data Splitting

In DeepCOP, researchers have split the aforementioned dataset into 10 randomly selected folds to perform 10-fold cross-validation for each cell line. This approach ensures every compound-gene combination is unique per fold. However, it does not accommodate the fact that each drug is repeated by the number of landmark genes. Conversely, each gene is repeated by the number of compounds. Therefore, a model trained on randomly split 9 folds, has already encountered the input elements (compound and gene) for the remaining fold, separately. This leads to complications that may cause over-fitting, for the reasons that we further addressed in the discussion section. For the sake of the completeness of this study, we have also repeated our experiments in this format which will be called "random-split" moving forward.

Cold-Drug splitting method divides the compound data into 10 folds, then populates each fold with the gene data. This ensures the drugs in the test fold are brand new for the trained models. We named this method of splitting "cold-drug-split". For transfer learning, the source model is trained on a 95%-5% random-split. Then we train the target cell line data on the cold-drug-split. We consider this splitting method to be the closest to real-life high-throughput testing.

Similar to cold-drug-split, we introduced Transfer-Drug splitting to counteract contamination of the test data. The main difference between the two splits is that this splitting method also eliminates the contamination between cell lines while transfer learning. On the last step of transfer learning on cold-drug-split, the compounds used in the training of the source model are removed from the test fold. This guarantees that the compounds in the test data are never-before-seen for the model. Going forward, this splitting method will be referred to as "transfer-drug-split".

2.4   Experiments

This study aims to justify the value of utilizing previously tested knowledge of cell lines in novel test domains. To be able to make a direct comparison with DeepCOP results, we have repeated the original experiments both with a random split and a transfer-drug split as a baseline. During these experiments, we also discovered that similar scores could be achieved with much smaller neural networks from the original study. The results of the experiments listed below have been achieved with a neural network that reduces the neuron count of the original 2 hidden layers to 400 (from 3155 of DeepCOP), while the rest of the network structure remains unchanged.

Based on the assumption that learned knowledge from cell lines could benefit others, we've opted to use network-based parameter sharing as our transfer learning method. Parameter sharing methods, transfer their learned knowledge between problems by keeping a part of or the whole network trained on the donor/source problem. Continuing the training on the receiver/target problem on the transferred network by either modifying the received weights or adding brand-new layers to train.

In this study, we trained a source model for every single cell line with 95% train and 5% validation split data. Then we saved the finalized weights of the source model and used them as the initial weights for training the target cell line model. We repeated this process for every cell line pair. Network structure and parameters were kept unchanged throughout experiments to ensure comparability. We selected the original six cell lines of the DeepCOP study as our source models because there was a huge falloff in the sample count after these six. The more knowledge we can acquire in the source problem makes for a stronger baseline for the target.

As our first objective, we trained target cell lines on the same random-split with DeepCOP. Evaluating our model on random-split resulted in average improvements of 4.51% for up-regulated and 4.52% for down-regulated models' AUC scores. Among up-regulated models, the maximum recorded betterment was on the NKDBA cell line when MCF7 was used as a source; which resulted in 15.73% improvement of the AUC score. As for down-regulated models, the maximum improvement was on the HL60 cell line with A375 as the source; that resulted in an added 12.73% for the AUC score.

A detailed view of the random-split experiments can be seen on the Table 2, for up and down-regulated model results. Each row represents the different target cell lines, and each column corresponds to different sources, while the "No-TL" (no transfer learning) column represents the results of the models when the model is trained on the same split, without a source model, on target cell line data. When the data is viewed as a whole, a clear trend emerges: The least amount of improvements are seen on the experiments that are trying to improve upon the cell lines we've selected as the source. This directly correlates to the number of samples each cell line possesses. For the remaining 17 target cell lines, the average gains for the AUC scores are 6.09% and 6.04% for up and down regulation models. While the scores are impressive, the random-split is the least realistic of the three. Transcriptomics datasets, like L1000, are subsets of gene perturbation measurements of wet-lab experiments. In these experiments, a chemical compound is tested on a cell line and the perturbations of the genes are measured simultaneously. Therefore, predicting a gene's perturbation by utilizing other gene's responses, is only useful in a situation where that specific gene perturbation value is lost. Which isn't useful for simulating high-throughput screening.

Apart from being unrealistic, this became a visible issue while we were trying to improve DeepCOP's scores on isolation with network optimization, for

Table 2. AUC scores of regulated genes on random-drug-split 10-fold data, rows and columns indicate target and source cell lines. The best results in a row are indicated in bold.

	Target cell ↓	Source cell No-TL	A375	A549	HT29	MCF7	PC3	VCAP
Up	A375	**0.8199**		0.8189	0.8190	0.8141	0.8167	0.8105
	A549	**0.8254**	0.8243		0.8228	0.8246	0.8244	0.8222
	BT20	0.7698	0.7975	**0.8015**	0.7994	0.8011	0.7987	0.7944
	HA1E	0.8281	**0.8298**	0.8293	0.8281	0.8260	0.8297	0.8251
	HCC515	0.8397	0.8405	0.8400	0.8403	0.8384	**0.8413**	0.8392
	HEK293T	0.8011	0.8549	0.8533	0.8431	0.8503	**0.8576**	0.8495
	HEPG2	0.8216	0.8548	0.8572	**0.8584**	0.8534	0.8517	0.8412
	HL60	0.8427	**0.8964**	0.8836	0.8928	0.8872	0.8852	0.8835
	HS578T	0.7556	0.7901	**0.7976**	0.7901	0.7909	0.7932	0.7859
	HT29	0.7904	**0.7966**	0.7902		0.7875	0.7899	0.7822
	HUH7	0.7505	0.8038	0.7998	**0.8072**	0.8048	0.8032	0.7987
	JURKAT	0.8071	0.8579	0.8493	**0.8602**	0.8029	0.8536	0.8452
	MCF10A	0.7733	**0.8054**	0.8002	0.8017	0.8013	0.7988	0.7928
	MCF7	0.8313	0.8291	0.8315	0.8293		**0.8327**	0.8295
	MDAMB231	0.7662	0.8207	0.8234	0.8214	0.8212	**0.8258**	0.8176
	NKDBA	0.6833	0.7876	0.7891	0.7864	**0.7908**	0.7891	0.7878
	NOMO1	0.7828	0.8013	**0.8278**	0.7485	0.7840	0.7816	0.7731
	PC3	**0.8327**	0.8253	0.8276	0.8248	0.8279		0.8268
	SKBR3	0.7655	0.7868	0.7943	0.7918	**0.7991**	0.7933	0.7855
	THP1	0.7296	0.7492	0.7986	0.7805	0.7887	0.7883	**0.8130**
	U266	0.7898	0.8146	0.8288	**0.8327**	0.7948	0.8307	0.8308
	U937	0.7572	0.8023	0.8019	**0.8085**	0.7721	0.7993	0.7898
	VCAP	**0.8471**	0.8457	0.8458	0.8450	0.8469	0.8466	
Down	A375	0.8239		0.8244	**0.8248**	0.8214	0.8201	0.8165
	A549	**0.8154**	0.8152		0.8132	0.8137	0.8153	0.8103
	BT20	0.7758	0.8187	0.8173	0.8164	**0.8267**	0.8225	0.8102
	HA1E	0.8384	**0.8403**	0.8380	0.8397	0.8382	0.8400	0.8342
	HCC515	0.8420	0.8444	0.8440	0.8449	0.8448	**0.8473**	0.8423
	HEK293T	0.8383	0.8835	0.8797	0.8766	0.8838	**0.8864**	0.8739
	HEPG2	0.8341	0.8635	0.8638	0.8636	**0.8645**	0.8600	0.8507
	HL60	0.7917	**0.8925**	0.8744	0.8881	0.8737	0.8739	0.8803
	HS578T	0.7843	0.8080	**0.8082**	0.8037	0.8063	0.8077	0.7993
	HT29	0.7974	**0.8032**	0.7954		0.7932	0.7960	0.7915
	HUH7	0.7682	0.7954	0.7953	**0.7988**	0.7963	0.7957	0.7816
	JURKAT	0.7917	**0.8781**	0.8506	0.8701	0.8591	0.8714	0.8422
	MCF10A	0.7955	0.8200	0.8192	0.8196	**0.8215**	0.8165	0.8178
	MCF7	**0.8430**	0.8425	0.8415	0.8414		0.8430	0.8395
	MDAMB231	0.7953	0.8395	0.8367	0.8345	**0.8431**	0.8397	0.8335
	NKDBA	0.7241	0.7948	0.7983	0.7914	**0.8002**	0.7967	0.7926
	NOMO1	0.7934	0.8044	0.7665	0.7420	**0.8467**	0.8044	0.6887
	PC3	0.8327	0.8322	0.8323	0.8314	**0.8345**		0.8320
	SKBR3	0.7951	0.8233	0.8225	0.8255	**0.8292**	0.8203	0.8208
	THP1	0.7590	0.7945	0.8156	0.7439	**0.8399**	0.7845	0.7082
	U266	0.7765	0.8192	0.8076	0.8217	0.8344	0.8241	**0.8345**
	U937	0.7569	**0.8050**	0.7642	0.8025	0.7370	0.7168	0.7705
	VCAP	0.8564	0.8554	0.8541	0.8539	**0.8570**	0.8561	

a stronger baseline. Our experiments showed minimal change in evaluation, even for major changes in the network structure. Upon further investigation, we deduced that the almost static but low error rate was limited by the data itself. While producing impressive results, the neural network itself wasn't modeling the data correctly, and instead was basically training on the test data, due to the repetitions in the dataset. This was also the reason behind the change in the layer sizes since smaller layers could produce similar results faster.

To eliminate the compound repetition, we've introduced the cold-drug-split. Repeating the original methodology with this new split resulted in 23.05% lower AUC scores on average. These results can be seen on the No-TL columns of the Table 3. The most improvement for the up-regulated models was on the JURKAT cell line when A375 cell line data was used as the source; which boosted the AUC score by 22.81%. For down-regulated, it was on the HCC515 cell line by 14.38% when the PC3 was used as the source. The results of transfer learning experiments on cold-drug-split can be seen on Table 3. As mentioned before, we regard cold-drug-split as the most realistic method of the three. Experiments on this split resulted in average improvements of 9.70% and 8.29% on AUC scores for up and down-regulated models, respectively.

The second splitting method we introduced, transfer-drug-split, while a bit unrealistic compared to cold-drug-split, posed an important challenge to the model training. We've re-tested the models we trained in cold-drug-split by removing the compounds that also were tested on the source cell line from the target test splits, producing a testing environment in which the model was tested purely tested on its ability to process new compounds. On transfer-drug-split, the AUC scores on average improved by 1.42% and -0.73% for up and down-regulated models. However, the maximum AUC gains were comparable to the ones on the other splits. For up-regulated, training the JURKAT cell line on top of the A375 resulted in 19.88% improved AUC. Among down-regulated it was HS578T which improved its AUC score by 6.74% when trained after MCF7.

Detailed AUC scores of transfer-drug-split experiments can be seen on Table 4, for up and down-regulated model results.

3   Discussion

3.1   Best Improvements

When we look at the top 10 most improved AUC scores in Table 5, several trends emerge that we can comment on.

Firstly, every experiment on the table is an up differential expression (DE) model. If we were to take an average of every up, and down differential expression experiments separately, we can see the up regulated experiments are more effected than down regulated ones. This can be correlated to the greater up regulated sample counts compared to the downs.

Another visible trend is in the splits. Other than one exception, every split in the table is either from a cold-drug-split or a transfer-drug-split experiment. This is mainly because of the 23% decrease in the AUC values when we'd switched

Table 3. AUC scores of regulated genes on cold-drug-split 10-fold data, rows and columns indicate target and source cell lines. The best results in a row are indicated in bold.

| | Target cell ↓ | Source cell | | | | | | |
		No-TL	A375	A549	HT29	MCF7	PC3	VCAP
Up	A375	0.6145		0.6633	0.6499	0.6558	**0.6652**	0.6304
	A549	0.5864	0.5944		0.5851	0.6294	**0.6445**	0.6145
	BT20	0.5952	0.5460	0.6316	0.5801	**0.6553**	0.6268	0.6013
	HA1E	0.6220	0.6601	0.6701	0.6482	0.6627	**0.6859**	0.6666
	HCC515	0.6136	0.6401	0.6761	0.6507	0.6679	**0.6970**	0.6664
	HEK293T	0.6165	**0.6971**	0.6238	0.6698	0.6543	0.6348	0.6466
	HEPG2	0.6096	0.7297	0.7192	0.6761	0.6893	**0.7388**	0.6224
	HL60	0.6063	0.6183	0.5397	**0.6665**	0.5670	0.5671	0.5604
	HS578T	0.5762	0.5796	0.6509	0.6306	**0.6725**	0.6436	0.6307
	HT29	0.6197	**0.6892**	0.6756		0.6742	0.6719	0.6374
	HUH7	0.6428	0.6197	0.6856	0.6488	0.6749	**0.6980**	0.6679
	JURKAT	0.5558	**0.6826**	0.5527	0.5816	0.5898	0.6307	0.6205
	MCF10A	0.6434	0.6131	0.6360	0.6291	**0.6594**	0.6460	0.6323
	MCF7	0.6059	0.6151	0.6569	0.6100		**0.6752**	0.6477
	MDAMB231	0.6191	0.5859	0.6300	0.6138	**0.6896**	0.6586	0.6288
	NKDBA	0.6121	0.5950	0.6267	0.6130	**0.6647**	0.6091	0.6129
	NOMO1	0.5888	0.5100	0.5758	0.5689	0.5590	**0.5920**	0.4933
	PC3	0.6055	0.6153	0.6453	0.6074	**0.6644**		0.6386
	SKBR3	0.6057	0.5599	0.6161	0.5757	**0.6575**	0.6311	0.5835
	THP1	0.5849	0.5427	0.5922	0.5841	**0.6019**	0.5848	0.5697
	U266	**0.6430**	0.6557	0.6408	0.6136	0.6035	0.6249	0.5553
	U937	0.5908	0.5800	0.6002	**0.6067**	0.5710	0.6046	0.5772
	VCAP	0.5956	0.5970	0.6238	0.5924	0.6281	**0.6387**	
Down	A375	0.6228		0.6648	0.6575	0.6563	**0.6671**	0.6317
	A549	0.5799	0.5884		0.5933	0.6309	**0.6352**	0.6162
	BT20	0.6236	0.6222	0.6620	0.6303	**0.7064**	0.6697	0.6188
	HA1E	0.6331	0.6685	0.6673	0.6505	0.6693	**0.6954**	0.6723
	HCC515	0.6184	0.6440	0.6836	0.6488	0.6885	**0.7073**	0.6776
	HEK293T	0.6982	0.7408	0.7752	0.7292	**0.7781**	0.6995	0.7610
	HEPG2	0.6653	**0.7457**	0.7450	0.7039	0.7415	0.7421	0.6554
	HL60	**0.7314**	0.6375	0.6507	0.6811	0.6235	0.6327	0.6659
	HS578T	0.6121	0.6203	0.6621	0.6469	**0.6964**	0.6575	0.6374
	HT29	0.6199	**0.6969**	0.6709		0.6742	0.6718	0.6396
	HUH7	0.6469	0.6543	0.6766	0.6777	**0.6955**	0.6708	0.6783
	JURKAT	0.6679	**0.7213**	0.6766	0.6820	0.5887	0.6649	0.6359
	MCF10A	0.6355	0.6396	0.6510	0.6559	**0.6805**	0.6800	0.6469
	MCF7	0.6148	0.6240	0.6600	0.6207		**0.6950**	0.6575
	MDAMB231	0.6595	0.6323	0.6702	0.6395	**0.7080**	0.6845	0.6370
	NKDBA	0.6320	0.6387	0.6364	0.6289	**0.6673**	0.6345	0.6252
	NOMO1	0.5725	0.5049	0.5858	0.5596	0.5649	**0.6268**	0.5099
	PC3	0.6118	0.6166	0.6526	0.6209	**0.6740**		0.6489
	SKBR3	0.6472	0.6325	0.6320	0.6474	**0.6937**	0.6545	0.6116
	THP1	0.6326	0.5687	0.5944	0.5802	**0.6413**	0.6338	0.5806
	U266	0.6799	0.6907	0.7053	0.6524	0.6506	**0.7065**	0.5438
	U937	0.5641	0.5860	0.5903	0.5786	0.5697	0.5750	**0.5913**
	VCAP	0.5965	0.6014	0.6197	0.6007	0.6272	**0.6458**	

Table 4. AUC scores of regulated genes on transfer-drug-split 10-fold data, rows and columns indicate target and source cell lines. The best results in a row are indicated in bold.

	Target cell ↓	Source cell						
		No-TL	A375	A549	HT29	MCF7	PC3	VCAP
Up	A375	**0.6145**		0.6065	0.5943	0.5933	0.6060	0.5767
	A549	**0.5864**	0.5414		0.5354	0.5711	0.5780	0.5572
	BT20	0.5952	0.5156	0.5765	0.5440	**0.6019**	0.5729	0.5409
	HA1E	0.6220	0.5979	0.6096	0.5913	0.6059	**0.6252**	0.6085
	HCC515	0.6136	0.5843	0.6164	0.5899	0.6155	**0.6381**	0.6169
	HEK293T	0.6165	**0.6302**	0.5973	0.5891	0.5685	0.5517	0.5673
	HEPG2	0.6096	0.6504	0.6458	0.6255	0.6302	**0.6517**	0.5811
	HL60	0.6063	0.5978	0.5479	**0.6268**	0.5572	0.5543	0.5590
	HS578T	0.5762	0.5426	0.5796	0.5746	**0.6263**	0.5851	0.5655
	HT29	0.6197	**0.6223**	0.6076		0.6028	0.5999	0.5781
	HUH7	**0.6428**	0.5984	0.6334	0.6157	0.6274	0.6221	0.5978
	JURKAT	0.5558	**0.6663**	0.6485	0.6325	0.6208	0.6652	0.6300
	MCF10A	**0.6434**	0.5687	0.5845	0.5827	0.6160	0.6005	0.5722
	MCF7	0.6059	0.5612	0.5896	0.5569		**0.6139**	0.5857
	MDAMB231	0.6191	0.5545	0.5905	0.5852	**0.6397**	0.6074	0.5700
	NKDBA	0.6121	0.5408	0.5623	0.5565	**0.6205**	0.5665	0.5797
	NOMO1	**0.5888**	0.5472	0.4782	0.4862	0.4978	0.5132	0.4282
	PC3	0.6055	0.5619	0.5874	0.5554	**0.6061**		0.5835
	SKBR3	0.6057	0.5306	0.5651	0.5460	**0.6196**	0.5798	0.5416
	THP1	**0.5849**	0.5095	0.5489	0.5360	0.5417	0.5522	0.4967
	U266	0.6430	**0.6619**	0.6252	0.5920	0.5915	0.6056	0.5308
	U937	**0.5968**	0.5570	0.5632	0.5792	0.5665	0.5739	0.5360
	VCAP	**0.5956**	0.5446	0.5680	0.5419	0.5755	0.5845	
Down	A375	**0.6228**		0.6085	0.6005	0.5962	0.6085	0.5765
	A549	**0.5799**	0.5376		0.5403	0.5727	0.5719	0.5594
	BT20	0.6236	0.5764	0.5992	0.5851	**0.6353**	0.6149	0.5696
	HA1E	0.6331	0.6029	0.6081	0.5890	0.6085	**0.6337**	0.6155
	HCC515	0.6184	0.5854	0.6166	0.5870	0.6239	**0.6455**	0.6270
	HEK293T	**0.6982**	0.6496	0.5940	0.5941	0.6015	0.6014	0.6125
	HEPG2	0.6653	**0.6693**	0.6693	0.6476	0.6639	0.6611	0.6072
	HL60	**0.7314**	0.6355	0.6215	0.6722	0.6274	0.6164	0.6266
	HS578T	0.6121	0.5725	0.6025	0.5900	**0.6534**	0.6029	0.5771
	HT29	0.6199	**0.6274**	0.6050		0.6046	0.6039	0.5761
	HUH7	**0.6469**	0.6113	0.6150	0.6275	0.6397	0.6126	0.6026
	JURKAT	0.7107	**0.7162**	0.6795	0.6728	0.6581	0.6953	0.6088
	MCF10A	**0.6355**	0.5980	0.6067	0.6163	0.6281	0.6200	0.6011
	MCF7	0.6148	0.5686	0.5962	0.5646		**0.6200**	0.5938
	MDAMB231	0.6595	0.5882	0.6082	0.6025	**0.6615**	0.6188	0.5855
	NKDBA	**0.6320**	0.5843	0.5739	0.5785	0.6219	0.5668	0.5589
	NOMO1	**0.5725**	0.4693	0.5309	0.4847	0.5083	0.5448	0.4489
	PC3	0.6118	0.5634	0.5925	0.5655	**0.6156**		0.5940
	SKBR3	0.6472	0.5858	0.5971	0.6041	**0.6495**	0.6131	0.5767
	THP1	**0.6326**	0.5500	0.5382	0.5443	0.5967	0.5946	0.5165
	U266	**0.6799**	0.6535	0.6438	0.5995	0.6150	0.6452	0.5164
	U937	0.5641	0.5605	0.5575	0.5747	**0.5837**	0.5476	0.5779
	VCAP	**0.5965**	0.5462	0.5637	0.5464	0.5753	0.5888	

to cold-drug-split. It is easier to improve upon on a worse baseline. Also, the complications in the random-drug-split makes it harder to improve its scores, of which we will discuss in the next section.

Lastly, two target cell lines dominate the top 10: JURKAT, and HEPG2. Interestingly, the reason behind them are polar opposites. For HEPG2, similar improvements are not visible in the transfer-drug-split experiments, therefore the benefits of transfer learning must be coming from the same drugs that are also tested on the source cell line. For the JURKAT cell line, the average improvement goes up by 63% when we switch to transfer-drug-split, which eliminates drugs tested on the source cell line. This points to better generalization for the target, and greater transferred knowledge from the source cell line.

Table 5. Transfer learning experiments that showed the most improvements for the direction of differential expression (DE) and split.

	Source - Target	Improvement (DE, split)
1	A375 - JURKAT	22.81% (Up, cold)
2	PC3 - HEPG2	21.19% (Up, cold)
3	A375 - JURKAT	19.88% (Up, transfer)
4	A375 - HEPG2	19.70% (Up, cold)
5	A549 - JURKAT	19.69% (Up, transfer)
6	PC3 - JURKAT	19.68% (Up, transfer)
7	A549 - HEPG2	17.98% (Up, cold)
8	MCF7 - HS578T	16.71% (Up, cold)
9	A549 - JURKAT	16.69% (Up, transfer)
10	MCF7 - NKDBA	15.73% (Up, random)

3.2 Complications of Using Random Split

The main idea behind DeepCOP is simple, yet effective: Utilizing differentiable characteristics of outputs lets us treat multiple genes' perturbation values as a single objective. This method populates the amount of data for each compound, retains the relation between individual genes, and gives each output a new meaning. However, for this theory to simulate real-life occurrences, the population should be done after the required validation split. To further demonstrate as an example; the THP1 cell line included in this study contains 18 different compounds. From the original data, we get 978 gene perturbations for each compound. After populating this data, we end up with 17,604 samples. However, we only have 18 unique compounds and 978 unique gene descriptors. Splitting this dataset into 10 random folds almost guarantees the possibility of data leakage.

There are two causes for this data leakage; duplicate genes, and compounds. In the L1000 dataset, an experiment corresponds to one compound, and its gene perturbation effects on a cell line. After the data processing step, we have ended up with the same compound repeated in 978 samples to predict each gene separately. Randomly splitting this data means separating the gene outputs of a single experiment into different folds. It also implies that our model is learning to predict individual gene perturbations from the outcomes of other genes, for the same compound. This is an unrealistic and trivial task, since every gene perturbation is measured simultaneously for that experiment.

To counteract the data leakage caused by gene repetition, we would have to implement a transfer-gene split, where we would split 978 genes into different folds and populate the folds with the compounds. However, this splitting method is the polar opposite of the objective of HTS, since we're trying to simulate an untested compound's effects on existing genes and not the other way around. Therefore, can be ignored for this study.

3.3   Random-Split in Source Model Training

In this study, we have trained our source models on a random 95%-5% train-validation split with early stopping. From our previous remarks about random-split, the credibility of these source models should also be questioned.

For our initial experiments, we were using the non-TL models we've trained for the random-split experiments as source models. When the problem of random-split arose, we've switched our source models to use 100% of the source data. This resulted in worse evaluations for the target model, due to the source network not being optimized for such a task. In an effort to minimize the negative effects of data leakage, while keeping the benefits of early stopping; we've decided on the 95%-5% random split. It should be noted that the 95%-5% split still negatively affects the training of the source models, and for a state-of-the-art product; source models should be first optimized on a compound-based split and trained on 100% of the source data.

3.4   Splitting Up and Down Regulations

In L1000, gene perturbations can be split into 3 categories; up-regulated, neutral, and down-regulated. Multi-class classification is a special case of classification problems and is usually harder to model compared to binary classification problems.

DeepCOP and subsequently this study divides what normally is a multi-class classification problem into 2 binary classifications. While this widely-used practice makes the data easier to model, it also comes at a cost of lost knowledge.

Specifically, in this application, the relation between up and down-regulated outputs is lost, because our binary classifications are "actively up-regulated to not significantly up-regulated" and "actively down-regulated to not significantly down-regulated". Training an ideal for the first problem would require a greater penalty to classify an actively down-regulated sample as actively up-regulated than to classify a non-regulated sample as one; and vice versa for the second problem.

Modeling the problem as multi-class showed that the features are not descriptive enough to model the added difficulty, at least for this type of neural network. The most obvious solution would be using a custom loss function that uses the results of an oppositely-regulated problem. Another possible solution could be transfer learning. Utilizing the weights of up-regulated models in down-regulated models, or modeling up and down-regulation as subnetworks of the same neural network, has the potential to utilize the lost knowledge.

4   Conclusion

In this study, we tried to exhibit the benefit of using the natural genetic similarities in between cell lines for chemogenomic machine learning. While doing so, we have introduced 2 splitting methods to DeepCOP to better evaluate the strength of its methodology. Based upon the initial study of DeepCOP, our results have shown improvements of 10.65% on average for the introduced colddrug-split. While there is a definite improvement in the results, this study should be treated as a simple demonstration, and can be further optimized for even better results. As it stands, this study is a testament for the usage of transfer learning in chemogenomics, and a demonstration on how it can be utilized. Moving forward, we're planning on implementing other methods of transfer learning, applying transfer learning on more than 2 cell line combinations, and optimize them to further illustrate the optimum possible result out of this methodology.

References

1. Bredel, M., Jacoby, E.: Chemogenomics: an emerging strategy for rapid target and drug discovery. Nat. Rev. Genet. **5**(4), 262–275 (2004)
2. Gene Ontology Consortium, et al.: The gene ontology (GO) database and informatics resource. Nucleic Acids Res. **32**(suppl_1), D258–D261 (2004)
3. Gobbi, A., Poppinger, D.: Genetic optimization of combinatorial libraries. Biotechnol. Bioeng. **61**(1), 47–54 (1998)
4. Li, H., et al.: Modern deep learning in bioinformatics. J. Mol. Cell Biol. **12**(11), 823–827 (2020)
5. Li, Y., Huang, C., Ding, L., Li, Z., Pan, Y., Gao, X.: Deep learning in bioinformatics: Introduction, application, and perspective in the big data era. Methods **166**, 4–21 (2019)
6. RDKit: Open-source cheminformatics. http://www.rdkit.org. Accessed Mar 2021
7. Rogers, D., Hahn, M.: Extended-connectivity fingerprints. J. Chem. Inf. Model. **50**(5), 742–754 (2010)
8. Subramanian, A., et al.: A next generation connectivity map: L1000 platform and the first 1,000,000 profiles. Cell **171**(6), 1437–1452 (2017)
9. Tang, B., Pan, Z., Yin, K., Khateeb, A.: Recent advances of deep learning in bioinformatics and computational biology. Front. Genet. **10**, 214 (2019)
10. Woo, G., Fernandez, M., Hsing, M., Lack, N.A., Cavga, A.D., Cherkasov, A.: DeepCOP: deep learning-based approach to predict gene regulating effects of small molecules. Bioinformatics **36**(3), 813–818 (2020)

Transfer Learning with Jukebox for Music Source Separation

Wadhah Zai El Amri$^{(\boxtimes)}$, Oliver Tautz, Helge Ritter, and Andrew Melnik

Bielefeld University, Bielefeld, Germany
wadhah.zai.papers@gmail.com, helge@techfak.uni-bielefeld.de

Abstract. In this work, we demonstrate how a publicly available, pre-trained *Jukebox* model can be adapted for the problem of audio source separation from a single mixed audio channel. Our neural network architecture, which is using transfer learning, is quick to train and the results demonstrate performance comparable to other state-of-the-art approaches that require a lot more compute resources, training data, and time. We provide an open-source code implementation of our architecture (https://github.com/wzaielamri/unmix).

1 Introduction and Related Work

Source separation is an important issue in many fields such as audio processing, image processing [9], EEG [8,10], etc. Music source separation from mixed audio is a challenging problem, especially when the source itself should be learned from a dataset of examples. Additionally, such models are expensive to train from scratch. We tested our model on the MUSDB18-HQ [14] dataset which supplies full songs with ground truth stems of 'bass', 'drums', 'vocals' and 'other', which includes instruments such as guitars, synths, etc. The task is to separate a mixed audio channel into the separately recorded instruments, called stems here. Most baseline models in the Music Demixing Challenge 2021 [11] used masking of input transformed to the frequency domain by short-time Fourier transformation such as UMX [18]. This older technique transforms the waveform into a three dimensional input that can be viewed as a picture. The model then computes a 'mask' which substracts parts of the audio in frequency domain before transforming back to listenable audio. *Demucs* [1] on the other hand showed a successful approach that works in waveform domain, where an autoencoder, based on a bidirectional long short-term memory network, is used.

This success of such a solution (using waveforms) encouraged us to adapt *Jukebox* [3], a powerful, generative model using multiple, deep Vector Quantized-Variational Autoencoders (VQ-VAE) [12] to automatically generate real sounding music, and using its publicly available pre-trained weights for the task.

Transfer learning helped deep learning models reach new heights in many domains, such as natural language processing [2,13] and computer vision [4,5].

The original version of this chapter was revised: an error in name of a co-author was corrected. The correction to this chapter is available at
https://doi.org/10.1007/978-3-031-08337-2_42

© IFIP International Federation for Information Processing 2022, corrected publication 2022
Published by Springer Nature Switzerland AG 2022
I. Maglogiannis et al. (Eds.): AIAI 2022, IFIP AICT 647, pp. 426–433, 2022.
https://doi.org/10.1007/978-3-031-08337-2_35

Although relatively unexplored for the audio domain, [7] proved feature representation learned on speech data could be used to classify sound events. Their results verify that cross-acoustic transfer learning performs significantly better than a baseline trained from scratch. TRILL [16] showed great results of pre-training deep learning models with an unsupervised task on a big dataset of speech samples. Its learned representations exceeded SOTA performance on several downstream tasks with datasets of limited size.

We take a similar approach that is heavily based on *Jukebox* [3]. It uses multiple VQ-VAEs to compress raw audio into discrete codes. They are trained self-supervised, on a large dataset of about 1.2 million songs, needing the compute power of 256 V100 to train in an acceptable time. Our experiments show that *Jukebox's* learned representations can be used for the task of source separation.

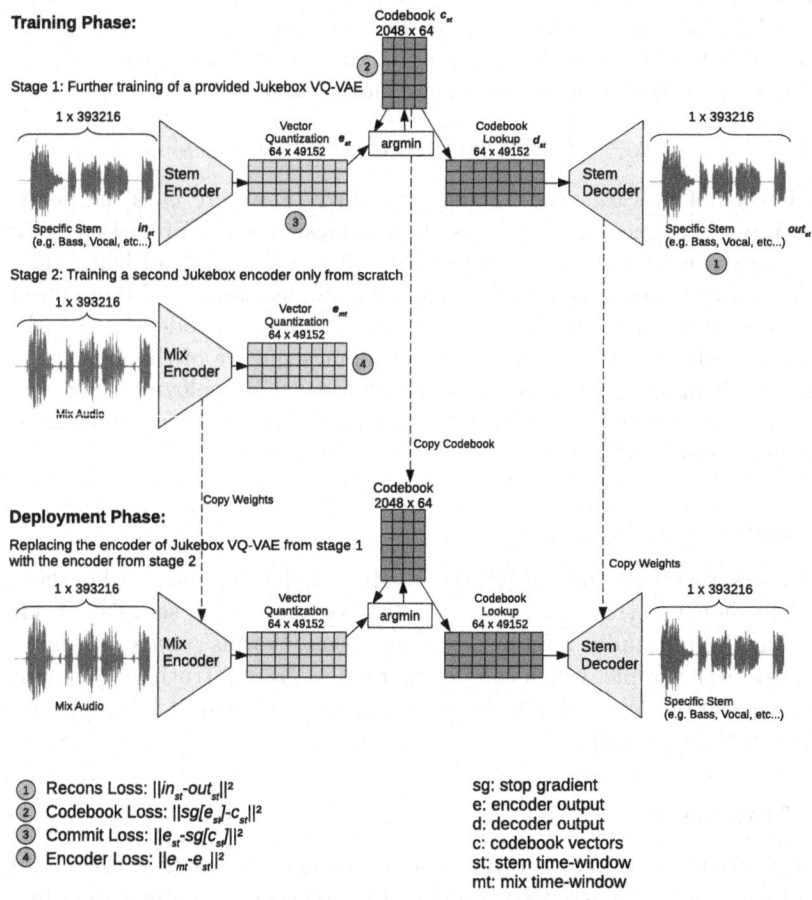

Fig. 1. Visualization of the proposed transfer learning model architecture.

2   Method

2.1   Architecture

Our architecture utilizes the default *Jukebox's* [3] variant of the publicly available pre-trained VQ-VAE model. *Jukebox* uses three separated VQ-VAEs. We use only the smallest one with the strongest compression, due to the low resource usage. It employs dilated 1-D convolutions in multiple residual blocks to find a less complex sequence representation of music. An audio sequence x_t gets mapped by an encoder E_1 to a latent space $e_t = E_1(x_t)$ of 64 dimensions so that it can be mapped to the closest prototype vector in a collection C of vectors called *codebook*. These 2048 prototype vectors, denoted c_{st}, are learned in training and help to form a high-quality representation.

The rate of compression for a sequence is called the hop length, for which a value of 8 is used. It depends on the stride values of the convolutional layers. We set the stride value to 2 as well as the downsampling to 3. All other values remain as defined in [3]. After mapping to the codebook, a decoder D aims to reconstruct the original sequence. In summary, Eq. (1)

$$y_t = D(argmin_c(\|E_1(x_t) - c)\|) \text{ for } c \in C \tag{1}$$

describes a full forward pass through the VQ-VAE, where y_t is the prediction for an input sequence x_t and $\|.\|$ is the euclidean norm. For further technical details on the used VQ-VAE architecture, refer to the paper of Dhariwal et al. [3]. The model is fine-tuned on data for one stem, learning good representations for a single instrument. In addition, we train a second encoder E_2, identical to the one already mentioned, to project an input sequence of the mixture to the space already known by the codebook and decoder. For deployment, the encoder of the VQ-VAE is switched with the second one, effectively mapping from the full mixture to one stem.

2.2   Data

Our models are trained on the MUSDB18-HQ [14] dataset, also used in the music demixing challenge [11]. It consists of 150 full-length songs, sampled at 44KHz, providing the full audio mixture and four stems, 'vocals', 'bass', 'drums', and 'other' for each sample, which can be regarded as ground truth in the context of source separation. We train on the full train set composed of 100 songs, testing is done on the remaining 50.

2.3   Training

For each stem i = 1 ... 4, we train a model in two phases (see Fig. 1). In the first phase, the model is trained on data that present the chosen stem in isolation (i.e. not embedded in a mixture). This produces a VQ-VAE with a "single stem encoder" (SE_i) that can map a single stem into a good latent representation, followed by a "stem decoder" (SD_i) tuned to reconstruct the input after the "discretization bottleneck" as faithfully as possible. Training of each VQ-VAE is based on the same three losses as chosen in the original Jukebox paper [3]: $L = L_{recons} + L_{codebook} + \beta L_{commit}$. However, our final goal is to process each stem when it is part of a mixture of all four stems. Such embedding will introduce distortion of each stem, requiring to replace each single stem encoder SE_i from phase 1 by a corresponding "mixture stem encoder" (ME_i) that is trained in phase 2, to map its changed (mixture embedded) stem i input onto the representation (stem-i codebook prototypes) created in phase by the SE_i-SD_i encoder-decoder pair. So, for each stem i (now omitting index i in the following) for each training sample (x_{mt}: the sequence of the mixed audio, x_{st}: the sequence of stem audio), we feed x_{st}, to the already trained encoder SE, producing e_{st}. Separately, the full mixture x_{mt} is passed through the new encoder ME, yielding e_{mt}. Now, we can backpropagate through ME using MSE loss $||e_{st} - e_{mt}||^2$ (keeping SE fixed throughout phase 2). It would also be possible to train E2 end-to-end, similar to training phase 1. This could be done in two ways, freezing the weights of the rest of the VQ-VAE or fine-tuning further. With frozen weights, the best reachable performance would be identical to our current approach, but training time would be increased. Continuing to fine-tune would most probably lead to more source bleeding because the embeddings no longer represent only the stem they were trained on in training phase 1, so we decided against training end-to-end.

Finally, we obtain our mixture-adapted final VQ-VAE by concatenating the trained mixture stem encoder ME with the stem decoder SD. Note that this procedure will be carried out for each of the four stems, yielding four correspondingly optimized "stem mixture encoder-decoders" that together provide our decomposition of the mixture input into its stem constituents. On a more technical note, in both training phases and deployment, the data is processed chunk-wise, with a size of about 9 s.

For a clear overview of the content of this section, refer to Fig. 1. All conducted experiments that will be defined in the next section were computed on two Tesla GPUs with 16 Gb each. The length of each input sequence is equal to 393216 data points as used by *Jukebox*. The batch size is equal to 4.

$$SDR_{stem} = 10 \log_{10} \frac{\sum_n ||s(n)||^2 + \epsilon}{\sum_n ||s(n) - \hat{s}(n)||^2 + \epsilon} \tag{2}$$

To benchmark the conducted experiments, signal-to-distortion ratio (SDR) metric is used, which is a common metric in other SOTA papers [1,6,15,17,18]. It is computed by Eq. (2), as stated in [11], where $s(n)$ is the values of the ground truth and $\hat{s}(n)$ depicts the values of the prediction. A small value $\epsilon = 10^{-7}$ is added to avoid division by zero. 'Total' SDR is the mean SDR for all stems (Table 1).

Table 1. Comparison of SDR values per stem and in total for three different versions of our approach.

SDR values					
Method	Drum	Bass	Other	Vocal	Total
Our approach (i)	4.925	4.073	2.695	5.060	4.188
Our approach trained from scratch (ii)	−0.002	−0.087	−0.026	0.00	−0.028
Our approach without finetuning (iii)	1.06	−1.072	0.79	0.33	0.279

Table 2. Comparison of SDR values per stem and in total. Our approach outperforms both the *ScaledMixturePredictor*, the basic baseline in the Music Demixing Challenge [11] and *Wave-U-Net* [17], a classic approach of source seperation in the waveform domain while *Demucs* [1] achieves current SOTA performance on the Dataset.

SDR values					
Method	Drum	Bass	Other	Vocal	Total
DEMUCS	6.509	6.470	4.018	6.496	5.873
Our approach	4.925	4.073	2.695	5.060	4.188
Wave-U-Net	4.22	3.21	2.25	3.25	3.23
ScaledMixturePredictor	0.578	0.745	1.136	1.090	0.887

3   Experiments and Results

The main key point of this paper consists of demonstrating that it is possible to get decent audio quality by using transfer learning. For this, we did three different experiments (i), (ii), and (iii) on the four audio stems. In experiment (i) we trained each audio stem's stem encoder SE from scratch without using any pretraining values. For the second experiment (ii) we trained the SE's with initial weights chosen as the pre-trained weights of Jukebox. Experiment (iii) is conducted to show the impact of fine-tuning the SE. We skip fine-tuning in training phase 1 and use the weights of Jukebox as is and train a ME like in the other phases.

For all these VQ-VAE, we pick the checkpoint 80K and train the corresponding mixture encoders ME in phase 2. For these, and in both experiments (i) (ii) and (iii), we initialized their weights randomly. For the first experiment, we found out that all results are bad, and no good audio quality is reached for the extracted stems. The SDR values are equal to or near 0 for all four stems. For the second experiment, the model converges after 32 h of training in total on two Tesla GPU units with 16 GB of VRAM each. (iii) shows that fine-tuning in phase 1 is important.

Figure 2 demonstrates decent SDR values for networks trained with pre-trained weights in comparison to others trained with randomly initialized weights from scratch. It can also be deduced that in order to get fairly good SDR values, it is enough to train until early checkpoint values, such as 20K. Then, the checkpoint 20K is reached after 16 h for each of the two models on two Tesla GPUs. Table 2 gives a comparison of different approaches for audio signal separation. Here, our approach achieves comparable results when benchmarked against other state-of-the-art networks.

In terms of deployment, we need 0.73 s of CPU processing time for an audio chunk of 8.91 s per stem, which translates into an RTF (Real-Time Factor) of 0.082. That seems quick, but the current implementation of our model takes an audio chunk of 8.91 s. As with most approaches to audio source separation, direct online processing is not possible. However, a single code vector of the VQ-VAE represents a sliding window of an input vector of 49152 timesteps, which corresponds to about 1s of audio with a sampling rate of 44.1k. So, we think that an adapted architecture could be more flexible.

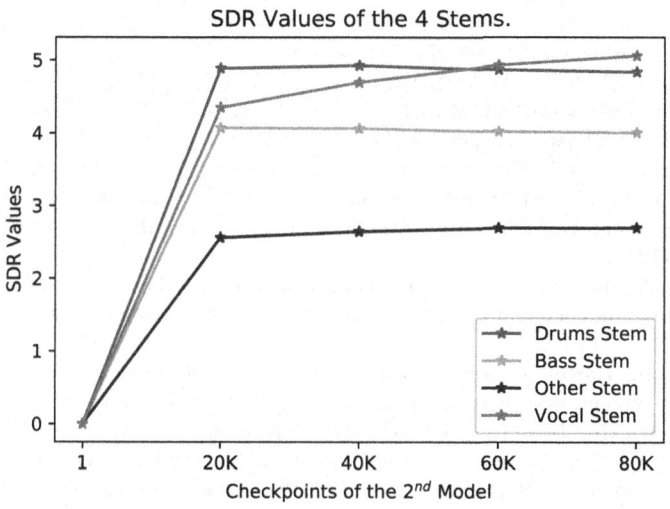

Fig. 2. SDR results of the 4 audio signal stems for the second experiment.

4 Conclusion

We demonstrate how transfer learning can be used for a problem of audio signal processing, in particular for the separation of an audio signal from a single mixed audio channel into four different stems: 'drums', 'bass', 'vocals', and 'other'. We show that it is possible to be successful with a small data set and relatively short training time on just two GPUs by fine-tuning pre-trained weights of *Jukebox* [3]. Similar results could not be achieved in a comparable timeframe when training from scratch or without fine-tuning, showing the potential for reduced training times and improving results through the use of transfer learning in the audio domain.

References

1. Défossez, A., Usunier, N., Bottou, L., Bach, F.R.: Demucs: deep extractor for music sources with extra unlabeled data remixed. CoRR abs/1909.01174 (2019). http://arxiv.org/abs/1909.01174
2. Devlin, J., Chang, M., Lee, K., Toutanova, K.: BERT: pre-training of deep bidirectional transformers for language understanding. CoRR abs/1810.04805 (2018). http://arxiv.org/abs/1810.04805
3. Dhariwal, P., Jun, H., Payne, C., Kim, J.W., Radford, A., Sutskever, I.: Jukebox: a generative model for music (2020)
4. Gao, Y., Mosalam, K.M.: Deep transfer learning for image-based structural damage recognition: deep transfer learning for image-based structural damage recognition. Comput. Aided Civ. Infrastruct. Eng. 33(9), 748–768 (2018)
5. Han, D., Liu, Q., Fan, W.: A new image classification method using CNN transfer learning and web data augmentation. Exp. Syst. Appl. 95, 43–56 (2018). https://doi.org/10.1016/j.eswa.2017.11.028. https://www.sciencedirect.com/science/article/pii/S0957417417307844
6. Hennequin, R., Khlif, A., Voituret, F., Moussallam, M.: Spleeter: a fast and efficient music source separation tool with pre-trained models. J. Open Source Softw. 5(50), 2154 (2020). https://doi.org/10.21105/joss.02154
7. Lim, H., Kim, M.J., Kim, H.: Cross-acoustic transfer learning for sound event classification. In: 2016 IEEE International Conference on Acoustics, Speech and Signal Processing (ICASSP), pp. 2504–2508 (2016). https://doi.org/10.1109/ICASSP.2016.7472128
8. Melnik, A., Hairston, W.D., Ferris, D.P., König, P.: EEG correlates of sensorimotor processing: independent components involved in sensory and motor processing. Sci. Rep. 7(1), 1–15 (2017)
9. Melnik, A., Harter, A., Limberg, C., Rana, K., Sünderhauf, N., Ritter, H.: Critic guided segmentation of rewarding objects in first-person views. In: Edelkamp, S., Möller, R., Rueckert, E. (eds.) KI 2021: Advances in Artificial Intelligence: 44th German Conference on AI, Virtual Event, 27 September–1 October 2021, Proceedings, pp. 338–348. Springer, Cham (2021). https://doi.org/10.1007/978-3-030-87626-5_25
10. Melnik, A., et al.: Systems, subjects, sessions: to what extent do these factors influence EEG data? Front. Hum. Neurosci. 11, 150 (2017)
11. Mitsufuji, Y., Fabbro, G., Uhlich, S., Stöter, F.R.: Music demixing challenge 2021 (2021). https://doi.org/10.48550/ARXIV.2108.13559. https://arxiv.org/abs/2108.13559
12. van den Oord, A., Vinyals, O., Kavukcuoglu, K.: Neural discrete representation learning. CoRR abs/1711.00937 (2017). http://arxiv.org/abs/1711.00937
13. Raffel, C., et al.: Exploring the limits of transfer learning with a unified text-to-text transformer. CoRR abs/1910.10683 (2019). http://arxiv.org/abs/1910.10683
14. Rafii, Z., Liutkus, A., Stöter, F.R., Mimilakis, S.I., Bittner, R.: MUSDB18-HQ - an uncompressed version of MUSDB18 (December 2019). https://doi.org/10.5281/zenodo.3338373
15. Sawata, R., Uhlich, S., Takahashi, S., Mitsufuji, Y.: All for one and one for all: improving music separation by bridging networks (2021)
16. Shor, J., et al.: Towards learning a universal non-semantic representation of speech. In: Interspeech 2020 (October 2020). https://doi.org/10.21437/interspeech.2020-1242

17. Stoller, D., Ewert, S., Dixon, S.: Wave-U-Net: a multi-scale neural network for end-to-end audio source separation (2018)
18. Stöter, F.R., Uhlich, S., Liutkus, A., Mitsufuji, Y.: Open-Unmix - a reference implementation for music source separation. J. Open Source Softw. 4(41), 1667 (2019). https://doi.org/10.21105/joss.01667

Unsupervised Modeling

An Inductive System Monitoring Approach for GNSS Activation

Shahrooz Abghari[1]([✉]) [ID], Veselka Boeva[1]([✉]) [ID], Emiliano Casalicchio[1] [ID],
and Peter Exner[2] [ID]

[1] Blekinge Institute of Technology, Karlskrona, Sweden
{shahrooz.abghari,veselka.boeva,emiliano.casalicchio}@bth.se
[2] Sony R&D Center Lund Laboratory, Lund, Sweden
peter.exner@sony.com

Abstract. In this paper, we propose a Global Navigation Satellite System (GNSS) component activation model for mobile tracking devices that automatically detects indoor/outdoor environments using the radio signals received from Long-Term Evolution (LTE) base stations. We use an Inductive System Monitoring (ISM) technique to model environmental scenarios captured by a smart tracker via extracting clusters of corresponding value ranges from LTE base stations' signal strength. The ISM-based model is built by using the tracker's historical data labeled with GPS coordinates. The built model is further refined by applying it to additional data without GPS location collected by the same device. This procedure allows us to identify the clusters that describe semi-outdoor scenarios. In that way, the model discriminates between two outdoor environmental categories: open outdoor and semi-outdoor. The proposed ISM-based GNSS activation approach is studied and evaluated on a real-world dataset contains radio signal measurements collected by five smart trackers and their geographical location in various environmental scenarios.

Keywords: Environmental context detection · GNSS signal · Inductive system monitoring · Clustering analysis

1 Introduction

Global Navigation Satellite System (GNSS) is a positioning technique that can be used for detecting the current position of a portable smart device. It utilizes any satellite constellation capable of providing Positioning, Navigation, and Timing (PNT) services on a global or regional basis. The localization of devices such as smartphones and trackers in outdoor areas typically relies on GNSS such as

This work is part of the Sony RAP 2020 Project "Distributed and Adaptive Edge-based AI Models for Sensor Networks". We thank Hannes Bergkvist (Sony R&D Center Lund Laboratory) for his contribution to the data collection.

ⓒ IFIP International Federation for Information Processing 2022
Published by Springer Nature Switzerland AG 2022
I. Maglogiannis et al. (Eds.): AIAI 2022, IFIP AICT 647, pp. 437–449, 2022.
https://doi.org/10.1007/978-3-031-08337-2_36

the Global Positioning System (GPS), which is known to perform well in open sky environments. However, these devices may operate in any environment, e.g., open outdoors, semi-outdoors, and indoors. In addition, battery power is a limitation for any portable smart device such as trackers or smartphones. Therefore, detecting the devices' environment and providing context-aware information in various scenarios can be helpful and lead to battery-saving solutions.

A review of existing GNSS and onboard vision-based solutions for environmental context detection has been conducted in [5]. The main finding of this work is that most of the existing context-aware solutions are based on one type of sensor (GNSS or vision) and are designed basically to perform sensor management in binary indoor/outdoor situations. Other recent works studying indoor/outdoor detection methods based on Machine Learning (ML) techniques are [4,6,7,13,15,16]. For example, in [15] the authors investigate a wide range of supervised ML algorithms for detecting four types of indoor/outdoor environments based on an approach using the Global System for Mobile communications (GSM) signal strength. The main idea is that different environmental scenarios lead to different signal strength characteristics. By learning various signal strength characteristics would be possible to determine the smart device's surrounding environment. GNSS measurements from Android smartphones are leveraged in [16] to detect indoor/outdoor complex environments. The authors extract spatial geometry distribution, time sequence, and statistical features from the GNSS measurements through Android smart mobile devices. Supervised ML algorithms are then used to predict indoor/outdoor status, which is interpreted as the observations of the Hidden Markov Model (HMM) to detect the transition between indoor/outdoor in complex scenarios. A similar solution to detect environmental context is proposed in [7]. In [4], an approach is introduced that uses ensemble learning methods such as Random Forest (RF) and AdaBoost to detect indoor/outdoor environments according to the different daily activities of users. Souza et al. [13], propose an interesting approach that integrates supervised and unsupervised ML techniques for indoor/outdoor detection.

In this paper, in contrast to the most published ML-based indoor/outdoor detection methods, we propose using a clustering technique to build a GNSS component activation model. Namely, the proposed approach is based on the Inductive System Monitoring (ISM) method introduced in [8]. Our ISM-based indoor/outdoor detection approach, similar to the idea studied in [15] uses the cellular signal strength to detect the environment. In this context, an ISM model of a given smart device can be created by using the device's historical data marked with geographic locations. The model is built by extracting clusters of related value ranges for the neighboring Long-Term Evolution (LTE) base stations' signal strength. The built model is further refined by using the remaining data without GPS location to discriminate between open outdoor and semi-outdoor scenarios. Each cluster models a specific environmental scenario by defining a range of allowable values for each cellular base station in a given input vector. In that way, our model not only supplies the user with easily interpretable representations of the device's environmental scenarios, but it is also small as it has modest requirements with respect to storage and computations.

2 Related Work

According to [16] the existing indoor/outdoor detection methods can be classified into two main groups: fixed detection rules or threshold-based techniques and ML-based techniques. While approaches in the first group use fixed detection rules and thresholds, making them difficult to adapt to different environments and devices, techniques in the second group use ML algorithms to detect indoor/outdoor status based on features extracted from devices. Since the approach proposed in this study belongs to the second group, ML-based indoor/outdoor environment detection techniques are reviewed in this section.

In [3], an approach, entitled SenseMe, uses the C4.5 algorithm on data generated from GPS, gyroscope, accelerometer, and Bluetooth to module the sensed environmental context, as well as the context-aware location. In [14], the authors proposed a sound-based indoor/outdoor detection method that utilizes binary classification of the environment's acoustic reverberation features. Reverte et al. [11] employed a binary classification technique on the Received Signal Strength Indicator (RSSI) from 802.11 access points to identify a pedestrian's indoor or outdoor status. Ashraf et al. [2] proposed MagIO, a solution that utilizes magnetic field signals sensed by smartphones for detecting indoor/outdoor states. Magnetic field features are classified with different ML algorithms, including Support Vector Machines (SVM), gradient booster machines, RF, k-nearest neighbor, and decision trees. In [15], the authors applied an ML algorithm to classify the neighboring GSM base station's signal in different environments and identify the users' current context by signal recognition. Radu et al. [9] propose to detect indoor/outdoor context by employing co-training according to the feature of light, magnetic, and cell sensors. The proposed solution can automatically learn the characteristics of new environments and devices, thus providing a detection accuracy that exceeds 90% even in unfamiliar circumstances. Multiple contextual features are also used in [1], which leveraged J48 and other ML algorithms to detect the indoor/outdoor state with high accuracy. In [12], an indoor and outdoor classification system that relies solely on light measurements is introduced. More specifically, the system measures ultraviolet light, color temperature, luminosity, and red, green, blue, and clear components of light at 1-minute intervals. Three ML algorithms, SVM, artificial neural network, and bagged tree, are trained and tested on these measurements. A multi-sensor deep learning model to predict the indoor/outdoor state has been proposed in [17]. An interesting indoor/outdoor detection solution that integrates unsupervised and supervised algorithms and relies on the location, location accuracy, and signal strength is proposed in [13].

Most of the approaches reviewed above propose solutions that use supervised ML techniques and demonstrate higher performance on datasets coming from the same environments/devices as those used for the model training than on new environments/devices. Exceptions are the semi-supervised learning app-roach proposed in [9] and the hybrid approach, HybridIO, introduced by Souza et al. [13]. The former method can conduct online updates of a Naive Bayes clas-sifier to previously unseen environments by applying co-training. The HybridIO, on the other hand, utilizes a supervised technique only when the clustering is not able to separate the data well into two (indoor vs. outdoor) groups. Many of the proposed indoor/outdoor detection solutions require a variety of sensors to identify the user's environmental context. In contrast to the most state-of-the-art indoor/outdoor detection methods, our proposed approach builds an ISM-based GNSS activation model that can discriminate between outdoor and indoor envi-ronments and characterizes the most typical outdoor environmental scenarios of a given portable smart device.

3   Methodology

3.1   An Inductive System Monitoring Approach

An ISM method, introduced in [8], provides a technique to automatically produce a health monitoring knowledge base for a given system. Historical datasets are used to extract general clusters of nominal data to characterize the typical system behavior. The system is monitored by comparing real-time operational data with these clusters. The main focus is to build a clustering model using available historical data by considering low and high vectors representing the boundary of each cluster. The low and high vectors are formed by selecting the minimum and maximum values of features by considering all data samples assigned to each cluster. In this case, the first data sample will be considered as a singleton cluster. Every other input data sample is compared to the currently available clusters to identify the closest cluster to it. The distance between a data sample and a cluster's centroid can be measured by computing the Euclidean distance. In the current context, the cluster's centroid is calculated by creating a vector from the average of the low and high values for each cluster's feature. For each new training input data sample, the IMS algorithm finds the closest cluster in the current clustering solution. Then it is determined whether the data sample is contained in the bounding rectangle defined by that cluster's low and high vectors or if it is close enough to be incorporated into the cluster.

3.2   The Proposed ISM-Based Approach for GNSS Activation

In this study, we propose a novel GNSS activation approach based on the method developed by Iverson in [8]. The ISM-based GNSS activation model is built in two steps. Initially, the ISM technique (Algorithm 1) is applied to the device's historical data marked with GPS coordinates to create clusters that model dif-ferent environmental scenarios. In the second step, the built ISM model is refined by applying Algorithm 2 to the remaining device's data without GPS location. This procedure allows for identifying those clusters that describe semi-outdoor scenarios. Thus, the built ISM-based model discriminates between two outdoor environmental categories: open outdoor and semi-outdoor. The clusters could be further analyzed and grouped based on their similarities by including additional information on location characteristics such as the city center, suburb, or rural area.

Algorithm 1: ISM Model

Data: data contains seven (un)sorted signal strengths and the number of available cells, and a distance threshold
Result: low_high, centers, labels

1 Create an empty list of labels w.r.t to the size of data;
2 Assign the first sample to the cluster 0;
3 Set the sample to be the centroid of the cluster;
4 Set the low and high vectors to be the sample itself;
5 **for** *sample 1 to n* **do**
6   Compute each sample's Euclidean distance from the available centroids and identify the closest cluster;
7   **if** *the sample is between the low and high vectors of the closest clusters* **then**
8 | Assign the sample to that cluster;
9   **else if** *the Euclidean distance of the sample is less than the threshold (=* 4.0) **then**
10   Assign the sample to that cluster;
11   Update the low and high vectors by computing the min and max vectors;
12   Update the centroid by averaging the low and high vectors;
13   **else**
14   Create a new cluster and assign the sample to it;
15   Consider the low and high vectors to be the sample itself and append it to the list of available low and high vectors;
16   Set the sample to be the centroid of the cluster and append it to the list of available centroids;
17   **end**
18 **end**

Our motivation to use the ISM approach [8] for building a GNSS component activation model is to get a better insight into the indoor/outdoor localization problem through data exploration and extraction of environmental scenarios' patterns. In addition, we search for a solution that can run on the device and quickly adapt to a new environment without the need to completely retrain the built model. The aim is to create a model that can identify the availability of GPS coverage with the help of a cellular network. The model created by applying the ISM algorithm (Algorithm 1) describes its environment through nested clusters. Namely, it consists of two categories, standing for open outdoor and semi-outdoor, being outer clusters, each one containing nested clusters modeling the corresponding category's typical environmental scenarios. Each inner cluster is represented by its low and high feature vectors, which facilitates its interpretation, visualization, and comparison with other clusters that represent environmental scenarios from the same category or the other. Note that the indoor environmental scenarios are not present in the built ISM-based GNSS activation model. In that way, during the monitoring phase (Algorithm 2), all data samples that do not fit any of the nested clusters of the two categories are interpreted as belonging to the indoor environment. All these keep the model small, having modest requirements with respect to storage and computations.

Algorithm 2: ISM Monitor

Data: data contains seven (un)sorted signal strengths and the number of available cells, low and high vectors, and centroids

Result: labeled data

1 Create an empty list of labels w.r.t to the size of data;

2 **for** *sample 0 to n* **do**

3 | Compute each sample's Euclidean distance from the available centroids and identify the closest cluster;

4 | **if** *the sample is between the low and high vectors of the closest clusters* **then**

5 | | Assign the sample to that cluster;

6 | **end**

7 **end**

---

4   Experimental Design

4.1   Dataset

The participants in the data collection process were equipped with trackers to record data during normal daily activities. The trackers are based on a Nordic Semiconductors nRF52832 paired with a Quectel BG96 for integrated GNSS positioning and cellular connectivity capabilities. The modem used for LTE connectivity is based on a Qualcomm mdm9206. The trackers are held in hand by participants or placed in a pocket or backpack.

During data collection, the trackers were configured to capture data within a 1-second interval, recording cellular network parameters along with positioning parameters. Cellular parameters included signal strength, channel quality, and bandwidth descriptors, while positioning parameters consisted of latitude and longitude coordinates. Parameters from the serving cell station to which the trackers were connected and neighboring cell stations were recorded. Participants were instructed to collect data from indoors and outdoors while considering corner cases, such as overpasses and building corners, and varying the type of building and areas visited, such as commercial, residential, and industrial. No other constraints were given regarding collection patterns, and participants were told to walk freely as they would normally. Data collection took place over two months, and in total more than 707k samples amounting to 200 hours data were collected.

4.2   Data Preprocessing

Among the available data features, we chose the signal strengths of six neighboring cells and the serving cell, together with the trackers' longitude and latitude. The trackers' GPS was enabled during data collection. As a result, these two columns might be empty based on the unavailability of GPS signals. In addition, we considered the number of available cells visible by the tracker at each time, t. The data further was labeled based on the availability of the GPS coverage into class 0 in the presence of GPS coverage and class -1 otherwise. Table 1 summarizes the total number of samples and percentages of samples with/without GPS coverage for each tracker.

Table 1. Collected data samples by five trackers

Tracker	No. of samples	GPS coverage(%)	
		With	Without
d1	176 528	59.79	40.21
d2	136 290	61.17	38.83
d3	129 342	66.75	33.25
d4	129 707	64.91	35.09
d5	135 476	65.15	34.85
Total	707 343		

For each tracker, we used class 0 to build a tracker's model and class -1 to check the model's performance in predicting whether GPS should be activated. For both training and testing, only eight features, i.e., the signal strengths of the six neighboring cells and the serving cell, and the number of available cells were considered. The signal strengths collected by the trackers are between 0 and 63. This range translates into -111 and -48 dBm by subtracting 111 from each value, representing the weakest and strongest signals. As the signal strengths are in the range $[0, 63]$, we fill in the missing signal strengths with a significant negative value, i.e., -100. Finally, all eight features are standardized by removing the mean and scaling to unit variance using z-score, calculated by the following equation $z = (x - \bar{x})/\sigma$, where $\bar{x}$ represents the mean of the samples and σ is the standard deviation of the samples.

4.3   Evaluation Metrics

We apply a symmetric external validation index, *Rand Index (RI)*, to evaluate the pairwise similarity between built models for different trackers. RI [10] measures the similarity between pairs of models considering the level of agreement between the two. RI is calculated as the ratio between the number of agreeing pairs and the total number of pairs. The RI score is bound between 0 and 1. A score close to 0 represents random labeling, and 1 stands for a perfect match. We also use *accuracy* to evaluate the performance of the built models in classifying data samples into classes 0 and 1, standing for the presence and absence of GPS coverage, respectively.

5   Results and Discussion

We performed three experiments using data collected by five trackers. In *Experiment 1*, we applied 10-fold cross-validation on the data collected by each tracker, i.e., nine parts of the data with GPS coverage were used for training, while the 10th part together with all the data without GPS coverage were used for testing. We explored shuffling the data with GPS coverage in another setup before applying 10-fold cross-validation. In addition, either the collected signals strengths by the trackers were sorted in descending order, or they were left as initially received. In total, a combination of four different setups was studied. Each setup was performed three times. Figure 1 summarizes the obtained results. The main finding is that sorting the collected signals' strengths by the trackers in the unshuffled scenario led to lower number of clusters and higher average accuracy for most trackers.

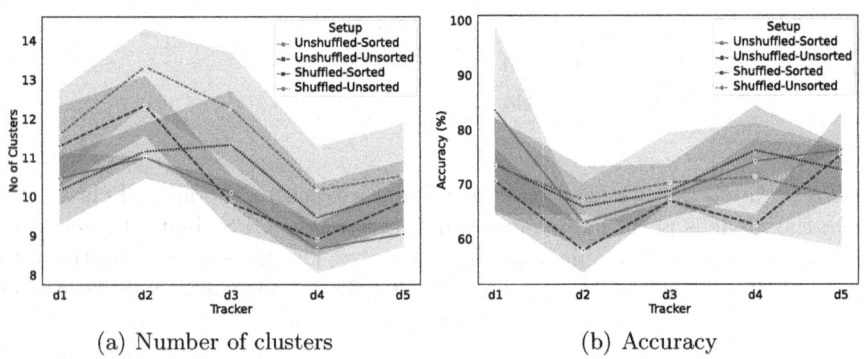

(a) Number of clusters   (b) Accuracy

Fig. 1. *Experiment 1* – Results of the 3-time 10-fold cross-validation. The dark and bright colors represent the mean and standard deviation, respectively.

Table 2 represents the built model for tracker d1 in fold 9 with unshuffled and sorted setups in *Experiment 1*. The used training data contains 94 981 data samples with GPS coverage, and the test data contains 81 541 data samples, where 10 553 samples have GPS coverage, and 70 988 do not have GPS coverage. This model contains 11 clusters. Each cluster in Table 2 is described by the minimum and maximum number of cells, the total number of samples, the number of samples with and without GPS coverage, and their percentages.

Table 2. *Experiment 1* – Built model with accuracy 99.89% in fold 9 for tracker d1 (unshuffled data samples and sorted signal strengths)

Cluster	Total	GPS coverage		No GPS coverage		Cells	
		Count	%	Count	%	Min	Max
0	17 991	17 910 (1 552)	99.55	81	0.45	4	7
1	374	374 (31)	100.00	0	0.00	3	3
2	762	762 (76)	100.00	0	0.00	2	2
3	53 704	53 704 (3 769)	100.00	0	0.00	5	7
4	5 524	5 524 (302)	100.00	0	0.00	4	4
5	97	97 (5)	100.00	0	0.00	1	1
6	1 145	1 145 (101)	100.00	0	0.00	3	3
7	95	95 (10)	100.00	0	0.00	1	1
8	15 905	15 905 (1 736)	100.00	0	0.00	4	5
9	484	484 (301)	100.00	0	0.00	4	4
10	9 522	9 522 (2 658)	100.00	0	0.00	7	7
−1	70 919	12 (12)	0.02	70 907	99.98	1	7

After performing the test, most of the data with GPS coverage fitted into clusters 3, 10, 8, and 0. The parenthesized numbers under GPS Coverage, Count column, in Table 2 represent test data with GPS coverage. Regarding the data without GPS coverage, 99.98% of the data did not match any clusters except 81 data samples that fit into cluster 0. Therefore, this cluster is considered to represent a semi-outdoor scenario.

In *Experiment 2*, we used the data with GPS coverage collected by each tracker to build a model representing the tracker's behavior. For testing, we used data without GPS coverage. Table 3 represents the accuracy of the models for each tracker with and without sorting the signal strengths. As one can notice, overall the models' accuracy of all trackers, except d5, is higher while the signal strengths are sorted. Therefore, we used the models with sorted signals for the third experiment.

As an example, we present in Table 4 the statistics regarding the tracker d2 model, which achieved the lowest accuracy among other models with the signal strengths sorted. As one can see, the built model contains 11 clusters, where cluster 0 represents the largest cluster with 52 099 data samples with GPS coverage and cluster 6 with only 28 data samples stands for the smallest cluster. After applying the model to the test samples, which only consist of data without GPS coverage, three clusters (0, 3, and 7) are identified as ones modeling semi-outdoor scenarios. Note that all these three clusters have something in common, namely the minimum and maximum number of cells in all are between 5 and 7. On the other hand, approximately 57% of the samples are not fitted into any clusters, suggesting the tracker's GPS should not be turned on. Another interesting observation was that when the minimum and the maximum number

Table 3. *Experiment 2* – Model's accuracy on data without GPS coverage for sorted and unsorted trackers' signal strengths

Model	Accuracy (%)	
	Sorted signals	Unsorted signals
M-d1	99.89	64.44
M-d2	57.15	49.82
M-d3	61.49	60.40
M-d4	68.81	56.04
M-d5	71.94	72.83

of cells for a cluster is in a range of $[4, 7]$ or $[5, 7]$, it represents a semi-outdoor scenario.

Table 4. *Experiment 2* – Built model with accuracy 57.15% for tracker d2 (sorted signal strengths)

Cluster	Total	GPS coverage		No GPS coverage		Cells	
		Count	%	Count	%	Min	Max
0	70 236	52 099	74.18	18 137	25.82	5	7
1	1 793	1 793	100.00	0	0.00	4	4
2	258	258	100.00	0	0.00	3	3
3	19 872	15 947	80.25	3 925	19.75	5	7
4	101	101	100.00	0	0.00	1	1
5	68	68	100.00	0	0.00	2	2
6	28	28	100.00	0	0.00	1	1
7	12 427	11 811	95.04	616	4.96	5	7
8	724	724	100.00	0	0.00	4	4
9	264	264	100.00	0	0.00	3	3
10	273	273	100.00	0	0.00	2	2
−1	30 246	0	0.00	30 246	100.00	1	7

In *Experiment 1*, the accuracy of the models is evaluated based on data with and without GPS coverage. In contrast, in *Experiment 2*, we studied how well a tracker's model can classify samples without GPS coverage collected by the same tracker. As can be observed in Table 3, the most precise model in the case where signal strengths are sorted belongs to the tracker d1, while the tracker d2 generates the least accurate model in both scenarios.

In *Experiment 3*, we applied each tracker's model to the data collected by the other four trackers. This experiment aimed to show to what extent the built model for a specific tracker can be used for accurate predictions on the data samples (with and without GPS coverage) collected by another tracker. Table 5 shows the performance of each model on other trackers' data. As one can see, the results vary, e.g., the tracker d1 model, denoted by M-d1, achieved an accuracy of 55.71% on the tracker d4 data. On the other hand, M-d4 attained an accuracy of 42.68% on the tracker d1 data and performed much better (51.89%) on the tracker d5 data. Overall, M-d2 achieved the best accuracy on the tracker d3 data (65.27%). In addition, both M-d3 and M-d4 achieved their highest performance on the tracker d5 data compared to other trackers' data.

Table 5. *Experiment 3* – Models' accuracy (%) on the collected data by other tracker's (sorted signal strengths)

	d1	d2	d3	d4	d5
M-d1	–	35.41	30.69	**55.71**	33.33
M-d2	54.58	–	**65.27**	38.27	62.14
M-d3	56.58	48.93	–	45.98	**64.59**
M-d4	42.68	51.23	46.73	–	**51.89**
M-d5	**54.56**	48.75	51.53	39.56	–

Tracker d1 data was collected within 56 days from the city center and a small rural area. On the other hand, other trackers' data was collected within 27 days and only limited to the city center. In addition, all five trackers were only used together for 24 days, explaining the different performances of the models. According to a domain expert, the tracks' model performance variation may also be due to trackers' orientation.

As part of *Experiment 3*, we also performed a pairwise comparison of the built model (see Table 6). For this reason, we used RI to measure the similarity between two models by considering the level of agreement between them. RI scores close to 1 represent perfect agreements between the two models in clustering pairs of data samples together, while scores close to 0 explain strong disagreements among the models. As can be seen, M-d2 and M-d3 achieved the highest level of agreement, 0.77. In addition, both of these models received RI scores of 0.71 and 0.73 when compared with M-d5, respectively.

Table 6. *Experiment 3* – Similarity of the models in terms of RI score

	M-d1	M-d2	M-d3	M-d4
M-d2	0.49			
M-d3	0.49	**0.77**		
M-d4	0.53	0.52	0.52	
M-d5	0.48	**0.71**	**0.73**	0.53

6   Conclusions and Future Work

In this paper, we have proposed a novel GNSS component activation model that automatically detects indoor/outdoor environments. We used radio signals received from LTE base stations to build an ISM-based model that describes different environmental scenarios captured by a smart tracker. The built model is capable of discriminating between two outdoor environmental categories: open outdoor and semi-outdoor. During the monitoring phase, data samples that do not fit any of the clusters of these two categories are interpreted to belong to the indoor environment. In that way, the model is kept small, with modest requirements regarding storage and computations.

We have evaluated the proposed ISM-based GNSS activation model on real-world data provided by a partner company in three different experiments. The obtained results have been analyzed, and interesting patterns about the GNSS activation problem have been extracted. For example, the models built on sorted and unshuffled data have shown higher performance. The proposed model supplies the user with easily interpretable representations of the environmental scenarios. These representations can be further analyzed to gain additional knowledge for further refinement of the built model. Our ISM-based model has produced a high accuracy result (99.89%) for the tracker trained on the largest dataset covering the longest period. This confirms that the quantity and quality of the training data matter for the model performance.

The built ISM model can easily be adapted to new environments by applying the same learning procedure to newly arrived data as the one used for the initial building of the model. This is one of the directions that is planned to be explored in the future. Another ambition is to develop an integration technique that can create an overall ISM model from ones built on different devices/locations.

References

1. Anagnostopoulos, T., Garcia, J.C., Goncalves, J., Ferreira, D., Hosio, S., Kostakos, V.: Environmental exposure assessment using indoor/outdoor detection on smartphones. Pers. Ubiquit. Comput. **21**(4), 761–773 (2017). https://doi.org/10.1007/s00779-017-1028-y
2. Ashraf, I., Hur, S., Park, Y.: MagIO: magnetic field strength based indoor- outdoor detection with a commercial smartphone. Micromachines **9**(10), 534 (2018). https://doi.org/10.3390/mi9100534
3. Bhargava, P., et al.: Senseme: a system for continuous, on-device, and multidimensional context and activity recognition. In: MobiQuitous (2014)
4. Esmaeili Kelishomi, A., Garmabaki, A.H.S., Bahaghighat, M., Dong, J.: Mobile user indoor-outdoor detection through physical daily activities. Sensors **19**(3), 511 (2019)
5. Feriol, F., Vivet, D., Watanabe, Y.: A review of environmental context detection for navigation based on multiple sensors. Sensors **20**(16), 4532 (2020)
6. Gao, H., Groves, P.D.: Environmental context detection for adaptive navigation using GNSS measurements from a smartphone. Navigation **65**(1), 99–116 (2018)

7. Gao, H., Groves, P.D.: Context detection for advanced self-aware navigation using smartphone sensors. arXiv arXiv:2005.07539 (Signal Processing) (2020)
8. Iverson, D.L.: Inductive system health monitoring. In: IC-AI, pp. 605–611 (2004)
9. Radu, V., Katsikouli, P., Sarkar, R., Marina, M.K.: A semi-supervised learning approach for robust indoor-outdoor detection with smartphones. In: Proceedings of the 12th ACM Conference on Embedded Network Sensor Systems, pp. 280–294 (2014)
10. Rand, W.M.: Objective criteria for the evaluation of clustering methods. J. Am. Stat. Assoc. **66**(336), 846–850 (1971)
11. Reverte, Ó.C., de Teruel, P.E.L., Ruiz, A.: WiFiBoost: a terminal-based method for detection of indoor/outdoor places. In: MobiQuitous (2014)
12. Rhudy, M.B., et al.: Indoor and outdoor classification using light measurements and machine learning. Appl. Artif. Intell. **24**, 1–14 (2021)
13. Souza, R.P., et al.: A big data-driven hybrid solution to the indoor-outdoor detection problem. Big Data Res. **24**, 100194 (2021)
14. Sung, R., Jung, S.H., Han, D.: Sound based indoor and outdoor environment detection for seamless positioning handover. ICT Exp. **1**(3), 106–109 (2015)
15. Wang, W., Chang, Q., Li, Q., Shi, Z., Chen, W.: Indoor-outdoor detection using a smart phone sensor. Sensors **16**(10), 1563 (2016)
16. Zhu, Y., et al.: A fast indoor/outdoor transition detection algorithm based on machine learning. Sensors **19**(4), 786 (2019)
17. Zhu, Y., Luo, H., Zhao, F., Chen, R.: Indoor/outdoor switching detection using multisensor DenseNet and LSTM. IEEE IoT J. **8**(3), 1544–1556 (2021)

Client Segmentation of Mobile Payment Parking Data Using Machine Learning

Ilze Andersone[1]([⊠]), Agris Ņikitenko[1], Valdis Bergs[2], and Uldis Jansons[2]

[1] Riga Technical University, Riga, Latvia
ilze.andersone@rtu.lv
[2] SIA Mobilly, Riga, Latvia

Abstract. This paper addresses the analysis of mobile payment parking data for client segmentation. The transaction data transformation into client-specific attributes is performed from the company data set to achieve the goal. Two clustering algorithms – K-Means and DBScan – are compared for multiple data subsets. For the clustering result interpretation, decision tree representation is used. As a result, the most appropriate combination of the clustering algorithm, its parameters and attribute combination is determined.

Keywords: Client segmentation · Clustering · Mobile payments · Parking

1 Introduction

The client segmentation from the historical data is a relevant research object for many companies, as it can give multiple benefits – help to choose an appropriate marketing strategy [1–3], assist in the creation of personalized offers to the existing clients [4], as well as help to understand the clients better and/or react to their potential needs in a timely manner [5]. Since the company offers multiple services, client clustering can also benefit from identifying their most essential services and how they relate to their customer base. In our case study, the company offers several services through mobile payments, emphasizing client parking data.

A lot of research has been done on the parking data, but it mostly focuses on the assistance in assisting in finding parking spots where geographical information is available [6–10]. Sometimes specific topics are addressed – such as autonomous vehicle parking [11] or smart parking [12]. Some papers address individual parking behaviour [13, 14], but it is mainly done only to simulate parking space availability.

The goal of the client segmentation in our research is to identify the primary client groups from the historical data of their mobile payment information so that the most appropriate marketing strategies and loyalty programs can be developed without overwhelming the clients with irrelevant offers. E.g., clients who mostly park inexpensive parking places would have different needs from those that only ever use public transport (buses or trains).

I. Maglogiannis et al. (Eds.): AIAI 2022, IFIP AICT 647, pp. 450–459, 2022.
https://doi.org/10.1007/978-3-031-08337-2_37

Though some client groups can be identified by proposing hypotheses and then statistically confirming or rejecting them, often the data can be overwhelming to analyze manually, and some essential client segments can quickly go unidentified.

2 Data Collection and Preprocessing

The data set used in our research contains the service, payment, and temporal data of 19 million individual transactions during the time period from January 2017 to August 2019. Mobilly [15] collected the data from a mobile payment service provider in Latvia. All the client data was anonymized to ensure EU data privacy standards.

The data set contains information about various services that can be paid for through the mobile phone app – parking, bus and train tickets, theatre tickets, and donations. Even though the company offers various services, parking is the most important business component; only the parking data subset was analyzed in detail. Both the data preprocessing and analysis was performed in Jupyter notebook environment using Python programming language.

The tables contain the transaction data about payments that clients make for the received services (payments/costs) as well as data about the funds they store in their accounts (income). This data differs significantly from other data sets used for parking analysis [6–10] in that it doesn't contain location data, but the emphasis is instead on payments and various services. Most transactions in the data set relate to parking in various cost parking zones, but there are also transactions related to other mobile payment services.

2.1 Attribute Extraction

As the transaction data does not contain any aggregated information about the clients, additional data aggregation is necessary to achieve the goal of client segmentation. Several groups of attributes are extracted from the data set that represents various characteristics of the clients:

- Absolute measures – this group contains attributes representing comprehensive data about the clients during the analyzed period, e.g., Total payment amount over two years and eight months.
- Average measures – this group contains attributes representing averaged data about the client (usually monthly), e.g., Average payment for parking in one month.
- Relative measures – this group contains attributes representing some relative relationship of two other attributes, e.g., Rate of parking payments compared to total costs.

An exhaustive list of attributes is given in Table 1. *Costs* represent the client's amount for services, while *income* shows how much the client has paid in his account. Different parking zones are available with standard zones on the streets (A zone is the most expensive and D zone is the cheapest) and parking places with plot-specific costs (e.g., parking zones by supermarkets or private properties). Clients can make payments for the services as individuals or company funds (represented by *private payment rate*).

Table 1. The measures extracted from the data set

Absolute measures	Average measures	Relative measures
Total months	Avg costs/month	Private payment rate
Total costs	Avg payment count/month	Parking rate
Total payment count	Avg amount paid	A parking rate
Vehicle count	Avg income/month	B parking rate
Total income	Avg income count/month	C parking rate
Total income count		D parking rate
Total parking expenses		Other parking rates
Different service count		

2.2 Data Preprocessing

Most machine learning algorithms benefit from the preprocessing of data. To prepare the data for the segmentation, the following steps are performed:

1. Missing value handling.
2. Removal of extreme values in the data.
3. Data standardization.
4. Principal Component Analysis for data dimensionality reduction.

Missing Value Identification
The original data set is of high quality, and none of the records in the tables contain null or NaN values. However, clients who have never used parking services lack corresponding vehicle counts, parking rates, and other parking-related information. For those clients, the missing values are replaced with zeros.

Removal of Extreme Values in the Data
Extreme values are removed to further adapt the data for the clustering part of the outliers. This approach has significant benefits because large clients are considered a completely separate group and receive individual offers when they are a target of marketing strategies. Additionally, if their data is left in the data set, the data analysis is made significantly more difficult due to the skewing of the data. As an example, consider Fig. 1.

On the left, the histogram of the client total active months is shown, and it is no surprise that there are many new clients (1 month active), but a significant part of clients have also been active for a longer time. However, a histogram of total costs is shown on the right side of Fig. 1. Although almost all clients are on the far left side of the histogram, some exceptions (large corporate clients) skew the histogram significantly.

To reduce the problem of outliers, some values are removed from the dataset by computing the 1st and 3rd Quartiles of the dataset (values 0.1 and 0.9) and removing all values below lower fence (1st Quartile $-$ 1.5 Interquartile range) and above upper fence

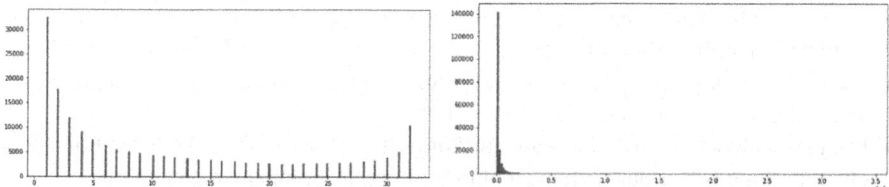

Fig. 1. Histograms of two attribute values. Left: Total month histogram; Right: Total costs histogram.

(3rd Quartile $+$ 1.5 Interquartile range). For most attributes, no values are removed – only some absolute and average measures are affected.

Data Standardization
The Minmax scaling method is chosen for the data standardization, which transforms all attribute values in the range [0; 1]. While the Minmax scaling method is sensitive to data extremes and outliers, the data extreme removal in the previous preprocessing step reduces this problem and, at the same time, allows it to retain the natural scale of relative attributes.

Principal Component Analysis
The data set doesn't contain any categorical data; therefore, Principal Component Analysis (PCA) reduces data set dimensionality, which extracts the essential details from the data and represents them as a reduced set of variables called principal components [16]. PCA is performed for each data subset separately.

3   Experimental Results

Two different clustering methods are chosen for the experiments: K-Means and DBScan. Each of these algorithms has its advantages and drawbacks, and their comparison is beneficial when the data characteristics are unknown.

K-Means is a well-known clustering method, and it is often used for client segmentation [17–20]. It is a partition-based algorithm that considers the centre of the data points as a centre of the cluster. It has high computational efficiency, but it has several drawbacks – it is unable to detect non-convex shapes in the data, and it is sensitive to cluster count, which is a required parameter for this algorithm [21].

As an alternative to K-Means clustering DBScan algorithm can be used for client data segmentation [17, 22, 23]. DBScan is a density-based clustering method requiring two parameters – the radius of the neighbourhood and the minimum number of neighbour points. Compared to K-Means, DBScan is efficient when the data shape is non-convex, but the results suffer when the data density is not balanced [21].

To compare how different attribute groups impact the client segmentation, five attribute subsets are used for the experiments (refer to Table 1 for contents of each attribute group):

- Data set with all attributes. Ideally, this group would have comparable segmentation results with attribute subsets.
- Data set with only absolute measure attributes. Represents general information about clients but contains no specific parking data.
- Data set with only relative measure attributes. It primarily contains information about client parking behaviour with the addition of private/company payment rates.
- Data set with only average measure attributes. Represents how much and how often, on average, the payments are made.
- Data set with a selected subset of attributes. All relative and average attributes are included here, along with some absolute attributes that contain information not represented in any other attribute groups – total months, vehicle count and different service count.

All five attribute subsets are used and compared for each clustering algorithm. For the implementation, Jupyter notebook was used [24] that provides a simple and interactive way to process data and develop live code.

3.1   K-Means Clustering

The only parameter for K-Means clustering is the cluster count. To find the best cluster count for each attribute subset Silhouette coefficient for 2–15 clusters was calculated. The silhouette coefficient represents how close points in one cluster are to points in another cluster [25]. It can take values [−1; 1] where value close to 1 indicates points being far away from each other (good for clustering), 0 – points from different clusters are close and negative values – possible assignment of points to wrong clusters.

Each data point in Fig. 2 represents an average value of 3 clustering attempts.

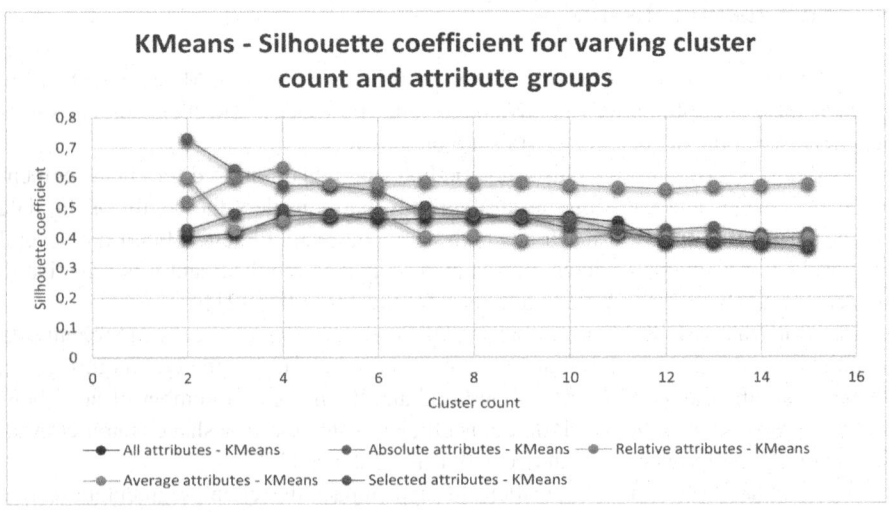

Fig. 2. K-Means clustering results for 2–15 clusters in five data subsets

Although they indicate the clustering quality, the overall highest Silhouette score does not guarantee that it is the best clustering result. The decision trees were used on the cluster count with highest Silhouette scores for each attribute group to interpret clustering results. Illustrations of decision trees are given in Fig. 3.

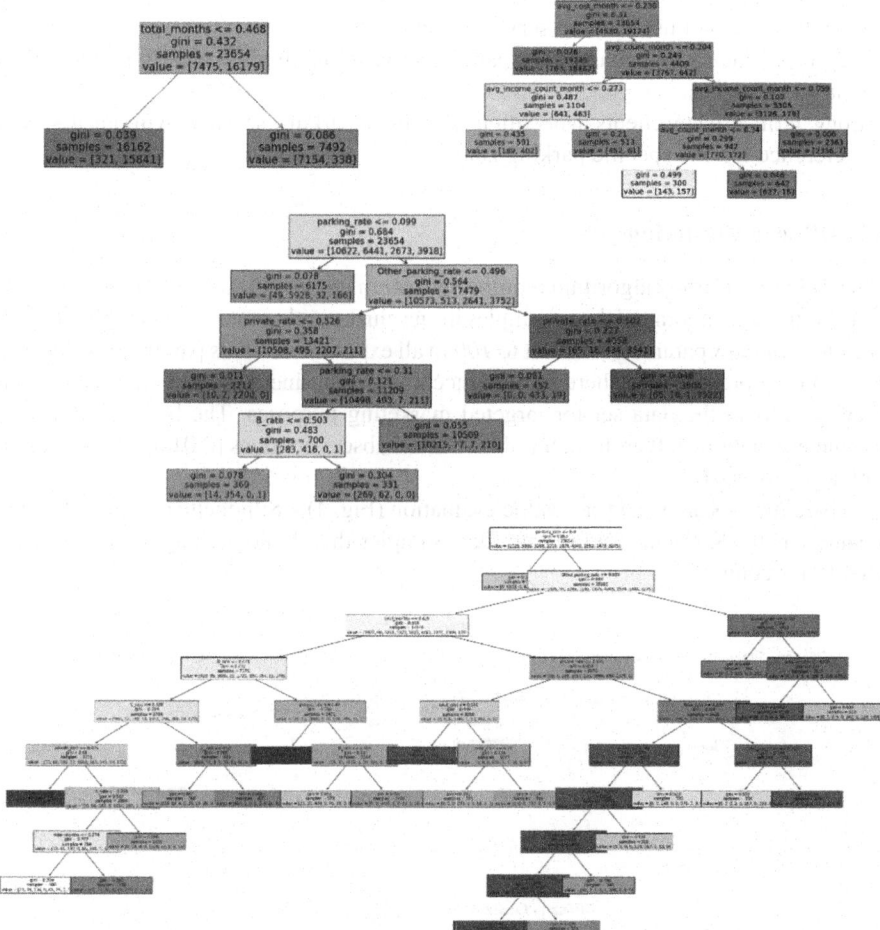

Fig. 3. Visual representation of decision trees for best Silhouette scores in each attribute group. Colours indicate data subset belongs to a particular class. Top left: Absolute measures – 2 clusters; Top right: Average measures – 2 clusters; Middle: Relative measures – 4 clusters. Bottom: All attributes – 9 clusters (also included as additional file for readability). The decision tree for Selected attributes is not included (it has similar characteristics to All attribute classification).

When each decision tree is analyzed in detail, it can be concluded that there is little new knowledge to be found about clients in decision trees with only two classes: Absolute attributes clustering (Fig. 3 top left) divides the clients by one attribute only – total months they have been active, and Average attribute clustering (Fig. 3 top middle) does the same by average costs per month (further classification has an impact on a very small part of data set).

More meaningful results are given by Relative, All and Selected attribute datasets with 4, 9 and 7 clusters as highest Silhouette scores. E.g., some client group examples that can be found in the decision tree analysis are (Fig. 3 bottom):

- Clients who don't use parking services at all.
- Corporate clients who mainly use parking services and mainly park in parking plots instead of streets.
- Long term private clients who often use street parking services without a strong preference for one specific parking zone.

3.2 DBScan Clustering

The DBScan clustering algorithm requires two parameters – *min_samples* that characterize the minimum amount of data examples in any cluster and ε – radius of neighbourhood. The *min_samples* parameter was set to *100* in all experiments. This parameter value was based on the premise that there is little incentive for businesses to identify very small client groups in the data set for targeted marketing purposes. The best value of ε is completely unknown; therefore, for all five data subsets, ε values [0.01–0.3] were tested with a step of 0.01.

Three metrics are used for ε value evaluation (Fig. 4) – Silhouette coefficient (same meaning as for K-Means), noise rate (data samples that do not belong to any clusters) and cluster count.

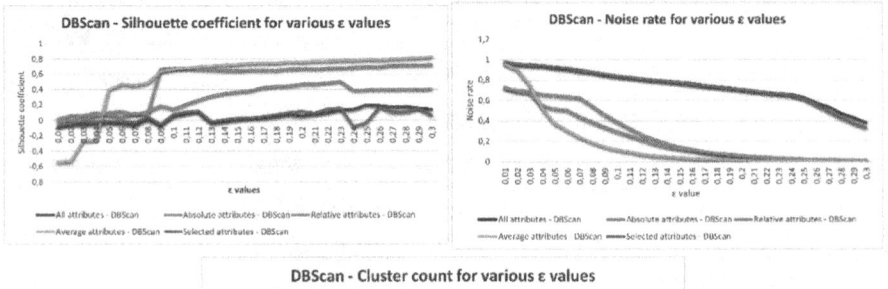

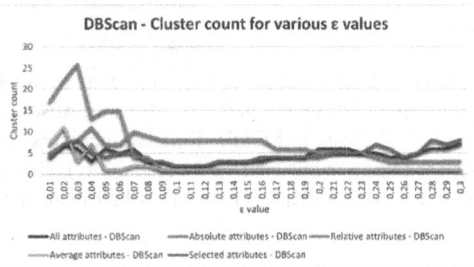

Fig. 4. DBScan clustering results in five data subsets for ε values [0.01–0.3]. Top left: Silhouette coefficient; Top right: Noise rate; Bottom: Cluster count.

The three metrics in Fig. 4 must be analyzed together to make any conclusions. While one metric in separation may show promising results for a particular ε value and data subset combination, in many cases, other metrics demonstrate that the acquired result is poor. The metric results for the five data subsets can be interpreted in the following way:

- All attributes. Cluster count, in this case, is irrelevant. The Silhouette scores (<0.2) and noise rates (>0.4) are consistently poor for all ε values.
- Absolute attributes. The combination of Silhouette scores (>0.6) and noise rates (<0.1) are suitable for ε values 0.17 and higher. However, cluster count shows that only one cluster is left for the average attribute subset, which is useless for business purposes.
- Relative attributes. Relative attributes have a relatively high Silhouette score (0.5) and noise rate (0.03) combination for ε value 0.23. The cluster count for this ε value is 5, which warrants further analysis of this parameter and data subset combination.
- Average attributes. Similar to absolute attributes, there is a range of ε values (0.1 and higher) that have a good combination of Silhouette scores (>0.6) and noise rates (<0.1). However, there is only one cluster left for this ε parameter range as before.
- Selected attributes. Like all attribute data sets, the metric results for the selected data subset are consistently poor through all tested ε values.

The overall conclusion about the DBScan results for all five attribute sets is that only the relative attribute subset gives any results considered for additional analysis. By far, the largest identified group is clients who use private funds and park at least sometimes. No significant new information about the clients is found by interpreting the results with a decision tree (Fig. 5).

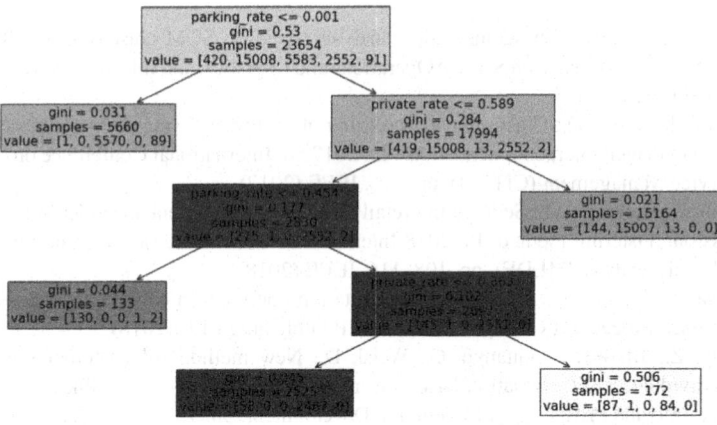

Fig. 5. Visual representation of decision tree for DBScan epsilon 0.23 (Relative attributes)

4 Conclusions

In this research, mobile payment company data was analyzed to target client segmentation. For this purpose, three attribute types (absolute, average and relative) were extracted from the company transaction data, five data subsets were created, and two clustering algorithms – K-Means and DBScan – were compared with different parameters to find the most suitable approach for the acquisition of new information.

Based on the K-Means clustering results with different parameters on five data subsets, it was concluded that although the highest Silhouette scores were acquired in the Absolute, Average and Relative data sets separately, the decision tree interpretation of the clustering gives more meaningful results for All attributes and Selected attributes, where decision tree analysis can yield useful information about the client groups and their proportion in the data set. Unfortunately, no meaningful results were acquired with the DBScan algorithm in any data subsets.

As future work, use of geographical data to support parking suggestions based on the history of user preferences is suggested. This would allow to identify overall client behaviour and give individualized parking suggestions based on regular parking behaviour history. E.g. suggestions of cheaper or safer parking places might not be important for clients who consistently park in the same spots, but more relevant to clients who often park in unfamiliar places.

Acknowledgement. The research leading to these results has received funding from the project "Competence Centre of Information and Communication Technologies" of EU Structural funds, contract No. 1.2.1.1/18/A/003 signed between IT Competence Centre and Central Finance and Contracting Agency, Research No. 1.3 "Research, development prototyping of financial analysis tool based on document management system".

References

1. Li, Y., Lin, F.: Customer segmentation analysis based on SOM clustering. In: 2008 IEEE International Conference on Service Operations and Logistics, and Informatics, vol. 1, pp. 15–19. IEEE (2008)
2. Maryani, I., Riana, D.: Clustering and profiling of customers using RFM for customer relationship management recommendations. In: 2017 5th International Conference on Cyber and IT Service Management (CITSM), pp. 1–6. IEEE (2017)
3. Yoseph, F., Heikkila, M.: Segmenting retail customers with an enhanced RFM and a hybrid regression/clustering method. In: 2018 International Conference on Machine Learning and Data Engineering (iCMLDE), pp. 108–116. IEEE (2018)
4. Mihova, V., Pavlov, V.: A customer segmentation approach in commercial banks. In: AIP Conference Proceedings, vol. 2025, no. 1. AIP Publishing LLC (2018)
5. Yuping, Z., Jílková, P., Guanyu, C., Weisl, D.: New methods of customer segmentation and individual credit evaluation based on machine learning. In: New Silk Road: Business Cooperation and Prospective of Economic Development, pp. 925–931. Atlantis Press (2020)
6. Alsafery, W., Alturki, B., Reiff-Marganiec, S., Jambi, K.: Smart car parking system solution for the internet of things in smart cities. In: 2018 1st International Conference on Computer Applications & Information Security (ICCAIS), pp. 1–5. IEEE (2018)
7. Pflügler, C., Köhn, T., Schreieck, M., Wiesche, M., Krcmar, H.: Predicting the availability of parking spaces with publicly available data. Informatik (2016)
8. Rong, Y., Xu, Z., Yan, R., Ma, X.: Du-parking: spatio-temporal big data tells you realtime parking availability. In: Proceedings of the 24th ACM SIGKDD International Conference on Knowledge Discovery & Data Mining, pp. 646–654 (2018)

9. Liu, K.S., Gao, J., Wu, X., Lin, S.: On-street parking guidance with real-time sensing data for smart cities. In: 2018 15th Annual IEEE International Conference on Sensing, Communication, and Networking (SECON), pp. 1–9. IEEE (2018)
10. Hilvert, O., Toledo, T., Bekhor, S.: Framework and model for parking decisions. Transp. Res. Rec. **2319**(1), 30–38 (2012)
11. Millard-Ball, A.: The autonomous vehicle parking problem. Transp. Policy **75**, 99–108 (2019)
12. Piovesan, N., Turi, L., Toigo, E., Martinez, B., Rossi, M.: Data analytics for smart parking applications. Sensors **16**(10), 1575 (2016)
13. Bonsall, P., Palmer, I.: Modelling drivers' car parking behaviour using data from a travel choice simulator. Transp. Res. Part C Emerg. Technol. **12**(5), 321–347 (2004)
14. Gomari, S., Knoth, C., Antoniou, C.: Cluster analysis of parking behaviour: a case study in Munich. Transp. Res. Procedia **52**, 485–492 (2021)
15. Mobilly, SIA. https://mobilly.lv/en/about-mobilly/. Accessed June 2021
16. Abdi, H., Williams, L.J.: Principal component analysis. Wiley Interdiscip. Rev. Comput. Stat. **2**(4), 433–459 (2010)
17. Monalisa, S., Kurnia, F.: Analysis of DBSCAN and K-means algorithm for evaluating outlier on RFM model of customer behaviour. Telkomnika **17**(1), 110–117 (2019)
18. Ezenkwu, C.P., Ozuomba, S., Kalu, C.: Application of K-means algorithm for efficient customer segmentation: a strategy for targeted customer services (2015)
19. Ye, L., Qiu-ru, C., Hai-xu, X., Yi-jun, L., Zhi-min, Y.: Telecom customer segmentation with K-means clustering. In: 2012 7th International Conference on Computer Science & Education (ICCSE), pp. 648–651. IEEE (2012)
20. Kansal, T., Bahuguna, S., Singh, V., Choudhury, T.: Customer segmentation using K-means clustering. In: 2018 International Conference on Computational Techniques, Electronics and Mechanical Systems (CTEMS), pp. 135–139. IEEE (2018)
21. Xu, D., Tian, Y.: A comprehensive survey of clustering algorithms. Ann. Data Sci. **2**(2), 165–193 (2015)
22. Zakrzewska, D., Murlewski, J.: Clustering algorithms for bank customer segmentation. In: 5th International Conference on Intelligent Systems Design and Applications (ISDA 2005), pp. 197–202. IEEE (2005)
23. Wang, X., et al.: Electricity market customer segmentation based on DBSCAN and k-means:—a case on Yunnan electricity market. In: 2020 Asia Energy and Electrical Engineering Symposium (AEEES), pp. 869–874. IEEE (2020)
24. Project Jupyter. https://jupyter.org/. Accessed Feb 2022
25. Kaufman, L., Rousseeuw, P.J.: Finding Groups in Data: An Introduction to Cluster Analysis, vol. 344. Wiley, Hoboken (2009)

Determining Column Numbers in Résumés with Clustering

Şeref Recep Keskin[1]($\boxtimes$), Yavuz Balı[1]($\boxtimes$), Günce Keziban Orman[2],
F. Serhan Daniş[2], and Sultan N. Turhan[2]

[1] Kariyer.net Ümraniye, İstanbul, Turkey
{seref.keskin,yavuz.bali}@kariyer.net
[2] Department of Computer Engineering, Galatasaray University, İstanbul, Turkey
{korman,sdanis,sturhan}@gsu.edu.tr

Abstract. In the recruitment process, the workload of manual résumé reviews is quite time consuming for the recruiters. This review process can benefit from Artificial Intelligent-aided intelligent systems to extract the actual meaning within the résumés and structure their forms. However, writing résumés has no standards, and the personalized structure of each received résumé makes this task highly challenging. This work is dedicated to tackling a part of this issue on structuring résumés. More specifically, we firstly focus on finding the column number of any résumé since once the main parts of the résumé are separated, the subdivisions can easily be analysed. This study, thus, formalizes the problem of finding columns of a résumé as a clustering problem. The experiments are performed on a data set of custom Turkish résumés having up to two-columns, on which we apply two algorithms: K-means and Density-based spatial clustering of applications with noise. As a result of the experiments, we observe that an optimal cluster size relates strongly to the valid column number. Our method is not limited to résumés but can be applied to any unstructured textual data.

Keywords: Information Extraction · Résumé Parse · DBSCAN · K-means

1 Introduction

The process of selectively structuring and combining implicitly or directly specified contents in textual data is called "Information Extraction" (IE) [7]. IE can be rule-based or model-based. One of the most recent famous IE problems is the information extraction from documents [2]. With the increasing data processing power, researchers are more confident in tackling IE tasks related to documents or texts. Résumés are regarded as valuable documents for document extraction with their varying structures and rich content. IE from résumés is the process of automatically generating or extracting specific phrases or meanings. Because manually assessing résumés is a time-consuming and labor-intensive task for recruiters, this process has a significant positive impact on the review process.

I. Maglogiannis et al. (Eds.): AIAI 2022, IFIP AICT 647, pp. 460–471, 2022.
https://doi.org/10.1007/978-3-031-08337-2_38

As Turkey's largest employment platform since 1999, Kariyer.net brings together job seekers and employers online with new generation technologies in job search and recruitment processes. On the platform offered by Kariyer.net, candidates are required to fill in various fields such as education information, past work experience, and personal information during registration. Besides, users can upload their free-style résumés to the system. These résumés are stored unprocessed in Kariyer.net databases. The unprocessed free-style résumés in PDF or other formats uploaded to the system by users will be called *unstructured*. After being exposed to IE procesdures, the data are stored with a particular hierarchy in the Kariyer.net database and will called *structured data*. It is essential to convert unstructured data into structured form since structured résumés allow IE processes. In this work, we are interested in this issue. More than 700,000 free-style unstructured résumés have been uploaded to the Kariyer.net database by users. Collecting information from each of these résumés, storing them in the database of the existing system with the human factor, and finally making them structured both cost time and are prone to errors. The main motivation of this work is to reduce this effort by proposing an automated system to replace any manual task of structuring. Additionally, this study aims to integrate the candidates into the Kariyer.net system by using the information obtained from these fields of the résumés in different formats [1]. The information extracted from a résumé is highly beneficial in terms of matching the candidate's qualifications with the right job by better analyzing them. We expect to increase the performance of further résumé-related operations, especially the job-candidate matching accuracy.

There is not a consensus about the résumé format and layout, that is to say, each résumé might have a different formatting style. This, of course, makes it difficult to develop an automatic structuring system working efficiently for any résumé format. The first difficulty of the process is that résumés in different file formats such as documents (DOC), portable file format (PDF), or any image format (PNG, JPEG, etc.) should be transferred to the computer environment as a text structure. Secondly, different layouts of the résumé files should be converted to a common format. For instance, because résumés are composed of different structures and the information is in different columns on a page, the extracted texts can mix with each other. In addition, the information in the extracted texts should be separated in a meaningful way. More clearly, the information should be separated and divided into the necessary information groups. In this study, we are specifically interested in this second difficulty. We concentrate on determining the number of columns in the résumés in order to provide a meaningful text extraction in the résumés containing different column numbers. By determining the number of columns in the résumés, it will be ensured that the extracted texts are separated into appropriate sections. Thus, the texts will be prevented from being mixed in the extraction stage.

In the literature, the IE operations from the résumé texts are carried out by using regular expressions, natural language processing, machine learning methods, and named entity recognition [4,6]. These works primarily seek to extract the semantic meaning of documents or to make use of this type of information. However, there are only a few works that focus on the process of structuring itself. For instance, Tobing et al. examine the résumés in the Indonesian language [12]. In this study, different models of header segmentation were used for separating different segments such as personal information, work experience, etc. In a sense of the dedication of segmentation, this work can be similar to our aim. However, we are explicitly interested in determining the number of columns in this study. To the best of our knowledge, our work has originality due to the specific area of interest.

The rest of this paper is organized as follows. In Sect. 2, we introduce the data set that is used in this study in detail, and in Sect. 3, we describe the methods used in this study. In Sect. 4, we give a discussion about different approaches. Finally, in Sect. 5, we conclude our paper.

2 Data Set

In this work, we use the real résumés that are intended for job applications. Along with the standard templates available on the Internet, the applicants are observed to create their résumés in various forms. Free form résumés result with a set of different font faces, colors and types. This wide variety of résumé forms constitutes a challenge when transforming their unstructured form into a structured one. We handle the résumé data sets in both PDF and any image format, which are converted into free form texts by parsing the documents. Two different formed examples of résumés are given in Fig. 1. In Fig. 1a, a single-column résumé is shown while the sample résumé in Fig. 1b has two columns.

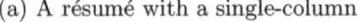
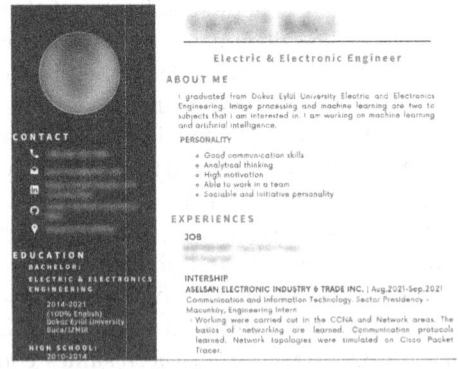

(a) A résumé with a single-column   (b) A résumé with two-columns

Fig. 1. Sample Résumés

This work uses use 1018 résumés of the format PDF. The résumés are extracted from Kariyer.net, which stores both the unstructured résumés uploaded by the candidates and the résumés constructed by filling in some structured forms. The résumés uploaded directly to the system might have different formats and styles, with one-, two-, or three-columns, different headers, or writing details. We rigorously selected the experiment samples to reflect the true natural variety of the original database; that is, the data set consists of résumés with one- or two-columns. Moreover, the samples are manually labeled with their column sizes. There are almost 685 and 333 samples having one- and two-columns respectively.

Table 1. Descriptions of properties expressing texts

Parameter	Explanation
x_0	Left corners x coordinate
y_0	Top corners y coordinate
x_1	Right corners x coordinate
y_1	Bottom corners y coordinate
Words	The output of text extraction

We aim to process and digitize the textual documents in various forms so that their outlines can be determined and structured. The unstructured but digitized intermediate text portions are obtained. They allow to catch the words containing the text and image content of the document page. It represents the hierarchical information structure of the document page, consisting of blocks, lines, spaces, and characters, each with its own sub-dictionary. We describe the features and explanations used in this study in Table 1. The geometric information of a text portion can be seen in Fig. 2.

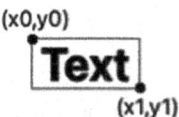

Fig. 2. Representation of coordinate parameters in the sample picture

In the obtained dictionary, unwanted data may occur due to the whitespace characters in the résumés, so the data without text is cleared from the dictionary. Additionally, the page that each text belongs to is added. After all cleaning and preprocessing steps, the features of the résumés are represented with a data frame table. A representative sample of such data is shown in Table 2. The coordinate information and text information of the extracted texts are obtained in the table.

In Fig. 3, a scatter plot of the x_0 coordinates of the detected texts are shown in order for two sample résumés with one- and two-columns. We observe that

Table 2. Parsed Résumé Dataframe

	x_0	y_0	x_1	y_1	Words	Page_number
10	24.959	223.092	494.355	240.014	Education \n	1
11	33.720	240.522	116.180	303.062	University \n(Ba...	1
12	173.779	242.209	518.020	300.038	İzmir University...	1
13	33.720	309.882	108.500	358.381	University \n(Ba...	1
14	173.779	311.653	517.298	355.477	İzmir University...	1

the text are concentrated in one region for the résumés with a single-column (see Fig. 3a), and for the samples with two-columns, two distinct regions are easily separable (see Fig. 3b). Similar behavior for x_0 coordinates is observed in many résumés examined.

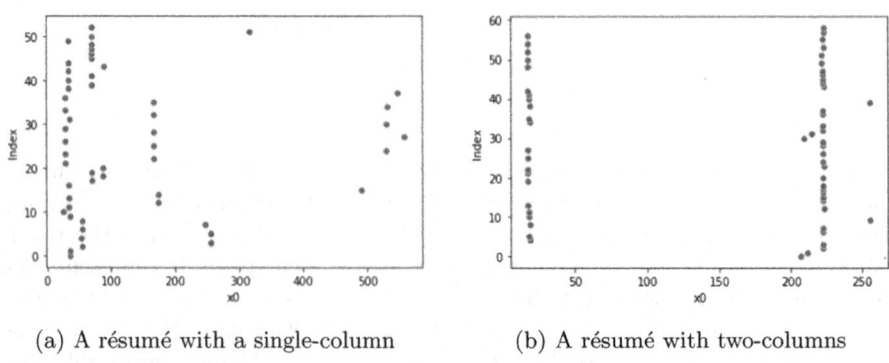

(a) A résumé with a single-column   (b) A résumé with two-columns

Fig. 3. Scatter plot of x_0 coordinates of sample résumés

3 Methodology

To determine the number of columns, we focus on the coordinate information of the texts parsed from the résumés. From this point of view, the problem is handled as an analytical problem, which examines the coordinates of the parsed data. Accordingly, x_0 and y_0 represent the starting points for a text portion, while x_1 and y_1 represent the endpoints. For languages written from left to right, x_0 coordinate information is considered as a feature representing the beginning parts of the writing in the résumés. We assume that for the texts that belong to the same paragraph, only the y_0 information changes whereas the x_0 information remain in a certain tolerance margin. In the case of more than one-column, the x_0 coordinate is considered as a feature that indicates the starting positions of the text. In this case, it makes sense to use x_0 coordinates in languages written from left to right to determine the number of columns.

In this way, the problem of determining the number of columns in the résumés with different forms turns into a clustering problem of x_0 values extracted from the résumés. Closer x_0 values will be grouped to form rows starting in the same column based on clustering. Once the column number determination problem is considered as a clustering problem of x_0 values, we can employ several clustering solutions such as partitioning methods, hierarchical methods, density-based methods, etc. However, many clustering methods cannot determine the number of clusters automatically. The well-known K-means approach needs post-processing methods such as elbow or silhouette while the algorithm of the Density-Based Spatial Clustering of Applications with Noise (DBSCAN) [8], which has a proven performance on analyzing geographic data, can determine the number of clusters while clustering the data simultaneously. x_0 values show the coordinates on a text, similar to geographic coordinates. In the following subsections we first explain the details of clustering-related approaches, then we give the details of our problem setting and how we use the clustering techniques for determining the different columns.

3.1 K-means Algorithm

K-means clustering method is a method of partitioning a data group into clusters in the specified number of data sets [9]. It is one of the unsupervised machine learning techniques. Clustering operations aim to maximize the similarities between the data in a cluster and minimize the similarities between the clusters. It is a widespread method in the data mining world. The specified number of clusters is significant for the algorithm. The algorithm divides all the data into the specified number of clusters. Specifying too many or too few clusters can lead to meaningless data partitioning. The elbow or silhouette methods can determine the optimal number of clusters [11].

3.2 Elbow Method

Each number of clusters calculates the sum of the squares of the distances from the center of the cluster to which the data is included [13]. This calculation is also called Within-Cluster-Sum of Squared Errors (WSS). When the graph of the calculated values for each cluster number is drawn, a graph is formed as shown in Fig. 4. In the graph, the elbow point where the difference between the totals starts to decrease is indicated as the most appropriate number of clusters for K-means.

3.3 Silhouette Method

The silhouette method is a method that provides the most appropriate number of clusters and interpretation of consistency between data clusters. The method calculates the silhouette coefficients of each point, which measures how similar a point is to its cluster compared to other clusters. We evaluate the classification

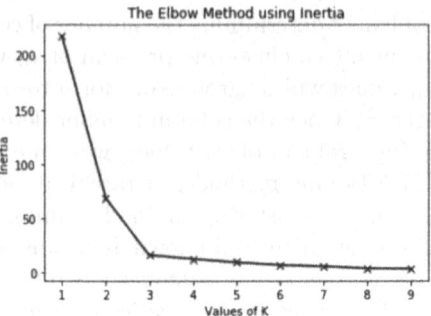

Fig. 4. Example of an elbow graph.

performance of each data point with silhouette coefficients. The formula for calculating the silhouette coefficient is given in Eq. 1. In this equation, $a(i)$ is the average distance function of a point from all other points in the same cluster [10]. $b(i)$ is the average distance function from all points in the other cluster closest to the cluster to which a point belongs. The distance calculation functions $a(i)$ and $b(i)$ can be used as Euclidean distance, Manhattan distance, Etc., any other distance metric.

$$s(i) = \frac{b(i) - a(i)}{max(a(i), b(i))} \tag{1}$$

The silhouette coefficient ranges from -1 to $+1$. A high positive value indicates that the data matches well with the cluster to which it belongs, and a low negative value indicates that the data is poorly matched with the cluster to which it belongs. Considering all the data, the fact that most of the silhouette coefficients of the data have a high value indicates that the clustering is appropriate. Most of the silhouette coefficients have low or negative values, indicating that the number of clusters is low or high.

3.4 DBSCAN Algorithm

DBSCAN algorithm is a clustering algorithm that depends on the neighborhood of data points in two or multidimensional space. Since the data is handled from a spatial point of view, it is mostly used in the analysis of spatial data. In the original work of Ester et al. [5], it is accredited as "A density-based algorithm for discovering clusters in large spatial databases with noise". DBSCAN produces successful results in large-volume databases, even when clusters are separated in arbitrary ways.

Unlike K-means algorithm, it does not require the number of clusters to be specified beforehand. It is also an outlier-resistant algorithm. Given a set of points in space, the algorithm aggregates points that are highly close and marks data points below a certain threshold in low-density regions as outliers. It contains two different parameter inputs distance ε and minPoint. ε specifies how close the points must be to be considered part of a set. Euclidean distance is commonly used to measure the distance between two points. However, different distance methods can also be used. If the distance between two data points is less than or equal to the ε value, it means that the point is considered a neighbor. minPoint is the minimum number of points to create a dense region. For a region to form a dense region, a data point must contain at least as many points as specified by the number of minPoints within the distance specified in the ε value. The minimum value for minPoint should be 3.

In DBSCAN, for clustering purposes, points are divided into three groups core points, reachable points, and outliers [3]. A data point is a core point if it contains as many data points as minPoints, including itself, within the epsilon distance. Points that are not core points within the area of a core point are called adjacent points and reachable points. Data that do not seed points and fall outside the areas of the seed points are called outliers. The seed points form a cluster together with the reachable points covered by the points. Each cluster contains at least one core point.

The data generated by the parsed résumés constitute an applicable data set for the DBSCAN Algorithm. Font, size, coordinate, etc., properties of the texts in the résumé are extracted in blocks. Coordinate information of text blocks creates point data in the 2D coordinate plane. The number of text blocks clustered on the page can be determined using the DBSCAN Algorithm. The number of clusters detected can give information about the number of columns in the résumé.

3.5   Column Detection via Clustering

We induced the problem of finding the different columns of a résumé to the problem of optimal clustering of x_0 coordinates of read text in résumés. In a real-world data set, we distinguish that some résumés have well-separated two-columns while some of them have vaguely separated ones. Thus, in our case, it is not certain that any clustering algorithm can easily detect the different segments, i.e. columns. We cannot find the best clustering of x_0 values in polynomial time because clustering is an NP-hard problem. That is why we need to choose one of the clustering approaches that gives the best results of all. Since clustering is an unsupervised problem by nature, and since the document column detection problem has never been studied from this perspective before, we do not know the most suitable algorithm yet. For this reason, we suggest using a supervised approach to find the clustering technique with the best performance for our case. That is why the numbers of the columns in our résumé set are labeled manually.

Among DBSCAN, K-means with elbow and K-means with silhouette, we choose the one that finds the correct column numbers for the labelled set. After preparing the data for the study and performing the calculations with the methods used in the experiment, we used multiple success metrics dedicated to measuring the performance of supervised modelling to monitor the results of this study. These metrics are accuracy, recall, precision, and F1-score. We used a confusion matrix to find these numbers. Here, our main purpose is to build an experimental setup for further similar studies.

4   Experiments and Results

This section describes the parameters of the experiments and reports the results performed with different methodologies. We also elaborate on the evaluation of the results. The results of three different methods, including DBSCAN, elbow and silhouette, were evaluated. It were tested with a total of 1018 résumé file, consisting of 685 single-column and 333 double-column résumés. The positions of x_0 are clustered by the K-means algorithm choosing a certain number of clusters. In order to decide the number of k, the number of clusters, in K-means, we use the elbow and silhouette methods as described in Sect. 3.

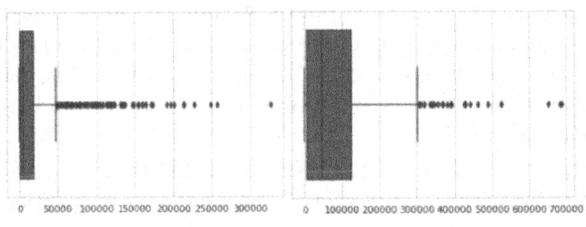

(a) Single-column samples   (b) Two-column samples

Fig. 5. Box plot of WSS scores of the elbow method

In Fig. 5a and 5b, the box-plots of WSS scores obtained by the elbow method for all résumés in the data set are shown for one- and two-column résumés respectively. According to these results, it is observed that there is no threshold value that can clearly distinguish one- and two-column résumés. On the other hand, for the best performance, a single-column résumé estimate can be given for résumés with a WSS below 50000 and a two-column résumé for résumés with a WSS above 50000.

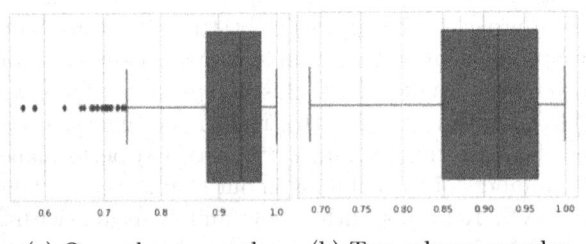

(a) One-column samples   (b) Two-column samples

Fig. 6. Box plot of the silhouette scores

We also report the scores obtained by the silhouette method according to the number of columns, as given in Fig. 6a and 6b. These results can be interpreted as a clear range of values cannot be observed for parsing one-column and two-column résumés. As in the elbow method, there is a range of values covering similar silhouette scores for both types of résumés. However, it can be determine that it includes résumés with one-column above a 0.95 silhouette score and six two-columns with a 0.95 silhouette score to ensure the highest accuracy.

With the estimation made by the DBSCAN algorithm on the x_0 coordinate values, we directly determine the column number of a résumé. The results obtained in the experiment performed on the test data are shown in Table 3. A high accuracy value was achieved with an accuracy rate of 83%. However, low accuracy was obtained for the double-column résumés. Accordingly, the F1-score 72% value was obtained.

Table 3. Column number determination performances

Method	Test accuracy	F1-score	Recall	Precision
DBSCAN	**83%**	**72%**	**68%**	**77%**
Elbow	75%	57%	49%	66%
Silhouette	57%	43%	49%	38%

Table 3 summarizes the column number estimation performances of three clustering strategies. The DBSCAN algorithm clearly outperforms the other K-means based strategies: silhouette and elbow methods. Moreover, Fig. 7 shows the confusion matrix results for each method. The success of the confusion matrix according to each label was examined. It is seen that DBSCAN achieved a success rate of 90.07% in single-column résumés and 67.56% in two-column résumés. It is seen that the Silhouette method reaches a success rate of 87.88% in single-column résumés and 49.24% in two-column résumés. On the other hand, the Elbow method has a success rate of 61.16% in single-column résumés and 48.94% in two-column résumés. Considering those results, all three methods outperform single-column resumes. Especially the DBSCAN method shows considerably high performance for single-column resumes. Nevertheless, all methods' performances seem to be one step behind when finding two-column.

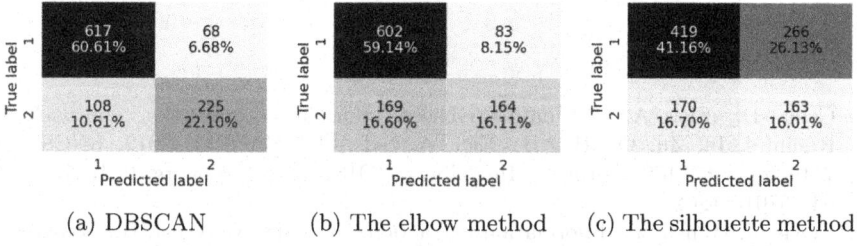

(a) DBSCAN   (b) The elbow method   (c) The silhouette method

Fig. 7. Confusion matrices with respect to column numbers

The performance of the single-column résumés is usually higher. This study shows that the DBSCAN algorithm, with which the results are compared, performs much better than the elbow and silhouette methods. However, examining the confusion matrix in detail, we notice that the success of discovering two-columns résumés is low.

5   Conclusion

This study focuses on determining the number of columns for transforming the unstructured documents into structured ones. We employ the clustering methods to determine the number of columns. The performances of three different methods, K-means with the silhouette method, K-means with the elbow method and DBSCAN algorithm, on the data set are compared. When the discrete data of the elbow and silhouette methods on the data set are examined, a parsing threshold value could not be determined for the résumés with one- and two-columns. In this case, a threshold value that gives the best performance is determined empirically.

Although DBSCAN performance is acceptable, it is not sufficient to determine the number of columns in documents. When the résumés are examined, we observe that the information is transferred under the relevant headings. Accordingly, the headings contain information about the column number of a résumé. As an extension to this work, the heading information (semantic and positional information) can be employed to determine the headers and the number of columns at the same time. In this way, we presume that the success rates can be increased to reasonable rates for the résumé parse task. Although the study was carried out on résumés, the proposed methods are independent of résumés and can be used on different textual documents. In addition, since the logic on which the study is based is on the clustering of the coordinates where the texts are located, it is independent of the language. It can be used for any language. Also, the right-to-left or left-to-right spelling of the text does not affect the method.

There are several different clustering approaches (model-based, spectral, hierarchical, etc.) and different metrics for finding optimal clustering numbers (gap statistics, modularity, etc.) besides the ones which are used in this work. They can also be added to evaluate the performance of these approaches on this specific problem in further studies.

References

1. Çelik, D., Elçi, A.: An ontology-based information extraction approach for Résumés. In: Zu, Q., Hu, B., Elçi, A. (eds.) ICPCA/SWS 2012. LNCS, vol. 7719, pp. 165–179. Springer, Heidelberg (2013). https://doi.org/10.1007/978-3-642-37015-1_14
2. Cowie, J., Wilks, Y.: Information extraction. In: Dale, R., Moisl, H., Somers, H. (eds.) Handbook of Natural Language Processing, pp. 241–260. Marcel Dekker Inc., USA (2000)

3. Daranda, A., Dzemyda, G.: Novel machine learning approach for self-aware prediction based on the contextual reasoning. Int. J. Comput. Commun. Control **16**(4), 1–15 (2021)
4. Das, P., Pandey, M., Rautaray, S.S.: A cv parser model using entity extraction process and big data tools. Int. J. Inf. Technol. Comput. Sci. (2018)
5. Ester, M., Kriegel, H.P., Sander, J., Xu, X.: A density-based algorithm for discovering clusters in large spatial databases with noise. In: Proceedings of the Second International Conference on Knowledge Discovery and Data Mining, KDD'96, pp. 226–231. AAAI Press (1996)
6. Gaur, B., Saluja, G.S., Sivakumar, H.B., Singh, S.: Semi-supervised deep learning based named entity recognition model to parse education section of resumes. Neural Comput. Appl. **33**, 5705–5718 (2021)
7. Grishman, R.: Information extraction. IEEE Intell. Syst. **30**(5), 8–15 (2015)
8. Li, J., Han, X., Jiang, J., Hu, Y., Liu, L.: An efficient clustering method for dbscan geographic spatio-temporal large data with improved parameter optimization. Int. Arch. Photogram. Remote Sens. Spatial Inf. Sci. **42**, 581–584 (2020)
9. Oyelade, O.J., Oladipupo, O.O., Obagbuwa, I.C.: Application of k means clustering algorithm for prediction of students academic performance (2010)
10. Rousseeuw, P.J.: Silhouettes: a graphical aid to the interpretation and validation of cluster analysis. J. Comput. Appl. Math. **20**, 53–65 (1987)
11. Shi, C., Wei, B., Wei, S., Wang, W., Liu, H., Liu, J.: A quantitative discriminant method of elbow point for the optimal number of clusters in clustering algorithm. EURASIP J. Wirel. Commun. Netw. **2021**(1), 1–16 (2021). https://doi.org/10.1186/s13638-021-01910-w
12. Tobing, B.C.L., Suhendra, I.R., Halim, C.: Catapa resume parser: end to end Indonesian resume extraction. In: Proceedings of the 2019 3rd International Conference on Natural Language Processing and Information Retrieval, NLPIR 2019, pp. 68–74. Association for Computing Machinery, New York (2019)
13. Yuan, C., Yang, H.: Research on k-value selection method of k-means clustering algorithm. J **2**(2), 226–235 (2019)

High Rank Self-Organising Maps for Image Fingerprinting

Anthony Benjamin Kolenic and Duncan Anthony Coulter$^{(\boxtimes)}$ ⓘ

University of Johannesburg, Corner of Kingsway and University Roads,
Auckland Park, Johannesburg, South Africa
dcoulter@uj.ac.za

Abstract. Image fingerprinting is the act of generating a unique digest for an image. Unlike cryptographical hashing, slight differences in the input to the hashing function do not create significant differences in the digest. This property makes image fingerprinting useful in identifying near-duplicates of an input image. This paper describes a novel technique for generating an image fingerprint using Self-Organising Maps (SOM) with ranks higher than 2. The method is compared to a selection of more traditional fingerprinting algorithms and against a further variation on the proposed technique using a more conventional rank 2 Self-Organising Map.

Keywords: Self-Organising Map · Image fingerprinting · Duplicate detection · Artificial intelligence

1 Introduction

The fingerprinting of an image is a valuable way to identify similar and duplicate images within a set of images. Therefore, fingerprinting can be used as a tool with which we can classify and group unknown images that are not yet within the set. While it is tempting to equate hashing to fingerprinting, they are two different techniques. The critical difference is that minor differences in the input in the hashing input lead to significant changes in the resulting digest. In contrast, in fingerprinting, small changes in the input lead to small changes in the resulting digest [3]. Although both techniques produce smaller digests than the original data in the image.

Rephrasing the generation process as a noise-resistant way to generate a unique digest with lower dimensionality than the original input helps identify where Self Organising Maps (SOMs) can be helpful. Self Organising Maps are commonly used for dimensionality reduction to aid with the visualization of large data sets and how the data within large data sets interact. SOMs achieve this by providing easy to consume visuals such as u-matrices and heat maps. Another critical aspect of a SOM is that it clusters similar data together, thus providing the second property required for a fingerprinting algorithm: Noise and rotation resilience [6].

© IFIP International Federation for Information Processing 2022
Published by Springer Nature Switzerland AG 2022
I. Maglogiannis et al. (Eds.): AIAI 2022, IFIP AICT 647, pp. 472–483, 2022.
https://doi.org/10.1007/978-3-031-08337-2_39

This paper will provide background into Self Organising Maps and explore the applications of higher rank Self Organising Maps. Then, building on the background, the concept of using SOMs for the fingerprinting of images will be outlined. After this, the technique will be compared to pre-existing Self Organising Map libraries and tested against well-known data sets. Finally, recommendations will be made on how the technique can be improved and the direction of possible future work. This technique aims to provide a novel manner in which an image can be fingerprinted using SOMs.

2 Self Organising Maps

Self Organising Maps (SOMs) are a form of artificial neural network (ANN) created by Dr Teuvo Kohonen. Self Organising Maps are also known as Kohonen Maps for this reason. While SOMs are a form of ANN, they have noticeable differences in their learning process, structure, and training method as opposed to Feed-Forward ANNs and Multi-Layer Perceptron ANNs. Whilst most ANNs are trained using corrective learning, SOMs take the approach of competitive learning. Competitive learning is utilised as it is better suited for unsupervised tasks, which SOMs are traditionally used for [5]. Structurally, the nodes of an ANN are represented by an activation function that changes output based on the input provided, whereas a SOM is a lattice of nodes that cluster around features. Each of these nodes contains a vector which is adjusted through the training process. The training process is briefly discussed in the next paragraph and in more detail in the method section. It is essential, at this stage, to take note that while the nodes are usually represented on a 2D grid lattice, the dimensionality of the lattice can be increased [4]. To visualise how one would represent a SOM on a higher dimension lattice, refer to Fig. 1.

As previously mentioned, SOMs are trained using a competitive learning approach. While this approach is discussed in more detail in the method section, this paragraph will provide a high-level overview of the basic training and operation of a Self Organising Map. The first step is to determine the initial parameters of a SOM. These parameters include the length of each node's vector and the dimensions of the SOM. The length of each node's vector can be thought of as the weights for each node. They are initialised to random values before training can begin. Since SOMs are represented as a lattice, each node has neighbours that form its neighbourhood, where the neighbourhood is traditionally defined with a neighbourhood function such as Moore's neighbourhood that has been extended for Chebyshev distances greater than 1. Determining the dimension of a SOM is also important and will determine how many nodes there are in the SOM.

Once all the nodes have been initialised with random values, training can commence. Training is the process where a random item is selected from the input data and presented in vector form to the self-organising map to find the node in the SOM whose vector has the smallest Euclidean distance to that of the input vector. Using this vector, known as the Best Matching Unit (BMU), all the nodes in the neighbourhood of the BMU are updated by pulling their vectors closer to the BMU in regard to their vector's Euclidean distance to the BMU. This process is repeated for a set number of iterations. Once the SOM has converged, an image is created. This image is known as a u-matrix and illustrates the average distance of a node to its adjacent nodes.

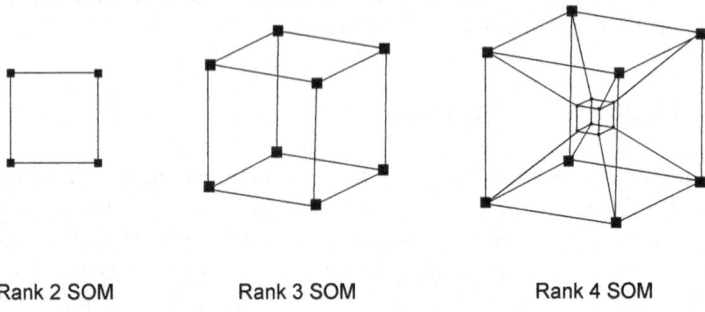

Rank 2 SOM   Rank 3 SOM   Rank 4 SOM

Fig. 1. Effect of increasing rank on a Self-Organising Map

The above sections mainly deal with self-organising maps in 2 spatial dimensions but allude to the fact that SOMs can be extended to work in higher spatial dimensions. This next section will discuss the properties of SOMs in higher spatial dimensions and the considerations that need to be kept in mind when extending SOMs [8]. When working with SOMs, the different interpretations of the word "dimension" can lead to confusion. To prevent this confusion, the paper will use the word rank (An abstract description of a vector) to describe the manipulation of a SOM in higher spatial dimensions. When increasing the rank of the SOM, there are important properties to note.

Interestingly, the dimensionality reduction is inversely proportional to the rank. Another property is that the distance between nodes decreases when keeping the number of nodes constant and increasing the rank. Shown below in Fig. 2 is an example of these properties applied to the IRIS data set, which has four attributes per value:

- sepal length in cm
- sepal width in cm
- petal length in cm
- petal width in cm

Increasing the rank of a SOM does come with unique challenges that need to be overcome. Firstly the creation of easy to view and understandable outputs, and secondly, the shapes that allow for the generation of regular honeycombs.

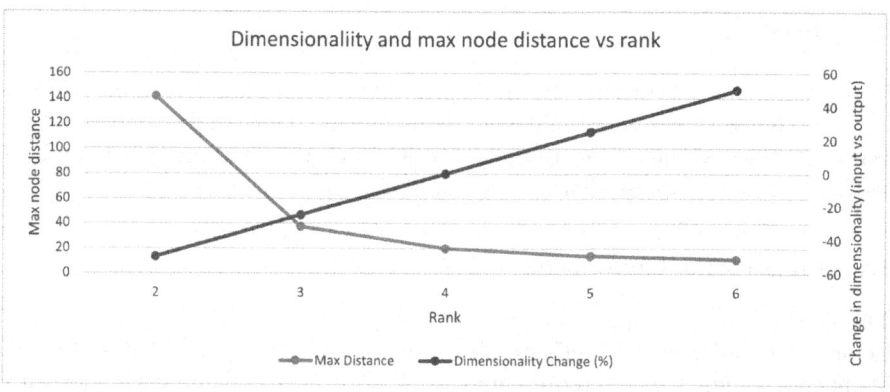

Fig. 2. Relationship between the rank of a SOM and the reduction in dimensionality of the data as well as the decrease of the maximum distance between the indices of the nodes as the rank increases and node count remains constant. The node count being 10,000 in this case

A SOMs primary use case allows the visualization and clustering of data that cannot be understood easily. The difficulty of understanding the data arises from problems such as large quantities of data or high dimensionality of the data. When increasing the rank of the SOM, it loses its ability to make data with a high dimension easy to understand visually. Although, colours and shapes can be used over an interval to minimize this impact. However, increasing the rank is not advised when working with data that has to be viewed by a human. This rule of thumb is reinforced by the fact that while it is easy to visualize a square or cube, it is difficult to visualize its four dimension analogue, the tesseract and nearly impossible to visualize a 5D hypercube, especially on a 2D surface such as a monitor or piece of paper.

A further technical problem comes with the structure of a Self-Organizing Map. SOMs can be thought of as a mathematical regular honeycomb. A regular honeycomb is the tiling/tessellation of regular convex polygons/polyhedrons so that there are no gaps and overlap. With rank two, the nodes can be thought of as the vertices in an equilateral triangle, a square or a hexagon where each node would have 3, 4, or 6 direct neighbours, respectively. Rank 3 only has one regular honeycomb, the cubic honeycomb, where each node would have six direct neighbours. From rank five onwards, it means the only shape each node can take is that of a hypercube [2]. This fact is important as it directly speaks to why the paper uses squares and their higher-dimensional analogues as the basis for the shape of the SOM.

3   Method

Presented below is a method for fingerprinting a set of images for quickly identifying duplicates and potentially classifying images. The technique involves two
main processes, namely, the training of a SOM to generate fingerprints and the
testing of fingerprints to identify near similarities.

3.1   Fingerprint Generation

The creation of an image's fingerprint is done using a Self Organising Map.
Before one can train the self-organising map, the input images must first be
segmented. These images represented as $N \times N$ array of numbers between 0
and 1 are segmented into $M \times M$ blocks for processing within the SOM, where
$N \bmod M = 0$ and $N, M \neq 0$. The segmenting of the input images into the
same size blocks helps cluster images that have similarities in certain areas, like
ID photos on a white background. The dimension of the vectors, also known as
the weights, within the SOM will equal M^2. Pseudocode for this algorithm is
provided in Algorithm 1.

> **input** : An *image* of size $N \times N$
> **input** : The segment size represented by M
> **output:** A list of $(\frac{N}{M})^2$ segments
>
> 1 **if** $N \bmod M = 0$ **then**
> 2 $results \leftarrow []$;
> 3 $numSegments \leftarrow \frac{N}{M}$;
> 4   **for** r *in numSegments* **do**
> 5   **for** c *in numSegments* **do**
> 6 $x \leftarrow c \times M$;
> 7 $y \leftarrow r \times M$;
> 8   append *image* segment at point $(x, y, x + M, y + M)$ to *results*;
> 9   **end**
> 10   **end**
> 11   **return** *result*;
> 12 **else**
> 13   display error and exit
> 14 **end**

Algorithm 1: Input pre-processing

Training of the SOM is performed by firstly initializing the P^r SOM where r
is the rank of the SOM, and P is the side length. In the SOM, each node, which
is represented by a vector of length M^2, is initialized with random values. Once
the SOM has been initialized, the training can commence by performing a set of
instructions n number of times. A random image segment is selected from the
input list and flatted into a $1 \times M^2$ vector on each training iteration. This vector

is fed into the SOM, where it is presented to each node within the map. This input process allows the SOM to identify which node is most similar to the input vector. Determining the similarity is done via a similarity metric such as the L^2 norm between the input vector and the weight of a node. Once the most similar node has been identified, the node's neighbours can be adjusted to cluster around the node. The reach and proportion of clustering is reduced as more iterations are performed. While the training remains the same with increasing rank, as mentioned before, the number of neighbours to a node increases. Pseudocode for this algorithm can be found in Algorithm 2.

---

input : The number of training iterations represented by n
input : The side length of the SOM represented by P
input : The rank of the SOM represented by r
input : A list of training segments $segmentList$
output: A trained self organsing map

1   $result \leftarrow$ randomly instantiate SOM of rank r;
2   **for** $iteration$ in n **do**
3     $sample \leftarrow$ selectRandomSegment($segmentList$);
4     $bmuIndex \leftarrow$ getIndexOfClosestNode($result$, $sample$);
5     $range \leftarrow maxRange \times \frac{iteration}{n}$;
6     $learningRate \leftarrow maxLearningRate \times \frac{iteration}{n}$;
7   **for** $node$ in $result$ $where$ $distance$ $between$ $node$ and $sample$ < $range$ **do**
8 | $node \leftarrow node + (sample - node) \times learningRate$;
9   **end**
10 **end**
11 **return** result

Algorithm 2: Self-Organising Map Training

After the SOM has converged, the creation of the fingerprints can be performed. The creation of the fingerprints is done by presenting all of the input data in order to the SOM and storing the index of the most similar weight into a list which is then flattened. Looking at a rank 2 SOM where an input image of size 4×4 is broken into segments of size 2 ($N = 4$ and $M = 2$), the result is four segments that, once flattened, have a size equal to M^2. If each segment is presented to the SOM because it is of rank two, the resulting index, the closest nodes index, will have two components. These components are appended to a list creating a set that contains $\{x_1, y_1, x_2, y_2, x_3, y_3, x_4, y_4\}$, where each x and y value correspond to an index in the SOM. The length of the digest would be equivalent to the number of segments multiplied by the rank of the SOM and represents the fingerprint. The length of this fingerprint is represented by k. Pseudocode is provided by Algorithm 3:

---

input : A *inputlist* of length l that contains image segments represented
          by vectors of length M^2
input : A *SOM* of rank r that is pre-trained, where the node weights are
          of length M^2
output: A vector of length $l \times r$

1 *result* ← [];
2 **for** *chunk in inputlist* **do**
3   *bmuIndex* ← getIndexOfClosestNode();
4   **for** *index in bmuIndex* **do**
5 | append *index* to *result*
6   **end**
7 **end**

Algorithm 3: Fingerprint generation

3.2 Fingerprint Comparison

Comparing generated fingerprints of the training data and input data is straightforward. First, the input image is converted into a grid of segments as outlined
above. Then, each input segment is presented to the SOM, and a fingerprint
for the input is generated. A vector of length k represents this fingerprint. This
vector can then be compared to the list of previous vectors to determine which
fingerprint is the most similar. In this paper, multiple techniques are used, and
the results are presented below. The techniques used to find similar fingerprints
are distance metrics such as the Euclidean distance, Cosine distance, Manhattan
distance, as well as k-nearest neighbours.

4 Results

The initial step of the creation of this novel technique was to implement a standard SOM and compare it to a well-established framework such as SuSi [7] to
ensure the underlying SOM is behaving as expected. Below is a comparison of
a rank 2 SOM, the custom implementation and using the SuSi framework. The
IRIS dataset was chosen for these comparisons as it is a well-understood dataset,
and the u-matrix is distinct. Figure 3 compares the custom implementation to
SuSi. This comparison demonstrates that the u-matrices are similar between the
implementations. It also shows a clear divide in the dataset, proving that the
SOM is behaving as expected. Following the previous comparison, another comparison is performed with the technique against itself to compare the training
times at different ranks.

    The times were taken as the average training time between 5 runs for rank
2–5 using the IRIS dataset, the number of nodes within the SOM is $n^r \approx 15625$
where r is the rank of the SOM (Fig. 4). To account for approximating the nodes,
the training time can be adjusted using the formula $r \times$ (actual node count ÷
desired node count) where r is the rank. The result of this adjustment can also

be seen in Fig. 4. Both comparisons use an epoch of 10000 for the number of training iterations and Euclidean distance for the distance metric. The number of nodes was chosen as 15625 as roots between 2 and 5 for 15625 have minimal rounding errors. Finally, there is a subsection that deals with the MNIST section.

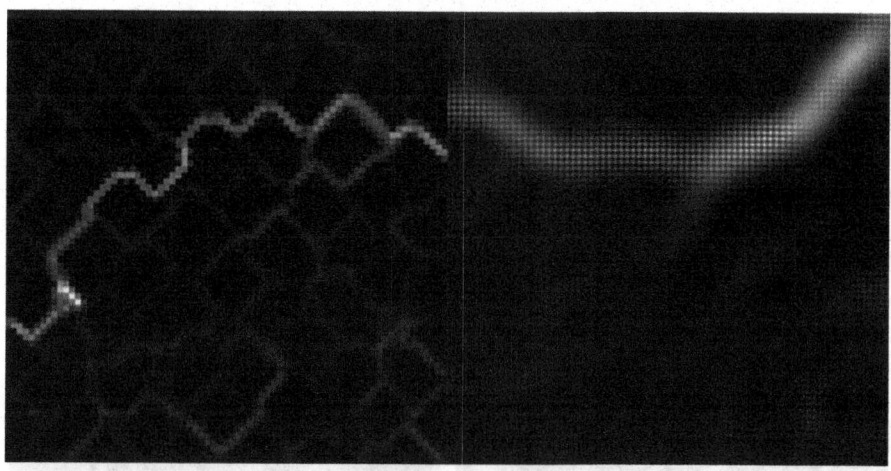

Fig. 3. Comparison between u-matrices generated on the IRIS dataset by the custom and SuSi implementations respectively.

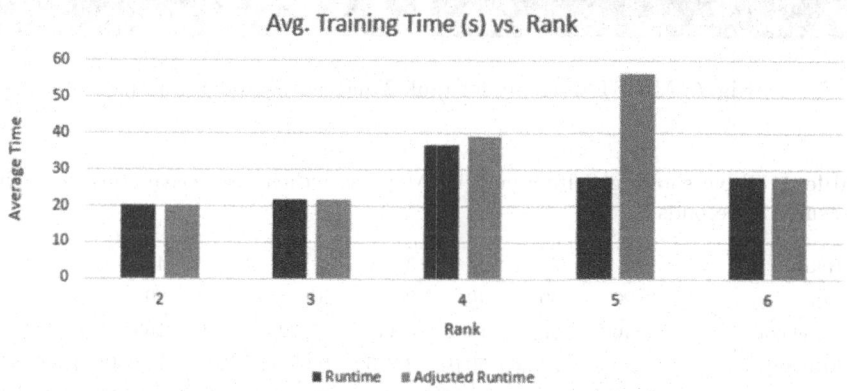

Fig. 4. The relation between a Self-Organising Map's rank and its training time measured in seconds

4.1 MNIST

The MNIST dataset was chosen as the initial test data for the fingerprint generation. MNIST was chosen as it is a well studied, freely available image dataset that is in greyscale, and the training and testing data is already split. Figure 5 shows the u-matrix of the Self-Organising Map when trained on a rank 2 SOM and a rank 3 SOM where the u-matrix is taken as slices of the SOM. Table 1 that follows shows the average training times, image fingerprinting error rate, and accuracy of image recognition using different distance metrics with respect to different sized SOM with different ranks.

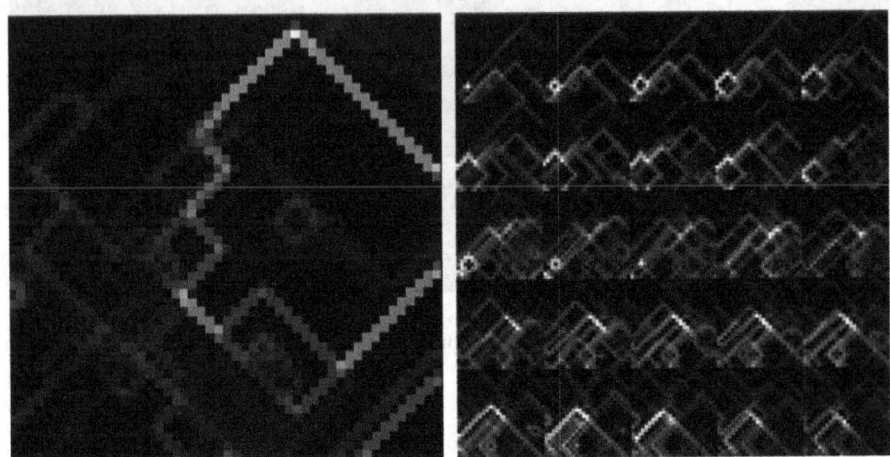

Fig. 5. MNIST u-matrix for rank 2 and 3 Self-Organising map

Table 1. Table showing Self-Organising Maps and their respective statistics. Time measured in seconds

Rank	2	2	2	3	3	3	4	4
Size	20	30	40	20	30	40	20	30
Node count	400	900	1600	8000	27000	64000	160000	810000
Training time	10.95	24.26	50.04	345.52	1068.92	2722.0	7239.08	37017.87
Fingerprinting time	687.89	1065.8	873.53	1342.13	3128.96	3364.83	6803.05	11863.93
Recognition time	524.53	349.15	572.33	924.13	1359.02	1863.06	2864.44	6634.27
Fingerprint error	18%	19%	17%	15%	16%	18%	27%	23%
Euclidean accuracy	65.20	65.00	62.70	70.10	64.00	64.30	62.70	62.40
Hamming accuracy	72.20	71.00	72.50	74.00	69.30	70.70	65.00	68.20
Manhattan accuracy	70.20	68.20	66.00	75.10	66.60	67.80	64.30	64.60

Interpreting the results from the table above, it is evident that the algorithm does better than randomly guessing if the images are the same. The accuracy also increases with training time but struggles to outpace the exponential growth of the node count. Thus, the best performing set of parameters was a SOM of rank 3 with a size of 20. Using this variable composition leads to a modest training time with better accuracy than other configurations. The following table (Table 2) compares the defined technique to modern image hashing methods. The algorithms being compared are average, perceptual, difference, and wavelet hashing. Looking at the values in the table, there is potential in using SOMs for image fingerprinting. This potential is evident in image recognition, where two images are similar, but the traditional hashes are too dissimilar.

Table 2. Table showing the accuracy and error of current image fingerprinting techniques

Technique	Fingerprint error	Recognition accuracy
Average hashing	0.15%	83.6%
Perceptual hashing	0.00%	81.5%
Difference hashing	0.00%	79.1%
Wavelet hashing	0.55%	62.0%

4.2 Noise Resilience

When fingerprinting, the technique must be noise resilient, as detail can be lost through compression, resizing, or watermarks. To demonstrate this technique's noise resilience, a set of 100 images that are the same size are used as input. Their fingerprints are compared to the same images but with noise applied in the form of loss of detail through compression and resizing, blurring, sharpening, changed pixel intensities or watermarks. Figure 6 demonstrates the different noise techniques and is followed by Table 3 with performance metrics.

Table 3. Effect of noise to image fingerprinting

	Blur	Sharpen	Smooth	Distorted	Watermark
Correct	93	98	96	95	77
Incorrect	7	2	4	5	23
Accuracy	93%	98%	96%	95%	77%

Fig. 6. Various noise filters that can be applied

5   Conclusion

In conclusion, this is a feasible technique for the fingerprinting of images. The noise-resilience of the technique ensures it would work with slightly altered images. Examples of alterations are watermarks or loss of detail through resizing and compression. While it can also perform image recognition, more research is required to improve the accuracy of the technique so that it can be competitive against techniques such as convolutional neural networks (one of the more commonly employed ANN architectures in the domain of image recognition problems) [1]. The main drawback of the technique is that training the SOM requires data similar to the images that will be fingerprinted, and training can be a time-consuming process. Future work on this topic could lead to new methods that decrease run times of the technique as well as increase fingerprinting accuracy. The applications of future work on this technique could also lead to improved image recognition and malware detection.

References

1. Bhandare, A., et al.: Applications of convolutional neural networks. Int. J. Comput. Sci. Inf. Technol. **7**, 2206–2215 (2016). ISSN 0975-9646. https://ijcsit.com/docs/Volume%207/vol7issue5/ijcsit20160705014.pdf
2. Coxeter, H.S.M.: Regular Polytopes, 3rd edn., pp. 58–73. Dover Publication Inc., New York (1973). 292296

3. Du, L., Ho, A.T.S., Cong, R.: Perceptual hashing for image authentication: a survey. Sig. Process. Image Commun. **81**, 115713 (2020). ISSN 0923-5965. https://doi.org/10.1016/j.image.2019.115713. http://www.sciencedirect.com/science/article/pii/S0923596519301286
4. Kohonen, T.: The basic SOM. In: Self-Organizing Maps, pp. 105–176. Springer, Heidelberg (2001). ISBN 978-3-642-56927-2. https://doi.org/10.1007/978-3-642-56927-2_3
5. Kohonen, T.: Variants of SOM. In: Self-Organizing Maps, pp. 191–243. Springer, Heidelberg (2001). ISBN 978-3-642-56927-2. https://doi.org/10.1007/978-3-642-56927-2_5
6. Polsterer, K.L., Gieseke, F., Doser, B.: PINK: parallelized rotation and flipping INvariant Kohonen maps (October 2019). ascl: 1910.001
7. Riese, F.M., Keller, S., Hinz, S.: Supervised and semi-supervised self-organizing maps for regression and classification focusing on hyperspectral data. Remote Sens. **12**(1), 7 (2019). rs12010007. https://doi.org/10.3390/rs12010007
8. Seiffert, U., Michaelis, B.: Multi-dimensional self-organizing maps on massively parallel hardware. In: Advances in Self-Organising Maps. Springer, London (2001). https://doi.org/10.1007/978-1-4471-0715-6_23

Implicit Maximum Likelihood Clustering

Georgios Vardakas and Aristidis Likas[(✉)]

Department of Computer Science and Engineering, University of Ioannina,
45110 Ioannina, Greece
g.vardakas@uoi.gr, arly@cs.uoi.gr

Abstract. Clustering is a popular unsupervised machine learning and data mining problem defined as a process of assigning objects to groups so that objects in the same group are similar to each other and differ from objects in other groups. In this paper, a data clustering method is proposed that is based on unsupervised training of a generative neural network using the technique of Implicit Maximum Likelihood Estimation (IMLE). Given a dataset, IMLE is an unsupervised method that trains a neural network that takes random noise as input and produces synthetic data samples whose distribution is close to the original data. We have developed an appropriate adaptation of the IMLE generative approach that also achieves clustering of the dataset. The proposed clustering method has been evaluated on several popular datasets of various types and complexity yielding promising results.

Keywords: Clustering · Neural networks · Implicit likelihood maximization · Synthetic data generation

1 Introduction

Clustering is one type of unsupervised learning and is defined as a process of partitioning a set of objects into groups (called clusters), so that the data in the same group share common characteristics [1,9,20]. It is one of the most important and popular problems in machine learning and data mining with numerous applications in computer science and many other scientific and technological areas [5,8]. Due to its particular importance, clustering is a well-studied problem and numerous approaches have been proposed that can be generally classified as hierarchical (divisive or agglomerative), model-based (e.g. k-means [14], mixture models [1]) and density-based (e.g. DBSCAN [3], DensityPeaks [18]).

A wide family of model-based approaches can be considered as Maximum Likelihood (ML) clustering methods. Such techniques construct a statistical generative model of the data by training a parametric probability density function model in order to maximize the likelihood of the data. The most popular approach is based on mixture models, where the underlying density model is a mixture of distributions. Once the mixture model has been trained, a clustering solution can be directly obtained by assuming that each component distribution

I. Maglogiannis et al. (Eds.): AIAI 2022, IFIP AICT 647, pp. 484–495, 2022.
https://doi.org/10.1007/978-3-031-08337-2_40

corresponds to a cluster and computing the posterior probability $P(k|x)$ that each data object x has been generated from the k-th component distribution. Then each data point x is assigned to the cluster k with maximum posterior probability. In the case where the component distributions are Gaussian, the well-known Gaussian mixture model (GMM) is obtained. An important issue to be stressed is that training neural network models for maximum likelihood clustering is considered a difficult task [16].

In this work, we aim to achieve generative maximum likelihood clustering based on neural networks, by exploiting a recently proposed method of *Implicit Maximum Likelihood Estimation* (IMLE) [13]. Given a set of data objects X, this method uses a neural network (called generator) that takes random input vectors and produces synthetic samples in the data space. By minimizing an appropriate objective, the network is trained so the distribution of samples resembles the data distribution. A notable issue is that it is proved that this training procedure maximizes the likelihood of the dataset without explicitly computing the likelihood.

Our proposed clustering method appropriately adapts the IMLE approach in order to achieve maximum likelihood clustering based on neural networks. As it will be explained, the modification occurs both in the way that the random input vectors are generated and in the way that representative synthetic samples are selected in order to be used for training. The method finally provides both a neural generator of synthetic samples that resemble the objects of dataset X as well as a partitioning of X into clusters.

The organization of the paper is the following. In Sect. 2 the IMLE method is described, while in Sect. 3 the proposed IMLE clustering method is presented and explained. Section 4 presents comparative experimental results on various datasets, while Sect. 5 provides conclusions and directions for future research.

2 Generative Modeling Using IMLE

Suppose we are given a dataset $X = \{x_1, ..., x_N\}$ where $x_i \in \mathbb{R}^d$. The Implicit Maximum Likelihood Estimation (IMLE) [13] approach assumes a neural network $\mathcal{G}_\theta$ with m inputs, d outputs and parameter vector (weights) θ. This network (called generator) takes as input a random vector $z \in \mathbb{R}^m$ usually sampled from the Normal distribution and produces a sample $s^\theta \in \mathbb{R}^d$, i.e., $s^\theta = \mathcal{G}_\theta(z)$ (see Fig. 2a).

IMLE trains the generator so that it can generate synthetic samples s^θ that resemble the real data x. It is a simple generative method that under certain conditions is equivalent to maximum likelihood estimation. This is surprising given that the IMLE objective does not explicitly contain any log-likelihood term and training neural networks using maximum likelihood is considered a difficult task [16].

At each IMLE iteration a sampling procedure takes place where a set of L random input vectors (called latent variables) are drawn from the Normal distribution $z_i \sim \mathcal{N}(0, \sigma^2)$ and used for the computation of the synthetic samples

$s_i^\theta = \mathcal{G}_\theta(z_i)$ $(i = 1, \ldots, L)$. Then, for each real data example x_i $(i = 1, \ldots, N)$, its representative sample $r_i^\theta \in S^\theta$ is computed via an application of the nearest neighbor search (NNS) in S^θ based on Euclidean distance, i.e. $r_i^\theta = NNS(x_i, S^\theta)$. The generator parameters θ are updated in order to minimize the following IMLE objective function:

$$\hat{\theta}_{IMLE} = argmin_\theta \sum_{i=1}^{n} ||r_i^\theta - x_i||_2^2 \tag{1}$$

IMLE training is summarized in Fig. 1. It is obvious that IMLE is very simple to implement. Moreover, it does not suffer from mode collapse, vanishing gradients or training instability, unlike popular deep generative methods such as, for example, GANs [7]. Mode collapses do not occur since the loss ensures that each data example is represented by at least one sample. Gradients do not vanish because the gradient of the distance between a data example and its representative sample does not become zero unless they coincide. Training is stable because the IMLE estimator is the solution to a simple minimization problem. Finally, it can be used both in the case of small and large datasets.

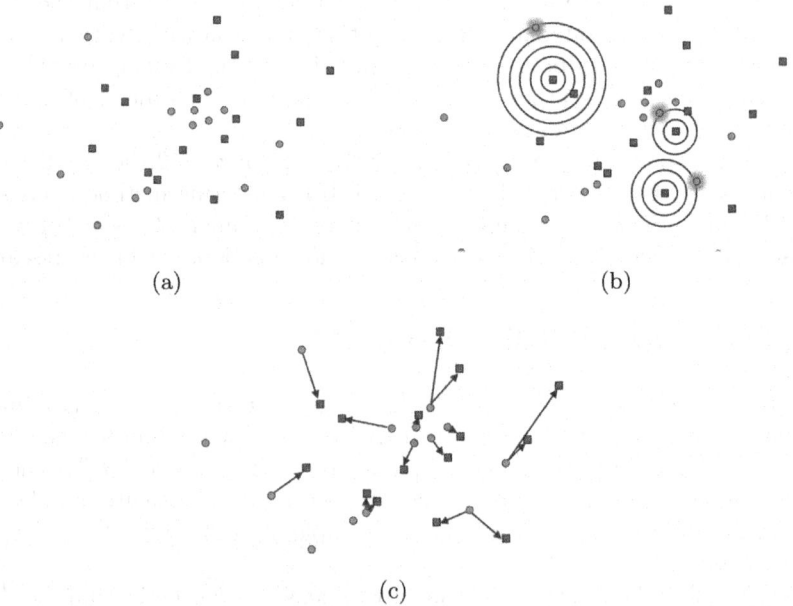

(a)   (b)

(c)

Fig. 1. (a) The data points are represented by squares and the samples by circles. (b) For each data point the nearest sample is found. (c) Minimize the IMLE objective.

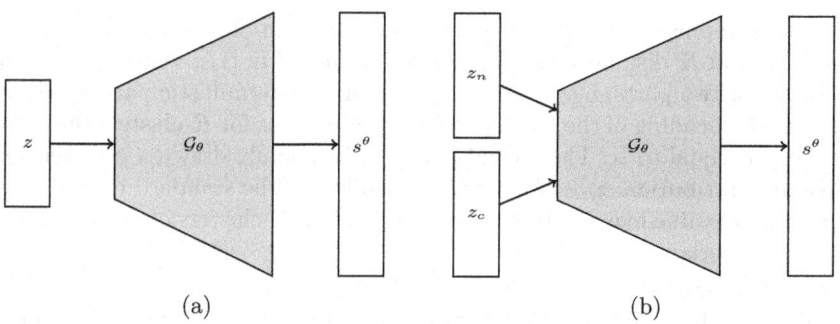

(a)   (b)

Fig. 2. (a) IMLE general architecture. (b) IMLE clustering architecture.

3 Clustering Based on IMLE

In this work, we propose a modification of the IMLE method in order to achieve not only synthetic data generation but also clustering of the original dataset X. More precisely, we introduce two basic algorithmic modifications to the IMLE framework namely: (i) a cluster-friendly sampling prior to generate random input vectors z_i and (ii) the two-stage nearest neighbor search algorithm to determine the representative sample $r_i^\theta \in S^\theta$ for a data point x_i. The two issues are explained below.

An important observation is that each data point x can be associated with the input vector z that generated the representative sample r^θ of x. Therefore, except for the correspondence (x, r^θ), the correspondence (x, z) (where $r^\theta = G_\theta(z)$)) can be defined and it will be exploited in our clustering method.

3.1 Cluster Friendly Input Distribution

In the original IMLE method, the input random vectors z belong to a single cluster since they are drawn from a multivariate m-dimensional Normal distribution. However, it can be observed that, if the original data x_i form distinct clusters, the corresponding input vectors also demonstrate a clustering tendency in the sense that similar data points x_i correspond to input vectors z_i that are close.

Based on this observation, if we assume that the random input vectors are drawn from a mixture model (i.e. from K distinct distributions), then a clustering of the original dataset X can be obtained: each data point x_i can be assigned to the cluster from which its corresponding input vector has been drawn. Therefore in the proposed method, the single Normal distribution is replaced by K non-overlapping distributions, with the k-th distribution responsible for the generation of the subset Z_k of input vectors assigned to cluster k. The most obvious first choice is a mixture of K m-dimensional Gaussian distributions. However, this choice requires the specification of the centers and covariances of K Gaussian distributions which are well separated.

A more sophisticated mechanism for generating m-dimensional random vectors that form K disjoint clusters has been proposed in [17], where input vector z consists of two parts, i.e. $z = (z_c, z_n)$. The first deterministic part z_c which is the one-hot encoding of the corresponding cluster, thus for K clusters the dimension of z_c is equal to K. The second part z_n is randomly drawn a p-dimensional Gaussian distribution: $z_n \sim \mathcal{N}(0, \sigma^2 I)$. In addition, the standard deviation σ is set to a small value like $\sigma = 0.10$ to ensure that the K clusters of random vectors Z_k do not overlap.

In summary, in order to generate an input vector $z = (z_c, z_n)$ of cluster k, we set z_c equal to the one-hot encoding of k and draw z_n from $\mathcal{N}(0, \sigma^2 I)$. By sampling an equal number of vectors for each cluster k the set of random input vectors Z is created at each iteration which is partitioned into disjoint subsets Z_k each one containing the random input vectors for cluster k $(k = 1, \ldots, K)$. Additionally, since $s^\theta = G_\theta(z)$, the set S^θ of computed samples is partitioned into K disjoint clusters S_k^θ. Consequently, the original dataset X can be partitioned into K clusters by assigning each x_i to the cluster of its representative r_i^θ, i.e. if $r_i^\theta \in S_k^\theta$ then x_i is assigned to cluster k.

3.2 Two-Stage Nearest Neighbor Search for Determining Data Representatives

As we already mentioned, for each data point x_i, the IMLE method performs a nearest neighbor search in the entire set of the generated samples S^θ to locate the representative sample $r_i^\theta \in S^\theta$ that is used in the IMLE objective (Eq. 1). We have empirically observed that clustering performance can be improved if we modify this strategy in order to take into account that samples s^θ are partitioned into subsets S_k^θ.

To take this information into account, we first compute the centroid c_k of each subset S_k^θ. Then we assign a data point x_i to the cluster l whose centroid c_l is nearest to x_i based on Euclidean distance. Then instead of determining the representative sample for x_i through nearest neighbor search over the entire set of samples S^θ, we confine the nearest neighbor search to the specific subset S_l^θ that contains the samples of cluster l. Therefore, $\hat{r}_i^\theta = NNS(x_i, S_l^\theta)$.

$$\hat{\theta} := argmin_\theta \sum_{i=1}^{n} ||\hat{r}_i^\theta - x_i||_2^2 \tag{2}$$

The proposed IMLE clustering method is presented in the Algorithm 1. Note that the gradient-based updates can use any standard gradient-based learning rule with the most popular choice being the Adam optimizer [10].

Algorithm 1. IMLE clustering algorithm

Require: Data X, number of clusters K
1: Specify the network architecture $\mathcal{G}_\theta$, the number of samples L, the number of iterations T
2: **for** $t \leftarrow 1$ to T **do**
3:     Sample K clusters of random input vectors $Z = \{z_1, ..., z_L\}$, where $z = (z_n, z_c)$. Let Z_k the subset corresponding to cluster k.
4:     Generate samples $\{s_1^\theta, ..., s_L^\theta\}$, where $s_i^\theta = \mathcal{G}_\theta(z_i)$. Let S_k^θ the subset corresponding to cluster k.
5:     For every S_k^θ compute the corresponding centroid c_k.
6:     For each x_i find $\hat{r}_i^\theta$ with the two-stage nearest neighbor search.
7:     Update the parameters θ of the generator network by descending its stochastic gradient:

$$\nabla_\theta \sum_{i=1}^n \|\hat{r}_i^\theta - x_i\|_2^2 \tag{3}$$

8: **end for**
9: Find the final clustering by assigning each x_i based on the nearest sample centroid c_l.
10: Return the final network parameters θ^* and the clustering solution.

Table 1. Main characteristics of the tested datasets.

Dataset	Instances	Features	Classes
Images			
Fashion-Mnist	60000	784	10
Mnist	60000	784	10
Olivetti	400	4096	40
Tabular			
10x_73k	73233	720	8
Australian	690	14	2
Dermatology	366	34	6
Ecoli	336	7	8
Iris	150	4	3
Pendigits	10992	16	10
Wine	178	13	3

4 Experiments

4.1 Datasets

In order to evaluate the proposed clustering method, several datasets have been considered. More specifically, we have conducted experiments on three image datasets and seven tabular datasets. In Table 1, we present the characteristics of the datasets used in our study. In all experiments, the number of clusters K was set equal to the number of classes of each dataset. All data are normalized in $[0, 1]$.

- **Fashion-MNIST** [19] dataset consists 60,000 training samples of grayscale images describing a fashion product. Each sample is a 784 image associated with a label from ten classes.
- **MNIST** [12] dataset consists of 60,000 training samples of grayscale images of handwritten digits. Each sample is a 784 image and it is associated with a label from ten classes.
- **Olivetti** [6] is a face database of 40 individuals with ten 4096 grayscale images per individual. For some individuals, the images were taken at different times, varying the lighting, facial expressions (open/closed eyes, smiling/not smiling) and facial details (glasses/no glasses). All the images were taken against a dark homogeneous background with the subjects in an upright, frontal position (with tolerance for some side movement).
- **10x_73k** [21] dataset consists of 73233 RNA-transcripts belonging to 8 different cell types. The 720 genes with the highest variances across the cells were selected to reduce the data dimensionality. The data set is sparse, since the data matrix has about 40% zero values.
- **Australian** [2] two-class dataset is composed of 690 credit card applications. Each sample is described by 14-dimensional feature vector.
- **Dermatology** [2] six-class dataset is composed of 366 patient records that suffer from six different types of the Eryhemato-Squamous disease. Each patient is described by a 34-dimensional vector, containing clinical and histopathological features.
- **Ecoli** [2] includes 336 proteins from the E.coli bacterium and seven attributes, calculated from the amino acid sequences, are provided. Proteins belong to eight categories according to their cellular localization sites.
- **Iris** [2] dataset contains three classes of 50 instances each, where each class refers to a type of iris plant. Each sample is described by a 4-dimensional vector, corresponding to the length and the width of the sepals and petals, in centimeters.
- **Pendigits** [2] dataset consists of 10992 writing samples from 44 different writers, in total 10992 written samples. Each sample is a 16-dimensional vector, containing pixel coordinates associated with a label from ten classes.
- **Wine** [2] tree-class dataset consists of 178 samples of chemical analysis of wines. Each sample is described by a 13-dimensional feature vector.

4.2   Neural Network Architecture

The networks are trained using the Adam optimizer with learning rate $n = 10^{-4}$ and coefficients $b_1 = 0.5$ and $b_2 = 0.9$. The dimension of z_c is the set equal to the number of classes in the dataset. We used Leaky Relu activations (LRelu) with leak $= 0.2$ and Batch Normalization (BN) and we trained the generator for 2000

Table 2. Network architecture for each dataset.

Dataset	Input (z_n, z_c)	Hidden {1, 2}	Output
Images			
Fashion-MNIST	(10, 10)	FC 256 LReLU BN	FC 784 Sigmoid
MNIST	(10, 10)	FC 256 LReLU BN	FC 784 Sigmoid
Olivetti	(10, 40)	FC 256 LReLU BN	FC 4096 Sigmoid
Tabular			
10x_73k	(10, 8)	FC 256 LReLU BN	FC 720 Sigmoid
Australian	(5, 2)	FC 256 LReLU BN	FC 14 Sigmoid
Dermatology	(5, 6)	FC 256 LReLU BN	FC 34 Sigmoid
Ecoli	(2, 8)	FC 256 LReLU BN	FC 7 Sigmoid
Iris	(2, 3)	FC 256 LReLU BN	FC 4 Sigmoid
Pendigits	(5, 10)	FC 256 LReLU BN	FC 16 Sigmoid
Wine	(2, 3)	FC 256 LReLU BN	FC 3 Sigmoid

Table 3. Selected batch size per datasets.

Dataset	Instances	Batch size	#Batches
Images			
Fashion-Mnist	60000	1024	58
Mnist	60000	1024	58
Olivetti	400	400	1
Tabular			
10x_73k	73233	1024	71
Australian	690	690	1
Dermatology	366	366	1
Ecoli	336	336	1
Iris	150	150	1
Pendigits	10992	1024	10
Wine	178	178	1

epochs for all datasets. The hidden layers are the same for all networks. It is necessary to adjust the input and the output layers based on the given dataset. The details of the network architectures are presented in Table 2. The number of synthetic samples generated was chosen to be equal to twice the number of data ($L = 2N$) in all cases. In Table 3 we present the selected batch size per dataset.

4.3   Evaluation Metrics

It is necessary to mention that since clustering is an unsupervised problem, we ensured that all algorithms are unaware of the true category of the data. In order to evaluate the results of the clustering methods, we use the standard evaluation metrics which assume that a ground truth clustering is available. For all algorithms, the number of clusters is set to the number of ground-truth categories [15] and assumes ground truth that cluster labels coincide with class labels. The first evaluation metric is Clustering Accuracy (ACC):

$$ACC = \max_m \frac{\sum\limits_{i=1}^{n} I(y_i = m(c_i))}{n} \tag{4}$$

where $I(x) = 1$ if x is true and 0 otherwise, y_i is the ground-truth label, c_i is the cluster assignment generated by the clustering algorithm, and m is a mapping function which ranges over all possible one-to-one mappings between assignments and labels. This metric finds the best matching between cluster assignments from a clustering method and the ground truth. It is worth noting that the optimal mapping function can be efficiently computed by the Hungarian algorithm [11]. The second evaluation metric is the Normalized Mutual Information (NMI) defined as [4]:

$$NMI(Y, C) = \frac{2 \times I(Y, C)}{H(Y) + H(C)} \tag{5}$$

where Y denotes the ground-truth labels, C denotes the clusters labels, I is the mutual information metric and H the entropy.

4.4   Experimental Results

In our experimental study, the proposed IMLE clustering method was compared in all datasets against k-means and the typical maximum likelihood clustering method which is the Gaussian Mixture Model (GMM). It should be noted that GMMs with diagonal covariance has been considered. Since all compared methods depend on initialization, we executed each algorithm 10 times with random initialization and provide in Table 4 the average and standard deviation for ACC and NMI.

It can be observed that the IMLE clustering approach outperforms the typical methods in the case of large datasets with structured data (images) in most cases. For small datasets, it is superior in some cases, while in the remaining cases it demonstrates comparable performance. It should be emphasized that the method does not necessarily require large datasets to be trained as happens with deep clustering methods (like clusterGAN [17]) that cannot be employed to cluster datasets with few data. This major advantage of our method is inherited from the IMLE approach and makes the method applicable in all clustering problems.

Table 4. Experimental results on several datasets. Bold numbers indicate the best average performance for each dataset.

Dataset	Algorithm	ACC	NMI
	Images		
Fashion-MNIST	IMLE clustering	**0.56** ± 0.05	**0.51** ± 0.02
	K-means	0.52 ± 0.02	0.47 ± 0.01
	GMM	0.52 ± 0.02	0.48 ± 0.02
MNIST	IMLE clustering	**0.55** ± 0.02	0.48 ± 0.02
	K-means	0.51 ± 0.03	0.48 ± 0.02
	GMM	0.51 ± 0.03	**0.49** ± 0.02
Olivetti-Faces	IMLE clustering	**0.56** ± 0.03	**0.77** ± 0.01
	K-means	0.52 ± 0.02	0.74 ± 0.01
	GMM	0.35 ± 0.03	0.62 ± 0.03
	Tabular		
10x_73k	IMLE clustering	0.53 ± 0.03	0.49 ± 0.03
	K-means	**0.54** ± 0.05	0.55 ± 0.04
	GMM	**0.54** ± 0.04	**0.58** ± 0.01
Australian	IMLE clustering	**0.77** ± 0.07	**0.25** ± 0.14
	K-means	0.73 ± 0.13	0.23 ± 0.18
	GMM	0.67 ± 0.11	0.12 ± 0.12
Dermatology	IMLE clustering	**0.73** ± 0.05	**0.80** ± 0.04
	K-means	0.68 ± 0.13	**0.80** ± 0.06
	GMM	0.70 ± 0.04	0.70 ± 0.04
Ecoli	IMLE clustering	0.56 ± 0.03	0.56 ± 0.03
	K-means	0.52 ± 0.05	0.56 ± 0.03
	GMM	**0.58** ± 0.08	**0.60** ± 0.03
Iris	IMLE clustering	0.89 ± 0.01	0.74 ± 0.02
	K-means	0.82 ± 0.10	0.70 ± 0.05
	GMM	**0.92** ± 0.00	**0.80** ± 0.00
Pendigits	IMLE clustering	**0.70** ± 0.03	0.66 ± 0.03
	K-means	0.69 ± 0.04	**0.69** ± 0.01
	GMM	0.58 ± 0.03	0.58 ± 0.03
Wine	IMLE clustering	**0.94** ± 0.01	**0.82** ± 0.02
	K-means	0.92 ± 0.08	0.80 ± 0.08
	GMM	**0.94** ± 0.03	**0.82** ± 0.06

5   Conclusions

We have proposed a data clustering method that is based on training a generative neural network using the technique of Implicit Maximum Likelihood Estimation (IMLE). In IMLE a neural network is trained that takes as input random noise and produces synthetic data similar to the data in the training set. We have appropriately modified the IMLE method by combining the generative process with a clustering procedure in order to perform clustering of the data in the training set. The proposed method has provided good clustering results on several datasets of various sizes and dimensionality.

Future research could focus on the detailed experimental investigation of the performance of the method and its sensitivity to various parameters such as the network architecture and the number of synthetic samples. Alternative mixture distributions for the random inputs could also be examined. Finally, it would be interesting to consider the use of a second neural network that will be trained to implement the inverse mapping of the generator network, i.e. it will take a synthetic sample as input and will provide as output the corresponding random input vector.

Acknowledgements. This research was supported by project "Dioni: Computing Infrastructure for Big-Data Processing and Analysis" (MIS No. 5047222) co-funded by European Union (ERDF) and Greece through Operational Program "Competitiveness, Entrepreneurship and Innovation", NSRF 2014-2020.

References

1. Bishop, C.M.: Pattern recognition and machine learning, Springer (2006)
2. Dua, D., Graff, C.: UCI machine learning repository (2017). http://archive.ics.uci.edu/ml
3. Ester, M., Kriegel, H.P., Sander, J., Xu, X., et al.: A density-based algorithm for discovering clusters in large spatial databases with noise. In: KDD, vol. 96, pp. 226–231 (1996)
4. Estévez, P.A., Tesmer, M., Perez, C.A., Zurada, J.M.: Normalized mutual information feature selection. IEEE Trans. Neural Netw. **20**(2), 189–201 (2009)
5. Filippone, M., Camastra, F., Masulli, F., Rovetta, S.: A survey of kernel and spectral methods for clustering. Pattern Recogn. **41**(1), 176–190 (2008)
6. Frey, B.J., Dueck, D.: Clustering by passing messages between data points. Science **315**(5814), 972–976 (2007)
7. Goodfellow, I., et al.: Generative adversarial nets. In: Advances in Neural Information Processing Systems, pp. 2672–2680 (2014)
8. Jain, A.K.: Data clustering: 50 years beyond k-means. Pattern Recogn. Lett. **31**(8), 651–666 (2010)
9. Jain, A.K., Murty, M.N., Flynn, P.J.: Data clustering: a review. ACM Comput. Surv. (CSUR) **31**(3), 264–323 (1999)
10. Kingma, D.P., Ba, J.: Adam: a method for stochastic optimization. arXiv preprint arXiv:1412.6980 (2014)
11. Kuhn, H.W.: The Hungarian method for the assignment problem. Nav. Res. Logist. (NRL) **52**(1), 7–21 (2005)

12. LeCun, Y., Cortes, C.: MNIST handwritten digit database (2010). http://yann. lecun.com/exdb/mnist/
13. Li, K., Malik, J.: Implicit maximum likelihood estimation. arXiv preprint arXiv:1809.09087 (2018)
14. MacQueen, J., et al.: Some methods for classification and analysis of multivariate observations. In: Proceedings of the 5th Berkeley Symposium on Mathematical Statistics and Probability, Oakland, CA, USA, vol. 1, pp. 281–297 (1967)
15. Min, E., Guo, X., Liu, Q., Zhang, G., Cui, J., Long, J.: A survey of clustering with deep learning: From the perspective of network architecture. IEEE Access **6**, 39501–39514 (2018)
16. Mohamed, S., Lakshminarayanan, B.: Learning in implicit generative models. arXiv preprint arXiv:1610.03483 (2016)
17. Mukherjee, S., Asnani, H., Lin, E., Kannan, S.: ClusterGAN: latent space clustering in generative adversarial networks. In: Proceedings of the AAAI Conference on Artificial Intelligence, vol. 33, pp. 4610–4617 (2019)
18. Rodriguez, A., Laio, A.: Clustering by fast search and find of density peaks. Science **344**(6191), 1492–1496 (2014)
19. Xiao, H., Rasul, K., Vollgraf, R.: Fashion-MNIST: a novel image dataset for benchmarking machine learning algorithms. arXiv preprint arXiv:1708.07747 (2017)
20. Xu, R., Wunsch, D.: Clustering, vol. 10. Wiley (2008)
21. Zheng, G.X., et al.: Massively parallel digital transcriptional profiling of single cells. Nat. Commun. **8**(1), 1–12 (2017)

Query Driven Data Subspace Mapping

Panagiotis Fountas[1]([✉])[iD], Maria Papathanasaki[1][iD], Kostas Kolomvatsos[1][iD],
and Christos Anagnostopoulos[2][iD]

[1] Department of Informatics and Telecommunications, University of Thessaly,
Papasiopoulou 2-4, 35131 Lamia, Greece
{pfountas,mpapathanasaki,kostasks}@uth.gr
[2] School of Computing Science, University of Glasgow, Lilybank Gardens 18,
G12 8RZ Glasgow, UK
christos.anagnostopoulos@glasgow.ac.uk

Abstract. The increased use of multiple types of smart devices in several application domains, opens the pathways for the collection of humongous volumes of data. At the same time, the need for processing of only a subset of these data by applications in order to quickly conclude tasks execution and knowledge extraction, has resulted in the adoption of a very high number of queries set into distributed datasets. As a result, a significant process is the efficient response to these queries both in terms of time and the appropriate data. In this paper, we present a hierarchical query-driven clustering approach, for performing efficient data mapping in remote datasets for the management of future queries. Our work differs from other current methods in the sense that it combines a Query-Based Learning (QBL) model with a hierarchical clustering in the same methodology. The performance of the proposed model is assessed by a set of experimental scenarios while we present the relevant numerical outcomes.

Keywords: Data mapping · Data management · Query-based learning · Hierarchical clustering · Data retrieval

1 Introduction

In the era of the intense increase of data collection and production, analysts have to cope with a massive amount of datasets which are spread across multiple locations. As a consequence, several challenges have emerged for data management and information retrieval. Data mapping is the process of combining data from various sources into a particular dataset storing it in a consistent manner. This procedure is essential in various processing activities including data migration, data integration, etc. One of the major challenges, when data management is the case, is the estimation of the appropriate responses to requests for processing performed in the minimum possible time. Such requests are, usually, formulated in the form of queries defining specific constraints and conditions for data retrieval.

© IFIP International Federation for Information Processing 2022
Published by Springer Nature Switzerland AG 2022
I. Maglogiannis et al. (Eds.): AIAI 2022, IFIP AICT 647, pp. 496–508, 2022.
https://doi.org/10.1007/978-3-031-08337-2_41

Queries are reported by streams to processing nodes that may be present at various locations being directly connected with smart devices. Devices are 'responsible' to collect data and report them feeding the geo-distributed datasets (DDSs).

In the current effort, we present a hierarchical clustering model adopted to detect the proper data for executing queries delivered to a server (SV) in the minimum time. We elaborate on a model which takes into consideration the data requested by a number of historical queries to detect and collect those that a future query may require avoiding to 'scan' the entire dataset. The proposed model performs two different types of clustering: (i) a fuzzy clustering using the Fuzzy C-Means (FCM) algorithm, and (ii) a hard clustering using K-Means (KM) algorithm. Both methods are adopted to group similar queries based on the data they request. When a new query arrives, the proposed model checks to find the most similar clusters. We also involve into our model a mechanism which concludes the overlap of the 'data area' of interest between two queries. We consider a set $DS = \{DS_1, \ldots, DS_w\}$ of DDSs and a SV. We also assume that a group Z_i of devices present in the Internet of Things (IoT) infrastructure is connected with a DDS DS_i such that each Z_i is connected with only one DS_i. IoT devices collect and report data into the respective DS_i in the form of multivariate vectors; $X_j^t = [x_1^t, \ldots, x_d^t]$, where the index j expresses the IoT device reporting X_j^t and the index t shows the time instance that X_j^t is reported. Additionally, d is the number of dimensions of X_j^t. DDSs receive X_j^t and store them in the appropriate format to be the subject of further processing activities. The SV receives queries $Q = \{q_1, q_2, \ldots\}$ from applications and users. We consider that every vector can be represented as a point in the d-dimensional space. q_i requires a number Φ of points as a response and can contain range selection operators for one or more dimensions. This means that q_i can create the boundaries of the area in which the requested data are located. Apparently, the SV has to detect the appropriate data to formulate the final responses to the incoming queries.

The novelty of this paper is that we combine the QBL [12,13] with a hierarchical clustering scheme into a model that is able to predict which data should be retrieved for similar future queries. The following list reports on the contributions of our work: **(i)** We propose a hierarchical clustering-based model combining two different types of clustering methods for the detection of the appropriate data that correspond to queries requests in the minimum possible time and with the minimum error; **(ii)** We adopt QBL to retrieve the appropriate data for the incoming queries while relying on the retrieved data of previously executed queries; **(iii)** We argue on an data overlap metric between the 'areas' of the incoming queries to detect the existence of common data points between past and future queries' requests.

The rest of the paper is organized as follows. Section 2 reports on the related work while Sect. 3 elaborates on the preliminary information before we present our model. Section 4 discusses the proposed model and Sect. 5 presents the adopted experimental evaluation approach. Finally, Sect. 6 concludes this paper by presenting our future research plans.

2   Related Work

Any data management process consists of an important factor for the effectiveness of various tasks like as the generation of analytics upon a specific dataset. The research community has proposed several models and mechanisms for the improvement of various data management processes.

The authors of [1] present a solution for assigning queries and tasks in the appropriate edge computing nodes to reduce the response time. For this purpose, the authors propose a method for the estimation of the computational burden, that an allocation of a query will add to a node. Also, the authors develop an ensemble similarity scheme, responsible to deliver the complexity class for each query or task and a probabilistic decision-making model. In [2], the authors define the concept of a Query Controller (QC) that assigns each query into a processor. Based on this model, they develop a framework for query assignment which involves two learning schemes, i.e., a Reinforcement Learning (RL) and a clustering scheme. In [3], the authors introduce an adaptive, reciprocity-based Machine Learning mechanism, to estimate the answers of a variety of aggregate queries (AQs). The mechanism learns from past analytical-query patterns while the authors develop solutions to correspond in changes in queries' requests. In [4], the authors discuss the Data Canopy framework, adopted to reduce the time needed to compute the statistical information of a dataset. The proposed framework is a smart cache designed for statistical exploratory analysis. It calculates and caches the fundamental primitives of statistical measures, thus, it composes results for future queries without having to return to the base data. The authors of [5] propose WANalytics, a geo-distributed system that copes with the Wide-Area Big Data problem, a challenge that concerns the supporting rich Directed Acyclic Graphs (DAGs) of computation over globally distributed data. WANalytics is formed by two major parts. The first one is a runtime layer that distributes user DAGs around data centers, and the other part pertains to a workload analyzer that constantly checks and improves the user workload.

The difference of our work compared to other efforts in the domain, is that we do not focus on the query allocation problem to nodes that exhibit a low load and a high processing speed, but on the creation of query clusters that share similar data requests. We do not deal with storing aggregates to synthesize answers for future queries, but we detect what historical queries are similar to the future ones, and return the historical responses as answer to the future queries. In addition, we deviate from approaches that propose solutions for the minimization of the required bandwidth, and we focus on the accuracy of the final results and the time requirements for delivering the outcome and not on the network performance. This is because we consider that queries do not require too many network resources to be reported and responded.

3   Preliminaries

K-Means Algorithm. K-Means algorithm (KM) is one of the most popular unsupervised clustering models. It groups the given data into K clusters trying to minimize the following objective function: $J = \sum_{i=1}^{K} \sum_{p \in C_i} \|p - c_i\|^2$. The minimization of the discussed equation is equivalent to the minimization of the distance between points in a cluster C_i with the centroid c_i. We consider a set $D = \{\vec{p}_1, \ldots, \vec{p}_n\}$ which consists of n vectors considered as a d-dimensional points. KM has the goal of splitting the n vectors into K clusters, where K $\leq n$ should be defined in advance. The steps of the KM are as follows [6,8,9]: (i) K points from D are randomly selected to be the centroids of clusters; (ii) In the second step, the algorithm computes for every point in D the distance from the available centroids. Afterwards, every data point is assigned to the closest cluster; (iii) The algorithm recalculates the centroids of each cluster' adopting the mean of the cluster members; (iv) The algorithm iterates to the second step till the stopping condition is true. For instance, a specific number of iterations l could be chosen. We have to notice that the cluster centroids could be virtual data points. The time complexity of KM depends on three parameters; the number of data vectors n, the number of clusters K and the number of iterations l that the algorithm needs to cluster the data. Consequently, the time complexity is $O(n \cdot K \cdot l)$ [6].

Fuzzy C-Means. FCM algorithm is a fuzzy clustering algorithm which assigns each data point to a cluster according to a membership value $u_{gi} \in [0,1]$ (g is the index of every data vector). u_{gi} indicates the correlation between a data point and the cluster center c_i, thus, the data point is assigned to the cluster with the highest membership value [7]. Given D, the FCM results a $n \times \varGamma$ matrix **U** which includes the membership values for each data point, and a set $C = \{C_1, C_2, C_3, \ldots, C_\varGamma\}$ of clusters with centroids $\{c_1, c_2, c_3, \ldots, c_\varGamma\}$. The FCM requires three parameters: (i) the fuzzier $m \in [1, \infty)$ that controls the fuzziness of the clustering; (ii) the number of clusters $\varGamma$ and; (iii) the stopping criterion value $\beta \in [0,1]$. The FCM intends to minimize the following objective function: $J_m = \sum_{i=1}^{\varGamma} \sum_{g=1}^{n} (u_{gi})^m \cdot \|p_g - c_i\|^2$. The steps of the algorithm are referred below [8–11]: (i) Choose of the parameters m,$\varGamma$,β; (ii) Initialize the membership matrix **U**; (iii) Calculate the centers of every cluster in C; (iv) Update the membership matrix **U**; (v) Repeat steps (iii), (iv) until the divergence is less than β; (vi) Output **U**,C. The following equations are adopted to deliver u_{gi} and c_i:

$$u_{gi} = \frac{1}{\sum_{j=1}^{\varGamma} \left\{ \frac{\|p_g - c_i\|}{\|p_g - c_j\|} \right\}^{\frac{2}{m-1}}} \tag{1}$$

$$c_i = \frac{\sum_{g=1}^{n} (u_{gi})^m \cdot p_g}{\sum_{g=1}^{n} (u_{gi})^m} \tag{2}$$

4 The Proposed Approach

We elaborate on the proposed model adopted to limit the time for providing responses to the incoming queries by incorporating statistical information retrieved by past queries. We call our model Hierarchical Mixed Clustering Model (HMCM). HMCM comprises two phases: (i) the 'warm up' phase and; (ii) the 'performance' phase. The 'warm up' phase consists of two stages; the preparation stage and the hierarchical clustering execution stage. In the preparation stage, when a query is reported to the SV, the HMCM performs a sequential scan of the entire database to determine the suitable data points. When a z number of queries have been sent to SV, the HMCM proceeds to the second stage of the 'warm up' phase. In this second stage, the hierarchical clustering execution stage, a hierarchical clustering is performed to create clusters and subclusters upon historical queries, which will take part of the 'performance' phase. The performance phase targets to map the appropriate data as the response to a future incoming query. Initially, the HMCM adopts the FCM to create the aforementioned set of clusters C upon z queries. Afterwards, the model divides every cluster further into a set of $N_{C_i} = \{S_1, S_2, \ldots, S_M\}$ using the KM algorithm. In the 'performance' phase, the HMCM is activated every time a query is reported to the SV. More specifically, the proposed model uses a similarity metric, to identify the top-r clusters whose members have the same data requests as the incoming query. Then, the HMCM utilizes again a correlation/similarity metric to identify, for each of the top-r clusters, the top-ℓ subclusters. Therefore, we focus only on groups of queries that have the most relevant data requests to the incoming query. In our implementation, we adopt the Euclidean Distance to realize the similarity/correlation metric. Moreover, we propose the adoption of an overlapping metric to detect the 'matching' between the data requests of queries. We consider that every query is represented by the area of points that targets to receive the final response. The Area Overlap Metric (AOM) is provided by the following equation:

$$AOM(q_{inc}, q_{member}) = \frac{q_{inc} \cap q_{member}}{incoming \ query \ area} \tag{3}$$

In the above equation, the numerator is the overlap area between two queries. q_{inc} is the incoming query while q_{member} depicts the queries in top-ℓ subclusters of every cluster present on the top-r list. The denominator is the area where the requested data may be present. The AOM indicates the percentage of the q_{inc} area which is covered by the area of q_{member} queries. The HMCM, after the detection of the appropriate clusters and subclusters, examines the members of the detected subclusters, to find those queries q_{member} where the AOM between them and the q_{inc} exceeds a pre-defined threshold θ. Afterwards, the HMCM retrieves only the data points that belong to the q_{member} queries, which satisfy the aforementioned condition. The q_{member} queries selection approach, gives the HMCM the ability to 'avoid' queries that belong into the top-ℓ subclusters of top-r clusters but they do not require data from the common area. This approach also allows the HMCM to ignore queries with which the q_{inc} shares a common area, but the AOM realization does not exceed θ. Algorithm 1 presents the steps adopted by the HMCM model to deliver the final outcomes.

For comparison purposes, we elaborate on two additional methods. We call the first as the Baseline Method (BM). BM is executed every time that a query is reported locally and scans the entire dataset, selecting data that satisfy the query. This approach identifies all the required data points and is the theoretical optimal threshold in terms of error. However, scanning all data in the DDSs for every query, it is a time consuming process. The second method is called Hard Clustering Based Method (HCBM) and is based on the clustering of 'similar' queries that the SV receives during a period of W time instances. Initially, the HCBM is trained over z incoming queries (the training phase), using the BM to identify the data required for their execution and, then, utilizes KM to cluster them. When a query is sent to the SV, the HCBM is 'triggered' and uses a correlation/similarity metric to find the top-r similar clusters to the incoming query. The HCBM uses the top-r clusters that have been detected to retrieve data points that satisfy the incoming query.

Algorithm 1. Pseudocode of the HMCM algorithm

D: The set of data

1: $counter = 0$
2: **while** $counter \leq z$ **do**
3:     Receive q_{inc}
4:     $counter + +$
5:     reponse = ScanDataset()
6:     Q.add(q_{inc})
7: **end while**
8: C = PerformFCM(Q)
9: **for** $C_i \in C$ **do**
10:     N_{C_i} =ExecuteKMeans(C_i)
11: **end for**
12: **while** true **do**
13:     Receive q_{inc}
14:     Top$r$CIds=FindTop$r$SimilarClusters(C,q_{inc})
15:     **for** ω in Top$r$CIds **do**
16:         TopℓSIds= FindTopℓSimilarSubspaces(N_{C_ω}, q_{inc})
17:         **for** j in TopℓSIds **do**
18:             DetectedData=DetectedData $\cup$ FindDataThatSatisfyQueryUsingAOM(q_{inc})
19:         **end for**
20:     **end for**
21:     Send(DetectedData)
22: **end while**

---

5   Experimental Setup and Evaluation

The experimental evaluation of the proposed model relies on the Query Analytics Workloads Dataset[1]. The dataset contains range/radius query workloads from Gaussian distributions over a real dataset. In our experiments, we focus on range queries, and are based on the file Range Queries Aggregates to create three datasets which are named Warming Dataset (D_W), Dataset of two-dimensional points (D_{2d}) and Test dataset (D_T). Each range query is stored in the following format $\{X, Y, Xr, Yr, Count, SUM, AVG\}$. However, we take into consideration only the first four attributes which refer to the range query.

---

[1] http://archive.ics.uci.edu/ml/datasets/Query+Analytics+Workloads+Dataset.

The first two attributes are the coordinates for the x-axis and y-axis for the center of a 'data rectangle', respectively. The third and fourth attributes represent the ranges of the first two attributes. The D_W consists of $1,000$ queries of the format $q_i = \{X_i, Y_i, Xr_i, Yr_i\}$. We randomly generate for each q_i a number $\delta_i \in [20, 30]$ of two-dimensional data points which are located inside the rectangle of q_i. The total number of two-dimensional points is equal to $24,923$ and constitutes the D_{2d} dataset. The last dataset D_T contains $\psi = 1,000$ incoming Range queries with the same distribution and format with the D_W. Our goal is to confirm that the proposed model has the ability to detect the data that an incoming query requests. We adopt the D_W to 'train' the HCBM and HMCM models while the D_T is used to test the performance of BM, HCBM and HMCM.

We evaluate the described models for both, the error levels and the time that they need to detect the correct data. The evaluation relies on the metrics of Precision (PRE), Recall (REC), Accuracy (ACC), False Positive Rate (FPR) and F1-score (FSC) as they ae realized by the calculation of True Positives (TP), True Negatives (TN), False Positives (FP), False Negatives (FN). We define as TP the number of data that an incoming query q_i demands being correctly detected while TN is the number of data that the q_i does not demand and the model correctly rejects them. On the other hand, FP is the number of data that the q_i does not demand but the model retrieves them, and FN is the number of data that the q_i demands but the model does not detect them. The equations that realize PRE, REC, ACC, FPR and FSC are defined as follows: $PRE =$ TP/(TP+FP); $REC =$ TP/(TP+FN); $ACC =$ (TP+TN)/(TP+TN+FP+FN); $FPR =$ FP/(FP+TN); $FSC =$ (2 · TP)/(2 · TP+FP+FN). The required time for each query is represented τ. The aforementioned metrics are used to calculate the performance of models for each q_i. However, the performance of the models has to be estimated over all the incoming queries, thus, we utilize the mean values of the aforementioned metrics. We also calculate the mean time that every model requires to detect the appropriate data which satisfy the incoming queries. The following equation holds true:

$$\mu_{\Omega_i} = \frac{\sum_{q_i \in D_T} \Omega_i}{\psi}, \Omega \in \{PRE, REC, ACC, FPR, FSC, \tau\} \tag{4}$$

The models have the best performance when μ_{ACC}, μ_{PRE}, μ_{REC}, μ_{FSC} reach the unity and μ_{FPR}, μ_τ are close to zero. In our experiments, we pay significant attention on μ_{FPR} and μ_τ as the former gives the average rate of data that the models retrieve but the incoming queries do not demand them, while the latter gives the mean time that our methods require to respond into the incoming queries. We present the performance of the proposed models for different number of clusters regardless the method adopted to deliver them, i.e., HMCM or HCBM. We have to mention that in our plots and especially for the error metrics, we do not consider the BM model because it detects all the required data with no error since it scans the entire dataset and consists of the theoretical optimal model.

In Fig. 1, we compare the HMCM and the HCBM when they create 24 clusters. As we can see, the HMCM exhibits the best performance for all metrics except the μ_{REC} where the two models have the same performance. The dominance of the HMCM is clearly revealed from the Fig. 2 where the mean time that the HMCM needs to respond to the incoming queries is significantly less than the BM method and much less than the HCBM.

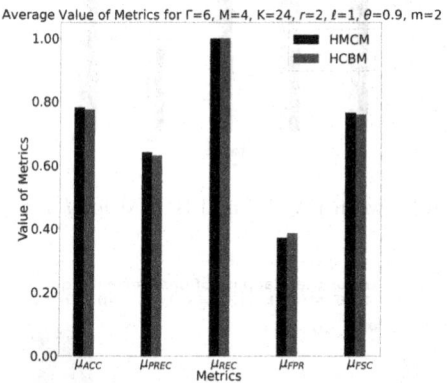

Fig. 1. Comparison between HMCM and HCBM for $\Gamma = 6$, $M = 4$ and $K = 24$

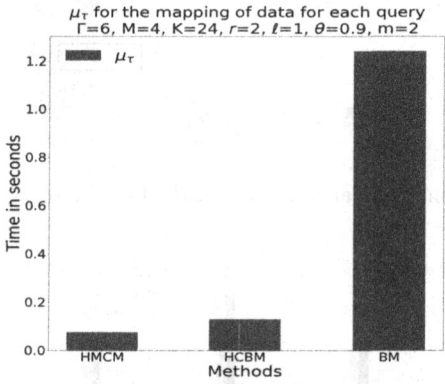

Fig. 2. Average Time comparison between the models for $\Gamma = 6$, $M = 4$, $K = 24$

Figure 3 shows the comparison of the HMCM and the HCBM for 42 clusters. We observe that the HMCM overcomes the HCBM for all metrics except the μ_{REC}, where the HMCM has slightly lower performance than the HCBM. Nevertheless, both μ_{FSC} and μ_{FPR} confirm that the HMCM has better performance when the estimation error is in our focus. Figure 4 strengthens the conclusion that we deduce from Fig. 4 since the HMCM achieves better performance than the HCBM in less conclusion time.

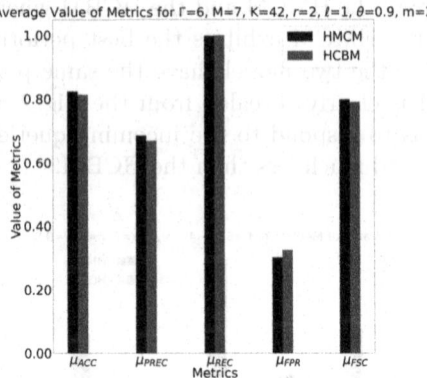

Fig. 3. Comparison between HMCM and HCBM for $\Gamma = 6$, M = 7 and K = 42

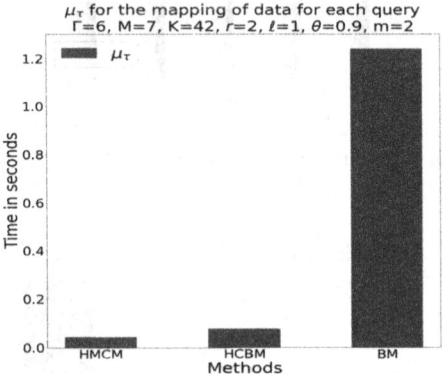

Fig. 4. Average Time comparison between the models for $\Gamma = 6$, M = 7, K = 42

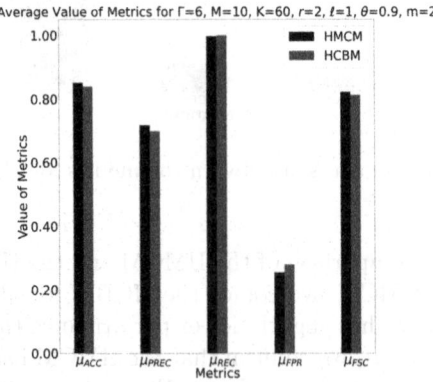

Fig. 5. Comparison between HMCM and HCBM for $\Gamma = 6$, M = 10 and K = 60

In Figs. 5 and 6, the comparison of error and time metrics is presented between the models for 60 clusters, respectively. In Fig. 5, same as in the previous performance outcomes, the HMCM has better performance then the HCBM in the majority of the error metrics. As far as the time metric concerns, the HMCM maps the data in less time than the other models, as it is presented by Fig. 6. Again, in the most important metrics for inferring the conclusion of the designation of the best model, the HMCM clearly outperforms the HCBM.

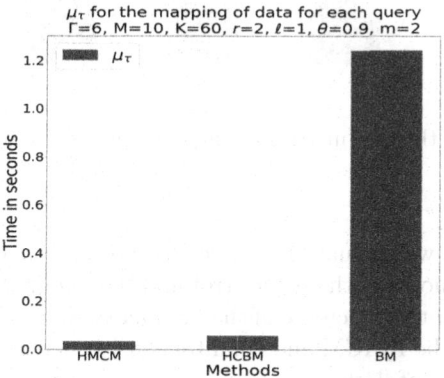

Fig. 6. Average Time comparison between the models for $\Gamma = 6$, $M = 10$, $K = 60$

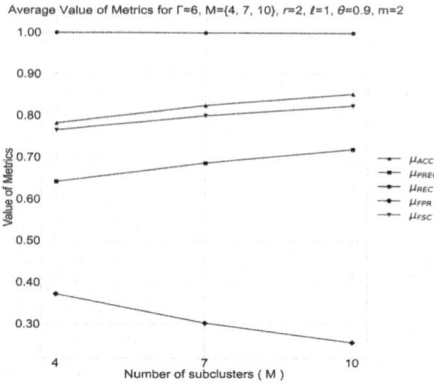

Fig. 7. Performance of error metrics for different number of subclusters in the HMCM

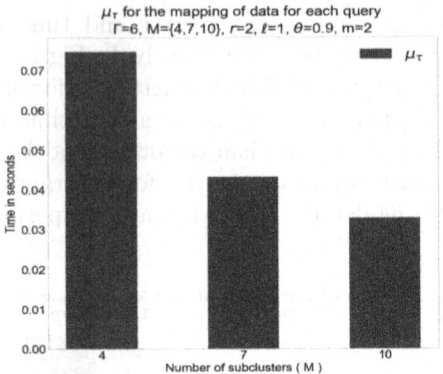

Fig. 8. Comparison of the time metric for different number of subclusters in the HMCM

In Figs. 7 and 8, we evaluate the effect of the number of subclusters in the performance of our model both for the error and the required conclusion time. We can easily observe that the increase of the number of subclusters clearly improves the performance of the HMCM and simultaneously decreases the mean required time for the mapping of data.

Figures 9 and 10 present the effect of the increase of clusters in error and time metrics for the HMCM. We notice that the higher the number of clusters, the better the performance becomes, while the mean time is affected in the opposite direction.

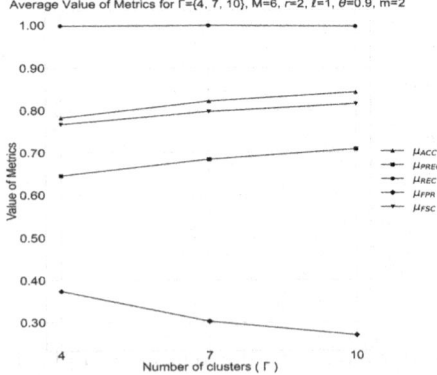

Fig. 9. Performance metrics for different number of clusters in the HMCM

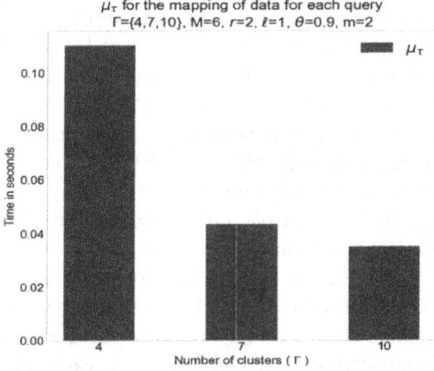

Fig. 10. Comparison of the time metric for different number of clusters in the HMCM

6 Conclusions and Future Work

Data mapping is a significant data management process which plays an important role in many application domains. This process becomes more complex when the data are geo-distributed. Data mapping can be improved if we can identify relations between the data in the DDSs and the defined queries. In this paper, we focus on the efficient data mapping and propose a solution for an effective mapping in the minimum possible time. We are based on the answers of past queries, and propose a hierarchical clustering scheme, which groups them, relying on the similarity of their data requests. Also, we involve a mechanism for the calculation of the matching data area between two queries. Hence, we create small groups of queries with similar data requests and try to benefit from the exclusion of non-similar groups with an incoming query to reduce the response time. A future extension of this work could be the incorporation of a more complex methodology for the improvement of both error and time metrics. We could also adopt a deep learning model that will be able to be adapted on continuous changes in queries requirements.

References

1. Kolomvatsos, K., Anagnostopoulos, C.: A probabilistic model for assigning queries at the edge. Computing **102**(4), 865–892 (2019). https://doi.org/10.1007/s00607-019-00767-8
2. Kolomvatsos, K., Anagnostopoulos, C.: Reinforcement learning for predictive analytics in smart cities. Informatics **4**(3), 16 (2017). https://doi.org/10.3390/informatics4030016
3. Savva, F., Anagnostopoulos, C., Triantafillou, P.: Adaptive learning of aggregate analytics under dynamic workloads. Futur. Gener. Comput. Syst. **109**, 317–330 (2020)

4. Wasay, A., Wei, X., Dayan, N., Idreos, S.: Data canopy. In: Proceedings of the 2017 ACM International Conference on Management of Data (2017)

5. Vulimiri, A., et al.: WANalytics. In: Proceedings of the 2015 ACM SIGMOD International Conference on Management of Data (2015)

6. Na, S., Xumin, L., Yong, G.: Research on k-means clustering algorithm: an improved k-means clustering algorithm. In: 2010 3rd International Symposium on Intelligent Information Technology and Security Informatics (2010)

7. Schwämmle, V., Jensen, O.: A simple and fast method to determine the parameters for fuzzy c-means cluster analysis. Bioinformatics 26, 2841–2848 (2010)

8. Etehadtavakol, M., Sadri, S., Ng, E.: Application of K- and fuzzy c-means for color segmentation of thermal infrared breast images. J. Med. Syst. 34, 35–42 (2008)

9. Jamel, A.M., Akay, B.: A survey and systematic categorization of parallel k-means and fuzzy-c-means algorithms. Comput. Syst. Sci. Eng. 34, 259–281 (2019)

10. Gupta, R., Muttoo, S.K., Pal, S.K.: Fuzzy c-means clustering and particle swarm optimization based scheme for common service center location allocation. Appl. Intell. 47(3), 624–643 (2017). https://doi.org/10.1007/s10489-017-0917-0

11. Stetco, A., Zeng, X., Keane, J.: Fuzzy c-means++: fuzzy c-means with effective seeding initialization. Exp. Syst. Appl. 42, 7541–7548 (2015)

12. Chang, R., Hsu, H., Lin, S., Chang, C., Ho, J.: Query-based learning for dynamic particle swarm optimization. IEEE Access. 5, 7648–7658 (2017)

13. Albishre, K., Li, Y., Xu, Y., Huang, W.: Query-based unsupervised learning for improving social media search. World Wide Web 23(3), 1791–1809 (2019). https://doi.org/10.1007/s11280-019-00747-0

Correction to: Transfer Learning with Jukebox for Music Source Separation

Wadhah Zai El Amri, Oliver Tautz, Helge Ritter, and Andrew Melnik

Correction to:
Chapter "Transfer Learning with Jukebox for Music Source Separation" in: I. Maglogiannis et al. (Eds.): *Artificial Intelligence Applications and Innovations,* **IFIP AICT 647, https://doi.org/10.1007/978-3-031-08337-2_35**

In an older version of this paper, there was an error in the name of the author Wadhah Zai El Amri. The name was incorrectly written as "El Amri, W.Z.", instead of "Zai El Amri, W.". This has been corrected.

The updated version of this chapter can be found at
https://doi.org/10.1007/978-3-031-08337-2_35

Published by Springer Nature Switzerland AG 2022
I. Maglogiannis et al. (Eds.): AIAI 2022, IFIP AICT 647, p. C1, 2022.
https://doi.org/10.1007/978-3-031-08337-2_42

Author Index

Printed in the United States
by Baker & Taylor Publisher Services